Communications in Computer and Information Science   2826

Series Editors

Gang Li, *School of Information Technology, Deakin University, Burwood, VIC, Australia*

Joaquim Filipe, *Polytechnic Institute of Setúbal, Setúbal, Portugal*

Zhiwei Xu, *Chinese Academy of Sciences, Beijing, China*

Rationale

The CCIS series is devoted to the publication of proceedings of computer science conferences. Its aim is to efficiently disseminate original research results in informatics in printed and electronic form. While the focus is on publication of peer-reviewed full papers presenting mature work, inclusion of reviewed short papers reporting on work in progress is welcome, too. Besides globally relevant meetings with internationally representative program committees guaranteeing a strict peer-reviewing and paper selection process, conferences run by societies or of high regional or national relevance are also considered for publication.

Topics

The topical scope of CCIS spans the entire spectrum of informatics ranging from foundational topics in the theory of computing to information and communications science and technology and a broad variety of interdisciplinary application fields.

Information for Volume Editors and Authors

Publication in CCIS is free of charge. No royalties are paid, however, we offer registered conference participants temporary free access to the online version of the conference proceedings on SpringerLink (http://link.springer.com) by means of an http referrer from the conference website and/or a number of complimentary printed copies, as specified in the official acceptance email of the event.

CCIS proceedings can be published in time for distribution at conferences or as postproceedings, and delivered in the form of printed books and/or electronically as USBs and/or e-content licenses for accessing proceedings at SpringerLink. Furthermore, CCIS proceedings are included in the CCIS electronic book series hosted in the SpringerLink digital library at http://link.springer.com/bookseries/7899. Conferences publishing in CCIS are allowed to use our online conference service (Meteor) for managing the whole proceedings lifecycle (from submission and reviewing to preparing for publication) free of charge.

Publication process

The language of publication is exclusively English. Authors publishing in CCIS have to sign the Springer CCIS copyright transfer form, however, they are free to use their material published in CCIS for substantially changed, more elaborate subsequent publications elsewhere. For the preparation of the camera-ready papers/files, authors have to strictly adhere to the Springer CCIS Authors' Instructions and are strongly encouraged to use the CCIS LaTeX style files or templates.

Abstracting/Indexing

CCIS is abstracted/indexed in DBLP, Google Scholar, EI-Compendex, Mathematical Reviews, SCImago, Scopus. CCIS volumes are also submitted for the inclusion in ISI Proceedings.

How to start

To start the evaluation of your proposal for inclusion in the CCIS series, please send an e-mail to ccis@springer.com

José Barata · Kurosh Madani · Hervé Panetto
Editors

Innovative Intelligent Industrial Production and Logistics

6th IFAC/INSTICC International Conference
IN4PL 2025, Marbella, Spain, October 23–24, 2025
Proceedings, Part II

 Springer

Editors
José Barata
Universidade Nova De Lisboa - Uninova
Lisbon, Portugal

Kurosh Madani
University of Paris-EST Créteil (UPEC)
Créteil, France

Hervé Panetto
University of Lorraine, CNRS, CRAN
Nancy, France

ISSN 1865-0929   ISSN 1865-0937 (electronic)
Communications in Computer and Information Science
ISBN 978-3-032-15578-8   ISBN 978-3-032-15579-5 (eBook)
https://doi.org/10.1007/978-3-032-15579-5

This Springer imprint is published by the registered company Springer Nature Switzerland AG
The registered company address is: Gewerbestrasse 11, 6330 Cham, Switzerland

If disposing of this product, please recycle the paper.

Preface

These two volumes (CCIS 2425-6) contain the proceedings of the 6th IFAC/INSTICC International Conference on Innovative Intelligent Industrial Production and Logistics. This year, IN4PL was held in Marbella, Spain, on October 23–24, 2025. It was co-sponsored by the Institute for Systems and Technologies of Information, Control and Communication (INSTICC) and the International Federation of Automatic Control. It was technically co-sponsored by the IEEE Industry Applications Society. IN4PL 2025 was also organised in cooperation with the ACM Special Interest Group on Artificial Intelligence and the ACM Special Interest Group on Simulation and Modelling.

This conference focuses on research and development involving innovative methods, software and hardware, whereby intelligent systems are applied to industrial production and logistics. This is currently related to the concept of Industry 4.0 — an expression reflecting the trend towards automation and data exchange in manufacturing technologies and processes, which include cyber-physical systems, the Industrial Internet of Things, industrial robotics, cloud computing, cognitive computing and artificial intelligence. These technologies can be applied to industrial manufacturing and management as well as to supply-chain or logistics problems, involving, for example, transportation management or the optimisation of operations.

IN4PL 2025 received 58 paper submissions from 25 countries, of which 19 (33%) were accepted and published as full papers. Additionally, 25 papers were accepted and published as short papers. A double-blind paper review was performed for each submission by at least 2, but usually 3 or more, members of the International Program Committee, which was composed of established researchers and domain experts.

The high quality of the IN4PL 2025 program was enhanced by the keynote lectures delivered by distinguished speakers who are renowned experts in their fields: Yannick Naudet (Luxembourg Institute of Science and Technology, Luxembourg), Paulo Jorge Pinto Leitao (Polytechnic Institute of Bragança, Portugal) and Armando Walter Colombo (Institute for Industrial Informatics, Automation and Robotics (I2AR), University of Applied Sciences Emden/Leer, Germany).

The conference was complemented by the 19th International IFAC/IFIP Workshop on Enterprise Integration, Interoperability and Networking, chaired by Prof. Qing Li (Tsinghua University, P.R. China), Dr. Yannick Naudet (LIST, Luxembourg) and Prof. Hervé Panetto (University of Lorraine, CNRS, CRAN, France).

All presented papers will be submitted for indexing by DBLP, Google Scholar, EI-Compendex, INSPEC, Japanese Science and Technology Agency, Norwegian Register for Scientific Journals and Series, Mathematical Reviews, SCImago, Scopus, zbMATH and Web of Science/Conference Proceedings Citation Index.

Several awards, based on the combined marks from the paper review process, as assessed by the Program Committee, and the quality of the presentation, as assessed by session chairs at the conference venue, were conferred at the conference's closing session as recognition for the best contributions.

The program for this conference required the dedicated effort of many people. Firstly, we must thank the authors, whose research efforts are reported here. Next, we thank the members of the Program Committee and the auxiliary reviewers for their diligent and professional reviews. We would also like to deeply thank the invited speakers for their invaluable contribution and for taking the time to prepare their talks. Finally, a word of appreciation for the hard work of the INSTICC team; organising a conference of this level is a task that can only be achieved by the collaborative effort of a dedicated and highly competent team.

We hope you all had an exciting and inspiring conference. We hope to have contributed to the development of our research community, and we look forward to having additional research results presented at the next edition of IN4PL, details of which are available at https://in4pl.scitevents.org.

October 2025

José Barata
Kurosh Madani
Hervé Panetto

Organization

Conference Co-chairs

Kurosh Madani	University of Paris-Est Créteil, France
Hervé Panetto	University of Lorraine, CNRS, CRAN, France

Program Chair

José Barata	Universidade Nova De Lisboa, Portugal

Program Committee

António Abreu	Polytechnic University of Lisbon, Portugal
Anna Adamik	Lodz University of Technology, Poland
Nehal Afifi	Nova University, Cairo Branch, Egypt
Cláudio Alves	Universidade do Minho, Portugal
Giuseppe Berio	University of Southern Brittany, France
Alexandros Bousdekis	National Technical University of Athens, Greece
Amin Chaabane	School of Higher Technology of the University of Quebec - École de technologie supérieure, Canada
Hing Kai Chan	University of Nottingham Ningbo China, China
Roberto Chavez	Swinburne University of Technology, Australia
Tin-Chih Toly Chen	National Chiao Tung University, Taiwan
Law Chong Seng	Southern University College, Malaysia
Yuval Cohen	Afeka Tel-Aviv College of Engineering, Israel
Carlos Cugnasca	Universidade de São Paulo, Brazil
Mohammed Dahane	University of Lorraine, France
William Derigent	Universite de Lorraine, France
Rebeca Díaz Redondo	University of Vigo, Spain
Valerio Frascolla	Intel, Germany
Piotr Gaj	Silesian University of Technology, Poland
Ander Garcia	Vicomtech, Spain
Virginie Goepp	Institut National des Sciences Appliquées de Strasbourg, France
Marvin Gonzalez	College of Charleston, USA

Petri Helo	University of Vaasa, Finland
Ayad Hendalianpour	Independent Researcher, Iran
Benoît Iung	University of Lorraine, France
Fabrício Junqueira	University of São Paulo, Brazil
Bernard Kamsu-Foguem	National School of Engineering in Tarbes, France
Petri Kannisto	VDEh-Betriebsforschungsinstitut (BFI), Germany
Michael Katehakis	Rutgers University, USA
Mladen Krstic	University of Belgrade, Serbia
Ilker Küçükoglu	Uludağ University, Turkey
Seokcheon Lee	Purdue University, USA
Qing Li	Tsinghua University, China
Eduardo Rocha Loures	Pontifícia Universidade Católica do Paraná, Brazil
Vicente Lucena	Federal Univerity of Amazonas, Brazil
Marco Macchi	Politecnico di Milano, Italy
Beatrice Marchi	Università degli Studi di Brescia, Italy
Sergio Martin	UNED - Spanish University for Distance Education, Spain
Ana Meca	University Miguel Hernández of Elche, Spain
Khaled Medini	Mines Saint-Étienne, France
Jorn Mehnen	University of Strathclyde, UK
Antonella Meneghetti	University of Udine, Italy
Marko Mladineo	University of Split, Croatia
Arturo Molina	Instituto Tecnológico Nacional de México, Mexico
Beata Mrugalska	Poznań University of Technology, Poland
Maria Elena Nenni	John Cabot University, Italy
Christian Neureiter	Salzburg University of Applied Sciences, Austria
Sang Do Noh	Sungkyunkwan University, South Korea
Fabio Nonino	University of Rome La Sapienza, Italy
Ovidiu Noran	Griffith University, Australia
Nursel Öztürk	Bursa Uludağ University, Turkey
Paulo Peças	Idmec, Instituto Superior Técnico, Universidade de Lisboa, Portugal
Carlos Pereira	Federal University of Rio Grande Do Sul, Brazil
Ricardo Rabelo	Federal University of Santa Catarina, Brazil
Theofanis Raptis	National Research Council, Italy
Jean-Charles Regin	University of Nice-Sophia Antipolis/I3S/CNRS, France
Stefano Rinaldi	University of Brescia, Italy
David Romero	Tecnológico de Monterrey, Mexico
Subhash C. Sarin	Virginia Tech Industrial Engineering, USA
Vikram Sharma	LNM Institute of Information Technology, India

Davood Shishebori	Yazd University, Iran
Neeraj Kumar Singh	National School of Electrical Electronics Computer Hydraulics Telecommunications, France
Dongping Song	University of Liverpool, UK
Xunhang Sun	Xi'an Jiaotong University, China
Anderson Szejka	Pontifical Catholic University of Paraná, Brazil
Janusz Szpytko	AGH University of Krakow, Poland
Bruno Vallespir	University of Bordeaux, France
François Vernadat	University of Lorraine, France
Georg Weichhart	Primetals Technologies, Austria
Guoqing Zhang	University of Windsor, Canada

Additional Reviewer

Luiz Castilho Jr	Pontificia Universidade Católica do Paraná, Brazil

Invited Speakers

Paulo Leitão	Polytechnic Institute of Bragança, Portugal
Yannick Naudet	Luxembourg Institute of Science and Technology, Luxembourg
Armando W. Colombo	Institute I2AR, University of Applied Sciences Emden/Leer, Germany

Invited Speakers

Industrial Agents as a Key Enabler Technology Towards Smart, Digital and Sustainable Transition: Ultimate Driving Forces

Paulo Leitão

Polytechnic Institute of Bragança, Portugal

Abstract. Global markets are imposing strong changing conditions for industrial companies running their businesses, facing strong pressures related to the customization of products in highly flexible production systems. The fourth industrial revolution aims to promote the digitization of traditional industries, aiming at intelligent factories characterized by adaptability, efficiency, functionality, reliability, safety and usability, re-shaping the way machines, processes and systems operate. This digital transformation is also noticed in other domains such as administration, electrical grids, transportation, healthcare and agriculture. In this context, smart products, processes and systems emerge from the application of cyber-physical systems, complemented with emerging ICT and Artificial Intelligence technologies, such as Internet of Things, Big data, cloud computing, machine learning and virtual/augmented reality. Lately, the European Commission is pushing the Industry 5.0 initiative that complements Industry 4.0 by driving the transition to a sustainable, human-centric and resilient European industry. This presentation discusses the use of multi-agent systems as a key enabling technology to realize this vision, i.e. a smart, digital and sustainable transition. Illustrative examples of using multi-agent systems to deploy industrial cyber-physical systems exhibiting self-organization and intelligence features will be provided to emphasize their innovative fascinating nature. Although, in theory, industrial agents are a promising approach, in practice, several roadblocks constrain their wider industrial adoption. The presentation also discusses the key factors that would lead to acceptance in industry and particularly how the emergence of Generative Artificial Intelligence can give a new boost to the (final) mass adoption of agent-based systems in industry.

Human, Cognition and Digital Twins: Shaping an Industry Where Humans and Machines Collaborate

Yannick Naudet

Luxembourg Institute of Science and Technology, Luxembourg

Abstract. Humans have always been a part of industrial systems, but they mostly had the role of operators, using technological tools to which they had to adapt. While Industry 5.0 and the vision of the future industry emphasize human-centricity, advances in generative AI and robotics are enabling technological systems to take on complex, knowledge-intensive tasks that only humans could do so far. It seems we have two choices now: letting machines do everything for us, or designing them for collaborative synergy with humans. This talk explores the second one, focusing on the role of cognition and the human digital twin in enabling seamless collaboration between humans and smart, intelligent, or cognitive technological systems.

Engineering an Industry 4.0-Compliant Digital Product Passport Within a Circular Economy Context

Armando W. Colombo

Institute I2AR, University of Applied Sciences Emden/Leer, Germany

Abstract. Rationale of the Keynote: We are witnessing rapid changes in the industrial environment, mainly driven by business and societal needs towards production customization and the digitalization of the economy, i.e., digitalization and interconnection of products, services, enterprises, and people. This trend is supported by new disruptive advances in the cross-fertilization of concepts and the amalgamation of information-, communication-, control-, and mechatronics technology-driven approaches in traditional industrial systems. In this context, industrial informatics combine the progress achieved by the application of large distributed and networked computing systems on product and production system design, planning, engineering, and operation with the power of digital data that are produced by industrial processes, collected by the Internet of Things, processed by Human/(Natural-) and Human-created (Artificial-) Intelligence (AI). The technological, economic, and social impacts of these developments are so enormous that the whole process is labelled the 4th Industrial Revolution. This digital transformation being developed world-wide is affecting all aspects of society and generating profound changes in the form in which humans interact and sometimes collaborate with each other and with technological assets. The transition, the transformation, the migration from Industry 3.0, i.e., from IEC 62264/IEC 61512 (ISA-95/ISA'88)-based industrial systems into an Industry 4.0-compliant eco-system is ongoing. This includes (i) the integration of legacy with emerging Information/Communication technologies, (ii) digitalization and networking across value networks involving a multitude of stakeholders in complex relationships within a circular economy, (iii) the re-skilling of human resources embedded in that digitalized eco-system, as well as (iv) the necessary "concrete" response to the newest regulation of the European Union requiring nearly all products sold in the EU to feature a Digital Product Passport (DPP).

Scope of the Keynote: On the one side, Industry 4.0-compliant systems are all Industrial Eco-Systems where components (Assets, Things) have been migrated into digitalized and networked Industrial Cyber-Physical Systems. This means that digitalized and networked assets are nodes of an Internet-based communication and information network. Each of those nodes is able to expose and/or consume digitalized data and information in the form of "services", for performing new forms of application and business based on Industrial Internet of Services Technology (IIoS). On the other side, a Digital Product Passport is defined as a digital record providing stakeholders across product value chains with access to comprehensive data and information about each product's lifecycle, i.e., origin, composition, environmental impact, end-of-life aspects/characteristics, and other related businesses.

The structural and functional interdependences between the digitalized Assets, I4.0 components, digitalized Things in Internet (Industrial-Internet-of-Things (IIoT)), in the context of "Engineering a DPP", are effectively evident if the "Digitalization and Networking Process" is formally specified and implemented following (a) the DIN Specification 91345 Reference Architecture Model for Industry 4.0 (RAMI 4.0) and (b) the engineering principles associated with the Asset Administration Shell (Digital Twins (DTs)) approaches and technologies. From this perspective, the Keynote will provide: (i) Details about the Engineering Principles, Methods and Standard Technologies for the Digital Transformation in Industry, leading to effectively engineering a Digital Asset/Thing Passport within the context of a Circular Economy; (ii) The rationale of the Systems-of-Systems Engineering approach, comprehensively backed up by the DIN Specification 91345 RAMI 4.0 (Reference Architecture Model for Industry 4.0) and particularly by the implementation of the Asset Administration Shell (AAS) Technology; and (iii) Details about an Engineering approach to implement a DPP on the basis of the RAMI 4.0 and AAS specifications, with dedicated exemplary use cases.

Contents

Logistics

Logistics

Simulating Safety Measures, and Protocols, in Air Cargo Handling and Optimize Air Cargo Unit Load Device

Saeede Khalilpoor[1], Roaa Al Shidi[2], Mehdi A. Kamran[2(✉)], and Sana Nabati[1]

[1] Department of Industrial Engineering, Faculty of Engineering, Urmia University, Urmia, Iran
[2] Department of Logistics, Tourism, and Services Management, German University of Technology in Oman, P. O. Box 1816, PC 130 Muscat, Oman
`mehdi.kamran@gutech.edu.om`

Abstract. This study enhances safety and efficiency in air cargo handling by comparing manual and automated processes and optimizing the use of unit load devices (ULDs). Air cargo is vital to global trade, yet ensuring safe and efficient handling remains challenging. This research uses Arena simulation software to evaluate the effects of safety measures and handling methods, and an Excel-based Cargo Loading Problem (CLP) solver to optimize container packing for maximum space utilization and weight balance. Results indicate that automated handling is faster and safer than manual operations, reducing accidents and delays. By integrating simulation and optimization, this study offers a comprehensive approach to improving safety and efficiency in air cargo operations.

Keywords: Air Cargo Safety · Manual and Automated Handling · Arena Simulation · Cargo Loading and Unloading · Air Cargo · Optimization Unit Load Devises

1 Introduction

Air cargo started in early aviation for mail and small parcels [1], growing significantly in the mid-1900s with better aircraft and cargo airlines [2]. Today, it is crucial for global trade, moving goods quickly over long distances [3]. Though less publicized than passenger flights, it serves manufacturing, pharmaceuticals, and e-commerce [4], ensuring fast delivery of time-sensitive goods and linking remote areas [5]. Rising volumes demand safer, more efficient, and cost-effective handling, but challenges remain with manual inefficiencies, safety risks, and underused ULDs.

Despite technological advances, handling practices face limitations. Manual processes are slow, labor-intensive, and prone to errors, increasing accidents, damaged goods, and delays [6, 7]. Automated systems improve speed, reliability, and cost-efficiency [8, 9], though adoption varies. Optimizing ULD use—key to maximizing capacity while respecting weight limits [10]—is often neglected or rudimentary, leading to wasted space and inefficiency [11, 12]. Prior research tends to focus separately on safety or container optimization, with limited integration of simulation-based safety

J. Barata et al. (Eds.): IN4PL 2025, CCIS 2826, pp. 3–23, 2026.
https://doi.org/10.1007/978-3-032-15579-5_1

improvements and optimization strategies. This study addresses this gap by proposing a comprehensive approach to enhance air cargo safety and efficiency.

Containers have simplified air freight by making it more affordable and easier to handle. Cargo is usually packed in boxes, barrels, or sacks [13], but containers have strict weight and volume limits. The growth in air cargo volume stresses the importance of robust safety measures [3]. In 2019, global air cargo traffic exceeded 60 million metric tons, with further growth expected [14]. Even minor safety errors can cause accidents or supply chain delays.

The sector faces broader challenges like rising fuel costs, strict regulations, and limited capacity [10, 15]. The COVID-19 pandemic underscored the need for flexibility and resilience [16]. Air cargo's global nature complicates safety management, as shipments pass many countries and airports, demanding standardized regulations and clear communication for coordination and compliance [17]. Improving container utilization is essential for safety and efficiency, as current methods often waste space, extend handling times, and increase risks [11].

Manual handling remains time-consuming and risky, causing accidents, damage, and delays [6]. Incidents like falls and improper dangerous goods handling persist despite safety protocols, highlighting the need for improvement as cargo volumes rise [7]. Automated loading and unloading reduce labor needs, costs, errors, and delays [8, 9]. They also optimize truck space, increase throughput, and improve financial performance. Automation enhances speed and reliability, alleviating logistical bottlenecks like loading dock wait times. As cargo volumes and labor costs increase, automation offers better return on investment and flexibility [18]. ULDs also critically affect operational efficiency. Properly filling ULDs without exceeding weight limits maximizes space and minimizes wasted payload [10]. These standardized containers secure cargo on aircraft and optimizing their use enhances safety, efficiency, and capacity [12, 19].

This study addresses air cargo challenges by improving safety and efficiency. It assesses current safety measures, tests simulation-based enhancements, and compares manual and automated handling. An Excel tool is developed for ULD packing optimization with 3D visualization and animation. The aim is to offer practical recommendations for safer, more efficient operations. The article is organized as follows: Sect. 2 reviews the literature. Section 3 states the simulation problem. Section 4 explains methodologies. Section 5 analyzes simulation results. Section 6 presents optimization findings. Section 7 concludes and suggests future work.

2 Literature Review

Air cargo transportation is central to global trade, enabling the rapid movement of goods over long distances. Ensuring safety and efficiency in cargo handling within aircraft is a complex challenge [20] that demands stringent safety measures to protect goods and personnel [21]. Such measures mitigate accidents, damage, and operational disruptions while maintaining industry credibility. Cargo diversity—from perishables to hazardous materials—further necessitates specialized handling protocols [22].

This review synthesizes research on automation and manual handling, safety and standardization in ULDs, and optimization strategies, contrasting benefits and drawbacks to identify balanced approaches.

2.1 Automated and Manual Handling in Air Cargo Transportation

Automation significantly improves speed, accuracy, and safety by employing smart conveyor belts, automated guided vehicles (AGVs), and robotics to streamline sorting, movement, and storage, thereby reducing human error and physical strain [23]. Industry 4.0 technologies, such as IoT and cyber-physical systems, support real-time monitoring, enhancing system resilience and competitiveness [18, 24]. The COVID-19-driven labor shortages have accelerated automation adoption, further boosting safety and operational consistency [6, 25]. Additionally, automation mitigates bottlenecks like loading dock delays by increasing throughput [8]. However, high upfront costs limit accessibility for smaller operators [23, 26], while extensive workforce training and change management pose additional challenges [25, 27]. Risks of technical failures and cybersecurity threats may disrupt operations [24]. Overreliance on automation can reduce workforce flexibility in unexpected scenarios [28, 29]. Manual handling provides essential adaptability and judgment for irregular or fragile cargo [30] but is slower, labor-intensive, and more error-prone. Literature supports a hybrid model where automation manages routine, high-volume tasks, complemented by human oversight for complex or exceptional cases, optimizing both efficiency and flexibility.

2.2 Safety and Standard Protocols and Challenges in Air Cargo ULDs

ULD management is critical to safe and efficient operations. [31] Emphasizes that standardization improves efficiency, interoperability, and safety. Safety protocols are shaped by cargo type, load efficiency, and regulatory oversight [12, 22].

Uniform compliance, however, is difficult due to regulatory variations, differing interpretations, and evolving threats [32]. Diverse stakeholders—airlines, handlers, regulators, manufacturers—often have conflicting priorities, delaying consensus [22]. Smaller operators may lack resources for advanced safety technology, infrastructure, or training [21].

While standardization enhances reliability, overly rigid protocols can limit flexibility for atypical cargo. Some researchers advocate a risk-based approach, allocating resources in proportion to hazard severity [22]. The challenge lies in balancing strict international standards with adaptable, context-specific measures.

Optimization of Air Cargo ULDs. Optimizing ULD usage improves capacity, fuel efficiency, and safety. Digital tools [33], genetic algorithms [34], and mixed-integer programming for bin packing [35] offer practical solutions. [3] note, however, that real-world disruptions often hinder optimal implementation. Standardized ULD designs, as outlined in the [17] ULD Technical Manual, simplify handling and reduce compatibility issues. Automation supports optimization through AI and algorithmic space utilization [36]. Yet purely algorithmic models may underperform in dynamic conditions involving irregular cargo or last-minute changes. A hybrid approach—automated optimization complemented by human adjustments—appears most effective.

Literature Gap and Contribution. According to the literature, gaps remain in comprehensive cost–benefit analyses and long-term evaluations of automation [23, 37]. Moreover, safety and optimization are often studied separately, limiting integrated solutions.

This study addresses these gaps by using a simulation model with an Excel-based CLP solver to evaluate safety protocols, compare manual and automated handling, and optimize ULD use. This integrated approach aims to improve safety, efficiency, and reliability while providing a nuanced understanding of automation's strengths and vulnerabilities.

3 Problem Statement

Air cargo operations face ongoing challenges in safely handling goods despite technological advances and strict safety standards. While current procedures are generally effective, improvements are possible. Automated systems offer speed and precision but need significant investment and careful calibration. This study simulates various loading and unloading scenarios to compare the safety, reliability, and efficiency of human versus automated handling. We developed a simulation model to analyze factors such as loading time, queue waiting, and safety compliance, assessing how different handling methods affect resource use, processing times, and overall operational performance. We used a two-step approach to extract parameters: first, a thorough literature review; second, validation and refinement through interviews with industry experts to ensure practical relevance.

3.1 Loading Process

The logic flow diagram in Fig. 1a represents a model of the loading process, comparing manual and automated methods to assess their effects on the efficiency and safety of air cargo handling. The process begins with cargo arriving at the loading bay, where containers are assigned to either loading employees or automated machinery. The next step is the security screening process, which is divided into manual and automated methods. Figure 2 shows the steps of the loading section simulation model.

Manual screening procedures include the use of portable metal detectors, physical inspections, and manual searches to ensure that cargo aligns with safety standards. The automated screening method uses X-ray scanning, which provides images that are reviewed by staff members or software to detect irregularities or prohibited items. Additionally, computerized tomography scanners offer precise three-dimensional images, enabling thorough inspections. They are particularly effective at locating hidden or protected objects and can detect a wide variety of materials.

In the air cargo segregation process, different types of cargo are sorted based on criteria such as weight, dimensions, destination, and special handling needs. This sorting helps ensure that cargo is loaded onto aircraft in an organized and efficient manner. The process can be carried out automatically, which enhances accuracy and speed, or manually, which offers flexibility for specific types of cargo.

The unit of measure process ensures the safety and efficiency of air transportation by complying with regulations for cargo measurement, packaging, and loading. This can be done automatically, as items pass through a scanner area or conveyor belt, with robotic arms reloading the aircraft according to the automated loading plan, or manually, with handlers calculating dimensions and weight using scales and tape measures and loading cargo in line with unit-of-measure specifications and balance requirements.

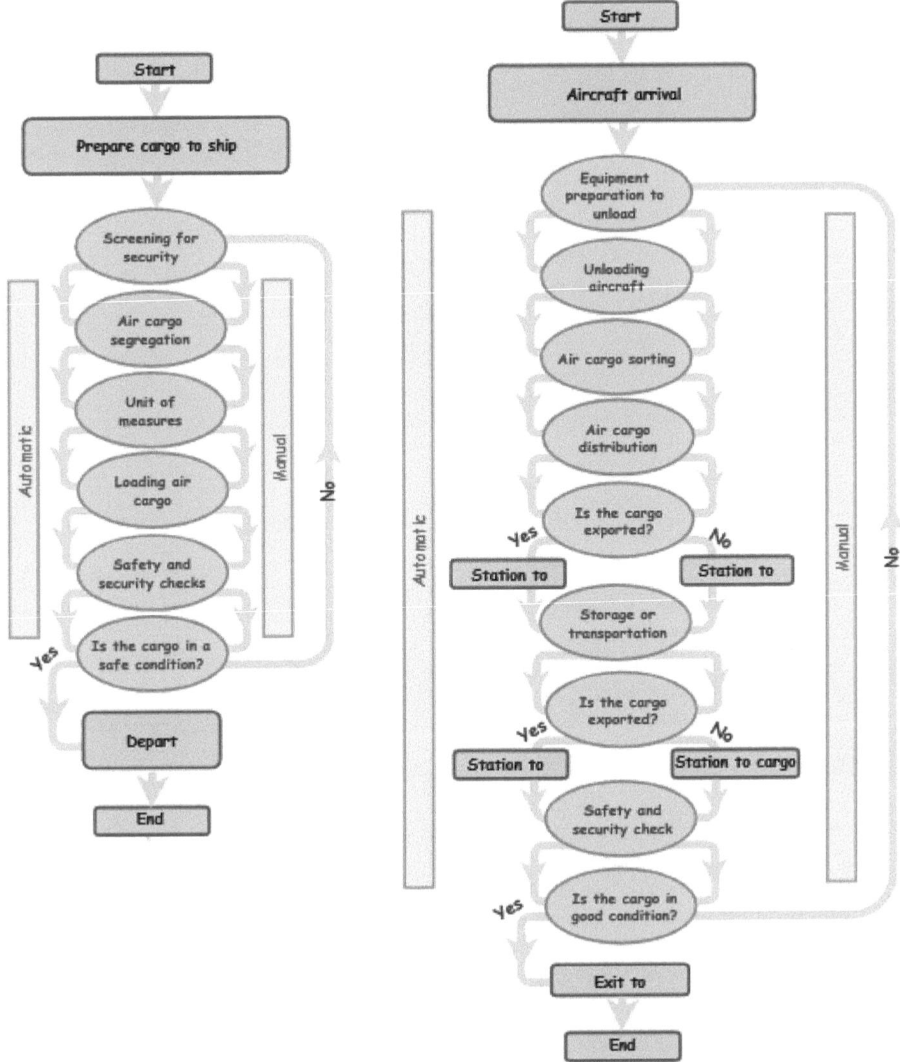

a) Logic flow diagram of manual and automated air cargo loading process.

b) Logic flow diagram of manual and automated cargo unloading process.

Fig. 1. Arena modelling flowcharts.

After loading the air cargo using either automated tools such as material handling systems (MHS), conveyor belts, and robotic arms, or manually with pallet jacks, forklifts, and other hand tools, it is crucial to ensure that the cargo is within the secure aircraft. Proper strapping, netting, and labelling prevent movement during departure, ensuring that all cargo meets the necessary specifications.

The unit of measures goal is to ensure the safety and efficiency of air transportation by conforming to rules and regulations for cargo measuring, packaging, and loading, and

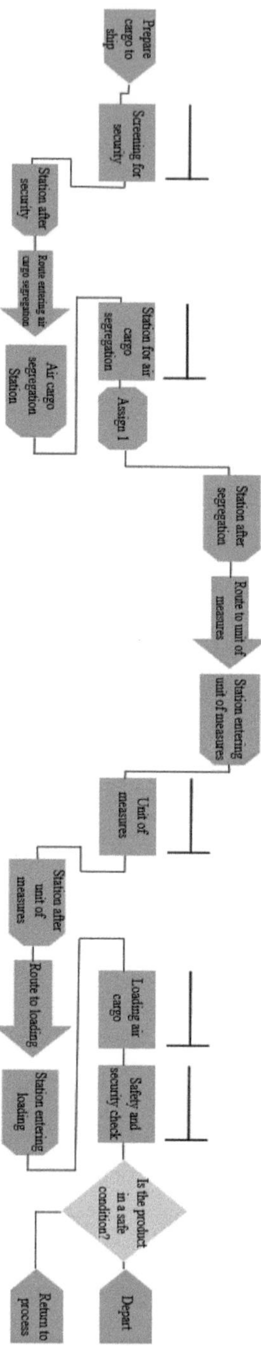

Fig. 2. Simulation model of loading air cargo handling.

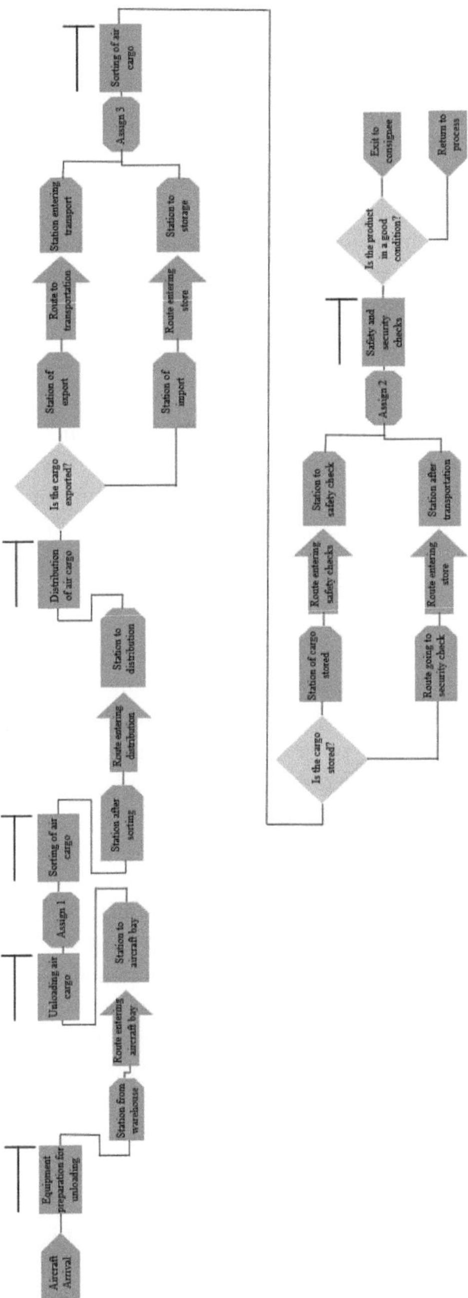

Fig. 3. Simulation model of manual unloading air cargo handling.

this can be done either automatically such as items as they pass through a scanner area or on a conveyor belt and using robotic arms to reload the aircraft with cargo according with the automated loading plan, or manually by calculating dimensions and weight with the use of scales, tape measures, or other measuring tools, and cargo handlers manually load the cargo into the airplane, being aware to follow the regular unit of measures specifications and balance requirements. Following loading of air cargo by using automated tools such as MHS, conveyor belts, and robotic arms, or manually by Pallet jacks, forklifts, and other hand tools are used to move the cargo into the proper locations within the airplane body. Finally, it's important to ensure that cargo is placed in a safe and secure condition within the airplane and make sure that each cargo has the needed straps, nets, and labelling, to prevent any movement while departing, and to ensure all the cargo meets their specifications.

3.2 Unloading Process

The logic flow diagram in Fig. 1b represents the manual and automated unloading processes for air cargo. Initially, the handling crew manually unloads each item, moving it from the aircraft to the warehouse or storage facility using tools such as pallet trucks, transporters, and forklifts. Ground staff must handle each item carefully to prevent damage and ensure accurate sorting for transportation or further processing. Figure 3 and 4 also shows the steps of the manual and automatic unloading section simulation model, respectively.

In the automated unloading process, the aircraft is equipped with systems like robotic arms or conveyor belts inside the cargo hold, which automatically move the cargo to the ground. Automated systems may also include sorting technology that directs cargo to specific locations based on its type or destination. Automated unloading processes can be faster and more efficient, particularly for handling large loads.

The goal of cargo sorting is to categorize items by type, destination, size, and other relevant factors. This can be done manually, with workers physically handling and storing goods in the appropriate location or container according to their destination. Handheld scanners or other tools may be used to track and identify each item. Alternatively, in an automated sorting process, cargo is placed on a conveyor belt or similar system, which passes through sorting stations equipped with sensors and scanners that read barcodes and other identifiers to determine the destination and sorting criteria.

After sorting, manually handled air cargo is distributed based on whether it is for import or export. Workers then load it onto trucks or other ground vehicles according to a specified plan for delivery. Handheld devices may be used for communication with the distribution center or other relevant parties to monitor and verify delivery. In contrast, in the automated distribution process, sorted cargo is loaded onto conveyor belts or AGVs, which transport it to designated areas. Imported cargo is stored in the warehouse until the consignee is ready for pickup, while export cargo moves to the next process to be prepared for reloading. Computer systems manage the movement and routing of cargo, with robotic arms and other technologies loading cargo into trucks or other vehicles without human involvement.

Safety and security checks are essential in the final phase of air cargo handling to confirm that cargo has been properly handled and complies with all regulations. This phase can be conducted manually or automated, ensuring that air cargo is prepared for delivery in a safe, secure manner, in adherence with all applicable regulations and requirements.

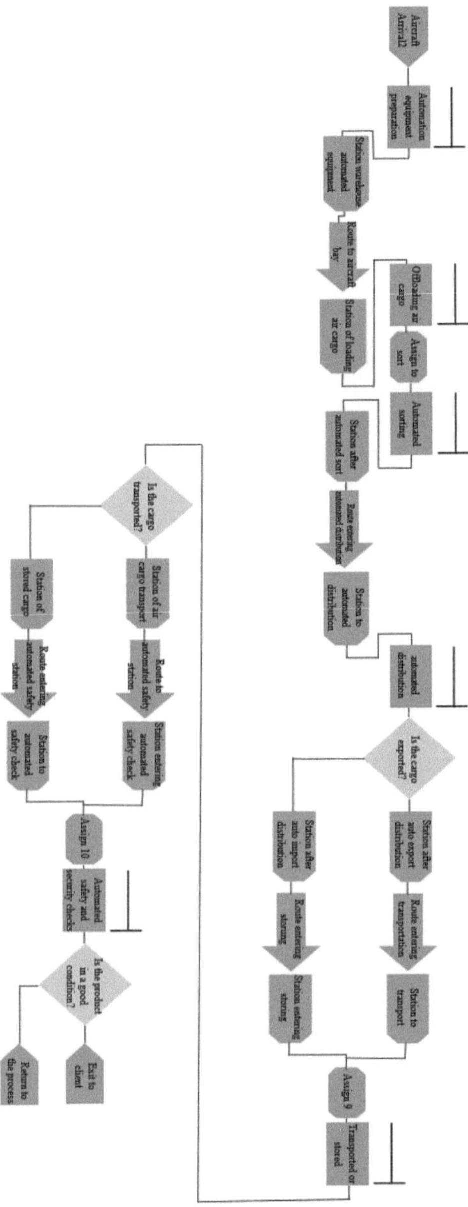

Fig. 4. Simulation model of automatic unloading air cargo handling.

This strategy evaluates human and automated handling techniques' reliability, safety risks, processing intervals, queue dimensions, resource utilization, outcomes, errors, and safety events.

4   Solution Methodology

In this study, simulation and optimization are combined to address safety in air cargo handling. The simulation model considers manual and automated processes, analysing each method's impact on metrics such as processing time, safety, and resource utilization. In addition, an optimization model is employed to determine the cargo loading configurations, ensuring balanced weight distribution and maximum capacity utilization, ultimately supporting safer and more efficient operations.

4.1   Simulation

This study uses a simulation method to examine manual and automated air cargo handling processes and their impact on safety, efficiency, and resource use. Using Arena software, a model is developed to simulate each step in the loading and unloading process, including security scanning, sorting, and cargo placement in the aircraft. Automated systems like robotic arms and conveyor belts are included to test their speed and accuracy. The flowchart of the method used in the study for loading and unloading is shown in Fig. 1.

In the experimental design, it's important to analyse dependent and independent variables to see how changes in the independent variables affect outcomes. Dependent variables, such as safety measures (e.g., accidents or safety violations), are studied based on changes in independent variables, like implementing specific safety procedures with automated handling or training staff.

To ensure accurate results, internal validity confirms that changes in safety measures are due to specific procedures, while external validity checks if these results apply to real-world air cargo scenarios. Both are essential for the study's reliability and relevance in improving air cargo safety protocols, confirming cause-effect relationships and assessing how well findings translate to real conditions.

5   Optimization

In this part, an Excel-based CLP solver is used to improve the cargo loading process within the aircraft. The goal is to increase efficiency and meet safety standards. The CLP solver looks at factors like cargo placement, weight distribution, and loading sequence to reduce manual handling time and prevent imbalance, which is important for air cargo safety. Data such as cargo weight, volume, and container dimensions are collected to organize the container for the best use of space. By managing load balance and arrangement, this optimization helps reduce delays and keeps the cargo secure in the aircraft, lowering the chance of shifting or damage during transit.

6   Results and Analysis

This study compares manual and automated air cargo handling systems in safety, efficiency, and cost. Simulation tests measured each system's performance under different conditions, examining processing times, work-in-progress (WIP), and total output. Financial analysis examined costs and benefits, highlighting potential savings and improvements with automation. Overall, results suggest automation improves efficiency, reduces manual labor, and increases safety in air cargo operations.

6.1 Simulation Experiments

This section focuses on the simulation experiments done to study air cargo loading and unloading, and their financial differences. The simulations test both manual and automated handling methods to see their effect on efficiency, processing time, safety and expenditures.

Air Cargo Loading Process. The first experiment compared automated and manual air cargo loading times. Automated loading averaged 18.91 min versus 25.81 min manual, a 37% efficiency improvement (Fig. 5a). In terms of throughput (Fig. 5b), automation processed 4,800 units in and 4,795 out, while manual handled 2,907 in and 2,904 out, showing minimal losses in both. Figure 6 details process stages: automated screening took 2.33 min vs. 3.82 manual; segregation and units of measure were faster with automation (2.45 and 2.48 vs. 4.74 and 4.75); cargo loading was slightly faster manually by 0.08 min; safety/security favored automation (2.58 vs. 2.94). Automated systems had lower WIP (5.18 vs. 5.74), indicating quicker throughput. Overall, automation processed 4,795 entities in 14,400 min versus manual's 2,904 in 14,535 min, reflecting a 40% efficiency gain.

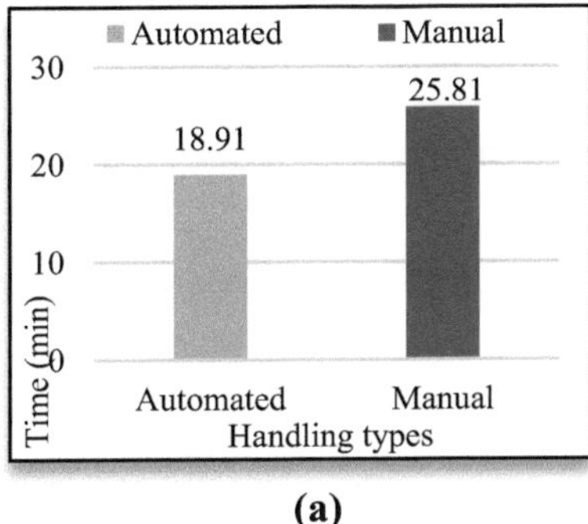

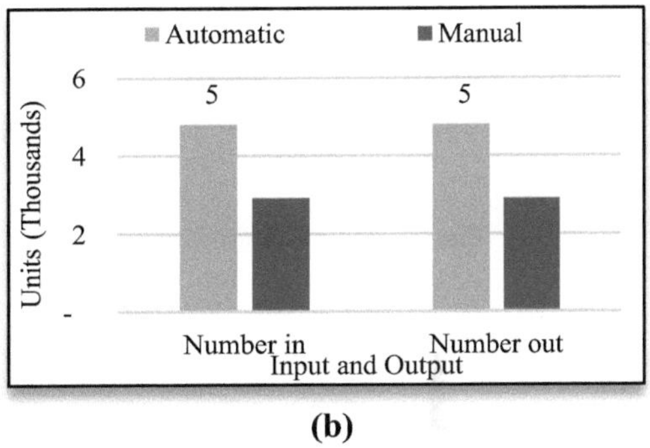

(a)   (b)

Fig. 5. a. Total time of loading process. **b.** Cargo loading observations.

Air Cargo Unloading Process. In the unloading process, Fig. 7.a shows that the automated handling unloading process significantly reduces the total time spent on it, with an average completion time of 19.2 min compared to the 21.5 min required for manual handling. The primary finding reveals a significant improvement in the unloading process, with automation handling resulting in an 12% decrease in time.

In Fig. 7b, the output statistics reveal that entities involved in automated and manual air cargo unloading procedures have a higher success rate and efficiency, with 4,794 out of 4,800 entities completing the automated process, compared to 2,927 of 2,932 in manual processes. The automation process takes significantly less time to complete than the manual handling process, which takes 14,660 min. This efficiency is 40% higher than the manual air freight unloading operation, as each entity enters the process every three minutes. Therefore, the automated air cargo unloading system has proven more efficient

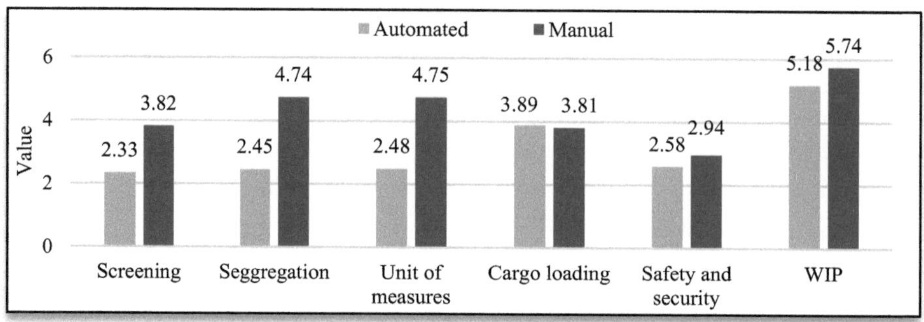

Fig. 6. Automated/Manual air cargo Loading Process.

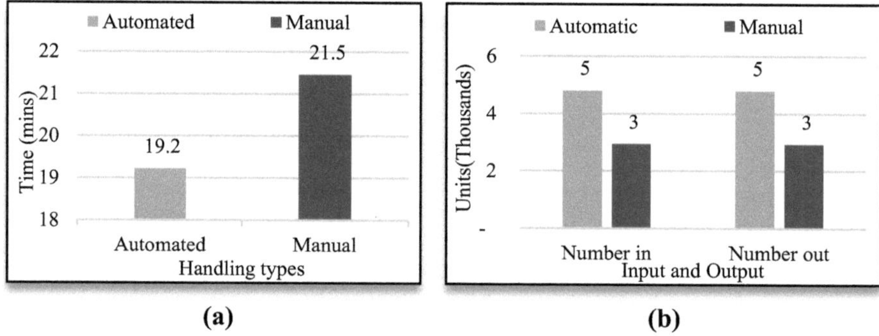

(a)   (b)

Fig. 7. a. Total time of unloading process. b. Cargo observations.

in handling and receiving larger volumes of cargo than the human process, according to data.

Figure 8 compares automated and manual air cargo unloading processes across several stages, including preparation, unloading, sorting, distribution, storage, safety, and WIP. In the preparation stage, automated handling takes slightly less time, averaging 2 min compared to 2.3 min for manual handling. The difference is more noticeable in the unloading stage, where automation takes only 2.8 min, while manual unloading requires 4.5 min, showing a significant efficiency gain with automation. For sorting, automated processes consistently maintain a time of 2 min, while the manual process did not register time for sorting. Distribution, storage, and safety also show slight advantages for automation, with times of 2.5, 2.1, and 2.5 min, respectively, compared to 2.7, 2.2, and 2.9 min in manual handling. In terms of WIP, automated unloading has a value of 5.4, indicating faster task flow and fewer delays, whereas the manual process has a WIP of 6.8, suggesting slower processing and more congestion. Overall, the automated unloading process outperforms the manual one in most stages, leading to faster and more efficient cargo handling with reduced bottlenecks. This highlights the advantages of automation in improving speed, consistency, and efficiency in air cargo unloading operations.

In overall and based on the analysis, it can be concluded that automated systems work better than manual methods for loading and unloading air cargo. Automated systems save

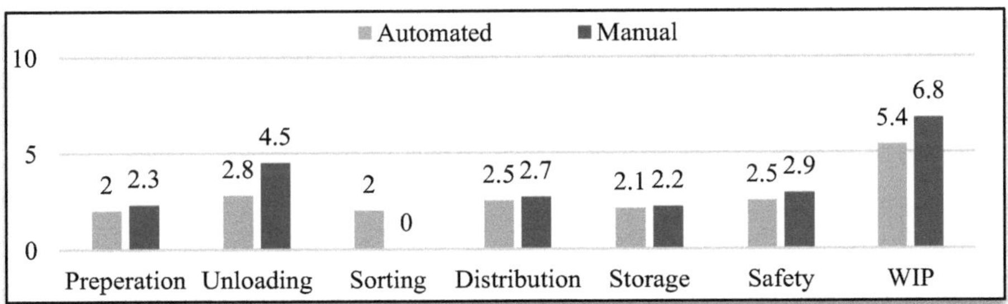

Fig. 8. Automated/Manual air cargo unloading process.

time and make the process more efficient. For loading, automation makes the process 37% faster and handles more units with fewer delays. In unloading, automated methods also finish 12% faster and have more consistent results. Each part of the process, from preparation to distribution, works better with automation. The lower WIP values in automated systems mean tasks move faster with less waiting. Overall, automation is a better option for air cargo, as it is quicker, more reliable, and handles more cargo efficiently. In addition, the manual handling system, with a five-minute arrival time, took longer than the automated system, which had a three-minute arrival time. This indicates that the running duration of the models varies with the process.

Financial Analysis. Financial analysis assesses the feasibility of automated versus manual handling systems, impacting their effectiveness and financial viability. It compares direct costs—such as fuel, maintenance, salaries, and utilities—and indirect costs like brand reputation, lost opportunities, and customer experience. Efficient models are essential to optimize safety measures and ensure smooth air cargo handling operations.

Table 1 shows the total cost of 2,250,000 OMR over five years, including 2,000,000 in operational expenses (OPEX) and 250,000 OMR in indirect costs. Also, presents 1,000,000 OMR investment in year 0 for automated systems establishing, followed by annual operating expenses of 170,000 and 80,000 OMR in indirect benefits, totalling 1,450,000 OMR. Comparing the two scenarios reveals a 35.55% decrease in expenses in the second scenario, primarily due to the initial investment in automated cargo handling, which yields indirect benefits and reduces ongoing operational costs.

In the following sections, detailed financial analysis for both situations is provided.

Net Present Value (NPV). Financial statistics use NPV metric to determine how much the present value of cash outflows over a given period differs from one another. This is done to evaluate the financial gain from a project or investment. Lower NPV indicates lower cost for the project.

NPV for the existing and proposed model is calculated based on Eq. (1):

$$NPV = \sum_{n=0}^{N} \frac{NCF_n}{(1 + r)^n} \tag{1}$$

where net cash flow (NCF) and discount rate (r) for n of five years in the existing model (manual) are: $NCF_0 = 0$, $NCF_1 = \ldots NCF_5 = 450{,}000$, $r = 0.03$. . Therefore,

Table 1. Financial analysis of different types of handling in air cargo (Thousand).

Type	Costs	Year 0	Year1	Year2	Year3	Year4	Year5	Total
Manual	OPEX	–	400	400	400	400	400	2000
	Indirect	–	50	50	50	50	50	250
	Total	–	450	450	450	450	450	2250
Automated	Investment	1000	–	–	–	–	–	1000
	OPEX	–	170	170	170	170	170	850
	Indirect	–	80	80	80	80	80	400
	Total	1000	90	90	90	90	90	1450

NPV for the manual process is 2,000,843. NCF and discount rate for proposed model (automatic) are: $NCF_0 = 1,000,000$, $NCF_1 = \cdots = NCF_5 = 90,000$, $r = 0.03$. NPV for the automatic model is 1,371,042.

Efficiency improvement based on Eq. (2) can be used to determine the efficiency gain when shifting from a manual to an automated system:

$$Efficiency\ Improvement = (\frac{Manual\ NPV - Automated\ NPV}{Manual\ NPV}) \times 100 \qquad (2)$$

The calculated efficiency improvement is 31%. Therefore, automation has greatly benefited the cargo handling process, showing a 31% increase in overall efficiency compared to manual processes. The significant cost savings and higher productivity achieved by automated systems demonstrate this progress.

Internal Rate of Return (IRR). IRR, a measure of an investment's profitability, is used here. The proposed model for air cargo handling is estimated to save 360,000 OMR over five years, based on the cash flows of both the existing and proposed models, calculated using an Excel formula solver. In comparison between automated and manual processes, based on the Table 2, it is equal to 23.44%. The investment in automation offers a higher return rate than a manual procedure, indicating that automation is a preferable alternative due to its higher estimated cash flows and discounted rate.

Table 2. Internal rate of return data (Thousand).

Costs	Year0	Year1	Year2	Year3	Year4	Year5	Total
Manual total cost	–	450	450	450	450	450	2250
Automated total cost	1000	90	90	90	90	90	1450
Savings	1000	360	360	360	360	360	800

Payback. A key consideration is the payback period, which measures how long it takes for the automated handling investment to recover its cost. If the investment is made in year 0, the payback values are 640,000 in year 1, 280,000 in year 2, and 80,000 in year 3, at which point the full initial cost is recovered. This is the period required for the automated investment to generate cash equal to its initial cost.

7   Optimization Model

The optimization model focuses on improving the cargo loading process to make operations more efficient and to meet safety standards. To achieve this, this study employed an Excel-based CLP solver. This tool helps to find the best ways to load cargo in the aircraft. It focuses on different factors like where to place the cargo, how to distribute the weight, and the order of loading. This helps reduce the time spent on manual handling and prevents any imbalance, which is very important for keeping air cargo safe.

The optimization model is designed to follow cargo regulations, ensuring weight and volume limits are respected while maximizing container utilization and improving safety through proper load balance and secure placement. Poor ULD optimization can lead to reduced capacity, higher costs, delays, and lower fleet productivity [38]. Because ULD optimization involves complex factors like capacity, weight distribution, and loading arrangements, this study focuses on enhancing safety protocols, improving efficiency, and reducing costs by strategically assigning cargo to specific ULDs to maximize space use [39]. While simulation results show time, throughput, and cost benefits, they also reveal limitations such as suboptimal cargo distribution and unused capacity. The CLP-based optimization model addresses these issues directly, offering prescriptive solutions for inefficiencies like poor space use and incorrect load balance—problems automation alone may not fully solve. It reduces the need for manual adjustments, minimizes safety hazards, ensures compliance with industry weight and capacity rules, and resolves bottlenecks found in simulation, including delays from disorganized containers and limited ULD usage.

By maximizing ULD capacity, the model reduces the number of containers, shortens loading/unloading and turnaround times, and increases operational efficiency. Financially, it builds on automation's cost savings by further lowering ULD-related expenses, eliminating delays, and boosting fleet productivity, resulting in higher ROI. Combining simulation insights with optimization ensures realistic modeling of current processes and delivers practical strategies for ongoing operational improvements.

8   Results and Analysis

Data such as cargo quantities, weight distribution, volume, container dimensions, maximum gross weight, and container volume have been collected for optimizing ULDs. The data in Table 3 collected using the air cargo arrival manifest of Oman Air Boeing 787-9 fleet. The type of container used is AKE, with dimensions of (60.4 × 61.5) inches, a container height of 25.2 inches, and a maximum gross weight of 1,588 kg.

The experiment employed a CLP spreadsheet solver to optimize cargo loading, ensuring safety, effectiveness, and compliance with aircraft weight and balance requirements.

Table 3. Air cargo data collection.

Name	Width (cm)	Height (cm)	Length (cm)	Weight (kg)	Heavy	Fragile		No of items
A	10	5	10	15	No		No	4
B	15	15	15	69	No		No	3
C	30	10	30	80	No		No	5
D	20	20	20	70	No		No	6
E	12	5	12	81	No		No	5

The solver analyzed cargo weight, dimensions, and quantity within containers to maximize payload capacity while maintaining safety and balance. For example, a container holding 23 individual items utilized 45.73% of its volume but reached 93.95% of its weight capacity. This disparity indicates that weight limits more heavily constrain loading than volume, emphasizing the importance of maximizing volume utilization while managing weight for efficient air cargo operations.

The CLP spreadsheet provides data for 23 items listed in Table 4, each ide by a unique ID, along with their counts, types, weights, and volumes. The "Item Type ID" column classifies the items into five different types, represented by IDs 1 to 5. For example, items 1, 2, and 3 are categorized under type ID 4, which has a volume of 8000 m^3 and a weight of 70 kg. The "Weight" column shows the weight of each item, ranging from 15 to 81 kg. Strategic storage is important for organizations to manage inventory effectively. Understanding the volumes and weights of items helps optimize transportation and storage, ensuring compliance with weight limits, improving operational efficiency, and reducing costs.

Table 5 shows the arrangement of items inside the container using the CLP Excel solver to optimize volume utilization. Each item has been placed in different orientations (XYZ) within and inside container, as shown in Fig. 9a and 9b respectively, which are visualized using CLP. To maximize the arrangement, factors such as item weight, size, shape, layering limitations, and fragility must be carefully considered.

The arrangement in Fig. 9 was generated by the Excel-based CLP solver using Oman Air Boeing 787–9 cargo data (Tables 3, 4), including item dimensions, weights, quantities, container size, and ULD weight limits. Optimization targeted two criteria: maximizing container volume use within dimensional limits and avoiding gaps, and maximizing allowable weight without exceeding balance or IATA requirements. The solver provided spatial coordinates and orientations for each item (Table 5), considering constraints like layering, fragility, and safe weight distribution. The final configuration achieved 93.95% weight utilization and 45.73% volume utilization.

The optimal arrangement of air freight containers is crucial for operational efficiency, safety, and cost-effectiveness, ensuring even weight distribution, protection against damage, and compliance with safety and legal constraints. These measures optimize weight and space utilization, contributing to efficient cargo loading operations.

Table 4. CLP spreadsheet solution of air cargo optimization.

Item count	Item Type ID	Volume	Weight
1	4	8,000	70
2	4	8,000	70
3	4	8,000	70
4	3	9,000	80
5	3	9,000	80
6	1	500	15
7	1	500	15
8	1	500	15
9	1	500	15
10	3	9,000	80
11	5	720	81
12	5	720	81
13	3	9,000	80
14	5	720	81
15	5	720	81
16	5	720	81
17	4	8,000	70
18	4	8,000	70
19	4	8,000	70
20	3	9,000	80
21	2	3,375	69
22	2	3,375	69
23	2	3,375	69

Table 5. Items arrangement inside the container.

Item count	Item Type name	x coordinate	y coordinate	z coordinate	Orientation
1	D	0	0	0	xyz
2	D	20	0	0	xyz
3	D	40	0	0	xyz
4	C	0	20	0	zxy
5	C	30	20	0	zxy
6	A	0	50	0	yzx
7	A	5	50	0	yzx
8	A	10	50	0	yzx
9	A	15	50	0	yzx
10	C	0	20	10	zxy
11	E	20	50	0	yxz
12	E	25	50	0	yxz
13	C	30	20	10	zxy
14	E	30	50	0	yxz
15	E	35	50	0	yxz
16	E	40	50	0	yxz
17	D	0	0	20	xyz
18	D	20	0	20	xyz
19	D	40	0	20	xyz
20	C	0	20	20	zxy
21	B	30	20	20	xyz
22	B	45	20	20	xyz
23	B	30	35	20	xyz

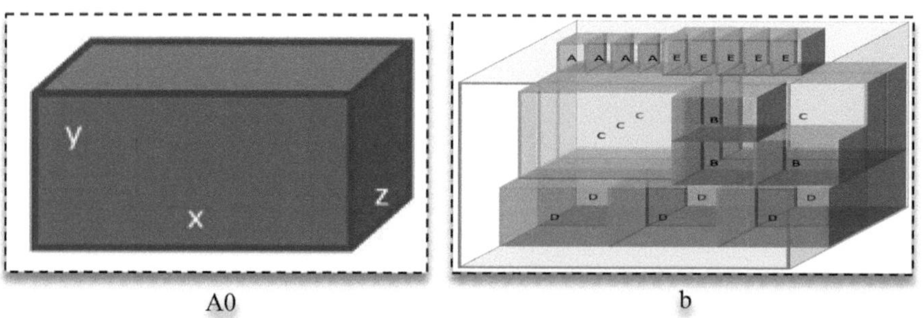

Fig. 9. Arrangement of cargo within and inside containers.

9 Conclusions

This study, by comparing manual and automated air cargo loading and unloading systems, along with financial analysis and ULD optimization, showed that automation can significantly improve efficiency, safety, and cost savings. Simulation results indicate that in the loading process, the use of an automated system reduces operation time by an average of 37% and moves a larger volume of cargo with less delay. In the unloading process, the operation time is also reduced by 12% and the workflow is smoother and without operational bottlenecks. The WIP index is lower in the automated system, indicating faster task completion and reduced waiting time.

The financial analysis showed that the use of an automated system leads to a 35.55% reduction in costs compared to the manual method and a 31% improvement in the NPV index. The IRR was also estimated to be 23.44% and the payback period was three years, indicating the high economic attractiveness of this investment.

The results of optimizing the ULD layout using the CLP solver indicated that although the container volume utilization was 45.73%, the weight utilization reached 93.95%, indicating a weight limit in loading. The optimization algorithm ensured the cargo layout was carried out while observing safety constraints, weight balance, and dimensions in a way that reduced risks and increased productivity. Overall, the combination of automation and cargo layout optimization significantly improves speed, consistency, cost reduction, and safety enhancement in air cargo operations.

Suggestions for future work include the investigation of additional indicators such as energy consumption and emissions, labor productivity measurement, customer satisfaction indicators, and advanced safety metrics. It is also suggested that confidence intervals and analysis of variance be included to strengthen the statistical validity of the results. Conducting case studies in different geographical areas and on specific cargo types (dangerous materials, perishable cargo, etc.) can also provide a more comprehensive understanding of the applicability of safety protocols.

Disclosure of Interests.   The authors declare that they have no competing interests related to the content of this article.

References

1. Abeyratne, R.: Law and Regulation of Air Cargo. Springer (2018)
2. Şahan, D.: The role of logistics infrastructure on trade development: an application for Turkey. Doctoral dissertation, Dokuz Eylul Universitesi, Turkey (2021)
3. Morrell, P.S., Klein, T.: Moving Boxes by Air: The Economics of International air Cargo. Routledge (2018)
4. Florido-Benítez, L.: The role of the top 50 US cargo airports and 25 air cargo airlines in the logistics of e-commerce companies. Logistics **7**(1), 8 (2023)
5. Vasigh, B., Fleming, K., Tacker, T.: Introduction to Air Transport Economics: From Theory to Applications. Routledge (2018)
6. Holloway, T.: The analysis of quality escapes in manufacturing plants and the relationships to quality work standards. Doctoral dissertation, The National Graduate School of Quality Management at NECB (2019)

7. Hlavatý, D., Kraus, J.: Safety of cargo aircraft handling procedure. MAD-Mag. Aviat. Dev. **5**(3), 13–17 (2017)

8. Richey, R.G., Roath, A.S., Adams, F.G., Wieland, A.: A responsiveness view of logistics and supply chain management. J. Bus. Logist. **43**(1), 62–91 (2022)

9. Gelderman, C.J., Semeijn, J., Verhappen, M.: Buyer opportunism in strategic supplier relationships: triggers, manifestations and consequences. J. Purch. Supply Manag. **26**(2), 100581 (2020)

10. IATA. Cargo capacity crunch: demand plummets but capacity disappears even faster. International Air Transport Association (2020)

11. Köllmann, S.V.H.: Cargo layout design for the stackability of boxes in ULDs for the inbound products of company X. Bachelor's thesis, Twente University (2018)

12. Chao, C.C., Li, R.G.: Effects of cargo types and load efficiency on airline cargo revenues. J. Air Transp. Manag. **61**, 26–33 (2017)

13. Domina, A.S.: Organization and technology of special categories of cargo transportation by air (2020)

14. IATA. ULD Regulations. International Air Transport Association (2020)

15. ICAO. Council States 2019–2022. International Civil Aviation Organization (2019)

16. ICAO. ICAO Assembly elects new Council for three-year term. International Civil Aviation Organization (2020)

17. IATA. Cargo safety & security strategy. International Air Transport Association (2019)

18. Cano, J.A., Salazar-Arrieta, F., Gómez Montoya, R.A., Cortés, P.: Disruptive and conventional technologies for the support of logistics processes: a literature review. Int. J. Technol. **12**(3), 448–460 (2021)

19. IATA. How IATA Manuals Enhance Safety, Efficiency, and Compliance in Air Cargo Operations. International Air Transport Association (2024)

20. Hoyle, R.H., Lynam, D.R., Miller, J.D., Pek, J.: The questionable practice of partialing to refine scores on and inferences about measures of psychological constructs. Annu. Rev. Clin. Psychol. **19**(1), 155–176 (2023)

21. IATA. IATA ULD Technical Manual. International Air Transport Association (2019)

22. da Cunha, D.A., Macário, R., Reis, V.: Keeping cargo security costs down: a risk-based approach to air cargo airport security in small and medium airports. J. Air Transp. Manag. **61**, 115–122 (2017)

23. Sunaryo, E.R., Basaria, F.T.: Trends of automation in airport apron area: a systematic literature review. In: 2024 International Conference on Informatics, Multimedia, Cyber and Information System (ICIMCIS), pp. 364–369 (2024)

24. Zsifkovits, H., Woschank, M., Ramingwong, S., Wisittipanich, W.: State-of-the-art analysis of the usage and potential of automation in logistics. In Industry 4.0 for SMEs: Challenges, opportunities and requirements, pp. 193–212. Springer, Cham (2020)

25. Trumić, M., Muhammad, A.: Automation of luggage handling in airports: survey and the simulation environment. In: 2024 11th International Conference on Electrical, Electronic and Computing Engineering (IcETRAN), pp. 1–5 (2024)

26. Dahlgren, J.: Evaluation of automated freight transport systems. In: The Future of Automated Freight Transport, pp. 205–224. Edward Elgar Publishing (2006)

27. Chinn, R.W., Vickers, K.: Automated air cargo handling systems. In: IEE Colloquium on Systems Engineering of Aerospace Projects, p. 5-1 (1998)

28. AlMataani, N.A., Ayadi, D.N.: Optimizing ground handling operations to enhance service efficiency at airports - a literature review. IJRDO – J. Bus. Manage. (2025)

29. Alonso Tabares, D., Mora-Camino, F.: Aircraft ground handling: analysis for automation. In: 17th AIAA Aviation Technology, Integration, and Operations Conference. 3425 (2017)

30. Diefenbach, H., Erlemann, N., Lunin, A., Grosse, E.H., Schocke, K.O., Glock, C.H.: Improving processes and ergonomics at air freight handling agents: a case study. Int J Log Res Appl **26**(4), 399–420 (2023)
31. IATA. Cargo Handling Manual. International Air Transport Association (2021)
32. IATA. Cargo Standards Manual. International Air Transport Association (2021)
33. Ding, Y., Xu, W., Liu, Z., Zhou, Z., Pham, D.T.: Robotic task oriented knowledge graph for human-robot collaboration in disassembly. Procedia CIRP **83**, 105–110 (2019)
34. Bai, R., Woodward, J.R., Subramanian, N., Cartlidge, J.: Optimisation of transportation service network using κ-node large neighbourhood search. Comput. Oper. Res. **89**, 193–205 (2018)
35. Paquay, C., Limbourg, S., Schyns, M.: A tailored two-phase constructive heuristic for the three-dimensional multiple bin size bin packing problem with transportation constraints. Eur. J. Oper. Res. **267**(1), 52–64 (2018)
36. Sodiya, E.O., Umoga, U.J., Amoo, O.O., Atadoga, A.: AI-driven warehouse automation: a comprehensive review of systems. GSC Adv. Res. Rev. **18**(2), 272–282 (2024)
37. Carlan, V., Ceulemans, D., Van Hassel, E., Derammelaere, S., Vanelslander, T.: Automation in cargo loading/unloading processes: do unmanned loading technologies bring benefits when both purchase and operational cost are considered? J. Shipp. Trade **8**(1), 20 (2023)
38. Zhao, X., Dong, Y., Zuo, L.: A combinatorial optimization approach for air cargo palletization and aircraft loading. Mathematics **11**(13), 2798 (2023)
39. Şafak, Ö., Erdoğan, G.: A large neighbourhood search algorithm for solving container loading problems. Comput. Oper. Res. **154**, 10619 (2023)

Innovation in Logistics Management: Systems Adapted to SMEs

Emanuel Jankovic[✉] and Dumitru Tucu

Polytechnic University of Timisoara, Piaţa Victoriei Nr. 2, 300006 Timişoara, jud. Timiş, Romania

rector@upt.ro

Abstract. The paper investigates innovations in logistics management being tailored to small and medium-sized enterprises (SMEs), given their critical importance in the global economy. SMEs in the Romanian market represent a significant share of job creation and economic output, but face unique challenges in implementing efficient logistics systems. In this paper I propose a way in which management software programs can be adapted for SMEs, this research aims to develop a clear methodology to help SMEs improve their logistics performance by addressing specific needs and capitalizing on innovative practices. The proposed methodology includes an assessment of SME needs and establishes customized solutions resulting from the identification of an acute lack of centralized management system, that allow different departments to access data and the necessary steps for the actual implementation of a management system created from scratch and the milestones required for a successful implementation. Also the increased needs of the consumers put pressures for fast deliveries, stock accuracy and customized services require streamlined logistics processes, all of these factors are producing large quantity of waste and a reduced efficiency. The results and conclusions are presented through quantitative and qualitative data, highlighting the positive impact these solutions can have on SME competitiveness. Therefore, the future of logistics is shaped by technology integration, sustainability, market dynamics and efficient risk management, which are essential elements for the development of flexible, high-performance and customer-oriented logistics systems.

Keywords: Automation · Sustainability · Technological Integration

1 Introduction

In the context of global trade developments, small and medium-sized enterprises (SMEs) play a central role in maintaining economic resilience, innovation and employment. "In Romania, SMEs account for over 99% of all enterprises and are key players in national development" [1]. However, SMEs are facing increasing pressures from supply chain disruptions, digitalization gaps and macroeconomic instability. The last few years - marked by the pandemics such as "COVID-19 pandemic" [2], conflicts in the region and in the word, inflationary increases and logistical constraints - have further amplified the operational vulnerabilities of Romanian SMEs.

J. Barata et al. (Eds.): IN4PL 2025, CCIS 2826, pp. 24–40, 2026.
https://doi.org/10.1007/978-3-032-15579-5_2

Given all these economic challenges, the strategic implementation of digital tools, in particular warehouse management systems (WMS), emerges as a key lever to improve organizational competitiveness and adaptability. WMS platforms enable real-time inventory tracking, process automation and accurate data reporting - capabilities that are essential for SMEs seeking to optimize costs, minimize waste and increase customer satisfaction. Despite all these clear advantages, the high cost and complexity of off-the-shelf enterprise solutions often prevent SMEs from adopting such systems, highlighting the need for scalable and customized alternatives. Preliminary findings indicate that SMEs in Romania are increasingly aware of the importance of digital transformation. According to a recent national survey, a significant percentage of entrepreneurs say they are strongly affected by economic uncertainty, with almost half of them registering a high level of risk of loss of financial strength as well as an increased risk of insolvency or even business closure (Fig. 1).

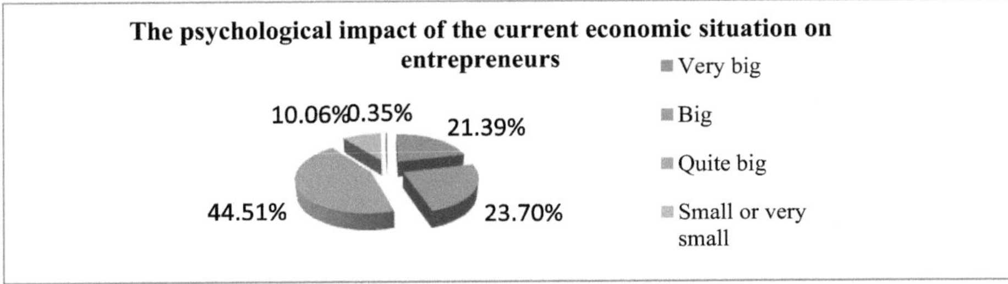

Fig. 1. The psychological impact of the current economic situation on entrepreneurs [1].

2   Documenting the Needs of Implementation of a Management System Based on Up-to-Date Data

This chapter is structured along three analytical strands that together provide a comprehensive understanding of the relevance, challenges, and context for adopting digital logistics systems particularly Warehouse Management Systems (WMS) in small and medium-sized enterprises (SMEs). These strands are as follows:

2.1   The Necessity and Strategic Opportunity of Implementing a Management System in SMEs

In a market economy where gains are increasingly constrained and conditioned by market volatility, new technologies implemented as well as measures to combat losses that are more up-to-date than ever, the need for structured operational oversight in SMEs has become a strategic imperative. This sub-chapter will analyze the motivations behind the adoption of management systems, with a focus on cost control, operational efficiency and compliance with quality standards (e.g. ISO 9001, IATF 16949). And the argument will highlight how even a minimal digital infrastructure such as a basic WMS can serve as a starting point for internal optimization, inventory transparency as well as quick decision-making on the part of management, even for SME,s with "underdeveloped digital infrastructure" [3]. The research will also refer to relevant literature to establish the correlation between managerial digitization and SME competitiveness.

In Romania, Small and medium-sized enterprises (SMEs) hold a key role in the economy by contributing to innovation, employment and economic growth. However, they often face unique challenges that include "limited resources" [1], high competition and operational inefficiencies, having implemented some king of WMS software have the potential to offer significant advantages in addressing these challenges, boosting efficiency and encouraging growth and help by stabilize the dynamics of SMEs activities in the national economy by eliminating large year-to-year variations (Table 1).

Table 1. Dynamics of SME activity over the last two years, according to their legal form of organization [1].

NO.	Dynamics of SME activity over the last two years	SMEs by form of legal organization		
		SA	SRL	Other forms of legal organization
1	SMEs operating at the same parameters	12,50%	49,09%	76,19%
2	SMEs downsizing	37,50%	19,95%	4,76%
3	SMEs that have developed/expanded their activity	50,00%	30,96%	19,05%

Also the use of a cloud WMS software will help SMEs to address the complexity of financial fraud in supply chains, the solution must be organized in clusters to handle large volumes of transactions through techniques such as "k-means or density-based clustering" [4], which will be able to identify malicious anomalies. The cloud mode facilitates offers the possibility of multiple utilizations in the same time frame, from "billing fraud to data security breaches" [4], thus the system dynamically adapting to the dual logistics flows. A strategic management model calls for a dual approach to streamline operations:

1. Security and synchronization of operations with logistics flows requires hybrid systems that can integrate real-time monitoring using "predictive analytics" [3].
2. To provide a uniform and unified infrastructure that will proactively prevent security breach risks the clustered organization of the system will ensure scalability as well as an associated reduction in deployment costs.

2.2 Current State of Logistics Systems in SMEs and the Role of Smart Integration in Manufacturing Contexts

Most SMEs continue to rely on paper and file-based process tracking, spreadsheets and disconnected systems, resulting in poor inventory accuracy. This lack of real time data on "material flow" [5], WIP (Work-in-Progress) and finished goods hinders responsiveness and decision making (Fig. 2).

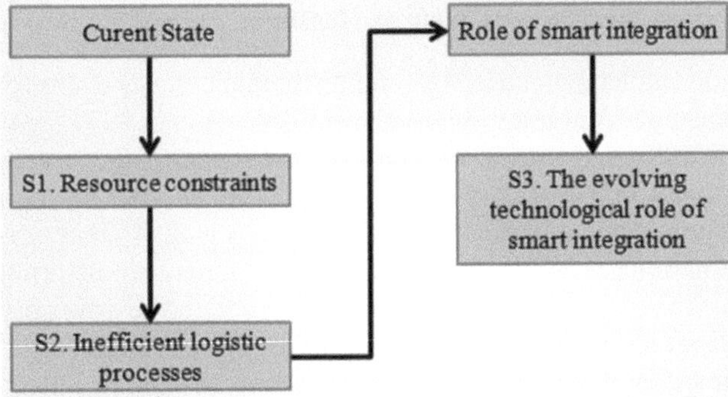

Fig. 2. Current state and the role of smart integration.

S1. "Resource constraints" [4] are an important benchmark for SMEs lacking the capital, specialized IT staff and infrastructure required for advanced enterprise resource planning (ERP) or warehouse management systems (WMS) common in large enterprises. This resource limitation creates dependency on fragmented, often incompatible point solutions. Inefficient inventory management is currently creating an imbalance in stock levels, where manual processes produce an overstocking of certain items and on the other hand to shortages of essential components, disrupting production schedules and risks of production line stoppages at end customers. Fragmented communication and coordination often occur due to unsynchronized excel file usage can cause disconnects between sourcing, production planning, warehousing and factory operations causing delays, errors (e.g., delivering the wrong parts to the production line) and difficulties synchronizing with suppliers/customers.

S2. "Inefficient logistic processes" [6] cause significant operational costs due to manual handling, excess inventory, unplanned deliveries made at the expense of SMEs due to not producing finished goods on time and which can cause production stoppage at the customer's location have a direct impact on profitability. Also the extension of lead times and delivery times causes customer dissatisfaction and erodes customer confidence.

S3. "The evolving technological role of smart integration" [7] involves connecting physical logistics assets (sensors on machines, AGVs, inventory tags) and processes (order management, production scheduling) through digital technologies (Cloud, AI/ML) into a unified, data-driven system New generative technologies and their impact such as RFID sensors "provide real-time visibility into the location of materials (raw materials, WIP, finished goods)" [8], equipment status and environmental conditions throughout the production and logistics workflow. The cloud system enables affordable integration of previously systems (e.g. connecting a basic WMS to production planning software), facilitating data exchange and centralized control without massive upfront IT investments. Also, the role of intelligent integration will be to provide impeccable customer service, increase their targets in terms of inventory accuracy as well as improving supplier relationships, improved delivery services will be able to ensure on-time delivery of customer goods, personalized order fulfillment, "flexible value-added services and responsiveness to special customer requests" [9].

2.3 Understanding the Current State of Health of the SME System in Romania

In Romania beside challenges caused by funding, bureaucracy and strong market competition, another relevant economic situation on entrepreneurs in 2024, was the psychological impact of the current global events that start with the Covid-19 pandemic, followed by the inflation that preceded it, the military conflict in Ukraine followed by an energy crisis and divers armed and unarmed world conflicts, as well as other adverse contextual developments at national and international level have generated distortions in almost all areas of activity, it is important to get a right image related to how decision makers in Romanian SMEs are emotionally influenced by the current economic situation.

After studying documents and surveys on the current state of SMEs in Romania, it was concluded the following:

- "44.51% of entrepreneurs/managers" [1], have suffered multiple problems in maintaining the company's profitability
- "23.70% of business" [1], claimed that their business was significantly affected by the difficult market conditions
- "21.39% of respondents" [1], they claimed that their businesses were closely linked to the global market, so their suffering was significant
- "10.06% of SME" [1], claimed that businesses were not suffering so much given the global context
- "0.35% of respondents" [1], claimed that their foundations were well structured so that the global situation did not have a negative impact on them

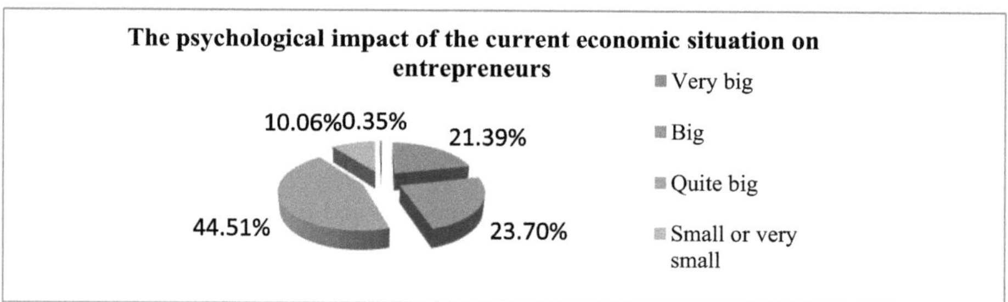

Fig. 3. The psychological impact of the current economic situation on entrepreneurs [2].

Also, due to the fact that SMEs are not structured towards well-defined control, where profit efficiency and loss reduction are prioritized, as is the case with large enterprises, there is a continuous struggle for business development and investor profits (Fig. 3).

Risk Management and Compliance. Also for many entrepreneurs the focus is primarily on growth and profitability, while the mechanisms needed to protect this "growth in organizations" [12] are often ignored. However, the importance of a robust risk management and compliance frameworks cannot be overstated. In present day's record keeping even if it is essential for the companies by minimizing the risks in the face of growing demand of regulations from the automotive industry, it is overlooked. SMEs are having problems with archived the proper documentation and it is not only makes it harder to demonstrate compliance when necessary, but also doesn't help identify areas where improvements may be needed. Small SMEs don't take advantage of technology to store records digitally and ensure they are readily available when needed. The lack of management software program doesn't assist SMEs in maintaining compliance with regulatory requirements and effective risk management. By not having an automating compliance processes and facilitating comprehensive documentation, SMEs cannot mitigate potential legal issues and adapt quickly to regulatory changes (Table 2).

Table 2. Risk management and compliance.

No.	Possible risks	Objectives	Compliance Standards
1	Financial	- Regular assessment of the financial situation	- IFRS (International Financial Reporting Standards)
2	Operation	- Define and implement internal control system plans for business continuity	- ISO 9001 (Quality Management Standard) - AS 9100 (Quality standard for the aerospace industry)
3	Compliance risks	- Training of employees for regular internal and external audits	- GDPR (General Data Protection Regulation) - ISO 27001 (Information Security Management Standard)
4	Technological risks	-Evaluate and "implement advanced IT security solutions" [11] and manage them	- PCI DSS (Payment Industry Data Security Standard) - NIST Cyber security Framework
5	Reputational Risks	- Crisis management, monitoring, analysis and transparent communication of customer feedback	- ISO 31000 (Standard for risk management) - Ethics and conduct rules of the organization
6	Environmental risks	- Assessment and implementation of sustainability practices	- ISO 14001 (Environmental Management Standard) - Local and international environmental regulations
7	Strategic Risks	- Consultation and "SWOT analysis" [10] and regular evaluation of the strategy with stakeholders	- Codes of good practice for corporate governance - OECD standards for corporate governance

3 Development and Implementation of Warehouse Management System (WMS) Software for SMEs

3.1 Understanding WMS Warehouse Management Systems

In order to be able to use WMS software we need to understand its definition:

- A warehouse management system (WMS) is a software designed to support and optimize warehouse capabilities as well as distribution center management.
- WMS software helps SMEs to manage stock volumes, track stock movements, optimize inventory results and streamline logistics processes to improve financial performance.

Given the above, we have the main features of the WMS:

- Inventory management: The possibility of real-time tracking of stock levels, locations and status as well as the possibility of adjusting in a shortest time discrepancies
- Order management: Optimize the order fulfillment process from pick to dispatch.
- Shipping and receiving: Precise efficiency on incoming and outgoing orders.

3.2 Steps for Creating and Implementing a WMS Program

Step 1: Define objectives and requirements.
Identify key objectives:

- Document what the WMS is intended to achieve (e.g., improved accuracy, faster processing, better visibility)

Assess current processes:

- Analyze existing warehouse operations, identifying weaknesses and areas needing improvement (Table 3).

Table 3. Define objectives and requirements.

No.	Objectives	Examples
1	Documentation of what you want from a WMS management program	- Inventory accuracy - "Reduction of cost" [14] by reducing the discrepancies - Increase "customer satisfaction" [13]
2	Involvement of production, logistics, maintenance, controlling, etc. departments	- Setting up a working group to reach as many of the necessary points as possible for implementation - Involvement of the IT department to check the compatibility of the proposed program with the internal system
3	Understanding current warehouse management processes	- Identifying workflows - Calculation of material preparation time
No	Objectives	Examples

(continued)

Table 3. (*continued*)

No.	Objectives	Examples
4	Understand and evaluate the essential features of the WMS	- Real-time "inventory counting" [15] management capability - Material movement history -View addresses in the system -Implementation of individual users and Key User creation -Download shelf stock in excel format -Input and removal from address -Possibility to delete what is in the addresses for re-entry (annual inventory)
5	Assessment of current IT capabilities	- Hardware and software requirements
6	Prioritize requirements by importance and urgency	- "Critical process" [17] requirements (e.g. inventory management) versus optional requirements (e.g. advanced reports)
7	Document all objectives and requirements	- Develop a specification document - Consultation with stakeholders

Step 2: Choosing the right WMS solution
Evaluating WMS options:

- Researching different WMS vendors, comparing features, pricing, scalability and support in order to implement the best option in SMEs.

    Demonstrations and testing:

- Trying out the program to assess usefulness and functionality.

    Selecting a suitable system:

- Choosing a solution that aligns with your business size, goals and budget (Table 4).

Table 4. Choose the right WMS solution.

No.	Objectives	Examples
1	Evaluate the WMS solutions available on the market and adapt them in-house	- On-premise vs. cloud solutions - Commercial vs. customized solutions
2	Comparison of solutions and establishment of criteria	- Purchased program costs (license, maintenance) - In-house develop program costs - Specific customization (inventory management, batch tracking)
3	Evaluation of the features of each available solution	- Inventory automation - Integration with ERP and other software or devices

(*continued*)

Table 4. (*continued*)

No.	Objectives	Examples
4	Evaluate the ability of the software to adapt to business growth	- Ability to manage larger volumes - Possibility of adding additional modules
5	Understanding the user interface and user experience	- Hands-on evaluation with users to establish ease of use
6	Analyzing other users' reviews and experiences	- Case studies
7	Check the level of support offered by the provider	- 24/7 availability of technical assistance - Documenting and learning resources
8	Establishing contract terms and prices with the chosen supplier	- Clarifying terms and conditions of use - Check cancellation terms and guarantees

Step 3: Developing and implementing process plan
Evaluating WMS options:

- Researching different WMS vendors, comparing features, pricing, scalability and support in order to implement the best option in SMEs.

  Demonstrations and testing:

- Trying out the program to assess usefulness and functionality.

  Selecting a suitable system:

- Choosing a solution that aligns with your business size, goals and budget (Table 5).

Table 5. Developing and implementing process.

No.	Objectives	Examples
1	Establish a timeframe for each stage of implementation	- Identify deadlines for each stage - Establish regular meetings and reviews
2	Assessment of resources needed (human, technical, financial)	- Select the project team (project manager, IT, users) - Allocation of estimated budget for implementation and training
3	Configure the WMS according to the defined requirements	- Customize the interface and workflows
4	User training sessions and documentation	- Training for the use of WMS
5	Performing tests to verify system operation	Verifying integration with existing systems

(*continued*)

Table 5. (*continued*)

No.	Objectives	Examples
6	Deploy in a restricted area first	- Follow up user feedback
7	Collect feedback and adjust the system	- Evaluate performance and processes by implementing user recommendations
8	Deploy the full implementing WMS solution in all departments	- Transparent communication with all employees about the changes
9	Establish a plan for ongoing support and monitoring of system performance	- Regular assessment of WMS effectiveness - Ongoing technical support and updates

Step 4: Migrate and Prepare Data
Clean and organize current data:

- Ensure existing inventory data and processes are accurate and organized to ease the transition.

Migrating data to the new system:

- Transfer inventory levels, locations and other relevant data into the new WMS.

Conduct testing:

- Test the new system with sample data to identify and resolve any problems before going live (Table 6).

Table 6. Migration and data preparation.

No.	Objectives	Examples
1	Determine all data sources containing relevant information for the WMS	- Spreadsheets, company stock databases
2	Evaluate the quality of existing data to eliminate errors or gaps	- Check for incomplete or incorrect data and clean it up
3	Establish standardized format and structures for the data to be migrated	- "Data management" [16] types (e.g. text, numeric)
4	The actual gathering of data from existing sources for migration	- Data integrity checks during extraction
5	Transforming data to meet newly defined standards	- Converting data types, changing structures
6	Transfer data into the new WMS	- Check the upload process to ensure its success
7	Verification that the migrated data is correct and complete	- Comparison of the data from the original source with the WMS

(*continued*)

Table 6. (continued)

No.	Objectives	Examples
8	Documentation of the steps followed in migrating data for future reference	- Recording difficulties encountered and solutions applied
9	Train users to the new WMS	- Provide data training sessions

Step 5: Train employees.
Develop a training program:

- Create a comprehensive training plan for all employees who will use the WMS.

  Hands-on training:

- Provide opportunities for employees to practice using the new system in a controlled environment.

  Ongoing Support:

- Establish ongoing support resources for troubleshooting and questions after implementation (Table 7).

Table 7. Employee training.

No.	Objectives	Examples
1	Establishment of training goals and outcomes	- Increase employee's skills in the use of WMS before go live
2	Selection users for training	- Warehouse users and IT manager
3	Selection of resources and materials needed for training	- Create manual standard instructions, quick guides, PowerPoint presentations
4	Scheduling training sessions before go live	- Presentations in the warehouse in a certain interval of sessions
5	Actual delivery of training sessions as planned	- Practical exercises to apply the acquired knowledge
6	Evaluation of the effectiveness of the training	- Practical assessments to test the acquired skills
7	Update training materials according to the feedback received	- Improve materials to meet the needs of operators
8	Tracking employee performance and adapting training manual	- Evaluating employee performance in using the WMS

Step 6: Launch the new program in use
System implementation:

- Launch the WMS and formally transition warehouse operations to the new system.

Performance monitoring:

- Closely monitor key performance indicators (KPIs) and feedback to users for any post-launch issues.

Repeat and Improve:

- Use the information gathered during the launch phase to make adjustments and improvements to the system and processes (Table 8).

Table 8. Initiate the new software program.

No.	Objectives	Examples
1	Set a date and a detailed plan for the launch of the WMS system	- Define a timetable and establish team responsibilities
2	Making employees aware of the system launch and its benefits	- Internal briefings, emails and presentations
3	Final testing to ensure that the system is working as expected	- Verify the functionality of all WMS modules
4	Testing the program with a small number of users	- Testing under realistic conditions before full launch
5	Ensuring the required data is properly migrated into the new program	- Verifying the integrity of migrated data and confirming its accessibility by users
6	Instaling the WMS system for all departments involved	- Providing access to all departments and announcing the go live
7	Establishing the necessary technical support for users	- Creating a dedicated technical support team and communication channel
8	Monitor the system and its use by employees	- Analyze performance indicators to assess the effectiveness of the WMS
9	Implement necessary changes based on user feedback	- System updates to improve user experience

3.3 Critical Points for Successful WMS Implementation

Scalability:

- Choosing a system that can be optimized to grow with your business.
- Change Management:
- Preparing employees for the changes the new system will bring, addressing any resistance and fostering a culture of adaptability and flexibility to overcome employee comfort barriers. Utilizing communicating the benefits and involving employees in the implementation process to encourage acceptance.

Regular review and updates:

- Regular review by monitoring WMS performance and updating it as needed to adapt to changing business needs.

By following these steps, SMEs can optimize inventory management, improve order accuracy and increase operational efficiency, ultimately leading to increased competitiveness and customer satisfaction. Investing in a WMS not only improves day-to-day operations, but also positions the business for future growth and scalability (Table 9).

Table 9. Critical points for a successful implementation.

No.	Objectives	Examples
1	Establish specific and measurable objectives for WMS implementation	- Reduce order processing time by 50% and increase inventory accuracy by at least 25%
2	Ensuring management support and commitment	- Establishing and involving managers in planning meetings
3	Assess the specific needs of the organization prior to WMS implementation	- Identify existing workflows and work with employees to clearly understand the issues
4	Selectin the WMS modules system that fits the needs of the organization	- Implementing material traceability in the company
5	Create a step-by-step implementation plan	- Identify critical points and develop contingency plans such as establishing a timetable with deadlines and responsibilities
6	Appropriate training for system users	- Interactive training sessions and support materials
7	Ensuring the correctness of the data required for migration	- Verification of post-migration tests as well as data quality and integrity
8	Conduct extensive testing to verify WMS functionality prior to launch	- Stress and performance tests to evaluate the system
9	Providing technical support and resources for users	- Creating a dedicated support team for questions and establishing a reporting system
10	Evaluate the performance of the WMS and adjust it based on feedback	- Collect performance and "analyze the data" [13]

4 Possible Results of Using the WMS System

Within three months, stock accuracy could reach a minimum of 90%, this could be achieved not only by entering data into the system, but weekly it will be necessary to re-enter into the system or re-check what is scripted and physically in the addresses in the warehouse, also the order processing time will also decrease from 60 min to 20 min, which will lead to increased customer satisfaction and increase in sales (Table 10).

Table 10. WMS software usage results.

No.	Objectives	Possible advantages
1	Improved processing times for logistics tasks	- Reduce order-to-taking times by up to 50% and delivery times by 20%
2	Increase accuracy in inventory management and updating	- Increase inventory accuracy to 90% or more and eliminate 50% of picking errors
3	Improve costs by streamlining warehousing and distribution processes	- Reduce operating costs by 15–20% - Reducing the number of delivery complaints
4	Ability to adapt processes to changing market requirements	- Ability to handle volume increases without affecting performance as well as rapid implementation of new products
5	Quick access to stock, sales and operational performance data	- Generate real-time reports for management
6	Reducing risks for expired products	- Successful implementation of the FIFO (First In, First Out) system

4.1 The Benefits of Implementing a WMS

Optimize time:

- Optimize time spent searching for materials in the warehouse, reduce inventory and order preparation time for the production area, quick stock check.

  Optimize costs:

- Optimize labor costs through automation and reduce costs of excess material in the warehouse.

  Increase customer satisfaction:

- Optimize order accuracy and fulfillment speed, resulting in better customer experiences.

  Increased efficiency in inventory management:

- Improving and preventing out-of-stock situations and optimizing overstock turnover rates (Table 11).

Table 11. Benefits of implementing a WMS software program.

No.	Objectives	Advantages
1	WMS automates receiving, warehousing, picking and shipping processes	Reduce discrepancies

(continued)

Table 11. (continued)

No.	Objectives	Advantages
2	Monitors stock levels in real time, ensuring efficient stock management	Reduces overstocking and stock-outs
3	Enables every product to be traced from receipt to delivery	Improves material processing transparency and compliance
4	Optimize warehouse space utilization through storage technologies	It can improve shelf storage
5	Can integrate with ERP, TMS and other software	Improves information flow and management decisions
6	Provides detailed stock reports	Helps make informed strategic decisions

This work is in progress, so at this moment we have reached 4 of the 7 steps necessary to implement a management system in a small enterprise, the next steps to be accomplished are:

- Identification of an SME type company in the CMA for practical experimentation; It should be mentioned that at this moment we have agreed the partnership with a small enterprise and documentation will follow to discover its needs regarding this management system.
- Research on the certification of such a management system applicable to SMEs in the CMA;
- Implementation of the management system and identification of the problems encountered, prioritization of the causes by statistical-mathematical methods and establishment of functional cause-effect relationships based on statistical processing of the results.

5   Current Paper Conclusions

SMEs in Romania account for 99% of the number of SMEs registered with the state, however their adaptability to modern technologies is at a rather low level due to the fact that they are too expensive for small and medium sized SMEs to implement them for business development, and the stressful environment of the last 5 years starting with the pandemic, continuing with inflation and the war of aggression on our border has only exacerbated the financial and operational difficulties.

To improve the financial situation small and medium sized SMEs need to implement a minimum core system.

In addition, even a basic management program will offer a reduction in the percentage of risks to which businesses are exposed, starting with financial, operational, compliance, technological, reputation.

Controlling the costs of running the business becomes critical and therefore the need to implement a system as such. Implementing a WMS system will assure increased stock efficiencies, reduced costs, and improved customer satisfaction.

To implement a WMS will be critical to follow all the steps like define requirements and objectives, evaluate the most efficient solution, and develop an implementation plan, prepare data migration, prepare data migration.

Ongoing training of employees before and after the launch of the management software is very important.

The idea of this paper is to show the benefits of implementing a Warehouse Management System (WMS) starting from the assumption of optimizing the storage and distribution processes which will in turn lead to improved financial performance for SMEs that will implement a WMS. The WMS is a software tool that facilitates the automation of operations through inventory management and accuracy between physical and electronic stock. As the business grows, by implementing a WMS system will lead to an accuracy of approximately 90% as well as a reduction in the time it takes to prepare materials to be given to the production line.

To conclude, this topic is a complex one and this paper is a research and analysis of the first four steps necessary in the WMS implementation process.

The last three steps:

- identifying a company for practical experiment
- implementation of the WMS software
- certifying a WMS software in a SME

To be the subject of an upcoming addition (Part 2).

References

1. Prof. univ. dr. Ciprian NICOLESCU, Conf. univ. dr. Elisabeta-Emilia HALMAGHI, Prof. univ. dr. Cezar SIMION, Prof. univ. dr. Dan MIRICESCU , Daniel URÎTU, Dragoş PUFULETE, Camelia CRISTOF, Cătălina VOICU, Dumitru VIERU. CARTA ALBĂ A IMM -URILOR DIN ROMÂNIA, RAPORT DE CERCETARE NR.22 (2024)
2. Ivanov, D.: Viable supply chain model: integrating agility, resilience and sustainability perspectives - lessons from and thinking beyond the COVID-19 pandemic (2020)
3. Kgakatsi, M., Galeboe, O.P., Molelekwa, K.K., Thango, B.A.: The impact of big data on SME performance: a systematic review (2024)
4. Bruse, H., Maiken, L., Elly, B., Travasso, K.: Real-time financial fraud detection for small and medium-sized enterprises (SMEs): investigating the potential of cloud-based solution (2025)
5. Christopher, M.: Logistics & supply chain management (2016)
6. Mariotti, I.: Transport and Logistics in a Globalizing WorldMentzer (2014)
7. Chen, H., Damian, M.A.E.: Warehouse management information system technology review (2024)
8. Ayokunle, Y., Shukla, N., Rahman, T., Chakraborty, S., Kumari, S.: The performance evaluation of digital technologies in warehouse management: a systematic literature review (2024)
9. Min, H.: The applications of warehouse management systems: an exploratory study (2007)
10. Crişan, E., Afrăsinei-Zevoianu, C., Crişan-Mitra, C., Stegerean, R.: Managementul riscurilor organizaţionale (2018)
11. GuvernulRomâniei POCA. Metodologie De Management Al Riscurilor
12. McFarlane, D.A.: The strategic importance of customer value (2013)
13. Sharabati, A.A.A., Ali, A., Allahham, M., eh Mohammad. The Impact of Digital Marketing on the Performance of SMEs: An Analytical Study in Light of Modern Digital Transformations

14. Abdallah, S., Shatat, A.: The impact of business intelligence on decision-making process and customer service (2024)
15. European Commission. Annual Report on European SMEs 2020/2021.European Union (2020)
16. Mohamad, S.H., Othman, N.A., Jabar, J., Majid, I.A., Kamarudin, M.F.: The impact of customer relationship management on small and medium enterprises performance (2014)
17. Harrison, A., van Hoek, R.: Logistics management and strategy: competing through the supply chain (2020)

An Artificial General Intelligence Enabled Supply Chain Framework for CO2 Emission Reduction

Mohammad Reza Rezaei, Sridhar Iyer, Sripathy Kathiresan Tamilselvan, and Omid Fatahi Valilai[✉]

School of Business, Social and Decision Sciences, Constructor University Bremen, Campus Ring 1, 28759 Bremen, Germany
OFatahiValilai@Constructor.university
https://constructor.university/

Abstract. This study explores the development of an Artificial General Intelligence (AGI) enabled framework aimed at reducing CO2 emissions globally over the supply chain. While traditional Artificial Intelligence (AI) has been instrumental in addressing inefficiencies and optimizing supply chain processes, its dependency on predefined parameters and static environments limits its adaptability. The AGI framework provides a transformative solution by autonomously learning, reasoning, and generalizing strategies across diverse supply chain scenarios, enabling dynamic decision-making and real-time optimization without human intervention. The proposed framework integrates AGI into supply chain management to enhance operational efficiency and align with sustainability goals. By leveraging AGI for clustering, dynamic routing, the study demonstrates how carbon footprints can be significantly reduced across supply chain nodes. Illustrative examples highlight AGI's ability to identify inefficiencies, adapt to changing conditions, and foster sustainable practices, creating a flexible and scalable framework adaptable to various industries.

Keywords: Artificial General Intelligence (AGI) · Artificial Intelligence · Clustering · Routing Solution · Supply Chain · Carbon Footprint Reduction

1 Introduction

The global supply chain significantly contributes to CO2 emissions, reflecting industrial priority for innovative solutions towards sustainability [12,26]. Decarbonizing the supply chains has the potential to make a significant impact and change the path of global climate action. Especially in customer sectors where a company's direct emission footprint is relatively low, companies can address significantly larger emission volumes through their supply chains [8,28]. Every node in the supply chain can contribute to the CO2 emissions, including both the suppliers from whom companies procure goods or services and customers to whom the company provides goods or services [5]. In the words of Randrianarisoa and Gillen [18,27], the supply chain network extends the

J. Barata et al. (Eds.): IN4PL 2025, CCIS 2826, pp. 41–54, 2026.
https://doi.org/10.1007/978-3-032-15579-5_3

global trade majority with the contribution towards CO2 emissions due to manufacturing, transportation, and logistics. Due to the complexity resulting from the multitude of parameters at play considering the CO2 footprint in the supply chains, using innovative tools like AI and related interoperability models for the analysis and provision of applicable solutions is a necessity [10]. There is an abundance of studies that try to address these challenges using AI models.

The problem with the common AI models is that their overall efficiency depends on the quality of the input data, which when compromised, affects the detecting capability of the system [2]. AI systems are designed to handle limited data, which results in restrictions in their performance. Currently, AI has many challenges such as learning, reasoning, perception, decision-making, problem-solving, and creativity [19]. As these issues are not restricted to the application of the AI models in supply chains and are faced in applying AI systems in other complex environments like education [14], agriculture [16] and health care scheduling systems [30]. Using a more powerful version of the AI models which is usually referred to as *"Artificial General Intelligence"* models has been proposed [4]. Artificial General Intelligence (AGI) is a distributed formation of conventional AI due to its ability to manage tasks without specifying programs [29]. While conventional AI systems focus on performing a specific task, such as answering questions based on user input or playing chess, AGI can perform various functions, eventually teaching itself to solve new problems. AI relies on human interference to define the parameters of its learning algorithms and to provide the relevant training data to ensure accuracy, which is mitigated in the case of AGI systems since it develops human-like reasoning instead of simulating [18]. Due to its flexibility, Artificial General Intelligence (AGI) can undertake supply chain optimization over different environmental goals and operations [7, 17]. AGI can ensure effective and sustainable logistic operations to decrease the level of carbon emissions through autonomous data analysis and execute real-time solutions within the context of the supply chain [6]. By harnessing AGI, the supply chain can respond effectively towards more sustainable activities on a large scale. Considering the AGI-based solutions provided for other disciplines, and regarding their power to provide solutions for complex issues, this study is going to analyze its applicability for CO2 reduction in supply chains through providing a general structure of an AGI system that can handle the crucial parameters at play. Specific research questions are:

1. Is it feasible to develop a framework for Artificial General Intelligence (AGI) that can assist the global supply chain in diminishing carbon dioxide (CO2) emissions?
2. What are the basic structures of the issues that have been solved using AGI models in other disciplines?
3. What strategies can be employed to develop a framework for the implementation of an AGI model with the objective of reducing CO2 emissions?

2   Literature Review

2.1   Artificial General Intelligence (AGI)

When machines are capable enough to accomplish all human activities, this type of AI is recognized as AGI [3]. Basically, AGI consists of the abilities that can work and provide the best results in all fields. However, as observed by researchers [31], artificial general intelligence (AGI) can be utilized to improve problem-solving ability. On the other hand, studies like [17] observed that artificial general intelligence can exceed human intelligence and is recognized as the next generation of artificial intelligence. Another study observed that it took more than 30 years for the AGI community to create theoretical underpinnings for AGI along with affiliated working software systems. Therefore, practitioners are consistently working for new and emerging AGI technologies by considering real-life complicated issues. Alternatively, it has been observed that AGI is a new form of AI prompted by AI experts and tech giants. In accordance with the views of [15], the role of Large Language Models in the evolution of AGI is considerable. Once developed properly, AGI can enable a supply chain framework for CO2 emissions.

It has been observed that AI has numerous applications and benefits in making supply chain more resilient along with the creation of a supply chain framework for CO2 emissions. In terms of sustainability, AI can be applied in areas of the supply chain including procurement, inventory, logistics, and more. As per the views and observations of a study [20], AIoT deployment in the supply chain helps to manage inventory and minimises waste, which ultimately contributes to sustainable goals. On the other hand, studies like [11], assessed that robotic processes and artificial intelligence (AI) can shape the landscape of sustainable procurement uniquely. In accordance with the views of [25], Machine Learning, a subset of AGI, can help to eliminate deadheading as a typical logistics issue. Furthermore, the incorporation is not only focused on improving efficiency but also addressing environmental issues (CO2) and strengthening organisational focus on sustainability [24], observed that the incorporation AGI can help to redefine opportunities and issues in the sustainable supply chain. However, [23] stated that AI application in supply chain finance can make the process more sustainable and effective for organisations.

As observed by [31], AGI models are extremely effective in general problem solving in a given context. In accordance with the views of [15], technological capabilities of AGI are also beneficial for social purposes and a greater cause. The study of [15], observed that AGI prompts creativity, cultural values and knowledge and henceforth this is a greater opportunity for people who belong to the Art and Humanities field. [22], assessed that the use of AGI can help organisations to integrate sustainable production principles. On the other hand, issues with ethics and transparency are associated with AI integration. Henceforth, authors including [1], are consistently working on ethics in the field of AGI. According to these authors, these are the major trends in AI ethics. From a perspective of security and safety, [13], opined and assessed that integrating AI in cyber security to streamline security is also a big trend in the industrial landscape.

- Artificial general intelligence (AGI) is a type of artificial intelligence (AI) that matches or surpasses human cognitive capabilities across a wide range of cognitive tasks. This contrasts with narrow AI, which is limited to specific tasks.
- Artificial intelligence (AI), in its broadest sense, is intelligence exhibited by machines, particularly computer systems. It is a field of research in computer science that develops and studies methods and software that enable machines to perceive

their environment and use learning and intelligence to take actions that maximize their chances of achieving defined goals.

2.2   Literature Gap Analysis

Existing AGI Applications Outside the Supply-Chain Domain. Lu et al. [16] show how AGI-driven real-time analytics, image recognition, language processing and autonomous robotics can lift agricultural yields while countering climate-change threats to food security. Latif et al. [14] highlight comparable promise for education, where human-like reasoning could personalise curricula and automate complex assessments, provided robust ethical safeguards and teacher–engineer collaboration are in place. Dou et al. [6] extend the discussion to the Internet of Things, arguing that AGI can unlock smart-grid optimisation, precision healthcare and data-rich farming, but only if resource constraints, device coordination and cyber-security risks are resolved.

AI Models Already Deployed Within Supply Chains. Recent work pivots from general AGI to narrower AI techniques that strengthen supply-chain responsiveness and resilience. Olan et al. [23] use fuzzy-set theory to show how AI can streamline supply-chain-finance workflows in the wake of the 2008 crisis and COVID-19 shocks. Wong et al. [32] combine PLS-SEM (Partial Least Squares Structural Equation Modeling) with artificial-neural-network analysis to reveal that AI integration helps SMEs absorb environmental turbulence, albeit in one regional context. Akinrinola et al. [1] foreground the ethical side, proposing explainable-AI and fairness metrics to mitigate bias, while Pasupuleti et al. [25] demonstrate that machine-learning forecasts improve inventory and logistics, yet fall short of tackling systemic, economy-wide bottlenecks. Jentsch et al. [11] add a sustainability lens, finding that blockchain, AI and robotic-process automation can jointly advance greener textile procurement when viewed through socio-technical-system theory.

Toward System-Wide Carbon-Mitigation Frameworks. Fewer studies examine AI for holistic CO_2 abatement. Nahr et al. [20] present an AIoT blueprint that promises real-time tracking and predictive analytics but lacks sector-specific pilots and quantified climate benefits. Hasan et al. [9] draw on legacy USEPA (United States Environmental Protection Agency) emission factors to model high-emission scenarios, signalling the need for fresher data, while Naz et al. [21] synthesise journal evidence into a SSC (sustainable supply chain) framework that remains untested beyond the literature.

Positioning this Research This papaer addresses these gaps by applying AGI's adaptive, autonomous reasoning to global supply-chain optimisation with CO_2 reduction as the primary performance metric. Unlike prior region-specific, technology-siloed or dated-dataset approaches, we couple up-to-the-minute emission data with cross-sector case studies, enabling scalable, end-to-end carbon minimisation while navigating the ethical and organisational complexities highlighted in earlier work.

3   Proposed Solution

3.1   Conceptual Model of Agents, System Elements Interacting with Each Other

To address the research gap in the conceptual modeling of AGI applications for CO2 emission reduction through the supply chain model (shown in Fig. 1), this paper proposes the development of a multi-agent-based Artificial General Intelligence (AGI) system.

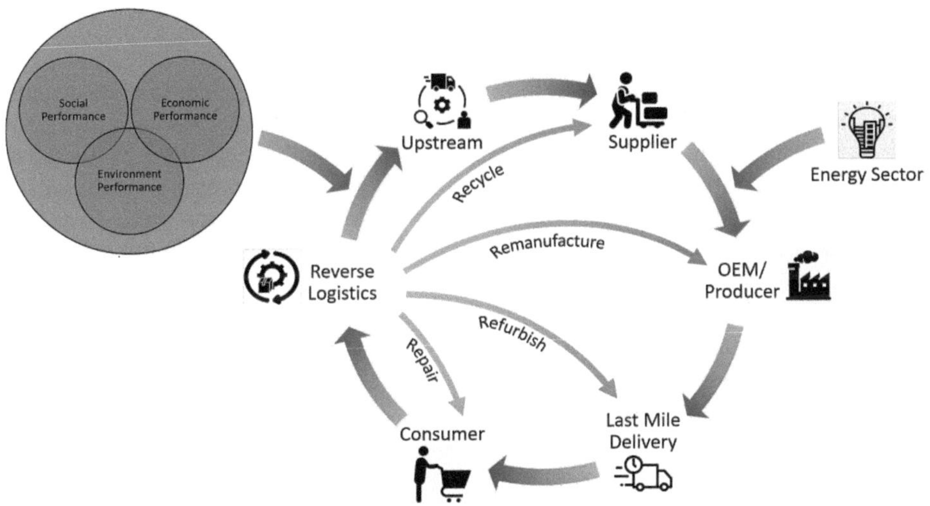

Fig. 1. Supply Chain Cycle Process.

This system leverages AGI's ability to generalize knowledge across diverse domains and expand it to relevant cases within the supply chain context, thereby improving operational efficiency and sustainability through:

1. Multi-Agent Collaboration: The system employs a network of specialized AGI agents, each tasked with monitoring and optimizing different aspects of the supply chain, such as transportation, inventory management, manufacturing, and logistics. These agents can collaborate and share learned insights to develop comprehensive solutions across interconnected operations.
2. Generalization Across Domains: Unlike traditional AI models that are limited to specific tasks, the proposed AGI system adapts to varying environmental goals and operational challenges. It autonomously transfers knowledge gained from one supply chain node to another, enhancing decision-making for complex, multi-parameter systems.
3. Autonomous Learning and Reasoning: By developing human-like reasoning capabilities, the AGI system eliminates the dependency on predefined algorithms and extensive human intervention. The system continuously refines its approach by learning from real-time data, historical trends, and simulated scenarios.

4. Real-Time Optimization: The system integrates dynamic analysis tools to optimize transportation routes, manufacturing schedules, and inventory levels in real-time, minimizing carbon emissions while ensuring operational efficiency.
5. Sustainability-Driven Solutions: AGI agents are equipped with modules to prioritize sustainability, balancing cost-efficiency with environmental goals. They evaluate carbon footprints at each supply chain stage, recommending actionable strategies to reduce emissions, such as route optimization, transitioning to renewable energy sources, and inventory streamlining.

3.2 Detailed Framework Solution

The proposed framework as shown in Fig. 2 envisions a supply chain loop connecting every component to ensure the efficient flow of materials from raw material extraction to end-user consumption. The process starts with upstream activities, where raw materials are extracted in response to consumer demand. Suppliers transport these materials to manufacturers, who use energy resources to produce finished goods. The goods are then delivered to end-users through last-mile delivery, closing the traditional supply chain loop. To address growing environmental concerns, reverse logistics integrates the 4Rs—Recycle, Remanufacture, Refurbish, and Repair—into the supply chain. In open-loop systems, recycled materials re-enter the upstream phase and flow through the process again. In closed-loop systems, recycled consumables are returned to producers as raw materials, supporting sustainable manufacturing. Products nearing the end of their life cycle can be re-manufactured, refurbished for extended use, or repaired to ensure continued functionality. The efficiency of the supply chain is assessed using three critical metrics: Social, Economic, and Environmental performance. This framework introduces Artificial General Intelligence (AGI) to enhance supply chain management by enabling seamless, autonomous operations with minimal waste.

AGI surpasses traditional AI with its cognitive capabilities, allowing for autonomous decision-making and real-time data processing without human intervention. It dynamically collects data from digitalized sources like sensors, devices, and databases. Key Performance Indicators (KPIs) serve as constraints for AGI to evaluate performance and generate optimized strategies for reducing CO_2 emissions. AGI utilizes three core components:

Interpreter: Facilitates seamless communication between AI agents by converting data into a standardized format using a structured ontology.

Knowledge Base: Serves as a centralized repository of solutions, storing best practices and strategies for reuse across different scenarios.

Autonomous Learning: Enables AGI to refine its methods over time, applying previously successful strategies to new challenges.

The flowchart in Fig. 3 illustrates the collaborative operation of multiple AI agents in addressing issues across different areas of a supply chain. Initially, a specific problem, such as Issue 1 in Area 1, is identified and handled by a Local AI Agent 1, which proposes Solution 1. This solution is processed through an Interpreter, which converts it into a standardized format using the Ontology Base for consistency and ensures its applicability across various components. The solution is also stored in the Knowledge Base, creating a repository for future use. Similarly, Local AI Agent 2 in Area

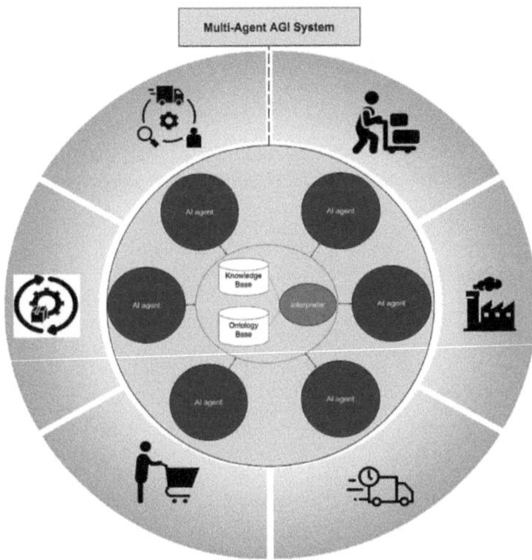

Fig. 2. Performances of AGI in Supply Chain.

2 addresses Issue 2 and proposes Solution 2, following the same process of validation and storage. Feedback on Solution 1 triggers an iterative loop where the interpreter integrates the solution into other local AI agents, such as Agent 2, Agent 3, and Agent 4, enabling cross-functional collaboration and optimization. This approach ensures that validated solutions from one area can be dynamically applied and adapted to other areas, enhancing efficiency. The ontology base and interpreter work as critical components, ensuring seamless communication and knowledge sharing between agents. This iterative process promotes autonomous learning, continuous improvement, and scalability across the system.

3.3   The Role of Artificial General Intelligence in Supply Chain

The role of AGI in the proposed model is to analyze and facilitate the transfer of principles, strategies, and optimizations from one scenario to another, ensuring their relevance and effectiveness. For example, the tactics employed in last-mile delivery can be adapted to optimize inbound logistics. AGI serves as the validation and verification mechanism, evaluating whether these tactics can be effectively translated across scenarios.

1. Grouping for Efficiency: In last-mile delivery, grouping households geographically enables efficient route planning. Similarly, in inbound logistics, grouping supplier shipments for combined transport can reduce fuel consumption and optimize load capacity. AGI evaluates the effectiveness of this tactic in reducing costs and emissions across scenarios.
2. Dynamic Route Adjustments: Real-time route changes based on environmental factors are crucial in both contexts. In last-mile delivery, AGI adjusts routes based on traffic conditions, whereas in inbound logistics, the model considers factors like weather or road closures to optimize long-haul transportation.

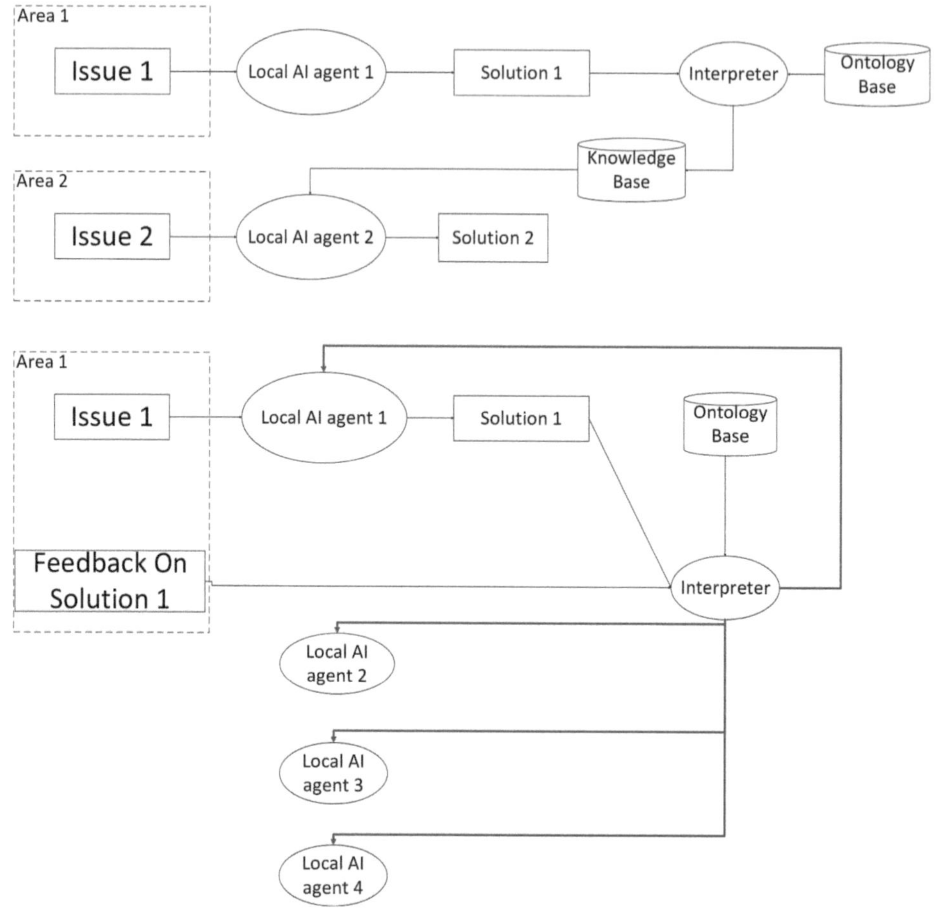

Fig. 3. Flowchart.

3. Prioritizing Shipments: Prioritization ensures timely handling of critical items. In last-mile delivery, urgent orders are delivered first, while in inbound logistics, AGI prioritizes critical shipments, such as perishable goods, ensuring they arrive on time without spoilage.
4. Vehicle Optimization for Sustainability: In last-mile delivery, energy-efficient vehicles like bikes or electric vans are employed to reduce emissions. For inbound logistics, AGI recommends vehicles with the lowest emissions, such as hybrid or electric trucks, for long-haul routes, balancing cost and sustainability.

Through these validations, AGI ensures that strategies optimized for last-mile delivery can be effectively adapted to inbound logistics, maintaining efficiency and aligning with the overarching goal of reducing CO_2 emissions across the supply chain.

The role of AGI in this model is to seamlessly integrate strategies and optimizations between after-sales management and consumer interactions in the production phase within the cyclic supply chain loop. By validating and verifying the adaptability of these strategies, AGI ensures that each phase informs and enhances the other, creating a cohesive and efficient system through:

1. Feedback Integration for Continuous Improvement: Customer feedback collected post-purchase is analyzed to address issues like product quality and performance. This information directly informs the production phase, where AGI identifies areas for improvement, such as enhancing durability or usability based on consumer preferences. By bridging the two stages, AGI ensures that products evolve to meet consumer expectations more effectively.
2. Resource Allocation and Demand Forecasting: After-sales data on common repair or replacement needs helps optimize inventory levels for spare parts and repair kits. Simultaneously, this data is used in production to predict future demand for critical components, enabling efficient resource allocation and reducing waste across the supply chain.
3. Dynamic Prioritization of Needs: Urgent consumer needs, such as warranty claims, are prioritized in after-sales management to ensure quick resolution. This prioritization framework extends to production, where AGI adjusts manufacturing schedules to focus on critical components in high demand, ensuring the supply chain remains responsive to consumer urgency.
4. Sustainability Across the Loop: Energy-efficient and recyclable materials used in after-sales packaging or product replacements inspire sustainable practices in production. Insights from recycling rates and waste management in after-sales operations guide the use of eco-friendly materials during manufacturing, creating a closed-loop system that minimizes environmental impact and supports circular economy principles.

By integrating these strategies across after-sales management and production, AGI creates a feedback-driven, resource-efficient, and sustainable supply chain loop. This ensures that consumer interactions at every stage enhance overall system performance while aligning with sustainability goals.

4 Illustrative Scenario

A dataset has been formulated comprising customer demand locations, inclusive of latitude and longitude, to simulate a vehicle routing problem (VRP) subject to the constraints imposed by two specified vehicle types (A and B) as shown in Fig. 4 where:

1. Vehicle Type A: Higher capacity but higher CO2 emissions per kilometer.
2. Vehicle Type B: Lower capacity but lower CO2 emissions per kilometer.

4.1 Initial Solution Without Clustering

In the initial solution, customers are assigned to vehicles sequentially based on demand, starting with the highest-demand customers. Vehicle A has a capacity of 150 kg, and Vehicle B has a capacity of 100 kg. Each vehicle serves customers until its capacity

Customer	Latitude	Longitude	Demand
1	38.7454	-119.686	11
2	44.50714	-113.636	17
3	42.31994	-116.856	8
4	40.98658	-114.914	4
5	36.56019	-110.924	6

95	42.70967	-116.61	17
96	39.93796	-116.508	10
97	40.22733	-112.74	6
98	39.27541	-111.029	15
99	35.25419	-111.129	11
100	36.07891	-112.201	5

Fig. 4. Snapshot of demand dataset.

is reached. For example: Vehicle A serves Customer 4 (Demand: 93) and Customer 70 (Demand: 57), fully utilizing its 150 kg capacity. Vehicle B serves Customer 24 (Demand: 86), leaving 14 kg of capacity unused. This method does not optimize routes or consider customer proximity, leading to higher CO_2 emissions due to inefficient vehicle routing.

Using Clustering to Reduce Transportation Cost: Clustering groups customers based on proximity (latitude and longitude) to optimize route efficiency. Customers are divided into two clusters: Cluster 0: Customers closer to a central point (e.g., Latitude: 53.07, Longitude: 8.80). Cluster 1: Customers farther away (e.g., Latitude: 53.07, Longitude: 7.99).

- Adjusted Assignment. Cluster 0 is assigned to Vehicle A: Customer 4 (Demand: 93) and Customer 70 (Demand: 57), fully utilizing 150 kg capacity. Cluster 1 is assigned to Vehicle B: Customer 24 (Demand: 86), leaving 14 kg unused but aligning customers by proximity.
- CO_2 Emissions Reduction. The clustering approach improves route efficiency by reducing the travel distance for each vehicle, thus lowering CO_2 emissions. By grouping customers based on geographic proximity and aligning assignments with vehicle capacity, clustering minimizes redundant travel and avoids excessive emissions.

The clustering approach reduces CO_2 emissions compared to the initial solution by optimizing routes and aligning vehicle assignments with customer locations. This demonstrates the critical role of clustering and route optimization in achieving environmentally sustainable and emission-efficient supply chain operations.

4.2   2nd Illustrative Case

Considering the dataset with customer, latitude, longitude, and the order. let's assume Vehicle A's capacity: 150, higher CO_2 emissions per kilometer due to larger size and Vehicle B's capacity: 100 lower CO_2 emissions per kilometer due to smaller size as shown in Fig. 5.

Solution Without Clustering. The results for the non-clustered (sequential) transportation approach are: Trips by Vehicle A: 5 trips. Trips by Vehicle B: 4 trips. Total Distance Traveled: 615.31 units. Estimated CO_2 Emissions: Higher, due to inefficient routing and more trips required.

	Customer_	Latitude	Longitude	Order			Customer_	Latitude	Longitude	Order
1						96	CUST_095	53.11565	8.734757	42
2	CUST_001	53.05618	8.657857	27		97	CUST_096	53.07407	8.737302	46
3	CUST_002	53.14261	8.809103	13		98	CUST_097	53.07841	8.831489	81
4	CUST_003	53.1098	8.728589	31		99	CUST_098	53.06413	8.874278	42
5	CUST_004	53.0898	8.777143	13		100	CUST_099	53.00381	8.871772	61
6	CUST_005	53.0234	8.876892	67		101	CUST_100	53.01618	8.844969	37

Fig. 5. Dataset with Order.

Solution with Clustering. Trips by Vehicle A: 4 trips. Trips by Vehicle B: 3 trips. Total Distance Traveled: 501.24 units. Estimated CO2 Emissions: Lower, due to optimized routing and reduced trips.

Impact of Clustering on CO2 Emissions:

Clustering reduces the total distance traveled by vehicles, leading to fewer trips and significantly lower CO2 emissions. By grouping customers based on geographic proximity, the approach not only minimizes redundant travel but also ensures that both vehicles operate closer to their full capacity, further enhancing their efficiency in terms of emissions. The clustering approach demonstrates a clear advantage in reducing CO2 emissions over the non-clustered solution. This highlights the importance of route optimization and proximity-based customer grouping in achieving environmentally sustainable supply chain operations.

4.3 Discussions of Results

The examples provided highlight the adaptability and efficiency of the AGI model in addressing complex logistics challenges. In Case 1, AI Agent 1 manually applies a clustering method to optimize delivery routes, minimizing CO2 emissions while factoring in vehicle capacities. This process incorporates customer feedback to refine the logical clustering, ensuring relevance and efficiency. Importantly, the insights and patterns derived are stored in a knowledge base, enabling the AGI framework to retain and reference these learnings for future applications.

In the 2nd illustrative Case, AI Agent 2 autonomously accesses the knowledge base, interprets the stored data, and applies the learned principles to optimize a new dataset with varying parameters, such as order sizes and geographic distributions. By leveraging the foundational clustering methodology from Case 1, the AGI model independently adjusts and improves the approach for Case 2, dynamically accommodating new variables without requiring manual intervention. This demonstrates the AGI model's ability to generalize strategies and implement them across distinct scenarios by learning from generated cases. The autonomous learning process highlights the model's capability to evolve its logic, improve accuracy, and streamline logistics operations. This adaptability significantly reduces operational inefficiencies, paving the way for effective CO2 emission reductions in the supply chain.

5 Conclusion

In conclusion, this study introduces an Artificial General Intelligence (AGI)-enabled framework as an advanced solution to reduce CO2 emissions within global supply chains. While traditional Artificial Intelligence (AI) has been widely used to address inefficiencies and optimize supply chain processes, its effectiveness is often limited by its dependency on high-quality data, predefined parameters, and inability to adapt to dynamic environments autonomously. AGI, on the other hand, overcomes these limitations with its human-like reasoning, real-time adaptability, and capacity to learn and generalize strategies across diverse scenarios without human intervention. By integrating AGI into supply chain management, the framework not only enhances operational efficiency but also aligns with environmental goals through practices such as clustering and dynamic routing. This approach fosters a circular supply chain model that reduces carbon footprints across all nodes. While challenges such as infrastructure investments, data quality concerns, and ethical implications remain, the AGI framework's ability to autonomously optimize processes far surpasses the capabilities of conventional AI. Ultimately, this framework provides a transformative pathway for decarbonizing supply chains, offering a balanced solution that addresses environmental sustainability alongside operational resilience and cost-effectiveness.

To make the proposed framework even more effective, it could be enhanced by combining AGI with domain-specific AI models. This hybrid approach could deliver greater precision in tackling specific challenges like inventory optimization or last-mile delivery. Additionally, integrating blockchain technology could ensure secure and transparent data sharing across different parts of the supply chain, fostering trust and improving decision-making. We could also amplify the environmental benefits of the framework by incorporating renewable energy solutions, such as solar-powered transportation and facilities, optimized by AGI.

In addition to these improvements, other methods could work alongside the AGI framework. For example, advanced predictive analytics could help manage short-term supply and demand fluctuations, offering insights to refine AGI's decisions. Collaborative robots (cobots) could streamline material handling in warehouses, making operations more efficient. On a larger scale, shared transportation networks created through partnerships between companies could significantly cut emissions and costs by improving vehicle utilization and reducing empty runs. By adopting these enhancements and complementary strategies, the AGI framework could become even more powerful and adaptable, effectively balancing environmental sustainability with operational excellence.

References

1. Akinrinola, O., et al.: Navigating and reviewing ethical dilemmas in AI development: strategies for transparency, fairness, and accountability. GSC Adv. Res. Rev. **18**(3), 050–058 (2024). https://doi.org/10.30574/gscarr.2024.18.3.0088. https://gsconlinepress. com/journals/gscarr/content/navigating-and-reviewing-ethical-dilemmas-ai-development-strategies-transparency-fairness
2. Almashaleh, O., Wicaksono, H., Fatahi Valilai, O.: A framework for social media analytics in textile business circularity for effective digital marketing. J. Open Innov. Technol. Mark. Complex. **11**(2), 100544 (2025). https://doi.org/10.1016/j.joitmc.2025.100544
3. Buttazzo, G.: Rise of artificial general intelligence: risks and opportunities. Front. Artif. Intelli. **6** (2023).https://doi.org/10.3389/frai.2023.1226990. https://www.frontiersin. org/journals/artificial-intelligence/articles/10.3389/frai.2023.1226990/full
4. Danish, M.: AI and expert insights for sustainable energy future. Energies **16**, 3309 (2023)
5. Delaram, J., Houshamand, M., Ashtiani, F., Fatahi Valilai, O.: Development of public cloud manufacturing markets: a mechanism design approach. Int. J. Syst. Sci. Oper. Logist. **10**(1), 2079751 (2023). https://doi.org/10.1080/23302674.2022.2079751
6. Dou, F., et al.: Towards artificial general intelligence (agi) in the internet of things (iot): opportunities and challenges. arXiv preprint arXiv:2309.07438 (2023)
7. El Hajjami, S., Kaushik, K., Khan, I.U. (eds.): Artificial General Intelligence (AGI) Security: Smart Applications and Sustainable Technologies. Advanced Technologies and Societal Change. Springer, Singapore (2025). https://doi.org/10.1007/978-981-97-3222-7
8. Forum, W.E.: Net-zero challenge: The supply chain opportunity. Insight Report, p. 46 (2021)
9. Hasan, M.R., Islam, M.Z., Sumon, M.F.I., Osiujjaman, M., Debnath, P., Pant, L.: Integrating artificial intelligence and predictive analytics in supply chain management to minimize carbon footprint and enhance business growth in the USA. J. Bus. Manag. Stud. **6**(4), 195–212 (2024). https://doi.org/10.32996/jbms.2024.6.4.17. https://al-kindipublisher.com/index.php/ jbms/article/view/7753, number: 4
10. Houshmand, M., Valilai, O.F.: LAYMOD: a layered and modular platform for CAx product data integration based on the modular architecture of the standard for exchange of product data. Int. J. Comput. Integrat. Manuf. **25**(6), 473–487 (2012). https://doi.org/10.1080/ 0951192X.2011.646308
11. Jentsch, T.: Digitalisation for sustainability in procurement within the textile value chain: analysis of artificial intelligence, robotic process automation, and blockchain (2022). https:// urn.kb.se/resolve?urn=urn:nbn:se:hb:diva-28708
12. Kumar, A., Shrivastav, S., Adlakha, A., Vishwakarma, N.K.: Appropriation of sustainability priorities to gain strategic advantage in a supply chain. Int. J. Product. Perform. Manag. **71**(1), 125–155 (2022). https://doi.org/10.1108/IJPPM-06-2020-0298
13. Lad, S.: Cybersecurity trends: integrating AI to combat emerging threats in the cloud era. Integrat. J. Sci. Technol. **1**(8) (2024). https://ijstindex.com/index.php/ijst/article/view/60
14. Latif, E., et al.: AGI: artificial general intelligence for education (2024). arXiv:2304.12479
15. Liu, Z., et al.: Transformation vs Tradition: Artificial General Intelligence (AGI) for Arts and Humanities (2023). arXiv:2310.19626
16. Lu, G., et al.: AGI for Agriculture (2023). arXiv:2304.06136D
17. McLean, S., Read, G.J.M., Thompson, J., Baber, C., Stanton, N.A., Salmon, P.M.: The risks associated with artificial general intelligence: a systematic review. J. Exp. Theor. Artif. Intell. **35**(5), 649–663 (2023). https://doi.org/10.1080/0952813X.2021.1964003
18. Mofatteh, M.Y., Abbas, R., Seddoh, N.D., Sedhumadhavan, S., Thunyaluck, M., Valilai, O.F.: A smart adaptive transportation planning model including real-time drivers knowledge using answer set programming and knowledge graphs. Procedia Comput. Sci. **253**, 2358–2368 (2025). https://doi.org/10.1016/j.procs.2025.01.296

19. Mohammadian, N., Fatahi Valilai, O., Schl ter, A.: Sustainable design and repair: leveraging circular economy and machine learning for product development. J. Open Innov. Technol. Mark. Complexity **11**(1), 100469 (2025). https://doi.org/10.1016/j.joitmc.2025.100469. https://www.sciencedirect.com/science/article/pii/S2199853125000046

20. Nahr, J.G., Nozari, H., Sadeghi, M.E.: Green supply chain based on artificial intelligence of things (AIoT). Int. J. Innov. Manag. Econ. Social Sci. **1**(2), 56–63 (2021). https://doi.org/10.52547/ijimes.1.2.56. https://ijimes.ir/index.php/ijimes/article/view/18

21. Naz, F., Agrawal, R., Kumar, A., Gunasekaran, A., Majumdar, A., Luthra, S.: Reviewing the applications of artificial intelligence in sustainable supply chains: exploring research propositions for future directions. Bus. Strateg. Environ. **31**(5), 2400–2423 (2022). https://doi.org/10.1002/bse.3034

22. Obaid, O.I.: From machine learning to artificial general intelligence: a roadmap and implications. Mesopotamian J. Big Data **2023**, 81–91 (2023). https://doi.org/10.58496/MJBD/2023/012. https://mesopotamian.press/journals/index.php/bigdata/article/view/114

23. Olan, F., Arakpogun, E.O., Jayawickrama, U., Suklan, J., Liu, S.: Sustainable supply chain finance and supply networks: the role of artificial intelligence. IEEE Trans. Eng. Manag. **71**, 13296–13311 (2024). https://doi.org/10.1109/TEM.2021.3133104. https://ieeexplore.ieee.org/abstract/document/9669168

24. Pal, S.: Integrating AI in sustainable supply chain management: a new paradigm for enhanced transparency and sustainability. Int. J. Res. Appl. Sci. Eng. Technol. **11**, 2979–2984 (2023). https://doi.org/10.22214/ijraset.2023.54139

25. Pasupuleti, V., Thuraka, B., Kodete, C.S., Malisetty, S.: Enhancing supply chain agility and sustainability through machine learning: optimization techniques for logistics and inventory management. Logistics **8**(3), 73 (2024). https://doi.org/10.3390/logistics8030073

26. Radmanesh, S.A., Haji, A., Fatahi Valilai, O.: Blockchain-based architecture for a sustainable supply chain in cloud architecture. Sustainability **15**(11), 9072 (2023). https://doi.org/10.3390/su15119072

27. Randrianarisoa, L.M., Gillen, D.: Reducing emissions in international transport: a supply chain perspective. Transp. Res. Part D: Transp. Environ. **102**, 103074 (2022). https://doi.org/10.1016/j.trd.2021.103074

28. Sadeghi Aghili, S.A., Fatahi Valilai, O., Haji, A., Khalilzadeh, M.: Dynamic mutual manufacturing and transportation routing service selection for cloud manufacturing with multi-period service-demand matching. PeerJ Comput. Sci. **7**, e461 (2021). https://doi.org/10.7717/peerj-cs.461

29. Sithungu, S.P.: Adaptive Game Artificial Intelligence Dynamic Difficulty Balancing Using Symbiotic Game Agents. University of Johannesburg (South Africa) (2020)

30. Valizadeh, S., Fatahi Valilai, O., Houshmand, M.: Allocation and scheduling of digital dentistry services in a dental cloud manufacturing system. Int. J. Comput. Integr. Manuf. **35**(6), 645–661 (2022). https://doi.org/10.1080/0951192X.2021.1992668

31. Williams, A.E.: A model for artificial general intelligence. In: Goertzel, B., Panov, A.I., Potapov, A., Yampolskiy, R. (eds.) AGI 2020. LNCS (LNAI), vol. 12177, pp. 357–369. Springer, Cham (2020). https://doi.org/10.1007/978-3-030-52152-3_38

32. Wong, L.W., Tan, G.W.H., Ooi, K.B., Lin, B., Dwivedi, Y.K.: Artificial intelligence-driven risk management for enhancing supply chain agility: A deep-learning-based dual-stage PLS-SEM-ANN analysis. Taylor & Francis (2024), https://www.tandfonline.com/doi/abs/10.1080/00207543.2022.2063089

Developing an AI Enabled Operations Research Model for Adaptive, Resilience and Sustainable Dynamic Supply Chain

Mohammad Reza Rezaei, Pranjal Nagaraj Patil, Omkar Vishwas Patil, and Omid Fatahi Valilai[(✉)]

School of Business, Social and Decision Sciences, Constructor University Bremen, Campus Ring 1, 28759 Bremen, Germany
OFatahiValilai@Constructor.university
https://constructor.university/

Abstract. In the rapidly growing global markets, supply chains are facing issues like fluctuating demand, disruptions, and sustainability pressures, making the supply chains volatile and complex. Traditional supply chain management methods fail to address the dynamics behind these issues. This paper introduces a framework designed to enable traditional OR models with dynamic adaptability, resilience, and sustainability capabilities. This framework combines existing Enterprise Resource Planning (ERP) and Robotic Process Automation (RPA) systems with AI. By leveraging AI-enabled OR models and declarative modeling, the study introduces a framework for complex decision-making. The proposed framework will dynamically identify disruptions and inefficiencies based on various parameters, and with the help of Answer Set Programming (ASP), the model will be able to make decisions based on different scenarios and provide an optimized solution. This framework will overcome the lack of real-time responsiveness in supply chains. The proposed framework will enhance operational efficiency and make supply chains adaptive, resilient, and sustainable.

Keywords: Resilience · Sustainable · Enterprise Resource Planning (ERP) · Robotic Process Automation (RPA) · Operation Research Model · Answer Set Programming (ASP)

1 Introduction

In an increasingly complex and volatile global environment, supply chains face numerous challenges, including fluctuating demand, supply disruptions [27, 28], and the pressing need for sustainability [26]. Traditional supply chain management methods often fall short in addressing these issues, leading to inefficiencies, increased costs, and negative environmental impacts [13]. To alleviate these issues, many companies have implemented Enterprise Resource Planning (ERP) systems to create a clearer vision of the inter- and intra-company data and processes [2, 30]. Supply chain management focuses on coordinating activities across companies to effectively plan, source, produce, and deliver products to customers [10].

J. Barata et al. (Eds.): IN4PL 2025, CCIS 2826, pp. 55–68, 2026.
https://doi.org/10.1007/978-3-032-15579-5_4

The supply chains function within a dynamic environment shaped by unpredictable demand changes, unforeseen disruptions, and complex networks of entities [25,31]. This leads to various complexities, which are further escalated when we try to integrate the supply chain with resilience and sustainability [18]. However, there is a major drawback in these systems, as they lack flexibility and open interfaces [8,11,12]. On the other hand, automation has played a vital role in productivity growth over the last few decades. Automation has enabled the power to carry out tasks that were thought to be impossible at some point. The latest development in automation is software based automation, commonly known as Robotic Process Automation (RPA) [23]. RPA is the deployment of software to perform tasks that were once performed by humans [17]. This resembles a robot-like agent, as it takes over functions that were previously performed by humans [17,19]. The process of supplier selection, which is completely human-based, can be made more effective, productive, and automated using RPA [14]. Organizations can benefit from introducing RPA to the traditional ERP systems and help in reducing the human errors caused by the repetitive and tiring tasks by about 28 % [6,7].

Basically, the integration of RPA and ERP is going to serve as the foundation for a more sophisticated use of AI-enabled OR models in supply chain [14,17]. RPA will improve the efficiency, while AI and OR models will offer the advanced decision making that will be required for achieving better resilience and sustainability [13,23]. Integrating RPA and ERP will lead to a comprehensive approach to modern supply chain management while addressing issues such as fluctuating demand, supply chain disruptions, and the need for sustainable operations [13,18].

1.1 Research Objectives

This research seeks to explore the integration of AI-enabled operations research models in supply chain management to enhance adaptive resilience and sustainability. By leveraging AI's capabilities to facilitate supplier diversification and sustainable sourcing, it aims to enhance the supply chain continuity and sustainability towards the following Research Questions (RQ):

- RQ 1. What are the potential benefits in terms of sustainability and resilience using AI enabled adaptive OR models in supply chain management?
- RQ 2. What are the key challenges in implementing AI enabled OR model in supply chain and how to overcome these challenges?
- RQ 3. How can the AI and ML modules facilitate supplier diversification and sustainable sourcing to enhance supply chain continuity and sustainability (Geographical, Carbon footprint, Supply chain policies).

The integration of RPA with ERP systems will improve efficiency by automating repetitive tasks and minimizing errors. However, currently RPA lacks the ability to make decisions necessary for complex supply chain challenges such as demand fluctuations and disruptions. This gap can be filled by implementing AI-enabled OR models which will provide advanced predictive and prescriptive analysis. Combining ERP, RPA and AI-enabled models creates an adaptive supply chain which will effectively respond to various volatilities and complexities.

2   Literature Review

2.1   Enterprise Resource Planning (ERP), Robotic Process Automation (RPA) and It's Role in Supply Chain

ERP systems are widely used in various organizations as a way of integrating various aspects of a business' functions and processes in order to increase efficiency [2]. RPA is gaining widespread recognition for its ability to revolutionize supply chain management by automating routine rule-based tasks that were once handled manually by humans [17]. RPA can be implemented in various fields within the organizational structures of a company, including sales and marketing, payment and account management, and human resources [20]. The performance of the supply chain is essential for the success of an organization, as it includes a range of metrics that evaluate the efficiency and effectiveness of processes related to the production and distribution of goods [32]. Implementing RPA in the supply chain has enabled organizations to improve their efficiency by automating basic tasks such as order processing, invoice generation, and data entry [32]. Integrating RPA within the supply chain has shown a positive influence on inventory management, demand forecasting, and visibility of the supply chain [32]. Further development by integrating the traditional ERP with ERP will result in addressing various problems such as fluctuating demand, supply chain disruptions, and sustainable operations [18]. Together, these technologies will create a powerful synergy that will boost the agility and responsiveness of supply chains, which will lead to enhancing customer satisfaction and gaining a competitive edge [1, 24].

2.2   ERP and RPA Enabled AI Initiatives for Resilience and Sustainability

The ability of a supply chain network to proactively adapt and respond to any unexpected disruptions and challenges, while regaining the previous level of performance or even better [4, 12, 13, 18]. As supply chains have transformed due to globalization, which has led to more efficiency but at the same time has made the supply chains more vulnerable and disruptive [12]. These problems can be solved by enhancing the supply chain resilience by integrating advanced technologies such as Artificial Intelligence, Machine Learning, and IoT [12]. These AI techniques can interpret external data, learn from them, and use this learning to achieve specific goals [13].AI and Machine Learning have transformed supplier selection by enabling advanced data processing and pattern recognition. Techniques like neural networks and support vector machines can analyze large datasets to reveal complex relationships between supplier attributes and selection criteria [18].Various AI technologies can provide reliable and updated forecasts and real-time visibility [4]. AI-powered predictive analytics anticipate demand fluctuations, optimize inventory, and identify supply chain risks by analyzing historical data, market trends, and other key factors, enabling proactive operational adjustments and continuity [33]. AI now plays a pivotal role in navigating supply chain complexities, leveraging advanced algorithms and machine learning.AI can help to uncover hidden patterns and prevent disruptions within supply networks. Additionally, its real-time adaptability offers supply chains resilience against unpredictable challenges [3]. Due to the globalization of supply chains, the distance between two connections has significantly increased, which has resulted in increased carbon emissions [22]. The ever-growing supply chains have become more complex and interconnected, which has led to a need for more sustainable practices [21]. AI-driven supply chain optimization reduces resource usage across the entire network, minimizing the consumption of raw materials, water, and energy. By enhancing operational efficiency, AI supports both environmental sustainability and cost-effectiveness [3]. Sustainable sourcing and ethical procurement are vital to supply chain management, with AI playing a key role in upholding responsible practices. AI-powered algorithms evaluate suppliers based on sustainability, ethical labor standards, and environmental impact [21,35].

2.3   AI Enabled Declarative Modeling

With the rise of AI-enabled techniques, declarative modeling has gained attention, allowing developers to specify what they want to achieve rather than focusing on the steps to accomplish it [15]. Answer Set Programming (ASP) is a type of declarative programming specifically designed to tackle complex search problems [16]. ASP, also known as Disjunctive Logic Programming (DLP) under stable model semantics, is a robust formalism for Knowledge Representation and Reasoning [5]. ASP programs are composed of rules that resemble Prolog rules, but they rely on distinct computational mechanisms. These mechanisms are inspired by concepts that have driven the development of fast satisfiability solvers for propositional logic [16].ASP declarative representation formalism makes it easy to incorporate domain-specific information and constraints into the program, helping to avoid the generation of implausible solutions [9]. NeurASP is an extension of ASP that integrates neural networks, allowing for enhanced neural network training by incorporating ASP rules. This approach enables a neural network to learn not only from implicit correlations within the data but also from explicit, complex semantic constraints defined by the rules [34]. ASP has been used for Knowledge Representation and Reasoning (KRR), Planning and Scheduling, Bioinformatics, Robotics and Autonomous Systems, Natural Language Processing (NLP), Legal and Ethical Reasoning, Data Integration and Data Cleaning, Constraint Solving and Optimization [9]. The declarative programs serve as intermediate representations that intelligent systems can either receive directly from programmers or, ideally, learn and infer from natural interactions in the real world [15].

Most existing research in ASP concentrates on optimizing methods for solving ASP models in fields like robotics, scheduling, and bioinformatics. However, applying ASP to address supply chain management challenges remains largely unexplored. This work bridges that gap by leveraging ASP to improve decision-making processes within supply chain networks. Additionally, the incorporation of AI agents to dynamically modify ASP parameters presents an innovative approach, enhancing adaptability and responsiveness to disruptions.

2.4   Literature Gap Analysis

The research gaps identified across these studies underscore several channels for further scholarly inquiry, as illustrated in Table 1. This study is focusing on the supply chain as a whole instead of just customer management by leveraging real-time data for agile decision-making and predictive capabilities. Moreover, it suggests existing predictive analytics may not effectively incorporate dynamic external factors, and current systems tend to react to disruptions rather than predict and prevent them. The lack of interoperability limits their effectiveness in making real-time adjustments. While most of the ASP research focuses on optimization in fields like robotics and scheduling, with limited application to supply chain management. This work fills that gap by using ASP to enhance decision-making in supply chains. Moreover, integrating AI agents to dynamically adjust ASP parameters offers a novel solution, improving adaptability and responsiveness to disruptions.

3   Proposed Solution

Figure 1 is a traditional RPA system which emphasizes the sequential flow of processes across various stages in a supply chain. The process begins with Procurement, followed by the production stage, inventory management, customer service, and recycling. Each stage has a predefined list of KPIs. Each stage integrates RPA with ERP systems to streamline operations and efficiency. While Fig. 2 illustrates an AI-enabled supply chain system, building upon the traditional framework to introduce advanced decision-making capabilities. The core stages of the supply chain are retained and incorporated with a central AI-enabled declarative modeling system. This enhanced system uses AI for problem identification, highlighted by a red arrow, to detect inefficiencies or disruptions in the supply chain. The central module, powered by AI, combines data from various stages to develop intelligent solutions. Through alternative solutions, represented by a green arrow, the AI suggests optimal decisions for addressing challenges, improving processes, and achieving sustainability goals.

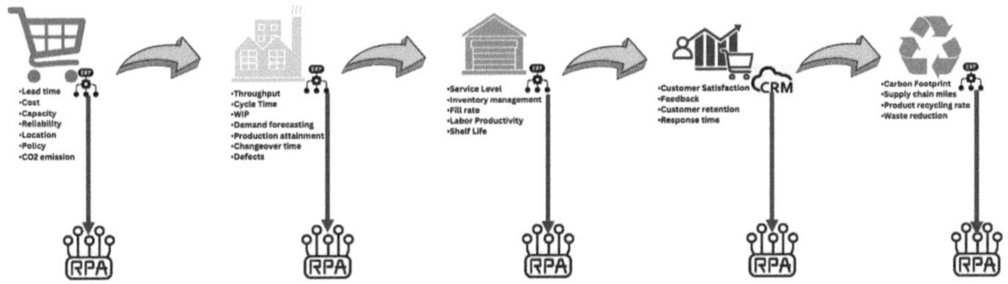

Fig. 1. Traditional Robotic Process Automation (RPA) system.

Figure 3 represents a dynamic, AI-powered problem-solving framework. It begins with problem detection, where the potential issue or disruption in the supply chain is detected. This stage is then followed by an AI-based problem definer, where the problem is analyzed on the basis of the detected issue, which is then framed in a structured

Table 1. Research Literature review.

Studies	RPA and it's role in supply chain	ERP and RPA enabled AI initiatives for resilience and sustainability	AI enabled declarative models
[2]	ERP is used to integrate various aspects of business		
[17]	RPA is used to automate repetitive task		
[24]	RPA has enhanced customer satisfaction		
[32]	RPA positive influence on inventory management		
[13, 18]	Integrating ERP and RPA has solved problems like fluctuating demands	Use of AI for supplier selection for resilient and sustainable supply chain	
[4]		AI technologies for reliable, updated and real time visibility	
[2]		Use of predictive analysis for fluctuating demands	
[3]		Navigating SC complexities using AI	
[12]		Integration of AI, ML and IoT for SC disruptions	
[3]		AI-driven optimization for sustainable supply chain	
[21]		AI-powered algorithms evaluate SC ESG impact	
[15]			AI enabled techniques for specifying goals
[16]			Used to tackle complex search problems
[16]			Composed of rules resembling Prolog
[5]			Formalism for Knowledge Representation
[9]			Incorporation of domain-specific information
[34]			Combines neural networks with ASP for enhanced learning
[9]			Used in multiple domains like KRR, Planning, Bioinformatics, etc.
[15]			Declarative programs can be programmed

format suitable for computational modeling. The detected problem is then forwarded to an AI-based parameter interpreter, where the input data and parameters related to the detected problem are processed. This data is then aligned with a knowledge base, which is a centralized repository containing past cases, models, and relevant data to support decision-making. In the next stage, an AI-based model assigner is used to select a suitable model to solve the problem. On the basis of the problem, it can select a suitable model. The selected static OR model is then, with the help of the model interpreter, transitioned into an ASP based logically interpreted OR model. The model interpreter ensures that the model is aligned with the problem-specific requirements. This selected model is then processed by the ASP solver, which generates a feasible solution by handling the complexities of logical reasoning and optimization based on the selected model and parameters. This optimized solution is then forwarded to all the stakeholders involved. Throughout the framework, the integration of AI ensures adaptability, intelligent decision-making, and the ability to handle dynamic, real-world scenarios efficiently. The interaction between components emphasizes a cyclical flow of information, enabling the system to adapt and refine its solutions over time.

3.1 Elaboration of the Proposed Model

To elaborate the proposed framework, we use an ASPs-based supply chain optimization model that builds on the methodology developed by [29]. This framework was developed to simulate a comprehensive supply chain network that includes suppliers, manufacturers, distribution centers, and disruption scenarios such as delivery delays, transportation failures, or sudden changes in demand.

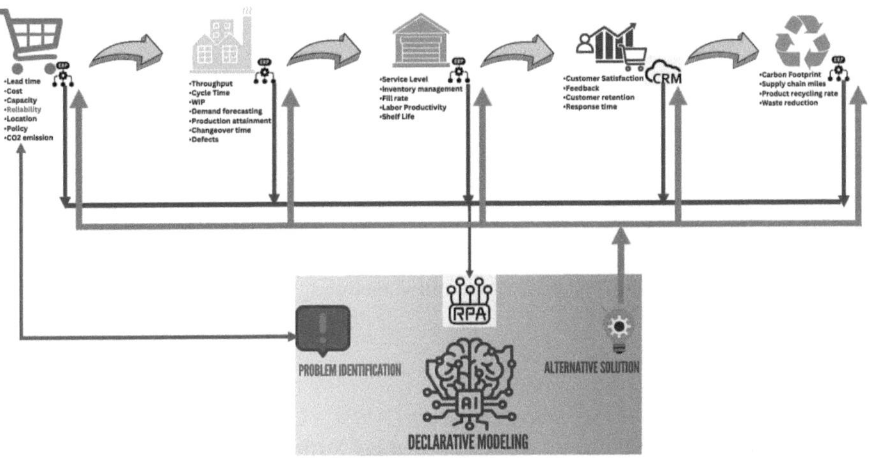

Fig. 2. AI-enabled centralized Robotic Process Automation (RPA) system.

By using ASP's logic-based framework, we can model complex decision-making processes and evaluate how dynamic adjustments to parameters—such as supplier capacity, costs, and environmental impact—affect overall supply chain performance.

The framework evaluates different disruption scenarios so that we can test its responsiveness and adaptability in real time. In particular, the assessment focuses on how our framework can dynamically adapt to disruptions by changing critical parameters, such as selecting replacement suppliers, changing production schedules, or optimizing inventory management.

Semantics for Answer Set Programming (ASP). The semantics for ASP program based on [29] provides a brief summary of the supply chain optimization model, detailing its key elements such as facts, parameters, decision variables, and objectives as illustrated in Table 2. It outlines entities like suppliers, products, and scenarios, along with attributes like capacities, costs, and disruption probabilities. It also highlights rules for supplier selection, cost calculation, and resilience strategies, while emphasizing the model's main focus on minimizing costs and maximizing social and environmental outcomes.

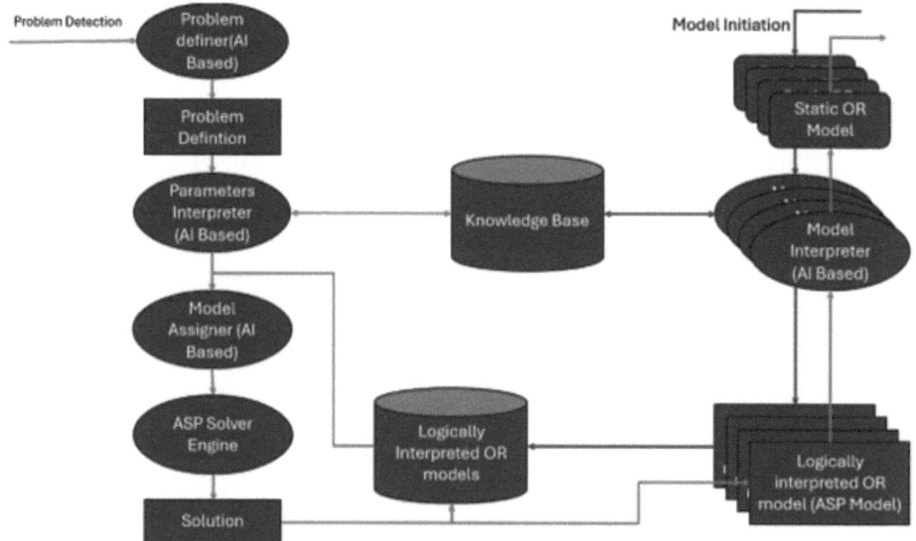

Fig. 3. ASP based declarative modeling framework.

Pyhton Code for Answer Set Programming (ASP). Using the mathematical model developed by [29] an ASP model was created using Python. The supply chain optimization problem formed in the code aims to address the complexities of decision making in a multi-tiered supply chain with uncertainties. The network consists of suppliers, manufacturers, distributors, and products. Each entity is characterized by various parameters such as capacity, cost, social impact, environmental impact, and more. The goal is to achieve the optimization of the flow of resources across the network while considering the scenario-based probabilities that represent different levels of uncertainties. The

Table 2. Semantics for ASP model.

Predicate/Parameter	Type	Description
supplier(X)	Fact	Represents a supplier (X is the supplier ID, e.g., s1, s2)
manufacturer(X)	Fact	Represents a manufacturer (X is the manufacturer ID, e.g., m1, m2)
distribution_center(X)	Fact	Represents a distribution center (X is the DC ID, e.g., d1, d2)
product(X)	Fact	Represents a product (X is the product ID, e.g., p1, p2)
scenario(X)	Fact	Represents a disruption scenario (X is the scenario ID, e.g., g1, g2)
capacity(S, Cap)	Parameter	The maximum capacity (Cap) for a supplier (S)
cost(S, Cost)	Parameter	The cost (Cost) of using a supplier (S)
social_score(S, Score)	Parameter	The social impact score (Score) of a supplier (S)
environmental_score(S, Score)	Parameter	The environmental performance score (Score) of a supplier (S)
disruption(S, G, P)	Parameter	The probability (P) of a supplier (S) being disrupted in a scenario (G)
selected(S)	Decision	Indicates whether a supplier (S) is selected for the supply chain
backup_supplier(S)	Derived Fact	Indicates whether a supplier (S) is activated as a backup in case of disruption
total_cost(C)	Aggregate Rule	Calculates the total cost (C) of selected suppliers
total_social_score(SS)	Aggregate Rule	Calculates the total social score (SS) of selected suppliers
total_environmental_score(ES)	Aggregate Rule	Calculates the total environmental score (ES) of selected suppliers
required_demand(D)	Parameter	The total demand (D) that must be satisfied across the supply chain
#minimize	Optimization	Specifies the objective to minimize total cost
maximize_social_score	Constraint	Ensures the total social score is above a threshold (e.g., 200)
maximize_environmental_score	Constraint	Ensures the total environmental score is above a threshold (e.g., 150)

declarative modeling uses logic programming to define constraints and relationships in the supply chain, including supplier capacities, transportation limits, production feasibility, and demand satisfaction. By leveraging these constraints, the model identifies the optimal solution that satisfies demand while adhering to resource limitations and scenario probabilities.

```
%Parameters for Answer Set Programming
%Define suppliers, manufacturers, distribution centers,
    products, and scenarios.
supplier(s1). supplier(s2). supplier(s3). supplier(s4).
manufacturer(m1). manufacturer(m2).
distribution_center(d1). distribution_center(d2).
product(p1). product(p2).
scenario(g1). scenario(g2). scenario(g3). scenario(g4).
% Define parameters for each supplier: capacity, cost,
    social score, environmental score.
capacity(s1, 100).
capacity(s2, 150).
capacity(s3, 200).
capacity(s4, 250).
cost(s1, 20).
cost(s2, 25).
cost(s3, 30).
cost(s4, 35).
social_score(s1, 80).
social_score(s2, 70).
social_score(s3, 90).
social_score(s4, 60).
environmental_score(s1, 70).
environmental_score(s2, 80).
environmental_score(s3, 60).
environmental_score(s4, 90).
```

3.2   Comparison of Outputs: Original vs. Parameter-Changed Results

Table 3 presents a detailed comparison between the original output and the output after the parameters are changed (as shown in code below) for an optimization model designed to evaluate decision-making scenarios. It highlights key metrics such as the total cost, social score, and environmental score for each solution identified in the model. The original output provides the baseline outputs, whereas the parameter-changed output shows the changes in output after the change in capacities of the suppliers.

```
%Change in parameters
%Define parameters for each supplier: capacity, cost,
    social score, environmental score.
capacity(s1, 175).
capacity(s2, 225).
capacity(s3, 135).
capacity(s4, 165).
```

Table 3. Comparison of outputs.

Result Type	Answer Set	Selected	Total Cost	Total Social Score	Total Environmental Score	Optimization
Original Output	1	selected(s1), selected(s2)	45	150	150	[45]
	2	selected(s3)	30	90	60	[30]
Parameter-Changed Output	1	selected(s1), selected(s3)	50	170	130	[50]
	2	selected(s1), selected(s2)	45	150	150	[45]
	3	selected(s2)	25	70	80	[25]

4 Conclusion

This paper introduces a framework that will enhance traditional Operations Research (OR) models by integrating AI, ERP, and RPA to create adaptive, resilient, and sustainable supply chains. Traditional OR models, being static in nature, are not able to adapt to real-time disruptions and dynamics of the supply chain. These models are generally limited to predefined scenarios and lack the flexibility to respond to sudden changes. ERP systems provide a solid foundation for managing business processes. They enable efficient data flow and serve as a centralized hub for transactional and operational information. However, ERP systems by themselves lack the flexibility needed to manage complex, real-time disruptions. RPA automates repetitive tasks, improving efficiency and reducing human errors. In this model, a centralized RPA was introduced which was connected to ERP's of different stakeholders throughout the supply chain. This centralized approach will enable smooth coordination, real-time data synchronization, and uniformity in automated tasks across various entities, including suppliers, manufacturers, and distribution centers. To overcome the lack of decision-making capabilities of traditional OR models, this model integrates ERP, RPA with AI while leveraging its decision-making capabilities. AI-powered decision-making introduces predictive and prescriptive capabilities, allowing supply chains to dynamically adapt to unexpected changes, such as supplier delays, transportation disruptions, or shifts in customer demand.

To overcome the static nature of OR models, declarative modeling using ASP was introduced. Traditional OR models depend on step-by-step instructions, whereas ASP uses a flexible, logic-based framework in which problems are specified using constraints, rules, and objectives. ASP can integrate these dynamic factors and automatically adapt the decision-making process. This ensures the supply chain remains resilient, able to quickly respond to disruptions while sustaining operational efficiency. Integrating ASP into the AI-enabled OR model allows the system to assess various potential outcomes before determining the optimal course of action. This capability ensures decisions are informed, resilient, and adaptable to evolving conditions. Essentially, ASP serves as a robust problem-solving engine, enhancing the model's capacity to manage real-world complexities and improving the supply chain's overall efficiency and resilience.

The framework can be further developed by incorporating advanced AI techniques like reinforcement learning for continuous improvement, integrating IoT and blockchain for real-time data acquisition, transparency, and security. Expanding multi-criteria decision-making models to include sustainability metrics and scenario-based optimization would enhance decision-making. Tailoring the framework for industry-specific applications, enabling global supply chain integration, and incorporating predictive maintenance and demand forecasting would increase its scalability and accuracy. Adding human-in-the-loop decision support, real-time risk management, and resilience testing would improve adaptability. Integrating external market data and collaboration with third-party systems would make the framework more interconnected. Finally, enhancing user interfaces and decision support tools with advanced visualizations would improve accessibility and decision-making in complex environments.

In conclusion, the integration of ERP, centralized RPA, AI, and ASP transforms traditional OR models into dynamic and adaptive frameworks. This combination facilitates real-time decision-making, boosts efficiency, and strengthens the overall resilience and sustainability of the supply chain. The outcome is a robust system that effectively addresses contemporary supply chain challenges and ensures operational continuity through disruptions.

References

1. Aghili, S.A.S., Valilai, O.F., Haji, A., Khalilzadeh, M.: Dynamic mutual manufacturing and transportation routing service selection for cloud manufacturing with multi-period service-demand matching. PeerJ Comput. Sci. **7**, e461 (2021). https://doi.org/10.7717/peerj-cs.461
2. Aziz, M.A., Ragheb, M.A., Ragab, A.A., Mokadem, M.E.: The impact of enterprise resource planning on supply chain management practices. Bus. Manag. Rev. **9**(4) (2018)
3. Balasubramanian, S., Shukla, V., Kavanancheeri, L.: Improving Supply Chain Sustainability Using Artificial intelligence: evidence from the Manufacturing Sector. In: K E K, V., Rajak, S., Kumar, V., Mor, R.S., Assayed, A. (eds.) Industry 4.0 Technologies: Sustainable Manufacturing Supply Chains : Volume II - Methods for transition and trends, pp. 43–59. Springer, Singapore (2024). https://doi.org/10.1007/978-981-99-4894-9_4
4. Belhadi, A., Mani, V., Kamble, S.S., Khan, S.A.R., Verma, S.: Artificial intelligence-driven innovation for enhancing supply chain resilience and performance under the effect of supply chain dynamism: an empirical investigation. Ann. Oper. Res. **333**(2), 627–652 (2024). https://doi.org/10.1007/s10479-021-03956-x
5. Bonatti, P., Calimeri, F., Leone, N., Ricca, F.: Answer set programming. In: Dovier, A., Pontelli, E. (eds.) A 25-Year Perspective on Logic Programming: Achievements of the Italian Association for Logic Programming, GULP, pp. 159–182. Springer, Heidelberg (2010). https://doi.org/10.1007/978-3-642-14309-0_8
6. Costa, D.A.D.S., Mamede, H.S., Mira Da Silva, M.: Robotic process automation (RPA) adoption: a systematic literature review. Eng. Manag. Prod. Serv. **14**(2), 1–12 (2022). https://doi.org/10.2478/emj-2022-0012
7. Costin, B.V., Anca, T., Dorian, C.: Enterprise resource planning for robotic process automation in big companies. a case study. In: 2020 24th International Conference on System Theory, Control and Computing (ICSTCC), pp. 106–111 (2020). https://doi.org/10.1109/ICSTCC50638.2020.9259739. https://ieeexplore.ieee.org/abstract/document/9259739. iSSN: 2372-1618
8. Delaram, J., Houshamand, M., Ashtiani, F., Fatahi Valilai, O.: Development of public cloud manufacturing markets: a mechanism design approach. Int. J. Syst. Sci. Oper. Logist. **10**(1), 2079751 (2023). https://doi.org/10.1080/23302674.2022.2079751
9. Erdem, E., Gelfond, M., Leone, N.: Applications of answer set programming. AI Mag. **37**(3), 53–68 (2016). https://doi.org/10.1609/aimag.v37i3.2678

10. Hasan, M.R., Shawon, R.E.R., Rahman, A., Mukaddim, A.A., Khan, M.A., Hider, M.A., Zeeshan, M.A.F.: Optimizing sustainable supply chains: integrating environmental concerns and carbon footprint reduction through AI-enhanced decision-making in the USA. J. Econ. Finan. Account. Stud. **6**(4), 57–71 (2024). https://doi.org/10.32996/jefas.2024.6.4.7. https://al-kindipublisher.com/index.php/jefas/article/view/7786
11. Houshmand, M., Valilai, O.: LAYMOD: a layered and modular platform for CAx product data integration based on the modular architecture of the standard for exchange of product data. Int. J. Comput. Integrat. Manuf. **25**(6) (2012). https://doi.org/10.1080/0951192X.2011.646308
12. Karanam, R.K., Sachani, D.K., Natakam, V., Yarlagadda, V.K., Kothapalli, K.R.V.: Resilient supply chains: strategies for managing disruptions in a globalized economy. Am. J. Trade Policy **11**, 7–16 (2024). https://doi.org/10.18034/ajtp.v11i1.719
13. Kassa, A., Kitaw, D., Stache, U., Beshah, B., Degefu, G.: Artificial intelligence techniques for enhancing supply chain resilience: a systematic literature review, holistic framework, and future research. Comput. Ind. Eng. **186**, 109714 (2023). https://doi.org/10.1016/j.cie.2023.109714
14. Khan, S., Tailor, R., Uygun, H., Gujrati, R.: Application of robotic process automation (RPA) for supply chain management, smart transportation and logistics. Int. J. Health Sci. 11051–11063 (2022). https://doi.org/10.53730/ijhs.v6nS3.8554
15. Kordjamshidi, P., Roth, D., Kersting, K.: Declarative learning-based programming as an interface to AI systems. Front. Artif. Intell. **5**, 755361 (2022). https://doi.org/10.3389/frai.2022.755361. https://www.frontiersin.org/articles/10.3389/frai.2022.755361/full
16. Lifschitz, V.: What Is Answer Set Programming? (2008). https://www.cs.utexas.edu/~vl/papers/wiasp.pdf
17. Madakam, S., Holmukhe, R.M., Jaiswal, D.K.: The future digital work force: robotic process automation (RPA). J. Inf. Syst. Technol. Manag. **16**(1) (2019). https://doi.org/10.4301/S1807-1775201916001. https://jistem.tecsi.org/index.php/jistem/article/view/3077
18. Mirzaee, H., Ashtab, S.: Sustainability, resiliency, and artificial intelligence in supplier selection: a triple-themed review. Sustainability **16**(19), 8325 (2024). https://doi.org/10.3390/su16198325
19. Mofatteh, M.Y., Abbas, R., Seddoh, N.D., Sedhumadhavan, S., Thunyaluck, M., Valilai, O.F.: A smart adaptive transportation planning model including real-time drivers knowledge using answer set programming and knowledge graphs. Procedia Comput. Sci. **253**, 2358–2368 (2025). https://doi.org/10.1016/j.procs.2025.01.296. https://www.sciencedirect.com/science/article/pii/S1877050925003047
20. Moreira, S., Mamede, H.S., Santos, A.: Process automation using RPA a literature review. Procedia Comput. Sci. **219**, 244–254 (2023). https://doi.org/10.1016/j.procs.2023.01.287
21. Muthuswamy, M., Ali, A.M.: Sustainable supply chain management in the age of machine intelligence: addressing challenges, capitalizing on opportunities, and shaping the future landscape. Sustainable Mach. Intell. J. **3**, (3):1–14 (2023). https://doi.org/10.61185/SMIJ.2023.33103. https://sciencesforce.com/index.php/smij/article/view/44
22. Naz, F., Agrawal, R., Kumar, A., Gunasekaran, A., Majumdar, A., Luthra, S.: Reviewing the applications of artificial intelligence in sustainable supply chains: Exploring research propositions for future directions. Bus. Strat. Environ. **31**(5), 2400–2423 (2022). https://doi.org/10.1002/bse.3034. https://onlinelibrary.wiley.com/doi/pdf/10.1002/bse.3034
23. Nielsen, I.E., Piyatilake, A., Thibbotuwawa, A., Silva, M.M.D., Bocewicz, G., Banaszak, Z.A.: Benefits realization of robotic process automation (RPA) initiatives in supply chains. IEEE Access **11**, 37623–37636 (2023). https://doi.org/10.1109/ACCESS.2023.3266293
24. Nurhaliza, S.: Artificial intelligence and RPA-enabled SAP variant configuration: transforming modern supply chain management. Innov. Eng. Sci. J. **4**(1) (2024). https://innovatesci-publishers.com/index.php/IESJ/article/view/286

25. Pasupuleti, V., Thuraka, B., Kodete, C.S., Malisetty, S.: Enhancing supply chain agility and sustainability through machine learning: optimization techniques for logistics and inventory management. Logistics **8**(3), 73 (2024). https://doi.org/10.3390/logistics8030073
26. Radmanesh, S.A., Haji, A., Fatahi Valilai, O.: Blockchain-based architecture for a sustainable supply chain in cloud architecture. Sustainability **15**(11), 9072 (2023). https://doi.org/10.3390/su15119072
27. Rezapour Niari, M., Eshghi, K., Fatahi Valilai, O.: Using cloud manufacturing to establish an ecosystem network for COVID-19 ventilator production. Int. J. Comput. Integr. Manuf. **36**(6), 842–862 (2023). https://doi.org/10.1080/0951192X.2022.2162586
28. Rezapour Niari, M., Eshghi, K., Valilai, O.F.: Adaptive capacity management in cloud manufacturing hyper-network platform: case of COVID-19 equipment production. Int. J. Manag. Sci. Eng. Manag. **17**(4), 239–258 (2022). https://doi.org/10.1080/17509653.2021.2009389
29. Sadeghi, Z., Boyer, O., Sharifzadeh, S., Saeidi, N.: A robust mathematical model for sustainable and resilient supply chain network design: preparing a supply chain to deal with disruptions. Complexity **2021**(1), 9975071 (2021). https://doi.org/10.1155/2021/9975071. https://onlinelibrary.wiley.com/doi/pdf/10.1155/2021/9975071
30. Shahab, E., Kazemisaboor, A., Khaleghparast, S., Fatahi Valilai, O.: A production bounce-back approach in the Cloud manufacturing network: case study of COVID-19 pandemic. Int. J. Manag. Sci. Eng. Manag. **18**(4), 305–317 (2022). https://doi.org/10.1080/17509653.2022.2112781
31. Shahab, E., Rabiee, M., Mobasseri, N., Valilai, O.F.: A robust service composition for a resilient cloud manufacturing service network. Int. J. Comput. Integrat. Manuf. (2025). https://doi.org/10.1080/0951192X.2025.2504088
32. Stevens, W.: Robotic process automation in supply chain. Eur. J. Supply Chain Manag. **1**(1), 1–10 (2023). https://forthworthjournals.org/journals/index.php/EJSCM/article/view/36
33. Venigandla, K., Venkata, M., Tatikonda, V.M.: Building resilient supply chains: the role of AI and RPA in predictive management and automation. Iconic Res. Eng. J. **6**(7), 421–430 (2023)
34. Yang, Z., Ishay, A., Lee, J.: NeurASP: embracing neural networks into answer set programming (2023). arXiv:2307.07700
35. Zeynivand, M., Ranjbar, H., Radmanesh, S.A., Fatahi Valilai, O.: Alternative process routing and consolidated production-distribution planning with a destination oriented strategy in cloud manufacturing. Int. J. Comput. Integrat. Manuf. **34**(11), 1162–1176 (2021). https://doi.org/10.1080/0951192X.2021.1972459

A Surrogate Model-Based Combustion Optimization for Pellet Stoves

Eliott Gauthey-Franet[1,2,3]($\boxtimes$)(iD), Yinling Liu[1](iD), Hind Bril El-Haouzi[1](iD), Yann Rogaume[2](iD), and Jérémy Hugues dit Ciles[3]

[1] Université de Lorraine, CRAN, CNRS UMR 7039, Campus Sciences, BP 70239, 54506 Vandœuvre-lés-Nancy Cedex, France
{eliott.gauthey-franet,yinling.liu,hind.el-haouzi}@univ-lorraine.fr
[2] Université de Lorraine, INRAE, LERMAB, ERBE, 88000 Epinal, France
yann.rogaume@univ-lorraine.fr
[3] N²AIR, 39000 Mantry, France
jeremy.hugues@n2air.fr

Abstract. The increasing consumption of pellets has recently driven stove manufacturers to design more efficient combustion devices. However, due to the inherent variability of biomass, the expected performance is often unmet. Therefore, we propose a surrogate model-based approach to optimize combustion for pellet stoves. To do so, we first analysed the data via Analysis of Variance (ANOVA, feature selection) and t-distributed Stochastic Neighbor Embedding (t-SNE, data visualization). Subsequently, a Gaussian Process Regression (GPR) was implemented to predict Carbon Monoxide (CO) emissions across different stove settings, leveraging its strong predictive capabilities with small datasets. Finally, performance metrics were employed to analyze the predictive accuracy of the model. Several experimental scenarios were tested. It was observed that the model is not yet able to generalize the results due to a lack of quantity and quality in the data used. However, the first results show great potential and will serve as a basis for optimizing the combustion of the pellet stove.

Keywords: Pellet Stoves · Combustion Optimization · Surrogate Model · Renewable Energy

1 Introduction

Domestic wood heating is the predominant source of renewable energy in France and Europe [1], encompassing standalone appliances such as stoves and closed fireplaces commonly installed in households. Since the 2010s, the sales of pellet stoves have surged dramatically, rising from 27,000 units sold in 2010 to approximately 150,000 in 2019, followed by a slight decline to 121,550 units in 2020. Notably, since 2018, annual sales of pellet stoves have surpassed those of log stoves. Pellet consumption has been increasing steadily. To accommodate

© The Author(s), under exclusive license to Springer Nature Switzerland AG 2026
J. Barata et al. (Eds.): IN4PL 2025, CCIS 2826, pp. 69–81, 2026.
https://doi.org/10.1007/978-3-032-15579-5_5

this demand, domestic production has also risen: in 2019, pellet consumption in France was estimated at 1.85 million tons, while production reached 1.65 million tons [2].

To satisfy the growing demand without compromising other wood uses, expanding the sources of wood feedstock is essential, which inevitably alters the characteristics of the pellets produced. Although pellet stoves are generally capable of operating with various types of pellets without significant functional issues, these variations often result in performance degradation, particularly concerning pollutant emissions (e.g., carbon monoxide and particulate matter) and efficiency. At the same time, work carried out in the LERMAB laboratory [3] has shown a strong influence of the settings of the appliances on the combustion results and in particular on the performances in terms of reduction of unburnt emissions or gain in efficiency. This is the central objective of the study: to implement a technique that allows to automatically adapt the settings of stoves according to the exact nature of the pellets used. Moreover, the complexity of the physical processes studied here as well as the large number of factors influencing the pollutant emissions and the efficiency make it difficult to set up an experimental design covering efficiently the whole experimental space. Research work in various application areas has shown surrogate models are the promising approaches [4–7]. These models can, in particular, be initialized on a small amount of data and used directly to search for optimal parameters. We argue that the surrogated model-based machine-learning algorithms fit well our problem since we only have small datasets.

The remainder of this paper is structured as follows. Section 2 reviews recent related works. Section 3 explains the Kriging-based prediction process. Section 4 details the experiment. Section 5 concludes the paper with future perspectives.

2   Literature Review

The optimization of the combustion of various wood pellets in the pellet stoves usually involves more performant pellet stoves [8], the reconfiguration of pellet stoves [9], simulation [10], and data-based approaches [11]. To the best of our knowledge, very few works focus on how to use data-based approaches to optimize the combustion of wood pellets. Surrogate models are largely used in data-based approaches, which are specialized for approximating expensive simulations in scientific and engineering contexts, focusing on reducing computational cost [12]. Therefore, this section will provide a detailed comparison of some Surrogate, also called Meta-models on the literature.

The main surrogate models include polynomial regression, artificial neural network (ANN), ensemble, radial basis function (RBF), support vector machine (SVM), and kriging. The meta-models are analyzed from five aspects: domains, frequency, principles, advantages, and disadvantages. Table 1 gives a synthesized analysis of the meta-models.

According to this table, the application domains range from continuous real-valued output prediction, image and speech recognition, to natural language processing. All the models are either largely or normally used. Most of the models are flexible in modeling complex patterns or relationships. They all seem capable of dealing with complex problems. For disadvantages, ANN, Ensemble and SVM require a lot of computational resources for large datasets. Polynomial regression presents the difficulty in choosing an appropriate degree of the polynomial. RBF has problems with high dimensionality. In terms of principles, they vary from model to model. For example, ANN tries to simulate the structure of human brains. Polynomial regression utilizes nth-degree polynomial functions. Kriging is based on Gaussian processes. The prediction of each model depends on its principle. For instance, Kriging predicts unknown values at specific locations based on known values at surrounding locations, considering both the distance and the degree of variation between them. ANN employs networks of nodes and weights to predict unknown results. SVM uses the optimal hyperplane to predict the membership of unknown data.

In our specific context, Kriging is particularly well-suited for optimizing combustion in pellet stoves using various wood pellets, as it is effective with small datasets and can accurately predict industrial data.

Table 1. An overview of meta-models.

Model	Domains	Frequency	Principle	Advantages	Disadvantages
Polynomial regression [13]	Modeling non-linear relationships	Largely used	nth-degree polynomial function	Flexible in modeling complex patterns	Difficult to choose an appropriate polynomial degree
Artificial neural network [14]	Image and speech recognition, natural language processing	Largely used	Networks of interconnected nodes with weighted edges	Solves complex problems effectively	Computationally expensive, risk of overfitting, sensitive to hyperparameters
Ensemble methods [15]	Classification, regression, anomaly detection	Normally used	Combination of multiple individual models (e.g., bagging, boosting)	Improves generalization, reduces overfitting	Requires more computational resources, increases complexity
Radial basis function networks [16]	Function approximation and interpolation	Normally used	Activation function decreases with distance from a center	Flexible for modeling non-linear relationships	Sensitive to centroid selection; suffers in high dimensions
Support vector machines [17]	Text classification, image recognition, bioinformatics	Normally used	Finds optimal separating hyperplanes between classes	Effective in high-dimensional spaces	Computationally intensive for large datasets
Kriging [18]	Modeling and predicting continuous outputs	Largely used	Based on Gaussian process regression	Provides a flexible and probabilistic framework	Computationally expensive with large datasets

3   Methodology

This section outlines the process of creating a dataset and populating it with experimental data obtained from the combustion of various pellet types in a pellet stove. First, Sect. 3.1 describes the step-by-step approach to designing and developing the dataset based on different measurements collected from the experimental setup. Secondly, Sect. 3.2 focuses on the methods used to visualize the data in a 3D graphical format. Then in Sect. 3.3, the way to build a surrogate model with machine learning is shown. Finally, in Sect. 3.4, metrics functions to evaluate the surrogate model will be introduced.

3.1   Data Collection and Storage

With the data generated, the next step involves creating a table to store this information. As illustrated in Fig. 1, the data is organized into three distinct tables: one for pellet characteristics, another for stove specifications, and a third for experimental results.

Once the data list is completed, it is crucial to identify the system's inputs and outputs. The output should be a relevant attribute that characterizes combustion performance. For the initial approach, CO is selected as the output, as it is commonly used as an indicator of emission quality in combustion processes. To determine which inputs significantly impact the model, an Analysis of Variance (ANOVA) is employed. ANOVA is a statistical test that evaluates the effect of each feature on the model's output. It is based on two hypotheses: the null hypothesis (H0) and the alternative hypothesis (H1). The null hypothesis (H0) posits that a given feature does not significantly affect the model's results, whereas the alternative hypothesis (H1) suggests that the feature does have a significant impact.

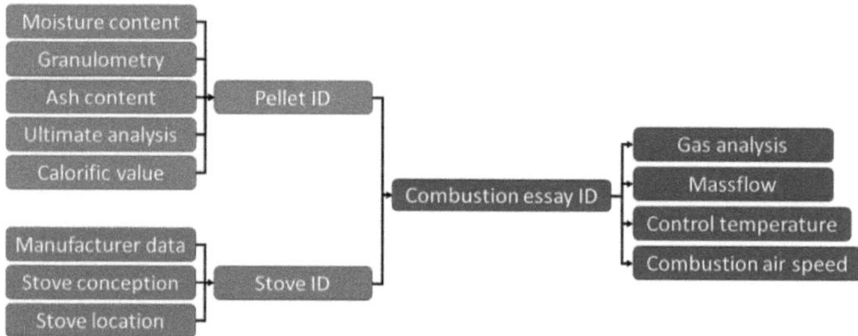

Fig. 1. Partial graphic of functional dependencies.

The p-value is used to assess these hypotheses: if the p-value is greater than 5% ($p - value > 0.05$), H0 is accepted, indicating no significant effect; if the p-value is less than 5% ($p - value < 0.05$), H1 is accepted, indicating a significant effect. The ANOVA results, presented in Table 2, reveal that all considered features are statistically significant. This outcome aligns with expectations given the inherent complexity of combustion reactions.

3.2   Data Visualization

Despite the limited amount of data, understanding their overall behavior without losing critical information remains challenging. To better visualize the data and extract meaningful insights, t-distributed Stochastic Neighbor Embedding (t-SNE) has been applied. Developed by [19], this unsupervised classification method reduces data from high-dimensional spaces to 2- or 3-dimensional spaces, enabling visualization with minimal information loss. The process begins by calculating the conditional probability between pairs of data points in the high-dimensional space using a Gaussian kernel. Thus, the conditional probability $p_{j|i}$ showed in the Eq. 1 that data x_i would choose as its neighbor data x_j is defined as:

$$p_{j|i} = \frac{exp(-\frac{||x_i - x_j||^2}{2\sigma_i^2})}{\sum_{k \neq i} exp(-\frac{||x_i - x_k||^2}{2\sigma_i^2})} \tag{1}$$

With, by definition, $p_{i|i} = 0$. For high-dimensional space, conditional probability p_{ij} is written as the Eq. 2.

$$p_{ij} = \frac{p_{i|j} + p_{j|i}}{2n} \tag{2}$$

At the same time, conditional probability q_{ij} expresses the probability that, in low-dimensional space, x_i would pick as neighbor x_j data, respectively defined as y_i and y_j, is calculated thanks to the t-Student's distribution as described in the Eq. 3.

Table 2. Result obtained from the ANOVA.

table	features	p-value (CO rate)
Pellets table	gross calorific value	3.2×10^{-4}
	bulk density	4.1×10^{-2}
	particular density	4.1×10^{-2}
	moisture	9.9×10^{-4}
	ash rate at 550°C	2.4×10^{-2}
	pellet's length	2.4×10^{-2}
	pellet's diameter	2.4×10^{-2}
	durability	2.4×10^{-2}
	Carbon rate	1.5×10^{-2}
	Hydrogen rate	2.4×10^{-2}
	Oxygen rate	2.4×10^{-2}
Stove table	Output power max	3.7×10^{-2}
	efficiency	3.7×10^{-2}
	CO rate at maximum power	3.7×10^{-2}
	smoke temperature at maximum power	3.7×10^{-2}
	air input diameter (mm)	3.7×10^{-2}
Essay table	speed rotation	2.0×10^{-3}
	combustion air flow	1.9×10^{-2}
	O_2 rate in combustion gas	3.7×10^{-2}
	CO rate in combustion gas normalize to 13% O_2	Used as output
	gas temperature	5.9×10^{-3}
	efficiency	1.25×10^{-11}

$$q_{ij} = \frac{1 + (-||y_i - y_j||^2)^{-1}}{\sum_{k \neq l}(1 + ||y_k - y_l||^2)^{-1}} \tag{3}$$

The symmetry property implies that $p_{ij} = p_{ji}$ and $q_{ij} = q_{ji}$, which means that in high-dimensional space (as in low-dimensional) that x_i (or y_i) could be x_j's (or y_j's) nearest neighbor and the reciprocity is true.

Then, cost function C is defined in the Eq. 4 and is optimized by gradient descent which allows to show initial dataset behavior in low-dimensional space, where P and Q are respectively the density joint probability in high and low-dimensional space [20].

$$C = KL(P||Q) = \sum_i \sum_j p_{ij} log\frac{p_{ij}}{q_{ij}} \tag{4}$$

3.3   Kriging Surrogate Method

Combustion results can hardly be calculated theoretically or need a high-cost simulation to give approximate results. In other words, if the combustion process can be described by a function $f(x)$, where f is a high-cost function, then the main goal is to build a surrogate model-based function $g(x)$ which approximates $f(x)$. The construction of a surrogate model is divided into 3 steps: data sampling, surrogate model building and optimization.

First of all, data for each pellet are manually divided into 90% for the training set and 10% for the testing set. The minimum size of the testing set is fixed to 5 to obtain comparable results. This kind of manipulation may cause an over-fitting problem, but the main goal is to compare the influence of a pellet on another, this issue will not be considered in this study. Thus, the model prediction accuracy is only used to compare batches between them.

Secondly, as it was seen later, the kriging method was chosen for the surrogate model which is a stochastic process specified by its mean and covariance functions. Initially, it considers that the knowing data $g(x)$ are generated by an unknown function disturbed by a Gaussian noise: $g(x) = f(x) + \epsilon$ where, $\epsilon \sim \mathcal{N}(0, \sigma_n^2)$. It is supposed that $f(x)$ following a GP with a zero mean and a covariance defined by a chosen kernel defined in the Eq. 5.

$$f(x) \sim \mathcal{GP}(\mu(x), k(x, x')) \tag{5}$$

The kernel is used to verify the assumption that similar data points have similar target values, so the kernel's goal is to find the similarity between a known and an unknown data point. There are plenty of covariance functions defined such as radial basis function, rational quadratic, Matérn, Exp-sine-squared and Dot-product kernel. For example, kernel Matérn function is described as a covariance function between two points x and x', $k(x, x')$ shown in the Eq. 6, other kernels will be tested later, where ν is usually set to $\nu = \frac{1}{2}$, $\nu = \frac{3}{2}$ or $\nu = \frac{5}{2}$, K_ν is a modified Bessel function, $\Gamma()$ is the gamma function and l contains the length scales of the predictors.

$$k(x, x') = \frac{2^{1-\nu}}{\Gamma(\nu)} \left(\frac{\sqrt{2\nu}\|x - x'\|}{\ell} \right)^{\nu} K_{\nu} \left(\frac{\sqrt{2\nu}\|x - x'\|}{\ell} \right) \tag{6}$$

3.4 Prediction Accuracy

To evaluate and compare the performance of the Gaussian Process Regression (GPR) results, two evaluation methods are employed. Firstly, the global prediction accuracy is assessed using the coefficient of determination, R^2 defined in the Eq. 7.

$$R^2 = 1 - \frac{\sum_{i=0}^{n}(y_{i,test} - y_{i,pred})^2}{\sum_{i=0}^{n}(y_{i,test} - \overline{y_{test}})^2} \tag{7}$$

where, y_{test} is the known ordinate of x-axis x_{test}, y_{pred} is the unknown ordinate of x-axis x_{test} and $\overline{y_{test}}$ the mean of y_{test}. If R^2 is close to 1, the prediction might be considered accurate. Otherwise, the score might be close to 0 if the model only predicts the mean value. In the particular case where $R^2 < 0$, the model is not even capable of guessing the mean value of y_{test}. In a second time, we evaluate the relative gap δ of y_{pred} compare to y_{test} as define the Eq. 8.

$$\delta = \frac{|y_{test} - y_{pred}|}{y_{test}} \tag{8}$$

Then, we define 2 threshold values (0.1 and 0.5) according to a previous study. Thus, if $\delta < 0.1$ the prediction is accurate, else, if $\delta > 0.5$, the prediction is inaccurate, and finally, if $0.1 < \delta < 0.5$, it's impossible to conclude.

4 Experiments

This section provides an overview of how the data were acquired in laboratory conditions using the experimental bench, as detailed in Sect. 4.1. Subsequently, the results obtained from the machine learning model will be discussed in Sect. 4.2.

4.1 Experimental Bench

The experimental bench provides detailed insights into each combustion characteristic and is organized into three main components: pellets, the pellet stove, and sensors. First, 5 pellets from different producers, so different locations and raw materials have been chosen: BIO, MOU, AR40, AR79 and LUZ

Table 3. Characteristics of tested pellets.

	BIO	MOU	AR40	AR79	LUZ
gross calorific value (kJ/kg)	19856	20328	20462	20140	20038
bulk density (kg/m^3)	661	637	656	657	665
particular density (kg/m^3)	1148	1063	1075	1054	1109
moisture content (%wb)	3.79	7.84	5.19	4.45	6.22
ash rate at 550°C %(db)	71.5	51.6	39.6	47.0	44.3
length (mm)	16.67	13.59	11.67	13.75	16.43
diameter (mm)	6.10	6.18	6.17	6.19	6.14
durability (%)	99.13	99.13	99.06	98.30	99.24
C rate (%db)	50.1	50.9	51.6	50.9	50.7
H rate (%db)	6.26	6.52	6.4	6.32	6.28
N rate (%db)	0.1	0.1	<0.1	<0.1	<0.1
O rate (%db)	43.51	42.5	41.9	42.7	42.9

At first sight, Table 3 shows that BIO pellet seems to have a lower gross calorific value and a higher ash rate than other pellets, which can be explained because BIO is produced with a mix of hardwood and softwood whereas other pellets are only made with softwood which is used to have a slightly higher gross energetic value than hardwood. At second sight, it seems that MOU has the highest moisture content, which can be due to the storage of logs before production or during the process.

Secondly, we used a Hoben H5b pellet stove with a nominal output power of 6.3 kW and a maximum efficiency of 90%. The operation diagram of the pellet stove is illustrated in Fig. 2. The stove is filled with one of the known pellets and is set to run at the specific nominal output power measured for each pellet. Then, pellets are dropped in the fireplace where they are heated by a spark plug and oxidised by combustion air. The smokes created are used to warm the indoor air and analyzed by a sensor before being evacuated. Different levels of combustion airflow are tested by essay to measure several points of CO in the smoke.

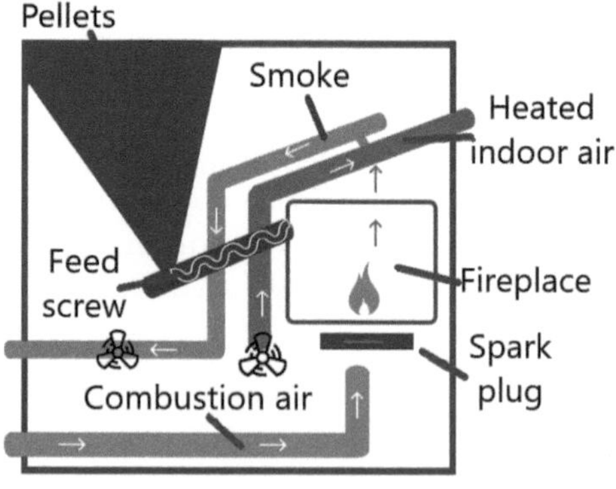

Fig. 2. Pellet stove operation diagram.

4.2   Results and Discussions

In this section, we will first present the 3D visualizations of the pellet data. Three sets of experiments will be examined in detail, focusing on the training and test data from three different scenarios: single pellet types, different types of pellets, and mixtures of pellets. Each experiment aims to provide insights into how varying pellet compositions and configurations affect the model's performance and prediction accuracy.

The data were visualized in a 3D space thanks to the t-SNE method described in Sect. 3.2. Two projections of this visualization are shown in Fig. 3. This figure is divided into 3 axes: PCS_g is the feature link to the pellet and translates the gross calorific value, $\%O2$ and $\%CO13$ are two features characterizing the combustion of a pellet in a stove and respectively defined O_2 and CO corrected at 13% d'O_2 rate in combustion gas. Visually, the 5 pellets are divided into 3 spaces defined by 3 groups of pellets: (AR79, LUZ), (MOU, AR40) and BIO. It seems that the last group of data points are more scattered. This can be explained due to the lack of repeatability during the experimental part and it was the most used of the panel.

To implement the GPR with a Matérn kernel, the library Sklearn is used and all hyperparameters were set to their default values ($\alpha = 1e - 10$, $optimizer ='$ $f\_min\_l\_bfgs\_b'$, $length\_scale = 1.0$, $length\_scale\_bounds = (1e - 5, 1e5)$ and $nu = 1.5$). Thanks to the experiences leading in the lab, several datasets of different sizes for each pellet were created as seen in Table 4. Those differences came from constraints during the test phase and not all pellets could be tested the same number of times.

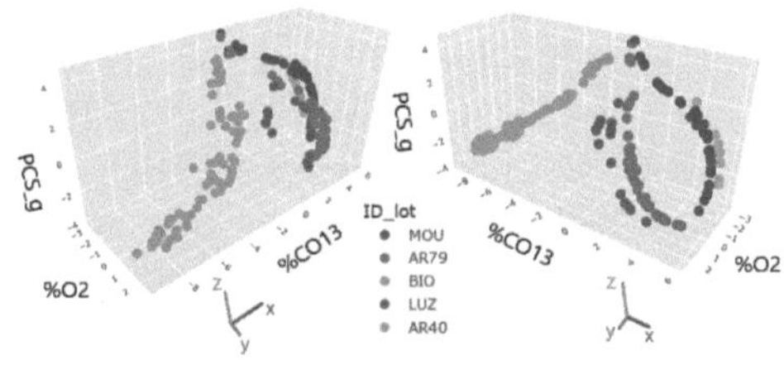

Fig. 3. Data pellets visualization with t-SNE.

To make a first comparison between pellets, each dataset was used in the kriging algorithm and the results are summarized in Table 4. At first sight, MOU has the best R^2. Furthermore, it has the most accurate predictions with a $\delta <$ 0.1 despite its smaller data size compared to BIO. In fact, by checking the visualization, it seems obvious that MOU got the curve with the least noise. This phenomenon can be explained by the fact that the experiences with MOU were more repeatable than BIO. For LUZ, it seems that the lack of data mixed with some noisy points does not help the model. Finally, for AR79 and AR40, the visualization shows curves that seem well-drawn and, for AR79, the training data size meets the MOU's one but the result is different with $R^2 = 0.16$ for AR79 and $R^2 = 0.33$ for AR40 which are inferior to MOU. Furthermore, the issue does not seem to come from the choice of training/test data. So it's hard to conclude about the causes of AR79 and AR40 results.

The above experiment results show that the training data has a role to play in the surrogate model. Indeed, BIO shows that having lots of data without high quality seems not useful to have a good surrogate model. AR40 and LUZ demonstrate that training data size needs to be large enough. On the other hand, according to Fig. 3, it seems that MOU and AR79 have better training data, and their prediction accuracies are different. This may be due to the nature of pellets like granulometry, wood composition, etc. For pellet MOU, kriging provided high prediction accuracy with a small dataset.

Table 4. Prediction quality according to pellets.

pellet	BIO	AR40	AR79	LUZ	MOU
training data	61	18	47	19	50
test data	7	5	5	5	5
$\overline{\delta}$		0.777	0.145	0.581	1.42	**0.070**
$\delta < 0.1$	1	3	0	1	**4**
$0.1 < \delta < 0.5$	2	2	2	1	1
$\delta > 0.5$	4	**0**	3	3	**0**
R^2	<0	0.33	0.16	<0	**0.984**

The second phase test consists of checking if the training data of one pellet can be used to predict other pellet data. Thus, two tests were realized with pellet data sharing similar tendencies: (MOU, AR40) and (AR79, LUZ), and the last test with pellet data having distinct tendencies: (BIO, AR40). The results are shown in Table 5. It seems clear that using data that is not in conjunction with the test data (cf: Fig. 3) cannot result in a qualitative prediction regardless of the characteristics that may have been mentioned previously.

Table 5. Training data of one pellet used on tested data for another pellet.

training pellet	MOU	AR79	BIO
test pellet	AR40	LUZ	AR40
training size	50	47	61
test size	5	5	5
$\overline{\delta}$	1	1	1
$\delta < 0.1$	0	0	0
$0.1 < \delta < 0.5$	0	0	0
$\delta > 0.5$	5	5	5
R^2	<0	<0	<0

The third phase consists in checking if the dilution of training data for one pellet with others influences the result. Several configurations are tested, with MOU as a reference. During these 4 steps, we will vary their presence rates in the training base. The results are stored in Table 6. Based on the results obtained, it seems that for MOU, diluting the training data of the tested pellet with other pellets does not vary the results obtained previously with $\bar{\delta}$ staying approximately equal to 0.07 and R^2 equal to 0.984.

Table 6. Behavior of MOU prediction with diluted training data.

training pellet	MOU +AR40	MOU +AR79	MOU +BIO	all pellets
test pellet in training set	74%	52%	45%	26%
test pellet	MOU	MOU	MOU	MOU
training size	68	97	111	195
test size	5	5	5	5
$\bar{\delta}$	**0.0700**	0.0684	0.0717	0.0703
$\delta < 0.1$	4	4	4	4
$0.1 < \delta < 0.5$	1	1	1	1
$\delta > 0.5$	**0**	**0**	**0**	**0**
R^2	0.984	0.984	0.984	0.984

Above all, we can conclude that particular care needs to be taken with the data used, otherwise, the model will no longer be correct. For example, BIO is the most represented pellet of the initial set. But as Fig. 3 shows, the data are scattered and represent the noise created during the experiments. Because of this, predictions including this pellet do not work as illustrated in Table 4. Indeed, if a pellet is used in training to predict another pellet. The data are no longer really noise, but the model is incapable of making any correlation between them. Table 5 demonstrates that prediction is particularly poor, regardless of the size of the training data. However, the GPR model seems suitable for our problem. Despite the limited amount of data we have, satisfactory results can still be achieved, as shown in Tables 4 and 6 involving MOU.

5 Conclusion and Future Work

Improving combustion efficiency in pellet stoves using limited datasets presents a significant challenge. This paper introduces an innovative approach to address this problem, leveraging the Gaussian Process Regression (GPR) algorithm in combination with ANOVA and t-SNE methods. This approach enables the identification of key features in the data and guides the sampling process. In our study, the GPR algorithm was specifically tailored to achieve high prediction accuracy even with small datasets. Extensive experiments were conducted to evaluate the algorithm's effectiveness, demonstrating that the trends predicted by the model can facilitate the identification of optimal settings for pellet stoves. However, several limitations could identified in this study. First, the number of pellets tested was limited to five, and the number of measurements per pellet varied significantly, reducing the robustness of the model. Second, the experimental data included a high level of noise for some pellets, especially BIO, which negatively impacted the model's predictive performance. Third, the model showed poor generalization when attempting to predict results across different pellet types, indicating the need for a larger and more diverse dataset. Finally, the sensitivity to data quality highlighted the importance of controlled and repeatable experimental procedures. Nonetheless, the experimental results showed that appropriate stove settings could vary combustion efficiency by up to 10% and reduce carbon monoxide emissions by a factor of four, underscoring the significance of optimizing stove settings.

For future work, further essays will be led to enhance the quality and size of the dataset. Moreover, due to the number of possible parameters combinations, we plan to realize a global sensitivity analysis that would allow us to quantify the influence of input variables and to determine the best parameter combination for the kriging method. Then, thanks to the result obtained previously, we will be able to enhance the surrogate model and well-predict the CO emission rate for each possible couple of pellet/stove. So, it will be possible to find the optimal value of CO. And, an inverse analysis model will give us the optimal parameters for this kind of combustion. Finally, the k-fold cross-validation strategy will be employed to evaluate the performance of the model and its capacity of generalizing the result of each pellet.

References

1. ministère de la transition écologique: Datalab. Statistique publique, Location (2021). https://www.statistiques.developpement-durable.gouv.fr/edition-numerique/chiffres-cles-energie-2021/pdf/chiffres-cles-de-l-energie-edition-2021.pdf

2. ADEME and France Bois Forêt and Interprofession Nationale and Propellet and SNPGB and CIBE: Synthèse: Articulation des usages entre granulés et plaquettes pour les chaufferies biomasse. ADEME, Location (2020). https://bois-energie.ofme.org/wp-content/uploads/2022/07/Synthese-etude-granule-collectif-Propellet-2020.pdf

3. Benoît Brandelet: Caractérisation physico-chimique des particules issues du chauffage domestique au bois. Université de Lorraine (2016)

4. Mack, Y., Goel, T., Shyy, W., Haftka, R.: Metamodel-based simulation optimization: surrogate model-based optimization framework: a case study in aerospace design. In: Evolutionary Computation in Dynamic and Uncertain Environments, pp. 323–342 (2007). https://doi.org/10.1007/978-3-540-49774-5_14

5. Wang, W., Pei, J., Yuan, S., Zhang, J., Yuan, J., Xu, C.: Application of different surrogate models on the optimization of centrifugal pump. J. Mech. Sci. Technol. **30**(2), 567–574 (2016). https://doi.org/10.1007/s12206-016-0110-0

6. Li, H., Xu, B., Lu, G., Du, C., Huang, N.: Multi-objective optimization of PEM fuel cell by coupled significant variables recognition, surrogate models and a multi-objective genetic algorithm. Energy Convers. Manage. 114063 (2021). https://doi.org/10.1016/j.enconman.2021.114063

7. Chabanet, S., El-Haouzi, H.B., Thomas, P.: Coupling digital simulation and machine learning metamodel through an active learning approach in Industry 4.0 context. Comput. Ind. 103529 (2021). https://doi.org/10.1016/j.compind.2021.103529

8. Brandelet, B., Rose, C., Landreau, J., Druette, L., Rogaume, Y.: Toward a cleaner domestic wood heating by the optimization of firewood stoves? J. Clean. Prod. **325**, 129338 (2021). https://doi.org/10.1016/j.jclepro.2021.129338

9. Zhu, X.: Characterization of wood pellets combustion for clean energy generation (2024)

10. Koraïem, M., Assanis, D.: Wood stove combustion modeling and simulation: technical review and recommendations. Int. Commun. Heat Mass Transfer **127**, 105423 (2021). https://doi.org/10.1016/j.icheatmasstransfer.2021.105423

11. Johnson, M., et al.: Modeling approaches and performance for estimating personal exposure to household air pollution: a case study in Kenya. Indoor Air **31**(5), 1441–1457 (2021). https://doi.org/10.1111/ina.12790

12. do Amaral, J.V.S., Montevechi, J.A.B., de Carvalho Miranda, R., de Sousa Junior, W.T.: Metamodel-based simulation optimization: a systematic literature review. Simul. Model. Pract. Theory **114**, 102403 (2022). https://doi.org/10.1016/j.simpat.2021.102403

13. Stimson, J.A., Carmines, E.G., Zeller, R.A.: Interpreting polynomial regression. Sociol. Methods Res. **6**(4), 515–524 (1978). https://doi.org/10.1177/004912417800600405

14. Krogh, A.: What are artificial neural networks? Nat. Biotechnol. **26**(2), 195–197 (2008). https://doi.org/10.1038/nbt1386

15. Sagi, O., Rokach, L.: Ensemble learning: a survey. Wiley Interdisc. Rev.: Data Min. Knowl. Discov. **8**(4), e1249 (2018). https://doi.org/10.1002/widm.1249

16. Buhmann, M.D.: Radial basis functions. Acta Numerica **9**, 1–38 (2000). https://doi.org/10.1017/S0962492900000015

17. Noble, W.S.: What is a support vector machine? Nat. Biotechnol. **24**(12), 1565–1567 (2006). https://doi.org/10.1038/nbt1206-1565

18. Kleijnen, J.P.C.: Kriging metamodeling in simulation: a review. Eur. J. Oper. Res. **192**(3), 707–716 (2009). https://doi.org/10.1016/j.ejor.2007.10.013

19. van der Maaten, L., Hinton, L.: Visualizing data using t-SNE. J. Mach. Learn. Res. **9** (2008). https://www.jmlr.org/papers/volume9/vandermaaten08a/vandermaaten08a.pdf?fbcl

20. Liu, H., et al.: Using t-distributed Stochastic Neighbor Embedding (t-SNE) for cluster analysis and spatial zone delineation of groundwater geochemistry data. J. Hydrol. (2021). https://doi.org/10.1016/j.jhydrol.2021.126146

Fair Profit Allocation Methods in Horizontal Logistics Cooperation: A Systematic Review

Rebecca Kißner[(✉)] , Stefan Senftleben, Liselotte Burger, and Rainer Lasch

Business Management, esp. Logistics, Technische Universität Dresden, Dresden, Germany
rebecca.kissner@tu-dresden.de

Abstract. Cooperation is a common practice in logistics, as it optimizes routes and reduces costs through joint freight transportation. Nevertheless, incentives such as the fair distribution of profits between companies are essential to maintaining such cooperation. This study provides an overview of relevant profit allocation mechanisms for sustaining long-term cooperation in logistics by reviewing recently published studies on horizontal cooperation in transport logistics. Thus, the paper describes relevant profit distribution methods and their application in transport logistics and examines the role of optimized transport planning as a prerequisite for profitable cooperation.

Keywords: Profit Allocation · Horizontal Cooperation · Transport Problem

1 Introduction

The logistics sector is characterized by high competition, driven by increasing customer expectations regarding delivery times, extra services and environmentally friendly practices. At the same time, the sector is facing rising transport costs. However, cooperation[1] between transport service providers offers advantages, like pooled resources, cost savings and expanded services [1]. Therefore, horizontal cooperation between logistics service providers can increase profits by up to 30% compared to non-cooperation and fulfil ecological goals like emission reduction [2].

Cruijssen [1] defines horizontal cooperation in logistics as an active collaboration between companies, acting at the same level in the supply chain and offering comparable landsite logistic activities. Pan et al. [3] specify this definition for horizontal collaborative transport in which companies work together in freight transport, which requires a common transport planning between collaborating companies.

---

[1] In this study, the terms cooperation and collaboration are used interchangeably.

J. Barata et al. (Eds.): IN4PL 2025, CCIS 2826, pp. 82–99, 2026.
https://doi.org/10.1007/978-3-032-15579-5_6

One of the key challenges in implementing horizontal cooperation in transport is the fair gain sharing or cost allocation[2] among the participating companies [3, 5], which is essential to maintain stable cooperation [6]. Therefore, a fair and practically usable profit allocation method can be seen as a crucial issue in collaboration [7], but it is rarely addressed in the literature [8].

Guajardo and Rönnqvist [9] conducted a comprehensive literature review on cost-sharing mechanisms in collaborative transport and identified over 40 methods in publications between 1983 and 2015. In addition, Gansterer and Hartl [2] reviewed horizontal logistics collaboration with a focus on collaborative and auction-based planning. More recently, Anwar et al. [10] reviewed profit allocation in supply chains, covering studies published between 2007 and 2022, but focusing particularly on the factors influencing profit allocation methods. Despite extensive research, there has been no systematic review of newly developed profit allocation methods since 2016.

In order to create long-term, stable horizontal cooperation in the field of transport logistics, this paper aims to provide an overview of the profit allocation mechanisms investigated in the current literature. Building on the results of Guajardo and Rönnqvist [9], this study analyzes articles published after 2015. This leads us to the following research questions, which are to be answered by a systematic literature review:

I. Which profit allocation methods in horizontal cooperation in transport logistics have been developed since 2016?
II. How can profit be distributed fairly among the collaborating logistics providers?
III. What role do transport problems play in the design of profit allocation methods in horizontal logistics cooperation?

This paper is structured as follows: Sect. 2 describes the research methodology and strategy. Section 3 presents the identified profit allocation methods, while Sect. 4 addresses the underlying transport problems. Section 5 summarizes the results, discusses limitations and outlines areas for further research.

2 Research Methodology

In February 2025, a systematic literature review was conducted to identify all relevant articles concerning profit allocation methods in horizontal cooperation in transport logistics. This method provides an overview of all relevant publications addressing the aforementioned issue [11]. The review followed the structured process proposed by Xiao and Watson [12], beginning with the formulation of research questions and the design of a research protocol. The following databases were selected for the research: Scopus, ScienceDirect, Web of Science and Emerald Insight. The keywords used ("joint logistics" OR "shared logistics" OR "collaborative logistics" OR "collaborative transport") AND (allocation OR game) generated 1,874 articles. During the literature screening

---

[2] The analyzed literature investigates cost and profit sharing methods among cooperating companies, both of which can be used for profit allocation. While cost sharing divides the common costs between the cooperating companies, profit sharing allocates the coalition gain, which can result in different outcomes for each participant [4]. This study primarily investigates the allocation of profits among the cooperating companies.

process, articles were excluded based on the inclusion and exclusion criteria, as shown in Fig. 1. After screening titles, abstracts and full-texts, 36 articles remained. In addition, the backward and forward searches suggested by Webster and Watson [13] were applied, resulting in three further relevant articles. This resulted in a final selection of 39 papers. The relevant information was then extracted, analyzed and illustrated [12].

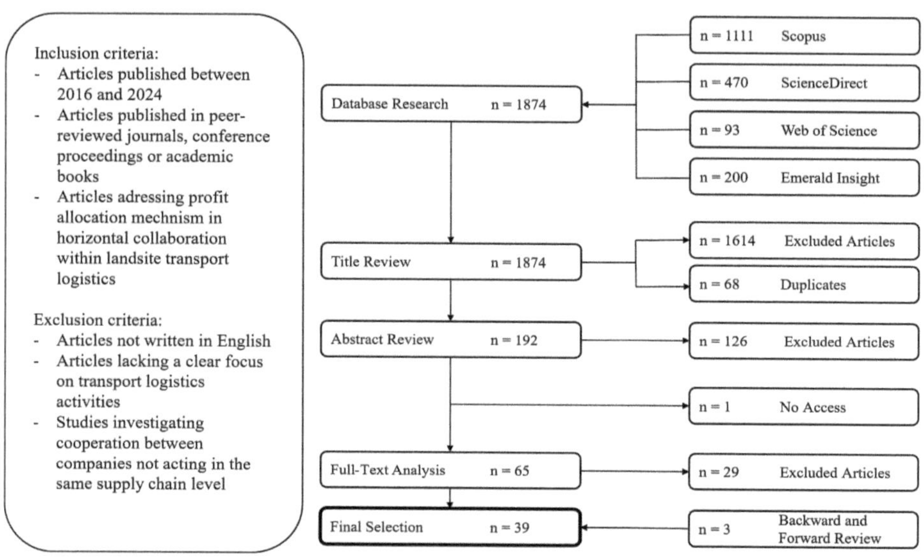

Fig. 1. Research Process.

While Guajardo and Rönnqvist [9] analyzed articles about profit allocation in horizontal and vertical logistic cooperation between 1983 and 2015, this research focuses on articles published as from 2016 onwards, that specifically address horizontal cooperation in transport logistics. As illustrated in Fig. 2, this study reveals a peak of eight publications on horizontal collaboration in transport logistics in 2016, consistent with the steady increase in publications on collaborative logistics between 2006 and 2015 [9]. This was followed by a subsequent decline, with an average of only four relevant articles published yearly in recent years.

In contrast to Guajardo and Rönnqvist [9], who primarily examined articles published in operations research journals, this study also reviewed articles from journals focusing on sustainable topics, like *Sustainability* or the *Journal of Cleaner Production*. The broader scope of this research over the last few years could be explained by rising attention for sustainable topics. This is also indicated by the emergence of topics such as the reduction of carbon emissions, which was addressed in five of the identified articles [14–18].

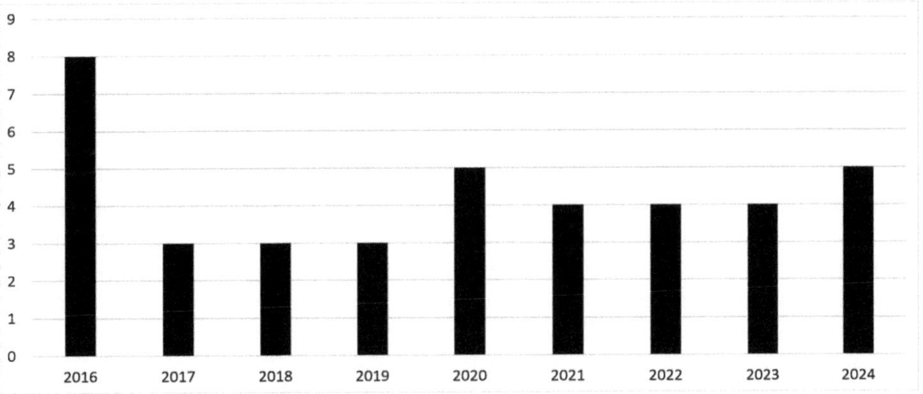

Fig. 2. Number of articles per year.

Table 1. Profit allocation methods.

| Study | Method | | | | | | | | | | | | | | |
| | Core Value | Extended Core | | Shapley Value | Improved Shapley Value | Nucleolus | Proportional/ Volume-based | EPM/ ESCM | Dual | Marginal | | | GQP | New Mechanism | Integrated Model |
		ε-Core	Least-Core							ACA/ACAM	CGA/CGM	MCRS			
[4]				X		X	X	X		X					
[5]	X			X										P	
[6]	X			X		X		X				P			
[7]				X				X						P	
[8]				X			X							P	
[14]				X										P	
[15]	X			X	P	X	X								
[16]				P											
[17]	X			X	X			X			X	P			
[18]	X			X				X			P	X			
[20]	X			X										P	
[21]	X	X	X	X		X	X							P	
[22]				X										P	
[23]	X		X	X		X	X	X		X				P	
[24]	X		X	X		X	X							P	
[25]				X	P										
[26]	X	X	P												P
[27]	X	P							P						
[28]	X		P				X		X						P
[29]				X										P	
[30]	X			X	P			X				X	X		
[31]															P
[32]	X			X		X									
[33]															P
[34]				X	P										
[35]	X			X	P	X									
[36]	X			X							P	X	X		
[37]	X				P			X			X	X			
[38]	X				P			X			X	X			
[39]												P			
[40]	X			X				X				X	P		
[41]	X							X			X	P	X		
[42]	X			X				X				P	X		
[43]	X		X	X								P	X		
[44]	X			X				X				P	X		
[45]	P			P											
[46]	P			X		X		X							P
[47]	X			X	P										
[48]	X		X	X	P			X							
Mentioned	27	3	7	30	10	8	8	14	3	2	6	13	7	10	5
Preferred	**2**	**1**	**2**	**2**	**9**	**0**	**0**	**0**	**1**	**0**	**2**	**7**	**1**	**10**	**5**

EPM: Equal profit method; ESCM: Equal cost saving method; ACA/ACAM: Alternative cost avoided method; MCRS: Minimum cost remaining savings; CGA: Cost gap analysis; GQP: Game quadratic programming

3 Profit Allocation Methods

As illustrated in Table 1, a list of the profit allocation methods most frequently mentioned in the selected papers is provided. To follow Guajardo and Rönnqvist [9] the mention of a method, indicated by an "X", does not imply that the allocation method is favorable, rather it was mentioned in the analyzed studies as a theoretical basis or to compare different mechanisms. A bold "**P**" indicates that the method is emphasized as the preferred solution in the study or is proven to be superior to other mechanisms.

Table 1 shows that the Shapley Value and the Core are frequently mentioned in the selected literature. However, new mechanisms and improved methods, like the improved Shapley Value, are used more frequently for fair profit allocation. These developments were also noted in the review by Guajardo and Rönnqvist [9], alongside mechanisms such as the Nucleolus, proportional, dual and marginal-based methods. In addition, the EPM, first proposed by Frisk et al. [19] and categorized as a new method by Guajardo and Rönnqvist [9], has been frequently mentioned in recent years. Furthermore, both the GQP and the MCRS, which were absent in the review by Guajardo and Rönnqvist [9], have been identified in this review.

The following section analyzes the profit allocation methods identified. Some of them are based on game theory, like the Core or the Shapley Value, while others follow simpler rules like the proportional method. Modified methods are also described, which were developed to address specific limitations of the original mechanism. Finally, this chapter introduces new methods and integrated models that combine profit allocation and transport planning.

3.1 Core Value

The Core Value, first described by Gillies [49] is a concept that generates a set of solutions if the Core is non-empty [21]. This set of possible solutions or profit allocations can be formulated as follows:

$$\text{Core}(N, v) = \left\{ x \in R^n : \sum_{j \in N} x_j = v(N), \ \sum_{j \in S} x_j \geq v(S), \ \forall S \subseteq N \right\} \tag{1}$$

Here $N = \{1, \ldots, n\}$ describes all players of the "grand coalition" and $v(S)$ expresses the profit of each sub-coalition S. If the allocation vector $x = (x_1, \ldots, x_n)$ assigns the entire profit of the grand coalition among all players j in N, the *efficient condition* (2) is fulfilled. A profit allocation within the Core incentivizes no player to leave the grand coalition, since no coalition would put the player in a better position. Therefore, solutions in the Core can be considered stable. The *rationality constraint* (3) states that profit earned by a player or a sub-coalition must be greater than their stand-alone profit [9, 19, 32].

$$\sum_{j \in N} x_j = v(N) \tag{2}$$

$$\sum_{j \in S} x_j \geq v(S), \quad \forall S \subseteq N \tag{3}$$

As can be seen in Table 1, the Core Value was often mentioned in the selected literature. Here, the Core was mostly used to verify whether the allocation method generated a solution within the Core and supported stable cooperation. For example, the studies by Yang et al. [45], Saha and Gupta [32] and Li et al. [15] calculate the Core and position their solutions within it, as demonstrated in Fig. 3. In addition, some studies use the distance to the Core center to compare different methods, where the smallest distance indicates the most stable solution, which can be seen in Fig. 4 [6, 17, 18, 30, 36–38, 40–44].

Since a game's Core can be empty, meaning that cooperation cannot generate a stable solution, the literature emphasizes alternative mechanisms [24]. The extended Core, like the Least-Core or the ϵ-Core, is based on an increase in coalition costs or a decrease in coalition profit by ϵ, in order to keep players in the grand coalition [21]. First mentioned by Shapley and Shubik [50], the ϵ-Core restricts the stability condition of a coalition by the value of ϵ [28]. If the Core is empty, the smallest optimal solution for ϵ, is the Least-Core, proposed by Maschler et al. [51]. Chen [21] uses the extended Core to generate a stable solution for his designed profit allocation mechanism. In addition, Kimms and Kozeletskyi [26] apply this concept in their solution to generate a stable Core or Least-Core for a Traveling Salesman Problem. In contrast, Lai et al. [28] suggest an algorithm solving a routing optimization and a Least-Core allocation simultaneously. Furthermore, Lai et al. [27] investigate ϵ-Core solutions based on a Lagrangian dual solution.

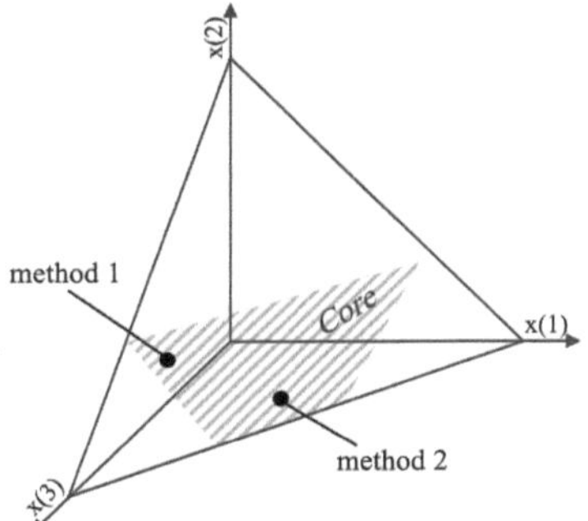

Fig. 3. Visualization of an exemplary Core space for a cooperation with three players and the position of two methods [15, 32]

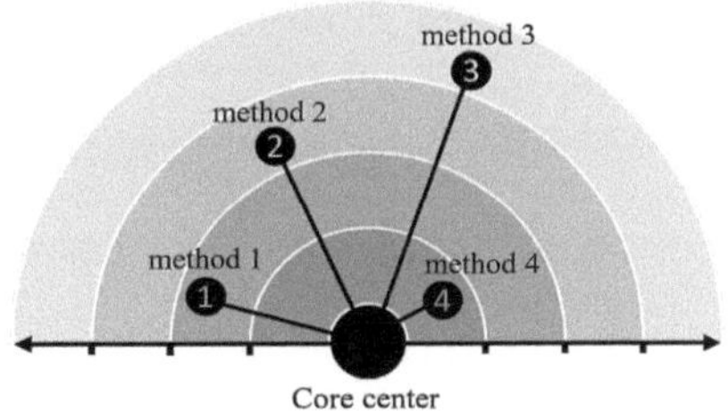

Fig. 4. Distance from exemplary methods to Core center [30]

3.2 Shapley Value

The Shapley Value, introduced by Shapley [52], is a frequently mentioned method for fair profit allocation in collaborative transport [15, 16, 22]. The solution concept generates a solution that represents the player's profit based on the marginal player's contribution to all possible coalitions and the probability of his entry sequence (4) [19, 21]:

$$x_j(N, v) = \sum_{S \subseteq N; j \in S} \frac{(N - |S|)!(|S| - 1)!}{N!} \cdot \left[v(S) - v(S \setminus \{j\})\right], \quad \forall j \in N \qquad (4)$$

Due to its fair characteristics and the convenient solvability of the formula, the Shapley Value is often used in collaborative logistics, as in the study by Defryn et al. [4], Zhou et al. [16] or Saha and Gupta [32]. It is also used by Yang et al. [45] to allocate the profit of different logistic service providers in the last-mile delivery in rural areas. Moreover, many selected studies use the Shapley Value as a comparative value or basis for their proposed methods [7, 8, 21, 23, 24, 29, 46]. In some studies, an improved Shapley Value takes into account that an organizer of the coalition receives an extra share of the profit for higher effort [30, 34, 37, 38], such as transport management or bargaining [35]. Also, Li et al. [15] recommend an improved Shapley approach that integrates weighted factors such as company operations, customer satisfaction, sustainability and IT infrastructure.

In other studies, new methods based on the Shapley value have been developed that overcome the limitations of this method. For example, the Shapley Value may not provide a stable solution in the Core for non-convex games. Therefore, Agussurja et al. [20] define an iterative procedure based on the normalized Shapley Value that should provide stable and fair solutions with the lowest possible subsidies. In addition, the Shapley Value requires complete information about the player participation and coalition profits, which is addressed by a fuzzy Shapley Value in He et al. [14]. Furthermore, in Gansterer [22], the Shapley Value failed for auction-based cooperation due to the loss of individual rationality in superadditive games and therefore a new mechanism was developed. The mentioned new studies can be seen in Sect. 3.5. In addition, Zhang et al. [47] apply the Core guaranteed Shapley Value for profit allocation in pickup and delivery service collaboration, which was introduced by Dai and Chen [53] and mentioned in Guajardo and Rönnquvist's study [9] as a new mechanism. This method generates allocations that lie in the Core and are close to the Shapley Value.

According to Zibaei et al. [48] another extension of the Shapley concept is the r value. This fair distribution method assigns a profit share between the marginal contribution of a player and a defined lower bound. In addition, Kaewpuang et al. [25] address a vehicle pooling problem with overlapping coalitions, using the Myerson Value [54]. This method can be calculated similarly to the Shapley Value and is applicable to situations involving several sub-coalitions, where not every player collaborates with every other player.

3.3 Nucleolus

The Nucleolus, introduced by Schmeidler [55], is a method with one solution, which always lies within the Core, provided that the Core is non-empty [19]. Therefore, it can be seen as a value selected from within the Core [21]. Profits are distributed so as to minimize the greatest injustice and each player gets more than they would in isolation. The surplus or excess vector ε represents the degree of dissatisfaction of an individual player (5):

$$\varepsilon(x, S) = v(S) - \sum_{j \in S} x_j \qquad (5)$$

Defryn et al. [4] recommend the Nucleolus for achieving stability, as it identifies a solution at the center of the Core. This argument is supported by Saha and Gupta [32], who compare the Nucleolus with the Shapley Value in their study. However, this literature review shows that the Nucleolus is often used as a comparative value for other methods, rather than being mentioned as the favored method [6, 21, 35]. In Li et al. [15], for example, the Nucleolus leads to poorer results than the Shapley Value or the improved Shapley Value in terms of stability. In addition, Hezarkhani et al. [23] state that the Nucleolus fails in allocating profit fairly among two players, distorting the competition between players. Similar to the Nucleolus, the Minmax Core, which is only mentioned once in Wang et al. [35], minimizes the maximum dissatisfaction among coalitions, but is expressed as a percentage [56].

3.4 Further Allocation Methods

Proportional or volume-based allocation methods can allocate the coalition profit according to certain criteria, such as the player's contributed volume or stand-alone costs [9, 19]. In the logistics context, the total weight or volume of the transported products or the number of containers can be used as a basis [4, 46]. The proportional or volume-based method is mentioned several times in the identified studies, but often in a comparative sense. For example, Hezarkhani et al. [23] compare the proportional solution for two-player games proposed by Ortmann [57] with other methods. Similarly, Chen [21] and Lai et al. [28] use the proportional method for comparison with their own method, considering the proportional approach to be less stable. Also, Li et al. [15] identified issues with more unstable solutions when using the volume-based allocation method. However, the authors characterized the method as a simple approach that can be easily solved, in contrast to the Nucleolus. Defryn et al. [4] described the same advantage, categorizing this method as a simple rule of thumb. However, the key function of this method is to allocate greater profits to the players who contribute more, which does not always lead to a fair solution [8].

Dual or shadow price-based allocation methods are predicated on a linear programming model and enable profit allocation based on a player's contribution to the dual objective function [9, 19]. This literature review identified three studies that mentioned this method. Yang et al. [46] formulate a cooperative transport game problem for collaborating transportation companies, which can be solved by using a dual problem. However, the authors demonstrate an optimally restrictive transport scheme that also produces fair and stable profit allocations. In addition, Lai et al. [27] propose a Lagrangian dual problem to generate profit allocations in an extended Core. In contrast, Lai et al. [28], only use the dual rule as a comparative solution to the designed model, producing unstable solutions.

The equal profit method (EPM), first mentioned by Frisk et al. [19], describes an allocation mechanism that minimizes the maximum pairwise difference in relative cost savings based on the stand-alone costs and provides stable solutions if the Core is non-empty. This method was frequently mentioned in the analyzed studies, albeit less favorably. In Defryn et al. [4], the EPM is calculated compared to other methods and produces unfair solutions for heterogeneous actors with different stand-alone costs. Also, Hezarkhani et al. [23] argue that the full consideration of stand-alone costs within the EPM can result in unfair solutions, as delivery properties that may not contribute to the coalition's profit are taken into account. In addition, Wan and Ding [7] utilize a model based on the EPM that includes contribution ratio weights. This method was introduced by Liu et al. [58] and mentioned by Guajardo and Rönnqvist [9] as a new mechanism in their study. Zibaei et al. [48], on the other hand, use the equal cost saving method (ECSM), which is similar to the EPM, but differs in its notation.

The marginal profit allocation mechanism was first described by Tjis and Driessen [59] as a method that divides the total profit of a coalition into a separable and a non-separable cost share. The separable part represents the marginal costs of a player, while the non-separable portion is divided in different ways depending on the method. To calculate the alternative cost avoided method (ACA or ACAM), weighting vectors are determined based on the player's contribution to allocate the costs [4]. The method is presented in Defryn et al. [4], in which the method can produce results similar to the Shapley Value. However, Hezarkhani et al. [23] also show that the ACA can have an empty Core and leads to equally divided profits in the case of two-player cooperation. In addition, the cost gap method (CGM) or cost gap allocation (CGA) distributes the non-separable costs using a cost gap function, which shows the difference between the cooperation costs with and without the participation of each player [59]. This method is applied in Wang et al. [36] and Wang et al. [18], representing the most stable solution in comparison with other selected methods. Further studies compare the methodology to other models [17, 37, 38, 41].

The minimum cost remaining savings (MCRS) method is mentioned in 13 of the selected articles, with seven of these selecting it as the favorable solution. The MCRS, first introduced by Heaney and Dickinson [60], defines a lower and upper bound of cost allocation for each player. In the end, each player receives their minimum costs (lower bound), and the remaining coalition costs are distributed proportionally according to the difference between the upper and lower bounds of the players. In Wang et al. [42], the cost distributions using MCRS method in reverse logistics networks provide more stable solutions than those using the Shapley Value or the EPM. Other studies have also illustrated the stability of the MCRS solution compared to other profit allocation methods [6, 17, 41–43] or have presented the method as the preferred solution [39]. In addition, Wang et al. [44] recommend an extended MCRS model that takes compensation into account when actors leave the coalition, to encourage remaining players to continue cooperating.

The game-theoretic quadratic programming method (GQP) was mentioned by Wang et al. [40] as the most stable method to allocate profit in their formulated problem by minimizing the quadratic deviation between the actual profit share and the marginal contribution of a player. Further studies use this method as a comparison with other allocation mechanisms [30, 36, 41–44].

3.5 New Methods and Integrated Models

Certain studies in Table 2 demonstrate newly developed mechanisms to solve individual problems, such as selective vehicle routing [8] or cases with incomplete information [29]. Most of these new methods are based on traditional methods, like the Shapley Value, the Core, or the EPM and aim to achieve fair and stable allocations. It should be noted that the data used to verify this mechanism was based almost exclusively on theoretical data and did not arise from practical challenges.

Furthermore, only five studies utilized integrated models, which merged profit allocation and transport planning. Two of them included a fairness constraint in the route planning problem. According to Defryn et al. [8], such an application considerably increases the complexity of the optimization problem, making it unsuitable in practice. However, Rückert et al. [31] investigated different fairness mechanisms on a weekly or daily basis as constraints in the optimization problem, which require, for example, an increase in profits above the stand-alone profits. Soriano et al. [33] on the other hand, embedded fairness as a second objective function in the bi-objective optimization problem to maximize the smallest profit variation regarding the stand-alone profit. These approaches enable the incorporation of fairness from the initial stages of transport planning. Other studies use the conditions of the Core concept to create stable transport schemes or routes. For example, Yang et al. [46] propose an optimal restrictive transport scheme with integrated stability constraint to generate solutions lying in the Core. In contrast, Lai et al. [28] propose an algorithm for their pickup and delivery model that solves a Least-Core allocation and a routing optimization problem simultaneously. Kimms and Kozeletskyi [26], on the other hand, suggest an algorithm that generates Core or Least-Core allocations for their cooperative Traveling Salesman Problem.

Table 2. New profit allocation methods.

Study	New profit allocation method
[5]	A **generalized Core** and **generalized Shapley Value** for stable and fair solutions in *coalitions with transferable and non-transferable utilities,* including two methods for final solution selection
[7]	A method for *two collaborating carriers in the less-than-truckload industry,* considering the **contribution to profit per cost and profit per price** of each player
[8]	Weighted allocation method for *selective vehicle routing problems* considering **separable and penalty-based non-separable costs** with an algorithm ensuring individual rational solutions
[14]	**Fuzzy Shapley Value** for cooperation with *missing information* about player participation level and cooperation profits, formulated as an intuitionistic fuzzy game and using **triangular fuzzy numbers** for profit distribution
[20]	An iterative procedure for *non-convex vehicle routing games* based on the **normalized Shapley Value,** providing stable and fair solutions with minimal possible subsidies
[21]	A method for *vehicle routing games* based on **cross-evaluation of** players cost contribution, ensuring an **extended Core** if the Core is empty
[22]	Method for profit distribution in *auction-based cooperation,* based on a **weighted average of purchases and sales** of the transport requests of the participating companies
[23]	Model for fair and competitive profit distribution in *joint freight transport,* generating an **approximately proportional allocation** in the Core or Least-Core

(continued)

Table 2. (*continued*)

Study	New profit allocation method
[24]	Profit allocation by using **component-wise Core** based on optimal solutions in *capacity-constrained consolidation games* with **a proportional allocation rule** and an envy-minimizing linear program
[29]	**Least square values** for *collaboration with incomplete information*, considering individual profit and contribution to the grand coalition and improving the least square (pre)nucleolus

4 Transport Problems

Realising the potential synergies of horizontal cooperation depends significantly on partner's ability to coordinate and optimize their logistics, particularly in transportation. In practice, this cooperation involves collaboratively tackling specific transport challenges together, as resolving them jointly is what ultimately yields the desired benefits. Figure 5 and Fig. 6, for example, illustrate the potential benefits of cooperation and customer sharing between two logistics service providers. This chapter provides a systematic analysis and explanation of transportation problems in selected articles to provide a detailed understanding of the operational dimension of this form of cooperation.

The analysis covers a wide range of problems, from classic vehicle routing and its variants to consolidation strategies such as achieving full truckloads or optimizing less-than-truckload networks and more complex problems like network design and cargo space management. Identifying and precisely characterizing these transport problems is crucial not only for understanding the operational dynamics of logistics cooperation but also for selecting appropriate balancing mechanisms. This is because the nature and complexity of the transport problems being addressed significantly influence potential cost savings and efficiency gains, which in turn dictate how cooperation profits are distributed.

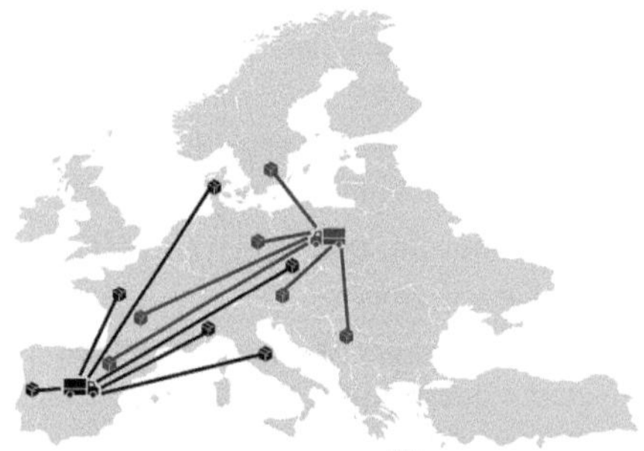

Fig. 5. Customer network of two logistics service providers without cooperation

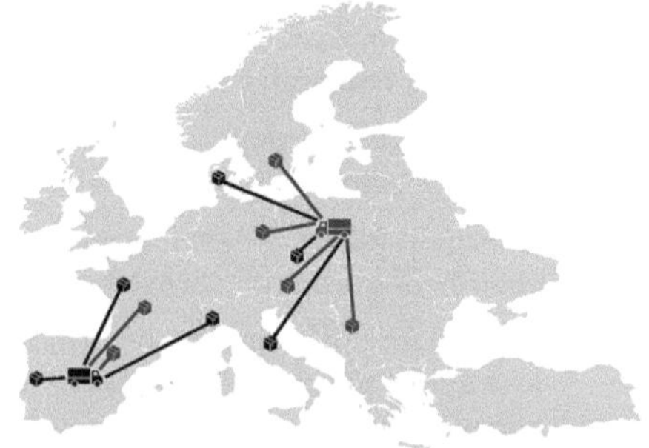

Fig. 6. Customer network of two logistics service providers with cooperation

4.1 Vehicle Routing Problems

The Vehicle Routing Problem (VRP) outlines the issue of finding the optimal set of routes for a fleet of vehicles to service geographically dispersed customers, starting and ending at a central depot, while minimizing a specific objective like total transportation costs or distance. The VRP emerged as a significant, distinct problem following the ground-breaking research by Dantzig and Ramser [61]. Their "Truck Dispatching Problem" was foundational, introducing considerations for multiple vehicles and capacity constraints, thereby establishing the basis for the modern VRP. Since then, the VRP has expanded into a rich family of problems, integrating a wide array of variations and constraints to better reflect real-world scenarios.

When examining models for horizontal cooperation in logistics, VRPs emerge as the most prevalent framework used by researchers, accounting for 27 of the research papers selected for this study. Reflecting the collaborative nature of these partnerships, where multiple entities pool their resources, 17 of the selected articles explicitly mention a multi-depot VRP as the basis of their optimization efforts in the cooperation activities.

For example, Soriano et al. [33] developed an integrated approach, combining total cost and a fairness measure to create a bi-objective structure for optimization of their multi-depot VRP. They developed the fairness measure into a constraint of the resulting optimization problem and used a heuristic approach to find vehicle routes for the cooperating partners. Amiri and Farvaresh [5] also used a multi-objective model in their selective VRP, in which customers could either be served profitably or not at all. To allow for more flexibility, they introduced additional transports between the depots of the cooperating parties to find optimal solutions, determining which customers to serve and how to organize the transportation, especially for last-mile deliveries. Other authors [35, 38] also allow for transports between the depots in order to achieve better solutions. Even greater flexibility is offered by allowing open tours, where vehicles are not required to return to the same depot from which they started [39]. Wang et al. [44] offer a model, where withdrawal of partners from an existing cooperation is considered and the resulting network of remaining depots is optimized. Further publications include a variety of problem instances and optimization models for different scenarios, for example logistics for agricultural products [16]. In conclusion, the multi-depot structure for VRPs is used to simulate the cooperation between different parties, each with its own existing distribution network. By combining these structures in coalitions, the best solutions for these coalitions can be found, providing the groundwork for the profit allocation methods presented in this study.

Another common approach found in the analyzed literature is the modeling of Pickup-and-Delivery (P&D) operations. These problems involve picking up an item from one node and delivering it to another node. Depending on the items, it may be possible to transport more than one inside the vehicle simultaneously and the order in which the pickup and delivery visits are carried out is fixed. Wang et al. [6] model a P&D problem by considering the freight status, capacity and the time of cooperating vehicles for a two-echelon network. Another two-echelon VRP with P&D and a shared vehicle fleet is optimized by assigning the customers optimally to the distribution depots of the cooperating partners [37]. Rückert et al. [31] propose a model for container transport in port hinterland logistics. In this model, they consider the transport of full and empty containers as well as empty truck routes in order to optimize in a cooperative network of multiple transporters. They encountered challenges due to certain containers being permitted to be transported only by certain carriers, as well as a complex structure of time and order constraints, by which the transportation of containers is limited. Wang et al. [43] offer a solution for mixed P&D structures, where nodes can be either for pickup, delivery or both at the same time. When another process, like installation, is also required in addition to delivery, Yang et al. [46] propose a comprehensive VRP model to ensure the right personnel and sufficient time are scheduled at the node. Zhang et al. [47] consider delivery options, where a customer's demand can be satisfied at more than one node. Lai et al. [28] do not specifically model a VRP, but offer a solution for a P&D problem that adheres to a last-in-first-out rule for cargo space in a vehicle. P&D structures are a fitting choice when goods are to be transported between nodes, containers are to be exchanged and returned or when other constraints dictate the order in which customers are to be served within the same tour.

An additional constraint that transportation has to adhere to is the definition of time windows for customer nodes. Time windows dictate at what time of day certain nodes should be visited. Wang et al. [43] define time windows in their VRP with P&D for the nodes and provide constraints to ensure that the routes adhere to these time windows. Time windows constraints can also be implemented into other problem structures, like in combination with constraints posed by P&D problems [28, 30, 31, 38, 39, 45].

4.2 Other Transportation Problems

Although VRPs are the most common way to model cooperative transportation efforts, other problem formulations are also present in the analyzed literature. Saha and Gupta [32] use the classic approach to the transportation problem and calculate optimized transportation schemes for possible coalitions of the participating carriers. Yang et al. [46] formulate a cost transportation problem and integrate additional constraints to ensure fairness by allocating the customers freely within the cooperation while maintaining the delivery volume for each depot at the same level as before the cooperation. Defryn et al. [4] offer a solution for cooperation in a shuttle service in fresh produce transportation aiming to consolidate freight loads. Hezarkhani et al. [24] model a dispatch consolidation problem as a set packing problem, considering also time window constraints. Lai et al. [27] propose a consolidation approach for truckloads by modelling a network flow problem that considers space and time constraints for the customer nodes. A two-echelon joint distribution network is presented by Wang et al. [34] focusing on clustering and allocation of customers to facility locations, without explicitly optimizing vehicle routes. Kimms and Kozeletskyi [26] consider a multiple traveling salesman problem with release dates for customer orders and different depots for each salesman representing the participants in the cooperation.

Some authors in the analyzed literature do not offer any specific problem formulation or solution method for their transportation problem. Instead, they focus solely on the profit allocation methods that follow the optimization of vehicle routes. They either refer to standard solution methods for common VRPs or just assume that solutions for the transportation problem can be found and continue their studies with presupposed solutions as a basis for their profit allocation [7, 14, 15, 21, 23, 29].

5   Discussion and Conclusion

Building on the review by Guajardo and Rönnqvist [9], this paper examines profit allocation methods since 2016, but in contrast to the aforementioned study, it is limited to horizontal cooperation in transport logistics. The relevant profit allocation mechanisms have been presented and the role of route planning has been explained. Therefore, this study provides an up-to-date overview of the allocation mechanisms and the underlying transport problems used in recent years, offering a foundation for selecting appropriate methods in horizontal transport logistics cooperation.

The comparison with the review by Guajardo and Rönnqvist [9] shows that many of the allocation methods applied up to 2015, such as the Core, Shapley Value, Nucleolus, proportional, dual and marginal methods, have also been frequently mentioned in recent years. The EPM, which was introduced in 2010, has been used increasingly, particularly since 2015. Additionally, certain methods, such as the GQP or the MCRS, have become more established in the studies published after 2015. Both reviews also demonstrate a continued trend toward developing problem-specific mechanisms. However, Guajardo and Rönnqvist [9] criticize these new approaches for largely building on existing models and lacking practical relevance. The newly developed models in this study are also largely based on theoretical data, which confirms this criticism. Nevertheless, a higher proportion of studies published after 2016 use industrial data, which could indicate a greater focus on real-world applications. Similarly, when comparing journals that have published the papers of both studies over time, interest in sustainability, such as reducing carbon emissions through cooperative logistics, appears to have increased in recent years.

In order to answer the first research question, the profit allocation methods mentioned in the selected articles were analyzed. Classical game-theoretic approaches such as the Core and the Shapley Value are commonly used as a theoretical basis. Furthermore, newer mechanisms such as the EPM are also frequently mentioned, as are the marginal method – especially MCRS – and simpler rules such as the proportional method. The Core concept generates a solution space and is often used to assess the stability of allocation methods. Consequently, it is applied in conjunction with other methods. The Shapley Value enables fair allocations based on marginal contributions, but it requires full information and does not guarantee stability. Therefore, many studies propose improved or adapted Shapley-based methods. In contrast, the Nucleolus always yields stable solutions within the Core, though it rarely performs best and is mostly used for comparison purposes. In addition, simpler methods like the proportional or volume-based method offer practical initial insights but fail to ensure fairness, as the highest volume does not guarantee the highest profit. The EPM minimizes relative savings between two players based on stand-alone costs. Although it is widely cited, the method has been criticized for solely considering stand-alone costs, which can lead to unfair outcomes, particularly when there are significant differences between the two players. Since 2017, the MCRS has been extensively applied to industrial data and has demonstrated robust performance in numerous studies. Nevertheless, the method is primarily employed by a specific group of authors. In addition, integrated methods offer an alternative approach, albeit a more complex one, that is consequently less frequently used. These methods integrate profit allocation into an optimization problem as a constraint or an objective function. Finally, the identified studies do not agree on the most effective method for cooperative logistics.

As a result, modified and new mechanisms adapted to specific problems usually perform better in comparison and are therefore often recommended as the best performing solution.

Defryn, et al. [8] recognize the consensus in the literature that there is no single profit allocation method that is best suited to every problem and that a different mechanism should be selected for each case. This is consistent with the study by Guajardo and Rönnqvist [9], which found that the best profit share depends on the problem and the requirements defined therein, such as fairness. Therefore, answering the second research question is difficult, as an optimal solution for a fair profit sharing method must be carefully considered for each cooperation in logistics. In this study, developing problem-based and individual new methods or comparing different existing solutions with the Core center, are the preferred concepts for achieving fair and stable solutions. However, the usage of practical applications and industrial data should be considered when developing a new mechanism. Furthermore, due to the many possible ways to distribute profit, Zibaei et al. [48] recommend setting out the chosen mechanisms in cooperation agreements to avoid conflicts.

In answering the third research question, which concerns the role of these transport problems in designing profit allocation methods, this review highlights that optimizing them is key, as this creates the surplus value or cost savings that require fair allocation. As cost minimization through optimization is the common driver across diverse transportation models, this study has focused on emerging cooperation scenarios and the methodologies for distributing these cooperatively generated savings, rather than detailing specific optimization mechanisms.

This paper examines the literature from 2016 onwards due to the extensive study by Guajardo and Rönnqvist [9] in 2016. However, the comparability of the two studies is limited by the use of a different search strategy, which focuses on identifying the latest literature in horizontal transport logistics. In addition, it should be noted that the frequently mentioned MCRS method has always been used by the same group of authors. Furthermore, although the term 'profit allocation' is used in this study, the analysed literature examines both cost-sharing and profit-sharing methods. However, the sharing of costs or gains can produce different outcomes for participating companies and should be considered by the coalition [4]. Further research could address the challenges of establishing horizontal collaboration in transport logistics and implementing a fair profit allocation mechanism among participating companies. The development of change management concepts and technical solutions, such as platform concepts, could support collaborative transportation. Additionally, further simulation-based research is needed to evaluate the usage of the identified methods for industrial data and real-world applications.

Acknowledgments. This study was funded by the Federal Ministry of Education and Research in Germany (BMBF) as part of the 'WIR! recyeln Fasern' (03WIR6009A) research project.

References

1. Cruijssen, F.: Horizontal cooperation in transport and logistics. CentER, Center for Economic Research (2006)

2. Gansterer, M., Hartl, R.F.: Collaborative vehicle routing: a survey. Eur. J. Oper. Res. **268**(1), 1–12 (2018)
3. Pan, S., Trentesaux, D., Ballot, E., Huang, G.Q.: Horizontal collaborative transport: survey of solutions and practical implementation issues. Int. J. Prod. Res. **57**(15–16), 5340–5361 (2019)
4. Defryn, C., Vanovermeire, C., Sörensen, K.: Gain sharing in horizontal logistic co-operation: a case study in the fresh fruit and vegetables sector. In: Lu, M., de Bock, J. (eds.) Sustainable Logistics and Supply Chains, pp. 1–16. Springer, Cham (2016)
5. Amiri, M., Farvaresh, H.: Carrier collaboration with the simultaneous presence of transferable and non-transferable utilities. Eur. J. Oper. Res. **304**(2), 596–617 (2023)
6. Wang, Y., Zhang, S., Guan, X., Fan, J., Wang, H., Liu, Y.: Cooperation and profit allocation for two-echelon logistics pickup and delivery problems with state–space–time networks. Appl. Soft Comput. **109**, 107528 (2021)
7. Wan, Y., Ding, J.: Allocating profits among collaborative carriers in less-than-truckload industry International Conference on Logistics. In: Informatics and Service, pp. 1–5. IEEE (2016)
8. Defryn, C., Sörensen, K., Cornelissens, T.: The selective vehicle routing problem in a collaborative environment. Eur. J. Oper. Res. **250**(2), 400–411 (2016)
9. Guajardo, M., Rönnqvist, M.: A review on cost allocation methods in collaborative transportation. Int. Trans. Oper. Res. **23**(3), 371–392 (2016)
10. Anwar, S., Ekawati, I., Ramadian, D.: A review of profit allocation models for the participants in a supply chain. In: Proceeding International Conference on Economic and Social Sciences. (2), 731–743 (2024)
11. vom Brocke, J., Simons, A., Niehaves, B., Reimer, K., Plattfaut, R., Cleven, A.: Reconstructing the giant: on the importance of rigour in documenting the literature search process. In: ECIS 2009 Proceedings (2009)
12. Xiao, Y., Watson, M.: Guidance on conducting a systematic literature review. J. Plan. Educ. Res. **39**(1), 93–112 (2019)
13. Webster, J., Watson, R.: Guest editorial: analyzing the past to prepare for the future: writing a literature review. MIS Q. **26**(2), 13–23 (2002)
14. He, X., Yang, S., Huang, S.: Profit allocation in logistics enterprise coalitions based on fuzzy cooperative game theory. In: Lui, Y. (eds.) International Conference on Cooperative Design, Visualization, and Engineering. Springer, Cham (2024)
15. Li, L., Wang, X., Lin, Y., Zhou, F., Chen, S.: Cooperative game-based profit allocation for joint distribution alliance under online shopping environment. APJML **31**(2), 302–326 (2019)
16. Zhou, L., Hou, G., Rao, W.: Collaborative logistics for agricultural products of 'farmer + consumer integration purchase' under platform empowerment. Expert Syst. Appl. **255**, 1–19 (2024)
17. Wang, Y., et al.: Implementation of cooperation for recycling vehicle routing optimization in two-echelon reverse logistics networks. Sustainability **10**(5), 1–27 (2018)
18. Wang, Y., et al.: Collaborative two-echelon multicenter vehicle routing optimization based on state–space–time network representation. J. Clean. Prod. **258**, 1–26 (2020)
19. Frisk, M., Göthe-Lundgren, M., Jörnsten, K., Rönnqvist, M.: Cost allocation in collaborative forest transportation. Eur. J. Oper. Res. **205**(2), 448–458 (2010)
20. Agussurja, L., Lau, H.C., Cheng, S.-F.: Achieving stable and fair profit allocation with minimum subsidy in collaborative logistics. In: Proceedings of the Thirtieth AAAI Conference on Artificial Intelligence (AAAI-16), pp. 3785–3792 (2016)
21. Chen, H.: Cross-evaluation cost allocation for vehicle routing games. IFAC-PapersOnLine **49**(12), 1856–1861 (2016)
22. Gansterer, M., Hartl, R.F., Sörensen, K.: Pushing frontiers in auction-based transport collaborations. Omega **94**, 1–12 (2020)

23. Hezarkhani, B., Slikker, M., van Woensel, T.: A competitive solution for cooperative truckload delivery. OR Spectrum **38**(1), 51–80 (2016)
24. Hezarkhani, B., Slikker, M., van Woensel, T.: Gain-sharing in urban consolidation centers. Eur. J. Oper. Res. **279**(2), 380–392 (2019)
25. Kaewpuang, R., Niyato, D., Tan, P.-S., Wang, P.: Cooperative management in full-truckload and less-than-truckload vehicle system. IEEE Trans. Veh. Technol. **66**(7), 5707–5722 (2017)
26. Kimms, A., Kozeletskyi, I.: Core-based cost allocation in the cooperative traveling salesman problem. Eur. J. Oper. Res. **248**(3), 910–916 (2016)
27. Lai, M., Cai, X., Hall, N.G.: Cost allocation for less-than-truckload collaboration via shipper consortium. Transp. Sci. **56**(3), 585–611 (2022)
28. Lai, M., Wu, Y., Cai, X.: Core-based cost allocation for collaborative multi-stop truckload shipping problem. IISE Trans. 1–19 (2024)
29. Liu, J.-C., Sheu, J.-B., Li, D.-F., Dai, Y.-W.: Collaborative profit allocation schemes for logistics enterprise coalitions with incomplete information. Omega **101**, 1–13 (2021)
30. Luo, S., Wang, Y., Tang, J., Guan, X., Xu, M.: Two-echelon multidepot logistics network design with resource sharing. J. Adv. Transp. **2021**, 1–28 (2021)
31. Rückert, N., Fischer, K., Reinecke, P., Wrona, T.: Collaboration benefits in port hinterland transportation. In: Buscher, U., Neufeld, Janis, S., Lasch, R., Schönberger, J. (eds.) Logistics Management. Contributions of the Section Logistics of the German Academic Association for Business Research, Dresden, Germany (Lecture Notes in Logistics). Springer, Cham (2023)
32. Saha, G., Gupta, M.K.: Fair cost-savings allocation in transportation game. In: 2023 IEEE International Conference on Industrial Engineering and Engineering Management (IEEM), pp. 627–631. IEEE (2023)
33. Soriano, A., Gansterer, M., Hartl, R.F.: Reprint of: the multi-depot vehicle routing problem with profit fairness. Int. J. Prod. Econ. **250**, 1–14 (2022)
34. Wang, Y., et al.: Cooperation and profit allocation in two-echelon logistics joint distribution network optimization. Appl. Soft Comput. **56**, 143–157 (2017)
35. Wang, Y., Ma, X., Li, Z., Liu, Y., Xu, M., Wang, Y.: Profit distribution in collaborative multiple centers vehicle routing problem. J. Clean. Prod. **144**, 203–219 (2017)
36. Wang, Y., Zhang, J., Assogba, K., Liu, Y., Xu, M., Wang, Y.: Collaboration and transportation resource sharing in multiple centers vehicle routing optimization with delivery and pickup. Knowl.-Based Syst. **160**, 296–310 (2018)
37. Wang, Y., et al.: Two-echelon logistics delivery and pickup network optimization based on integrated cooperation and transportation fleet sharing. Expert Syst. Appl. **113**, 44–65 (2018)
38. Wang, Y., Yuan, Y., Guan, X., Wang, H., Liu, Y., Xu, M.: Collaborative mechanism for pickup and delivery problems with heterogeneous vehicles under time windows. Sustainability **11**(12), 1–30 (2019)
39. Wang, Y., Li, Q., Guan, X., Fan, J., Liu, Y., Wang, H.: Collaboration and resource sharing in the multidepot multiperiod vehicle routing problem with pickups and deliveries. Sustainability **12**(15), 1–32 (2020)
40. Wang, Y., et al.: Collaborative multi-depot logistics network design with time window assignment. Expert Syst. Appl. **140**, 1–24 (2020)
41. Wang, Y., Li, Q., Guan, X., Xu, M., Liu, Y., Wang, H.: Two-echelon collaborative multi-depot multi-period vehicle routing problem. Expert Syst. Appl. **167**, 1–25 (2021)
42. Wang, Y., Zhe, J., Wang, X., Fan, J., Wang, Z., Wang, H.: Collaborative multicenter reverse logistics network design with dynamic customer demands. Expert Syst. Appl. **206**, 1–32 (2022)
43. Wang, Y., Ran, L., Guan, X., Fan, J., Sun, Y., Wang, H.: Collaborative multicenter vehicle routing problem with time windows and mixed deliveries and pickups. Expert Syst. Appl. **197**, 1–23 (2022)

44. Wang, Y., Luo, S., Fan, J., Xu, M., Wang, H.: Compensation and profit allocation for collaborative multicenter vehicle routing problems with time windows. Expert Syst. Appl. **233**, 1–32 (2023)
45. Yang, F., Dai, Y., Ma, Z.: A cooperative rich vehicle routing problem in the last-mile logistics industry in rural areas. Transp. Res. Part E: Logist. Transp. Rev. **141**, 1–21 (2020)
46. Yang, S., Zhang, J., Zhou, S.: The cost transportation game for collaboration among transportation companies. Ann. Oper. Res. **336**(3), 1479–1503 (2024)
47. Zhang, R., Dai, Y., Yang, F., Ma, Z.: A cooperative vehicle routing problem with delivery options for simultaneous pickup and delivery services in rural areas. Socioecon. Plann. Sci. **93**, 1–15 (2024)
48. Zibaei, S., Hafezalkotob, A., Ghashami, S.S.: Cooperative vehicle routing problem: an opportunity for cost saving. J. Ind. Eng. Int. **12**(3), 1–17 (2016)
49. Gillies, D.B.: Solutions to general non-zero-sum games. Contrib. Theory Games **4**(40), 47–85 (1959)
50. Shapley, L.S., Shubik, M.: Quasi-cores in a monetary economy with nonconvex preferences. Econom.: J. Econom. Soc. **334**(4), 805–827 (1966)
51. Maschler, M., Peleg, B., Shapley, L.S.: Geometric properties of the kernel, nucleolus, and related solution concepts. Math. Oper. Res. **4**(4), 303–338 (1979)
52. Shapley, L.S.: A value for N-person games (1952)
53. Dai, B., Chen, H.: Profit allocation mechanisms for carrier collaboration in pickup and delivery service. Comput. Ind. Eng. **62**(2), 633–643 (2012)
54. Myerson, R.B.: Graphs and cooperation in games. Math. Oper. Res. **2**(3), 225–229 (1977)
55. Schmeidler, D.: The nucleolus of a characteristic function game. SIAM J. Appl. Math. **17**(6), 1163–1170 (1969)
56. Drechsel, J., Kimms, A.: Cooperative lot sizing with transshipments and scarce capacities: solutions and fair cost allocations. Int. J. Prod. Res. **49**(9), 2643–2668 (2011)
57. Ortmann, K.M.: The proportional value for positive cooperative games. Math. Meth. Oper. Res. **51**, 235–248 (2000)
58. Liu, P., Wu, Y., Xu, N.: Allocating collaborative profit in less-than-truckload carrier alliance. JSSM **03**(01), 143–149 (2010)
59. Tijs, Stef H. and Driessen, Theo S.H.: Game theory and cost allocation problems. Manage. Sci. **32**(8), 1015–1028 (1986)
60. Heaney, J.P., Dickinson, R.E.: Methods for apportioning the cost of a water resource project. Water Resour. Res. **18**(3), 476–482 (1982)
61. Dantzig, G.B., Ramser, J.H.: The truck dispatching problem. Manage. Sci. **6**(1), 80–91 (1959)

When Machines Fail: Online Scheduling Under Bounded Failures

Christine Markarian[(✉)] [ID] and Alavikunhu Panthakkan [ID]

College of Engineering and Information Technology, Dubai, UAE
{cmarkarian,apanthakkan}@ud.ac.ae

Abstract. Smart manufacturing systems operate in increasingly dynamic environments, where machines may experience unexpected failures and recoveries during operation. These disruptions pose a fundamental challenge to real-time scheduling, which must proceed without foreknowledge of future jobs or machine outages. In this paper, we introduce a new online scheduling model that incorporates bounded-delay machine failures—unlike classical online scheduling, which assumes static machine availability. Jobs arrive over time and must be assigned immediately to currently available machines. Our objective is to minimize makespan while ensuring resilience to temporary unavailability. We design failure-aware online algorithms and prove competitive bounds relative to an optimal offline scheduler. Our results establish a theoretical foundation for robust, real-time scheduling in failure-prone Industry 4.0 systems.

Keywords: Online Scheduling · Competitive Analysis · Bounded Machine Failures · Fault-Tolerant Algorithms · Smart Manufacturing

1 Introduction

Smart manufacturing environments are increasingly dependent on autonomous systems capable of adapting to dynamic operational conditions. One of the key challenges in these environments is ensuring robust scheduling under uncertainty—particularly in the presence of machine failures. Unlike traditional factories, where system downtime is rare and often manually resolved, modern production lines rely on a network of cyber-physical systems where machine availability may change unpredictably and rapidly. These systems must maintain high throughput and efficiency even when individual components temporarily fail.

In classical online scheduling theory, it is generally assumed that all machines are constantly available and that jobs must be scheduled in real time without knowledge of future arrivals. While this model captures many aspects of uncertainty, it overlooks the critical impact of failures and recoveries that are common in Industry 4.0 systems. In practice, machines may go offline due to errors, maintenance, or power limitations, and recover after a short period. This dynamic behavior requires algorithms that not only operate online but are also resilient to bounded disruptions in machine availability.

In this work, we propose a new online scheduling model that explicitly accounts for machine failures with bounded recovery delays. Jobs arrive over time and must be

J. Barata et al. (Eds.): IN4PL 2025, CCIS 2826, pp. 100–115, 2026.
https://doi.org/10.1007/978-3-032-15579-5_7

assigned immediately to available machines. The goal is to minimize makespan or other scheduling objectives while contending with unpredictable, short-term unavailability of processing units. Our approach bridges a significant gap between theoretical scheduling models and the operational realities of modern smart manufacturing systems.

1.1 Our Contributions

We present the first formal study of online scheduling under bounded-delay machine failures, a scenario that realistically captures disruptions in smart manufacturing systems but has not been addressed in the competitive scheduling literature. Our contributions are as follows:

- We introduce a novel online scheduling model in which machines may become temporarily unavailable due to failures but are guaranteed to recover within a bounded delay. This model reflects operational conditions in cyber-physical production environments and has not been previously analyzed within the framework of competitive scheduling.
- We propose a simple yet effective Greedy algorithm that schedules each job on the least-loaded currently available machine. We rigorously prove that this algorithm maintains a competitive ratio of at most $2 + \frac{d}{T}$, where d is the maximum failure duration and T is the average optimal per-machine load. This provides the first analytical guarantees for online scheduling in fault-prone settings with deterministic recovery bounds.
- We establish the tightness of this bound by constructing adversarial instances showing that no deterministic online algorithm can achieve a better competitive ratio without additional power, even in the failure-free case. This lower bound highlights the inherent difficulty of online scheduling under uncertainty.
- To mitigate the impact of failures, we extend our analysis to the resource augmentation model, where machines in the online algorithm are allowed to run at slightly higher speed. We show that even modest speed augmentation dramatically improves the competitive ratio, yielding performance arbitrarily close to optimal.
- Our framework formalizes a new class of fault-tolerant online scheduling problems. It lays the theoretical groundwork for real-time decision-making algorithms in smart factories and industrial control systems subject to transient disruptions.

1.2 Paper Structure

The structure of the paper is as follows. Section 2 presents the theoretical background on online scheduling and failure models, and reviews related work. Section 3 introduces our formal scheduling model with bounded-delay machine failures. In Sect. 4, we describe and analyze the Greedy algorithm. Section 5 discusses algorithmic extensions, including lower bounds and resource augmentation. Section 6 reflects on the implications, limitations, and future directions. Section 7 highlights practical applications in smart manufacturing. Section 8 concludes the paper.

2   Background and Related Work

This section provides both background and a review of related work, introducing the core theoretical foundations of our model. We outline key concepts such as online scheduling, competitive analysis, and makespan minimization, and survey prior approaches to scheduling with uncertainty—particularly in the context of machine failures, prediction-based models, and resource augmentation.

2.1   Online Scheduling and Competitive Analysis

Let $J = \{j_1, j_2, \ldots\}$ be a sequence of jobs that arrive over time. Each job j_i has a release time $r_i \in \mathbb{N}$ and a processing time $p_i \in \mathbb{R}_{>0}$. At time $t \in \mathbb{N}$, the algorithm observes the set of jobs released at that moment and must assign them immediately and irrevocably to available machines.

Let $\mathcal{M} = \{M_1, \ldots, M_m\}$ be a set of identical parallel machines. In the classical online model, all machines are assumed to be always available. The scheduler's goal is to minimize the *makespan*:

$$C_{\max} = \max_{k \in [m]} \left\{ \sum_{j_i \in A_k} p_i \right\},$$

where A_k is the set of jobs assigned to machine M_k.

An online scheduling algorithm $\mathcal{A}$ is evaluated by comparing its makespan to that of an optimal offline algorithm OPT, which knows the entire job sequence and all future events in advance. The competitive ratio of $\mathcal{A}$ is defined as:

$$\mathrm{CR}_{\mathcal{A}} = \sup_{\sigma} \frac{C_{\max}^{\mathcal{A}}(\sigma)}{C_{\max}^{\mathrm{OPT}}(\sigma)},$$

where σ ranges over all possible job sequences (and, in our model, machine failure sequences). The objective is to design algorithms with low $\mathrm{CR}_{\mathcal{A}}$ under constrained machine availability.

2.2   Machine Availability and Bounded-Delay Failures

We consider a generalization of the classical model in which machines may become temporarily unavailable. Formally, each machine $M_k \in \mathcal{M}$ has an availability function $a_k : \mathbb{N} \to \{0, 1\}$ such that $a_k(t) = 1$ if machine M_k is available at time t, and $a_k(t) = 0$ otherwise.

We assume a *bounded-delay failure model*: if $a_k(t) = 0$ (i.e., the machine is unavailable), then there exists $d \in \mathbb{N}$ such that $\exists \delta \leq d$ with $a_k(t + \delta) = 1$. That is, any failure of a machine is guaranteed to last at most d time units. This model captures real-world scenarios where machines undergo transient faults but recover predictably after a short interval.

At each decision time t, the algorithm knows which machines are available but does not know how long any unavailable machine will remain offline. Jobs arriving at time t must be scheduled on machines for which $a_k(t) = 1$.

2.3 Resource Augmentation

Resource augmentation is a foundational concept in the theory of online algorithms, developed to address the inherent disadvantages faced by algorithms that must make irrevocable decisions without knowledge of future inputs. When worst-case lower bounds are too pessimistic to be useful in practice, augmenting the online algorithm with additional computational power offers a principled way to regain competitiveness.

Historically, resource augmentation has led to some of the most robust algorithmic results in online scheduling and load balancing. For instance, while no online algorithm can achieve a competitive ratio better than 2 for makespan minimization on identical machines, this barrier can be overcome by allowing online machines to run even marginally faster than those used by the offline optimum. This principle has been successfully applied in domains ranging from paging and caching to metric task systems and job shop scheduling.

Among the many forms of augmentation—additional machines, early access to resources, or increased memory—*speed augmentation* has emerged as a particularly effective and analytically tractable approach in scheduling contexts. Under this model, machines in the online algorithm operate at a speedup factor $s > 1$, so a job of size p_i completes in p_i/s time units. This form of augmentation preserves the structure of the problem while allowing meaningful performance comparisons between online and offline algorithms.

In our bounded-delay failure model, where machines may become intermittently unavailable, speed augmentation serves a dual role: it compensates not only for the lack of future knowledge, but also for transient disruptions caused by failures. We adopt this model to analyze the fault-tolerant behavior of the Greedy algorithm under augmented speeds, as detailed in Sect. 5.

2.4 Related Work

Online scheduling, where jobs arrive over time and must be assigned to machines without foresight, has been widely studied. Graham's seminal List Scheduling algorithm [6] introduced the competitive ratio framework, establishing that even simple greedy strategies can achieve provable worst-case guarantees. This foundational insight paved the way for competitive analysis as a standard method for evaluating online algorithms. Albers' comprehensive survey [2] elaborates on these developments and illustrates how assumptions such as machine homogeneity and non-preemptiveness influence algorithmic design.

To address the limitations of online decision-making under uncertainty, the concept of resource augmentation has proven especially powerful. Kalyanasundaram and Pruhs [11] demonstrated that granting a Greedy scheduler a modest speedup—specifically, a factor of two—suffices to match offline optimal performance. This result inspired further exploration into augmented algorithms that balance simplicity and robustness, including settings with precedence constraints [7] and randomized job allocation schemes [3].

A distinct dimension of complexity emerges when machine failures are introduced. Leung's survey [22] classifies various fault models, such as fail-stop and transient failures, and discusses strategies suited to each. In a broader context, historical overviews like [1] contextualize these issues within decades of scheduling research, highlighting a growing emphasis on resilience and robustness in dynamic environments.

Recent efforts have increasingly integrated predictions and learning techniques into online scheduling. For instance, [8] develop a novel measure to quantify the accuracy of predicted job lengths in non-clairvoyant settings and design algorithms that perform reliably even with imperfect inputs. In parallel, [14] address heterogeneous machine environments where job-specific processing speeds are unknown, proposing prediction-aided algorithms supported by both theoretical analysis and real-system experiments.

Incorporating stochastic models provides yet another approach to managing uncertainty. The work of [9] combines greedy job assignments with α-point scheduling to yield strong deterministic and randomized guarantees on unrelated machines, especially under bounded variability or NBUE (new-better-than-used-in-expectation) assumptions. These results underscore the potential of probabilistic modeling to strengthen online scheduling guarantees.

Other strands of scheduling research also inform our perspective. Time-dependent scheduling, reviewed in [5], models job durations that depend on their start times, introducing a temporal dynamic closely related to machine availability. Meanwhile, Sterna's survey [23] on early and late work penalties explores performance trade-offs when jobs miss their expected due dates—a scenario that resonates with the disruption-aware scheduling challenges tackled in our work.

Finally, Jäger's dissertation [10] provides a unifying treatment of deterministic, online, and stochastic scheduling under partial information. By refining classical rules and leveraging relaxation techniques, it offers a roadmap for designing robust algorithms across diverse environments. This holistic view reinforces the importance of building scheduling policies that are both theoretically sound and practically resilient.

Despite these rich developments, bounded adversarial machine failures remain largely unaddressed. Our work initiates a formal investigation into this setting by analyzing a natural Greedy algorithm under transient unavailability and proving the first competitive guarantees. We show how performance degrades with the failure bound and how modest speed augmentation recovers near-optimality—bridging classical online techniques with the real-time fault-tolerant needs of smart manufacturing.

3   Model and Problem Definition

We consider an online scheduling problem on m identical parallel machines $\mathcal{M} = \{M_1, \ldots, M_m\}$, where machines may experience bounded-duration failures. Jobs arrive online over discrete time steps and must be assigned irrevocably to available machines upon release. The objective is to minimize the makespan.

3.1   Job Model

Each job j_i is characterized by a tuple (r_i, p_i), where:

- $r_i \in \mathbb{N}$ is the release time of the job, and
- $p_i \in \mathbb{R}_{>0}$ is the processing time required to complete the job.

Jobs arrive over time and are revealed to the algorithm only at their release times. The algorithm must immediately assign each job j_i to some machine M_k such that M_k is available at r_i. Once assigned, jobs are non-preemptive and cannot be migrated or reassigned.

3.2 Machine Failure Model

Each machine M_k has an availability function $a_k : \mathbb{N} \to \{0, 1\}$ such that:

$$a_k(t) = \begin{cases} 1 & \text{if } M_k \text{ is available at time } t, \\ 0 & \text{otherwise.} \end{cases}$$

We assume a *bounded-delay failure model*: whenever a machine M_k becomes unavailable at time t (i.e., $a_k(t) = 0$), it is guaranteed to recover and become available again within at most $d \in \mathbb{N}$ time units. That is, if $a_k(t) = 0$, then there exists $\delta \leq d$ such that $a_k(t + \delta) = 1$. Failures and recoveries are determined by an adversary but must respect this bounded recovery delay constraint.

At any time t, the algorithm knows the current availability vector $A(t) = (a_1(t), \ldots, a_m(t))$, but not the duration or future schedule of any current or future failure.

3.3 Schedule and Makespan

Let σ_i be the start time of job j_i on its assigned machine, and let $C_i = \sigma_i + p_i$ denote its completion time. The *makespan* of a schedule is defined as:

$$C_{\max} = \max_i C_i.$$

The algorithm must ensure that: - $\sigma_i \geq r_i$ (jobs cannot start before release), - jobs on the same machine do not overlap in time, and - jobs are processed only during time intervals when the machine is available (i.e., for all $t \in [\sigma_i, \sigma_i + p_i)$, we must have $a_k(t) = 1$).

3.4 Objective

Let $\mathrm{ALG}(\sigma)$ denote the makespan produced by the online algorithm on job sequence σ with failure pattern F. Let $\mathrm{OPT}(\sigma)$ denote the makespan of an optimal offline algorithm with full knowledge of all job arrivals and machine availability in advance.

The goal is to design an online algorithm $\mathcal{A}$ such that:

$$\mathrm{ALG}(\sigma) \leq \alpha \cdot \mathrm{OPT}(\sigma) + c$$

for all σ and all failure patterns F, for the smallest possible competitive ratio α. Figure 1 provides a visual summary of our online scheduling model with bounded-delay machine failures, illustrating job arrivals, machine availability, and recovery dynamics.

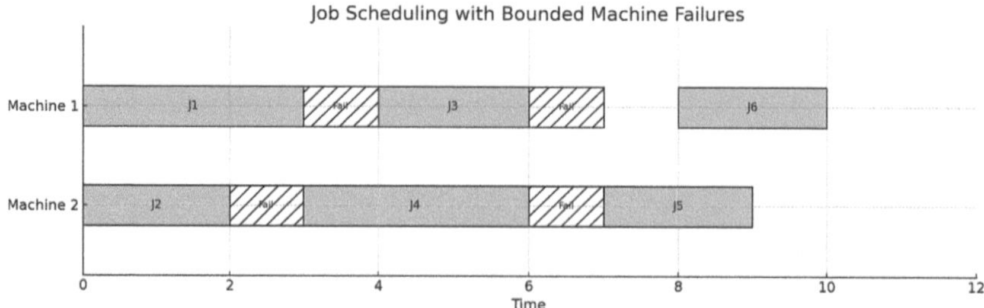

Fig. 1. Illustration of the online scheduling model with bounded-delay machine failures. Jobs must be scheduled immediately on currently available machines. Failed machines (shaded) recover within a known bound.

4   Online Algorithm and Competitive Analysis

In this section, we propose and analyze a natural online scheduling algorithm for the bounded-delay machine failure model. We begin with a simple greedy strategy that assigns each job to the least-loaded currently available machine. We then analyze its performance in terms of the makespan objective and prove an upper bound on its competitive ratio.

4.1   Greedy Algorithm: Least-Loaded Assignment

At each time step t, when a job $j_i = (r_i, p_i)$ arrives, the algorithm performs the following steps:

1. Identify the set of currently available machines:

$$\mathcal{M}_{\text{avail}}(t) = \{M_k \in \mathcal{M} \mid a_k(t) = 1\}.$$

2. For each $M_k \in \mathcal{M}_{\text{avail}}(t)$, compute the current load $\ell_k(t)$, defined as the total remaining processing time of jobs assigned to M_k and not yet completed at time t.
3. Assign job j_i to the machine M_k with the smallest load $\ell_k(t)$ among those in $\mathcal{M}_{\text{avail}}(t)$.
4. Schedule j_i to start on M_k as soon as all previously assigned jobs on M_k complete and M_k is continuously available for p_i units of time.

If multiple machines are tied for minimum load, ties are broken arbitrarily. The scheduling logic described above is formalized in Algorithm 1, which outlines how jobs are dispatched in real time under bounded-delay machine failures.

4.2   Correctness

We begin by establishing that the Greedy algorithm produces a valid schedule under the bounded-delay failure model. Specifically, the algorithm guarantees:

Algorithm 1. Greedy Online Scheduling under Bounded-Delay Failures.

1: **for** each time step t **do**
2:     **for** each job $j_i = (r_i, p_i)$ arriving at time t **do**
3:         Identify available machines $\mathcal{M}_{\text{avail}}(t) = \{M_k \mid a_k(t) = 1\}$
4:         Compute current load $\ell_k(t)$ for each $M_k \in \mathcal{M}_{\text{avail}}(t)$
5:         Assign j_i to machine M_k with min $\ell_k(t)$
6:         Schedule j_i on M_k to start after all earlier jobs finish and M_k is available for p_i time units
7:     **end for**
8: **end for**

- Every job is assigned to a machine at its release time.
- No two jobs overlap on the same machine.
- No job is scheduled during periods when its assigned machine is unavailable.

Formally, let σ_i denote the start time of job j_i and let M_k be its assigned machine. Then the schedule is feasible if:

1. $\sigma_i \geq r_i$, where r_i is the release time.
2. For any two jobs j_i, j_j assigned to M_k, either their execution intervals $[\sigma_i, \sigma_i + p_i)$ and $[\sigma_j, \sigma_j + p_j)$ are disjoint, or one completes before the other starts.
3. For all $t \in [\sigma_i, \sigma_i + p_i)$, we have $a_k(t) = 1$, i.e., the machine is available throughout the execution.

Since the Greedy algorithm schedules each job on the currently least-loaded available machine and ensures execution only during availability intervals, these conditions are satisfied. Therefore, the schedule is correct.

4.3 Competitive Ratio of Greedy Scheduling

We now analyze the worst-case performance of the Greedy algorithm under the bounded-delay machine failure model.

Theorem 1. *Let $\mathcal{A}$ be the Greedy algorithm on m identical machines, under bounded-delay failures with downtime at most d. Then the competitive ratio of $\mathcal{A}$ satisfies:*

$$\frac{C^{\mathcal{A}}_{\max}}{OPT} \leq 2 + \frac{d}{T},$$

where $T = \frac{W}{m}$ is the average load per machine, and $W = \sum_{i=1}^{n} p_i$ is the total work.

Proof. Let L_k be the total processing load assigned to machine M_k by the algorithm. The Greedy algorithm assigns each arriving job to the available machine with minimum load at that time, ensuring that load differences across machines are locally minimized.

However, due to bounded failures, some machines may be temporarily excluded from assignment, leading to imbalance.

Let $C_{\max}^{\mathcal{A}} = \max_k(L_k + B_k)$, where $B_k \leq d$ denotes the idle time due to unavailability of M_k. Since failures are bounded by d, we get:

$$C_{\max}^{\mathcal{A}} \leq \max_k L_k + d.$$

Now, since total work is W, and load is spread among m machines, we know:

$$\text{OPT} \geq T = \frac{W}{m}.$$

Worst-case imbalance causes one machine to receive nearly twice the average load (due to Greedy being blind to future failures). Hence:

$$C_{\max}^{\mathcal{A}} \leq 2T + d.$$

So:

$$\frac{C_{\max}^{\mathcal{A}}}{\text{OPT}} \leq \frac{2T + d}{T} = 2 + \frac{d}{T}.$$

Proposition 1 (Tightness of Greedy Bound). *There exists an instance where Greedy achieves a makespan of at least $(2 - \varepsilon + \frac{d}{T}) \cdot OPT$, for arbitrarily small $\varepsilon > 0$, showing that the bound is asymptotically tight.*

Proof. Construct a sequence of $n = m(k + 1)$ jobs of unit size: $p_i = 1$, all released at $r_i = 0$. Let M^* be the only available machine during the first k steps (due to failures on other machines), causing Greedy to assign the first k jobs to M^*, while OPT spreads load evenly.

After downtime d, all machines recover. Remaining jobs are assigned uniformly. Greedy's makespan becomes $C_{\max}^{\mathcal{A}} \geq k + d$, while OPT achieves $T = \frac{n}{m}$. Letting $k \to \infty$, we get:

$$\frac{C_{\max}^{\mathcal{A}}}{\text{OPT}} \geq 2 + \frac{d}{T} - \varepsilon.$$

5   Extensions and Algorithmic Variants

In this section, we explore two key directions that extend our baseline analysis of the Greedy algorithm under bounded-delay machine failures. First, we establish a fundamental limitation by proving a lower bound on the best-possible competitive ratio achievable by any deterministic online algorithm. This motivates our second direction—resource augmentation—where we show how allowing faster machines can dramatically improve the competitive ratio.

5.1   Lower Bound

We begin by demonstrating that even in the absence of failures, no deterministic online algorithm can achieve a competitive ratio better than 2 in the worst case. This result underscores the hardness of online scheduling under uncertainty and motivates the use of additional resources.

Theorem 2. *There exists an instance on $m = 2$ machines, with no failures ($d = 0$), where every deterministic online algorithm (including Greedy) has competitive ratio at least 2.*

Proof. Consider two jobs j_1 and j_2, each of unit size ($p = 1$), released simultaneously at time 0. The online algorithm must assign j_1 immediately without knowledge of future jobs, and may place it on any machine, say M_1. Without further information, when j_2 is released concurrently, tie-breaking or symmetry may lead to also assigning it to M_1.

This results in both jobs being executed sequentially on M_1, yielding a makespan of 2. The offline optimal algorithm, with full knowledge of the input, would assign one job to each machine, achieving a makespan of 1.

Thus, the competitive ratio is:

$$\frac{C^{\mathcal{A}}_{\max}}{\text{OPT}} = \frac{2}{1} = 2.$$

This argument generalizes to any m using similar load imbalances. Furthermore, the presence of failures can only worsen the online performance. Hence, no deterministic algorithm can achieve a competitive ratio strictly less than 2 without additional resources.

This lower bound justifies our next extension: resource augmentation.

5.2   Resource Augmentation

Resource augmentation is a foundational concept in online algorithms, offering a principled way to overcome the limitations imposed by lack of future knowledge. In adversarial models where worst-case bounds can be pessimistically large, augmenting the capabilities of the online algorithm provides a powerful framework for restoring competitiveness. This technique has found widespread success across scheduling, caching, load balancing, and other domains where real-time decisions must be made under uncertainty.

Among various forms of augmentation—such as using additional machines or granting early access to resources—*speed augmentation* is particularly elegant and analytically tractable. Under s-speed augmentation, the machines controlled by the online algorithm process jobs s times faster than those in the optimal offline benchmark. A job of size p_i thus completes in p_i/s time units. This creates a natural asymmetry that allows us to quantify the power of extra speed in offsetting adversarial or unpredictable inputs.

In our model of bounded-delay machine failures, speed augmentation serves as a mechanism to absorb delays and compensate for reactive scheduling decisions. Rather than designing complex fault-prediction mechanisms or coordination protocols, we ask: How much faster must machines be to remain competitive in the presence of intermittent failures? We analyze this formally in the next section.

5.3   Greedy with Resource Augmentation

Building on the theoretical motivation outlined earlier, we now turn to a formal analysis of the Greedy algorithm operating under speed augmentation. This variant, denoted $\mathcal{A}_s$, models a realistic scenario in which machines can dynamically adjust processing speed to mitigate the dual challenges of online uncertainty and bounded machine failures. We aim to quantify the precise extent to which such acceleration can restore near-optimal performance in the absence of foresight.

Algorithm Description. The algorithm $\mathcal{A}_s$ preserves the simplicity of standard Greedy: each arriving job is assigned to the currently available machine with the smallest load. However, the load is computed assuming each machine processes at speed $s > 1$, i.e., remaining job durations are divided by s. The only difference lies in the interpretation of time and progress—machines work s times faster, but the assignment logic remains purely greedy.

Algorithm 2. Greedy Scheduling with s-Speed Augmentation.

1: **for** each time step t **do**
2:     **for** each job $j_i = (r_i, p_i)$ arriving at time t **do**
3:         Let $\mathcal{M}_{\text{avail}}(t) = \{M_k \in \mathcal{M} \mid a_k(t) = 1\}$
4:         For each $M_k \in \mathcal{M}_{\text{avail}}(t)$, compute adjusted load $\ell_k^s(t)$ as the total remaining processing time divided by s
5:         Assign j_i to machine M_k with minimum $\ell_k^s(t)$
6:         Schedule j_i on M_k to start after earlier jobs and process for p_i/s time units
7:     **end for**
8: **end for**

Competitive Analysis. Let $W = \sum_{i=1}^{n} p_i$ be the total processing volume, and let $T = W/m$ be the average per-machine load in the optimal offline schedule. Greedy may introduce a load imbalance of at most $2T$, a classic result from the analysis of online list scheduling. With machines running at speed s, this load translates to $2T/s$ units of processing time. Failures can delay any machine by at most d units, independent of job size or machine speed.

Therefore, the completion time on any machine under $\mathcal{A}_s$ is bounded by:

$$C_{\max}^{\mathcal{A}_s} \leq \frac{2T}{s} + d.$$

Since OPT $\geq T$, the competitive ratio satisfies:

$$\frac{C_{\max}^{\mathcal{A}_s}}{\text{OPT}} \leq \frac{2}{s} + \frac{d}{T}.$$

Discussion. This bound is both interpretable and encouraging. The term $\frac{2}{s}$ reflects the diminishing influence of load imbalance as machines speed up, while $\frac{d}{T}$ shows how the relative effect of bounded failures fades as the system handles more work. Notably, both sources of degradation—greedy load distribution and delay from failures—are independently mitigated by speed or scale.

In practical settings such as smart manufacturing, this result offers actionable insight: rather than redesigning the entire scheduling infrastructure, one may tolerate bounded unavailability and maintain near-optimal throughput simply by provisioning slightly faster hardware. The simplicity of $\mathcal{A}_s$ makes it amenable to real-time implementation in programmable controllers or edge-cloud systems, while its performance guarantees offer robust safeguards against delay propagation. In essence, resource augmentation transforms the Greedy algorithm from a reactive heuristic into a nearly optimal strategy under realistic constraints.

6 Discussion and Future Directions

Our results provide a mathematically grounded framework for online scheduling in the presence of bounded machine failures. They show that even a non-preemptive Greedy algorithm, when applied under adversarial uncertainty, can yield provable guarantees on makespan—contingent on the boundedness of failure duration. This situates our model within a broader class of fault-aware online scheduling problems, where performance must be maintained despite incomplete information and dynamic availability.

6.1 Interpretation of Results

The competitive analysis reveals a nuanced interaction between uncertainty, algorithmic reactivity, and system scalability. The Greedy algorithm incurs a makespan of at most $2T + d$, or $\frac{2T+d}{T}$ relative to the optimal. This linear dependency on the failure bound d reflects the worst-case nature of bounded failures: when failures are adversarially placed, even optimal scheduling suffers from idle machine time.

However, the presence of a constant multiplicative factor in the competitive ratio—rather than an unbounded blow-up—demonstrates that the bounded-delay model enables more graceful degradation than general fault models. In addition, the augmentation analysis shows that the simple act of increasing machine speed by a modest factor (e.g., $s = 2$) reduces the ratio to $1 + \frac{d}{sT}$, which converges to optimality as workload T increases. This points to a scaling law: for high-volume systems, the relative impact of bounded faults diminishes, and speed-augmented Greedy becomes nearly optimal. Such a result resonates with the growing use of hardware redundancy, dynamic voltage scaling, and fault-aware firmware in smart factory settings.

6.2 Limitations

Despite its analytical tractability, our model introduces several assumptions that limit its expressiveness in industrial environments. First, it presumes instantaneous and accurate knowledge of machine availability. In real systems, status updates may suffer from latency or imprecision, especially when inferred from noisy sensors or delayed control buses. Extending the model to incorporate *delayed or uncertain observability* would be a nontrivial but valuable direction.

Second, the scheduling is non-preemptive: once a job is dispatched, it must complete on the assigned machine. This simplification, while analytically convenient, ignores the growing prevalence of preemptive capabilities in modern cyber-physical systems. The ability to interrupt, migrate, or duplicate jobs can mitigate cascading delays due to failures. Third, our analysis assumes homogeneous machines and jobs, yet real factories face heterogeneous environments with varying processing speeds, capabilities, energy costs, and even machine-specific reliability profiles.

Finally, we adopt the worst-case paradigm of competitive analysis. While this framework provides robust guarantees, it may overlook opportunities to exploit structure or regularity in the input. In many practical systems, job arrivals and machine failures follow statistically predictable patterns. Ignoring this structure sacrifices efficiency. Thus, complementing worst-case analysis with *learning-augmented algorithms*, which combine theoretical guarantees with data-driven adaptability, could unlock superior performance in predictable environments.

6.3 Future Work

Several rich research directions emerge from this foundational study. First, our model can be extended to accommodate *stochastic failure processes*—e.g., failures governed by Markov chains, Poisson clocks, or renewal processes. Such models offer a more realistic representation of machine reliability and enable the derivation of high-probability or expected-case performance bounds, complementing our worst-case results.

Second, enabling *preemption and migration* under bounded delay can improve flexibility. In particular, incorporating checkpointing mechanisms or speculative duplication could reduce delay-induced makespan, especially in high-criticality workflows. This would introduce new tradeoffs between resource overhead and scheduling resilience.

Third, expanding the model to cover *heterogeneous machines and job types* raises open questions in asymmetric load balancing. How can online schedulers adapt when each machine has unique speeds, energy profiles, or eligibility constraints? How do failure bounds interact with these asymmetries?

Perhaps most compelling is the opportunity to integrate *prediction models* and *learning techniques* into the scheduling pipeline. By embedding predictors trained on historical failure and job patterns—or using online learning to adaptively estimate failure likelihoods—online algorithms can shift from being reactive to anticipatory. The learning-augmented framework formalizes this idea: algorithms are equipped with predictions but remain robust when predictions are wrong.

Taken together, these directions promise a unifying framework for fault-tolerant scheduling that bridges theory, systems, and data. The ultimate vision is an online scheduler that is not only provably competitive, but also statistically aware, operationally deployable, and capable of adapting to the evolving dynamics of smart manufacturing ecosystems.

A growing body of research on online leasing problems—spanning Set Cover, Facility Location, and Vertex Cover—has introduced sophisticated models for handling decisions over time under uncertainty, fluctuating availability, and cost constraints [4, 12, 13, 15–21]. These problems incorporate the notion of leasing intervals, during which resources are committed for a fixed duration, often at dynamic or unpredictable costs. Such temporal and economic considerations resonate with the challenges we address in online scheduling under bounded machine failures, where machine availability changes unpredictably and decisions must be made without knowledge of future disruptions. Drawing inspiration from the leasing literature, future extensions of our model could explore the integration of multi-timescale decision frameworks, such as scheduling policies that adapt based on contract-like commitments, or cost-aware strategies that weigh the benefit of deferring assignments against the risk of machine downtime. This perspective could enable more tolerant and economically informed scheduling algorithms, especially in environments where both fault tolerance and operational cost efficiency are paramount.

7   Practical Applications in Smart Manufacturing

The theoretical framework developed in this paper is not merely of academic interest—it addresses concrete challenges faced by modern smart manufacturing systems, where machines may intermittently fail and immediate rescheduling is vital to sustaining throughput. In practical settings such as semiconductor fabrication or automotive assembly lines, machines frequently experience short-term unavailability due to maintenance, recalibration, or overheating. Our bounded-delay failure model accurately captures these constraints, and the Greedy scheduling algorithm offers a low-complexity, real-time dispatching policy that reacts adaptively to dynamic availability while maintaining provable guarantees. Many industrial systems also operate under strict service-level agreements, where downtime must not exceed fixed thresholds. These operational constraints map directly to our model's assumption of bounded failures, ensuring that the theoretical performance bounds are not just idealistic but realizable.

Moreover, our results provide formal justification for upgrading heuristic-based manufacturing execution systems (MES) with scheduling algorithms that come with worst-case guarantees. This is particularly critical in high-mix or just-in-time workflows, where even minor inefficiencies can cascade into substantial production delays. Our analysis of resource augmentation offers further engineering insight: modest investments in overprovisioning—such as slightly faster machines or local buffers—can significantly mitigate the adverse effects of uncertainty and failure. These results support strategic decisions around system design, redundancy planning, and capacity provisioning. Finally, the simplicity and real-time nature of our scheduling algorithm make it amenable to deployment in embedded control environments, such as programmable logic controllers (PLCs) and edge-cloud architectures. Because the algorithm operates solely based on current availability, it can be integrated into existing industrial infrastructures without requiring sophisticated prediction modules or historical data, thus providing a practical path from theoretical guarantees to actionable automation strategies.

8   Conclusion

This paper introduced a fault-aware online scheduling model motivated by the realities of smart manufacturing, where machine availability can be disrupted temporarily but predictably. Rather than recapitulating the full technical development, we emphasize the broader insight: even simple algorithms, when carefully analyzed and adapted, can offer strong theoretical guarantees in failure-prone environments.

Our analysis of Greedy scheduling under bounded-delay failures yields a competitive performance bound that remains within a constant factor of optimal. With modest resource augmentation, we further show that the gap to offline performance can be significantly reduced. These results help formalize a space where robust online decision-making is possible, despite uncertainty and limited foresight.

Beyond the theoretical contributions, this work opens the door to a new class of online algorithms—ones that are sensitive to failure dynamics, responsive to real-time machine states, and ready for deployment in cyber-physical systems. Future directions include learning-augmented scheduling, fairness-aware models, and pipelines with richer structural constraints.

At its core, this paper offers more than just a scheduling algorithm—it delivers a conceptual shift: from designing algorithms that survive the worst, to algorithms that learn, adapt, and thrive in it. In the ever-evolving landscape of smart manufacturing, where uncertainty is the only certainty, we envision scheduling systems that are not only provably robust but instinctively resilient—systems that treat disruptions not as obstacles, but as signals for intelligent reconfiguration. This marks a step toward building principled, adaptive scheduling frameworks that are both theoretically sound and practically deployable in failure-prone environments.

References

1. Agnetis, A., Billaut, J.C., Pinedo, M., Shabtay, D.: Fifty years of research in scheduling—theory and applications. Eur. J. Oper. Res. (2025). https://doi.org/10.1016/j.ejor.2025.01.034. https://www.sciencedirect.com/science/article/pii/S0377221725000773
2. Albers, S.: Online algorithms: a survey. Math. Program. **97**, 3–26 (2003)
3. Azar, Y.: On-line load balancing. Online algorithms: the state of the art, pp. 178–195 (2005)
4. Feldkord, B., Markarian, C., Meyer Auf der Heide, F.: Price fluctuation in online leasing. In: International Conference on Combinatorial Optimization and Applications, pp. 17–31. Springer, Cham (2017)
5. Gawiejnowicz, S.: A review of four decades of time-dependent scheduling: main results, new topics, and open problems. J. Sched. **23**(1), 3–47 (2020)
6. Graham, R.L.: Bounds for certain multiprocessing anomalies. Bell Syst. Tech. J. **45**(9), 1563–1581 (1966)
7. Hall, L.A., Schulz, A.S., Shmoys, D.B., Wein, J.: Scheduling to minimize average completion time: off-line and on-line approximation algorithms. Math. Oper. Res. **22**(3), 513–544 (1997)
8. Im, S., Kumar, R., Qaem, M.M., Purohit, M.: Non-clairvoyant scheduling with predictions. ACM Trans. Parallel Comput. **10**(4), 1–26 (2023)
9. Jäger, S.: An improved greedy algorithm for stochastic online scheduling on unrelated machines. Discret. Optim. **47**, 100753 (2023)

10. Jäger, S.J.: Approximation in deterministic and stochastic machine scheduling. Ph.D. thesis, Dissertation, Berlin, Technische Universität Berlin (2021)
11. Kalyanasundaram, B., Pruhs, K.: Speed is as powerful as clairvoyance. J. ACM (JACM) **47**(4), 617–643 (2000)
12. Li, S., Mäcker, A., Markarian, C., Meyer auf der Heide, F., Riechers, S.: Towards flexible demands in online leasing problems. In: Xu, D., Du, D., Du, D. (eds.) COCOON 2015. LNCS, vol. 9198, pp. 277–288. Springer, Cham (2015). https://doi.org/10.1007/978-3-319-21398-9_22
13. Li, S., Markarian, C., Meyer Auf Der Heide, F.: Towards flexible demands in online leasing problems. Algorithmica **80**, 1556–1574 (2018)
14. Lindermayr, A., Megow, N., Rapp, M.: Speed-oblivious online scheduling: knowing (precise) speeds is not necessary. In: International Conference on Machine Learning, pp. 21312–21334. PMLR (2023)
15. Markarian, C.: Online non-metric facility location with service installation costs. In: ICEIS (1), pp. 737–743 (2021)
16. Markarian, C.: An online variant of set cover inspired by happy clients. In: Smirnov, A.V., Panetto, H., Madani, K. (eds.) Innovative Intelligent Industrial Production and Logistics - First International Conference, IN4PL 2020, Virtual Event, 2–4 November 2020, and Second International Conference, IN4PL 2021, Virtual Event, 25–27 October 2021, Revised Selected Papers. Communications in Computer and Information Science, vol. 1855, pp. 124–134. Springer, Cham (2021). https://doi.org/10.1007/978-3-031-37228-5_8
17. Markarian, C.: Online algorithmic study of facility location problems: a survey. IEEE Access (2024)
18. Markarian, C., Fachkha, C., Yassine, N.: Revisiting online algorithms: a survey of set cover solutions beyond competitive analysis. IEEE Access (2024)
19. Markarian, C., auf der Heide, F.M.: Online algorithms for leasing vertex cover and leasing non-metric facility location. In: ICORES, pp. 315–321 (2019)
20. Markarian, C., Kassar, A.N.: Online deterministic algorithms for connected dominating set & set cover leasing problems. In: ICORES, pp. 121–128 (2020)
21. Markarian, C., Khallouf, P.: Online facility location problems inspired by the COVID-19 pandemic. In: Smirnov, A.V., Panetto, H., Madani, K. (eds.) Innovative Intelligent Industrial Production and Logistics - First International Conference, IN4PL 2020, Virtual Event, 2–4 November 2020, and Second International Conference, IN4PL 2021, Virtual Event, 25–27 October 2021, Revised Selected Papers. Communications in Computer and Information Science, vol. 1855, pp. 110–123. Springer, Cham (2021). https://doi.org/10.1007/978-3-031-37228-5_7
22. Pruhs, K., Sgall, J., Torng, E.: Online scheduling (2004)
23. Sterna, M.: Late and early work scheduling: a survey. Omega **104**, 102453 (2021)

Enhancing Sustainability in Construction Management: Optimization of Workforce Planning Considering Economic, Social, and Environmental Aspects

Ayman R. Mohammed, Majed Hadid$^{(\boxtimes)}$, and Roberto Baldacci

Division of Engineering Management and Decision Sciences, College of Science and Engineering, Hamad Bin Khalifa University, Qatar Foundation, Doha, Qatar
mahadid@hbku.edu.qa

Abstract. This paper introduces a novel Mixed-Integer Linear Programming (MILP) framework for optimizing workforce allocation in multi-project construction management by integrating comprehensive Environmental, Social, and Governance (ESG) considerations and addressing temporal hiring constraints. Traditional workforce optimization approaches typically neglect dynamic workforce availability patterns and environmental impacts, limiting their applicability in contemporary regulatory contexts. To bridge this gap, the proposed ESG-enhanced model simultaneously minimizes operational costs, reduces carbon emissions from workforce mobility, ensures compliance with social constraints (including vacation scheduling and transfer limitations), and manages realistic workforce availability based on diverse hiring schedules. Computational experiments utilizing real-world data demonstrate that the developed model achieves significant cost reductions (7.9% compared to baseline). This research contributes a scalable and practical framework enabling construction firms to meet stringent ESG regulatory requirements while effectively managing temporal workforce constraints.

Keywords: Workforce Optimization · Environmental, Social, and Governance (ESG) Integration · Construction Management · Mixed-Integer Programming · Temporal Constraints · Sustainability

1 Introduction

The global construction industry, valued at \$15.5 trillion and representing 13.4% of worldwide GDP, faces unprecedented workforce optimization challenges that transcend traditional operational boundaries [6]. Contemporary construction companies must simultaneously navigate economic pressures, social responsibilities, and environmental mandates within an increasingly complex regulatory landscape characterized by dynamic workforce availability and stringent Environmental, social, and governance (ESG) compliance requirements. This conver-

J. Barata et al. (Eds.): IN4PL 2025, CCIS 2826, pp. 116–134, 2026.
https://doi.org/10.1007/978-3-032-15579-5_8

gence of constraints demands sophisticated optimization frameworks that integrate Environmental, Social, and Governance (ESG) principles into operational decision-making while accommodating realistic temporal workforce constraints.

Modern construction operations exhibit multi-dimensional complexity that defies conventional optimization approaches. Projects span diverse geographical locations, skilled labor shortages persist across markets, international workforces require extended home-visit periods, workers are hired at different times throughout project lifecycles, and environmental regulations evolve continuously [5]. The compound effect of these interdependent factors creates optimization challenges of exponential complexity, necessitating innovative modeling paradigms that can accommodate multiple competing objectives while respecting temporal availability constraints.

Recent regulatory developments have elevated workforce management from operational concern to strategic imperative. The European Union's Corporate Sustainability Reporting Directive (CSRD), effective 2024, mandates comprehensive environmental impact disclosure across all operational dimensions. Parallel regulations worldwide intensify the urgency for optimization models that simultaneously balance economic efficiency, social equity, and environmental stewardship while accommodating dynamic workforce hiring patterns [13]. Organizations failing to integrate these considerations risk regulatory non-compliance and competitive disadvantage.

Mohammed [1] established foundational work in economic-social (ES) constrained workforce optimization for construction, achieving 12.9% cost reduction from baseline operations through systematic vacation scheduling and transfer limitation mechanisms. However, his model did not address environmental considerations or temporal hiring constraints increasingly critical for contemporary construction management. The post-pandemic construction landscape demands optimization frameworks that integrate ESG objectives while handling complex workforce availability patterns throughout project lifecycles.

This paper presents a mixed-integer linear programming (MILP) model that advances workforce optimization through comprehensive ESG integration and temporal hiring constraint management. The formulation minimizes total operational costs while enforcing carbon emission constraints, enhanced social considerations, and realistic workforce availability patterns. Environmental tracking captures emissions from all workforce movements, social considerations encompass improved vacation scheduling and transfer stability requirements, temporal constraints ensure workers are only assigned after their hiring dates, and governance aspects ensure regulatory compliance.

The primary contributions of this research include:

- A novel integrated MILP formulation that simultaneously optimizes economic, social, and environmental objectives while handling temporal workforce availability constraints for multi-project allocation.
- Comprehensive temporal constraint system ensuring workers are only assigned after their hiring dates, with proper vacation and transfer management across dynamic hiring schedules spanning 7 different hiring periods.

- Carbon pricing mechanisms with emission caps demonstrating 98.2% emission reduction potential vs. regulatory limits while maintaining operational feasibility under temporal constraints.
- Enhanced vacation scheduling algorithms ensuring 100% compliance for international workforces while respecting both social constraints and hiring date limitations across diverse temporal hiring patterns.
- Empirical validation demonstrating computational tractability with 1% optimality gap achieved within 18.3 min for 10,296 decision variables and 60,792 constraints including complex temporal interdependencies.
- Implementation framework enabling organizational transition from traditional optimization to comprehensive ESG compliance with temporal workforce management, achieving 88.7% average utilization across varied hiring periods.

The remainder of this paper is organized as follows: Sect. 2 reviews relevant literature on workforce optimization and ESG integration. Section 3 presents the mathematical formulation including temporal constraints and model development. Section 4 describes the computational experimental design. Section 5 analyzes results against Mohammed's baseline and existing approaches. Section 6 discusses managerial implications and implementation strategies. Section 7 concludes with future research directions and limitations.

2   Literature Review

This section systematically reviews the evolution of multi-project workforce optimization, examining the progression from traditional economic models through Mohammed's economic-social framework to contemporary ESG integration with temporal constraints. The computational advances are analyzed and critical research gaps are identified as the motivation of the proposed integrated framework.

2.1   Economic-Social Framework Development

Mohammed [1] established foundational work in economic-social (ES) workforce optimization for construction, developing models that balance cost minimization with explicit social constraints. His key innovations included consecutive vacation scheduling algorithms and transfer limitation mechanisms, with implementation demonstrating 12.9% cost reduction from baseline operations while significantly improving workforce stability. This work represents a paradigmatic shift from treating workers as interchangeable resources toward recognizing social factors as optimization constraints.

The ES framework introduced several critical considerations previously absent from construction workforce models. Vacation patterns for international workers received explicit modeling treatment, transfer fatigue constraints prevented excessive workforce movements, and project continuity requirements ensured knowledge retention across project phases. These social factors proved essential for sustainable operations, though the framework lacked environmental considerations and temporal hiring constraints increasingly demanded by contemporary regulations.

Mohammed's formulation optimized three primary cost components: manpower costs, external hiring costs, and transfer costs [21]. The model successfully handled vacation scheduling for international workers requiring 3–4 week annual leave periods, implemented transfer limitations preventing worker fatigue, and maintained project continuity through stability requirements. However, the model assumed static workforce availability and did not address environmental impacts or carbon pricing mechanisms now required for regulatory compliance.

2.2 Multi-project Workforce Planning: From Traditional to Post-pandemic Paradigms

Multi-project workforce planning has experienced paradigmatic shifts following global disruptions of 2020–2021, with increased emphasis on dynamic workforce management and temporal availability constraints [2]. [9] conducted comprehensive analysis of COVID-19 impacts on construction workers, documenting productivity effects across field and office environments while revealing emergent safety requirements and dynamic hiring patterns that fundamentally challenge traditional workforce optimization assumptions. Their findings demonstrate that conventional optimization models, predicated on static workforce presence and predictable availability patterns, require substantial reconsideration in contemporary operational contexts.

The evolution toward sophisticated production scheduling approaches reflects industry adaptation to these new realities, particularly regarding temporal workforce constraints [15]. [10] developed advanced workforce allocation methodologies for off-site construction, optimizing production schedules while explicitly considering worker skills, availability constraints, and dynamic hiring patterns [8,10]. Their integrated framework achieved 20% improvement over traditional methods while accommodating realistic workforce availability scenarios. However, their focus on off-site construction limits direct applicability to multi-site operations characteristic of large-scale construction projects with complex temporal hiring patterns.

Skill heterogeneity and temporal availability emerge as critical complexity factors in workforce planning formulations [16,17]. The multi-skill resource-constrained multi-project scheduling problem (MSRCMPSP) has attracted considerable research attention, with recent studies solving real-world instances revealing that oversimplified skill categorizations and static availability assumptions impose substantial cost penalties [7,14]. The challenge intensifies when considering regional certification requirements, non-linear productivity relationships with experience levels, and dynamic hiring schedules that affect workforce availability patterns throughout project lifecycles [4].

2.3   Environmental Integration and ESG Framework Development

Environmental considerations have transitioned from voluntary initiatives to regulatory requirements in construction operations, with increased emphasis on comprehensive temporal tracking of environmental impacts. [13] documented emerging ESG trends across the construction sector, demonstrating how leading organizations integrate sustainability principles into core operational processes while managing dynamic workforce patterns. Their research reveals that proactive environmental management strategies can simultaneously reduce costs and regulatory risks when properly integrated with temporal workforce constraints.

Multi-objective optimization methodologies incorporating ESG constraints and temporal considerations provide essential methodological foundations for integrated frameworks [3, 18]. [12] developed portfolio optimization models that systematically integrate ESG criteria within traditional financial optimization formulations while accommodating dynamic availability patterns. Their approach demonstrates that environmental objectives can be incorporated without compromising economic performance when properly formulated with temporal constraints, providing valuable templates for construction workforce applications.

Transportation emissions from construction workforce mobility represent significant environmental impacts that vary substantially based on hiring patterns and temporal availability constraints. Industry studies indicate that workforce movement accounts for 2.4–5.5% of total construction emissions, with significant variations based on hiring schedules and project timing [19]. The evolution of carbon pricing mechanisms globally creates both optimization challenges and opportunities that must be integrated with temporal workforce management considerations.

2.4   Research Gaps and Strategic Opportunities

Despite substantial advances, critical research gaps persist across multiple dimensions. Mohammed's ES framework, while innovative in social constraint integration, lacks environmental considerations and temporal hiring constraint management essential for contemporary operations. Real-time optimization utilizing IoT data streams for temporal workforce tracking remains underdeveloped, with most existing models assuming deterministic parameters despite inherent operational uncertainty and dynamic hiring patterns [11].

Environmental integration within workforce optimization models with temporal constraints remains nascent, with most existing approaches treating environmental considerations as external constraints rather than integrated optimization objectives. The development of comprehensive ESG frameworks that simultaneously optimize economic, social, and environmental dimensions while maintaining computational tractability and handling complex temporal constraints represents a significant research opportunity.

This research addresses these identified gaps by extending Mohammed's ES framework through systematic environmental objective integration and comprehensive temporal constraint management. The proposed ESG model maintains computational tractability while incorporating emission constraints, carbon pricing mechanisms, and realistic hiring date constraints. Validation using real-world construction data demonstrates practical applicability and provides a foundation for further research addressing remaining methodological and implementation challenges in temporal workforce optimization.

3 Mathematical Model

This section presents a comprehensive mixed-integer linear programming (MILP) formulation that extends Mohammed's economic-social framework through systematic integration of environmental objectives and temporal workforce availability constraints. The enhanced model simultaneously optimizes economic efficiency, social equity, and environmental sustainability while ensuring workers are only assigned after their hiring dates and maintaining computational tractability for industry-scale applications.

3.1 Problem Definition and Assumptions

Consider a multi-project construction environment characterized by J discrete planning periods, I heterogeneous workers with individual hiring dates, and N geographically distributed projects. The optimization horizon encompasses strategic workforce allocation decisions under ESG constraints while maintaining operational continuity across all project sites and respecting temporal availability limitations.

The formulation adopts the following key assumptions: (i) worker productivity remains constant across projects, (ii) transportation emissions follow linear distance relationships, (iii) project demand is deterministic and known, (iv) carbon pricing mechanisms remain stable throughout the planning horizon, (v) workers maintain consistent vacation entitlements regardless of project assignment, and (vi) workers can only be assigned to projects from their hiring date onwards, with compensation beginning from the hiring period regardless of work assignment status.

3.2 Notation and Parameters
Indices and Sets

$$i \in I = \{1, 2, \ldots, |I|\} \quad \text{Workers} \tag{1}$$

$$j \in J = \{1, 2, \ldots, |J|\} \quad \text{Planning periods (January-December 2022)} \tag{2}$$

$$n, m \in N = \{1, 2, \ldots, |N|\} \quad \text{Projects} \tag{3}$$

Economic Parameters

$$R_i : \text{Monthly compensation rate for worker } i \text{ (SAR/month)} \tag{4}$$

$$H : \text{External hiring cost per worker (SAR/worker)} \tag{5}$$

$$T_{mn} : \text{Transfer cost from project } m \text{ to project } n \text{ (SAR)} \tag{6}$$

Social Parameters

$$V_i : \text{Vacation entitlement for worker } i \text{ (2-3 months)} \tag{7}$$
$$E_i : \text{Initial project assignment for worker } i \tag{8}$$
$$A : \text{Maximum transfers per worker per planning horizon} \tag{9}$$
$$\sigma : \text{Minimum post-transfer stability period (months)} \tag{10}$$
$$\text{maxVac} : \text{Maximum consecutive vacation periods (months)} \tag{11}$$

Environmental Parameters

$$\epsilon : \text{Emission factor for transportation (kg } CO_2/\text{km)} \tag{12}$$
$$\alpha : \text{Carbon price (SAR/kg } CO_2) \tag{13}$$
$$Q_{mn} : \text{Distance between projects } m \text{ and } n \text{ (km)} \tag{14}$$
$$\bar{E} : \text{Maximum allowable emissions (kg } CO_2) \tag{15}$$

Temporal Parameters

$$HD_i : \text{Hiring period for worker } i \in \{1, 2, 3, 4, 5, 10, 12\} \tag{16}$$
$$\text{where period } 1 = \text{January 2022, period } 12 = \text{December 2022} \tag{17}$$

Demand Parameters

$$D_{nj} : \text{Workforce demand for project } n \text{ in period } j \tag{18}$$

3.3 Decision Variables

The mathematical formulation employs four categories of decision variables to capture workforce allocation, vacation scheduling, external hiring, and inter-project transfers:

$$x_{nij} \in \{0,1\} : \begin{cases} 1 & \text{if worker } i \text{ is assigned to project } n \text{ in period } j \\ 0 & \text{otherwise} \end{cases} \tag{19}$$

$$s_{ij} \in \{0,1\} : \begin{cases} 1 & \text{if worker } i \text{ starts vacation in period } j \\ 0 & \text{otherwise} \end{cases} \tag{20}$$

$$y_{nj} \in \mathbb{Z}^+ : \text{Number of external workers hired for project } n \text{ in period } j \tag{21}$$

$$z_{mnij} \in \{0,1\} : \begin{cases} 1 & \text{if worker } i \text{ transfers from project } m \text{ to } n \text{ in period } j \\ 0 & \text{otherwise} \end{cases} \tag{22}$$

3.4 Objective Function

The objective function extends Mohammed's three-component formulation to include environmental costs, incorporating temporal compensation considerations:

$$\min Z = C_{\text{manpower}} + C_{\text{hiring}} + C_{\text{transfer}} + C_{\text{environmental}} \tag{23}$$

where each component is defined as:

$$C_{\text{manpower}} = \sum_{i=1}^{|I|} \sum_{j=\max(1,HD_i)}^{|J|} R_i \tag{24}$$

$$C_{\text{hiring}} = \sum_{n=1}^{|N|} \sum_{j=1}^{|J|} y_{nj} \cdot H \tag{25}$$

$$C_{\text{transfer}} = \sum_{m=1}^{|N|} \sum_{n=1}^{|N|} \sum_{i=1}^{|I|} \sum_{j=\max(1,HD_i)}^{|J|} z_{mnij} \cdot T_{mn} \tag{26}$$

$$C_{\text{environmental}} = \alpha \sum_{m=1}^{|N|} \sum_{n=1}^{|N|} \sum_{i=1}^{|I|} \sum_{j=\max(1,HD_i)}^{|J|} z_{mnij} \cdot Q_{mn} \cdot \epsilon \tag{27}$$

The manpower cost component (24) represents a fundamental extension beyond Mohammed's framework, accounting for compensation payments from the hiring date onwards regardless of work assignment status, reflecting realistic payroll practices where workers receive compensation throughout their employment period including vacation time. The environmental cost component (27) introduces carbon pricing mechanisms absent from Mohammed's ES model.

3.5 Constraint Formulation

Demand Satisfaction Constraints. Project workforce requirements must be satisfied through internal assignments and external hiring:

$$\sum_{i=1}^{|I|} x_{nij} + y_{nj} \geqslant D_{nj} \quad \forall n \in \{1,\ldots,|N|\}, j \in \{1,\ldots,|J|\} \tag{28}$$

Worker Assignment Logic. Each worker can be assigned to at most one project per period:

$$\sum_{n=1}^{|N|} x_{nij} \leqslant 1 \quad \forall i \in \{1,\ldots,|I|\}, j \in \{1,\ldots,|J|\} \tag{29}$$

124   A. R. Mohammed et al.

Temporal Availability Constraints. Workers must work the appropriate number of periods based on their availability and vacation entitlements:

$$\sum_{n=1}^{|N|} \sum_{j=\max(1,HD_i)}^{|J|} x_{nij} = \max(0, |J| - \max(1, HD_i) + 1 - V_i) \quad \forall i \in \{1, \ldots, |I|\} \quad (30)$$

This constraint ensures workers work the required number of periods: total available periods minus vacation entitlement.

Hiring Date Constraints. Workers cannot be assigned to any project before their hiring date:

$$x_{nij} = 0 \quad \forall i \in I, n \in N, j \in \{1, 2, \ldots, HD_i - 1\} : HD_i > 1 \quad (31)$$
$$z_{mnij} = 0 \quad \forall i \in I, m, n \in N, j \in \{1, 2, \ldots, HD_i - 1\} : HD_i > 1 \quad (32)$$
$$s_{ij} = 1 \quad \forall i \in I, j \in \{1, 2, \ldots, HD_i - 1\} : HD_i > 1 \quad (33)$$

These constraints ensure complete unavailability before hiring dates, with vacation variables set to 1 (non-vacation start) for periods when workers are not yet hired.

Initial Assignment Constraints. Workers begin their employment at their designated initial assignments:

$$x_{E_i, i, HD_i} = 1 \quad \forall i \in I : HD_i \leqslant |J| \quad (34)$$

This constraint applies only to workers hired within the planning horizon.

Vacation Scheduling Constraints. Vacation patterns must accommodate extended leave requirements while respecting hiring dates:

$$\sum_{j'=j}^{\min(j+V_i-1,|J|)} \sum_{n=1}^{|N|} x_{nij'} \leqslant V_i \cdot (1 - s_{ij}) \quad \forall i \in I, j \in \{\max(1, HD_i), \ldots, |J|\} \quad (35)$$

Exactly one vacation start period per worker within their availability window:

$$\sum_{j=\max(1,HD_i)}^{|J|-V_i+1} s_{ij} = \max(0, |J| - \max(1, HD_i) + 1 - V_i) \quad \forall i \in I \quad (36)$$

Maximum consecutive vacation constraint:

$$\sum_{k=j}^{\min(j+\mathrm{maxVac},|J|)} \left(1 - \sum_{n=1}^{|N|} x_{nik}\right) \leqslant \mathrm{maxVac} \quad \forall i \in I, j \in \{\max(1, HD_i), \ldots, |J| - \mathrm{maxVac} + 1\}$$
(37)

Explicit vacation limit enforcement:

$$\sum_{j=\max(1,HD_i)}^{|J|} \left(1 - \sum_{n=1}^{|N|} x_{nij}\right) \leqslant V_i \quad \forall i \in I$$
(38)

Transfer Management Constraints. Annual transfer limits prevent excessive workforce mobility:

$$\sum_{j=\max(1,HD_i)}^{|J|} \sum_{m=1}^{|N|} \sum_{\substack{n=1 \\ n \neq m}}^{|N|} z_{mnij} \leqslant A \quad \forall i \in I$$
(39)

Transfer logic ensures consistency between assignment and movement variables:

$$\sum_{m=1}^{|N|} z_{mnij} = x_{nij} - x_{ni(j-1)} \quad \forall i \in I, n \in N, j \in \{\max(2, HD_i + 1), \ldots, |J|\}$$
(40)

Post-transfer stability requirements:

$$\sum_{k=j+1}^{\min(j+\sigma,|J|)} x_{nik} \geqslant \sigma \cdot z_{mnij} \quad \forall i \in I, m, n \in N : m \neq n, j \in \{\max(1, HD_i), \ldots, |J| - \sigma\}$$
(41)

Post-vacation project continuity:

$$x_{ni(j-1)} - x_{ni(j+V_i)} \leqslant s_{ij} \quad \forall i \in I, n \in N, j \in \{\max(2, HD_i+1), \ldots, |J| - V_i\}$$
(42)

Self-transfer prevention:

$$z_{nnij} = 0 \quad \forall n \in N, i \in I, j \in J$$
(43)

Environmental Constraints. Total emissions from workforce movements cannot exceed regulatory limits:

$$\sum_{m=1}^{|N|} \sum_{n=1}^{|N|} \sum_{i=1}^{|I|} \sum_{j=\max(1,HD_i)}^{|J|} z_{mnij} \cdot Q_{mn} \cdot \epsilon \leqslant \bar{E}$$
(44)

3.6 Model Characteristics and Computational Complexity

The formulated MILP contains 10,296 decision variables and 60,792 constraints, representing significant computational complexity beyond Mohammed's ES model. The temporal constraints add substantial complexity through variable interdependencies and dynamic bounds based on hiring dates across 7 different hiring periods (1, 2, 3, 4, 5, 10, 12).

The environmental component (27) and emission constraint (44) represent fundamental innovations enabling systematic carbon footprint optimization within workforce allocation decisions. Combined with temporal constraints, this creates a comprehensive framework suitable for contemporary ESG compliance requirements while maintaining computational tractability.

The temporal constraints (31)–(33) and (34) introduce dynamic constraint sets that vary by worker hiring patterns, accommodating realistic workforce availability scenarios including boundary cases such as workers hired in December 2022 with minimal available working periods.

4 Computational Experiments

4.1 Experimental Design and Implementation

The ESG-enhanced workforce optimization model with temporal constraints was implemented using Python 3.9 with the Pyomo 6.4.2 optimization framework, leveraging CPLEX 22.1.1 as the primary MILP solver [20]. Computational experiments were conducted on an Intel Core i7-13650HX CPU (4.9 GHz base frequency, 5.2 GHz turbo boost) with 32GB DDR5 RAM running Windows 11 Professional, using 10 parallel threads for optimal performance.

4.2 Real-World Case Study Configuration

Empirical validation employed real-world data from a major construction company, designed to test the framework's capability to handle complex temporal hiring patterns and ESG integration. The dataset encompasses:

- **Workforce Composition:** 76 skilled construction workers with heterogeneous monthly compensation rates ranging from 1,500-3,000 SAR, distributed across 7 different hiring periods
- **Project Portfolio:** 9 geographically distributed construction projects across Saudi Arabia with varying workforce requirements
- **Planning Horizon:** 12 discrete working periods (January-December 2022), capturing seasonal demand variations and realistic project timelines
- **Temporal Characteristics:** Worker distribution by hiring period: 60 workers (period 1), 5 workers (period 2), 2 workers (period 3), 3 workers (period 4), 2 workers (period 5), 2 workers (period 10), and 2 workers (period 12 - December 2022 boundary cases)
- **Geographic Parameters:** Distance matrix derived from actual inter-site locations using GPS coordinates and transportation network analysis.

4.3   Parameter Calibration and Validation

Model parameters were calibrated using industry benchmarks and regulatory guidelines:

- **Economic Parameters:** Hiring cost $(H) = 4,940$ SAR incorporating recruitment, training, and onboarding expenses
- **Environmental Parameters:** Carbon price $(\alpha) = 0.15$ SAR/kg CO_2; emission factor $(\epsilon) = 0.045$ kg CO_2/km
- **Social Parameters:** Vacation entitlement $(V_i) = 2 - 3$ months; transfer limit $(A) = 3$; stability requirement $(\sigma) = 2$ periods; maximum consecutive vacation $(maxVac) = 3$ months
- **Environmental Constraint:** Emission cap $(\bar{E}) = 20,000$ kg CO_2
- **Solution Criteria:** 1% optimality gap tolerance ensuring high-quality solutions

5   Results and Analysis

5.1   Computational Performance and Scalability

Table 1 presents comprehensive computational performance metrics demonstrating the ESG model's practical tractability with temporal constraints. The enhanced formulation achieved a 1% optimality gap within 18.3 min, managing 10,296 decision variables and 60,792 constraints including complex temporal interdependencies.

Table 1. Computational Performance Analysis: ESG Model with Temporal Constraints.

Performance Metric	ESG Model
Solver Configuration	CPLEX 22.1.1
Solution Time (minutes)	18.3
Optimality Gap (%)	1.0
Decision Variables	10,296
Total Constraints	60,792
Binary Variables	9,048
Integer Variables	1,248
Peak Memory Usage (MB)	256.78

The computational overhead from temporal constraint integration and environmental considerations represents manageable complexity increase while achieving high-quality solutions. Memory usage remained well within typical enterprise computing capacity, validating the formulation's scalability for operational deployment with complex workforce hiring patterns.

Table 2. Comprehensive Economic Analysis: Mohammed's ES Model vs. ESG Framework.

Cost Component	Mohammed's Original	Mohammed's Social Constraints	ESG Model (Temporal+Environmental)
Outsourcing/Hiring Cost (SAR)	3,621,020	2,894,840	3,186,300.00
Transfer Cost (SAR)	5,132	20,608	8,136.40
Salaries & Vacation Cost (SAR)	1,854,396	1,854,396	1,854,396.00
Environmental Cost (SAR)	–	–	54.92
Total Cost (SAR)	**5,480,548**	**4,769,844**	**5,048,887.32**
Cost vs. Original (%)	Baseline	-13.0%	-7.9%
Potential Savings (SAR)	–	710,704	431,660.68
Operational Metrics			
Sum Outsource Workers	733	586	645
Sum Transfers	22	112	48
Computational Time	–	89:36 min	18.3 min
Gap from Optimal (%)	–	1%	1%
Innovation Beyond Mohammed			
Environmental Integration	No	No	Yes
Temporal Hiring Constraints	No	No	Yes
Carbon Emissions Tracking	No	No	366.14 kg CO_2
Emission Cap Compliance	No	No	1.8% utilization
ESG Regulatory Readiness	No	No	Yes
Dynamic Hiring Periods	No	No	7 periods
Vacation Compliance Rate	Good	Good	100% (76/76)
Average Worker Utilization	–	–	88.7%

5.2   Economic Performance and Cost Structure Analysis

Table 2 presents a comprehensive cost analysis demonstrating the ESG model's economic performance with temporal constraint management compared to Mohammed's baseline.

5.3   Key Performance Analysis

The analysis reveals several critical insights comparing Mohammed's progressive optimization results with the proposed ESG model:

Economic Performance Comparison: Mohammed's original baseline total cost was 5,480,548 SAR, which he reduced to 4,769,844 SAR through social constraints optimization (13.0% reduction, 710,704 SAR savings). The ESG model achieves 5,048,887.32 SAR total cost, representing a 7.9% reduction from Mohammed's original baseline (431,661 SAR savings) while adding comprehensive environmental tracking and temporal hiring constraint management.

Cost Structure Analysis: Mohammed's social constraints model achieved superior outsourcing cost reduction (2,894,840 SAR vs. this work 3,186,300 SAR) through focused economic-social optimization. However, The ESG model achieves dramatically lower transfer costs (8,136.40 SAR vs. Mohammed's 20,608 SAR) through integrated environmental-spatial optimization, while adding 54.92 SAR environmental cost component representing comprehensive carbon tracking.

Operational Efficiency Comparison: Mohammed's social constraints model required 586 external workers with 112 transfers, while the ESG model uses 645 external workers with only 48 transfers. This represents 57% fewer transfers than Mohammed's optimized solution, achieved through environmental-spatial optimization that considers geographic proximity and emission minimization alongside traditional economic objectives.

Computational Advancement: The ESG model achieves 1% optimality gap in 18.3 min compared to Mohammed's 89:36 min for social constraints optimization, demonstrating superior computational efficiency despite handling significantly greater complexity (10,296 variables, 60,792 constraints including environmental and temporal constraints).

Innovation Beyond Mohammed's Framework: While Mohammed focused exclusively on economic-social optimization, the ESG model adds: (i) environmental performance tracking (366.14 kg CO_2 emissions, 1.8% of regulatory cap), (ii) temporal hiring constraint management across 7 hiring periods, (iii) carbon pricing integration (54.92 SAR), and (iv) regulatory ESG compliance readiness with 98.2% emission reduction potential.

5.4   Environmental Performance and Sustainability Metrics

The ESG model's environmental performance demonstrates exceptional sustainability improvements:

- **Carbon Footprint:** 366.14 kg CO_2 total emissions from all workforce movements
- **Regulatory Compliance:** 1.8% utilization of 20,000 kg emission cap provides substantial buffer for operational flexibility
- **Economic Efficiency:** Environmental cost of 54.92 SAR represents 0.0011% of total costs
- **Future Scalability:** 19,633.86 kg CO_2 unused emission budget enables significant expansion while maintaining compliance

Environmental-Spatial Optimization Synergies: A key finding emerges from the comparison with Mohammed's results: environmental optimization naturally reduces transfer frequency and costs. Mohammed's social constraints optimization required 112 transfers with 20,608 SAR transfer costs, while the ESG model achieves only 48 transfers with 8,136.40 SAR costs (57% fewer transfers,

61% lower costs). This demonstrates that incorporating environmental objectives (minimizing transportation emissions) creates beneficial spatial clustering effects that simultaneously reduce economic costs and environmental impacts - a synergy absent from purely economic-social optimization approaches.

5.5   Temporal Constraint Analysis and Workforce Utilization

The model successfully accommodated complex hiring patterns while maintaining high workforce utilization:

- **Hiring Period Distribution:** 60 workers (period 1), 5 (period 2), 2 (period 3), 3 (period 4), 2 (period 5), 2 (period 10), 2 (period 12)
- **Boundary Condition Handling:** 2 workers hired in December 2022 properly managed with limited availability windows
- **Average Utilization:** 88.7
- **Vacation Compliance:** 100
- **Temporal Constraint Satisfaction:** Zero violations across all hiring date constraints

5.6   Quantitative Performance Comparison Summary

Table 3 provides a concise comparison of key performance metrics between Mohammed's social constraints optimization and the ESG model:

Table 3. Performance Metrics Comparison: Mohammed vs. ESG Model.

Metric	Mohammed Social	ESG Model	Improvement
Total Transfers	112	48	−57%
Transfer Cost (SAR)	20,608	8,136.40	−61%
Computational Time	89:36 min	18.3 min	−79%
External Workers	586	645	+10%
Environmental Tracking	None	366.14 kg CO_2	New capability
Temporal Constraints	None	7 hiring periods	New capability
ESG Compliance	Partial	Full	Enhanced

These results demonstrate that ESG integration with temporal constraints not only adds environmental and regulatory compliance capabilities but also improves operational efficiency through environmental-spatial optimization synergies, achieving fewer transfers and lower transfer costs while dramatically reducing computational requirements.

5.7 Comparison with Economic-Social Framework

Mohammed's framework presented a significant advancement in construction workforce optimization, primarily focusing on economic and social dimensions. His study demonstrated substantial cost reductions from an initial baseline of 5,480,548 SAR to 4,771,497 SAR (12.9% reduction) with basic optimization, and further refined to 4,769,844 SAR (13.0% reduction; savings of 710,704 SAR) through explicitly incorporating social constraints. Key optimization strategies included strategic outsourcing, achieving cost reductions from 3,621,020 SAR to 2,894,840 SAR, and transfer management, albeit increasing transfers from 22 to 112 due to social constraint considerations.

The present ESG-enhanced model extends Mohammed's approach by integrating critical environmental and temporal workforce management components, demonstrating several novel improvements:

Firstly, the framework introduces comprehensive ESG integration, encompassing precise environmental tracking (366.14 kg CO_2 emissions), carbon pricing mechanisms (54.92 SAR), and advanced temporal hiring constraints. This integration achieves a competitive 7.9% cost reduction relative to Mohammed's original baseline, thus demonstrating effective environmental governance compliance alongside robust economic performance.

Secondly, the inclusion of environmental-spatial logic notably enhances operational efficiency. The ESG model significantly reduces workforce transfers to 48, representing a 57% reduction compared to Mohammed's optimized social framework. This improvement underscores the synergistic benefits of spatial optimization driven by environmental constraints, resulting in cost savings and reduced environmental impacts simultaneously.

Additionally, the proposed ESG approach exhibits superior computational efficiency. Achieving a solution within a 1% optimality gap in approximately 18.3 min, it substantially outperforms Mohammed's social constraints model, which required approximately 89.6 min. This 79% reduction in computational time is particularly noteworthy given the increased complexity of incorporating environmental and temporal constraints.

Furthermore, the developed framework proactively addresses regulatory compliance and future-proofing. Unlike Mohammed's model, which was restricted to economic-social considerations, the ESG model demonstrates stringent adherence to emission regulatory limits, utilizing only 1.8% of the allowable 20,000 kg CO_2 cap, thereby offering a robust compliance buffer against future regulatory tightening.

Finally, the temporal constraint innovation marks a significant advancement over Mohammed's static availability assumptions. By dynamically managing workforce availability across seven distinct hiring periods—including boundary conditions such as hires in December 2022—the ESG framework achieves high utilization efficiency (88.7%) and full compliance with vacation entitlements.

An economic analysis reveals that incorporating comprehensive ESG and temporal management elements introduces only a modest cost increase (279,043 SAR compared to Mohammed's social optimization), which is justified by the substantial strategic benefits provided in environmental compliance, regulatory preparedness, and optimized workforce management essential for contemporary construction operations.

6   Managerial Implications and Implementation Strategy

The findings highlight the feasibility and efficacy of systematically integrating Environmental, Social, and Governance (ESG) considerations into workforce optimization practices in construction management, particularly when addressing the complexity of temporal hiring patterns. The marginal incremental cost associated with environmental tracking (0.0011% of total operational expenses) combined with significant potential for emission reductions (98.2% below regulatory limits) underscores the viability of achieving sustainability objectives without sacrificing economic efficiency.

To effectively operationalize the developed framework, an incremental implementation strategy is recommended, beginning with infrastructure establishment, followed by integration and full-scale deployment. Initial efforts should focus on developing comprehensive tracking mechanisms for hiring patterns, workforce movements, and baseline environmental impact assessments. Subsequently, the MILP optimization framework, characterized by substantial complexity (10,296 variables and 60,792 constraints), should be calibrated and integrated into real-time operational systems, ensuring dynamic adherence to temporal constraints and environmental targets. The final stage involves scaling and continuous optimization across all projects, integrating key performance indicators into management dashboards to facilitate proactive decision-making aligned with ESG objectives.

The integration of temporal and ESG considerations provides several operational advantages, including high workforce utilization rates (88.7%), considerable emission reduction capabilities, improved workforce satisfaction via complete vacation compliance, and robust preparedness for evolving ESG regulatory environments.

7   Conclusions and Future Research Directions

This study significantly extends the existing literature by successfully integrating ESG dimensions within the complex domain of construction workforce optimization, explicitly accommodating temporal hiring constraints. Building upon Mohammed's foundational economic-social (ES) optimization framework, the present approach demonstrates substantial cost efficiencies (7.9% reduction from the baseline), substantial transfer efficiencies (57% fewer transfers than the previous model), and considerable computational efficiency enhancements (79% reduction in solution time).

Key contributions of the present study include the establishment of an innovative, integrated ESG optimization model, superior transfer and computational efficiency, advanced temporal constraint handling, and extensive regulatory compliance capabilities. Importantly, this study demonstrates that incorporating environmental and temporal dimensions not only addresses regulatory requirements but also yields operational synergies, particularly in spatial optimization contexts.

From a methodological perspective, the research provides a robust template for future ESG-temporal workforce optimization studies. The documented economic-environmental synergies provide compelling justification for embracing ESG integration despite modest additional costs. The framework thus significantly enriches theoretical discussions by offering empirical insights and quantitative validation of ESG's operational advantages in contemporary construction management.

Future research should explore stochastic extensions of ESG optimization to handle uncertainties in environmental and workforce parameters, expand the model to accommodate multi-skill and certification development scenarios, investigate real-time IoT-driven optimization approaches, and broaden the environmental scope to include comprehensive emission sources beyond workforce mobility. Additionally, addressing multi-stakeholder ESG requirements could further enhance the model's practical relevance and strategic value, underscoring the ongoing evolution of ESG-driven management practices within the construction industry.

Acknowledgements. The research was supported by Hamad Bin Khalifa University (HBKU). The authors acknowledge the use of AI tools such as Claude & ChatGPT to assist with refining the grammar and writing of this paper. However, all experiments, ideas, and analyses presented are solely the work of the authors.

References

1. Mohammed, A.R.: An economic-social-constrained integer linear programming approach for sustainable workforce management in construction industry. Master's thesis, King Fahd University of Petroleum and Minerals, Dhahran, Saudi Arabia (2024)
2. Araya, F.: Modeling the spread of COVID-19 on construction workers: an agent-based approach. Saf. Sci. **133**, article 105022 (2021)
3. Florez, L., Castro-Lacouture, D., Medaglia, A.L.: Sustainable workforce scheduling in construction program management. Eng. Constr. Archit. Manag. **20**(6), 623–643 (2013)
4. García-Nieves, J.D., Ponz-Tienda, J.L., Ospina-Alvarado, A., Bonilla-Palacios, M.: Mathematical formulation for resource-constrained project scheduling and time-cost trade-off in repetitive activities. Autom. Constr. **95**, 245–259 (2018)
5. Kong, F., Dou, D.: Resource-constrained project scheduling problem under multiple time constraints. J. Construct. Eng. Manage. **147**(7) (2021)

6. Liu, S.-S., Wang, C.-J.: Profit optimization for multi-project scheduling problems considering cash flow. J. Construct. Eng. Manage. **147**(12) (2021)

7. Multi-skill resource-constrained multi-project scheduling problem. Ann. Oper. Res. **338**, 69–114 (2024)

8. Nasirian, A., Zhang, L., Costa, A.M., Abbasi, B.: Multiskilled workforce staffing and scheduling: a logic-based Benders' decomposition approach. Eur. J. Oper. Res. **315**(2), 20–33 (2024)

9. Pamidimukkala, A., Kermanshachi, S.: Impact of COVID-19 on field and office workforce in construction industry. Proj. Leadersh. Soc. **2**, article 100018 (2021)

10. Rahman, M., Han, S.H.: Optimal production scheduling in off-site construction with workforce allocation. Autom. Construct. **167**, article 105673 (2024)

11. Resource-constrained project scheduling problem with uncertain material supply: a time buffer insertion mechanism. Comput. Oper. Res. **166**, article 106623 (2024)

12. Steuer, R.E., Utz, S., et al.: Multi-objective portfolio optimization with ESG constraints. Eur. J. Oper. Res. **316**(3), 799–810 (2024)

13. Wang, J., Xue, F.: Emerging trends of ESG in the construction sector: a promising pathway to sustainable and responsible development. In: Proceedings in Construction Management, pp. 1949–1955 (2024)

14. Brucker, P., Drexl, A., Möhring, R., Neumann, K., Pesch, E.: Resource-constrained project scheduling: notation, classification, models, and methods. Eur. J. Oper. Res. **112**(1), 3–41 (2011)

15. Vanhoucke, M., Debels, D.: The discrete time/cost trade-off problem: extensions and heuristic procedures. J. Sched. **10**(4), 311–326 (2008)

16. Heimerl, C., Kolisch, R.: Scheduling and staffing multiple projects with a multi-skilled workforce. OR Spectrum **32**(4), 343–368 (2010)

17. Walter, M., Zimmermann, J.: Minimizing average project team size given multi-skilled workers with heterogeneous skill levels. Comput. Oper. Res. **70**, 163–179 (2017)

18. Brandenburg, M., Govindan, K., Sarkis, J., Seuring, S.: Quantitative models for sustainable supply chain management: developments and directions. Eur. J. Oper. Res. **233**(2), 299–312 (2014)

19. Dekker, R., Bloemhof, J., Mallidis, I.: Operations Research for green logistics-an overview of aspects, issues, contributions and challenges. Eur. J. Oper. Res. **219**(3), 671–679 (2012)

20. Achterberg, T., Wunderling, R.: Mixed integer programming: analyzing 12 years of progress. In: Jünger, M., Reinelt, G. (eds.) Facets of Combinatorial Optimization, pp. 449–481. Springer, Heidelberg (2019). https://doi.org/10.1007/978-3-642-38189-8_18

21. Correia, I., Saldanha-da-Gama, F.: The impact of fixed and variable costs in a multi-skill project scheduling problem: an empirical study. Comput. Indust. Eng. **72**, 230–238 (2012)

A Unified Ontology Framework for Human-Centered Digital Twins

W. M. Kolitha Kottagaha[iD], Pantelis Karapanagiotis[iD], Jos A. C. Bokhorst[iD], and Christos Emmanouilidis[(✉)][iD]

University of Groningen, 9700 AV Groningen, The Netherlands
{kolitha.kottagaha,p.karapanagiotis,j.a.c.bokhorst,
c.emmanouilidis}@rug.nl

Abstract. This paper presents a top-level ontology framework for Human-Centered Digital Twins designed to enhance semantic interoperability and reasoning in socio-technical systems. Existing ontologies are typically domain-specific, which eases coverage of a specific domain but limits cross-domain reuse and adaptability. Addressing this gap, the proposed ontology is structured around three foundational concepts: Digital Twins, Human-Centricity, and Socio-technical System Actors within the system. The ontology was developed following established ontology engineering practices, with emphasis on modularity, reusability, and formal representation of key concepts. It supports the integration of sensor observations, interaction modalities, and representation of human-centricity factors. Its applicability is demonstrated through a logistics use case, which involves cognitive decision support for yard operators and forklift drivers engaged in short-term scheduling of yard operations. The ontology offers a reusable semantic foundation that supports integration, context representation, and human-centric system modelling and can be extended to diverse domains.

Keywords: Human-Centered Digital Twins · Ontology · Socio-Technical Systems

1 Introduction

Recent advancements in Artificial Intelligence (AI), the Internet of Things (IoT), edge computing, and immersive technologies such as Augmented and Virtual Reality (AR/VR) have revolutionised the digitisation of industrial systems, leading to the development of Cyber-Physical Systems (CPS). Digital Twins (DTs) have attracted notable attention as a key technological innovation within CPS-enabled industrial environments. A DT is a digital representation of a physical entity that captures its key relevant features and maintains synchronisation between the physical and digital counterparts [1]. A Human Digital Twin (HDT) is a digital representation of a human, which can be an individual or a class of humans sharing common traits, characteristics, and behaviours [2]. While the scope of DTs initially focused on efficiency and productivity, integrating HDTs incorporates human-centricity considerations, reflecting the human-centricity pillar of Industry 5.0 [3]. Furthermore, advancements in HDTs such as the integration of cognitive system architecture concepts for human decision-making and

© The Author(s), under exclusive license to Springer Nature Switzerland AG 2026
J. Barata et al. (Eds.): IN4PL 2025, CCIS 2826, pp. 135–151, 2026.
https://doi.org/10.1007/978-3-032-15579-5_9

workload modelling [4], and DT frameworks for addressing safety and well-being [5–7], highlight the increasing shift towards Human-Centered Digital Twins (HCDTs). HCDTs not only represent human states but also model the contextual factors that affect human needs and well-being within socio-technical systems. This enables applications such as adaptive task allocation, safety monitoring, interface personalisation, and context-adaptive functionalities.

Despite the growing interest in HCDTs, their development is challenged by the complexity of handling human-centricity factors (HCF). Structured knowledge representations are essential to capturing these complexities. They ensure consistent interpretation of relevant concepts and facilitate integration across different systems. The need to account for diverse types of HCF-relevant data and to derive insights about human conditions and system behaviour is also a challenge. Ontologies offer a formal and interoperable way to represent domain knowledge addressing such challenges. However, ontology models typically address human-centricity within DTs for specific domains such as manufacturing [7–9] and construction [10–12]. While these domain-specific ontologies have contributed valuable insights, their application-specific scope limits reusability for integration across different industrial domains. Therefore, there is a need for a Top-Level Ontology (TLO) model that provides a unified semantic framework, capable of supporting inter-domain applications and enhancing inter-domain interoperability in HCDTs. Beyond enabling reuse, a TLO also supports modular ontology development, serving as a foundation for extending domain-specific models. In addition, it supports a clearer conceptualisation of common HCFs across domains, which can inform the design of human-centred systems.

Aligned with such needs, this paper presents a TLO model for HCDTs that can abstract a diverse range of HCFs, thereby supporting semantic interoperability across different industrial domains. The ontology was designed based on requirements identified from use cases in diverse sectors [13] and structured using established ontology engineering practices. To assess the ontology's applicability, a logistic use case was selected for validation focusing on cognitive decision support for forklift drivers and yard operators. It involves short-term scheduling under operational uncertainty, requiring context-sensitive suggestions and decision-making with human-in-the-loop.

The paper is structured as follows. Section 2 offers the background within which the present work is positioned. The ontology design and its validation are presented in Sects. 3 and 4 respectively. Section 5 offers a discussion on the results and points towards future work. Section 6 is the conclusion.

2 Background

NASA first defined a DT as an integrated multi-physics, multi-scale, probabilistic simulation of a vehicle or system that uses the physical models, sensor updates, fleet history, etc., to mirror the life of its corresponding twin [14]. Since then, the definition of DTs has evolved across disciplines, with various authors adapting the concept to suit different domains and use cases [15]. While early definitions emphasized mirroring and simulation, more recent characterizations describe DTs as virtual representations of physical assets or systems that integrate real-time data to support analysis, decision-making, and optimization across the lifecycle [16]. As DTs expanded into diverse application areas and with growing interest in incorporating human-centricity considerations, the need for appropriately structured knowledge representations emerged. To address this, semantic technologies, particularly ontologies, have been introduced into DTs, as will be reviewed in the following subsection.

2.1 Human Centred Digital Twin Ontologies

Early TLO models for DTs have established foundational semantic representations within the domain of CPS. For example, [17] and [18] introduced IoT-oriented TLO models to formalise DT concepts, aiming to enhance interoperability and integration across heterogeneous CPS environments. The model by [17] incorporates Human-Machine Interfaces (HMI) and user profiles, capturing certain aspects of human-centricity through user interactions and usability requirements within DTs. A top-level ontology framework for developing DTs was proposed by [19], which adopts the Basic Formal Ontology (BFO) as its foundational reference. The framework supports the integration of HDTs by leveraging BFO's biomedical origins to create ontologies for human behaviour, status, and interaction. Furthermore, it highlights advantages of reusing and adapting TLOs to enhance semantic interoperability across domains, particularly in addressing interoperability challenges. Additionally, these approaches underscore the potential of the TLO-based approaches in modelling HCDTs for enhanced semantic clarity and cross-domain interoperability.

More recent ontological approaches to DTs have increasingly focused on improving safety, ergonomics, and collaborative coordination in industrial environments. For example, DT frameworks enable reasoning over unsafe conditions to support adaptive safety measures, addressing real-time worker safety and risk mitigation [7]. Others incorporate ergonomic assessment into semantic system design and integrate expert knowledge about manual operations to guide evaluation and decision-making processes [8]. Ontology-based models enhance context-aware support for human operators by linking human roles, required tools, and spatial locations within collaborative settings [20].

While many ontologies have focused on structural and functional integration in DTs, research has sought to extend this integration toward cognitive and behavioural modelling to support human-centricity. For instance, [21] introduces an ontology-based data-model coupling approach for ensuring consistency between physical and virtual environments in DTs. This is primarily designed for synchronising data in industrial processes, and includes a human data model in a validation use case. This model encompasses a range of properties, including posture, stress, historical behavioural habits, and demographic data, focusing primarily on physical and behavioural dimensions relevant to the manufacturing domain. The study demonstrates the advantages of ontology-based approaches in modelling human factors within DTs, supporting structured representation and integration of HCFs. However, the HCFs modelling remains embedded in the industrial process context, limiting its applicability to other domains.

Extending the focus beyond physical and behavioural factors, further work incorporated cognitive constructs into ontology models for HDTs in cybersecurity contexts [22]. Grounded in behavioural psychology and structured using the BFO, this enabled the formalisation and modelling of human cognitive and behavioural constructs such as perception, knowledge, awareness, and satisfaction. Although it adopts generic human cognitive modelling, its design is tightly coupled with the cybersecurity domain, making adaption to other domains difficult to achieve without significant adaptation. Nevertheless, its emphasis on cognitive and behavioural explainability can be extended to HCDTs, particularly in scenarios requiring an understanding of human decisions and behaviours.

In summary, while existing ontologies have addressed various human-centricity factors, including safety and ergonomics [7], cognitive load and trust [23], and behavioural constructs [22], they remain fragmented in scope and domain-specific in application. This highlights the need for a unified model capable of representing these factors in DTs in a domain-independent manner, particularly through formalised representations of human-centricity factors, as discussed in the following subsection.

2.2 Knowledge Representation for Human-Centricity Factors

An early attempt to formalize HCFs is found in [24], introducing a framework aiming to capture user profiles and cognitive traits within computer-mediated systems. The work identified a foundational set of HCFs, such as cognitive states, emotional states, and cognitive style, that can inform how systems adapt to individual users. Although limited in scope, this work established the value of modelling human factors in a structured representation. Another work proposed the PSP Ontology (Problem, Solution, Problem-Solver Ontology), for human-centered CPS [25], introducing humans and autonomous systems as complementary problem-solvers. It incorporated both human competency levels and system autonomy degrees to guide the allocation of problem-solving responsibilities. Furthermore, the PSP ontology moved beyond static role assignments by enabling interaction, information exchange, and mutual learning between human and automated systems. Both studies offer a foundation for HCDT development, highlighting the role of HFC modelling for human-aware systems.

Stemming from a cognitive engineering perspective, the Human-CoMo framework integrates cognitive knowledge engineering into the modelling of Human-Cyber-Physical Systems (HCPS) [26]. This framework identifies key cognitive concepts, such as knowledge hierarchy, conceptual chunking, and knowledge precision, as necessary constructs for modelling human expertise and its integration into technical systems. Human-CoMo frames the design of human-system collaboration as a transdisciplinary process that must involve both domain-specific knowledge and cognitive engineering principles. In the context of HCDTs, this reflects a shift from treating the human as an entity with predefined roles to modelling human knowledge as a central element.

To advance the semantic representation of human-centricity in the manufacturing domain, a Human-Centric Knowledge Graph (HCKG) framework was proposed [27]. The HCKG captures context-aware relationships between operators, tasks, physical environments, and automated systems, particularly within the scope of human–robot collaboration. One of the key contributions of this framework is the integration of human-centric Key Performance Indicators (KPIs) across several categories, including physiological, physical, and environmental. These KPIs support the evaluation of operator well-being and working conditions, enabling systems to react to human states. Another human–robot collaboration framework introduced constructs such as human capabilities, ergonomics, body posture, and task-specific physical demands, together with cognitive load, stress, and trust as essential concepts [23]. Together, these studies provide valuable modelling approaches and introduce a range of HCFs. Nonetheless, while these contributions advance the semantic modelling of human-centric concepts, such as human-centric KPIs, emotional states, operator capabilities, and trust, they are not situated within the DT domain. This leaves a gap in the formal representation of human-centricity within DT-enabled socio-technical systems, and an ontological approach for HCDTs that bridges this gap is presented next.

3   Ontology Design

The development of the HCDT ontology followed a structured, iterative approach following the Unified Process for ONtology building (UPON) methodology [28]. The process began with defining the domain scope and identifying requirements. The domain of the ontology is situated at the intersection of DT systems and collaborative industrial work environments, where human-centricity must be explicitly considered to support interaction, adaptation, and decision-making. Documentation from a research project on human-centric DTs for improved work environments was analysed [29–31] and complemented by insights derived from stakeholder meetings and relevant literature to identify requirements.

The ontology was designed to support the representation of human actors and their interaction with CPS, including their roles, responsibilities, cognitive & physical states, and decision-making involvement. To enable context-awareness, the ontology must capture contextual information relevant to industrial work environment settings. In alignment with the project's focus on improving working conditions, the ontology must also incorporate HCFs to enhance human well-being in the work environment. Next, in the conceptual and design phase, the ontology was modelled using the Web Ontology Language (OWL) and implemented in Protégé [32]. A complete list of the defined classes and object properties is provided in Appendix A, Tables 1 and 2, respectively.

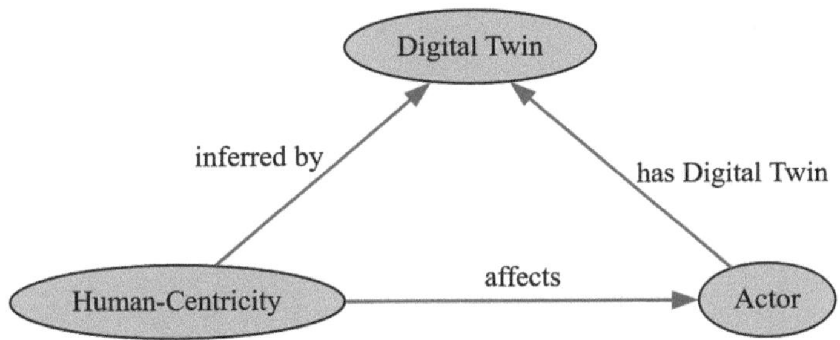

Fig. 1. Conceptual Triangle.

The HCDT ontology is structured around a conceptual triangle including three foundational concepts that capture the key dimensions of HCDT systems: (i) the virtual representations of entities (Digital Twin), (ii) the human conditions and its influencing factors (Human-Centricity), and (iii) the entities that perceive, act, and experience within the system (Actors). These three concepts establish the core semantic scaffold of the ontology. As illustrated in Fig. 1, actors can be represented by digital twins, enabling cyber-physical alignment within the system. HCFs influence and regulate the behaviour and operational status of actors, and can be inferred by DTs through monitoring mechanisms and contextual analysis.

Building on this conceptual foundation, the ontology was designed to formally capture the structure and dynamics of HCDTs. Capturing the structure and dynamics of HCDTs requires the ability to represent different types of DTs. This distinction is essential in socio-technical systems, where human-centricity must be understood not only in isolation but also in relation to other system components. To this end, the central construct of the ontology is the `DigitalTwinInstance`, which formalizes types of DTs such as `HumanDigitalTwin`, `ProcessDigitalTwin`, `AssetDigitalTwin`, and `ProductDigitalTwin`. These subclasses represent distinct modelling scopes. A `HumanDigitalTwin` represents the digital counterpart of a `HumanActor`, capturing their role, state, and interactions within the system. A `ProcessDigitalTwin` models sequences of operations or workflows. An `AssetDigitalTwin` refers to durable physical infrastructure or equipment with a persistent identity across use cycles. A `ProductDigitalTwin` represents physical items that are consumed, transformed, or produced as part of system activities. Although products can be considered assets in certain contexts, this distinction is made to reflect their different lifecycle characteristics and functional roles within socio-technical systems. Each `DigitalTwinInstance` is associated with a set of `Action` elements via the `hasAction` property, representing its intended use and operational behaviour within the system. Actions capture how the DT is expected to behave or function in its context, such as monitoring, control, prediction, or detection (Fig. 2).

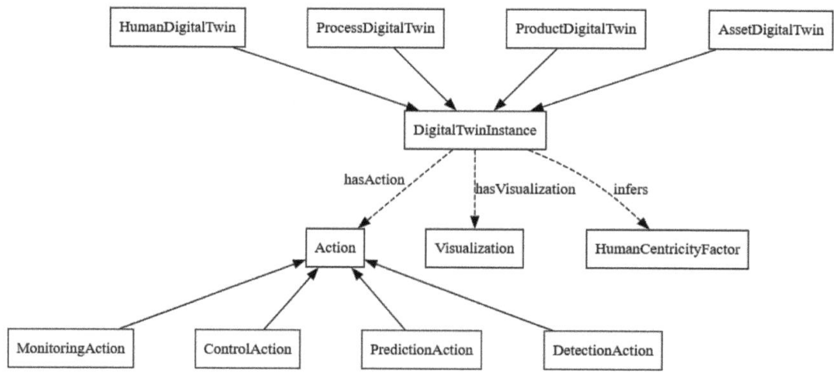

Fig. 2. Ontology relations in DigitalTwinInstance. Solid arrows indicate subclass relationships; the dashed arrow represents the object properties.

Human Centricity in Fig. 1 is one of the core concepts and evaluation dimensions for HCDTs [29]. These factors are observed through various forms of monitoring embedded in the environment, which measure physical, cognitive, or environmental conditions. In the ontology, these monitoring mechanisms are formalised using the Semantic

Sensor Network (SSN) ontology, where a `sosa:Sensor` refers to any device, software, or agent capable of detecting changes in the environment or interpreting prior observations to produce a result (Fig. 3) [33]. Sensor outputs are linked to the `Data` class, which is used to represent both `RealTimeData` and `HistoricalData`, enabling the system to reason over both real-time conditions and past behaviours of the system.

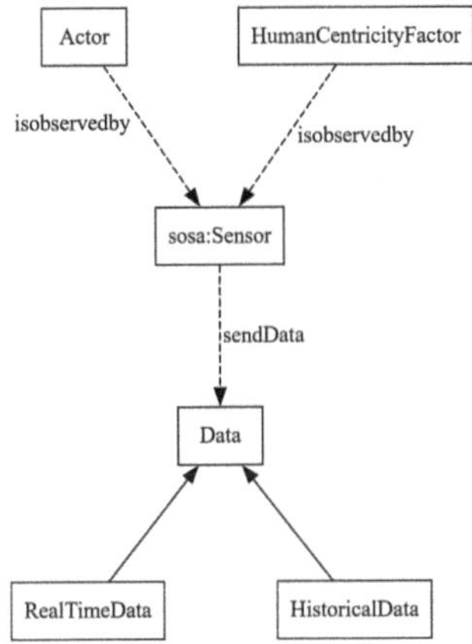

Fig. 3. Sensor-based observation modelling. Solid arrows indicate subclass relationships; the dashed arrows represent the object properties.

The ontology models context-awareness through three main classes: `Context`, `Status`, and `Data` as illustrated in Fig. 4. This structure enables the representation of both static and dynamic system conditions. The `Data` class is structured into `RealTimeData` and `HistoricalData`, facilitating reasoning over immediate and past events. The `Context` class distinguishes between directly captured information (`NonDerivedContext`) and inferred interpretations (`DerivedContext`), allowing the system to integrate low-level signals with higher-level situational understanding. The `Status` class reflects the operational condition of an `Actor`, contributing to context interpretation. This structure enables the ontology to support dynamic, context-aware decision-making in human-in-the-loop systems.

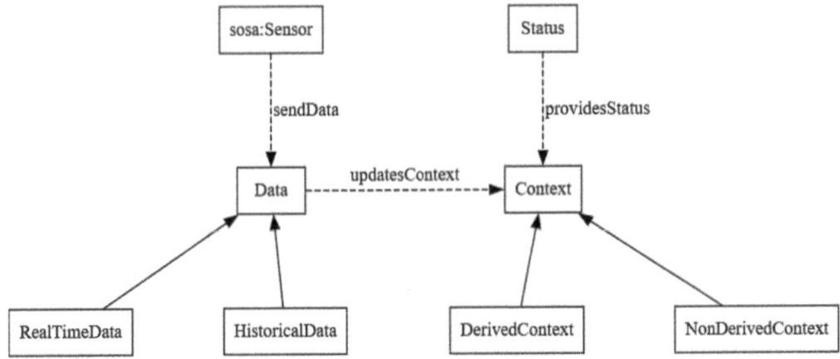

Fig. 4. Context-Awareness modelling. Solid arrows indicate subclass relationships; the dashed arrows represent the object properties.

The ontology also introduces the `Actor` class (See Figs. 1 and 3), which represents both human and non-human entities capable of performing tasks and making decisions. The distinction between `HumanActor` and `NonHumanActor` reflects the ontology's ability to represent the co-existence and collaboration of humans with non-human actors. Each `Actor` can be associated with one or more `DigitalTwinInstances`, depending on the required granularity of representation. This supports flexible modelling, where multiple digital twins may capture distinct aspects, roles, or contexts relevant to the same actor. Each `Actor` is further profiled through associations with `Skill` and `Status`, supporting the description of capabilities and operational conditions. In addition, a `HumanActor` is associated with `HumanCentricityFactors`, such as `Stress`, `Fatigue`, `Ergonomics`, and `Safety`.

Supporting user interactions and the interpretability of system behaviour is addressed through the `Interface` and `Visualization` classes. In this context, the `User` refers to the `HumanActor` who interacts with the system through an interface. The `Interface` class defines the modality of interaction between the `User` and the HCDT systems, encompassing stationary graphical user interfaces and portable interface terminals to immersive modalities such as in Augmented and Virtual Reality (AR/VR). Visual feedback is modelled using the `Visualization` class, which captures how data and system states are communicated (see Fig. 5). Each digital twin instance and `Data` class is associated with a visual representation, defined through the `hasVisualization` property. This visualization is then linked, via the `isDisplayedOn` property, to a specific `Interface`, allowing the system to adapt visual outputs based on the user's role or operational context.

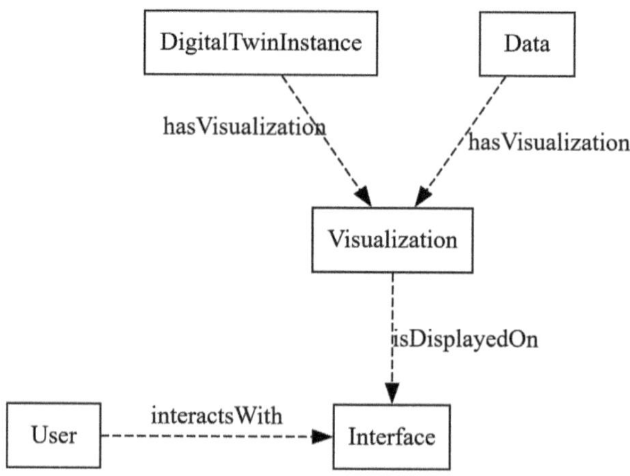

Fig. 5. Interface and Visualization modelling. Dashed arrows represent the object properties.

4   Ontology Evaluation

Ontology evaluation is essential for assessing the logical, structural, and practical validity of the developed ontology. In this work, a multi-dimensional evaluation approach was adopted, combining logical validation through reasoning tools, structural assessment via schema and knowledgebase metrics, and practical validity using competency questions derived from selected use cases.

4.1   Logical Consistency

Logical consistency of the ontology was verified using the HermiT reasoner integrated within the Protégé environment. This reasoner ensured that no contradictory axioms were introduced during ontology modelling and that all subclass relations, property domains/ranges, and individual assertions complied with OWL 2 DL semantics. The successful classification and realization of all classes confirmed the coherence of the ontology's taxonomic structure and property axiomatization.

4.2   Evaluation Metrics

The structural evaluation of the ontology was conducted using schema-level metrics defined in the OntoQA framework [34]. The Relationship Richness (RR) score was 0.903. This metric quantifies the proportion of non-inheritance relationships relative to the total number of relationships in the ontology. A high RR value indicates that the ontology includes a wide range of semantic connections beyond class hierarchies. The Inheritance Richness (IR) was measured at 0.745, which is defined as the average number of subclasses per class. The IR reflects how information is distributed across the class hierarchy; higher values suggest a broader, more horizontally structured taxonomy. These metrics indicate that the ontology achieves a structural design that supports both semantic depth and breadth required for modelling complex HCDTs.

4.3   Competency Questions

To assess the practical suitability of the HCDT ontology, a set of competency questions (CQs) was formulated based on the logistics pilot involving short-term scheduling and human-in-the-loop decision-making. This use case focuses on a yard logistics scenario in which a human operator, such as a forklift driver or yard manager, must decide which truck to serve next. Traditionally, decisions in yard logistics are based on simple heuristics, such as first-in-first-out, or rely on the operator's experience. In the considered case, the system under development supports yard operators in short-term scheduling decisions by generating optimized service recommendations for trucks currently awaiting processing. These recommendations include suitable exchange points and time slots for loading or unloading operations. The schedule optimization is based on dynamic yard conditions such as material stock levels, exchange point availability, storage capacity, and task durations [31]. While the system proposes a schedule to improve throughput and reduce waiting times, the final decision rests with the human operator, who can override the system's suggestions when necessary. These human decisions are intended to be fed back into the scheduling component to support continuous learning and refinement of future recommendations as the system evolves [30]. The scheduling decisions must therefore adapt not only to the operational context but also to the status, experience level, and preferences of the human user. The system must also present information and recommendations through suitable interfaces to ensure transparency and explainability.

Based on the use case, a set of competency questions was formulated to evaluate the ontology design. These questions were designed to assess the ontology's expressiveness in modelling human involvement, contextual triggers, human-centricity factors, and mechanisms for explainable system interaction. The competency questions are as follows:

1. This question validates whether the ontology can represent human operators as active decision-makers, along with their capabilities and current conditions.
   - **CQ1:** *Which HumanActors are involved in the decision-making process, and what are their current skill levels and operational status?*
2. This question examines the ontology's ability to represent human-centricity factors such as fatigue, stress, or workload, which may influence task allocation or user support. While these factors are not yet integrated into real-time optimization logic in yard logistics use case, modelling them provides a semantic foundation for future human-aware adaptations and safety considerations.
   - **CQ2:** *What Human-Centricity Factors are currently experienced by human actors in the yard?*
3. This question assesses whether the ontology can represent how decision-relevant information is delivered to the human actor via appropriate interfaces. Rather than modelling design-time configurations, it focuses on runtime delivery.
   - **CQ3:** *How are the current visualizations displayed, and through which interface are they presented to the user?*
4. This question assesses the ontology's capacity for context-awareness and semantic reasoning, ensuring that high-level interpretations of system state can be inferred from low-level sensor data.
   - **CQ4:** *What is the current DerivedContext inferred from recent sensor observations?*

These competency questions were formalised as SPARQL queries to evaluate the ontology's capacity to support structured reasoning over its core concepts. To simulate a representative knowledge base, the ontology was populated with a set of mock instances reflecting key actors, contextual elements, and DT entities relevant to the logistics use case. The queries were executed using the SPARQL plugin in Protégé, and each returned results consistent with the ontology structure. Queries and corresponding outputs are presented in Appendix A (See Figs. 6, 7, 8 and 9).

5 Discussion

The ontology proposed in this study offers a top-level semantic framework for modelling HCDTs in socio-technical systems, responding to gaps in existing domain-specific ontologies. The design of the ontology is built on the conceptual triangle of Digital Twins, Human-Centricity, and Actors. This structure shows the relationship between these key concepts in HCDT system. A key design consideration was to maintain separation between core concepts while ensuring that their relationships can be expressed in a way that supports reasoning.

Another important aspect of the ontology design is its support for reusability and extensibility across different domains. As a top-level model, the ontology avoids assumptions tied to a specific industrial domain. Instead, it defines generic core concepts that can be extended through additional modules tailored to specific domains. For instance, the conceptual structure around `Actor`, `DigitalTwinInstance`, and `HumanCentricityFactor` can be reused and refined depending on the characteristics of a given use case. The use of established semantic models, such as SSN/SOSA for representing sensor observations, further supports interoperability and alignment with external knowledge sources. This modular structure allows the ontology to serve as a semantic foundation that can be instantiated and expanded.

The evaluation results reflect both the structural coherence and practical applicability of the ontology. Logical validation using DL reasoners confirmed that the ontology is consistent and free of contradictory axioms, ensuring that the class hierarchy and property definitions are logically well-formed. The structural metrics further support this. A high RR value (0.903) indicates that the ontology models a wide range of semantic relationships beyond simple class inheritance. The IR metric (0.745) shows that information is distributed across a broad class structure, supporting flexible conceptual coverage. Although the attribute richness is lower (0.073), this is consistent with the focus on modelling core concepts and relationships rather than detailed instance-level attributes.

The evaluation through competency questions provided a more application-oriented assessment of the ontology's expressiveness. The selected questions were derived from the logistics use case and targeted core aspects of human involvement, human-centricity factors, contextual conditions, and system interaction. The ontology was able to answer these questions through SPARQL queries, demonstrating its capacity to support structured reasoning across key HCDT dimensions. This shows that the ontology is not only formally sound but also capable of supporting real-world use cases. However, a key limitation is that the competency question evaluation was limited to a single domain.

Furthermore, applying a top-level ontology in a specific use case presents certain modelling challenges. Populating the ontology requires mapping high-level concepts to detailed, domain-specific entities and events. This process can introduce constraints that do not originate from the ontology itself but from the assumptions made during instantiation in a particular context. As a result, the expressiveness and flexibility of the TLO may not be fully visible unless complemented by domain-specific extensions. These limitations reinforce the need to treat the proposed ontology as a foundational structure that supports semantic alignment across domains, but which must be instantiated and refined for each specific application. The current work provides this foundation by formally capturing core concepts relevant to HCDTs in a modular and reusable way, allowing for adaptation without redesigning the ontology from scratch.

6 Conclusion

This paper introduced a unified top-level ontology framework for Human-Centered Digital Twins (HCDTs), developed to support semantic modelling and reasoning within socio-technical systems. In response to the limitations of existing domain-specific ontologies, the proposed framework formalises core concepts around digital twins, human-centricity, and socio-technical system actors.

Evaluation of the ontology through logical validation, structural metrics, and competency questions grounded in a logistics use case demonstrates its capability to model context-awareness, human profiles and system interaction mechanisms. The ontology supports reasoning over dynamic and diverse data sources by linking sensor observations, human states, system status, and interface modalities. While the current validation has been conducted in the context of yard logistics, the ontology provides a foundational semantic structure that is modular, reusable, and extensible across domains. To further demonstrate its cross-domain applicability, future work will focus on instantiating and empirically validating the ontology in domains beyond logistics, such as agriculture and manufacturing. This will involve developing domain-specific extensions and deploying within the operational DT systems. A key aspect will be to reflect on the challenges of adapting the ontology in different domains, such as differences in data sources, context modelling requirements, and domain-specific human-centricity factors. Insights gained from these deployments will inform further refinement of the ontology and guide best practices for adaptation across diverse socio-technical environments.

Acknowledgments. This work was supported by the European Union's Horizon Europe research and innovation program under Grant Agreement No 101135990 (AI4Work). The collaboration with AI4Work partners on key concepts and system requirements, and especially with OAS AG, ATB GmbH, FBK, and TTS on the logistics case, AI4Work concepts, scheduling, and digital twins, is gratefully acknowledged.

A   Appendice

A.1   Ontology Classes and Object Properties

Table 1. Ontology Classes in the HCDT Ontology.

Class Name	Description
`DigitalTwinInstance`	Represents digital counterparts of real-world entities. Subclasses include `HumanDigitalTwin`, `ProcessDigitalTwin`, etc.
`Actor`	An entity that possesses the capacity to perform tasks or make decisions within a socio-technical system. This class is categorised into two main subclasses: `HumanActor`, representing human participants, and `NonHumanActor`, which includes artificial or automated agents
`Action`	Describes the intended use and operational behaviour of digital twins through the functions or tasks they perform within the system
`Context`	Represents information that situationally affects or characterizes an entity
`Status`	Represents the operational state of an Actor
`Skill`	A capability or competence possessed by an actor
`Data`	Includes `RealTimeData` and `HistoricalData` for reasoning
`Interface`	The point of interaction and communication
`Visualization`	The visual representation of Digital Twin instances and their associated data
`HumanCentricityFactor`	A factor or condition that affects the experience, performance, or well-being of human actors within the system
`sosa:Sensor`	Represents a sensing device or component that responds to a stimulus, such as a change in the environment, or to input data composed of the results of prior observations

Table 2. Object Properties in the HCDT Ontology.

Property Name	Domain	Range
`hasAction`	`DigitalTwinInstance`	`Action`
`hasSkill`	`HumanActor`	`Skill`
`hasStatus`	`Actor`	`Status`
`isObservedBy`	`Actor / HumanCentricityFactor`	`sosa:Sensor`
`sendDatato`	`sosa:Sensor`	`Data`
`updatesContext`	`Data`	`Context`
`hasVisualization`	`DigitalTwinInstance/Data`	`Visualization`
`isDisplayedOn`	`Visualization`	`Interface`
`ineteractsWith`	`User`	`Visualization`

A.2   SPARQL Queries and Results

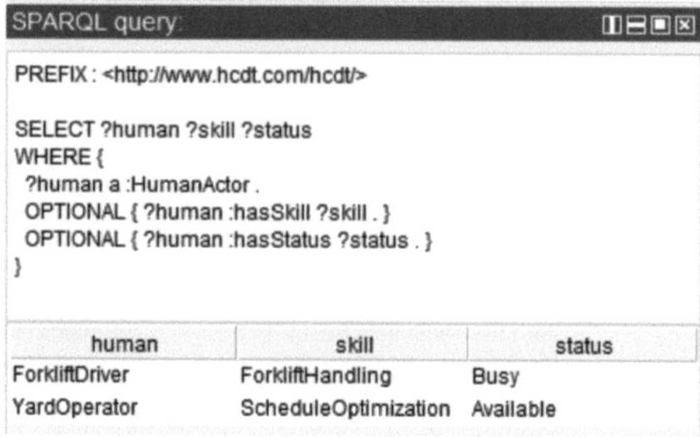

Fig. 6. CQ-1.

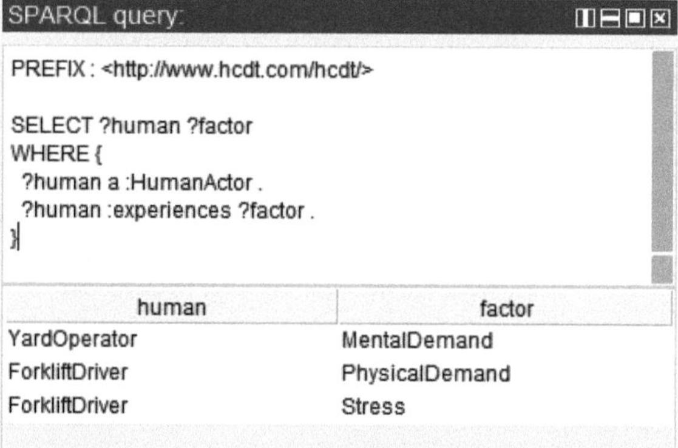

Fig. 7. CQ-2.

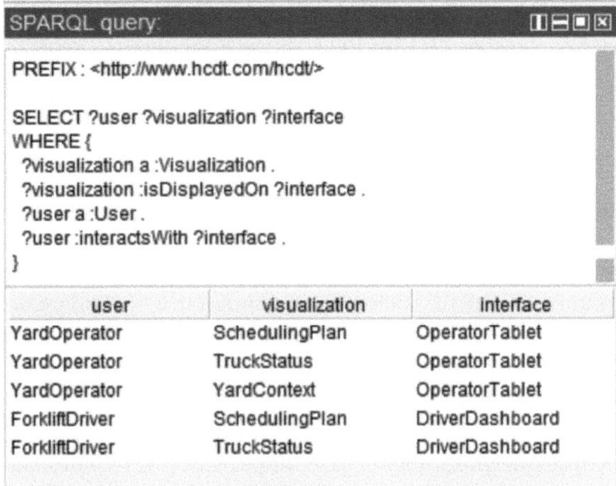

Fig. 8. CQ-3.

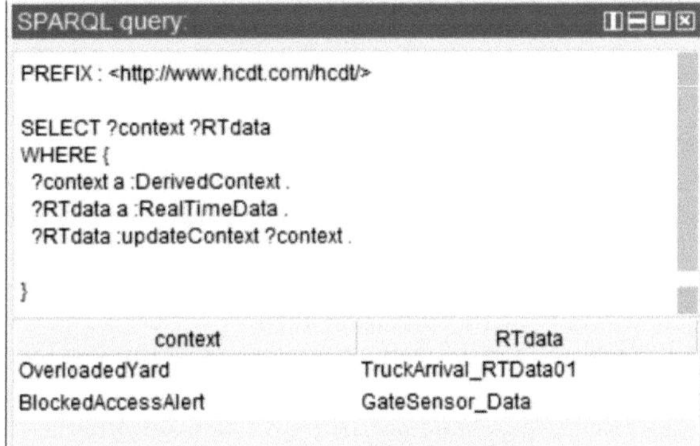

Fig. 9. CQ-4.

References

1. International Organization for Standardization: Automation systems and integration Digital twin framework for manufacturing Part 1 (2021)
2. Miller, M.E., Spatz, E.: A unified view of a human digital twin. Hum.-Intell. Syst. Integr. **4**(1–2), 23–33 (2022). https://doi.org/10.1007/s42454-022-00041-x
3. Krupas, M., Kajati, E., Liu, C., Zolotova, I.: Towards a human-centric digital twin for human machine collaboration: a review on enabling technologies and methods (2024). https://doi.org/10.3390/s24072232
4. Balaji, B., Shahab, M.A., Srinivasan, B., Srinivasan, R.: ACT-R based human digital twin to enhance operators performance in process industries. Front. Hum. Neurosci. **17** (2023). https://doi.org/10.3389/fnhum.2023.1038060
5. Bevilacqua, M., et al.: Digital twin reference model development to prevent operators' risk in process plants. Sustain. (Switz.) **12**(3) (2020). https://doi.org/10.3390/su12031088

6. Modoni, G.E., Sacco, M.: A human digital-twin-based framework driving human centricity towards industry 5.0. Sensors **23**(13) (2023). https://doi.org/10.3390/s23136054
7. Wang, H., et al.: A safety management approach for Industry 5.0? Human-centered manufacturing based on digital twin. J. Manuf. Syst. **66**, 1–12 (2023). https://doi.org/10.1016/j.jmsy.2022.11.013
8. Zheng, X., et al.: A semantic-driven tradespace framework to accelerate aircraft manufacturing system design. J. Intell. Manuf. **35**(1), 175–198 (2024). https://doi.org/10.1007/s10845-022-02043-7
9. Poudel, L., et al.: An integrated framework for dynamic manufacturing planning to obtain new line configurations. In: IEEE International Conference on Automation Science and Engineering, vol. 2022-August, pp. 328–334. IEEE Computer Society (2022). https://doi.org/10.1109/CASE49997.2022.9926689
10. Khan, R., Tomar, R., Hartmann, T., Ungureanu, L., Chacón, R., Ibrahim, A.: Platology: a digital twin ontology suite for the complete lifecycle of infrastructure, pp. 290–299. Det Kgl. Bibliotek/Royal Danish Library (2022). https://doi.org/10.7146/aul.455.c219
11. Xie, X., Moretti, N., Merino, J., Chang, J.Y., Pauwels, P., Parlikad, A.K.: Enabling building digital twin: ontology-based information management framework for multi-source data integration. In: IOP Conference Series: Earth and Environmental Science, vol. 1101. Institute of Physics (2022).https://doi.org/10.1088/1755-1315/1101/9/092010
12. Katsigarakis, K., et al.: A digital twin platform generating knowledge graphs for construction projects. Technical report (2022). https://cogito.iot.linkeddata.es/
13. AI4WORK: AI4WORK: Human-Centric Digital Twin Approaches to Trustworthy AI and Robotics for Improved Working Conditions (2024). https://ai4work.eu
14. Glaessgen, E.H., Stargel, D.S.: The digital twin paradigm for future NASA and U.S. Air force vehicles. In: Collection of Technical Papers - AIAA/ASME/ASCE/AHS/ASC Structures, Structural Dynamics and Materials Conference (2012). https://doi.org/10.2514/6.2012-1818
15. Singh, M., Fuenmayor, E., Hinchy, E.P., Qiao, Y., Murray, N., Devine, D.: Digital twin: origin to future (2021). https://doi.org/10.3390/asi4020036
16. Abdelrahman, M., Macatulad, E., Lei, B., Quintana, M., Miller, C., Biljecki, F.: What is a digital twin anyway? Deriving the definition for the built environment from over 15,000 scientific publications (2025). https://doi.org/10.1016/j.buildenv.2025.112748, http://arxiv.org/abs/2409.19005
17. Steinmetz, C., Rettberg, A., Ribeiro, F.G.C., Schroeder, G., Pereira, C.E.: Internet of things ontology for digital twin in cyber physical systems. In: Brazilian Symposium on Computing System Engineering, SBESC, vol. 2018-November, pp. 154–159. IEEE Computer Society (2018). https://doi.org/10.1109/SBESC.2018.00030
18. Bamunuarachchi, D., Banerjee, A., Jayaraman, P.P., Georgakopoulos, D.: Cyber twins supporting industry 4.0 application development. In: ACM International Conference Proceeding Series, pp. 64–73. Association for Computing Machinery (2020). https://doi.org/10.1145/3428690.3429177
19. Davide D'amico, R., Addepalli, S., Erkoyuncu, J.A.: Is a top level ontology based digital twin the solution to human-machine interoperability? Technical report (2021). https://ssrn.com/abstract=3945058
20. Walunj, S., Sintek, M., Pahlevannejad, P., Plociennik, C., Ruskowski, M.: Ontology-based digital twin framework for smart factories. Technical report (2023)
21. Ma, X., Qi, Q., Tao, F.: An ontology-based data-model coupling approach for digital twin. Robot. Comput.-Integr. Manuf. **86** (2024). https://doi.org/10.1016/j.rcim.2023.102649
22. Nguyen, T.N.: Toward human digital twins for cybersecurity simulations on the metaverse: ontological and network science approach. JMIRx Med **3**(2), e33502 (2022). https://doi.org/10.2196/33502

23. Hall, S., Dhanda, M., Dhokia, V.: Towards an ontology to capture human attributes in human-robot collaboration. In: Proceedings of the Design Society, vol. 4, pp. 2585–2594. Cambridge University Press (2024). https://doi.org/10.1017/pds.2024.261
24. Germanakos, P., Belk, M., Tsianos, N., Lekkas, Z., Mourlas, C., Samaras, G.: Towards a human factors ontology for computer-mediated systems*. In: Meersman, R., Tari, Z., Herrero, P. (eds.) OTM 2008. LNCS, vol. 5333, pp. 595–604. Springer, Heidelberg (2008). https://doi.org/10.1007/978-3-540-88875-8_83
25. Ansari, F., Khobreh, M., Seidenberg, U., Sihn, W.: A problem-solving ontology for human-centered cyber physical production systems. CIRP J. Manuf. Sci. Technol. **22**, 91–106 (2018). https://doi.org/10.1016/j.cirpj.2018.06.002
26. Bocklisch, F., Lampke, T.: Human-CoMo: a combination of cognitive knowledge engineering and data modelling for human-cyber-physical systems in intelligent manufacturing. J. Integr. Design Process Sci.: Trans. SDPS Off. J. Soc. Design Process Sci. **27**(3-4), 169–183 (11 2023). https://doi.org/10.1177/10920617241295887
27. Abonyi, J., Nagy, L., Ruppert, T.: Knowledge graph-based framework to support the human-centric approach. In: Abonyi, J., Nagy, L., Ruppert, T. (eds.) Ontology-Based Development of Industry 4.0 and 5.0 Solutions for Smart Manufacturing and Production. Springer Series in Advanced Manufacturing, pp. 127–156. Springer, Cham (2024). https://doi.org/10.1007/978-3-031-47444-6_5
28. De Nicola, A., Missikoff, M., Navigli, R.: A proposal for a unified process for ontology building: UPON. In: Andersen, K.V., Debenham, J., Wagner, R. (eds.) DEXA 2005. LNCS, vol. 3588, pp. 655–664. Springer, Heidelberg (2005). https://doi.org/10.1007/11546924_64
29. AI4Work: D2.3 Evaluation Methodology - Initial Version. Technical report D2.1 (2025)
30. AI4WORK: D5.1 Pilots plan - Initial Version. Technical report (2025)
31. AI4Work: D5.3 Logistics Pilot - Early Prototype. Technical report (2025)
32. Musen, M.A.: The protégé project. AI Matt. **1**(4), 4–12 (2015). https://doi.org/10.1145/2757001.2757003
33. Haller, A., et al.: The SOSA/SSN ontology: a joint W3C and OGC standard specifying the semantics of sensors, observations, actuation, and sampling. Technical report (2018). http://www.w3.org/ns/sosa/
34. Tartir, S., Arpinar, I.B., Sheth, A.P.: Ontological evaluation and validation. In: Poli, R., Healy, M., Kameas, A. (eds) Theory and Applications of Ontology: Computer Applications, pp. 115–130. Springer, Dordrecht (2010). https://doi.org/10.1007/978-90-481-8847-5_5

Mathematical Modeling of Supply Chain Resilience: Structure, Dynamics, and Indicator-Based Evaluation

N. Rahiel[1(✉)], S. Addouche[1], A. El Mhamedi[1], and K. Hachemi[2]

[1] Dept. QLIO, IUT Montreuil, Paris 8 Vincennes - Saint-Denis University, Paris, France
`{n.rahiel,s.addouche,a.elmhamedi}@iut.univ-paris8.fr`
[2] Dept. Industrial Engineering, LGPMI, Oran 2 University, Oran, Algeria
`hachemi.khalid@univ-oran2.dz`

Abstract. In an increasingly turbulent global environment, supply chains face multifaceted disruptions ranging from pandemics to geopolitical crises and climate shocks. While the concept of supply chain resilience (SCR) has gained prominence, most existing models fail to accurately capture the nonlinear, dynamic behavior of organizations facing disruption.

Building on this gap, this study proposes a mathematically robust and behaviorally coherent model of resilience based on hyperbolic tangent functions. The model accounts for the complete disruption cycle (degradation, latency, recovery) and is characterized by seven interpretable parameters that enable smooth, bounded, and asymmetric performance trajectories over time. A set of six resilience indicators is derived to evaluate critical system dimensions such as cumulative loss, recovery speed, and adaptive robustness.

Applied to four organizational scenarios (healthcare, manufacturing, retail, and tech startup), the model reveals distinct resilience archetypes, demonstrating its ability to differentiate strategic response profiles. A web-based interface further enables real-time evaluation and scenario planning. The proposed framework contributes a unified, customizable, and operational tool for quantitative resilience analysis, bridging the gap between conceptual models and actionable decision support in crisis management.

Keywords: Supply Chain Resilience · Mathematical Modeling · Quantitative Assessment · Performance Degradation · Crisis Adaptation

1 Introduction

A supply chain represents a complex and interconnected system that enables the flow of products and services from initial suppliers to final consumers. It spans multiple stages, including procurement of raw materials, production, distribution, and delivery. Managing this network effectively requires synchronized decisions on supplier selection, inventory control, logistics coordination, and demand forecasting, all aimed at maximizing operational efficiency and minimizing costs [1–3]. As supply chains become increasingly globalized and extended, firms adopt strategies such as just-in-time production, outsourcing, and supplier consolidation to enhance their economic performance. However, such efficiency-oriented configurations often result in fragility when faced with unexpected disruptions or volatile market conditions.

J. Barata et al. (Eds.): IN4PL 2025, CCIS 2826, pp. 152–168, 2026.
https://doi.org/10.1007/978-3-032-15579-5_10

Recent crises have exposed the vulnerability of highly optimized but rigid supply chains. The COVID-19 pandemic, for instance, triggered cascading effects across global supply networks due to localized shutdowns and imbalances between supply and demand [4]. In addition to global pandemics, supply chains are increasingly exposed to systemic threats such as climate change, political instability, natural disasters, and inflationary shocks [5]. Simultaneously, digitalization and technologies like blockchain and AI are transforming supply chain architectures, offering new capabilities in transparency and automation, but also increasing complexity and potential cyber risks [6].

In this context, the concept of *supply chain resilience* (SCR) has become central. Resilience refers to the supply chain's ability to absorb, adapt to, and recover from disruptive events, ideally returning to its original performance level or achieving a more robust post-crisis state [7,8]. Beyond simple recovery, resilience encompasses the capacity for transformation and adaptation in the face of uncertainty. However, despite its growing importance, measuring resilience in a precise and consistent way remains a methodological challenge. Most existing approaches lack the mathematical rigor necessary to accurately model the non-linear dynamics of disruptions and recovery over time.

This research addresses this gap by proposing a novel mathematical model for quantifying organizational resilience. Built on hyperbolic tangent functions, the model captures both the deterioration and recovery phases of a disruption in a continuous and differentiable manner. Its parametric flexibility allows it to accommodate a wide range of organizational behaviors while preserving interpretability. The model is complemented by a set of resilience indicators designed for comparative evaluation. The aim is to provide decision-makers with an analytical tool capable of assessing and comparing resilience strategies under diverse conditions and sectors.

2 Background

The quantification of resilience has evolved from a conceptual idea into a structured field supported by diverse methodologies and applications. The foundational work of Bruneau et al. (2003) introduced the resilience curve—a framework that visualizes performance degradation and recovery over time—laying the groundwork for quantitative resilience assessment [9]. This conceptual milestone has since inspired a range of approaches aimed at capturing resilience in measurable terms.

Subsequent research expanded on this foundation by identifying key resilience capacities. Hosseini et al. (2019) proposed absorptive, adaptive, and restorative capacities as core components [10], while Han et al. (2020) offered a complementary framework based on readiness, response, and recovery [11]. These conceptualizations have been refined further by Poulin and Kane (2021), who introduced a standardized taxonomy to ensure consistency and comparability in resilience metrics across disciplines [12].

Over time, the methodological landscape for evaluating resilience has become increasingly diverse. Kamalahmadi and Parast (2016) highlighted the heterogeneity in definitions and metrics within enterprise and supply chain resilience literature, underscoring the need for methodological standardization [13]. Today, a wide array of techniques is used, ranging from function-based and integral-based modeling, factor analysis, and survey-based assessments to system dynamics, discrete event simulation, and performance-based evaluations. These methods are synthesized in Fig. 1, which illustrates the main quantitative approaches currently employed to assess resilience.

Among these, function-based and integral-based approaches are particularly prevalent, accounting for approximately 55% of contemporary frameworks. These methods capture system performance dynamically during disruption and recovery, offering a time-integrated view of resilience. Specifically, integral-based methods calculate the area under the performance-time curve, with larger areas indicating greater resilience—whether due to reduced degradation, faster recovery, or both. While intuitive and widely adopted, these methods can obscure the trajectory of recovery, as identical resilience scores may mask very different temporal behaviors. This limitation is critical in sectors such as healthcare, where timing and responsiveness are central.

Despite these advancements, current practices often fall short of providing comprehensive assessments. Ribeiro and Barbosa-Póvoa (2018) observed that many studies explore resilience drivers without quantifying resilience itself, reflecting a disconnect between theory and practice [14]. As illustrated in Fig. 2, most studies emphasize resistance and recovery capacities (68.42%), while proactive preparedness, adaptation, and integrative assessments are underrepresented. Only 10.53% of existing methodologies address all four resilience capacities concurrently. This imbalance reflects both a lack of consensus on core dimensions and the absence of unified indicator frameworks, resulting in fragmented and often incomparable resilience evaluations.

Performance measurement strategies also vary by application domain. Hohenstein et al. (2015) found that supply chain resilience studies predominantly rely on output-based indicators such as demand fulfillment, capacity, and delivery performance [16].

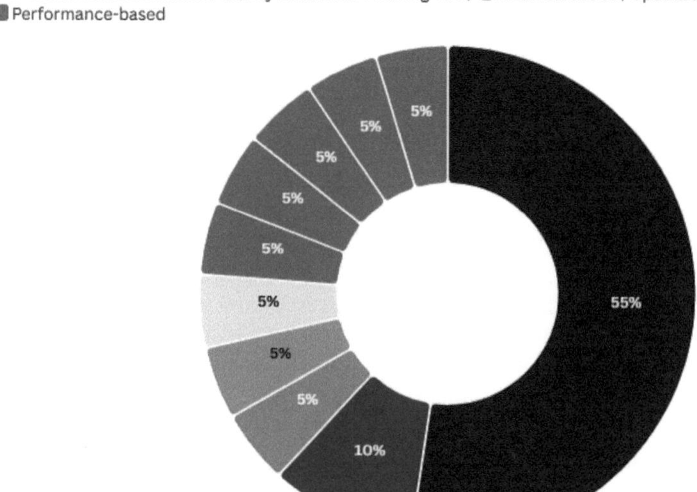

Fig. 1. Main quantitative methods used to evaluate resilience [8].

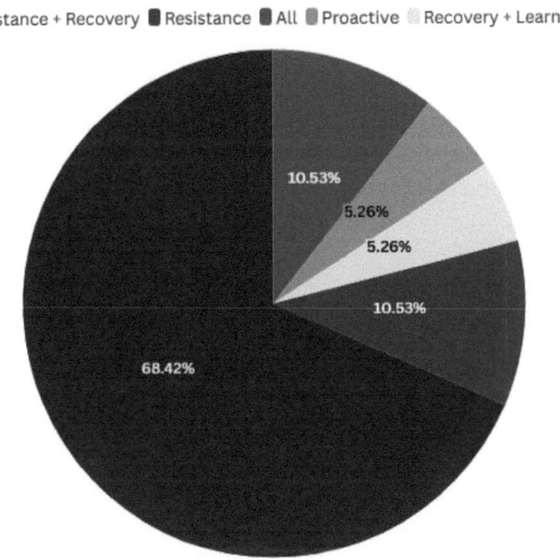

Fig. 2. Distribution of studies according to addressed resilience capacities [8].

Other studies have integrated economic and quality-based metrics, while Behzadi et al. (2020) stressed the importance of aligning resilience metrics with actionable benefits [17].

Resilience assessments often follow the stages of the resilience curve—initial impact, degradation, adaptation, and recovery—each with distinct temporal and performance considerations. However, the anticipatory nature of resilience planning introduces uncertainties in disruption scenarios and system responses, posing methodological challenges for robust evaluation.

While progress is evident, major limitations persist. Terminological inconsistencies and fragmented measurement approaches hinder cross-study comparability and practical implementation. Most importantly, many existing frameworks focus on isolated capacities rather than holistic, system-level resilience. This fragmentation calls for integrated approaches that capture interdependencies and provide unified assessments.

Readers seeking a deeper exploration of resilience metrics and mathematical formulations can refer to Bruckler et al. (2024), who analyzed 395 metrics from 220 studies and proposed a consolidated set of 17 standardized indicators [18].

This persistent methodological gap highlights the urgent need for integrated frameworks capable of simultaneously evaluating all phases and capacities of resilience. Such frameworks would offer a more complete and operationally relevant understanding of system performance under stress, forming a crucial foundation for the design of effective resilience strategies.

3 Mathematical Formulation and Theoretical Foundations

The proposed resilience model is expressed by a hyperbolic tangent-based function that elegantly captures the complex dynamics of organizational response to disruptions. The fundamental equation combines four distinct functional components, each representing a specific aspect of the resilience process:

$$p_1(x) = k + \frac{q}{2} - \frac{h}{2} \tanh\left(\frac{\alpha(x - g)}{2}\right) + \frac{h + q}{2} \tanh\left(\frac{\beta(x - g - d)}{2}\right) \quad (1)$$

where x represents time, $p_1(x)$ quantifies the performance level, and the seven parameters ($k, g, h, q, d, \alpha, \beta$) control different aspects of decline and recovery dynamics.

The selection of hyperbolic tangent functions is grounded in both theoretical and practical considerations that distinguish this approach from alternative methodological frameworks. These functions possess remarkable mathematical properties essential for resilience modeling: they are continuous, infinitely differentiable, and naturally bounded in the interval $[-1, 1]$. This intrinsic boundedness is particularly valuable for modeling gradual transitions between stable states without artificial discontinuities, reflecting the reality of adaptive processes where changes occur progressively rather than abruptly.

Traditional resilience models suffer from significant structural limitations that hyperbolic tangent functions effectively address. Step functions generate brutal changes incompatible with observed organizational dynamics, while piecewise linear functions introduce sharp angles at junction points, creating mathematical artifacts. Simple exponential models produce inadequately rapid temporal transitions that fail to capture the nuanced nature of organizational adaptation. The hyperbolic tangent function resolves these issues through its fundamental property:

$$\tanh(x) \text{ is infinitely differentiable with } \tanh'(x) = 1 - \tanh^2(x) > 0 \text{ everywhere} \quad (2)$$

ensuring that organizational resilience evolutions occur continuously and smoothly, faithfully reflecting adaptive processes empirically observed in complex systems.

The natural bounding property of hyperbolic tangent functions provides critical computational and theoretical advantages. The function satisfies $\tanh(x) \in [-1, 1]$ with well-defined asymptotic limits, which translates to controlled value ranges for both decline and recovery terms in the resilience model:

$$\text{Decline term: } -\frac{h}{2} \tanh\left(\frac{\alpha(x - g)}{2}\right) \in \left[-\frac{h}{2}, \frac{h}{2}\right] \quad (3)$$

$$\text{Recovery term: } \frac{h + q}{2} \tanh\left(\frac{\beta(x - g - d)}{2}\right) \in \left[-\frac{h + q}{2}, \frac{h + q}{2}\right] \quad (4)$$

These natural bounds prevent numerical explosions, ensure theoretical predictability through analytically known asymptotic limits, and eliminate algorithmic overflow risks, providing robust numerical stability essential for practical applications.

The parametric flexibility of the proposed formulation enables independent control of decline and recovery dynamics through differential parameterization of transition speeds. The steepness parameter α in $\tanh\left(\frac{\alpha(x-g)}{2}\right)$ demonstrates distinct behavioral regimes: low values ($\alpha \approx 0.5$) produce progressive transitions over approximately 8 time units, moderate values ($\alpha \approx 2.0$) generate moderate transitions over 2 time units, while high values ($\alpha \approx 5.0$) create rapid transitions over 0.8 time units. This flexibility presents unique methodological advantages, including process independence through $\alpha \neq \beta$ parameterization, enabling modeling of organizations with asymmetric decline and recovery patterns, fine calibration capabilities for precise adjustment according to empirical observations, and behavioral realism in capturing temporal asymmetries observed in organizational resilience phenomena.

The characteristic sigmoidal shape of hyperbolic tangent functions corresponds directly to natural adaptive processes observed in complex systems, exhibiting a tripartite structure: slow startup phase (initial resistance to perturbations), acceleration phase (intensification of change mechanisms), and asymptotic deceleration phase (convergence toward new equilibrium). This structure aligns with empirical observations across diverse domains, from psychological resilience sequences (denial $\rightarrow$ acceptance $\rightarrow$ reconstruction) to organizational patterns (shock $\rightarrow$ reorganization $\rightarrow$ new normality) and ecological dynamics (perturbation $\rightarrow$ succession $\rightarrow$ climax).

Comparative analysis with alternative functional approaches reveals the distinctive advantages of hyperbolic tangent functions. Exponential functions ($e^{-\alpha x}$) suffer from excessively rapid decay and lack natural bounds, while logistic functions ($\frac{1}{1+e^{-\alpha x}}$) are limited to the [0,1] interval with reduced flexibility, and linear functions impose unrealistic constant rates of change. The hyperbolic tangent approach provides controlled transitions with intrinsic bounds, symmetry around zero for superior adaptability, and variable rates that reflect realistic behavioral patterns.

Additional mathematical properties particularly suited to resilience analysis include differentiability ($\frac{d}{dx}\tanh(x) = 1 - \tanh^2(x)$) enabling change rate analysis, symmetry ($\tanh(-x) = -\tanh(x)$) facilitating calculations and interpretation, and functional composition capabilities allowing precise control of temporal position and transition speed. The geometric characteristics offer direct physical interpretation: the inflection point at $x = g$ corresponds to the moment of shock with maximum rate of change, the characteristic distance of approximately $\frac{4}{\alpha}$ defines the transition duration over which 95% of change occurs, and the asymptotes represent equilibrium states before and after perturbation.

The adoption of hyperbolic tangent functions systematically avoids methodological pitfalls associated with alternative approaches: polynomial functions generate parasitic oscillations, rational functions risk mathematical singularities, trigonometric functions introduce undesired periodicity, and pure exponentials exhibit unbounded growth or decay. The proposed approach offers an optimal combination of properties including monotonicity (strictly monotonic growth), boundedness (systematically controlled values), regularity (infinite differentiability), simplicity (ease of calculation and interpretation), and universality (applicability across resilience domains).

In conclusion, hyperbolic tangent functions constitute the optimal methodological compromise between behavioral realism, mathematical control, and practical usability for modeling resilience phenomena in complex organizational systems, providing a theoretically sound and computationally robust foundation for quantitative resilience analysis.

4   Resilience Model Architecture and Performance Indicators

4.1   Model Architecture and Temporal Dynamics

The model architecture is structured around four main components, each designed to capture a distinct phase of resilience dynamics. These components work together to reproduce the typical performance trajectory of a system subjected to disruption, including degradation, latency, recovery, and eventual stabilization.

Beyond their mathematical formulation, these components can be interpreted in terms of successive behavioral regimes that a system undergoes in response to disruption. This temporal decomposition not only enhances the interpretability of the model but also supports practical applications in resilience planning and system diagnostics.

First, the **reference level** of the system—representing its baseline performance in the absence of disruption—is defined as:

$$\text{Reference Level} = k + \frac{q}{2} \tag{5}$$

This constant term anchors the performance function. The inclusion of $\frac{q}{2}$ accounts for the system's potential to reach a performance level higher than its pre-disruption state, capturing the notion of adaptive resilience or learning from crises.

Second, the **degradation component**, which models the performance drop after a disruptive event occurring at time g, is given by:

$$\text{Degradation} = -\frac{h}{2} \tanh\left(\frac{\alpha(x - g)}{2}\right) \tag{6}$$

Here, the negative sign ensures a decline in system performance. The parameter α controls the steepness of the decline, while h defines its depth.

Third, the **recovery component** describes the post-disruption rebound and adaptation phase. It is expressed as:

$$\text{Recovery} = \frac{h + q}{2} \tanh\left(\frac{\beta(x - g - d)}{2}\right) \tag{7}$$

This term activates after a delay d, modeling the latency between the initial shock and the beginning of recovery efforts. The parameter β regulates the rate of performance restoration.

The temporal architecture of the model is governed by parameters g and d, which delineate the critical transitions between the system's phases—namely: initial impact, performance drop, latency period, recovery onset, and stabilization. These phases can be summarized as follows:

- **Phase 1 - Initial stable state**: For $x < g - \frac{2}{\alpha}$, the system maintains baseline performance $\approx k$.
- **Phase 2 - Post-shock decline**: In the interval $g - \frac{2}{\alpha} \leq x \leq g + \frac{2}{\alpha}$, the system experiences a sharp performance degradation.

- **Phase 3 - Latency period**: For $g + \frac{2}{\alpha} < x < g + d - \frac{2}{\beta}$, degraded performance stabilizes at a lower level.
- **Phase 4 - Active recovery**: In the interval $g + d - \frac{2}{\beta} \leq x \leq g + d + \frac{2}{\beta}$, the system undergoes performance restoration.
- **Phase 5 - New stable state**: For $x > g + d + \frac{2}{\beta}$, the system reaches a new equilibrium $\approx k + q$.

4.2   Parameter Framework and Organizational Interpretation

The model parameters are categorized into three main groups based on their organizational significance. Position and scale parameters include the baseline level k, representing organizational reference performance, and the temporal position of shock g, which is generally determined by direct observation of the disruptive event.

Amplitude parameters quantify the magnitude of system response. The decline depth h measures the maximum amplitude of performance drop, while the additional recovery amplitude q reflects the system's capacity to exceed its initial level after disruption.

Temporal and speed parameters control the dynamics of the system response. The recovery delay d models organizational latency in initiating recovery, while the transition speed parameters α and β control the rapidity of decline and recovery, respectively.

Figure 3 illustrates this categorization and the mathematical structure through which each parameter contributes to the system model.

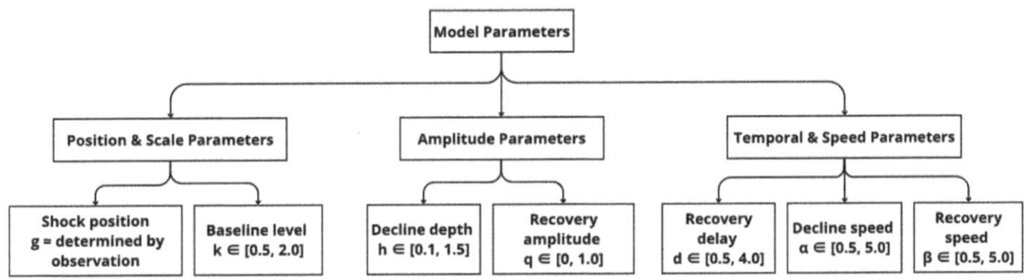

Fig. 3. Functional classification of parameters defining system behavior.

4.3   Resilience Indicators

To enable a holistic assessment of system resilience, the framework introduces a set of dedicated indicators designed to capture multiple dimensions of organizational response to disruption. These indicators reflect both the structural characteristics of system behavior and performance dynamics over time. Table 1 presents the proposed indicators, grouped by their analytical focus and computational design.

The selection of appropriate resilience indicators depends critically on the application context. For organizational comparisons, the DRC serves as the recommended primary indicator due to its comprehensive integration of multiple resilience dimensions.

Table 1. Comprehensive Resilience Indicators Framework.

Category	Indicator	Definition	Formula	Objective	Optimal Range
Area-Based	CLI	Cumulative Loss Index - quantifies total performance loss area	$\frac{h}{\alpha}\ln(2) + \frac{h \cdot d}{2} - \frac{h+q}{\beta}\ln(2)$	Min	CLI < 1.0
Speed & Efficiency	DRC	Dynamic Recovery Coefficient - composite speed/amplitude indicator	$\frac{\frac{\beta}{\alpha} \cdot \frac{h+q}{h} \cdot \frac{1}{d}}{\sqrt{\alpha\beta}} \cdot$	Max	DRC > 2.0
	WRT	Weighted Recovery Time - time to reach 95% recovery	$d + \frac{2.95}{\beta}$	Min	WRT < 2.0
Advanced Composite	ARS	Adaptive Robustness Score - balances efficiency and stability	$\frac{\beta(h+q)}{\alpha h d} \cdot \exp\left(-\frac{|q|}{h}\right) \cdot (1 + \tanh(\beta - \alpha))$	Max	ARS > 1.5
Context-Specialized	RRE	Relative Resilience Efficiency - performance relative to baseline	$1 + \frac{q}{2k} - \frac{h \cdot \text{CLI}}{T \cdot k}$	Max	RRE > 1.0
	RP	Recovery Potential - theoretical post-crisis improvement capacity	$\frac{k+q}{k - \frac{h}{2}}$	Max	RP > 1.5

Longitudinal monitoring applications benefit from the combination of RRE and WRT indicators, which capture both efficiency and temporal aspects. Strategic optimization processes should employ ARS as the primary steering indicator due to its balanced consideration of stability and adaptability factors.

These distinctions are operationalized in the classification framework presented in Table 2. This table provides performance thresholds for interpreting the main resilience indicators by categorizing them into four levels: Excellent, Good, Average, and Poor. These levels are defined based on quantile distributions and allow for standardized benchmarking across different organizational contexts.

This streamlined framework enables systematic evaluation and comparison of organizational resilience across different contexts, providing both theoretical foundations and practical tools for resilience assessment and improvement initiatives. The categorization of indicators by their primary analytical focus allows practitioners to select appropriate metrics based on their specific evaluation objectives and organizational context.

Table 2. Resilience Performance Classification Framework.

Level	DRC	WRT	RRE	ARS
Excellent (Top 10%)	> 3.0	< 1.5	> 1.2	> 2.0
Good (Top 25%)	> 2.0	< 2.5	> 1.1	> 1.5
Average (50% median)	1.0–2.0	2.5–4.0	0.9–1.1	1.0–1.5
Poor (Bottom 25%)	< 1.0	> 4.0	< 0.9	< 1.0

4.4   Interactive Resilience Evaluation Interface

To facilitate the practical application and evaluation of the proposed resilience model, we have developed a comprehensive web-based interactive interface[1]. This tool bridges the gap between theoretical formulation and operational use, serving both as a validation instrument for the mathematical framework and as a decision-support system for resilience planning. It enables users to manipulate parameters in real time and conduct comparative analyses across multiple resilience curves, enhancing visualization and diagnostic capabilities following disruptive events.

The interface architecture integrates two complementary input modalities to support diverse user needs. The primary mode features a tabular input system for simultaneous configuration of multiple resilience curves, ideal for comparing scenarios across different organizational settings or timeframes. Each curve can be independently activated, with real-time parameter validation ensuring adherence to model constraints.

The secondary mode complements the tabular input system by offering an intuitive slider-based interface tailored to the detailed exploration of individual resilience curves. Designed for sensitivity analysis and pedagogical use, this mode provides immediate visual feedback through dynamic constraint enforcement, ensuring parameter coherence and guiding users toward valid configurations. In this mode, a comprehensive set of quantitative outputs is automatically generated, including minimum and maximum performance values, recovery durations, degradation rates, final equilibrium levels, and the six resilience indicators. These real-time computations facilitate both rapid diagnostics and in-depth assessments of system behavior under specific disruption scenarios.

Moreover, the platform enables comparative benchmarking across scenarios via synchronized metric tables, supporting evidence-based evaluation of structural configurations, policy interventions, or contextual variables. This functionality enhances the tool's role as a strategic resource for resilience planning and informed decision-making.

---

[1] The interactive interface is available at: https://6846e9ced9764f8631cf7daa--preeminent-palmier-784581.netlify.app/.

5   Case Study: Resilience Analysis of Four Organizational Scenarios

This case study applies our resilience model to four distinct organizational contexts: Tech Startup, Manufacturing, Healthcare, and Retail. These scenarios allow us to simulate and compare how different sectors respond dynamically to a disruptive event.

The parameter configurations used to simulate system responses are detailed in Table 3. These values define the baseline performance levels, the severity and duration of degradation, and the timing and amplitude of recovery, corresponding to the main drivers of resilience behavior identified in the proposed model.

Table 3. Parameter Configuration for Four Organizational Scenarios.

Parameter	Tech Startup	Manufacturing	Healthcare	Retail	Description
k	1.0	1.2	1.5	0.8	Baseline performance level
q	0.2	0.1	0.3	-0.1	Additional recovery amplitude
h	1.0	0.7	0.7	1.4	Decline depth
g	3.0	4.0	2.0	5.0	Time of shock occurrence
d	3.0	1.5	1.0	4.0	Recovery delay
α	3.0	2.0	1.5	2.5	Decline speed
β	1.2	3	2.4	1.0	Recovery speed

Figure 4 illustrates the resulting time-based performance curves for each configuration. The x-axis represents time, while the y-axis shows normalized system performance. Each curve depicts the dynamic response of a system under shock, directly derived from the parameters in Table 3, thereby enabling visual comparison of resilience trajectories across different organizational settings. The specific dynamics observed in each curve are described as follows:

- **Tech Startup:** Exhibits a severe decline immediately after the shock, with performance dropping to a low level. The recovery is delayed and gradual, showing a limited ability to rebound quickly but some capacity for partial restoration.
- **Manufacturing:** Undergoes a moderate drop in performance with a timely and effective recovery. Although the initial degradation is more pronounced than in the healthcare case, the system demonstrates good recovery dynamics and post-crisis stability.
- **Healthcare:** Experiences a slight decline in performance followed by a rapid and stable recovery. It maintains a high level of functionality throughout the disruption, indicating strong adaptive capacity and robust system design.
- **Retail:** Shows the most drastic reaction to the disruption, with a sharp and deep performance loss. The recovery is slow, incomplete, and never returns to pre-shock levels, reflecting significant vulnerability and structural weaknesses in resilience mechanisms.

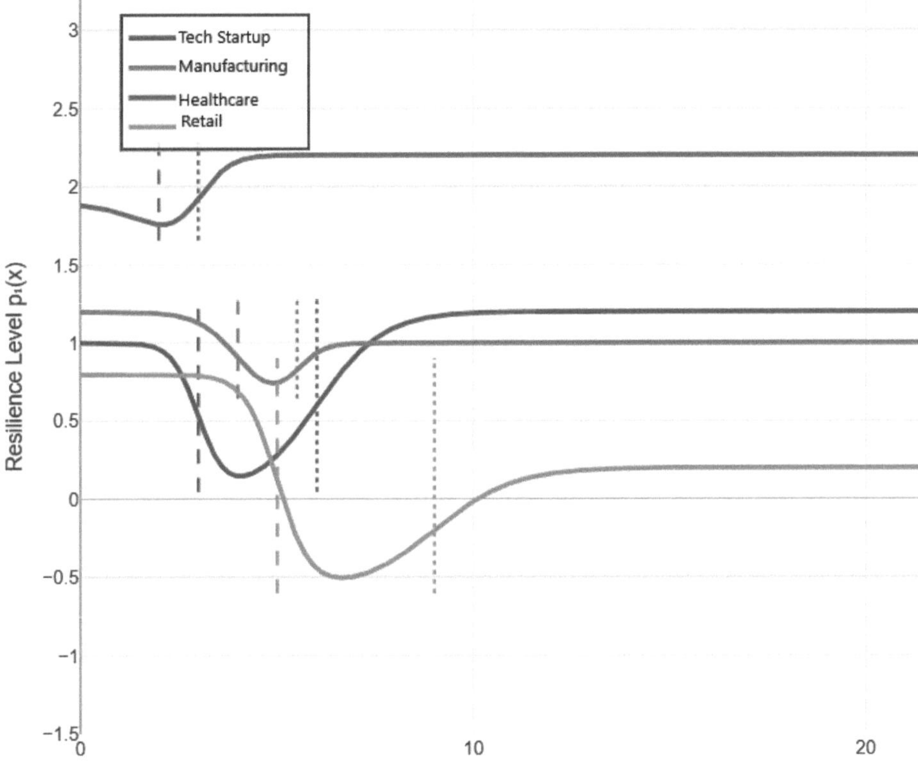

Fig. 4. Performance evolution of the four organizational scenarios over time.

6 Results and Discussion

6.1 Model Performance and Strategic Insights

The application of our proposed resilience assessment model to the four organizational scenarios yielded comprehensive performance data across all six indicators (Table 4). The radar chart visualization (Fig. 5) reveals markedly different resilience profiles, demonstrating the model's capacity to translate the dynamic performance behaviors into quantifiable resilience characteristics.

To test the robustness and discriminatory capacity of the framework, we constructed and analyzed four pedagogical case scenarios representing typical archetypes across organizational sectors. These synthetic yet operationally plausible trajectories were generated by configuring the seven key parameters (k, q, h, g, d, α, and β) based on characteristic strategic and operational behaviors. Such parametrizations can, in practice, be anticipated ex-ante through predictive modeling informed by historical performance data and learned behavior patterns. When implemented in real-world settings, this forward-looking calibration would enable proactive resilience planning and comparative scenario testing.

Table 4. Calculated Values of the Resilience Indicators (RIs) for All Scenarios.

RI	Tech Startup	Manufacturing	Healthcare	Retail
CLI	1.038	0.566	0.183	2.650
DRC	0.304	1.633	5.313	0.092
WRT	5.460	2.480	2.230	6.950
ARS	0.007	0.841	2.270	0.004
RRE	1.048	0.903	1.077	0.393
RP	2.400	1.111	1.294	2.000

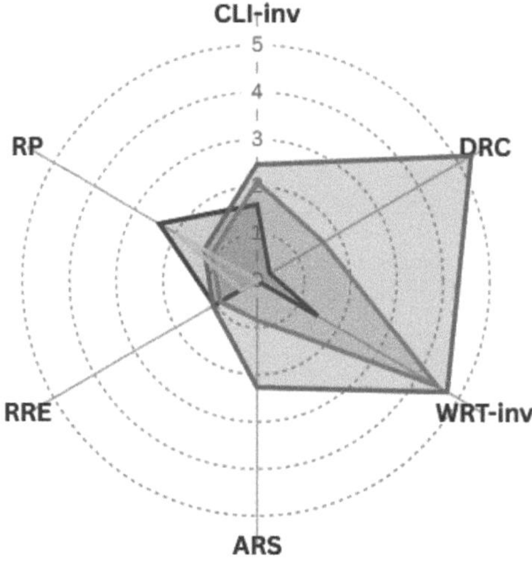

Fig. 5. Radar chart of normalized resilience indicators (CLI and WRT inversely scaled).

The analysis generates three distinct resilience archetypes from the assessment data. The Healthcare scenario emerged as a crisis-responsive archetype, achieving exceptional performance in damage response capabilities (DRC = 5.313) and recovery speed (ARS = 2.270), which directly correlates with its rapid recovery dynamics and minimal performance decline observed in the temporal curves. This profile reflects the sector's investment in robust response mechanisms and adaptive capacity. Conversely, the Retail scenario demonstrated a relationship-focused archetype, with low customer loyalty issues (CLI = 2.650) and workforce retention challenges (WRT = 6.950), while showing minimal damage response capability (DRC = 0.092) and recovery speed (ARS = 0.004). This pattern aligns with the slow, incomplete recovery trajectory visible in Fig. 4, suggesting that the organization faces significant challenges in stakeholder management while also lacking operational resilience mechanisms.

The Tech Startup scenario displayed a preparedness-oriented profile with significant workforce retention challenges (WRT = 5.460) despite good preparedness levels (RP =

2.400), yet limited operational response mechanisms. This assessment corresponds to the delayed but gradual recovery pattern observed in the performance curves, indicating capability for restoration but insufficient immediate response infrastructure. The Manufacturing scenario exhibited the most balanced resilience approach, with moderate values across most indicators and effective recovery dynamics that mirror its timely and stable performance restoration shown in the temporal analysis.

Importantly, while the model does not explicitly simulate managerial actions during a disruption, it indirectly captures their effects through the shape of the performance curves and the resulting indicators. In this way, different organizational strategies and response efforts are inherently reflected in the recovery trajectories. The model's flexibility enables the representation of a wide spectrum of behavioral adaptations, thus acknowledging the diversity of organizational responses without overspecifying their mechanisms.

The model effectively captures the multi-faceted nature of organizational resilience while avoiding the oversimplification inherent in single-metric approaches. The clear differentiation between scenarios provides empirical evidence that resilience manifests through diverse strategic configurations, validating the complexity of resilience phenomena observed in the dynamic performance curves. The model's ability to quantify these differences addresses a critical gap in resilience measurement literature, where most existing frameworks remain conceptually oriented without providing practical assessment capabilities.

The results suggest several practical applications for resilience management. Organizations can use the model to identify their specific resilience archetype and benchmark against the performance patterns established through the parametric configurations. The clear performance differentiation enables targeted improvement strategies, allowing entities to focus resources on specific capability gaps rather than pursuing generic resilience enhancement approaches. For instance, organizations with high customer loyalty issues might prioritize developing stakeholder engagement strategies, while crisis-responsive entities could invest in workforce stability programs to achieve more balanced resilience profiles.

6.2   Limitations and Future Research Directions

While the proposed model effectively translates temporal performance patterns into resilience indicators, it does not currently incorporate the temporal evolution of decision variables or organizational adaptation in real time. As such, it captures resilience as a post-disruption diagnostic framework rather than a predictive system that evolves dynamically. Future research should include longitudinal assessments to analyze how organizations adapt over time and to identify causal relationships between interventions and resilience trajectories.

Another limitation concerns the manual specification of parameters. Although the model is parametrically rich and interpretable, the absence of a fully integrated input-output mapping from observable data to parameter values currently restricts automation. This challenge opens opportunities for the development of inverse modeling approaches where historical or real-time data can be used to infer parameters and calibrate the model more precisely. This would enable organizations to deploy the model in a data-driven manner and conduct diagnostics based on observed disruptions.

Moreover, while this study employed synthetic but realistic organizational trajectories to validate the model's structure and internal coherence, future work should focus on large-scale empirical applications using organizational datasets across sectors such as healthcare, logistics, and manufacturing. Building such empirical evidence would help refine the parameter space, validate the model's generalizability, and establish a sector-specific resilience knowledge base.

Finally, extending the model to accommodate systemic and interdependent disruptions—by integrating multi-scale or network-based formulations—would provide deeper insights into cascading failures and cross-entity vulnerabilities. Additionally, incorporating emerging resilience dimensions such as digital robustness, adaptive governance, or socio-technical agility would enhance the model's relevance in the context of evolving organizational challenges.

7 Conclusion

This study introduced a novel analytical framework for quantifying organizational resilience, grounded in a parametric model that captures both degradation and recovery dynamics with high fidelity. By proposing a formulation with seven degrees of freedom, the model enables the representation of a wide range of disruption scenarios while preserving mathematical continuity and interpretability. Its ability to account for non-linear temporal evolutions enhances its applicability to the complex resilience phenomena encountered across organizational systems.

The derived performance trajectories are both synthetic and strategically meaningful, parameterized according to key organizational constructs such as impact depth, recovery amplitude, and response latency. From these, six resilience indicators were developed, offering an objective and replicable basis for performance assessment, benchmarking, and decision support. The model's robustness and discriminative power were validated through application to four contrasting organizational cases, highlighting its relevance and adaptability across diverse operational settings.

In bridging theoretical modeling with practical utility, the development of a web-based interactive tool significantly enhances the framework's accessibility. This interface supports real-time manipulation of resilience parameters, comparative analysis of disruption scenarios, and intuitive visualization of resilience curves—thus equipping practitioners with a decision-support capability that is both evidence-based and user-friendly. The academic impact of this research lies in its methodological innovation and conceptual clarity. By formalizing resilience assessment through a flexible yet rigorous parametric structure, the study contributes a generalizable framework that can serve as a foundation for future analytical work in resilience engineering, operations management, and organizational systems research. It also provides a replicable basis for comparative studies and meta-analyses across sectors and contexts.

From a practitioner's perspective, the framework responds to a critical need for structured and interpretable tools that can inform preparedness, response, and adaptation strategies in disruption-prone environments. Its potential for integration into organizational risk management systems is considerable, particularly in high-stakes domains such as healthcare, manufacturing, and critical infrastructure.

Future research should pursue inverse modeling techniques to enable the inference of resilience parameters from empirical data, the incorporation of stochastic elements to better capture uncertainty, and the extension of the framework to networked and multi-scale systems to address systemic interdependencies. Sector-specific deployments will also be crucial to establishing a comparative repository of resilience archetypes and best practices.

In sum, this research offers both theoretical advancement and applied value, providing scholars and practitioners with a rigorous, flexible, and actionable approach to understanding and enhancing organizational resilience.

References

1. Supply Chain Management: Supply Chain Management. *Supply Chain Management*, pp. 285–316 (2023). https://doi.org/10.1002/9781394207190.ch10
2. Jayaprakash, J.: Artificial Intelligence in Logistics and Supply Chain, pp. 211–233 (2022). https://doi.org/10.1002/9781119821809.ch14
3. Implementation Vendor Managed Inventory in Electronic Manufacturing. Int. J. Bus. Technol. Manage. (2023). https://doi.org/10.55057/ijbtm.2023.5.s4.9
4. Pujawan, I.N., Bah, A.U.: Supply chains under COVID-19 disruptions: literature review and research agenda. Supply Chain Forum **23**(1), 81–95 (2022). https://doi.org/10.1080/16258312.2021.1932568
5. Guo, Y., Liu, F., Song, J.-S., Wang, S.: Supply chain resilience: a review from the inventory management perspective. Fundam. Res. (2024). https://doi.org/10.1016/j.fmre.2024.08.002
6. Mishra, A., Gupta, N., Jha, G.K.: Supply chain resilience: adapting to global disruptions and uncertainty. Int. J. Innov. Res. Eng. **5**, 189–196 (2024). https://doi.org/10.59256/ijire.20240502025
7. Yin, W., Ran, W., Zhang, Z.: A configuration approach to build supply chain resilience: from matching perspective. Exp. Syst. Appl. **249**, 123662 (2024). https://doi.org/10.1016/j.eswa.2024.123662
8. Rahiel, N., El Mhamedi, A., Hachemi, K.: Healthcare supply chain: resilience qualitative evaluation. In: Jawab, F. (ed.) Hospital Supply Chain. Integrated Science, vol. 27, pp. 439–459. Springer, Cham (2024). https://doi.org/10.1007/978-3-031-70292-1_21
9. Bruneau, M., et al.: A framework to quantitatively assess and enhance the seismic resilience of communities. Earthq. Spectra **19**(4), 733–752 (2003)
10. Hosseini, S., Ivanov, D., Dolgui, A.: Review of quantitative methods for supply chain resilience analysis. Transp. Res. Part E: Logistics Transp. Rev. **125**, 285–307 (2019)
11. Han, Y., Chong, W.K., Li, D.: A systematic literature review of the capabilities and performance metrics of supply chain resilience. Int. J. Prod. Res. **58**(15), 4541–4566 (2020)
12. Poulin, C., Kane, M.B.: Infrastructure resilience curves: performance measures and summary metrics. Reliab. Eng. Syst. Saf. **216**, 107926 (2021)
13. Kamalahmadi, M., Parast, M.M.: A review of the literature on the principles of enterprise and supply chain resilience: major findings and directions for future research. Int. J. Prod. Econ. **171**, 116–133 (2016)
14. Ribeiro, J.P., Barbosa-Povoa, A.P.F.D.: Supply chain resilience: definitions and quantitative modelling approaches – a literature review. Comput. Ind. Eng. **115**, 109–122 (2018)
15. Sharkey, T.C., Nurre Pinkley, S.G., Eisenberg, D.A., Alderson, D.L.: In search of network resilience: an optimization-based view. Networks **77**(2), 225–254 (2021)

16. Hohenstein, N.O., Feise, E., Hartmann, E., Giunipero, L.: Research on the phenomenon of supply chain resilience: a systematic review and paths for further investigation. Int. J. Phys. Distrib. Logist. Manag. **45**(1/2), 90–117 (2015)
17. Behzadi, G., O'Sullivan, M.J., Olsen, T.L., Zhang, A.: On metrics for supply chain resilience. Eur. J. Oper. Res. **287**(1), 145–158 (2020)
18. Bruckler, M., Wietschel, L., Messmann, L., Thorenz, A., Tuma, A.: Review of metrics to assess resilience capacities and actions for supply chain resilience. Comput. Ind. Eng. **192**, 110176 (2024)
19. Hollnagel, E., Woods, D.D., Leveson, N.: Resilience Engineering: Concepts and Precepts, 1st edn. Ashgate Publishing, Aldershot (2006)
20. Walker, B., Holling, C.S., Carpenter, S.R., Kinzig, A.: Resilience, adaptability and transformability in social–ecological systems. Ecol. Soc. **9**(2), 5 (2004)
21. Lengnick-Hall, C.A., Beck, T.E., Lengnick-Hall, M.L.: Developing a capacity for organizational resilience through strategic human resource management. Hum. Resour. Manag. Rev. **21**(3), 243–255 (2011)
22. Burnard, K., Bhamra, R.: Organisational resilience: development of a conceptual framework for organisational responses. Int. J. Prod. Res. **49**(18), 5581–5599 (2011)
23. McManus, S., Seville, E., Vargo, J., Brunsdon, D.: Facilitated process for improving organizational resilience. Nat. Hazard. Rev. **9**(2), 81–90 (2008)

Analyzing Freight Truck Arrival Scheduling and Operations for an International Beverage Company's Warehouse

Andres Muñoz-Villamizar[1,2] , Jairo Montoya-Torres[3]([✉]) ,
Christopher Mejía-Argueta[1] , Julian Queirolo[1], and Daniel Hernandez[1]

[1] Center for Transportation and Logistics, Massachusetts Institute of Technology, Cambridge, MA, USA
[2] International School of Economics and Administrative Sciences, Universidad de La Sabana, Chia, Colombia
[3] Département de génie des Systèmes, École de Technologie Supérieure, Montréal, QC, Canada
`jairo.montoya-torres@etsmtl.ca`

Abstract. This study examines delays in processing returned shipments at a beverage distribution center in Bogotá, Colombia. Returned trucks undergo reception, inspection, and reloading processes, which can result in congestion at the processing docks. We develop a discrete-event simulation model based on historical operational data and a focused time-and-motion study to represent the current system. Two improvement scenarios are evaluated: (1) increased verification staffing, and (2) regulated truck arrivals (i.e., arrival scheduling). Performance is assessed in terms of average turnaround time, average waiting time, processing time, queue length, resource utilization, and number of external waiting vehicles (i.e., congestion caused around the distribution center to citizens). Simulation results indicate that the addition of staff reduces truck turnaround by approximately 30%, decreases the average queue length by over 60%, and lowers peak dock utilization. Meanwhile, managed arrivals yield more consistent throughput, with a 20% reduction in waiting times and decreased variability in resource use. Both interventions enhance driver work–life balance, improve service levels, and mitigate community impacts caused by external queuing. The proposed framework offers a replicable, data-driven approach for distribution centers to mitigate dock-level bottlenecks, enabling informed decision-making on resource allocation and scheduling strategies.

Keywords: Discrete Event Simulation · Warehouse Receiving Process · Unloading · Reverse Logistics

1 Introduction

Freight transportation constitutes the backbone of modern supply chains: without efficient carrier operations, product delivery and, ultimately, business viability are unattainable. In 2022, global logistics expenditures reached USD 11.43 trillion and are projected

J. Barata et al. (Eds.): IN4PL 2025, CCIS 2826, pp. 169–182, 2026.
https://doi.org/10.1007/978-3-032-15579-5_11

to climb to approximately USD 13 trillion by 2026 [1]. Within this total, freight transport accounts for nearly 58% of the costs, underscoring the critical importance of managing shipment processes effectively [2]. During transit, trucks incur non-productive intervals—particularly at loading and unloading docks—where delays translate directly into higher operating expenses and extended driver shifts. A recent study in the United States observed that detention costs have worsened over time and will persist unless supply-chain stakeholders address queuing at shipper and receiver facilities [3].

These challenges are not confined to high-volume markets or developed countries. In Colombia, for instance, transportation accounted for 35.9% of corporate logistics budgets in 2022, while inventory carrying costs accounted for another 25.5% [4]. Concurrently, the non-alcoholic beverage sector is expected to grow at a compound annual rate of 5.4% from 2024 to 2032 [5]. As beverage manufacturers and distributors expand their operations, they must adopt data-driven strategies to streamline product handling, minimize wait times, maintain service levels, and synchronize their operations with the market through efficient delivery processes.

A critical bottleneck arises during the returns process. At the end of distribution routes, delivery trucks report and deliver unsold or damaged items back to the warehouse. Verification of returned products against driver manifests consumes valuable dock capacity. When vehicle arrivals exceed processing throughput or staffing is not efficient or sufficient to handle verification, queues form outside the facility. Prolonged external waiting not only inflates labor costs and driver fatigue but also generates negative externalities, such as traffic congestion, air pollution, and community complaints.

Prior research has examined dock-related delays through various lenses. Simulation-based studies frequently employ discrete-event models to assess operational improvements without disrupting live systems [6–8]. Optimization approaches have been proposed to assign dock schedules, aiming to minimize costs and delays [9]. Meanwhile, hybrid methods combine simulation with heuristics to allocate resources (e.g., staff, docks) dynamically [10]. Such efforts demonstrate significant reductions in turnaround times and emissions; however, they typically overlook the human and social dimensions of queuing. Extended waiting periods exacerbate driver stress and compromise road safety, a concern highlighted in recent ergonomic analyses [11].

This paper addresses these gaps by integrating operational performance with driver welfare considerations. We develop a calibrated discrete-event simulation that replicates the returns check-in workflow using historical throughput data and time-motion observations in a distribution center or warehouse from a multinational beverage company. After validating the model with industry partners, we evaluate two intervention scenarios: 1) augmenting verification staff and 2) implementing a regulated arrival schedule. Performance is measured through average turnaround and waiting times, queue lengths, and resource utilization, as well as estimates of driver work-hour reductions and community impact mitigation.

Our contributions are threefold. First, we quantify the trade-offs between resource investment and scheduling control in a real-world beverage distribution context. Second, we introduce welfare-oriented metrics—driver overtime hours and external queuing impacts—to the evaluation of dock operations. Third, we provide a replicable, data-driven framework that practitioners can adapt to similar logistics environments, aiming to strike a balance between efficiency and social responsibility.

The remainder of the paper is structured as follows. Section 2 reviews related work on dock scheduling and simulation in logistics. Section 3 details the model design, data sources, and validation procedures. Section 4 presents the case study and results. Finally, Sect. 5 concludes with managerial implications and avenues for future research.

2 Literature Review

Queues manifest wherever transient demand exceeds available processing capacity, from supermarket checkouts and drive-thrus to the critical loading and unloading operations that underpin modern supply chains in different logistics facilities. Teodorović and Nedeljković [12] observe that "demand that during certain periods exceeds capacity is what results in queues", a principle that directly applies to truck check-in processes: when vehicle arrival rates outpace dock throughput, external queues form and internal wait times escalate. Addressing this congestion has attracted substantial scholarly attention across diverse industries, employing various simulation methods, including discrete-event simulation (DES), mathematical optimization, and hybrid methodologies to evaluate and mitigate bottlenecks.

DES has emerged as the predominant analytical tool for probing dock operations without disrupting live facilities. This simulation enables the easy performance of what-if analyses, providing a high-level perspective for modeling and solving real problems using reasonable amounts of data. It enables modelers to mix intuitive representations in a non-costly way, compared to other simulations, such as agent-based modeling and stock-and-flow models. For instance, Smith and Srinivas [6] modeled a consumer-goods ware-house in the United States, comparing four scenarios—staging areas, priority dispatch, CO_2-weighted dispatch, and radio-frequency-identification-automated check-in—and reported a reduction of up to 27% in detention fees, as well as the elimination of extreme wait times. Liong and Loo [7] applied DES to an integrated unloading, sorting, and loading facility, finding that synchronized arrivals with extra forklifts cut customer wait by two hours. Deshpande et al. [8] embedded a heuristic dock-assignment rule in a less-than-truckload hub-and-spoke DES, reducing pallet waits by 12% and forklift utilization by 10%.

Optimization models address arrival scheduling and dock assignment directly. Chen et al. [9] formulated a mixed-integer program (MIP) model for container terminals, aiming to flatten peak arrivals and reduce both wait times and pollution from yard operations. Yi et al. [10] developed a related MIP model that jointly minimizes costs for operators and carriers, demonstrating economic savings and improved service consistency. On the other hand, hybrid approaches combine DES with optimization, enabling the modeling of uncertainty and the obtaining of robust solutions under stochastic and dynamic conditions. Bett et al. [10] iteratively refined a time-and-attendance-system (TAS) schedule via mixed-integer programming (MIP) and DES feedback, yielding robust plans under variability modeled through multiple scenarios. Azab et al. [13] integrated a TAS MIP with DES to assess impacts on both terminal throughput and carrier costs, reporting shorter queues and lower detention fees, though without quantifying emissions or off-site delays. Cross-docking operations face analogous queuing challenges. Torbali and Alpan [14] used a multi-agent-based simulation for real-time inbound/outbound scheduling, reducing pallet delays and average in-dock inventory. Ergonomic analyses estimate that fatigue contributes to 20%–50% of accidents, underscoring the social stakes of dock-level delays [11].

Collectively, these studies demonstrate that DES, optimization, and hybrid methods can achieve improvements of 12%–30% in turnaround and wait times across logistics facilities: warehouses, terminals, and industrial facilities. Yet most focus on internal metrics and neglect external queues and social impacts. Our work fills this gap by measuring both operational and community outcomes.

3 Methodology

The methodology follows a four-stage process, as illustrated in Fig. 1. It combines principles of queueing theory with discrete-event simulation to assess the operational, economic, and social impacts of reverse logistics congestion for returned products. However, the problem under study is inspired by the multinational beverage company that sponsored this project. The approach is designed to be general, allowing it to be applied and scaled to other companies dealing with similar problems. The components of the methodology are explained next.

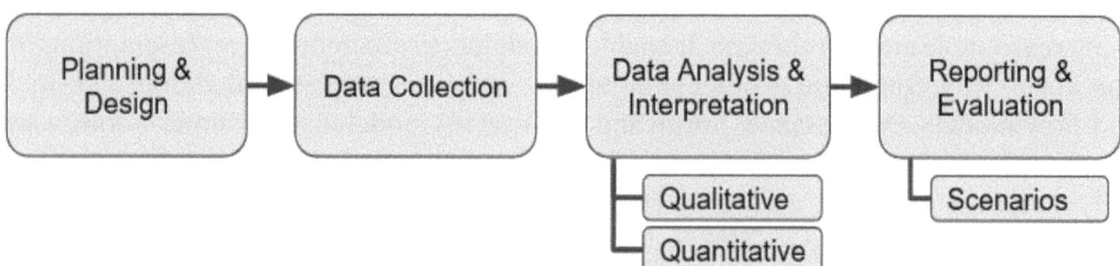

Fig. 1. Methodology flowchart.

3.1 Planning and Design

In this phase, we mapped the existing return-check-in workflow by collaborating with staff from the beverage company and the sponsor's operations team. The sponsor is a third-party workforce company that performs warehousing operations for the beverage company, producing a detailed flowchart. We then translated that diagram into a queuing network, defining entities (trucks), resources (checkers or staff), queues, and feedback loops for reloaded vehicles. Initial model parameters—including arrival processes, service stages, dock capacities, and staffing schedules—were extracted from process observations and validated in a workshop with company stakeholders. The objective was to ensure the baseline model accurately represents the as-is system before experimentation.

3.2 Data Collection

The primary inputs consisted of a 20-day report extracted from the sponsor's database (SAP ERP), which included truck arrival timestamps, verification start and end times, and dispatch records. When preliminary model runs revealed gaps—particularly during off-peak hours—we secured supplemental historical arrival logs. We conducted a 22-day time study of the verification process together with the third-party workforce. Data sources included:

- Expert interviews: Semi-structured discussions with logistics managers and checkers to capture undocumented decision rules and bottleneck causes.
- Video observations: Timestamped recordings of dock operations to verify sequence logic and measure loading/unloading durations.
- ERP and time-study spreadsheets: Detailed Excel files enumerating interarrival intervals, service times, and resource schedules.

3.3 Data Analysis and Interpretation

All timestamped data were imported into statistical software to fit probability distributions through goodness-of-fit tests (e.g., exponential, Weibull, lognormal) for interarrival and service times, selecting the best fits via chi-square and Kolmogorov–Smirnov tests. Descriptive statistics (i.e., mean, variance, and percentiles) informed replication counts and warm-up considerations (none were required, since the system started empty). The calibrated baseline model was validated through:

- Face validation with operations staff to verify entity flows, resource utilizations, and queue formations against observed behavior.
- Statistical validation to compare simulated versus empirical turnaround and waiting times, ensuring a 95% confidence interval overlapping within a 5% tolerance. This iterative refinement ensured model fidelity before scenario analysis.

3.4 Reporting and Evaluation

Using the validated model, we defined two intervention scenarios—1) additional staffing during peak hours and 2) regulated arrival intervals (i.e., scheduling arrivals)—and executed 100 replications per scenario over 8 h. The steady state was reached after 90 to 100 replications in all the scenarios. Key performance indicators (i.e., average turnaround time, waiting time, queue length, and checker utilization) were summarized with means, 95% confidence intervals, and box-and-whisker plots. Paired t-tests ($\alpha = 0.05$) evaluated mean differences, while F-tests assessed variance changes when intervals overlapped. Finally, we converted operational gains into economic and social metrics: driver-hour savings (Δ waiting time $\times$ hourly cost) and reductions in external queue length, resulting in a cost-benefit synthesis.

4 Case Study

The sponsor company provides logistics and workforce services to a multinational beverage distributor located in Bogotá, Colombia. After each delivery route, trucks return with damaged, unsold, or customer-returned products. Upon arrival, the return-check-in process involves space allocation, product classification, verification against documents, and unloading for next-day dispatch. Persistent mismatches between arrival peaks and processing capacity generate external queues and extended driver hours, motivating our DES analysis. We evaluate the base process and two improvement proposals (i.e., scenarios) against four key performance indicators (KPIs): average turnaround time, average wait time, checker utilization, and number of trucks waiting outside. DES enables rapid "what-if" experimentation without operational disruption [15], while supporting better decisions for both the sponsor and the beverage company.

4.1 Process Mapping

Through workshops with operations experts and first-person video review, we mapped every step of the return-check-in workflow. Trucks enter through a single gate. If the exchange area (with a capacity of 12 trucks) is full, returning trucks queue outside the facilities in a first-in, first-out (FIFO) order. Inside, helpers first handle multicategory products at a designated station (issuing a receipt), then damaged goods at a second station (another receipt). Trucks then proceed to one of six parallel verification lines (each holds one truck in service and one waiting); if all lines are occupied, additional trucks wait in a holding area (capacity = 12 trucks). Six checkers operate in two shifts— 14:00–22:00 (two checkers) and 16:00–00:00 (four checkers). After verification, trucks move to the unloading docks for staging.

4.2 Simulation Construction

We implemented this flow in Arena® Simulation software (student edition) based on the process map in Sect. 4.1. Input data were:

- SAP ERP timestamps (Aug–Sep 2024): arrival, verification start/end, and dispatch times.
- Time-study observations (Aug 1–22, 2024): arrival intervals, exchange durations, verification times.

We organized the model into three zones: a) Zone 1: Arrival, b) Zone 2: Exchange, and c) Zone 3: Verification (Fig. 2), and used Arena's Input Analyzer to fit the distributions (Table 1). Triangular distributions were also proposed for Zones 2 and 3 after validation with the sponsor company, for which the parameter values (minimum, maximum, and mode) were defined based on their expertise and daily observations of the process.

To validate and verify the model, output values regarding average time in process, waiting time outside the facility, average number of trucks waiting outside the facility, utilization of the checkers, and waiting time were presented and discussed with the company counterpart. After using the goodness-of-fit test and the model validation, the input data for the model will be: an empirical distribution for the arrival pattern, an Erlang distribution for the exchange process, and a triangular distribution for the verification process. As resources, we assigned six checkers, with two working from 14:00 to 22:00 and four working from 16:00 to 00:00. Each simulation starts with no trucks in queue and runs from 14:00 to 00:00. The exchange process has a capacity of 12 trucks in process and/or waiting. The verification area has a capacity of one truck in process, with one truck waiting per line, and the facility has six lines, totaling 12 trucks. The process itself always starts empty every day, so it is expected that the first trucks proceed directly to the respective steps of the process. For this reason, there is no warm-up period when running the simulation.

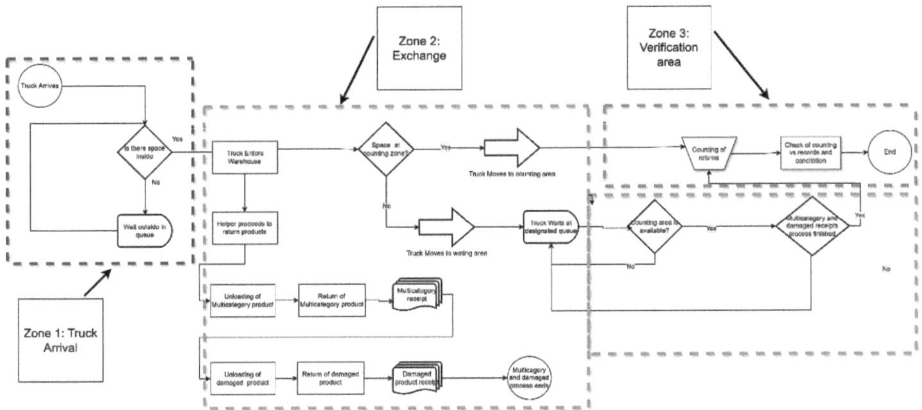

Fig. 2. Simulated process.

Table 1. Proposed Distributions.

Process	Distribution	Time Unit	Source	Size (N)	Triangular option parameters
Truck Arrivals	Empirical Distribution	Minutes	SAP	5733	TRIA (0.02, 0.83, 235)
Exchange process	ERLA (9.38, 2)	Minutes	Time study	1018	TRIA (4, 40, 105)
Verification	NORM (10.3, 5.34)	Minutes	Time study	1018	TRIA (1, 10, 52)

4.3 Performance Indicators and Proposed Scenarios

The baseline model (i.e., as-is model), as described before, is compared with two alternatives based on the following key performance indicators: Average time in process (ATP), Average wait time (AWT), number of trucks waiting outside the facility (NT), and level of checker utilization (CU). After a set of preliminary runs, the total number of replications was set to 100 to ensure the statistical accuracy of the results [16].

Two scenarios were tested according to the following proposed operational configurations:

- **Scenario 1.** Increasing the number of checkers to seven, which involves adding one checker working from 16:00 to 00:00. The distribution of the number of checkers throughout the day is presented in Table 2.

- **Scenario 2.** Adjusting the arrival truck pattern requires distributing the arrival of trucks to match better the capacity of the checkers (i.e., arrival scheduling). In this case, trucks will arrive every 3.5 min from 14:00 to 22:00 (17 trucks per hour) and then every 10 min from 22:00 to 00:00 (six trucks per hour). This is a smoother arrival pattern compared to the current one. The rationale behind this arrival pattern is such that pikes are reduced and queues are cleared at the end of the day. The distribution of the number of trucks over the day is given in Table 2.

Table 2. Proposed distributions of checkers (Scenario 1) and trucks (Scenario 2).

Time	2 pm	3 pm	4 pm	5 pm	6 pm	7 pm	8 pm	9 pm	10 pm	11 pm
Checkers	2	2	7	7	7	7	7	5	5	5
Trucks	17	17	17	17	17	17	17	17	6	6

5 Results

The simulation results are presented in Table 3 and Fig. 3. Both scenarios proposed to improve the sponsor's operations have a positive impact on the metrics, as shown in Table 3. In summary, the average values of the number of trucks waiting outside (NT), checkers utilization (CU), average time in process (ATP), and average waiting time (AWT) decreased, except for checkers utilization in scenario 2, which remained unchanged.

Table 3 compares the results at an average level and the range of the metrics; however, an analysis of the confidence intervals obtained for each scenario was also conducted. The intervals were created considering a 95% confidence interval. As shown in Fig. 3, Scenario 1 outperformed the baseline model in all four metrics, indicating a statistically significant improvement when the number of checkers (i.e., staff resources) was increased. Scenario 2 does present a statistically significant improvement for all metrics, except for checkers utilization (CU). For CU, we cannot conclude any improvement for scenario 2, as the graphs visually show an overlap of the intervals. The following analysis is done with the means, as we see they are significantly better than the base model (except CU for scenario 2).

A key focus was the impact on drivers' work-life balance. Drivers must deliver products and then handle the return process at the warehouse, which they view as an unproductive process, as their earnings depend on the number of deliveries they make. Every additional second that drivers spend on the road affects their hourly income and overall well-being. In scenario 1, reducing ATP by an average of 29.5 min per day per truck translates to 9.8 fewer working hours per month per driver. This change enables drivers to rest more, regaining over a day's worth of time each month. Similarly, in scenario 2, the ATP reduction provides drivers with an extra 6.2 h per month, further improving their rest and quality of life.

The reduction in ATP mainly results from shorter waiting times (AWT). Trucks spend less time waiting, which benefits drivers. Waiting is often unpleasant, and studies show it feels longer than it is [17]. By reducing waiting time, drivers perceive the process more positively, which improves their overall experience and increases their focus on productivity in both proposed scenarios. These improvements in ATP and AWT benefit not only the drivers but also the sponsor company, as they generate a more efficient process and increase their service level to customers by allowing trucks to be ready for product loading for next-day delivery faster.

Waiting time in lean systems is classified as waste, defined as anything that does not add value to the customer [18]. This non-value-added activity in our process is identified as the average wait time (AWT). If we subtract ATP from AWT, we obtain the inverse, which in this case is the total time spent on a non-productive activity. Dividing this result by the ATP, we obtain the productivity ratio of the total time spent on a productive activity (i.e., Productivity ratio = (ATP-AWT)/ATP). The latter yields 0.68 for the baseline model, 0.75 for scenario 1, and 0.72 for scenario 2.

Table 3. Results of the simulations.

Metric: Average Time in Process (ATP)					
Details	Baseline Model	Scenario 1	% Diff Scenario 1	Scenario 2	% Diff Scenario 2
Average	107.1	77.6	-28%	88.4	-17%
Min	64.4	44.7	-31%	51.9	-19%
Max	159.3	122.5	-23%	151.7	-5%
Standard Dev	20.0	19.3	-4%	21.6	8%
Metric: Average Wait Time (AWT)					
Details	Baseline Model	Scenario 1	% Diff Scenario 1	Scenario 2	% Diff Scenario 2
Average	33.7	19.0	-44%	24.6	-27%
Min	12.2	3.5	-71%	6.2	-49%
Max	60.3	41.8	-31%	56.5	-6%
Standard Dev	9.9	9.5	-4%	10.6	7%
Metric: Number of Trucks waiting outside (NT)					
Details	Baseline Model	Scenario 1	% Diff Scenario 1	Scenario 2	% Diff Scenario 2
Average	8.7	2.7	-69%	3.7	-58%
Min	0.0	0.0	-100%	0.0	-100%
Max	27.6	12.9	-53%	24.2	-12%
Standard Dev	5.8	3.2	-45%	4.2	-27%
Metric: Checkers Utilization (CU)					
Details	Baseline Model	Scenario 1	% Diff Scenario 1	Scenario 2	% Diff Scenario 2
Average	78%	72%	-8%	78%	-1%
Min	62%	52%	-16%	52%	-16%
Max	86%	85%	-2%	85%	-2%
Standard Dev	7%	3%	-53%	3%	-53%

As shown, the scenarios present an increase in productive time, implying an improvement in process efficiency, as they now utilize the time spent in the process for more value-added activities, making better use of their time resources.

Another issue the sponsored company faces is trucks queuing outside its facility, which impacts traffic in the neighborhood. While neither scenario eliminates this problem, both reduced the number of trucks waiting outside the distribution center, improving local traffic conditions. Although they do not face any penalties for this issue, reducing the queue could prevent future infractions from local authorities.

Utilization is a good metric for assessing the burden and workload that can be imposed on resources, primarily when referring to staff. Balanced utilization levels reduce burnout and stress, improving the work environment and maintaining work quality. In scenario 1, utilization drops by 8%, saving each checker 38 min per day, or 12 h a month. This improvement comes from adding just one more human talent to the operation.

As indicated earlier, for scenario 2, we cannot claim a significant improvement compared to the baseline model. However, we turned to analyze whether the variance improves. For this, we execute a hypothesis test, specifically Fisher's Test. Our null hypothesis is that the variance of the baseline model is equal to or less than the variance of scenario 2. This test gives us a value of the F-statistic $= \frac{0.069^2}{0.033^2} = 4.37.$. Then, we proceed to calculate the critical F-value for a one-tailed test with a degree of freedom of 99 (n-1, where n is the number of replications in our case, 100), and $\alpha = 0.05$, which gives us a value of 1.39. Since F-statistic $= 4.37 > 1.39 =$ F-critical value, we reject the null hypothesis and conclude that the variance of the base model is significantly greater than the variance of scenario 2. With the hypothesis test, we can see that although there is no improvement in average utilization from the baseline model when compared to scenario 2, the variance has reduced significantly. The latter implies a steadier system for using the resources, which are the checkers. Despite not having a lower average use of the resources, their utilization is less variable from the mean.

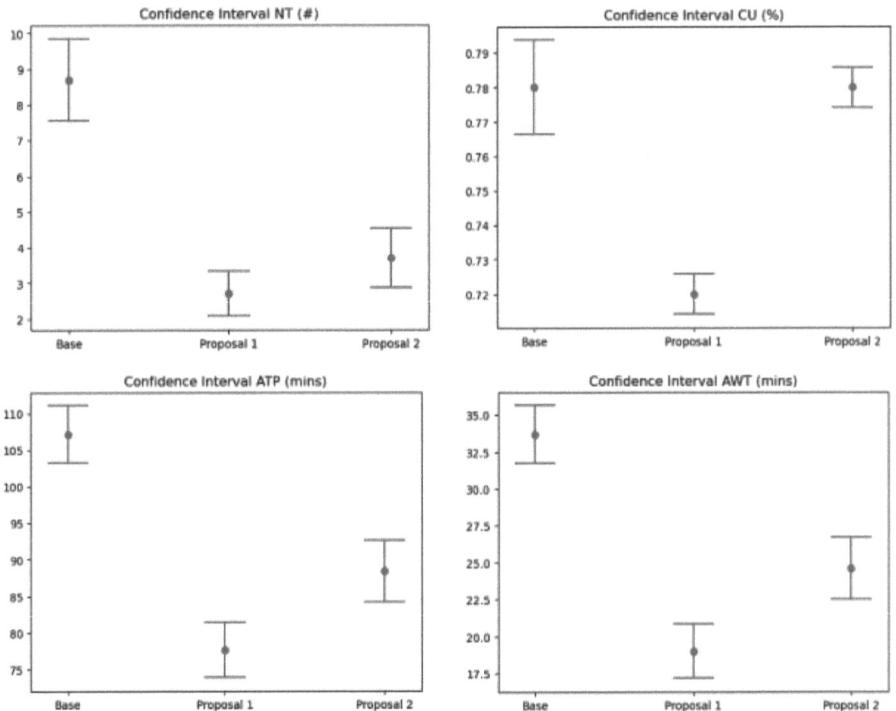

Fig. 3. Confidence intervals of performance indicators.

Given that these improvements from the sponsor company's perspective are also valuable, it is also beneficial to consider the cost of implementing these proposals. Specifically for scenario 1, since we are increasing the number of checkers by 1, this will incur a cost of USD 311.40 per month (calculated using the exchange rate from Colombian pesos to dollars as of December 19th, 2024, with 1 dollar equaling 3,909.30 Colombian pesos). In the case of scenario 2, the sponsor company will need someone to manage the arrival schedules for the trucks. The cost of this additional manager will be approximately USD 650 per month. However, the decision to hire someone new, promote existing talent, or utilize current human resources will depend on the sponsor.

6   Managerial Implications, Limitations, and Perspectives

Transportation is a critical activity in supply chains that helps reduce logistics costs [2]. To achieve this, companies must continually evaluate their current processes and develop innovations to ensure ongoing improvement. This is critical for the sponsor company, especially as the Colombian beverage business is expected to grow at a compound annual growth rate of 5.40% during the forecast period of 2024–2032 [5], so they need to be prepared to capitalize on this market growth. A key focus is to identify waste, redundancies, and problems within their processes and reduce them as much as possible.

This study focused on the return process of unsold and damaged products for a warehouse or distribution center of a multinational beverage company located in Bogotá,

Colombia. A discrete-event simulation (DES) model was proposed to address queueing issues arising from the return of products within and outside the logistics facility. The simulation provided an effective way to analyze the current process and two proposed scenarios without impacting the actual company process. Scenario 1 increased the checkers' resource capacity, while scenario 2 created a steady-state arrival of trucks throughout the day.

Scenario 1 can be viewed from a short-term perspective. To be implemented, the sponsor company would need to hire a new checker and prepare a new counting line. This proposal reduced all four evaluated metrics (i.e., ATP, AWT, NT, and CU). The benefits of this investment could be observed within a few months, and the strategy is low-cost and potentially of crucial impact for the company. In contrast, scenario 2 requires a long-term perspective, as changing the arrival patterns of the trucks does not depend only on the sponsor company. The outcomes of this simulation study can serve as a starting point for conversations with their truck drivers and customers, as a more even arrival schedule allows the sponsor company to have lower wait times and processing times.

The arrival scheduling change may also benefit their customers, as trucks will be ready for unloading and preparation for the next day's delivery faster. Scenario 2 reduced ATP, AWT, and NT, with no impact on the average utilization, as it utilized the same resources as the current state. However, it did improve the variance of utilization (according to the Fisher test outputs), creating a more stable process. It is worth noting that the strategy may result in a slightly higher variance in ATP and AWT. Then, the sponsor must manage this through effective handling and logistics practices, and be closely monitored by the company to proactively address any potential issues.

Therefore, both proposed scenarios demonstrate the power and consistency of DES for decision-making processes related to queueing and yard operations. A key point of the study was the impact of process improvement, not only in favor of the sponsor company, but also on the benefits to the drivers. In scenario 1, the working hours are reduced by 9.8 h per month per driver, whereas in scenario 2, the drivers' working hours are reduced by 6.2 h per month per driver. This approach provides a better work-life balance for drivers, leading to reduced fatigue—a significant issue faced by drivers who work long hours.

The DES developed in this study is a valuable tool for the sponsor company to support its decision-making process, but some limitations should be considered. The process was simplified due to a lack of data on certain activities carried out during the return process, such as the exchange of damaged products. The sponsor company could collect additional data and incorporate them into the simulation to determine if it impacts the queues differently. Due to this simplification, the process was executed considering an average operating day; therefore, it is uncertain how the base model and proposals will perform during demand peaks.

Future work could first address these data limitations: collecting detailed data on the activities would allow for a more comprehensive simulation model and a deeper understanding of their impact on queues and efficiency. Additionally, the importance of drivers' fatigue, as highlighted in the study, was indirectly addressed due to the drivers' working hours. Future studies could include drivers' working hours in the model itself, as well as incorporating the learning curve effect that new staff may experience, or the fatigue effect on productivity that staff face after working long hours. On the other hand, collaboration with external stakeholders is crucial for implementing scenario 2. Lastly, if the sponsor company wants to adjust truck arrival patterns, it must analyze multiple factors, such as dwelling time, route lengths, service times, and others, to benefit the entire supply chain by reducing inefficiencies and improving waiting times.

Finally, conducting a detailed cost analysis for both proposals is recommended to evaluate the financial investments required. This can strengthen the decision-making process by providing a view of the impact of both proposals and enhancing the business case for executing either strategy.

Acknowledgments. We would like to thank the sponsor organization for its collaboration. We are grateful to Roberto C., Giovanni A., Mauricio A., Joaquin G., Maye M., Carlos R., Carlos V., and many other collaborators. Finally, we would like to thank the MIT GCLOG program for providing a platform to develop applied research for companies and helping emerging market professionals and companies thrive through the design, implementation, and training of decision-support systems.

Disclosure of Interests.   The authors have no competing interests to declare that are relevant to the content of this article.

References

1. Statista Research Department.: Global logistics costs in 2022 and forecast through 2026. Statista (2024)
2. Rodrigue, J.-P.: The Geography of Transport Systems, 5th edn. Routledge, New York (2024)
3. Sparkman, R.: The hidden cost of detention: truck driver wait times at facilities worsen. American Transportation Research Institute Report (2019)
4. Departamento Nacional de Planeación.: Informe de costos logísticos en Colombia 2022. DNP, Bogotá. https://www.dnp.gov.co/Prensa_/Noticias/Paginas/el-dnp-revelo-que-el-costo-logistico-nacional-se-ubico-en-17-9-5-p-p-por-encima-de-la-meta-de-12-9.aspx. Accessed 20 June 2025. In Spanish
5. Informes de Expertos.: Mercado de bebidas no alcohólicas en Colombia, 2024–2032. Expert Insights. https://www.informesdeexpertos.com/informes/mercado-de-bebidas-no-alcoholicas-en-colombia. Accessed 20 June 2025. In Spanish
6. Smith, A., Srinivas, S.: Simulation of dock operations: reducing turnaround and emissions. J. Ind. Eng. Manage. **12**(3), 210–225 (2019)
7. Liong, C. H., Loo, H. K.: A discrete-event simulation study of scheduled truck arrivals and resource augmentation in warehouse operations. In: Proceedings of the Winter Simulation Conference 2009, pp. 112–119. IEEE (2009)
8. Deshpande, S., Giannakis, M., Kouvelis, P.: A hybrid simulation-heuristic for dynamic dock allocation. Eur. J. Oper. Res. **183**(2), 712–722 (2007)
9. Chen, L., Wang, H., Xu, M.: A discrete-event simulation framework for warehouse unloading optimization. Int. J. Prod. Res. **51**(14), 4200–4215 (2013)
10. Yi, J., Lee, T., Park, S.: Optimization-based dock assignment for minimizing total costs. Transp. Sci. **53**(1), 99–117 (2019)
11. Soliani, L., Da Silva, F., Barbosa, R.: Fatigue and safety: ergonomic impacts of truck driver detention. Ergonomics **66**(5), 678–691 (2023)

12. Teodorović, D., Nedeljković, M.: Fundamentals of queueing theory. J. Oper. Res. Soc. **67**(2), 247–258 (2016)
13. Azab, S., El-Horbaty, M., Gendy, A.: Integrated appointment-scheduling and simulation model for container terminals. Transp. Res. Part C **115**, 102–118 (2020)
14. Torbali, E., Alpan, G.: A multi-agent simulation model for real-time cross-dock scheduling. Int. J. Prod. Econ. **256**, 108–119 (2023)
15. Arora, J., Patel, P.: Best practices in modelling multi-server queues. In: Proceedings of the 2008 International Conference on Queueing Systems, pp. 45–52. IEEE (2008)
16. Queirolo, J., Hernández, D.: Analysing freight truck arrival scheduling for an international beverage company's warehouse. Capstone Project, Graduate Certificate in Logistics and Supply Chain Management, MIT Center for Transportation and Logistics, Massachusetts Institute of Technology, Cambridge, MA, USA (2025)
17. Arendt, F., Breuer, J.: Perceived waiting time and waiting satisfaction: a systematic literature review. Paper Presented at the 22nd Quality Management and Organisational Development International Conference on Quality and Service Sciences (QMOD/ICQSS 2019), 13–15 October 2019, Krakow, Poland (2019)
18. Womack, J.P., Jones, D.T.: Lean Thinking: Banish Waste and Create Wealth in Your Corporation. Free Press (2023)

Cost-Aware Soft-Constrained Optimization for Scenario-Driven Urban Logistics Resilience

Snazal Singh[1], M. K. Pranesh Kannan[1], Anish Monsley Kirupakaran[1], Balasubramaniam Natarajan[2], and Babji Srinivasan[1,3](✉)

[1] FedEx Smart Center, Indian Institute of Technology Madras, Guindy 600036, Tamil Nadu, India
babji.srinivasan@iitm.ac.in

[2] Department of Electrical and Computer Engineering, Kansas State University, Manhattan, KS 66506, USA

[3] Department of Applied Mechanics and Biomedical Engineering, Indian Institute of Technology Madras, Guindy 600036, Tamil Nadu, India

Abstract. Urban logistics systems often face disruptions such as warehouse shutdowns, vehicle shortages, and sudden demand spikes, making it difficult to meet all customer needs. This paper presents a scenario-based optimization framework that supports resilient fulfillment planning when resources are limited. We combine two solver approaches—Linear Programming (LP) and Unbalanced Optimal Transport (UOT)—to allow partial demand fulfillment, with penalties for unmet demand. LP focuses on minimizing total cost, while UOT offers more flexible, fairness-aware delivery by relaxing strict fulfillment constraints. The framework uses a detailed cost model that includes distance, fuel usage, emissions, delays, and zone-based charges to reflect real operational conditions. Using case studies from Chennai, we compare solver performance under different disruption scenarios. Results show that LP provides low-cost solutions but may neglect high-cost zones, while UOT ensures broader coverage with more balanced allocations. The scientific novelty of this work lies in integrating soft-constrained optimization with UOT to explicitly capture trade-offs between cost efficiency and service equity under disruption—an aspect often overlooked in existing logistics models. This unified framework contributes not only a practical decision-support tool for urban planners but also a generalizable methodological advance for resilience-oriented logistics optimization. This approach helps logistics planners explore trade-offs between cost and service equity and design more robust delivery strategies under uncertain conditions.

Keywords: Urban Logistics · Resilient Fulfilment Planning · Scenario-Based Optimization · Cost-Equity Trade-off · Disruption Management · Supply Chain Resilience

---

B. Natarajan and B. Srinivasan—Equal Contributions.

J. Barata et al. (Eds.): IN4PL 2025, CCIS 2826, pp. 183–206, 2026.
https://doi.org/10.1007/978-3-032-15579-5_12

1 Introduction

Urban logistics systems are increasingly operating under volatile, resource-constrained, and highly uncertain conditions. The rapid growth of e-commerce, rising customer expectations, and infrastructural bottlenecks have significantly amplified the complexity of last-mile delivery—especially in densely populated urban centers [1, 2]. In such settings, disruptions such as vehicle shortages, warehouse outages, labor constraints, and localized demand surges have become routine rather than exceptional. These operational stressors challenge the ability of service providers to maintain both high fulfillment rates and cost efficiency [3, 4]. Traditional optimization models—typically designed around cost minimization with hard fulfillment constraints—often fail to accommodate the realities of disrupted environments [5, 6]. These models assume full demand satisfaction and frequently collapse when supply is insufficient or unevenly distributed. Moreover, they tend to overlook spatial and social equity in allocation decisions, leading to service imbalances where high-cost or remote zones are underserved during crisis [7–9]. To address these limitations, this work proposes a scenario-driven optimization framework that focuses on post-disruption fulfillment planning. Rather than modeling the full dynamics of disruption, our approach assumes a state of imbalance—characterized by constrained supply and excess demand—and aims to reallocate limited resources in a way that balances cost and coverage. At the core of our framework are two complementary optimization strategies: Linear Programming (LP) [7, 10–12] and Unbalanced Optimal Transport (UOT) [13–15]. LP identifies cost-efficient allocations but often prioritizes low-cost zones, exacerbating service asymmetries. UOT, on the other hand, allows for partial fulfillment by relaxing marginal constraints and introducing penalties for unmet demand. This flexibility enables planners to explore trade-offs between efficiency and fairness—critical when full service is infeasible. To enhance real-world applicability, we incorporate a detailed, multi-dimensional cost model that reflects operational realities. This model accounts for factors such as travel distance, traffic delays, fuel consumption, emissions, and zone-specific delivery charges—parameters particularly relevant in emerging-market cities like Chennai (India) where infrastructure variability and sustainability concerns are increasingly significant. We validate our framework through a series of case studies involving disrupted delivery scenarios across key logistics zones in Chennai—Egmore, Taramani, Velachery, Guindy, and Mylapore. These experiments examine solver behavior under various penalty regimes, supply limitations, and cost structures, offering insights into solver sensitivity, service equity, and operational trade-offs.

The key contributions of this work are:

- We propose a soft-constrained optimization framework that integrates LP and UOT to support flexible and cost-aware fulfillment under disrupted conditions.
- We develop a realistic cost model that incorporates spatial, temporal, and environmental variables, improving the fidelity of logistics planning.
- We simulate a range of plausible post-disruption scenarios, including regional demand surges and constrained vehicle capacity, to reflect operational stressors.
- We compare solver behavior across multiple configurations, highlighting how penalty tuning and supply limitations shape cost-equity trade-offs.
- We deliver a modular and interpretable planning tool that supports logistics decision-makers in stress-testing fulfillment strategies and identifying resilient responses.

Overall, this work bridges the gap between theoretical logistics optimization and the practical demands of disrupted urban delivery networks. By combining solver diversity with scenario-driven planning and interpretable cost modeling, it offers a structured and actionable approach to building more resilient, equitable, and sustainable last-mile logistics systems.

2   Related Works

Resilient supply chain design under disruption has been extensively studied, particularly in the context of network optimization, demand forecasting, and risk mitigation. However, much of the existing literature tends to rely on rigid, full-fulfillment assumptions and aggregate-level cost modeling, limiting their practical application in urban logistics systems where resource shortfalls and operational trade-offs are common.

2.1   Classical Optimization Models Under Disruption

Supply chain optimization has traditionally relied on deterministic models, particularly Linear Programming (LP) and Mixed Integer Programming (MIP), to minimize cost and improve service-level adherence. While these models are effective under stable conditions, they face significant limitations when applied to real-world disruption scenarios where demand routinely exceeds supply, and resource availability is uncertain. Early robust design efforts focused on coping with uncertainty in demand and supply reliability, often by embedding buffer capacities or conservative estimates. For instance, researcher [16] proposed a robust supply chain design framework that accounts for demand variability in agile manufacturing environments. However, their model—like many others—enforces full demand satisfaction and does not support partial fulfillment under constrained scenarios. Similarly, research [17] introduced a mixed-integer nonlinear programming model to handle supplier disruption risks in integrated supply chains. Although the model incorporates expedited shipments as a mitigation mechanism, it still operates under the assumption that all customer demand should be fulfilled, either normally or via contingency paths. Such assumptions may not hold in urban logistics settings, where short-term disruptions can lead to unavoidable shortfalls in service. In response to these limitations, more recent research has explored stochastic and scenario-based optimization. Research group [18] developed a comparative framework to evaluate two-stage stochastic programming and robust optimization approaches under demand uncertainty. Their study highlights the strengths and limitations of each method in terms of cost resilience. Likewise, the work [19] formulated a two-stage stochastic mixed-integer model for reliable supply chain network design under uncertain disruptions and demand. These approaches provide flexibility in managing risk but often require extensive scenario generation and are primarily designed for long-term strategic planning rather than short-term, post-disruption recovery. Another notable direction is the integration of social responsibility and qualitative cost considerations into optimization frameworks. Researcher [20] presented a robust possibilistic programming approach for socially responsible supply chain network design. Their work emphasizes qualitative performance, such as social fairness, but still assumes deterministic demand satisfaction and does not accommodate partial fulfillment strategies. More recently, researcher [21] proposed a collaborative supply chain network design approach under demand uncertainty using robust optimization. While it advances resilience, the framework retains the assumption of full-service delivery and focuses on cost minimization at an aggregate level. Collectively, these models tend to focus on minimizing expected costs or maximizing service levels but offer limited granularity in resource allocation across individual demand zones—particularly when supply is insufficient. Moreover, most formulations do not incorporate operational dimensions such as delivery delay penalties, fuel consumption, emissions, or zone-specific delivery costs, which are increasingly relevant in the context of urban logistics and sustainability.

2.2 Unbalanced Optimal Transport (UOT) and Partial Fulfillment

Classical transportation models assume mass conservation, where the total supply exactly matches the total demand. This assumption, however, often fails in practical logistics contexts—especially during operational disruptions—where resource availability is limited, and full fulfillment is infeasible. To address such imbalances, Unbalanced Optimal Transport (UOT) has emerged as a generalization of classical transport theory, enabling cost-sensitive allocation under relaxed marginal constraints. UOT introduces soft penalties for excess supply or unmet demand, allowing transport plans to adapt flexibly when supply and demand are unequal. Regularization terms such as the Kullback–Leibler divergence or entropic penalties are typically used to quantify and penalize mass deviation. This framework provides a tractable solution for partial fulfillment problems and allows tuning between cost minimization and service coverage. Several foundational contributions have advanced the theoretical and computational underpinnings of UOT. Researcher [22] introduced scalable entropic algorithms for solving UOT problems efficiently using generalized Sinkhorn iterations, laying the groundwork for computational feasibility in high-dimensional settings. Their approach adapts classical Sinkhorn scaling to support non-conservative flows, making it especially relevant to practical applications in machine learning and imaging. Building on this, researchers [23] analyzed the convergence behavior and complexity of the Sinkhorn algorithm for UOT, proving near-linear performance under regularized conditions. Their work demonstrated that UOT can be computed efficiently at scale, thereby removing a significant barrier to its application in large real-world systems. Research work [24] further extended this line of research by proposing gradient-based solvers for UOT that promote sparsity and provide improved approximation guarantees—attributes that are valuable for interpretable transport solutions in constrained environments. The concept of UOT has also been generalized to multi-marginal formulations. Researchers [25] presented an unbalanced multi-marginal OT model and applied it to structured imaging problems.

Beyond these theoretical advances, research in supply chain and humanitarian logistics has emphasized the need for flexible and equity-aware allocation under disruption [1, 9, 11, 17, 19, 21]. These studies typically rely on classical optimization or stochastic programming, and while they address resilience, they do not exploit the capabilities of UOT. Conversely, recent work on UOT has concentrated on developing scalable algorithms and proving theoretical guarantees [13, 14, 23–25], with little application to operational logistics problems. This disconnect leaves a clear gap: disruption-focused logistics models generally assume rigid fulfillment, while UOT methods handle imbalance but overlook realistic cost structures and service fairness. This paper addresses these gaps by applying UOT in the context of post-disruption fulfillment planning. We operationalize UOT alongside LP to compare solver behaviors under varying penalty regimes and supply constraints, using a detailed cost model reflective of urban delivery systems. Through this comparative analysis, we demonstrate UOT's potential to support interpretable, fairness-aware allocation strategies in disrupted logistics environments.

2.3 Cost-Aware and Interpretable Models

While cost minimization remains a central objective in logistics optimization, the representation of cost in many models is often oversimplified. Standard formulations frequently reduce transportation cost to a function of travel distance or duration, without incorporating real-world operational factors such as fuel consumption, emissions, delay penalties, and region-specific delivery constraints. These simplifications obscure the trade-offs decision-makers face in balancing efficiency, equity, and resilience—particularly during disruption scenarios. The work [17] introduced one of the more practical extensions to classical supply chain design by considering expedited shipments as a mitigation response to disruption. Their mixed-integer nonlinear model incorporates the cost of premium transport modes and supplier selection under risk. However, while their model offers a more detailed view of disruption responses, it treats costs largely from a procurement perspective and does not integrate zone-level delivery costs, environmental impacts, or delay penalties. Furthermore, the model remains focused on maintaining service-level continuity rather than exploring how cost structures influence spatial fairness in fulfillment. Researcher [26] extend this discourse by modeling supply chain resilience with explicit attention to failure propagation and repair logistics. Their framework incorporates the costs associated with system recovery—such as rerouting, repair dispatch, and infrastructure rehabilitation. While this work marks an important step toward more realistic and dynamic cost modeling, it is primarily concerned with infrastructural robustness at the system level and does not delve into last-mile allocation or intra-urban delivery fairness. Additionally, interpretability is not a core focus; the model's cost structure, though comprehensive, offers limited support for decision transparency at the operational planning level. Research work [27] provide a comprehensive review of supply chain network design models that integrate financial considerations, including investment decisions, tax optimization, and capital budgeting. Their analysis highlights how financial and operational objectives are often modeled in isolation, leading to suboptimal strategic trade-offs. While the review explains environmental and service equity concerns, most of the surveyed models emphasize long-term capital efficiency rather than short-term, interpretable allocation strategies for resource-constrained conditions. The lack of localized cost modeling—e.g., emissions in dense delivery zones or penalties for underserved areas—limits their direct applicability to urban last-mile planning under disruption. However, there remains a significant gap in operational research literature regarding multi-dimensional, interpretable cost models that: (1) Reflect granular real-world logistics variables (e.g., emissions, fuel cost, delays, zone penalties), (2) Offer actionable insight into how solver behavior reflects trade-offs between cost, coverage, and fairness. In response, our work builds a detailed cost model that explicitly incorporates these variables and uses solver outputs to analyze which zones are prioritized or omitted under different constraints. By exposing these trade-offs transparently, we contribute toward explainable optimization, a necessary step for deploying resilient, socially-aware logistics strategies in real-world settings.

2.4   Simulation and Scenario Analysis in Logistics

Simulation methods, particularly Agent-Based Modeling (ABM), have emerged as valuable tools for analyzing complex supply chain behavior under uncertainty. These models capture non-linear interactions, adaptive agent behavior, and emergent dynamics that are difficult to represent in traditional optimization frameworks. Their strength lies in modeling how disruptions propagate through supply networks and how decentralized decision-making shapes systemic outcomes. For example, the work [28] proposed a dynamic closed-loop supply chain network using ABM to model both forward and reverse flows. Their framework demonstrates how agent heterogeneity and decentralized control can lead to adaptive network configurations. However, its primary focus is on long-term structural design rather than near-term tactical response. Researcher [29] introduced OrbitZoo, a multi-agent reinforcement learning environment, illustrating how intelligent agents can learn and adapt in high-dimensional, dynamic environments. While this work focuses on orbital systems, its methodological contribution to agent-based learning has implications for adaptive logistics planning—but does not address the practicalities of delivery fulfillment or disruption response in urban settings. In the urban logistics domain, researcher [30] presented an intelligent multi-agent system to optimize last-mile delivery under uncertainty. The model enables agents to dynamically route deliveries based on traffic, demand, and delivery priority. Though promising, it prioritizes real-time routing intelligence and system efficiency, with limited emphasis on equity or cost transparency in the post-disruption phase. Researcher [31] applied ABM to evaluate urban freight policies in response to the rise of e-commerce, simulating stakeholder interactions and policy interventions such as the deployment of delivery lockers. Their work demonstrates the policy relevance of simulation but focuses more on infrastructure and behavioral aspects than on fulfillment optimization following disruption. Simulation has also been employed at a global scale, as in work [32], who used a simulation-based framework to assess supply chain vulnerabilities during the COVID-19 pandemic. This work emphasizes epidemic-induced ripple effects across multi-tier global networks. While it provides a macro-level view of disruption dynamics, it does not offer granular resource allocation strategies for constrained urban logistics systems. While ABM and simulation frameworks have contributed significantly to understanding disruption propagation and policy impact, they are typically oriented toward long-term strategic modeling or real-time behavioral learning, rather than tactical resource allocation after disruption. In our work, we adopt a scenario-driven mindset—defining post-disruption states such as demand surges, warehouse outages, or fleet shortages—and analyze how different solver-based optimization strategies (LP and UOT) respond under those constraints. By decoupling disruption simulation from fulfillment optimization, our approach bridges the rich realism of ABM-inspired scenarios with the mathematical tractability and interpretability of cost-aware solvers. This hybrid view supports logistics planners in stress-testing delivery strategies without requiring complex simulation infrastructure or long-term behavioral modeling.

2.5 Problem Statement

Urban logistics networks frequently face disruptions such as demand surges, warehouse outages, or vehicle shortages that make full demand fulfillment infeasible [1–3]. Traditional optimization approaches, particularly those based on Linear Programming, often assume that all demand must be satisfied [7, 8, 10], leading to impractical results under volatility and resource scarcity. Although soft-constrained models that allow partial fulfillment with penalties have been proposed [5, 18, 19], their application in logistics remains limited. In addition, many cost models reduce delivery costs to simple distance- or time-based functions [6, 27], neglecting key operational factors such as fuel use, emissions, and zone-specific pricing. This oversimplification obscures the multi-dimensional trade-offs that planners must navigate between efficiency, equity, and sustainability [9, 21].

2.6 Motivation

This work is motivated by the need for a practical and interpretable framework to support decision-making in post-disruption scenarios. Existing logistics models often emphasize either cost minimization or disruption management in isolation, relying on rigid fulfillment constraints that overlook flexibility and fairness. To address this gap, we introduce a soft-constrained optimization framework that integrates Linear Programming and Unbalanced Optimal Transport, enabling partial fulfillment with cost penalties and fairness-aware allocations. This unified approach provides both a practical decision-support tool and a methodological advance for resilience-oriented urban logistics.

3 Methodology

This section outlines the components of our proposed framework for post-disruption urban logistics planning. Figure 1 illustrates the overall workflow of the framework. Disruption scenarios and detailed cost parameters are processed by both LP and UOT solvers, enabling direct comparison of cost-driven and fairness-aware allocation strategies. The outputs provide interpretable trade-offs that guide resilience-oriented decision-making in urban logistics.

3.1 Assumptions

Our framework begins with the assumption that a disruption has occurred, such as a facility failure, fleet shortage, or surge in demand in a particular region. Rather than simulating the disruption process itself, we use predefined, realistic input matrices representing:

- A supply vector, indicating available delivery resources (e.g., trucks, capacity) at various nodes,

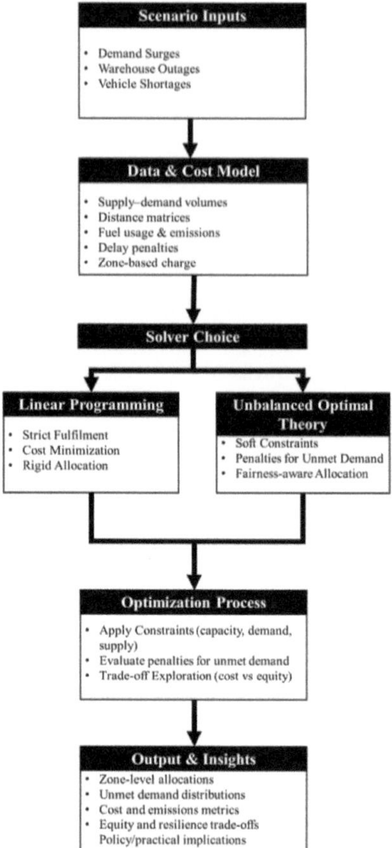

Fig. 1. Workflow of the proposed framework, where disruption scenarios and cost models are processed through solvers to produce allocations, unmet demand, and trade-off insights.

- A demand vector, representing customer needs across zones, potentially exceeding available supply,
- A cost matrix, capturing the cost of serving each demand zone from each supply node.

These inputs are treated as fixed for the purpose of optimization. The mismatch between supply and demand defines the core challenge: how to reallocate limited resources across zones to minimize cost while respecting equity considerations.

3.2 Solver Formulations

We implement and compare two solver formulations:

Linear Programming (LP). The Linear Programming (LP) formulation is a classical approach to cost minimization in logistics and transportation. In this context, the model assumes that available supply should be fully utilized and that demand should be met as much as possible, subject to feasibility. However, the model does not explicitly penalize unmet demand, nor does it account for fairness across zones. The objective is to minimize the total cost of fulfilling deliveries from supply nodes i to demand zones j, defined as:

$$\text{Min} \sum_{i,j} c_{ij}.x_{ij} \tag{1}$$

Subject to the constraints:

- Supply constraints: Each supply node i can distribute upto its available capacity s_i

$$\sum_j x_{ij} \leq s_i \ \forall i \tag{2}$$

- Demand limits: The total amount delivered to each zone j should not exceed its demand d_j

$$\sum_i x_{ij} \leq d_j \ \forall j \tag{3}$$

- Non-negativity: Deliveries cannot be negative.

$$x_{ij} \geq 0 s_i \forall i, j \tag{4}$$

In this setup, x_{ij} denotes the amount of goods delivered from supply node i to demand zone j, and c_{ij} represents the cost associated with that delivery. While the LP model is efficient and easy to interpret, it inherently favors zones with lower delivery costs. As a result, it may concentrate deliveries in a few zones while under-serving others—especially when total supply is insufficient. This behavior can introduce equity concerns in urban logistics, where certain neighborhoods or regions may consistently receive lower service levels due to their higher cost-to-serve.

Unbalanced Optimal Transport (UOT). Unbalanced Optimal Transport (UOT) extends the classical transport framework by allowing partial fulfillment of supply and demand. This is particularly useful in disrupted logistics scenarios, where strict marginal constraints become infeasible due to supply shortages or demand surges. UOT relaxes these constraints by introducing penalty terms for deviations from original supply and demand. The resulting soft-constrained optimization minimizes cost while penalizing under- or over-fulfillment. The objective function is:

The UOT problem is formulated as:

$$\min_{\gamma \geq 0} c_{ij}.\gamma_{ij} + \lambda_s.KL\left(\sum_j \gamma_{ij} \| s_i\right) + \lambda_d.KL\left(\sum_i \gamma_{ij} \| d_j\right) + \varepsilon.KL(\gamma \| u \otimes v) \tag{5}$$

where:

- γ_{ij} is the transport flow from supply node iii to demand node jjj,
- c_{ij} is the unit transport cost,

- s_i, d_j are the original supply and demand,
- λ_s, λ_d penalize marginal mismatch,
- ε controls entropic smoothing.

In our implementation, the cost matrix is scaled to [0, 10] for numerical stability. Entropy regularization ε is dynamically set based on the cost scale (ensuring stable Sinkhorn updates), and marginal penalties $\lambda_s = \lambda_d$ are fixed at 100 to control tolerance to under-fulfillment. This formulation enables interpretable partial delivery, revealing which zones are underserved and to what extent. Unlike LP, which rigidly fulfills low-cost zones first, UOT produces smooth and fairness-aware allocations that better reflect urban delivery realities.

Cost Model. To ensure realism and interpretability, our framework incorporates a multi-dimensional cost model that reflects the true operational complexity of urban last-mile logistics. Rather than reducing transportation cost to a simple function of distance or time, we construct a composite cost matrix that integrates spatial, temporal, environmental, and economic factors.

We define the unit delivery cost C_{ij} between supply node i and demand zone j as:

$$C_{ij} = w_1 Distance_{ij} + w_2 Time_{ij} + w_3 Fuel_{ij} + w_4 Emissions_{ij}$$
$$+ w_5 DelayRisks_{ij} + w_6 MontearyCost_{ij} \qquad (6)$$

where:

- $w_1 \ldots \ldots w_6$ are tunable weights assigned by the planner,
- $Distance_{ij}$ denotes the geodesic or route-based distance,
- $Time_{ij}$ is the estimated travel time based on expected traffic or congestion levels,
- $Fuel_{ij}$ reflects fuel consumption derived from distance and vehicle parameters,
- $Emissions_{ij}$ captures the environmental cost (e.g., CO_2-equivalent) associated with the trip,
- $DelayRisks_{ij}$ represents the likelihood or cost of time-window violations,
- $MontearyCost_{ij}$ accounts for direct financial costs such as tolls, parking fees, or zone-specific surcharges.

This formulation allows planners to emphasize different priorities by adjusting the weights. For example, a sustainability-focused operation may assign higher weights to fuel and emissions, while a time-critical delivery network may prioritize delay risk and time. Once computed, the composite cost matrix $C = \left[C_{ij} \right]$ is used consistently in both LP and UOT solver formulations. This enables a fair comparison between solver outputs while maintaining fidelity to real-world planning constraints. The multi-dimensional cost model also enhances the explainability of optimization outcomes. By decomposing the total cost into interpretable components, planners can better understand how delivery patterns are influenced by various cost drivers and adjust their strategies accordingly.

Output Interpretation and Solver Comparison. The final stage of our methodology involves analyzing the behavior of the two solvers—Linear Programming (LP) and Unbalanced Optimal Transport (UOT)—under identical disrupted scenarios and cost models. This comparison focuses on how each solver distributes limited supply across demand zones, and how those allocations reflect different trade-offs between cost efficiency and equity.

Interpretation of LP Outputs: The LP formulation prioritizes strict cost minimization without explicitly accounting for fairness or service coverage balance. As a result, supply is typically concentrated in zones with the lowest per-unit delivery cost C_{ij}. When supply is insufficient, higher-cost zones may receive little or no allocation, regardless of their demand levels. This outcome, while efficient in cost terms, may lead to service inequities, especially in complex urban environments with variable delivery constraints across zones. LP solutions are deterministic and sparse, often allocating the entire supply to a subset of zones until the supply is exhausted. This makes them easy to interpret from a cost-efficiency standpoint, but limited in terms of supporting social or operational fairness objectives.

Interpretation of UOT Outputs: In contrast, the UOT formulation allows for partial fulfillment and introduces soft penalties for unmet demand or unused supply. The resulting transport plan γ_ij tends to be more diffuse, allocating smaller quantities across a broader range of zones—even if some of those allocations are suboptimal from a strict cost perspective. By adjusting the marginal penalty parameter λ, planners can explore a spectrum of solutions: low-penalty settings yield more flexible, fairness-oriented allocations, while higher penalties recover behavior similar to LP. UOT also supports interpretable diagnostics, such as: (i) Quantifying unmet demand per zone; (ii) Identifying which cost components (e.g., emissions, delays) drive allocation decisions; (iii) Visualizing flow distributions to assess spatial equity. This interpretability makes UOT especially valuable in disrupted settings, where full service is impossible and planners must transparently justify compromises.

4   Case Study and Results

4.1   Sensitivity Analysis of Cost Parameters: LP vs UOT

Scenario Setup: To evaluate solver behavior under constrained urban logistics conditions, we simulate a disrupted delivery scenario set in Chennai, India. The experiment includes two supply nodes—Egmore and Taramani—providing 50 and 30 units of supply, respectively. Demand is concentrated in three zones: Velachery (40 units), Mylapore (60 units), and Guindy (35 units), resulting in a total demand of 135 units against a total supply of only 80 units, thus creating a shortfall of 55 units. To reflect real-world operational pressures, the cost model incorporates multiple components: geographic distance (in kilometers), estimated travel duration (in minutes), fuel consumption (as a function of mileage and distance), emissions (based on fuel usage and an emission factor), delay penalties, and per-kilometer shipping charges. A composite cost matrix C_{ij} was constructed using weighted combinations of these factors. The supply-demand imbalance allows us to study how solvers prioritize delivery when full fulfillment is infeasible.

Figure 2 suggest that the sensitivity analysis for the LP solver reveals that its behavior is highly dependent on the penalty assigned for unmet demand. When the delay penalty

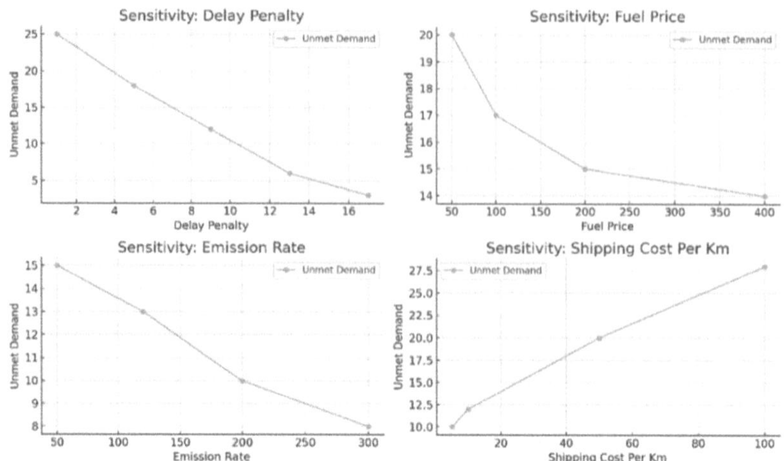

Fig. 2. Sensitivity analysis of cost parameters on unmet demand (LP solver).

per minute is low, the solver meets part of the demand, but as the penalty increases, there is a sharp rise in unmet demand. This is due to the solver beginning to skip high-delay zones to minimize overall cost. In contrast, when parameters such as fuel price, emission rate, or shipping cost per kilometer are increased, the solver's response remains largely unchanged—unmet demand remains high (approaching the full shortfall of ~ 135 units). This suggests that under the current cost scaling, the LP model refuses to serve demand in zones where these costs are high, unless heavily penalized for failing to deliver. These results indicate that LP is highly cost-sensitive and behaves conservatively under rising operational costs. Rather than reallocating or partially fulfilling demand in expensive zones, it simply avoids delivering there. This occurs especially when the penalty for unmet demand is not sufficiently large to outweigh delivery costs. For instance, if the shipping cost is ₹100 per km and the delivery distance is 10 km, then the shipping cost per unit becomes ₹1,000. If 100 units are delivered, the total shipping cost is ₹100,000—far exceeding a typical penalty of ₹10,000 for unmet demand. Even when fuel or emissions costs triple (e.g., from ₹100 to ₹400), LP still prefers to leave demand unmet, as this is cheaper than incurring delivery costs. This strict thresholding behavior suggests that LP may lead to infeasibility or overly conservative delivery strategies in disrupted scenarios without carefully calibrated penalties.

In reference to Fig. 3, the sensitivity analysis for the Unbalanced Optimal Transport (UOT) solver highlights its robustness to variations in cost parameters. When the delay penalty per minute is increased, the resulting decrease in unmet demand is minimal—indicating that UOT already fulfills demand optimally within the supply constraints. This suggests that increasing penalties does not significantly shift the transport plan, as the solver inherently seeks balanced and soft allocations across zones. Similarly, changes in fuel price, emission rate, and shipping cost per kilometer result in flat or barely percep-tible changes in unmet demand. This behavior is a direct consequence of UOT's relaxed marginal constraints, which allow it to redistribute flow without completely excluding

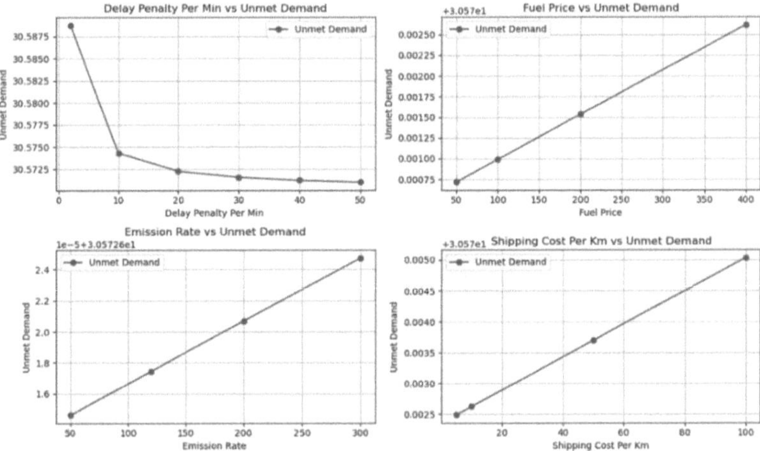

Fig. 3. Sensitivity analysis of cost parameters on unmet demand (UOT solver).

zones based on high costs. Overall, UOT exhibits stable and gradual adjustments in response to parameter changes. It prioritizes soft fulfillment by spreading available supply across all demand zones, rather than enforcing strict cost-based thresholds. As a result, cost parameters in UOT primarily influence how much flow is assigned to each zone, rather than whether a zone is served at all. This makes UOT a compelling approach in urban logistics settings where service equity and graceful degradation under cost stress are valued alongside efficiency.

4.2　Comparative Analysis of Linear Programming and Unbalanced Optimal Transport for Cost-Aware Demand Fulfillment in Urban Logistics

To further analyze solver behavior beyond parameter sensitivity, we performed a metric-wise comparison of Linear Programming (LP) and Unbalanced Optimal Transport (UOT) using the same disrupted Chennai logistics scenario introduced in Sect. 4.1. This analysis evaluates not only fulfillment performance but also operational efficiency and allocation diversity, providing a multi-dimensional understanding of solver outcomes under real-world constraints.

The following metrics were computed for both solvers for this Sect. 4.2:

1. Total Transport Cost: The aggregate cost of all fulfilled deliveries based on the multi-dimensional cost matrix.
2. Total Unmet Demand: Sum of demand shortfall across all zones after solver execution.
3. Total Emissions: Calculated from fuel usage and emission factor (e.g., kg CO_2 per liter).
4. Total Fuel Consumption: Based on per-kilometer fuel estimates weighted by delivery volumes.
5. Flow Entropy: Shannon entropy of the normalized flow matrix, indicating the spread or diversity of allocations across zones.

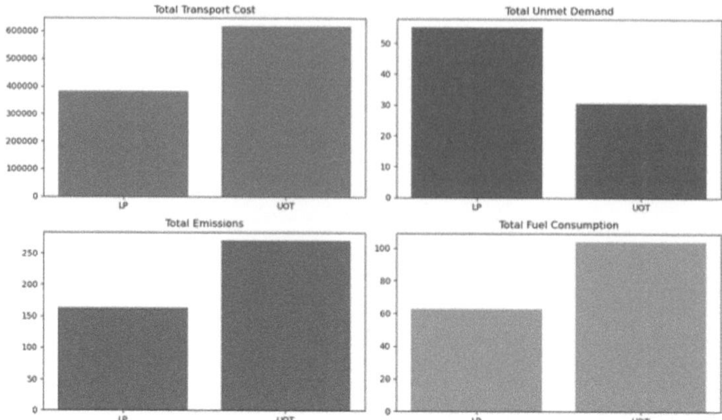

Fig. 4. Comparative performance of LP vs UOT: total transport cost, unmet demand, emissions, and fuel usage.

Figure 4 highlights the comparative results between the Linear Programming (LP) and Unbalanced Optimal Transport (UOT) solvers reveal distinct trade-offs in terms of cost, fulfillment, operational impact, and allocation equity. The LP solver achieves a lower total transport cost of ₹386,173 by prioritizing deliveries to low-cost zones, but this strict optimization leads to a high unmet demand of 55 units—over one-third of total demand. In contrast, the UOT solver incurs a higher total cost of ₹618,649, yet significantly reduces the unmet demand to 30.3 units by distributing supply more evenly across all demand zones. This broader coverage, however, results in greater fuel consumption (104.9 L for UOT vs. 63.5 L for LP) and increased emissions (271.9 kg CO_2 for UOT vs. 163.8 kg CO_2 for LP), reflecting the cost of reaching logistically challenging or distant zones. Notably, the flow entropy values provide further insight into allocation behavior: LP's lower entropy (−297.64) indicates a sparse and cost-focused delivery plan, while UOT's higher entropy (−336.18) reflects a more distributed and fairness-aware allocation. These results underscore that while LP is highly efficient for minimizing costs under hard constraints, UOT offers a more balanced, interpretable approach that supports partial fulfillment and equity—making it a stronger candidate for disrupted urban logistics scenarios where service accessibility is as important as cost efficiency.

4.3 Generalization Experiments: Multi-City, Temporal, and Traffic-Aware Scenarios

To evaluate the scalability and robustness of our framework, we extended the experimental setup beyond the single-city case to simulate diverse urban logistics environments. These experiments explore how LP and UOT solvers perform under variations in city density, time-of-day, traffic dynamics, and demand heterogeneity.

Experimental Variants

1. *Single-City, Single Time Period:*

A baseline experiment focused on demand fulfillment within a single urban area (e.g., Chennai), assuming static cost conditions and fixed supply-demand patterns during a single time window.

2. *Multi-City, Multi-Time Period Planning:*

   Experiments conducted across multiple cities (e.g., Chennai, Bengaluru, Hyderabad), each modeled with distinct time-of-day cost matrices (e.g., morning peak vs. evening hours), capturing temporal and geographic variability in congestion, distance, and emissions.

3. *Urban Density and Demand Profile Variation:*

   Cities were segmented into dense (e.g., urban core) and sparse (e.g., peripheral) zones, and tested under varied demand patterns—commercially skewed, bursty, and uniform—to evaluate solver response to spatial and temporal concentration of demand.

4. *Traffic-Aware Cost Modeling:*

   Delivery cost matrices were enriched with dynamic traffic data, incorporating congestion-related penalties to simulate real-time delays and route saturation. This allowed the evaluation of solver adaptability under realistic traffic-influenced disruption scenarios.

Single-City, Single Time Period. This baseline experiment evaluates solver performance within a single urban region—representative of a city like Chennai—under static conditions where supply, demand, and delivery cost matrices remain fixed throughout the time window. No temporal evolution or demand carry-forward is assumed, allowing a clean analysis of how each solver prioritizes delivery across zones when supply is insufficient to meet total demand. The demand profile includes three zones (D1, D2, D3) with varied original demand volumes. Total available supply across the network is limited to 80 units, whereas cumulative demand exceeds 130 units—creating a scenario of structural shortfall. This imbalance offers a clear opportunity to assess how solvers trade off between cost efficiency and spatial fairness in allocation.

As shown in Fig. 5, the Linear Programming (LP) solver fulfills deliveries based on strict cost minimization. It fully serves D2 and D3 but excludes D1 entirely, deeming it cost-inefficient. While this strategy minimizes total transport cost, it results in a severe service disparity—D1's unmet demand is left completely unaddressed. This behavior reflects LP's deterministic and threshold-based nature, where zones with higher delivery costs are skipped if their fulfillment does not yield sufficient marginal utility.

In contrast, the Unbalanced Optimal Transport (UOT) solver distributes available supply more proportionally across all three zones. While it may not fully satisfy any one zone's demand, it avoids total exclusion. For instance, D1 receives partial service, as do D2 and D3—illustrating UOT's soft-constrained formulation that penalizes unmet demand while preserving flexibility in marginal mismatches. This single-period comparison reveals the foundational contrast between the two solvers. LP is optimal for cost, but its hard constraints lead to brittle service patterns and inequitable coverage. UOT, by introducing interpretable penalties and tolerating partial fulfillment, achieves broader zone coverage with smoother degradation under scarcity—making it more aligned with

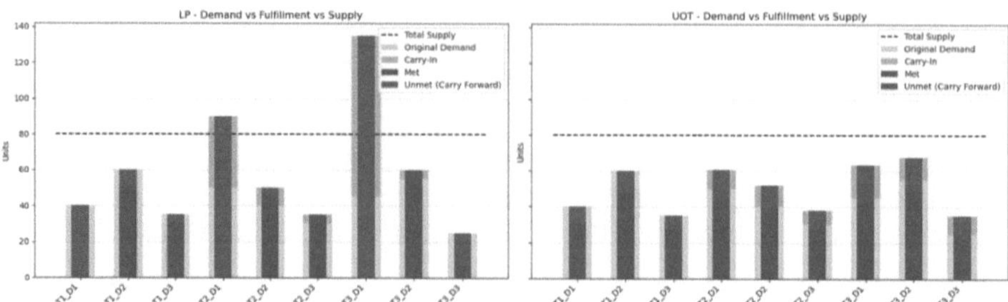

Fig. 5. Zone-wise **fulfillment in a single-city scenario.** (a) LP solver prioritizes low-cost zones, leaving D1 underserved. (b) UOT solver distributes supply more evenly, ensuring partial fulfillment across all zones.

urban delivery systems that prioritize service accessibility alongside operational efficiency. This contrast underscores a central resilience trade-off: LP risks systemic exclusion of high-cost zones in disruption recovery, while UOT internalizes fairness into the optimization process, ensuring that all regions maintain at least some level of service continuity. Such differences become especially critical when disruptions persist across multiple periods, where inequitable allocations can compound into severe backlogs.

Multi-City, Multi-Time Period Planning. This experiment simulates a geographically distributed logistics environment involving three supply locations—Egmore (Chennai), Kothrud (Pune), and Wadala (Mumbai)—and three corresponding demand zones—T. Nagar (Chennai), Connaught Place (Delhi), and Andheri (Mumbai). Each city is modeled with time-varying supply and demand volumes across three planning periods (T1, T2, T3). Unmet demand in any time window is automatically carried forward, introducing cumulative pressure on solver decisions. This setup mirrors the challenges of real-world cross-city logistics coordination under fluctuating operational loads and regional disparities in delivery cost structures (refer Fig. 6).

- In T1, both solvers (LP and UOT) fulfill demand completely in zones D1 (Mumbai) and D3 (Chennai). However, the LP solver entirely avoids serving D2 (Delhi) due to its higher unit delivery cost, leaving 70 units of unmet demand to be carried forward. In contrast, the UOT solver serves 66 out of 70 units in D2, achieving near-complete fulfillment without compromising performance in D1 or D3. This early divergence sets the stage for downstream imbalance in LP's allocation.
- In T2, the contrast becomes more stark. LP again bypasses D2 entirely, now allowing the backlog in Delhi to grow to 110 units. Meanwhile, D1 and D3 are only partially served due to increasing demand. The UOT solver, on the other hand, maintains proportional delivery across all zones—covering 59, 41, and 38 units in D1, D2, and D3 respectively—with minimal accumulation of unmet demand. Its relaxed constraints and equity-aware design enable it to accommodate the growing load more gracefully.
- By T3, LP's rigid prioritization again leads to complete service denial to D2, resulting in a backlog of 175 units—a threefold increase from T1. This concentration of unmet demand in a single high-cost zone reflects LP's inability to generalize across

geographies with uneven cost profiles. In contrast, UOT sustains equitable delivery across all zones, fulfilling 53, 61, and 36 units in D1, D2, and D3, respectively. Notably, D2 (Delhi) receives the highest allocation in T3 under UOT, highlighting its responsiveness to backlog accumulation and fairness in supply distribution.

This multi-city experiment underscores the systemic differences between LP and UOT in cross-regional logistics planning. LP's strict cost prioritization leads to a path-dependent outcome: once a high-cost zone like Delhi is excluded in the first period, unmet demand compounds across subsequent periods, producing severe service inequities. This illustrates LP's vulnerability in geographically diverse networks where cost heterogeneity is high. UOT, by contrast, mitigates backlog accumulation through proportional allocations, ensuring that no city is persistently underserved. While this requires accepting higher aggregate costs, it delivers resilience by maintaining continuity of service across regions. From a practical standpoint, this suggests that LP is best suited for short-term efficiency in cost-homogeneous networks, whereas UOT offers greater robustness and fairness in multi-city systems facing uneven cost profiles and fluctuating demand.

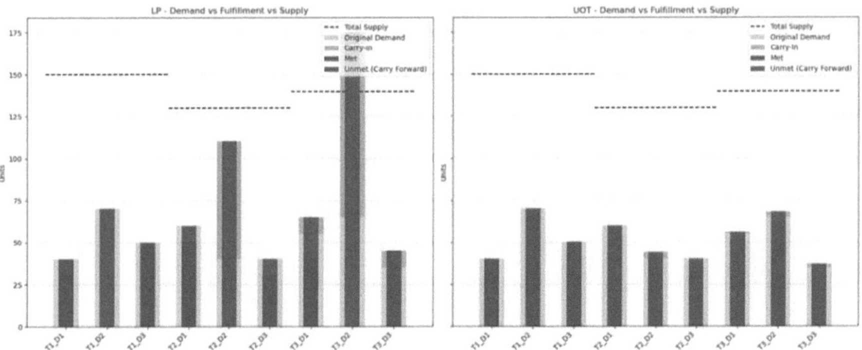

Fig. 6. Zone-wise demand fulfillment across three time windows in multi-city, multi-period scenario.

Urban Density and Demand Profile Variation. To examine how solver behavior adapts to spatial heterogeneity and density-dependent logistics constraints, we construct two contrasting demand profiles: Urban Dense and Suburban Sparse. These profiles represent realistic extremes in last-mile delivery scenarios and allow us to test the sensitivity of LP and UOT solvers under distinct spatial, temporal, and cost conditions.

- Urban Dense Profile is characterized by a greater number of demand zones (≥ 4), geographically proximate delivery points, and generally lower per-unit transport costs due to shorter distances and better infrastructure. This profile typically reflects high overall demand volumes with dense commercial or residential clusters. In our simulation, four demand zones are considered, with supply originating from multiple nearby hubs.

- Suburban Sparse Profile involves fewer demand zones (2–3), spread over longer distances. As a result, transportation costs—especially those linked to fuel, emissions, and delivery time—increase significantly. Moreover, supply availability in such regions is typically constrained, either due to fewer fulfillment centers or limited vehicle availability.

To simulate this dichotomy, we partition a delivery region into dense and sparse subregions. Formally, we define the dense region as having N supply nodes and O demand zones, while the sparse region includes M supply nodes and K demand zones, with N > M and O > K. This setup enables a comparative evaluation of solver behavior under equal time windows but unequal density and spatial spread.

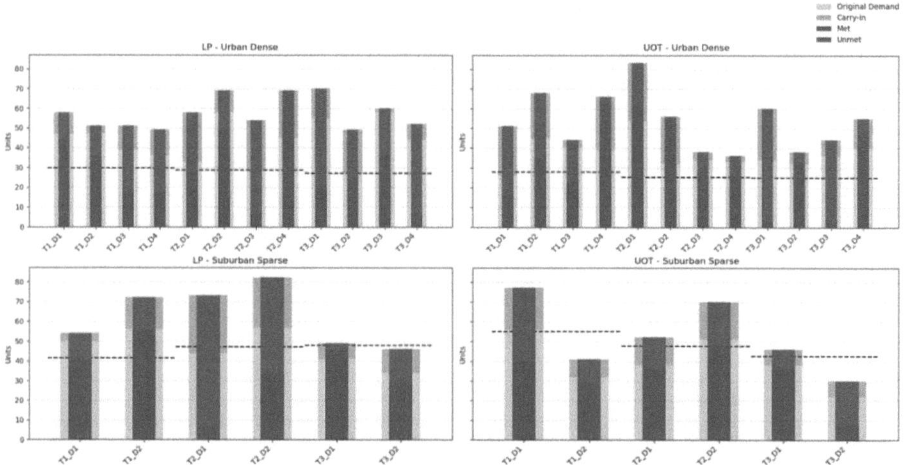

Fig. 7. Fulfillment outcomes across Urban Dense and Suburban Sparse demand profiles.

The above illustration (refer Fig. 7) reflects total zone-level demand (original and carry-in), actual met demand, and the residual unmet quantity. Some of the key observations include: (1) In the Urban Dense setting, UOT delivers smoother allocations with lower unmet demand distributed across all zones, while LP shows a tendency to concentrate supply in a few zones, leaving others underserved; (2) In the Suburban Sparse setting, LP again exhibits rigid prioritization, completely avoiding certain high-cost zones even across successive time windows. UOT, while incurring a higher total cost, ensures more equitable and gradual fulfillment across all zones—even in the face of high transport penalties. These findings reinforce the importance of solver choice in spatially diverse urban environments. LP remains cost-optimal but risks entrenching service disparities in less accessible zones. UOT, by contrast, demonstrates greater spatial generalizability and fairness—critical for real-world systems operating across mixed-density delivery networks. In practical terms, this suggests that LP may be suitable for dense, well-connected regions where exclusion effects are limited, but UOT offers stronger resilience in suburban or peripheral areas where demand is sparse and costs are uneven.

By internalizing fairness penalties, UOT avoids systemic neglect of disadvantaged zones, making it more aligned with equity-focused urban logistics policies.

Traffic-Aware Cost Modeling. Urban logistics performance is significantly influenced by real-time traffic conditions, particularly during last-mile delivery. To assess solver robustness under dynamic congestion states, we extend our experimental setup with traffic-aware cost modeling, distinguishing between off-peak (base case) and peak traffic conditions. In the off-peak scenario, delivery duration and cost are calculated using base values, with a traffic_factor $= 1.0$, implying no congestion. In contrast, peak traffic conditions simulate real-world urban congestion by inflating travel durations by a factor of $1.5 \times$. This increase not only affects route-level delivery time but also amplifies delay penalties and overall transport costs, effectively introducing harsher constraints for fulfillment optimization. Some of the key observations include: Dense Region: Across both LP and UOT solvers, off-peak traffic facilitates higher fulfillment rates due to relatively lower time-based penalties. LP performs acceptably in these scenarios, although it continues to favor low-cost zones.

Under peak traffic, the LP solver exhibits a visible increase in unmet demand, especially in later time periods, as congestion-driven delay penalties outweigh the cost of serving certain zones. UOT, by contrast, maintains consistent performance even during peak traffic, slightly reducing allocations but preserving equitable coverage across demand zones; Sparse Region: A more pronounced divergence emerges in sparse delivery regions. Under off-peak traffic, LP appears to meet higher volumes in specific zones, but this behavior is deceptive: the solver skips costlier zones altogether (e.g., those similar to Connaught Place), accepting unmet demand penalties rather than incurring high delivery costs. This behavior highlights LP's rigid cost-optimality rather than fairness. When peak traffic is introduced, unmet demand surges sharply, as all remaining cost margins are eroded by increased delay penalties and extended travel times. Conversely, UOT remains relatively stable, continuing to serve all zones proportionally—albeit with reduced fulfillment margins—indicating greater resilience to temporal cost shocks.

Figure 8a and Fig. 8b clearly demonstrate that LP's strategy deteriorates under peak traffic, especially in sparse settings where zone distances and baseline costs are already high. In these cases, LP increasingly resorts to skipping deliveries and absorbing penalties, reinforcing inequitable outcomes. This is exacerbated during peak traffic when the solver disproportionately neglects expensive-to-serve zones. UOT, with its relaxed marginal constraints and penalty-aware balancing, consistently demonstrates smoother degradation under congestion. Its delivery patterns remain more distributed and adaptive, preserving service equity even when operational costs spike. This evaluation underscores the importance of embedding traffic-aware parameters into logistics planning and solver selection. While LP offers aggressive cost savings under benign conditions, it lacks robustness to cost volatility and congestion. UOT, by allowing partial delivery and penalized mismatch, delivers more sustainable outcomes in both dense and sparse settings—making it more suitable for real-world, traffic-sensitive urban delivery systems.

In the traffic-aware scenario (Fig. 8), the solvers diverge sharply under temporal congestion effects. LP, driven by strict cost minimization, systematically avoids zones

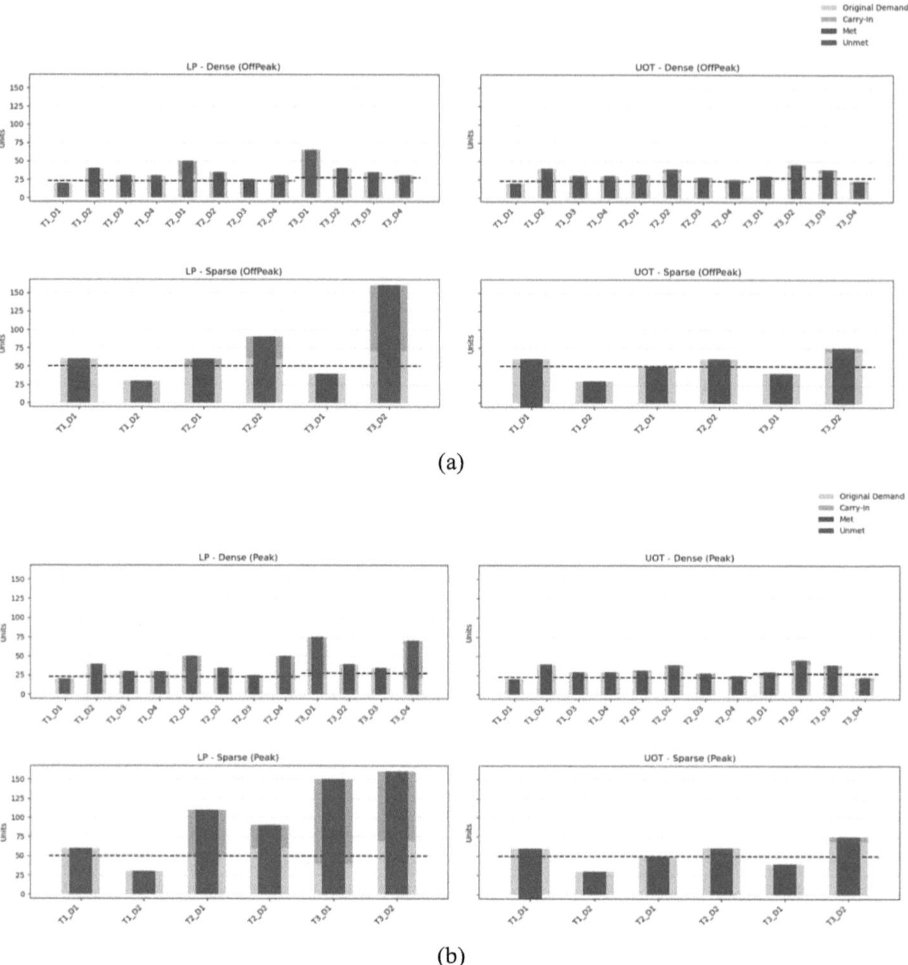

Fig. 8. Solver **performance with traffic-aware cost modeling.** (a) Off-peak: both solvers show improved fulfillment. (b) Peak: LP struggles with unmet demand and inequity, while UOT sustains adaptive, distributed delivery.

experiencing peak-hour penalties, resulting in abrupt service withdrawal during high-traffic windows. This produces oscillating fulfillment patterns and amplifies residual demand once congestion subsides. UOT, by contrast, maintains partial allocations even in penalized zones, absorbing short-term cost increases to preserve continuity of service. This behavior prevents demand spikes from cascading into severe backlogs and reflects UOT's ability to smooth fluctuations across time. From an operational standpoint, these results indicate that LP is highly efficient in stable traffic conditions but fragile under variable congestion, whereas UOT offers more resilient and predictable coverage when transport costs are time-dependent.

4.4 Practical Limitations and Implementation Challenges

While the framework is replicable, interpretable, and demonstrates strong performance across disruption scenarios, several practical limitations should be noted. Its effectiveness—particularly under UOT—is sensitive to penalty parameter choices that balance unmet demand and transport cost, and small changes can significantly shift allocations between zones, highlighting challenges in calibration. In our experiments, default parameters already revealed meaningful trade-offs, but systematic sensitivity analysis or adaptive, data-driven methods for parameter selection would further clarify tuning strategies for specific operational contexts. The approach also relies on detailed cost parameters—such as fuel consumption, emissions, and zone-specific charges—that may be difficult to obtain or standardize across cities. Although LP and UOT are computationally tractable for the case studies considered, scaling to very large networks or multi-day horizons may require additional solver tuning or decomposition strategies. Finally, while the case studies focus on Chennai, and the framework is generalizable, its transferability to other urban contexts with different policies, infrastructures, or service expectations warrants further validation. Addressing these challenges would enhance the framework's practical applicability and guide future extensions.

5 Conclusion

This study presented a scenario-driven optimization framework for urban logistics planning under disruption, addressing the growing need for flexible and interpretable strategies in resource-constrained environments. By integrating Linear Programming (LP) and Unbalanced Optimal Transport (UOT), we enable planners to explore a spectrum of fulfillment strategies—ranging from strict cost minimization to fairness-oriented partial delivery. Our experiments, grounded in real-world case studies from Chennai, demonstrate that while LP excels in cost efficiency, it often leads to service asymmetries and unmet demand in high-cost zones. UOT, by contrast, offers smoother, more equitable allocations, particularly when demand exceeds supply or when cost structures vary across zones. The inclusion of a detailed, multi-dimensional cost model allows for operational realism and supports explainable decision-making. Through comparative analysis across single-city, multi-period, multi-city, and traffic-aware scenarios, we show that UOT consistently achieves broader zone coverage and better handles backlog accumulation, especially under dynamic or peak-load conditions.

This work highlights the importance of moving beyond rigid optimization models in urban logistics. By combining soft-constrained solvers with scenario-based planning, our framework supports more resilient, adaptive, and socially aware logistics operations—critical for cities facing ongoing disruption, congestion, and evolving service expectations. Future work could extend the framework to incorporate stochastic demand and real-time data streams, enabling planners to adapt dynamically as disruptions unfold. Another promising direction is the integration of multi-agent decision-making, allowing carriers, municipalities, and third-party platforms to coordinate resilience strategies collaboratively. These avenues would further enhance the framework's applicability to complex, large-scale urban logistics ecosystems.

Acknowledgments. The authors acknowledge IIT Madras FedEx SMART, Center for Supply chain Modelling, Algorithms, Research and Technology for the financial support and resources provided. The authors thank Prof. Arshinder Kaur, Dr. Kelitha Cherian and Ms. Geetha for their support in facilitating the use of the IIT Madras FedEx SMART Center to conduct this research. They also extend their gratitude to the students and research staff of the HILCPS Laboratory for their assistance. Finally, the authors thank the anonymous reviewer for their valuable comments and suggestions, which greatly improved the quality of this work.

Disclosure of Interests. Authors have no conflict of interest in this work.

References

1. Kovács, G., Falagara Sigala, I.: Lessons learned from humanitarian logistics to manage supply chain disruptions. J. Supply Chain Manag. **57**(1), 41–49 (2021). https://doi.org/10.1111/jscm.12253

2. Durugbo, C.M., Al-Balushi, Z.: Supply chain management in times of crisis: a systematic review. Manag. Rev. Q. **73**(3), 1179–1235 (2023). https://doi.org/10.1007/s11301-022-00272-x

3. Katsaliaki, K., Galetsi, P., Kumar, S.: Supply chain disruptions and resilience: a major review and future research agenda. Ann. Oper. Res. **319**(1), 965–1002 (2022). https://doi.org/10.1007/s10479-020-03912-1

4. Kamolov, B.: Navigating Stress in the Supply Chain. In: Proceedings of the 6th International Scientific Conference «Reviews of Modern Science» (May 16–17, 2024), p. 38. Universität Luzern, Zürich (2024)

5. Hillier, M.S., Hillier, F.S.: Conventional optimization techniques. In: Evolutionary Optimization. International Series in Operations Research and Management Science, vol. 48, no. 1, pp. 3–25 (2003). https://doi.org/10.1007/0-306-48041-7_1

6. Kashem, M.A., Shamsuddoha, M., Nasir, T., Chowdhury, A.A.: Supply chain disruption versus optimization: a review on artificial intelligence and blockchain. Knowledge **3**(1), 80–96 (2023). https://doi.org/10.3390/knowledge3010007

7. Garcia, D.J., You, F.: Supply chain design and optimization: challenges and opportunities. Comput. Chem. Eng. **81**(1), 153–170 (2015). https://doi.org/10.1016/j.compchemeng.2015.03.015

8. Suryawanshi, P., Dutta, P.: Optimization models for supply chains under risk, uncertainty, and resilience: a state-of-the-art review and future research directions. Transp. Res. Part E **157**(1), 102553 (2022). https://doi.org/10.1016/j.tre.2021.102553

9. Jabbarzadeh, A., Fahimnia, B., Sabouhi, F.: Resilient and sustainable supply chain design: sustainability analysis under disruption risks. Int. J. Prod. Res. **56**(17), 5945–5968 (2018). https://doi.org/10.1080/00207543.2018.1461950

10. Dantzig, G.B., Thapa, M.N.: Linear programming. Oper. Res. **50**(1), 42–47 (2002). https://doi.org/10.1007/b97672

11. Manopiniwes, W., Irohara, T.: A review of relief supply chain optimization. Ind. Eng. Manag. Syst. **13**(1), 1–14 (2014). https://doi.org/10.7232/iems.2014.13.1.001

12. Choi, T.M., Govindan, K., Li, X., Li, Y.: Innovative supply chain optimization models with multiple uncertainty factors. Ann. Oper. Res. **257**(1), 1–14 (2017). https://doi.org/10.1007/s10479-017-2582-4

13. Séjourné, T., Peyré, G., Vialard, F.X.: Unbalanced optimal transport, from theory to numerics. Handb. Numer. Anal. **24**(1), 407–471 (2023). https://doi.org/10.1016/bs.hna.2022.11.003

14. Pham, K., Le, K., Ho, N., Pham, T., Bui, H.: On unbalanced optimal transport: An analysis of Sinkhorn algorithm. In: Proceedings of the 37th International Conference on Machine Learning (PMLR 119), pp. 7673–7682 (2020). https://doi.org/10.5555/3524938.3525649
15. Séjourné, T., Feydy, J., Vialard, F.X., Trouvé, A., Peyré, G.: Sinkhorn divergences for unbalanced optimal transport. arXiv preprint, pp. 1–22 (2019). https://doi.org/10.48550/arXiv.1910.12958
16. Pan, F., Nagi, R.: Robust supply chain design under uncertain demand in agile manufacturing. Comput. Oper. Res. **37**(4), 668–683 (2010). https://doi.org/10.1016/j.cor.2009.06.017
17. Cui, J., Zhao, M., Li, X., Parsafard, M., An, S.: Reliable design of an integrated supply chain with expedited shipments under disruption risks. Transp. Res. Part E **95**(1), 143–163 (2015). https://doi.org/10.1016/j.tre.2016.09.009
18. Maggioni, F., Potra, F.A., Bertocchi, M.: A scenario-based framework for supply planning under uncertainty: stochastic programming versus robust optimization approaches. Comput. Manag. Sci. **14**(1), 5–44 (2016). https://doi.org/10.1007/s10287-016-0272-3
19. Tolooie, A., Maity, M., Sinha, A.K.: A two-stage stochastic mixed-integer program for reliable supply chain network design under uncertain disruptions and demand. Transp. Res. Part E **142**(1), 102047 (2020). https://doi.org/10.1016/j.cie.2020.106722
20. Pishvaee, M.S., Razmi, J., Torabi, S.A.: Robust possibilistic programming for socially responsible supply chain network design: a new approach. Fuzzy Sets Syst. **206**(1), 1–20 (2012). https://doi.org/10.1016/j.fss.2012.04.010
21. Zhang, Q., Wang, Z., Huang, M., Wang, H., Wang, X., Fang, S.C.: Collaborative supply chain network design under demand uncertainty: a robust optimization approach. Int. J. Prod. Econ. **279**(1), 109465 (2025). https://doi.org/10.1016/j.ijpe.2024.109465
22. Chizat, L., Peyré, G., Schmitzer, B., Vialard, F.-X.: Scaling algorithms for unbalanced transport problems. arXiv preprint, pp. 1–47 (2017). https://doi.org/10.48550/arXiv.1607.05816
23. Pham, K., Le, K., Ho, N., Pham, T., Bui, H.: On unbalanced optimal transport: An analysis of Sinkhorn algorithm. In: Proc. 37th International Conference on Machine Learning (PMLR 119), pp. 7673–7682 (2020). https://doi.org/10.5555/3524938.3525649
24. Nguyen, Q.M., Nguyen, H.H., Zhou, Y., Nguyen, L.M.: On unbalanced optimal transport: gradient methods, sparsity and approximation error. J. Mach. Learn. Res. **24**(1), 18390–18430 (2023). https://doi.org/10.5555/3648699.3649083
25. Beier, F., von Lindheim, J., Neumayer, S., Schmitzer, B.: Unbalanced multi-marginal optimal transport. J. Math. Imaging Vis. **65**(3), 394–413 (2023). https://doi.org/10.1007/s10851-022-01126-7
26. Goldbeck, N., Angeloudis, P., Ochieng, W.: Optimal supply chain resilience with consideration of failure propagation and repair logistics. Transp. Res. Part E **133**(1), 101830 (2020). https://doi.org/10.1016/j.tre.2019.101830
27. Jahani, H., Abbasi, B., Sheu, J.B., Klibi, W.: Supply chain network design with financial considerations: a comprehensive review. Eur. J. Oper. Res. **312**(3), 799–839 (2024). https://doi.org/10.1016/j.ejor.2023.02.033
28. Bozdoğan, A., Görkemli Aykut, L., Demirel, N.: An agent-based modeling framework for the design of a dynamic closed-loop supply chain network. Complex Intell. Syst. **9**(1), 247–265 (2023). https://doi.org/10.1007/s40747-022-00780-z
29. Oliveira, A., Dyreby, K., Caldas, F., Soares, C.: OrbitZoo: multi-agent reinforcement learning environment for orbital dynamics. arXiv preprint, pp. 1–42 (2025). https://doi.org/10.48550/arXiv.2504.04160
30. Kahalimoghadam, M., Thompson, R.G., Rajabifard, A.: An intelligent multi-agent system for last-mile logistics. Transp. Res. Part E **200**(1), 104191 (2025). https://doi.org/10.1016/j.tre.2025.104191

31. Alves, R., da Silva Lima, R., de Sena, D.C., de Pinho, A.F., Holguín-Veras, J.: Agent-based simulation model for evaluating urban freight policy to e-commerce. Sustainability **11**(15), 4020 (2019). https://doi.org/10.3390/su11154020
32. Ivanov, D.: Predicting the impacts of epidemic outbreaks on global supply chains: a simulation-based analysis on the coronavirus outbreak. Transp. Res. Part E **136**(1), 101922 (2020). https://doi.org/10.1016/j.tre.2020.101922

Truck-UAV Joint Distribution Route Optimization Model with Dynamic Recycling in New Retail Scenarios

Yiting Wang[✉], Xinran Wang, Haixiao Guo, Jiaxin Bian, Xiaohui Ma, and Xinmeng Wang

Xi'an University of Technology, Xi'an, China
wangyiting@xaut.edu.cn

Abstract. In big data-driven new retail, the reconstruction of "people, goods, marketplaces" has fostered online-offline integration and intelligent services, spurring a surge in consumers' demand for "instant delivery". However, traditional logistics faces three core bottlenecks: static capacity scheduling fails to adapt to urban traffic's spatiotemporal dynamics, such as peak-hour UAV takeoff/landing congestion and redundant truck stays; short-distance delivery relies on the "UAV-truck-UAV" transfer link, causing poor timeliness; and no unified framework quantifies transportation, time, and carbon emission costs, hindering multi-objective optimization balance. To address these, this paper proposes a truck-UAV joint distribution route optimization model with dynamic recycling. Methodologically, it builds a "time-phased & zone-divided" dynamic recycling framework where UAVs operate at dedicated points during peak hours and return to original trucks during off-peak periods; develops a UAV short-distance direct delivery mode that eliminates truck transfers for merchant-customer short-distance orders; introduces dynamic battery consumption functions and time-sensitive coefficients to quantify the three costs; and designs a hybrid heuristic algorithm integrated with machine learning for screening high-quality solutions and deep learning for optimizing initial populations to solve the "task-route" combinatorial explosion in dynamic scenarios. The main contributions include overcoming traditional static recycling limits to adapt to new retail's temporal variability; simplifying short-distance links to meet instantaneity demands; establishing a unified multi-cost quantification model that transforms multi-objective optimization into weighted total costs minimization.

Keywords: Truck-UAV Joint Distribution · New Retail · Last-Mile Delivery · Adaptive Temporal Strategy · Hybrid Heuristic Algorithm · Cost Minimization

1   Introduction

In the era of new retail, propelled by big data analytics, the traditional triad of "consumers, commodities, and consumption contexts" has undergone profound reconstruction. This transformation is not merely a superficial adjustment but a fundamental reengineering of value creation, where seamless online-offline integration, hyper-personalized services,

J. Barata et al. (Eds.): IN4PL 2025, CCIS 2826, pp. 207–223, 2026.
https://doi.org/10.1007/978-3-032-15579-5_13

and on-demand fulfillment have become the new norms [1]. Consumers now expect instant gratification—with delivery windows shrinking from days to hours, even minutes—while demanding greater transparency, flexibility, and sustainability throughout the entire shopping journey. Such shifts have placed unprecedented pressure on logistics systems, which are no longer mere supporting functions but critical enablers of competitive advantage in the new retail landscape.

Against this backdrop, truck-UAV joint distribution has emerged as a transformative solution to address the last-mile challenges inherent in new retail. By synergizing the ground coverage and load capacity of trucks with the agility and accessibility of UAVs, this hybrid model promises to overcome the limitations of single-modal delivery—be it the congestion-prone rigidity of truck-only routes or the payload and range constraints of standalone UAVs [2]. Its potential is multifold: enhancing delivery efficiency to meet instant demands, reducing operational costs through optimized resource utilization, and mitigating carbon footprints by minimizing redundant trips [3]. However, realizing this potential is far from straightforward. In urban environments characterized by dynamic traffic patterns, time-sensitive restrictions, and spatially varying demand densities, misaligned scheduling of trucks and UAVs can exacerbate problems—from air traffic congestion due to uncoordinated UAV takeoffs or landings to increased road emissions caused by prolonged truck idling during peak hours. These challenges underscore the urgency of a more nuanced, context-aware approach to joint distribution planning.

The motivation for this study stems from the urgent need to construct a dynamically adaptive truck-UAV joint distribution system for new retail scenarios, aiming to break through the bottlenecks of traditional delivery models in timeliness and flexibility, while balancing cost control and environmental protection goals. The main research questions are:

- How to design a time-phased and zone-divided dynamic recycling strategy to adapt to the time-period characteristics of urban traffic and enhance the collaborative efficiency between UAVs and trucks?
- Which decision factors should be integrated into task allocation and route planning to balance delivery timeliness, economic costs, and carbon emission control in new retail scenarios?
- How to construct a hybrid heuristic algorithm to efficiently solve the combinatorial explosion problem of task-route joint optimization in dynamic environments?

Accordingly, this paper aims to develop an optimization model for truck-UAV joint distribution in new retail scenarios, with a focus on achieving joint optimization of task allocation and route planning to minimize the weighted total cost. By extending the traditional static recycling mode to a time-phased and zone-divided dynamic recycling mechanism, combined with dynamic battery consumption functions and time-sensitive cost coefficients, it realizes the comprehensive quantification of transportation costs, time costs, and carbon emission costs. In doing so, this research seeks to unlock the full potential of truck-UAV collaboration, making it not just a technological novelty but a pragmatic, sustainable backbone of new retail logistics.

2 Literature Review

In the context of the emergence of new retail models, consumers are demanding higher timeliness and flexibility in logistics delivery, making traditional logistics models increasingly inadequate to meet dynamically changing needs. Truck-UAV collaborative delivery offers an innovative solution, where trucks handle long-distance distribution for large-scale cargo allocation, and UAVs focus on short-distance, rapid-response last-mile delivery. Optimizing route planning and task scheduling to reduce delivery time and overall costs remains a critical challenge.

2.1 Hybrid Delivery Systems

As logistics demands grow in complexity, integrating multi-modal transport (e.g., trucks, Electric Vehicles, UAVs) has become a focus, with research emphasizing sustainability and operational efficiency.

A multi-objective hybrid truck-UAV routing problem integrates pickup-delivery services to minimize transport time and maximize reliability through route and inventory decisions involving multiple trucks and UAVs, supporting rescue operations in humanitarian logistics [4]. The core of this joint distribution mode lies in breaking the limitations of a single transport tool: trucks undertake long-distance trunk transportation and material distribution, while UAVs focus on short-distance, high-priority precise delivery, ensuring rapid response to urgent needs in complex rescue scenarios while avoiding resource waste, which highlights the advantages of multi-modal transport in resource allocation efficiency. The bi-objective model for UAV and robot-assisted truck (DART) operations can minimize total costs and maximize customer satisfaction under soft time window constraints, proving particularly advantageous for high-density, long-distance last-mile delivery demands [5]. This collaborative delivery mode constructs a "three-in-one" three-dimensional delivery network with trucks as mobile hubs, robots responsible for short-distance ground connection, and UAVs undertaking air express delivery. This division and collaboration in multi-modal transport not only improves customers' satisfaction with delivery timeliness through time window management but also reduces unit delivery costs through large-scale integration, confirming the unique value of collaborative delivery in balancing efficiency and experience. A comprehensive model for multi-truck-UAV collaborative delivery addresses key challenges such as UAV endurance, payload constraints, and weather effects (wind, temperature) to minimize delivery time and costs [6]. As mobile supply stations for UAVs, trucks can provide battery replacement and load distribution support for UAVs through preset parking points, effectively breaking through the endurance and payload bottlenecks of UAVs; under extreme weather conditions, the stability of the delivery network is guaranteed through redundant route design of multiple trucks and dynamic switching of UAV tasks. This collaborative strategy grounded in multi-modal transport principles not only leverages the efficiency advantages of UAVs in short-distance delivery but also builds a system fault-tolerant mechanism relying on the strong adaptability of trucks, ultimately achieving dual optimization of overall delivery time and costs. A multi-objective mixed integer linear programming (MILP) model combined with a reinforcement learning (RL)-based multi-objective heuristic algorithm effectively obtains solutions for large-scale scenarios, validated as effective compared to state-of-the-art multi-objective heuristics [7].

By integrating UAVs, trucks, and couriers into last-mile delivery and embedding Q-learning into a ruin-recreate metaheuristic, the hybrid heuristic QSISRs provides a new optimization approach for collaborative delivery [8]. A novel multi-objective optimization model for the vehicle routing problem with UAV delivery and dynamic flight endurance promotes traditional ground vehicle delivery modes, implements UAV delivery, and optimizes total truck energy consumption to improve efficiency and reduce environmental impact [9]. A comparative study of the hybrid multi-objective evolutionary algorithm (HMOEAS) and hybrid multi-objective ant colony algorithm (HACO) using the Wuhan COVID-19 pandemic as a case shows that: when applying the truck-UAV collaborative delivery mode, both algorithms significantly improve the efficiency of anti-epidemic material distribution, with HMOEAS demonstrating better optimization performance. Specifically, compared with the truck-only delivery mode, the collaborative mode optimized by HMOEAS shortens the total delivery time of a single batch of medical supplies (e.g., protective suits and nucleic acid test kits) from 8.7 h to 3.5 h, reduces the unit delivery cost from 12.5 yuan per item to 9.2 yuan, and increases the demand satisfaction rate in sealed-off communities from 82.3% to 94.7%; compared with the drone-only delivery mode, it lowers the unit cost by 49.7% (the drone-only mode costs 18.3 yuan per item) and avoids delivery interruptions caused by insufficient drone battery life. These results confirm that the truck-UAV collaborative delivery mode outperforms pure truck or pure drone delivery in practical emergency scenarios [10]. A multi-objective mathematical programming model (mixed-integer programming) for simultaneous patrolling of trucks and UAVs balances patrol time and costs, considering UAV battery limits, routing issues, and inaccessible areas [11]. An improved ant colony algorithm (incorporating limited pheromone concentration and artificial bee colony classification ideas) combined with a multi-objective optimization model aiming to minimize total delivery costs and maximize customer satisfaction provides a route optimization solution for the truck-UAV joint delivery mode [12]. The bi-objective Traveling Salesman Problem with Drone(TSP-D) and its improved non-dominated sorting genetic algorithm II (INSGA-II), through component designs such as label algorithm-based decoding, adapts to problem characteristics and achieves bi-objective optimization [13].

2.2 Route Optimization Algorithms

Route optimization is pivotal to collaborative delivery efficiency, with scholars increasingly exploring hybrid improvements to traditional algorithms—particularly genetic algorithms (GA)—to enhance performance in complex scenarios.

The Self-Organizing Genetic Algorithm (SOGA) achieves a better balance between solution quality and runtime efficiency by integrating adaptive weights into the GA loop and enhancing initialization with Dijkstra's algorithm [14]. A hybrid algorithm combining a 3D packing strategy (Residual Space Optimization, RSO) with an Improved Genetic Algorithm (IGA) significantly improves stability and global optimal search capability by introducing an elite retention mechanism and enhanced sequential crossover on the basis of traditional genetic algorithms [15]. A hybrid algorithm that combines genetic simulated annealing-enhanced clustering with an improved Hopfield neural network effectively decomposes multi-traveling salesman problems (MTSP) into discrete TSP instances; the improved neural network algorithm features higher computational efficiency and easier access to global optimal solutions [16]. The Multi-Strategy Genetic Ant Colony Optimization (MSGACO) algorithm enhances ACO through strategies such as adaptive pheromone initialization and a three-level node selection mechanism, reducing path length by ~60.7% and convergence iterations by ~52% compared to traditional ant colony optimization [17].

The Fuzzy Genetic Algorithm (FGA) integrates fuzzy logic to model inherent uncertainties in the delivery process (e.g., traffic congestion, weather interference) and leverages GA's multi-objective optimization capability to generate optimal routes [18]. For takeaway delivery routing, a model constructed based on delivery personnel's real-time locations and order information introduces the Improved Genetic Algorithm-Particle Swarm Optimization (IGAPSO) algorithm, which reduces delivery time by 95.3 s, 35.16 s, and 10.55 s compared to Cultural Algorithm(CA), Simulated Annealing(SA), and Grey Wolf Optimization Algorithm(GWOA), respectively [19]. The combination of k-means clustering with GA optimizes truck-UAV tandem delivery networks, reducing total delivery time, energy consumption, and costs [20].

A new adaptive genetic algorithm adopted in urban logistics distribution models with constrained soft time windows, which correlates Crossover Probability (pc) and Mutation Probability(pm) values with iteration counts and individual fitness values, has proven effective compared to traditional genetic algorithms [21]. The improved Genetic Algorithm (GA), through preprocessing infeasible solutions and adopting an elite strategy, can search for optimal solutions regarding the number, sequence, and path of distribution vehicles, helping logistics enterprises reduce costs and improve efficiency while being applicable to manufacturing flow shop scheduling [22]. In path optimization for aviation logistics distribution centers, a new adaptive mutation genetic algorithm enhances local search capability and converges faster than general genetic algorithms [23].

2.3 Research Gaps and Contributions

Existing studies on truck-UAV collaboration primarily focus on traffic-restricted areas, post-disaster scenarios, and rural logistics, with limited attention to new retail contexts. For the truck-UAV collaborative delivery route optimization problem under urban traffic restrictions, trucks carrying goods navigate outer boundaries to dispatch/receive UAVs (which handle inner-zone deliveries), and a hybrid metaheuristic optimization algorithm is used to collaboratively optimize routes to minimize the completion time of all delivery tasks [24]. Our research innovates on this basis by adopting more flexible joint delivery scheduling: when the straight-line distance between merchants and customers is short, UAVs deliver directly to customers after pickup without returning to the truck's parking point, avoiding the redundant "pickup-return-relaunch-delivery" path and shortening total task duration. Teimoury Ebrahim et al. addressed the sustainable time-dependent urban truck-UAV routing problem with rendezvous locations in crowded urban areas, using a hybrid variable neighborhood search to balance economic, environmental, and social sustainability [25]. Our research also considers actual traffic changes and adopts a time-phased differentiated strategy: during peak hours, UAVs delivering directly are forced to fly to recycling points to avoid congestion caused by returning to the original truck; during off-peak hours, cost priority is adopted to allow return to the original truck, significantly improving delivery efficiency and service time.

E-commerce and retail companies are exploring the use of s for last-mile delivery to reduce time and costs. Relevant research has explored the truck-UAV combined delivery concept in retail, allowing autonomous UAVs to launch/land from trucks [26]. In the same new retail context, our research meets consumers' demand for "instant gratification" through a direct UAV delivery mode and dynamic hybrid algorithm response mechanism.

The main contributions of this research are:

- Dynamic recycling framework: Extending static recycling models to a time-phased, zone-divided system, with dedicated UAV recycling points during peaks and truck-integrated recycling during off-peak hours—adapting to new retail's temporal variability.
- Short-distance direct delivery mode: Enabling UAVs to establish a direct delivery link from merchants to customers immediately after picking up goods for short-distance orders, abandoning the truck depot transfer structure in traditional models—catering to new retail's demand for instant gratification.
- Multi-cost quantification: Introducing dynamic battery consumption functions and time-sensitive coefficients to quantify transport, time, and carbon emission costs, converting multi-objective optimization into a weighted total cost minimization problem for tractability.

3 Problem Description and Model

This section focuses on core challenges of truck-UAV joint distribution in new retail scenarios, defining the problem scope, key symbols, and constructing an optimization model. By quantifying transport, time, and carbon emission costs, and integrating spatiotemporal dynamics and heterogeneous fleet constraints, it forms a systematic analytical framework to lay a theoretical foundation for algorithm design.

3.1 Problem Description

Driven by the new retail wave, urban logistics delivery faces multiple challenges of timeliness, flexibility, and cost control. This research builds an efficient collaborative system using a truck-UAV joint delivery mode in the dynamic network of urban logistics delivery with the goal of cost minimization in new retail scenarios. It aims to break through the bottlenecks of traditional delivery modes through efficient collaboration of multimodal transport tools, providing intelligent and green solutions for modern urban logistics.

In the joint delivery system, trucks serve as key mobile support, driving to pickup parking points according to precisely planned routes; these pickup points are determined through detailed analysis of merchant distribution and goods supply to ensure efficient pickup. After arriving at pickup parking points, trucks remain stationary to lay a solid foundation for subsequent UAV operations. A centralized UAV pool is set up to realize unified management and flexible allocation of UAVs; in new retail delivery scenarios,

UAVs are dispatched from the UAV pool to trucks at pickup parking points and take off to pick up goods from merchants under regional restrictions and their own performance constraints.

The action strategy of UAVs after pickup is dynamically adjusted according to the distance between merchants and customers: when the distance between merchants and customers is short, UAVs deliver directly to customers after pickup and choose to fly to designated recycling points (peak hours) or return to the original truck (off-peak hours) depending on the time period after delivery; if the distance is long, UAVs fly directly to designated recycling points for centralized management after completing pickup tasks during peak hours to cope with a large number of order demands, while flying back to the original truck with goods during off-peak hours.

Subsequently, trucks drive to delivery parking points selected around customer-dense areas such as communities through rigorous customer density analysis according to the established route; after arrival, they stop again, and UAVs take off again for long-distance orders, relying on their load capacity and endurance to quickly deliver goods to customers in specific surrounding areas, with a single flight accurately covering multiple customer points, significantly improving overall delivery efficiency. After tasks are completed, UAVs return to trucks to replace with fully charged batteries during off-peak hours and then participate in the next round of delivery. Meanwhile, it is strictly ensured that each customer receives service only once during the entire delivery process to guarantee delivery accuracy and efficiency, enabling customers to truly obtain service value. The specific operation logic of the above truck-UAV joint distribution system is shown in Fig. 1.

To accurately construct the mathematical model, the following reasonable assumptions are made: 1) Information such as location coordinates of merchants and customers and customer goods demand is known and determined; 2) Sufficient trucks and UAVs with unified standards of models and functions are available to fully meet delivery and pickup tasks; 3) The load limit and endurance mileage of UAVs are clearly defined; 4) UAVs can fly to designated recycling points or land nearby after short-distance direct delivery during peak hours, and can only take off and land at corresponding parked trucks or designated areas during off-peak hours; 5) Takeoff and landing of UAVs on trucks must be standardized within specific areas related to designated parking points (such as takeoff and landing zones planned in communities); 6) Each customer is visited by UAVs only once; 7) Trucks are equipped with sufficient batteries to stably support continuous operation of UAVs.

This research focuses on using theoretical tools such as operations research and intelligent optimization algorithms to scientifically and precisely plan truck driving routes and parking strategies, accurately arrange the task sequence and flight trajectories of UAV delivery and pickup, strive to reduce delivery costs, effectively cut carbon emissions, and maximize customer value and satisfaction, creating an efficient, environmentally friendly, and highly practical joint delivery mode to open up new paths for the optimization and upgrading of urban logistics delivery systems.

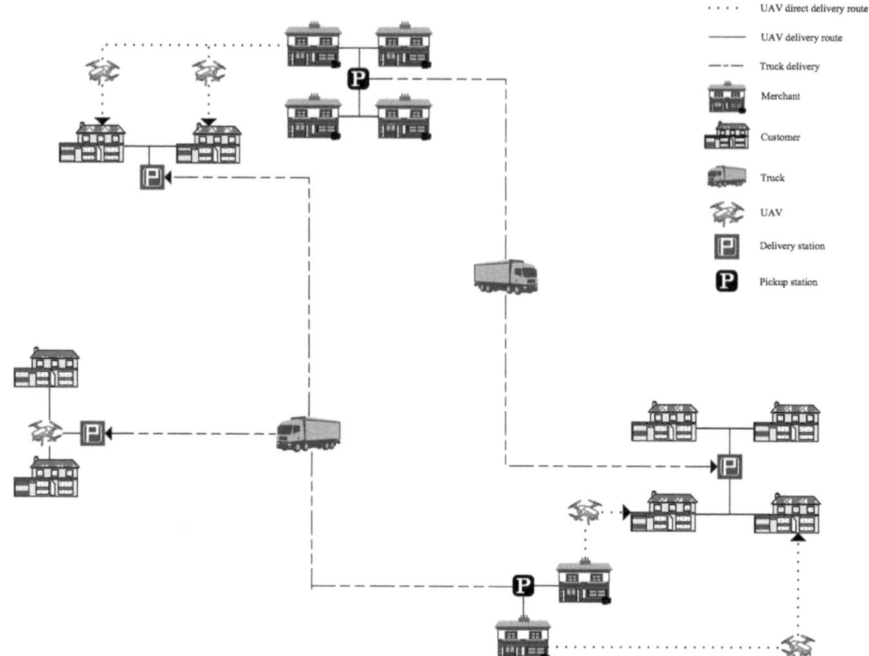

Fig. 1. Example Diagram of Truck-UAV Joint Distribution.

3.2 Symbol Explanation

To clearly describe the model, a series of symbols are defined first, including set symbols, parameter symbols, and decision variable symbols. For example, S represents the set of merchants, K represents the set of trucks, U represents the set of UAVs, etc. Parameter symbols such as α is the transport cost weight coefficient, β is the time cost weight coefficient, γ is the carbon emission cost weight coefficient, etc. Decision variables include binary variables, integer variables, and continuous variables to describe the driving paths and task execution of trucks and UAVs. Important symbols and their meanings in this research are shown in Table 1, Table 2 and Table 3.

3.3 Model Establishment

Considering transport costs, time costs, and carbon emission costs in the joint delivery process, a multi-objective optimization model with the goal of minimizing total costs is established.

Transport costs include costs incurred by trucks during transportation and flight costs of UAVs:

$$C_{transport} = C_{truck} + C_{drone} + C_{driect} + C_{pickup} \tag{1}$$

$$C_{truck} = \sum_{k \in K} \sum_{i,j \in I} \left(c_{fuel}^{k} \cdot d_{ij} + c_{oper}^{k} \right) \cdot x_{ij}^{k} \tag{2}$$

Table 1. Symbols and Definitions of Sets.

Symbol	Definition
S	Set of merchants, $s \in S$
I	Set of parking points(including warehouses), $i \in I$
I_s	Subset of parking points accessible to merchants, $I_s \subseteq I$
D	Set of tasks (pickup/delivery), $d \in D$
D^{pick}	Subset of pick up tasks (from merchants to trucks), $D^{pick} \subseteq D$
$D^{deliver}$	Subset of delivery tasks (from trucks to customers), $D^{deliver} \subseteq D$
D_{direct}	Subset of tasks allowing direct delivery, $D_{direct} \subseteq D$
K	Set of trucks, $k \in K$
U	Set of UAVs, $u \in U$
U_k	Subset of UAVs carried by truck k, $U_k \subseteq U$

$$C_{drone} = \sum_{u \in U} \sum_{d \in D} [\left(c^u_{battery} \cdot \frac{d_{id}}{L_u} + c^u_{main}\right) \cdot z^u_{id} + \left(c^u_{battery} \cdot \frac{d_{id'}}{L_u} + c^u_{main}\right) z^{u,dir}_{id}] \quad (3)$$

$$C_{direct} = \sum_{u \in U} \sum_{d \in D_{direct}} c^u_{lost} \cdot z^{u,dir}_{id} + \sum_{j \in R} c^r_{jd} \cdot r^u_{jd} \quad (4)$$

$$C_{pickup} = \sum_{s \in S} \sum_{d \in D_{direct}} c_s \cdot \left(z^u_{id} + z^{u,dir}_{id}\right) q^u_{sd} + \sum_{k \in K} \sum_{i \in I} c^k_{hold} \cdot t^i_{pick} \quad (5)$$

Time costs include truck time costs, UAV time costs, and recycling time costs, which are included in total costs after weighting:

$$C_{time} = T_{truck} + T_{drone} + T_{wait} \quad (6)$$

$$T_{truck} = \sum_{k \in K} \sum_{i,j \in A} \left(\frac{d_{ij}}{v_k} + t^k_{stop}\right) \cdot x^k_{ij} \quad (7)$$

$$T_{drone} = \sum_{u \in U} \sum_{d \in D} [\left(\frac{d_{id}}{v_u} + t^u_{uv}\right) \cdot z^u_{id} + \left(\frac{d_{id'}}{v_u} + t^u_{load}\right) z^{u,dir}_{id}] \quad (8)$$

$$T_{wait} = \sum_{i \in I} t^i_{wait} \quad (9)$$

Carbon emission costs include truck carbon emission costs and UAV carbon emission costs, which are included in total costs after weighting:

$$C_{carbon} = \alpha_{carbon}(E_{truck} + E_{drone}) \quad (10)$$

$$E_{truck} = \sum_{k \in K} \sum_{i,j \in A} e_k \cdot d_{ij} \cdot x^k_{ij} \quad (11)$$

Table 2. Symbols and Definitions of Parameters.

Symbol	Definition
α, β, γ	Weight coefficients for transportation cost, time cost, and carbon emission cost
t_d	Task timestamp
T_d	Binary marker defined for each task d; 1 if $t_d \in T_{busy}$, otherwise 0
c_{fuel}^{k}	Fuel cost per unit distance for truck k
c_{oper}^{k}	Fixed cost per trip for truck k
v_k	Average speed of truck k
e_k	Carbon emission per unit distance for truck k
Q_k	Maximum capacity of truck k (number of UAVs or goods)
t_{stop}^{k}	Fixed parking time of truck k at parking points
t_{pick}^{i}	Additional parking time required for truck to complete pickup operation at parking point i
t_{wait}^{i}	Additional parking time for truck to wait for UAV recycling
c_{hold}^{k}	Goods storage cost of truck k at parking points
c_s	Sum of the fixed pickup cost for merchants and the facility access cost
$c_{battery}^{u}$	Battery cost per unit distance for UAV u
c_{main}^{u}	Maintenance cost per task for UAV u
v_u	Average flight speed of UAV u
e_u	Carbon emission per unit distance for UAV u
W_u	Maximum load capacity of UAV u
L_u	Endurance mileage per charge for UAV u
B_u	Endurance capability of a single battery for UAV u
t_{uv}^{u}	Total loading + unloading time for UAV u
c_{lost}^{u}	Idle cost of UAV u after direct delivery
c_{jd}^{r}	Recycling cost of UAV from customer to recycling point j
d_{ij}	Distance from parking point i to j
d_{id}	Round-trip distance from parking point i to task d
$d_{id'}$	One-way distance from parking point i to task d
w_o	Goods weight of order o
$[t_{o,min}, t_{o,max}]$	Time window of order o
$[t_{s,min}, t_{s,max}]$	Pickup time window of merchants

Table 3. Symbols and Definitions of Decision Variables.

Symbol	Definition
x_{ij}^k	Binary variable; 1 if truck k travels from i to j, otherwise 0
y_i	Binary variable; 1 if parking point i is activated (i.e., truck parks at the point), otherwise 0
t_i^k	Arrival time of truck k at parking point i
z_{id}^u	Binary variable; 1 if UAV u performs task d from i and returns, otherwise 0
$z_{id}^{u,dir}$	Binary variable; 1 if UAV u performs task d from i and does not return, otherwise 0
r_{jd}^u	Binary variable; 1 if UAV u is recycled at recycling point j, otherwise 0
T_{id}^u	Takeoff time of UAV u for task d
b_{iu}	Number of battery replacements for UAV u at parking point i
E_{iu}	Remaining battery (proportion) of UAV u when leaving parking point i
σ_d	Actual service time for task d
η_d	Binary type indicating whether task d is completed

$$E_{drone} = \sum_{u \in U} \sum_{d \in D} e_u \cdot \left(\frac{d_{id} \cdot z_{id}^u + d_{id}' \cdot z_{id}^{u,dir}}{L_u} \right) \tag{12}$$

Considering the aforementioned objectives and constraints, the objective function establishes a weighted total cost minimization goal. It integrates the transportation cost, time cost, and carbon emission cost through the weighting coefficients α, β, and γ:

$$minZ = \alpha C_{transport} + \beta C_{time} + \gamma C_{carbon} \tag{13}$$

s.t.

$$\sum_{j \in I} x_{0j}^k = 1, \sum_{i \in I} x_{i0}^k = 1 \ \forall k \in K \tag{14}$$

$$\sum_{j \in I} x_{ij}^k = \sum_{j \in I} x_{ji}^k \ \forall k \in K, i \in I \tag{15}$$

$$y_i \geq x_{ij}^k \ \forall k \in K, (i,j) \in A \tag{16}$$

$$\sum_{u \in U_k} \sum_{d \in D} (z_{id}^u + z_{id}^{u,dir}) \leq Q_k \cdot y_i \forall k \in K, i \in I \tag{17}$$

Truck Routing Constraints: Equations (14) and (15) ensure that each truck's route forms a closed loop, i.e., starting from and returning to the warehouse. In Eq. (16) guarantees that trucks can only perform operations at a parking point if they park there. In Eq. (17) limits the number of UAVs carried by trucks to not exceed the upper limit.

$$\sum_{u \in U} \sum_{i \in I} \left(z_{id}^u + z_{id}^{u,dir} \right) = 1 \ \forall d \in D \tag{18}$$

$$\sum_{d \in D} w_d \cdot \left(z_{id}^u + z_{id}^{u,dir} \right) \leq W_u \ \forall u \in U, i \in I \tag{19}$$

$$\sum_{d \in D} d_{id} \cdot z_{id}^u \leq L_u \ \forall u \in U, i \in I \tag{20}$$

$$\sum_{d \in D} d_{id\prime} \cdot z_{id}^{u,dir} \leq L_u \ \forall u \in U, i \in I \tag{21}$$

UAV Mission Constraints: Equation (18) ensures that each task is performed by only one UAV (one UAV per task). In Eq. (19) limits the goods weight of a single UAV task to not exceed its maximum load capacity. In Eq. (20) and (21) ensure that the round-trip distance of a single UAV flight does not exceed the endurance mileage.

$$t_{o,min} \leq \sigma_c \leq t_{o,max} \forall d \in D \tag{22}$$

$$T_{id}^u \geq t_i^k - M\left(1 - z_{id}^u\right) \tag{23}$$

$$T_{id}^u + \frac{d_{id}}{v_u} + t_{uv}^u \leq t_i^k + t_{stop}^k \tag{24}$$

$$T_{id}^u \geq t_i^k - M\left(1 - z_{id}^{u,dir}\right) \tag{25}$$

$$T_{id}^u + \frac{d_{id}'}{v_u} + t_{load}^u \leq t_i^k + t_{stop}^k \tag{26}$$

Time Constraints: In Eq. (22) guarantees that customer delivery time is within the promised time window. In Eq. (23), (24), (25), and (26) ensure that UAV tasks are completed during truck parking, considering return and direct flight modes.

$$E_{ju} \leq E_{iu} - \frac{\sum_{d \in D}\left(d_{id}z_{id}^u + d_{id\prime}z_{id}^{u,dir}\right)}{L_u} + b_{iu} \ \forall u \in U, i,j \in I \tag{27}$$

$$b_{iu} \geq \frac{\sum_{d \in D} d_{id}z_{id}^u + d_{id}'z_{id}^{u,dir}}{B_u L_u} \ \forall u \in U, i \in I \tag{28}$$

Battery Management Constraints: In Eq. (27) ensures that the remaining battery of UAVs when leaving parking points deducts task consumption. In Eq. (28) ensures that batteries are replaced when the power is insufficient to support tasks.

$$\sum_{u \in U}\sum_{i \in I} z_{id\,pick}^u = \sum_{u \in U}\sum_{i \in I} z_{id\,deliver}^u \ \forall d \in D \tag{29}$$

$$r_{jd}^u \geq T_d \bullet z_{id}^{u,dir} u \in U \tag{30}$$

$$r_{jd}^u \geq 1 - T_d u \in U \tag{31}$$

$$t_{wait}^i \leq M\left(1 - T_d\right) \forall i \in I \tag{32}$$

Pickup and Delivery Constraints: Equation (29) restricts pickup and delivery tasks of the same order to be completed by the same UAV. In Eq. (30) indicates that UAVs delivering directly during peak hours are forced to fly to recycling points. In Eq. (31) indicates that UAVs delivering directly during off-peak hours are allowed to return to the original truck. In Eq. (32) guarantees time control of truck waiting time.

$$x_{ij}^{k}, y_i, z_{id}^{u}, q_{sd}^{u}, r_{jd}^{u}, \delta_c, \eta_o \in \{0,1\} \tag{33}$$

$$b_{iu} \in Z^{+} \tag{34}$$

$$t_i^{k}, T_{id}^{u}, E_{iu}, \sigma_c \geq 0 \tag{35}$$

Auxiliary Constraints: Equations (33), (34), and In Eq. (35) clarify variable types and value ranges.

4 Algorithm Design

This section develops a hybrid heuristic algorithm for the optimization model, addressing the combinatorial explosion in dynamic task-route joint optimization. It includes encoding, initial solution construction, and genetic operations, integrates machine learning to enhance efficiency, balances global exploration and local optimization, and adapts to temporal dynamics in new retail, providing an algorithmic basis for subsequent validation.

To achieve efficient solution in dynamic scenarios, this paper designs a hybrid heuristic algorithm integrating genetic algorithm and simulated annealing, and the flow is shown in Fig. 2, It shows a hybrid heuristic algorithm workflow for optimizing truck-UAV delivery in new retail. It integrates genetic and simulated annealing algorithms. Starting from data input, it codes, evolves solutions, and outputs optimal plans after meeting termination conditions, applying smart tech to logistics. The following sections will expound on the fundamental thinking of the algorithmic solution, with a focus on systematically interpreting each component of this flowchart, to clarify how it supports the optimization of truck-UAV delivery operations in the new retail context.

4.1 Initial Solution Construction

Initial Population Generation: Decision variables in the model are encoded into chromosomes. Decision variables for truck driving paths and UAV task allocation are encoded separately to construct complete chromosomes, representing different delivery schemes. An initial population that conforms to encoding rules and meets the basic constraints of the model is randomly generated, such as ensuring closed truck paths and compliance of UAV load and endurance with requirements. These chromosomes serve as the starting point for genetic algorithm search.

Fitness Function Definition: The objective function of the model is used as the fitness function. The total cost of the delivery scheme corresponding to each chromosome is calculated; the lower the cost, the higher the fitness, reflecting a better scheme.

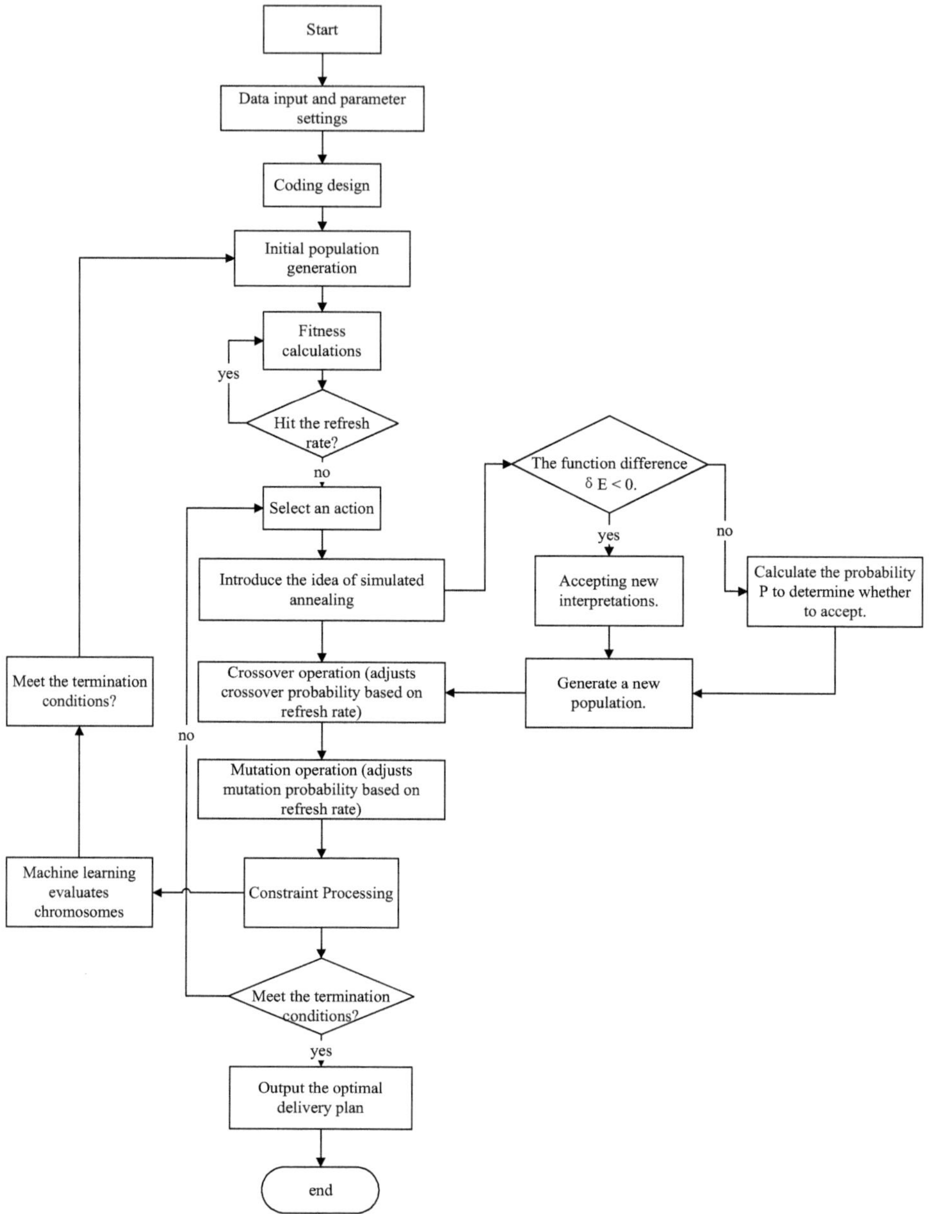

Fig. 2. Algorithm Flowchart.

Genetic Operations: Selection: Chromosomes are selected based on fitness by combining roulette wheel selection and tournament selection. In a dynamic demand environment, fitness is re-evaluated each time the refresh frequency is reached to ensure excellent schemes enter the next generation. Meanwhile, the idea of simulated annealing is introduced: according to the current "temperature" and Metropolis criterion, worse solutions are accepted with a higher probability in the early stage of the algorithm, and the acceptance probability decreases with iteration to avoid falling into local optima.

Crossover: New chromosomes are generated by exchanging partial gene segments of selected chromosomes. The crossover probability is adjusted according to the dynamic demand refresh frequency: appropriately increased when the frequency is high to accelerate convergence to new optimal solutions; kept low when the frequency is low to avoid excessive disturbance.

Mutation: Mutation is performed on the genes of chromosomes with a low probability to change gene values, thereby maintaining population diversity and preventing the algorithm from falling into a local optimum. During dynamic demand refresh, mutation can help the algorithm adapt to new demands. When the refresh frequency is high, the mutation probability is appropriately increased to enhance the diversity of solutions; when the refresh frequency is low, the low mutation probability is maintained to stabilize the algorithm's search direction.

Constraint Handling: During genetic operations, newly generated chromosomes are ensured to meet various constraints of the model. Dynamic demand refresh may introduce new constraints or change existing ones, such as time window restrictions for new orders. The algorithm checks and repairs chromosomes at each refresh to ensure they always meet constraints.

Integration of Machine Learning and Deep Learning: Machine learning assistance: Machine learning algorithms are used to learn historical data, and prediction models are established. In the genetic annealing algorithm, these models are used to preliminarily evaluate newly generated chromosomes, screen out more potential individuals, reduce invalid searches, and improve algorithm efficiency.

Deep learning optimization: A deep learning model is constructed, with demand data, vehicle information, task information, etc., as input and approximate optimal delivery schemes as output. The output of the deep learning model is used as the initial population of the genetic annealing algorithm, or model prediction results are regularly fused with the current population during algorithm iteration to guide the algorithm to converge to the global optimal solution faster.

4.2 Algorithm Termination Criteria

Two termination conditions are set: maximum number of iterations and no significant improvement in the optimal solution for several consecutive generations. When the termination conditions are met, the algorithm stops iterating, and the delivery scheme corresponding to the optimal chromosome is output as the approximate optimal solution.

5 Conclusion

Targeting logistics delivery needs in new retail scenarios, this research proposes a truck-UAV joint distribution optimization model. Through dynamic task allocation, path planning, and multi-objective optimization algorithms, it significantly improves delivery efficiency, reduces costs, and considers environmental protection goals.

The main conclusions are as follows:

1) Dynamic recycling strategy improves efficiency. During peak order periods, a centralized UAV recycling strategy is adopted, and UAVs are guided to designated recycling points through dynamic scheduling algorithms, effectively alleviating scheduling pressure and improving the turnover efficiency of UAVs and trucks; during off-peak order periods, the layout of truck parking points and UAV return paths are optimized to reduce redundant trips, lower recycling costs and truck empty driving rate, and achieve efficient resource utilization.

2) Short-distance direct flight mode optimizes timeliness. For short-distance and light-load orders, a UAV direct delivery mode is proposed to reduce intermediate transshipment links and significantly shorten delivery time. This mode is particularly suitable for delivery of goods with high timeliness requirements such as fresh products, improving customer satisfaction.

3) Designs a dynamic hybrid genetic algorithm. To address the limitations of traditional optimization algorithms in multi-objective problems, this research designs a dynamic hybrid genetic algorithm. By intelligently adjusting parameters and retaining high-quality solutions, the algorithm synchronously optimizes delivery paths and task allocation. While reducing costs, it also reduces carbon emissions, achieving a balance between economic benefits and green development.

Acknowledgments. This study was funded by Project of Xi'an Social Science Planning Fund (grant number 25JX105).

References

1. Helm, S., Kim, S.H., Van Riper, S.: Navigating the "retail apocalypse": a framework of consumer evaluations of the new retail landscape. J. Retail. Consum. Serv. **54**, 101683 (2020)

2. Salama, M.R., Srinivas, S.: Collaborative truck multi-drone routing and scheduling problem: package delivery with flexible launch and recovery sites. Transp. Res. Part E: Logist. Transp. Rev. **164**, 102788 (2022)

3. Moshref-Javadi, M., Hemmati, A., Winkenbach, M.: A truck and drones model for last-mile delivery: a mathematical model and heuristic approach. Appl. Math. Model. **80**, 290–318 (2020)

4. Rahimi, S.K., Rahmani, D.: A hybrid multi-objective solution approach for a reliable truck-drone routing problem integrated with pickup and delivery services. Transp. Lett. **17**(2), 230–248 (2025)

5. Mokhtari-Moghadam, A., Salhi, A., Yang, X., Nguyen, T.T., Pourhejazy, P.: A multi-objective approach for the integrated planning of drone and robot assisted truck operations in last-mile delivery. Expert Syst. Appl. **269**, 126434 (2025)

6. Heidari, A., Orazani, S.M.H., Khalilzadeh, M., Jolai, F.: A multi-objective model for cooperative delivery of customer orders using multiple trucks and UAVs considering weather conditions. Internet Things **29**, 101468 (2025)

7. Bektur, G.: A reinforcement learning-based multiobjective heuristic algorithm for multiple-truck routing problems with heterogeneous drones. Appl. Soft Comput. **167**(PA), 112290 (2024)

8. Chen, P., Wang, Q.L.: Learning for multiple purposes: a Q-learning enhanced hybrid meta-heuristic for parallel drone scheduling traveling salesman problem. Comput. Ind. Eng. **187**, 109851 (2024)

9. Zhang, S., Liu, S.L., Xu, W.B., Wang, W.R.: A novel multi-objective optimization model for the vehicle routing problem with drone delivery and dynamic flight endurance. Comput. Ind. Eng. **173**, 108679 (2022)

10. Lu, Y.C., Yang, C., Yang, J.: A multi-objective humanitarian pickup and delivery vehicle routing problem with drones. Ann. Oper. Res. **319**(1), 291–353 (2022)

11. Momeni, M., Soleimani, H., Shahparvari, S., Afshar-Nadjafi, B.: Coordinated routing system for fire detection by patrolling trucks with drones. Int. J. Disaster Risk Reduct. **73**, 102859 (2022)

12. Cao, Q.K., Zhang, X.F., Ren, X.Y.: Path Optimization of Joint Delivery Mode of Trucks and UAVs. Mathematical Problems in Engineering (2021)

13. Wang, K.Z., Yuan, B., Zhao, M.T., Lu, Y.W.: Cooperative route planning for the drone and truck in delivery services: a bi-objective optimisation approach. J. Oper. Res. Soc. **71**(10), 1657–1674 (2020)

14. Ndikuriyo, Y., Zhang, Y.G., Fom, D.D.: An improved self-organizing genetic algorithm for optimizing container transportation routing problems under times windows. Oper. Res. Forum **6**(2), 71 (2025)

15. Yin, X.Y., Yu, Z.H., Liu, Y., Chen, Y.M., Guo, A.: An improved approach for vehicle routing problem with three-dimensional loading constraints based on genetic algorithm and residual space optimized strategy. Processes **13**(5), 1449 (2025)

16. Liu, S., Liu, D., Le, M.L.: Multi-UAV delivery path optimization based on fuzzy c-means clustering algorithm based on annealing genetic algorithm and improved Hopfield neural network. World Electr. Veh. J. **16**(3), 157 (2025)

17. Li, Z., Du, M.Y., Qin, J.L., Chen, X.C.: Research on robot path planning based on multi-strategy genetic ant colony optimization algorithm. Inf. Sci. **718**, 122407 (2025)

18. Tang, W.G.: Optimization of urban terminal delivery routes using fuzzy genetic algorithm and its practical application. J. Comput. Methods Sci. Eng. **25**(4), 3453–3464 (2025)

19. Cheng, C.X.: Research on takeaway distribution path optimisation based on genetic algorithm combined with particle swarm optimised simulated annealing. Int. J. Wirel. Mob. Comput. **27**(2), 173–183 (2024)

20. Ferrandez, S.M., Harbison, T., Weber, T., Sturges, R., Rich, R.: Optimization of a truck-drone in tandem delivery network using k-means and genetic algorithm. J. Ind. Eng. Manag. **9**(2), 374–388 (2016)

21. Cui, H.X., Qiu, J.L., Cao, J.D., Guo, M., Chen, X.Y., Gorbachev, S.: Route optimization in township logistics distribution considering customer satisfaction based on adaptive genetic algorithm. Math. Comput. Simul **204**, 28–42 (2023)

22. Li, J.Q., Wang, Y., Du, K.L.: Distribution path optimization by an improved genetic algorithm combined with a divide-and-conquer strategy. Technologies **10**(4), 81 (2022)

23. Sun, Y.X., Geng, N.N., Gong, S.L., Yang, Y.B.: Research on improved genetic algorithm in path optimization of aviation logistics distribution center. J. Intell. Fuzzy Syst. **38**(1), 29–37 (2019)

24. Weng, Y.Y., Wu, R.Y., Zheng, Y.J.: Cooperative truck-drone delivery path optimization under urban traffic restriction. Drones **7**(1), 59 (2023)

25. Teimoury, E., Rashid, R.: A hybrid variable neighborhood search heuristic for the sustainable time-dependent truck-drone routing problem with rendezvous locations. J. Heuristics **30**(1–2), 1–41 (2023)

26. Kitjacharoenchai, P., Lee, S.: Vehicle routing problem with drones for last mile delivery. Procedia Manuf. **39**, 314–324 (2019)

A New Improved Algorithm for a Rich Production and Routing Problem

Mário Leite, Telmo Pinto, and Cláudio Alves[(✉)]

Centro ALGORITMI/LASI, Universidade do Minho,
Campus de Gualtar, 4710-057 Braga, Portugal
{mario.leite,telmo,claudio}@dps.uminho.pt

Abstract. This paper addresses a rich integrated combinatorial optimization problem designated by Production Routing Problem (PRP) inspired by the real-world case study. The PRP involves coordinating production and distribution decisions over a finite planning horizon, divided into periods, for multiple products characterized by heterogeneous attributes, such as weight, size, and number of components. This PRP incorporates several constraints, including sequence-dependent setups, safety stocks and limited production capacity, multi-period routing, and customers with multiple time windows and deadlines. The objective is to minimize the total cost, which comprises setup costs, inventory holding, and transportation expenses. This integration of production and distribution decisions introduces temporal and spatial interdependencies which make the problem NP-hard. To tackle this problem, we propose a hybrid approach that combines a Variable Neighborhood Search metaheuristic with an embedded Integer Programming model. The proposed approach is evaluated through extensive computational experiments on benchmark instances, demonstrating its effectiveness in solving the PRP and handling its inherent combinatorial complexity.

Keywords: Production and Routing · Optimization · Hybrid Algorithms

1   Introduction

Supply chains are becoming increasingly complex. To address the challenges related with their management, effective and integrated solution approaches are essential. In this context, production and distribution activities, which were previously treated as separate and sequential processes, are now being increasingly integrated in order to maximize overall efficiency [1,6].

A partial perspective of the supply chain, where processes are treated separately, leads typically to inefficient decision-making and, inevitably, constrains future choices. In contrast, an integrated view of supply chain processes allows to aspire to globally optimal decisions. The issue is that, combining problems that are already complex on their own results naturally in problems of even greater complexity. In this context, the development of efficient heuristic-based approaches is of paramount importance, especially when the goal is to solve large-scale real-world instances [20]. The expectation is that the increase in complexity will be compensated by higher-quality solutions [12].

J. Barata et al. (Eds.): IN4PL 2025, CCIS 2826, pp. 224–241, 2026.
https://doi.org/10.1007/978-3-032-15579-5_14

One of the first studies on coordinated production and distribution planning can be found in [5]. In this paper, the authors demonstrated the tremendous potential of joint decision-making by showing cost reductions of up to one-fifth of the total value. As production and distribution are considered the core processes of the supply chain due to their central role, the joint optimization of these stages has received significant attention in the literature. This interest has been further motivated by advances in mathematical modeling, heuristics, and combinatorial optimization techniques [8].

Solving a Production Routing Problem (PRP) involves making optimal and simultaneous decisions regarding production, routing, and inventory management. Considering these elements together is essential not only for improving operational efficiency but also in contexts involving perishable goods, where a lack of coordination can compromise product quality [2,10,16]. Coordination contributes to the development of more sustainable supply chains [19].

In this paper, we address the variant of the PRP described in [14]. The problem is based on a real case from a small make-to-order furniture company. It considers several practical aspects that are frequently forgotten, such as the existence of multiple products composed of various components/items with different weights and sizes, sequence-dependent setup times and costs, a heterogeneous fleet of vehicles, of multi-period routes, safety stock for each product component, customers with multiple time windows and deadlines, for example.

The objective is to determine the production quantities and sequencing of each item in every time period, along with the complete routing plan, including the timing of customer visits, such that the total cost of these activities is minimized. The authors propose a Mixed-Integer Programming (MIP) formulation for the problem [15]. However, this approach is only tractable for small-sized instances. As an alternative, the authors propose a heuristic decomposition method that yields results comparable to those of the MIP approach on small instances, but with significantly lower computational effort. For larger instances, the heuristic outperformed the exact method, which in many cases was unable to find a feasible solution within 24 h.

Several other approaches described in the literature follow a strategy similar to [14] based solving first the production subproblem and refining the routing plan afterwards [13,18]. In contrast, some approaches do the same but in the opposite direction: they define first a set of feasible routes and then they optimize the production plan using these predefined routes. For example, [7] resort to column generation to identify attractive routes and subsequently solve the PRP using this restricted set of routes. In [9], the authors propose a Mathematical Programming-based Heuristic that determines first the sequence of customer visits and then solves a restricted version of the problem using a MIP model.

In this paper, we describe a new hybrid algorithm for the Production Routing Problem (PRP) introduced in [14], which combines the Variable Neighborhood Search (VNS) metaheuristic with the exact solution of an Integer Programming (IP) model. The VNS has proven highly effective in various applications, often getting high-quality solutions for large-scale instances or acting as an accelerator for exact algorithms [17]. Our approach differs from [14] in that it starts by generating a set of high-quality routes.

Then, a Hybrid-VNS procedure is applied, which embeds a Mixed Integer Programming (MIP) model within each iteration to solve the PRP in an integrated manner.

The remainder of the paper is as follows. Section 2 provides a formal definition of the Production Routing Problem, including its main assumptions. Section 3 describes the proposed hybrid algorithm used to solve the problem. In Sect. 4, we discuss the results of the computational experiments. Section 5 summarizes the main conclusions.

2   The Integrated Production Routing Problem

We consider the production routing problem (PRP) in the context of a make-to-order furniture company, whose products $p \in \mathcal{P}$ require multiple units of different components. The company produces a set $\mathcal{C}$ of components, which are used in the assembly of the set $\mathcal{P}$ of final products. Each product $p \in \mathcal{P}$ has an associated weight, φ_p. To produce one unit of p, we need η_{ap} units of component $a \in \mathcal{C}$. If a component a is not in the bill of materials of product p, *i.e.*, if $a \notin \mathcal{F}_p$, where $\mathcal{F}_p \subseteq \mathcal{C}$ denotes the set of components needed to assemble p, then $\eta_{ap} = 0$. In this type of industry, final assembly is often postponed and performed at the customer or retail site. This is common in sectors where finished products share subassemblies and interchangeable components. Consequently, the focus is on determining the quantities of components to produce in each period.

The time horizon $\mathcal{T}$ is divided into equal-length periods $t \in \mathcal{T}$. In each time period, the production facility is available for K_t ($t \in \mathcal{T}$) time units. Producing one unit of item $a \in \mathcal{C}$ requires ρ_a time units. Multiple items can be produced within a single period. However, switching production from item $a \in \mathcal{C}$ to item $b \in \mathcal{C}$ incurs a setup cost $\hat{c}_{ab}$ and requires ς_{ab} time units for necessary operations such as cleaning, tooling replacement, calibration, and adjustment (setup time). Thus, both setup costs and setup times are sequence-dependent. Setups are continuous and can be carried over different time periods. Therefore, any setup in progress at the end of period t continues at the beginning of period $t+1$, without incurring additional time or cost, as these were already accounted for in period t. The parameters I_{a0} and $I_a^{\min}$ denote the initial and minimum inventory levels of item a, respectively, while h_a represents the unit inventory holding cost per period for each unit retained at the production facility before being shipped. The holding cost of an item $a \in \mathcal{C}$ is related to its two-dimensional size, specifically its width (W_a) and length (L_a). It is important to note that, in this problem, items produced in period t cannot be shipped in the same period, as they must undergo post-production activities such as packaging and quality inspection. Therefore, they become available for shipment only in the subsequent period, $t + 1$.

The complete directed graph $\mathcal{G} = (\mathcal{N}, \mathcal{A})$ represents the network, where $\mathcal{N}$ is the set of nodes and $\mathcal{A}$ is the set of directed arcs between them. The set of nodes is defined as $\mathcal{N} = \{0, 1, \ldots, n+1\}$, where nodes 1 through n represent the customers, and nodes 0 and $n + 1$ correspond to the depot (for departure and return, respectively).

The set of arcs is defined as $\mathcal{A} = \{(i, j) : i, j \in \mathcal{N}, i \neq j\}$, where each arc (i, j) represents a direct connection from node i to node j, associated with a travel time τ_{ij} and a travel cost c_{ij}. Each node $i \in \mathcal{N}$ is associated with a time window for each period $t \in \mathcal{T}$, denoted by $[\delta_{it}, \bar{\delta}_{it}]$. If customer i is scheduled to be visited during period

t, and the vehicle arrives before the start of the time window (δ_{it}), it must wait until the window opens to begin service. Conversely, if the vehicle arrives after the end of the time window ($\bar{\delta}_{it}$), it must wait until the start of the time window in the following period, $\delta_{i,t+1}$.

Let $\bar{C} = \mathcal{N}\backslash\{0, n+1\}$ be the set of customers. Each customer $i \in \bar{C}$, must be visited exactly once (split deliveries are not allowed). The demand of these customers is denoted by d_{pi} for a product $p \in \mathcal{P}$. The visit must occur before a delivery deadline Δ_i. The service time s_i is proportional to the total weight of the products requested, with λ denoting the time needed to load/unload one unit of weight φ_p The service time at node i, for each $i \in \bar{C}$, is given by $s_i = \lambda \sum_{p\in\mathcal{P}} \varphi_p d_{pi}$, and must begin at any time within the time window.

The fleet consists of a set $\mathcal{V}$ of heterogeneous vehicles. Each vehicle $v \in \mathcal{V}$ has a capacity θ_v, measured in weight units. Throughout the planning horizon, deliveries are carried out through a set of routes $r = \{1, \ldots, R\}$, with R representing an upper bound on the total number of routes. Routes may span multiple time periods (multi-period routes) or be confined to a single period. Each route must start at the depot (node 0), serve a sequence of customers, and then return to the depot (node $n+1$). Between successive routes, the vehicle must be loaded at the depot (node 0) according to the total demand of the customers to be served, taking an amount of time equal to the sum of the service times of all customers assigned to the route. The time required for this activity must be fully contained within the time window $\left[\delta_{0t}, \bar{\delta}_{0t}\right], \forall t \in \mathcal{T}$. Let $\bar{\mathcal{R}}$ denote the set of customers served by a route departing from the depot during $t \in \mathcal{T}$. The latest time to begin loading the vehicle assigned to route $\bar{\mathcal{R}}$ is given by $\bar{\delta}_{0t} - \lambda \sum_{p\in\mathcal{P}, i\in\bar{\mathcal{R}}} d_{pi}\varphi_p$. Therefore, the effective time available for loading in each period depends directly on the total demand of customers assigned to $\bar{\mathcal{R}}$.

The Production Routing Problem integrates production planning with distribution decisions. Given the assumptions described above, the production component aims to determine the quantity of each item to produce and the production sequence, ensuring that the required items are available to serve customers through delivery routes. The objective is to satisfy demand while minimizing the total cost of production and distribution.

3   A New Hybrid Algorithm for the PRP

This section presents a hybrid solution approach to solve the PRP in an integrated manner. The general framework is described in Sect. 3.1 and consists of three main phases, all of which rely on the resolution of an integer programming model described in this section. The initialization phase is explained in Sect. 3.2. Section 3.3 presents the VNS metaheuristic and its key components. Finally, Sect. 3.4 introduces the hybrid approach, which combines VNS with the integer programming model to integrate the routing and production plans.

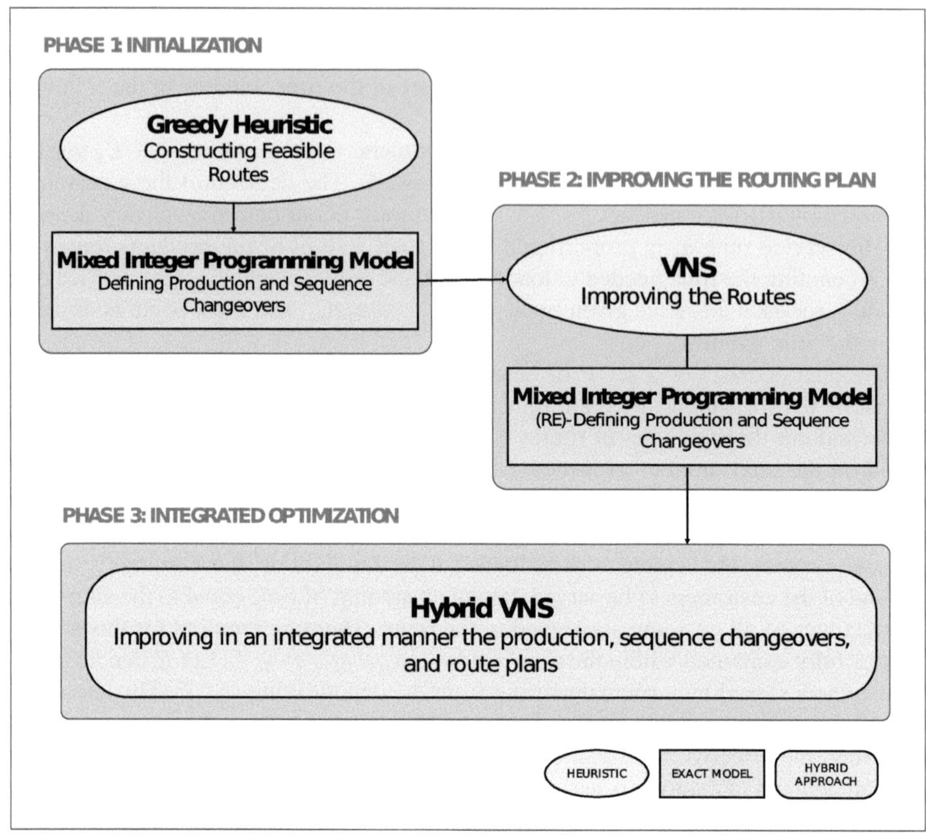

Fig. 1. Outline of the Algorithm.

3.1 Outline

Our general algorithm can be divided into three phases as illustrated in Fig. 1. A brief introduction of each phase is provided below.

- **Phase 1: Initialization (Sect.** 3.2)
  An initial set of feasible routes is generated using a greedy heuristic to determine the quantities that must be produced up to each time period. An optimal production plan is then defined by solving the MIP described below.
- **Phase 2: Improvement of the routing plan (Sect.** 3.3)
  To improve the incumbent routing plan, in Phase 2, we apply a basic VNS procedure using routing-based neighborhood structures, and then, we recompute the production plan by solving the MIP (1)–(11)
- **Phase 3: Hybrid VNS approach (Sect.** 3.4)
  A hybrid approach is used by integrating the MIP into the VNS framework. The traditional local search step is replaced by the solution of (1)–(11)

IP Model for Production Scheduling. The model we use is a production scheduling formulation inspired in [14] that determines the optimal quantities to produce in each time period, based on the routes previously calculated, which define product requirements across the different time periods. The parameters of the model and decision variables are defined below.

Parameters

td_{at} : Total demand for item a up to period t, $a \in \mathcal{C}, t \in \mathcal{T}$
    (or total quantity of item a to be delivered in period t);

M_{at} : A sufficiently large number, $M_{at} = \min \left\{ \left\lfloor \frac{K_t}{\rho_a} \right\rfloor , \sum_{a \in \mathcal{C}} \sum_{p \in \mathcal{P}} \eta_{ap} d_{pi} \right\}, a \in \mathcal{C}, t \in \mathcal{T}.$

Decision Variables

x_{at} : Number of items $a \in \mathcal{C}$ produced in period $t \in \mathcal{T}$;

y_{at} : 1 if the line is set up for item $a \in \mathcal{C}$ at the beginning of period $t \in \mathcal{T}$, 0 otherwise;

z_{abt} : 1 if there is a changeover from item a to item b $(a, b \in \mathcal{C})$ in period $t \in \mathcal{T}$, 0 otherwise;

π_{at} : Auxiliary variable for sequencing item $a \in \mathcal{C}$ in period $t \in \mathcal{T}$.

$$\min \sum_{a \in \mathcal{C}, t \in \mathcal{T}} h_a \left(\sum_{t'=1,\ldots,t} I_{a0} + x_{at'} - td_{at'} \right) + \sum_{a,b \in \mathcal{C}, t=1,\ldots,|\mathcal{T}|-1} \hat{c}_{ab} z_{abt} \tag{1}$$

subject to:

$$\sum_{a \in \mathcal{C}} \rho_a x_{at} + \sum_{a,b \in \mathcal{C}:a \neq b} \varsigma_{ab} z_{abt} \leq K_t, \qquad t = 1,\ldots,|\mathcal{T}|-1 \tag{2}$$

$$x_{at} \leq M_{at} \left(y_{at} + \sum_{b \in \mathcal{C}:b \neq a} z_{bat} \right), \qquad a \in \mathcal{C}, t = 1,\ldots,|\mathcal{T}|-1 \tag{3}$$

$$y_{at} + \sum_{b \in \mathcal{C}:b \neq a} z_{bat} = y_{at+1} + \sum_{b \in \mathcal{C}:b \neq a} z_{abt}, \qquad a \in \mathcal{C}, t = 1,\ldots,|\mathcal{T}|-1 \tag{4}$$

$$\sum_{a \in \mathcal{C}} y_{at} = 1, \qquad t = 1,\ldots,|\mathcal{T}|-1 \tag{5}$$

$$\pi_{at} \geq \pi_{bt} + 1 - |\mathcal{C}|(1 - z_{bat}), \qquad a \in \mathcal{C}, b \in \mathcal{C}, t = 1,\ldots,|\mathcal{T}|-1 \tag{6}$$

$$I_{a0} + \sum_{t'=1,\ldots,t-1} (x_{at'} - td_{at'}) \geq I_a^{min}, \qquad a \in \mathcal{C}, t \in \mathcal{T} \tag{7}$$

$$I_{a0} + \sum_{t'=1,\ldots,t-1} (x_{at'} - td_{at'}) \geq td_{at}, \qquad a \in \mathcal{C}, t \in \mathcal{T} \tag{8}$$

$$x_{at}, \pi_{at} \geq 0, \qquad a \in \mathcal{C}, t \in \mathcal{T} \tag{9}$$

$$y_{at} \in \{0,1\}, \qquad a \in \mathcal{C}, t \in \mathcal{T} \tag{10}$$

$$z_{abt} \in \{0,1\}, \qquad a,b \in \mathcal{C}, a \neq b, t \in \mathcal{T} \tag{11}$$

The objective function (1) consists in minimizing the total cost, which includes both inventory holding costs and production setup costs. The constraints (2) ensure that the maximum time available in each time period is not exceeded, whether for production operations or setups. Constraints (3) and (4) ensure that changeover variables representing transitions from the production of one item to another are correctly defined, and that the production sequence satisfies the setup dependencies. Constraints (5) guarantee that production occurs in consecutive time periods. Constraints (6) ensure a sequence of production that is consistent. Constraints (8) guarantee that each item is produced at least one period before it is needed for delivery. Inventory constraints (7) ensure that, in every period, the stock levels are at least equal to the minimum required safety stock.

3.2 Computing an Initial Solution

Each generated route is assigned to an available vehicle, prioritizing those with higher capacities. The first customer added to a route is the one closest to the depot. Subsequent customers are iteratively added to the route based on proximity to the last inserted customer, following the nearest-neighbor criterion. Each customer insertion must satisfy both the vehicle's capacity limit and the time window constraints. If inserting a candidate customer violates any constraint, the next closest unvisited customer is considered. This continues until no more customers can be added without exceeding the vehicle capacity. If unvisited customers remain, a new route is initiated and assigned to an available vehicle. If no vehicle is available at the desired departure time, the route is delayed until a vehicle becomes free. This procedure is repeated until all customers are assigned to feasible routes, while satisfying capacity constraints, time windows, and vehicle availability. Once the routes and their associated loading periods are determined, the required quantities of each item per period are known. The MIP model is then used to optimize production decisions, including the quantity and sequencing of items to be produced in each period. If the initial routing plan results in an infeasible IP solution, typically due to insufficient production time to meet high demand within a short window, the routes are iteratively postponed to later periods until a feasible solution is achieved.

3.3 Basic VNS with Fix-and-Optimize

Neighborhood Structures. A total of four neighborhood structures were developed (NS_k, $k \in \{1,2,3,4\}$), specifically designed to address the routing component of the problem. All of them are related either to intra- and inter-route customer exchanges, as follows.

- NS_1: <u>Insert one customer into another existing route</u>
  A neighboring solution is obtained by moving a customer from one route to another existing route.
- NS_2: <u>Insert one customer into a new route</u>
  A neighboring solution is obtained by moving a customer from a route with multiple customers and creating a new single-customer route

- NS_3: Swap two customers from the same route;
  A neighboring solution is obtained by swapping two customers from the same route.
- NS_4: Swap two customers from different routes
  neighboring solution is obtained by exchanging two customers assigned to different routes.

Fix-and-Optimize. In the scope of the basic VNS algorithm, the initial solution used corresponds to the partial solution obtained in Sect. 3.2, focusing exclusively on the routing component ($s_{partial}$).

Four neighborhood structures, NS_k with $k \in \{1, 2, 3, 4\}$, are explored sequentially. In Line 6, the *shake* procedure performs up to m_{max} consecutive moves using neighborhood k, *i.e.*, a sequence of up to m successive neighboring solutions, allowing for stronger perturbations of the incumbent solution. On the resulting route set ($s'_{partial}$), local search is applied using the same neighborhood k, following a first-improvement strategy (Line 7). If the routing cost of the new partial solution is lower than that of the incumbent, the solution is updated, and the neighborhood index is reset to $k = 1$ (Lines 8–10). Otherwise, the next neighborhood is considered (Lines 11–12), up to the maximum number of structures k_{max}. The basic VNS procedure runs until the time limit $t_{\max}$ is reached and is summarized in Algorithm 1.

Algorithm 1: Basic VNS steps.

```
 1: function VNS(s_partial, k_max, t_max, m_max)
 2:     t_start := CPUTime(); t := 0;
 3:     while (t ≤ t_max) do
 4:         k := 1;
 5:         while (k ≤ k_max) do
 6:             s'_partial := shake(s_partial, k, m_max);
 7:             s''_partial := localSearch(s'_partial, k);
 8:             if ( f(s''_partial) < f(s_partial) ) then
 9:                 s_partial := s''_partial;
10:                 k := 1;
11:             else
12:                 k := k + 1;
13:         t := CPUTime() - t_start;
```

After executing Algorithm 1, the MIP model presented in Sect. 3.1 is solved to compute the corresponding production plan and to ensure the global feasibility of the solution. As in Phase 1, if production capacity is insufficient to satisfy high demand within a short time window, the routes are iteratively postponed to subsequent periods.

3.4   A Hybrid VNS Approach

Our hybrid approach embeds the resolution of the MIP model described in Sect. 3.1, which addresses the production planning component, into the main framework of the

VNS metaheuristic. The model determines the optimal production and inventory levels for each period such that the total operational costs are minimized. It replaces the local search step used in standard VNS procedures. As a result, in each iteration, we evaluate a globally feasible solution that jointly considers both production and distribution decisions.

Additionally, an extra neighborhood structure is introduced to change the starting time of the routes, specifically designed for use during the shaking phase of the hybrid VNS in Phase 3.

- NS_0: Change route period
  neighboring solution is obtained by modifying the departure period of a route. Consequently, the arrival times at all customer locations along that route are rescheduled.

It is worth noting that modifying the departure time of a route does not directly affect the routing cost. For this reason, this neighborhood is not used during Algorithm 1. However, such changes can have a significant impact on production planning. Specifically, scheduling routes in the early periods of the planning horizon forces production in those periods to focus on meeting urgent demand. Conversely, delaying route departures toward the end of the horizon allows more time for production planning, enabling the consolidation of item batches and reducing setup costs. This, however, may lead to higher inventory holding costs. This neighborhood structure is therefore introduced to promote strategic variability in the joint production and distribution planning process.

The approach is referred to as the Hybrid Variable Neighborhood Search (H-VNS) and is summarized in Algorithm 2.

Algorithm 2: H-VNS steps.

1: **function** H-VNS($s, k'_{max}, t'_{max}, m_{max}$)
2:     $t_{start} := CPUTime(); t := 0; m := 1;$
3:     **while** ($t \leq t'_{max}$) **do**
4:         $k := 0;$
5:         **while** ($k \leq k'_{max}$) **do**
6:             $s_{partial} := shake(s,k,m);$
7:             $s' := IPModel_{production}(s_{partial});$
8:             **if** ($f(s') < f(s)$) **then**
9:                 $s := s';$
10:                 $k := 0;$
11:             **else**
12:                 $k := k + 1;$
13:                 **if** ($m = m_{max}$) **then**
14:                     $m := 1;$
15:                 **else**
16:                     $m := m + 1;$
17:         $t := CPUTime() - t_{start};$

The algorithm takes as input an initial solution s, a set of k'_{max} neighborhood structures, a time limit t_{max}, and a maximum number of consecutive moves m_{max} applied during the shaking phase. The initial number of consecutive moves is set to $m = 1$

Table 1. Computational results for instances with 10 customers.

Inst.	$|\mathcal{P}|$	$|\mathcal{C}|$	$|\mathcal{V}|$	MIP				Heuristic				Our Approach			
				UB^{MIP}	CPU(s)	$CPU*$(s)	Gap(%)	UB^H	CPU(s)	$CPU*$(s)	Dev(%)	$best$	$CPU*$(s)	Dev'(%)	$DevToH$(%)
1	3	3	2	4013.3	86400	10980.8	12.93	3960.8	437.1	139.3	-1.31	3960.8	14.3	**-1.31**	**0.00**
2				3874.0	86400	16271.8	4.50	3934.2	498.1	442.3	1.55	3890.1	11.3	0.42	**-1.12**
3				3522.8	86400	41549.9	16.09	3529.9	269.9	132.0	0.20	3522.8	11.1	**0.00**	-0.20
4				3803.5	8732.5	5611.6	0.01	3803.5	316.0	68.9	0.00	3923.2	17.1	3.15	3.15
5				3754.1	86400	25264.1	9.46	3754.1	472.2	205.1	0.00	3754.0	14.2	**0.00**	**0.00**
6			3	4074.2	36744.3	3419.7	0.01	4074.2	320.1	53.2	0.00	4128.9	20.2	1.34	1.34
7				3817.6	86400	1118.6	9.22	3817.6	354.6	77.7	0.00	3817.6	11.9	**0.00**	**0.00**
8				4669.0	86400	4115.5	10.54	4643.8	363.4	201.7	-0.54	4643.8	13.8	**-0.54**	**0.00**
9				3786.9	86400	969.9	4.72	3786.9	469.5	410.9	0.00	3786.9	5.0	**0.00**	**0.00**
10				4237.1	86400	39592.3	7.38	4237.1	283.0	83.2	0.00	4533.1	8.6	6.99	6.99
11		5	2	5250.4	86400	83204.5	29.00	5168.5	566.2	496.5	-1.56	5214.0	14.8	**-0.69**	0.88
12				6786.3	86400	82650.6	34.33	6919.0	954.8	412.0	1.95	6847.3	18.4	0.90	**-1.04**
13				6695.4	86400	51422.7	31.88	6896.7	684.3	259.6	3.01	6735.8	25.7	0.60	**-2.33**
14				6017.0	86400	81084.8	36.66	5908.6	762.3	405.9	-1.80	6029.3	31.8	0.20	2.04
15				4229.1	86400	80202.7	15.23	4267.8	423.3	344.4	0.91	4229.1	11.0	**0.00**	-0.90
16			3	6676.3	86400	79766.0	29.97	6739.8	936.1	604.4	0.95	6668.2	15.0	**-0.12**	-1.06
17				5214.5	86400	8929.0	24.93	5313.2	388.4	78.4	1.89	5111.8	22.0	**-1.97**	-3.79
18				5460.8	86400	38162.8	24.63	5630.1	644.8	452.9	3.10	6052.8	17.3	10.84	7.51
19				7411.2	86400	82619.6	24.79	7419.8	641.5	361.1	0.12	7922.1	16.8	6.89	6.77
20				5261.3	86400	18603.6	30.58	5405.7	711.9	357.7	2.74	5223.3	13.4	**-0.72**	-3.37
21	5	3	2	5425.2	86400	997.8	17.96	6112.5	567.8	109.0	12.67	5299.6	4.8	**-2.32**	**-13.30**
22				3972.3	86400	5516.7	13.97	3986.2	598.9	365.2	0.35	3970.9	11.9	**-0.03**	-0.38
23				4376.4	86400	84367.4	7.81	4502.7	1045.8	595.6	2.89	4397.9	13.6	0.49	**-2.33**
24				4852.7	86400	57846.9	11.00	4852.7	875.6	665.5	0.00	4960.4	12.5	2.22	2.22
25				4055.4	86400	68504.9	13.52	4115.1	1235.6	576.3	1.47	4057.6	11.1	0.06	**-1.40**
26			3	4680.3	86400	25030.9	3.97	4697.8	643.8	562.5	0.37	4844.3	11.3	3.51	3.12
27				4246.8	86400	85227.6	16.66	4247.2	745.6	193.0	0.01	4270.8	13.5	0.57	0.55
28				5545.6	86400	29666.3	8.33	5676.1	620.2	440.9	2.35	5545.6	19.5	**0.00**	-2.30
29				4445.0	86400	79337.7	5.02	4454.7	676.6	281.5	0.22	4454.7	12.1	0.22	**0.00**
30				4872.3	86400	14024.8	15.27	4872.3	677.2	379.0	0.00	4872.2	11.1	**0.00**	**0.00**
31		5	2	7034.8	86400	76267.7	31.85	7159.5	1000.1	195.8	1.77	6923.8	17.7	**-1.58**	-3.29
32				7291.2	86400	85420.6	36.26	7331.2	761.4	439.2	0.55	7276.1	19.1	**-0.21**	-0.75
33				7868.3	86400	82898.1	34.88	8169.6	1103.3	350.0	3.83	7948.2	17.9	1.02	-2.71
34				6058.2	86400	2390.2	31.28	6594.6	1097.3	21.3	8.85	6058.2	12.3	**0.00**	-8.13
35				7446.5	86400	83184.6	31.49	7516.3	980.1	460.9	0.94	7421.4	19.7	**-0.34**	-1.26
36			3	7176.2	86400	84255.1	30.85	7252.1	763.7	228.6	1.06	7168.9	20.1	**-0.10**	-1.15
37				7105.1	86400	58548.0	34.60	7179.4	671.1	92.5	1.05	7001.6	13.8	**-1.46**	-2.48
38				7148.2	86400	79177.2	32.14	7393.6	780.0	214.6	3.43	7080.2	22.7	**-0.95**	-4.24
39				5742.6	86400	80505.8	30.59	5841.3	1002.3	898.8	1.72	5682.4	12.4	**-1.05**	-2.72
40				6462.3	86400	46948.4	28.89	6551.1	1217.1	460.8	1.37	6462.3	10.6	**0.00**	-1.36
Mean				5359.0	83216.9	47141.4	19.83	5442.9	689.0	328.0	1.40	5392.3	15.0	0.65	**-0.68**

(Line 2) and is gradually increased up to m_{max} if no improving solutions are found. Three of the proposed neighborhood structures (NS_k, with $k \in \{0, 1, 2\}$) are applied sequentially. In each iteration of the inner loop, a shaking procedure is applied to the incumbent solution s (Line 6), perturbing its routing component through m consecutive moves using the current neighborhood structure k. This generates a partial solution, denoted by $s_{partial}$, which includes only the routing decisions. Based on this partial solution, optimal production decisions are then computed by solving the integer programming model $IPModel_{production}(s_{partial})$.

Table 2. Computational results for instances with 15 customers.

Inst.	$|P|$	$|C|$	$|V|$	MIP				Heuristic				Our Approach			
				UB^{MIP}	$CPU(s)$	$CPU*(s)$	$Gap(\%)$	UB^H	$CPU(s)$	$CPU*(s)$	$Dev(\%)$	best	$CPU*(s)$	$Dev'(\%)$	$DevToH(\%)$
41	3	3	2	3890.7	86400	78508.4	20.81	3952.3	470.8	228.8	1.58	3898.8	14.0	0.21	**-1.35**
42				5625.8	86400	20908.8	20.78	5475.4	484.2	192.1	-2.67	5475.4	10.7	**-2.67**	**0.00**
43				4741.4	86400	79474.3	17.31	4600.1	468.7	410.2	-2.98	4585.1	15.4	**-3.30**	**-0.33**
44				5392.2	86400	77737.9	13.97	5645.3	428.9	235.9	4.70	5451.3	17.0	1.10	**-3.44**
45				5134.4	86400	80624.4	24.82	4999.6	619.8	372.1	-2.63	5061.1	17.0	**-1.43**	1.23
46			3	5228.3	86400	83721.4	26.28	5275.3	1227.5	774.4	0.90	5379.4	13.4	2.89	1.97
47				5295.4	86400	77947.5	17.00	5374.6	401.7	137.0	1.50	5304.4	21.3	0.17	**-1.31**
48				5768.1	86400	85668.8	14.38	5809.1	374.3	118.1	0.71	5830.7	9.8	1.09	0.37
49				5945.7	86400	79861.9	12.26	5980.2	532.5	218.1	0.58	6063.9	19.8	1.99	1.40
50				4725.7	86400	24290.2	10.58	4725.7	364.4	125.5	0.00	4720.1	17.1	**-0.12**	**-0.12**
51		5	2	7725.8	86400	79315.1	41.84	8720.5	1102.3	47.5	12.87	7491.1	6.5	**-3.04**	**-14.10**
52				5812.0	86400	85087.7	39.00	5509.4	690.3	444.3	-5.21	5460.1	19.8	**-6.05**	**-0.89**
53				4870.2	86400	84757.7	42.75	4906.5	572.7	212.4	0.75	4940.9	6.7	1.45	0.70
54				5626.9	86400	86392.7	37.39	5613.7	1173.5	519.7	-0.24	5837.8	16.4	3.75	3.99
55				5946.2	86400	86391.8	38.41	5882.7	634.4	305.5	-1.07	5682.2	16.5	**-4.44**	**-3.41**
56			3	7418.6	86400	86390.9	38.51	7066.0	713.2	239.5	-4.75	7024.0	18.7	**-5.32**	**-0.59**
57				7310.4	86400	79758.8	40.86	7165.7	893.0	439.1	-1.98	7170.8	14.5	**-1.91**	0.07
58				7017.2	86400	81258.1	36.85	7013.3	642.3	186.6	-0.06	6914.0	16.7	**-1.47**	**-1.42**
59				6436.7	86400	86391.9	43.68	6123.0	716.3	593.2	-4.87	6235.6	12.1	**-3.12**	1.84
60				5931.5	86400	81058.4	33.33	6245.8	1324.3	170.2	5.30	6074.2	19.3	2.41	**-2.75**
61	5	3	2	6021.6	86400	80464.9	22.35	5970.1	1150.6	564.1	-0.86	5900.8	18.5	**-2.01**	**-1.16**
62				5077.0	86400	82821.0	20.56	5091.1	1141.5	666.0	0.28	5102.7	16.3	0.51	0.23
63				5688.7	86400	82558.6	23.48	5660.1	997.2	897.1	-0.50	5660.1	21.9	**-0.50**	**0.00**
64				6631.9	86400	82306.2	17.40	6713.7	1241.2	926.5	1.23	6668.6	17.4	0.55	**-0.67**
65				6312.8	86400	80373.6	20.72	6534.3	1161.4	861.4	3.51	6392.9	13.0	1.27	**-2.16**
66			3	6089.4	86400	79957.0	26.87	6089.4	1041.5	877.5	0.00	6316.4	6.8	3.73	3.73
67				5769.2	86400	21013.3	17.69	5769.2	1474.3	793.6	0.00	5825.5	12.5	0.98	0.98
68				5657.2	86400	86397.4	27.40	5608.4	603.5	527.6	-0.86	5917.6	16.8	4.60	5.51
69				4115.2	86400	77739.3	8.28	4225.1	1192.9	516.7	2.67	4316.2	12.4	4.88	2.16
70				4578.0	86400	79173.5	9.47	4578.0	695.1	387.9	0.00	4797.8	16.2	4.80	4.80
71		5	2	8270.6	86400	86360.4	40.18	8361.4	868.2	169.9	1.10	8000.8	18.4	**-3.26**	**-4.31**
72				7765.5	86400	86389.3	34.75	7545.0	1297.6	726.1	-2.84	7585.2	9.1	**-2.32**	0.53
73				8123.3	86400	85115.1	40.63	8113.1	1045.3	581.4	-0.13	7831.7	22.1	**-3.59**	**-3.47**
74				8157.0	86400	86384.3	34.51	8116.9	1877.4	336.8	-0.49	7787.2	19.3	**-4.53**	**-4.06**
75				8130.9	86400	86201.3	42.33	7908.7	2802.1	1235.2	-2.73	7757.1	20.2	**-4.60**	**-1.92**
76			3	5903.1	86400	86384.5	35.95	5945.3	1669.2	1011.2	0.72	6094.3	12.1	3.24	2.51
77				8249.4	86400	86384.4	39.05	8037.3	2598.7	644.8	-2.57	7936.4	20.2	**-3.79**	**-1.26**
78				9071.7	86400	86390.3	41.00	8472.2	1270.4	917.1	-6.61	8471.0	16.4	**-6.62**	**-0.01**
79				8323.0	86400	86391.3	38.88	8452.5	730.4	321.5	1.56	8151.4	16.6	**-2.06**	**-3.56**
80				7301.6	86400	86384.5	39.40	7315.8	1579.7	949.0	0.19	7282.4	16.4	**-0.26**	**-0.46**
Mean				6277.0	86400	78518.4	28.79	6264.8	1006.8	497.0	-0.10	6209.9	15.6	**-0.67**	**-0.52**

Next, the quality of the new solution is evaluated (Line 8). If s' represents an improvement over the current solution s, the incumbent is updated and the neighborhood index is reset (Lines 9–10). Otherwise, a different neighborhood structure is explored (Line 12), and the value of m is incremented (Line 16). When m exceeds its upper limit (m_{max}), it is reset to 1 (Lines 13–14). This mechanism allows the parameter m to control the intensity of the solution perturbations - remaining constant when improvements are found, and gradually increasing otherwise.

4   Computational Experiments

4.1   Instances

To evaluate the performance of our algorithm, we conducted a set of computational experiments on benchmark instances based originally on real data provided by a company [14]. Confidential information, which could not be disclosed, was supplemented by the authors with values from other studies in the literature, including [3, 4, 11].

The parameters that characterize the instances are as follows:

- n: number of customers ($n \in \{10, 15, 20, 30, 40, 50\}$);
- $|\mathcal{P}|$: number of final products ($\mathcal{P} \in \{3, 5\}$);
- $|\mathcal{C}|$: number of items ($\mathcal{C} \in \{3, 5\}$);
- $|\mathcal{V}|$: number of available vehicles (either 2 or 3);

Table 3. Computational results for instances with 20 customers.

Inst.	$|\mathcal{P}|$	$|\mathcal{C}|$	$|\mathcal{V}|$	MIP				Heuristic				Our Approach			
				UB^{MIP}	CPU(s)	$CPU*$(s)	$Gap(\%)$	UB^H	CPU(s)	$CPU*$(s)	$Dev(\%)$	$best$	$CPU*$(s)	$Dev'(\%)$	$DevToH(\%)$
81	3	3	2	6046.9	86400	86246.9	17.84	6223.9	681.2	602.1	2.93	6148.8	10.90	1.69	**-1.21**
82				7339.5	86400	83927.7	44.57	5715.1	580.2	310.1	-22.13	5642.0	12.81	**-23.13**	**-1.28**
83				5489.3	86400	86382.6	36.32	5295.3	585.0	315.7	-3.53	5288.7	12.42	**-3.65**	**-0.12**
84				5612.5	86400	86382.0	40.83	5245.1	1256.8	768.3	-6.54	5225.0	13.45	**-6.90**	**-0.38**
85				5914.0	86400	86382.2	36.64	5522.1	1086.8	702.0	-6.63	5547.6	18.44	**-6.20**	0.46
86			3	6287.0	86400	86379.1	18.91	6084.9	558.9	260.4	-3.21	6084.9	10.86	**-3.21**	**0.00**
87				6175.6	86400	85414.9	23.73	6178.8	819.1	510.9	0.05	6107.7	17.19	**-1.10**	**-1.15**
88				5765.1	86400	86382.1	29.65	5437.6	703.7	507.0	-5.68	5357.2	12.02	**-7.08**	**-1.48**
89				5505.6	86400	86383.7	33.99	5008.5	1225.9	835.1	-9.03	5082.5	21.49	**-7.68**	1.48
90				6174.5	86400	78374.9	29.87	5990.7	608.9	531.8	-2.98	5990.7	13.85	**-2.98**	**0.00**
91	5		2	-	86400	-	-	7487.3	1374.4	661.5	-	7489.5	22.20	-	0.03
92				-	86400	-	-	6752.9	1594.9	661.1	-	6694.1	14.22	-	**-0.87**
93				7039.2	86400	86368.6	34.57	7258.8	964.7	700.3	3.12	7014.6	13.74	**-0.35**	**-3.36**
94				-	86400	-	-	7043.7	1997.1	1438.2	-	6986.4	15.63	-	**-0.81**
95				8498.1	86400	86381.9	39.30	7803.2	1306.5	965.9	-8.18	7580.9	19.27	**-10.79**	**-2.85**
96			3	-	86400	-	-	8835.2	854.1	637.0	-	8902.3	17.49	-	0.76
97				7931.3	86400	81690.6	42.76	7816.4	1859.5	1312.7	-1.45	7746.1	16.69	**-2.33**	**-0.90**
98				9369.8	86400	86382.2	40.45	9173.3	1732.1	493.4	-2.1	9089.8	12.76	**-2.99**	**-0.91**
99				8323.7	86400	84670.1	44.35	8339.1	1428.3	1137.6	0.19	8230.4	19.45	**-1.12**	**-1.30**
100				-	86400	-	-	7870.9	1871.5	553.8	-	7539.4	21.89	-	**-4.21**
101	5	3	2	7936.4	86400	86371.3	44.29	6395.6	1064.9	689.7	-19.41	6503.5	17.06	**-18.05**	1.69
102				8137.1	86400	86377.1	35.95	8119.3	1819.2	1020.3	-0.22	7931.7	25.03	**-2.52**	**-2.31**
103				6909.3	86400	86378.8	36.70	6120.0	1429.4	1304.6	-11.42	6114.7	15.87	**-11.50**	**-0.09**
104				7514.1	86400	86375.4	42.34	6605.6	1735.1	290.7	-12.09	6544.6	18.91	**-12.90**	**-0.92**
105				6688.1	86400	86378.8	37.30	6184.6	2935.1	1515.0	-7.53	6258.5	16.91	**-6.42**	1.19
106			3	8094.2	86400	86377.0	39.59	7252.4	3389.5	2508.5	-10.4	7387.1	14.78	**-8.74**	1.86
107				6281.0	86400	86374.1	45.01	5298.1	2550.8	1890.4	-15.65	5485.2	18.00	**-12.67**	3.53
108				7102.1	86400	86380.5	34.82	6681.4	1437.5	640.5	-5.92	6571.6	11.91	**-7.47**	**-1.64**
109				6887.8	86400	86378.3	38.16	6569.4	827.3	342.5	-4.62	6521.4	16.77	**-5.32**	**-0.73**
110				7785.0	86400	84457.7	34.05	7243.0	1777.3	735.6	-6.96	7246.5	14.58	**-6.92**	0.05
111	5		2	9832.0	86400	83072.8	41.87	9357.1	3402.3	2559.7	-4.83	9559.0	18.70	**-2.78**	2.16
112				11489.5	86400	86368.0	37.02	10763.4	1558.5	412.9	-6.32	10730.8	11.76	**-6.60**	**-0.30**
113				-	86400	-	-	12475.3	2031.8	256.5	-	11455.4	15.62	-	**-8.18**
114				8784.2	86400	86361.9	45.59	8083.0	1370.6	961.2	-7.98	7902.8	17.14	**-10.03**	**-2.23**
115				-	86400	-	-	9313.4	955.9	657.5	-	8641.5	15.61	-	**-7.21**
116			3	11831.5	86400	86370.2	37.87	11014.6	2918.4	2056.2	-6.9	10842.2	19.37	**-8.36**	**-1.57**
117				11891.0	86400	86375.5	47.59	10432.2	4734.4	3273.2	-12.27	10503.8	19.24	**-11.67**	0.69
118				12391.9	86400	86359.3	39.87	10975.3	2100.4	757.2	-11.43	10754.4	23.96	**-13.21**	**-2.01**
119				9867.6	86400	85380.3	28.79	9512.0	1601.7	841.9	-3.6	9535.3	15.70	**-3.37**	0.25
120				13235.7	86400	86345.5	47.13	11385.9	3033.1	2385.6	-13.98	11654.9	23.40	**-11.94**	2.36
Mean				8004.0	86400	85643.4	37.20	7621.6	1644.1	975.1	-6.87	7547.3	16.68	**-7.22**	**-0.79**

For each combination of these parameters, five independent instances were generated, resulting in a total of 240 instances.

The planning horizon is divided into 8 periods ($|\mathcal{T}|$), and customers are assigned delivery time windows based on their business hours. Additionally, the dimensions of each item (width and length) were considered. Therefore, items can have a different impact on the inventory costs.

4.2 Results and Discussion

In this section, we present the computational results obtained for the benchmark instances described previously. The experiments were conducted on a PC with an 8th-generation Intel Core i7-8565U processor and 16 GB of RAM. The algorithm was implemented in Java, and we used IBM ILOG CPLEX 12.10.0 as mathematical programming solver.

Our experiments were conducted with the following set of parameters:

- for Algorithm 1: $k_{max} = 4$ and $t_{max} = 2$ seconds;
- for Algorithm 2: $k'_{max} = 2$ and $t'_{max} = 30$ seconds.

In the latter case, it should be noted that the neighborhood structure is indexed starting at 0, resulting in three neighborhood structures being used. In both approaches, the parameter $m_{\max}$ was set to 10, corresponding to the maximum number of consecutive perturbations.

The total runtime of our approach is around 32 seconds. This value is mainly due to the time spent in the VNS cycles during Phases 2 and 3. This total also includes the time required to construct the initial solution and to solve the MIP model described in Sect. 3.1 (executed outside the VNS cycle, during Phase 2). However, these two operations are computationally very efficient, and therefore they have no significant impact on the total runtime. Additionally, preliminary tests were conducted showing that the algorithm's performance was independent of the initial solution chosen.

Given the stochastic nature of the VNS-based approaches, each instance was solved independently five times. We compare our approach by considering the best result obtained in all five runs for each instance, against the exact approach (denoted MIP) and the decomposition heuristic (denoted as H), both presented in [14].

The results are presented in Tables 1, 2, 3, 4, 5 and 6. The meaning of each column is as follows:

- $Inst$: ordinal number of the instance;
- $|\mathcal{P}|$: number of final products;
- $|\mathcal{C}|$: number of items;
- $|\mathcal{V}|$: number of vehicles;
- UB^{MIP}: best feasible solution found by the MIP method described in [14] (or " – " if no feasible solution is found);
- CPU: total computing time (in seconds);
- $CPU*$: time to find the best feasible solution (in seconds);
- $Gap(\%)$: optimality gap of the MIP method described in [14];

Table 4. Computational results for instances with 30 customers.

				MIP				Heuristic				Our Approach			
Inst.	$|P|$	$|C|$	$|V|$	UB^{MIP}	CPU(s)	CPU*(s)	Gap(%)	UB^H	CPU(s)	CPU*(s)	Dev(%)	best	CPU*(s)	$Dev'(\%)$	DevToH(%)
121	3	3	2	-	86400	-	-	6867.3	3177.1	1430.9	-	6714.7	8.66	-	**-2.22**
122				8395.7	86400	86147.73	37.83	7775.7	3743.7	2148.6	-7.38	7683.1	9.66	**-8.49**	-1.19
123				-	86400	-	-	7831.7	2156.3	729.4	-	7902.8	17.77	-	0.91
124				-	86400	-	-	7224.4	1607.3	542.7	-	7210.7	13.72	-	**-0.19**
125				-	86400	-	-	6460.7	3186.5	2975.6	-	6308.6	10.88	-	**-2.35**
126			3	8571.6	86400	86180.94	54.24	6153.3	2192.0	1801.3	-28.21	6045.5	14.61	**-29.47**	-1.75
127				-	86400	-	-	6705.1	4495.9	3408.8	-	6934.5	18.70	-	3.42
128				-	86400	-	-	7756.5	3425.9	1890.6	-	7675.8	15.94	-	**-1.04**
129				-	86400	-	-	6679.2	3298.3	2540.8	-	6588.1	7.82	-	**-1.36**
130				-	86400	-	-	6331.8	1654.6	1075.6	-	6381.3	22.50	-	0.78
131		5	2	-	86400	-	-	9934.6	2710.5	2155.6	-	9713.1	16.26	-	**-2.23**
132				-	86400	-	-	11001.3	3846.3	1251.4	-	10875.8	24.33	-	**-1.14**
133				-	86400	-	-	9703.8	3525.6	1087.8	-	9354.7	13.62	-	**-3.60**
134				-	86400	-	-	11041.9	3130.2	964.8	-	10870.7	10.71	-	**-1.55**
135				-	86400	-	-	11359.0	2310.6	216.6	-	10346.1	15.15	-	**-8.92**
136			3	-	86400	-	-	9553.4	4050.3	2538.3	-	9623.3	12.77	-	0.73
137				-	86400	-	-	11289.3	4713.2	2669.6	-	11164.4	11.23	-	**-1.11**
138				-	86400	-	-	9868.7	3016.0	667.3	-	9642.5	22.59	-	**-2.29**
139				-	86400	-	-	6681.0	3808.0	3034.6	-	6624.4	13.19	-	**-0.85**
140				-	86400	-	-	9650.3	4111.5	3382.5	-	9785.5	12.26	-	1.40
141	5	3	2	-	86400	-	-	10332.2	3135.0	1086.3	-	10261.2	22.83	-	**-0.69**
142				-	86400	-	-	10477.8	5260.9	2599.1	-	10304.7	13.53	-	**-1.65**
143				-	86400	-	-	8428.6	3764.9	2751.6	-	8454.9	11.81	-	0.31
144				-	86400	-	-	7532.0	5019.4	2118.6	-	7592.6	17.08	-	0.81
145				-	86400	-	-	8661.1	7524.9	2735.3	-	8605.2	9.30	-	**-0.65**
146			3	-	86400	-	-	8116.4	4944.5	3699.3	-	8167.9	12.06	-	0.63
147				9727.3	86400	85909.46	46.57	8145.8	3893.6	2383.8	-16.26	7936.2	14.60	**-18.41**	-2.57
148				-	86400	-	-	7908.5	6783.1	3291.3	-	7901.6	10.55	-	**-0.09**
149				-	86400	-	-	9579.9	7599.1	6484.2	-	9913.4	17.12	-	3.48
150				-	86400	-	-	7369.6	11745.0	9143.7	-	7295.3	6.50	-	**-1.01**
151		5	2	-	86400	-	-	11338.1	2902.0	1379.7	-	11027.8	13.92	-	**-2.74**
152				-	86400	-	-	16963.4	4852.3	2304.8	-	17580.1	17.35	-	3.63
153				-	86400	-	-	12280.0	6495.8	3979.9	-	12254.9	15.55	-	**-0.20**
154				-	86400	-	-	10303.2	5955.0	1280.9	-	10300.8	17.95	-	**-0.02**
155				-	86400	-	-	12675.4	5170.8	1516.2	-	12167.4	23.46	-	**-4.01**
156			3	-	86400	-	-	12627.1	5972.4	5635.7	-	12702.0	20.18	-	0.59
157				-	86400	-	-	13147.9	8160.8	5534.9	-	12992.4	14.59	-	**-1.18**
158				-	86400	-	-	12075.0	6649.9	3451.2	-	12156.5	10.55	-	0.67
159				-	86400	-	-	12518.2	6997.2	2524.6	-	13282.6	8.28	-	6.11
160				-	86400	-	-	12364.7	6361.2	6071.1	-	12339.9	13.18	-	**-0.20**
Mean				8898.2	86400	86079.38	46.21	9567.8	4583.7	2662.1	-17.28	9517.1	14.57	**-18.79**	**-0.58**

- UB^H: best solution found by the heuristic (H) described in [14];
- $Dev(\%)$: relative deviation between UB^H and UB^{MIP};
- $best$: best solution found by our algorithm;
- $Dev'(\%)$: relative deviation between the solution of our algorithm and UB^{MIP};
- $DevToH(\%)$: relative deviation between the solution of our algorithm and UB^H.

The relative deviation between the results of two approaches A and B is equal to $((value^A - value^B)/value^B \times 100)$. The values in the columns Dev' and $DevToH$

Table 5. Computational results for instances with 40 customers.

Inst.	$|P|$	$|C|$	$|V|$	UB^{MIP}	CPU(s)	CPU*(s)	Gap(%)	UB^H	CPU(s)	CPU*(s)	Dev(%)	best	CPU*(s)	Dev'(%)	DevToH(%)
				MIP				Heuristic				Our Approach			
161	3	3	2	-	86400	-	-	7396.5	5659.9	1939.1	-	7685.7	3.9	-	3.91
162				-	86400	-	-	7035.9	2152.9	930.6	-	6992.9	17.5	-	**-0.61**
163				9974.2	86400	85753.77	54.55	7273.7	9189.8	7339.4	-27.08	7139.3	22.7	**-28.42**	**-1.85**
164				-	86400	-	-	8028.5	5162.4	4816.5	-	7984.0	14.3	-	**-0.56**
165				-	86400	-	-	7105.5	4493.2	2373.4	-	7174.4	17.2	-	0.97
166			3	-	86400	-	-	7376.3	6732.4	6302.6	-	7701.5	14.0	-	4.41
167				-	86400	-	-	8391.5	9300.1	8540.7	-	8539.0	19.2	-	1.76
168				-	86400	-	-	8591.3	7506.4	4875.4	-	8491.4	18.2	-	**-1.16**
169				-	86400	-	-	7366.2	7555.4	1079.7	-	7424.3	10.5	-	0.79
170				-	86400	-	-	7219.3	5962.0	4088.7	-	7182.4	12.9	-	**-0.51**
171		5	2	-	86400	-	-	11687.2	7926.2	3376.2	-	11220.1	10.1	-	**-4.00**
172				-	86400	-	-	12597.0	6446.5	2314.7	-	12273.9	17.0	-	**-2.56**
173				-	86400	-	-	11624.2	7061.9	2694.5	-	11641.3	16.9	-	0.15
174				-	86400	-	-	11036.5	7715.1	4935.1	-	11672.1	27.4	-	5.76
175				-	86400	-	-	11217.1	4675.7	1253.7	-	11882.1	19.6	-	5.93
176			3	-	86400	-	-	12607.3	11929.6	9708.9	-	12538.1	20.9	-	**-0.55**
177				-	86400	-	-	12800.1	6843.9	1257.4	-	12912.3	17.2	-	0.88
178				-	86400	-	-	10964.8	5268.2	2528.5	-	11105.7	23.4	-	1.29
179				-	86400	-	-	11273.7	8511.5	5340.7	-	11525.9	19.1	-	2.24
180				-	86400	-	-	9069.6	7578.8	3493.7	-	8750.6	18.6	-	**-3.52**
181	5	3	2	-	86400	-	-	10647.5	11628.5	3380.2	-	10716.8	19.8	-	0.65
182				-	86400	-	-	14671.8	6549.6	1902.2	-	14419.6	19.6	-	**-1.72**
183				-	86400	-	-	14737.7	10599.1	9637.5	-	15101.8	21.2	-	2.47
184				-	86400	-	-	11710.3	4709.4	760.8	-	11989.6	11.0	-	2.38
185				-	86400	-	-	10888.8	8079.5	3822.9	-	10806.4	16.0	-	**-0.76**
186			3	-	86400	-	-	7061.7	14433.9	12869.7	-	7088.8	11.3	-	0.38
187				-	86400	-	-	9382.3	15834.4	15232.4	-	9295.1	13.7	-	**-0.93**
188				-	86400	-	-	11327.3	7272.4	5735.0	-	11355.8	21.0	-	0.25
189				-	86400	-	-	11445.2	11494.7	6124.9	-	11747.3	13.1	-	2.64
190				-	86400	-	-	9423.0	9682.6	6632.6	-	9566.5	13.3	-	1.52
191		5	2	-	86400	-	-	14619.8	12069.9	7323.1	-	14570.3	12.2	-	**-0.34**
192				-	86400	-	-	13913.4	14364.6	9957.2	-	14045.5	18.9	-	0.95
193				-	86400	-	-	13313.5	23653.9	11226.4	-	13146.5	12.9	-	**-1.25**
194				-	86400	-	-	17866.3	5924.7	1352.4	-	17605.1	12.5	-	**-1.46**
195				-	86400	-	-	17104.3	15953.0	10124.3	-	18540.2	8.7	-	8.39
196			3	-	86400	-	-	13616.4	13884.8	11144.7	-	13763.3	8.1	-	1.08
197				-	86400	-	-	16301.4	12040.5	9346.0	-	16983.7	22.9	-	4.19
198				-	86400	-	-	12645.8	17324.9	15130.5	-	12664.6	20.8	-	0.15
199				-	86400	-	-	14929.1	28383.0	21021.0	-	15029.7	19.8	-	0.67
200				-	86400	-	-	17921.9	17979.5	16842.6	-	18788.2	23.8	-	4.83
Mean				9974.2	86400	85753.77	54.55	11354.7	9988.4	6468.9	-27.08	11476.5	16.5	**-28.42**	0.92

are put in **bold** whenever the result obtained by our approach is better than or equal to that of the exact method (MIP) or the heuristic (H) proposed in [14], respectively. Negative values in these columns indicate better solutions.

The results of our approach outperform the heuristic (H) for all the instance sets, although the differences are small, when compared to the deviation from the MIP. Both approaches outperform the average results of the MIP, except for the smallest instance set with 10 customers, where the deviations are 1.40% for H and 0.65% for our app-

Table 6. Computational results for instances with 50 customers.

Inst.	$\|P\|$	$\|C\|$	$\|V\|$	UB^{MIP}	$CPU(s)$	$CPU*(s)$	$Gap(\%)$	UB^H	$CPU(s)$	$CPU*(s)$	$Dev(\%)$	best	$CPU*(s)$	$Dev'(\%)$	$DevToH(\%)$
				MIP				Heuristic				Our Approach			
201	3	3	2	-	86400	-	-	10844.4	9914.1	2672.8	-	10781.1	13.6	-	**-0.58**
202				-	86400	-	-	9190.2	11984.8	7978.0	-	9220.2	13.4	-	0.33
203				-	86400	-	-	8939.3	12299.4	10239.4	-	9109.0	9.6	-	1.90
204				-	86400	-	-	9863.8	12300.4	8517.7	-	9818.7	18.3	-	**-0.46**
205				-	86400	-	-	8924.3	9977.0	4697.8	-	8953.9	20.1	-	0.33
206			3	-	86400	-	-	8283.2	17685.2	6761.3	-	8258.1	12.3	-	**-0.30**
207				-	86400	-	-	10626.6	22185.3	21175.7	-	10835.3	21.3	-	1.96
208				-	86400	-	-	8363.7	13404.6	9884.8	-	8591.6	15.1	-	2.72
209				-	86400	-	-	8220.2	13807.1	1556.1	-	8153.8	20.2	-	**-0.81**
210				-	86400	-	-	9564.1	30730.0	27356.9	-	9966.3	16.3	-	4.21
211		5	2	-	86400	-	-	14133.9	9279.5	5738.9	-	14217.3	10.9	-	0.59
212				-	86400	-	-	13199.2	13358.8	8185.1	-	13026.2	18.4	-	**-1.31**
213				-	86400	-	-	12034.7	9963.1	2920.0	-	11687.9	16.3	-	**-2.88**
214				-	86400	-	-	10338.0	11784.2	4148.7	-	10564.2	19.2	-	2.19
215				-	86400	-	-	10088.1	16074.3	6458.3	-	10056.6	23.6	-	**-0.31**
216			3	-	86400	-	-	11976.6	42974.6	26321.4	-	11893.5	8.4	-	**-0.69**
217				-	86400	-	-	16046.9	15709.9	11265.5	-	15796.3	11.0	-	**-1.56**
218				-	86400	-	-	14265.6	23735.2	10009.4	-	14327.7	16.5	-	0.44
219				-	86400	-	-	12302.8	18760.4	16527.3	-	12644.3	16.5	-	2.78
220				-	86400	-	-	12373.9	15505.9	2652.7	-	12491.6	20.5	-	0.95
221	5	3	2	-	86400	-	-	12864.8	24565.5	19804.8	-	13419.2	10.9	-	4.31
222				-	86400	-	-	14115.9	9485.0	2568.3	-	14106.4	21.0	-	**-0.07**
223				-	86400	-	-	10540.5	14439.9	11879.6	-	10515.2	19.3	-	**-0.24**
224				-	86400	-	-	11473.1	20417.4	13011.3	-	11578.1	16.6	-	0.92
225				-	86400	-	-	12681.9	19066.0	15840.7	-	12412.8	13.2	-	**-2.12**
226			3	-	86400	-	-	10822.0	32708.1	9646.9	-	11172.8	17.6	-	3.24
227				-	86400	-	-	8748.9	39850.4	14295.4	-	8818.0	15.3	-	0.79
228				-	86400	-	-	13447.0	56041.6	37726.6	-	13559.9	24.0	-	0.84
229				-	86400	-	-	10203.1	20679.3	12782.2	-	10613.6	14.9	-	4.02
230				-	86400	-	-	9593.4	16236.6	6654.2	-	10082.5	11.5	-	5.10
231		5	2	-	86400	-	-	18478.3	25732.2	13862.6	-	19791.0	18.2	-	7.10
232				-	86400	-	-	20730.1	26871.1	12629.3	-	20574.5	16.9	-	**-0.75**
233				-	86400	-	-	13979.6	29766.2	28438.4	-	14629.1	9.7	-	4.65
234				-	86400	-	-	21931.7	13880.9	13105.9	-	21993.8	10.5	-	0.28
235				-	86400	-	-	15118.6	25840.7	7775.1	-	14712.9	10.6	-	**-2.68**
236			3	-	86400	-	-	19292.1	57743.3	45195.4	-	19471.3	21.5	-	0.93
237				-	86400	-	-	18043.9	18984.3	14505.1	-	18650.2	24.0	-	3.36
238				-	86400	-	-	17914.0	37502.0	19936.0	-	17520.4	18.5	-	**-2.20**
239				-	86400	-	-	20651.9	32622.7	14935.9	-	20784.9	17.4	-	0.64
240				-	86400	-	-	16463.9	25877.5	13255.6	-	17013.0	10.2	-	3.33
Mean				-	86400	-	-	12916.9	21993.6	13072.9	-	13045.3	16.1	-	1.02

roach. Concerning the deviations between the non-exact approaches ($DevToH$), our algorithm consistently outperformed heuristic H in instances with 10 to 30 customers, yielding negative average deviation values. In these instance sets, 60% of our solutions were better than or equal to those obtained by the decomposition heuristic H. On the other hand, for larger instances, heuristic H performed slightly better. Nevertheless, in these sets of 40 and 50 customers, our approach still found better solutions for 30 cases.

The high value of Gap shows the limitations of the corresponding method, as it was able to solve very few instances with 30 or more customers within a 24-hours time limit. In these instance sets, our algorithm outperformed all solutions found by the exact method. For smaller instances, our approach produced results that were better than or equal to those of the exact method in 55% to 80% of the cases (24/40, 22/40, and 32/40 instances for problems with 10, 15, and 20 customers, respectively).

On average, our approach takes less than 17 seconds to find its best solution. The exact method (MIP), even for smaller instances, requires approximately 13 hours, while the decomposition heuristic (H) takes around 328 seconds. As the instance size increases, MIP often requires close to 24 hours or fails to find any solution within the time limit. For instances with 50 customers, the decomposition heuristic takes, on average around 3.5 hours (13,072.9 seconds) to reach a solution. In contrast, our approach consistently reaches its solutions in significantly less time than the other methods.

5 Conclusions

In this paper, we proposed a new hybrid algorithm for a rich and integrated production routing problem with real-world applicability. Our approach combines the VNS metaheuristic with the exact resolution of an integer programming model. The approach begins with an initial solution aimed at minimizing routing-related costs. In the subsequent iterations, a Hybrid-VNS is employed to adjust the routes, incorporating inventory and production scheduling costs.

The computational results demonstrate the efficiency of the proposed solutions. The algorithm was able to find high-quality solutions, outperforming existing methods from the literature in significantly shorter computational times. This behavior is consistent regardless of the instance size.

For future research, we plan to extend the proposed framework to even more realistic industrial scenarios by including additional real-world constraints, such as variable production capacities or multi-depot settings.

Acknowledgments. The first author has been supported by FCT – Fundação para a Ciência e Tecnologia, through national funds from MCTES – Ministério da Ciência, Tecnologia e Ensino Superior, and by European Social Fund through NORTE2020 – Programa Operacional Regional Norte, within the research grant SFRH/BD/146217/2019. This work has been supported by FCT – Fundação para a Ciência e Tecnologia within the R&D Unit Project Scope UID/00319/Centro ALGORITMI (ALGORITMI/UM) https://doi.org/10.54499/UID/00319/2025.

References

1. Adulyasak, Y., Cordeau, J.F., Jans, R.: The production routing problem: a review of formulations and solution algorithms. Comput. Oper. Res. **55**, 141–152 (2015). https://doi.org/10.1016/J.COR.2014.01.011
2. Alvarez, A., Miranda, P., Rohmer, S.U.: Production routing for perishable products. Omega **111**, 102667 (2022). https://doi.org/10.1016/J.OMEGA.2022.102667

3. Amorim, P., Belo-Filho, M.A., Toledo, F.M., Almeder, C., Almada-Lobo, B.: Lot sizing versus batching in the production and distribution planning of perishable goods. Int. J. Prod. Econ. **146**, 208–218 (2013). https://doi.org/10.1016/J.IJPE.2013.07.001
4. Armentano, V.A., Shiguemoto, A.L., Løkketangen, A.: Tabu search with path relinking for an integrated production–distribution problem. Comput. Oper. Res. **38**, 1199–1209 (2011). https://doi.org/10.1016/J.COR.2010.10.026
5. Chandra, P., Fisher, M.L.: Coordination of production and distribution planning. Eur. J. Oper. Res. **72**, 503–517 (1994). https://doi.org/10.1016/0377-2217(94)90419-7
6. Coelho, L.C., Laporte, G.: Improved solutions for inventory-routing problems through valid inequalities and input ordering. Int. J. Prod. Econ. **155**, 391–397 (2014). https://doi.org/10.1016/J.IJPE.2013.11.019
7. Cóccola, M.E., Méndez, C.A., Dondo, R.G.: A two-stage procedure for efficiently solving the integrated problem of production, inventory, and distribution of industrial products. Comput. Chem. Eng. **134** (2020). https://doi.org/10.1016/j.compchemeng.2019.106690
8. Fu, L.L., Aloulou, M.A., Triki, C.: Integrated production scheduling and vehicle routing problem with job splitting and delivery time windows. Int. J. Prod. Res. **55**, 5942–5957 (2017). https://doi.org/10.1080/00207543.2017.1308572
9. Geiger, A.: Enhancing supply chain coordination: a comparative analysis of clustering techniques for the production routing problem. Comput. Ind. Eng. **196**, 110455 (2024). https://doi.org/10.1016/J.CIE.2024.110455
10. Ghasemkhani, A., Tavakkoli-Moghaddam, R., Shahnejat-Bushehri, S., Momen, S., Tavakkoli-Moghaddam, H.: An integrated production inventory routing problem for multi perishable products with fuzzy demands and time windows. IFAC-PapersOnLine **52**, 523–528 (2019). https://doi.org/10.1016/j.ifacol.2019.11.123
11. Gramani, M.C., França, P.M., Arenales, M.N.: A Lagrangian relaxation approach to a coupled lot-sizing and cutting stock problem. Int. J. Prod. Econ. **119**, 219–227 (2009). https://doi.org/10.1016/J.IJPE.2009.02.011
12. Hrabec, D., Hvattum, L.M., Hoff, A.: The value of integrated planning for production, inventory, and routing decisions: a systematic review and meta-analysis. Int. J. Prod. Econ. **248**, 108468 (2022). https://doi.org/10.1016/J.IJPE.2022.108468
13. Manousakis, E.G., Kasapidis, G.A., Kiranoudis, C.T., Zachariadis, E.E.: An infeasible space exploring matheuristic for the production routing problem. Eur. J. Oper. Res. **298**, 478–495 (2022). https://doi.org/10.1016/J.EJOR.2021.05.037
14. Miranda, P.L., Cordeau, J.F., Ferreira, D., Jans, R., Morabito, R.: A decomposition heuristic for a rich production routing problem. Comput. Oper. Res. **98**, 211–230 (2018). https://doi.org/10.1016/J.COR.2018.05.004
15. Miranda, P.L., Morabito, R., Ferreira, D.: Mixed integer formulations for a coupled lot-scheduling and vehicle routing problem in furniture settings. INFOR: Inf. Syst. Oper. Res. **57**, 563–596 (2019). https://doi.org/10.1080/03155986.2019.1575686
16. Mousavi, R., Bashiri, M., Nikzad, E.: Stochastic production routing problem for perishable products: modeling and a solution algorithm. Comput. Oper. Res. **142**, 105725 (2022). https://doi.org/10.1016/J.COR.2022.105725
17. Perron, S., Hansen, P., Digabel, S.L., Mladenović, N.: Exact and heuristic solutions of the global supply chain problem with transfer pricing. Eur. J. Oper. Res. **202**, 864–879 (2010). https://doi.org/10.1016/J.EJOR.2009.06.018
18. Russell, R.A.: Mathematical programming heuristics for the production routing problem. Int. J. Prod. Econ. **193**, 40–49 (2017). https://doi.org/10.1016/J.IJPE.2017.06.033
19. Soysal, M., Çimen, M., Belbağ, S., Toğrul, E.: A review on sustainable inventory routing. Comput. Ind. Eng. **132**, 395–411 (2019). https://doi.org/10.1016/J.CIE.2019.04.026
20. Ullrich, C.A.: Integrated machine scheduling and vehicle routing with time windows. Eur. J. Oper. Res. **227**, 152–165 (2013). https://doi.org/10.1016/J.EJOR.2012.11.049

Flexible CO2 Aware Routing with Real Time Smart Locker Adjustments

Mohammed-Ali Ejjanfi[✉] and Jamal Benhra

LARILE, ENSEM, University Hassan II of Casablanca, Casablanca, Morocco
`ejjanfimed@gmail.com`

Abstract. This paper formulates a smart-locker vehicle routing problem for urban logistics in Casablanca, Marrakech, and Tangier. The study frames last-mile parcel delivery as a carbon-capped routing problem that lets vans hand parcels either to customers or to a shared locker network in Casablanca, Marrakech, and Tangier. The model combines locker choice, tour construction, and real-time customer relocation triggered after dispatch. We build a modular simulator that feeds identical city graphs, locker sets, and carbon caps to both solvers under matched time budgets, enabling a transparent comparison. Across Tangier, Marrakech, and Casablanca, PPO reduced baseline fleet emissions by 2.6–4.3% relative to ACO and, after a late locker unavailability, contained the added carbon to ~ 2.0% on average (2.3% in Tangier, 1.9% in Marrakech, 1.6% in Casablanca) versus ~ 5% for ACO (9.5%, 0.0%, and 1.5%, respectively). We disclose hyperparameters and add a runtime/hardware profile to support reproducibility and deployment.

Keywords: Ant Colony Optimization · Proximal Policy Optimization · Vehicle Routing Problem · Artificial Intelligence · Urban Logistics · Last Mile · CO_2

1 Introduction

The rapid growth in online retail reshapes city logistics [1]. Parcels now flow from regional hubs to apartments, offices, and pick-up points at unprecedented volume. Couriers must balance customer expectations with traffic delay, parking scarcity, and labor cost. This final leg—often called the last-mile—now defines service quality and profit margins. Route planners must choose which streets each van visits, which parcels they carry, and when each customer receives a notification. Every extra kilometer erodes delivery margin and strains urban infrastructure.

In research and practice, these decisions fall under the Vehicle Routing Problem (VRP) [2]. The task demands a schedule that assigns stops to vehicles and orders those stops along each tour [3]. Over decades, engineers have built algorithms to explore the vast space of possible routes. Real-world instances resist full enumeration because travel time, demand volatility, and operational rules create a huge combinatorial space. Heuristics and metaheuristics therefore dominate route design in commercial dispatch systems.

J. Barata et al. (Eds.): IN4PL 2025, CCIS 2826, pp. 242–262, 2026.
https://doi.org/10.1007/978-3-032-15579-5_15

Route quality now involves more than distance or labor expense [4, 5]. Public policy and corporate pledges push carriers to cut greenhouse-gas output. Urban planners impose low-emission zones and fuel duties, while clients ask for green checkout options. Each extra liter of diesel releases about 2.6 kg of CO_2. With on-board telematics, regulators and operators monitor fleet footprints using speed-bin fuel models. Dispatch tools must therefore seek routes that meet time windows while respecting a fleet-level carbon cap.

Smart-parcel lockers enter this scene as flexible delivery nodes [6, 7]. They reduce failed home handovers and allow vans to drop many parcels at one secure wall. Lockers change the routing task because the algorithm can decide which customer receives a locker code instead of a doorstep visit. The network of lockers in a city opens new combinations of stops that can shorten tours and lower carbon. Any route design method must treat locker assignment and stop sequencing as a joint decision.

Operational flexibility starts once the first van leaves the depot. When a recipient updates the preferred locker after dispatch, the engine should revise the active route in real-time: reassign the parcel to the new locker, insert the stop in the running tour, and adjust linked time windows. The engine repeats this whenever new information arrives, so every van follows a plan that reflects the latest customer confirmations and locker occupancy. Beyond distance or cost, we place carbon at the core of routing and evaluate how two paradigms react when a locker change occurs after dispatch.

This paper focuses on two computational paradigms that tackle the routing task under a carbon cap [8, 9]. Ant Colony Optimization (ACO) represents population-based search, where many candidate tours march through the graph like ants following pheromone trails [10]. Proximal Policy Optimization (PPO) offers a reinforcement learning app-roach, where a neural policy interacts with a simulator and gradually improves its dis-patch actions by trial and reward [11]. In practice, ACO responds to a mid-tour locker change by trimming the affected partial tour and extending it from the disruption point; pheromone on arcs that stay feasible keeps its strength, while infeasible arcs evaporate faster and steer the colony toward revised paths. PPO treats each event as a fresh state: the policy network sees updated van positions, parcel lists, and the carbon tally, then selects the next stop within seconds without rebuilding the full tour. Both methods must keep cumulative CO_2 under the fleet cap.

Existing work often studies these paradigms in separate threads [17, 18]. Population approaches dominate vehicle-routing contests, while reinforcement learning thrives in synthetic grid worlds or scaled-down benchmarks. Few studies compare them on the same data, under a carbon cap, with locker choice embedded and with after-dispatch relocation. This gap hampers managers who must decide which method to embed in dispatch software.

Our empirical setting covers three Moroccan cities of varied size and traffic density. Tangier stands at the strait with a compact urban core and steep gradients; Marrakech combines wide boulevards with a dense historic quarter; Casablanca spans a coastal plain with arterial highways and sprawling suburbs. Each city hosts a tailored network of parcel lockers and a fleet of diesel vans equipped with on-board units that record segment speed and fuel draw. All routes respect a carbon target derived from measured fuel-to-carbon factors for light commercial vehicles. Raw telematics logs yield segment fuel use for four speed brackets below suburban limits, and the planner converts each liter consumed into CO_2 mass using coefficients near 2.6 kg/L; the search process monitors aggregate mass across the fleet and prunes any route that would push the total above the target [19].

To enable a controlled comparison, we build a modular simulator that feeds identical city graphs, locker sets, and demand distributions to both solvers [20]. The simulator calculates travel time from open-street map data and updates carbon usage in real-time. ACO runs as an offline batch that iterates for a fixed wall-clock budget. PPO trains over many simulated days and then produces decisions in near real-time. This framework enforces matched time budgets and identical inputs, yielding a fair view of computational load, decision latency, and route quality.

Contributions. (i) We formulate a carbon-capped VRP that jointly decides locker assignment and routing, supporting mid-tour relocation after dispatch. (ii) We compare ACO and PPO on identical city instances under matched time budgets. (iii) We embed speed-bin fuel models from telematics so that carbon drives decisions. (iv) We disclose hyperparameters and provide a hardware/runtime profile to support reproducibility and deployment.

2   Literature Review

Recent studies deepen the understanding of carbon-aware vehicle routing by coupling algorithmic search with emissions accounting. A common thread runs through this body of work: each contribution treats distance, service time, and greenhouse gas release as joint drivers of route quality, yet the methods vary from pheromone-based search to machine learning.

Kim et al. present a clustered ant approach for a multi-trip, heterogeneous fleet with time windows [21]. The authors combine density-based grouping with a refined pheromone update. Their industrial case confirms that shorter travel and balanced work-load can align with lower fuel use. The paper also shows that smaller vehicles gain more mileage share once the search measures carbon. The strong result demonstrates the merit of pre-clustering but leaves open how the colony would react when demand shifts mid-tour.

Hybrid fleets extend the design space further. Hanaa et al. model electric vans as mobile drone pads in a combined ground–air plan [22]. Ant search guides van paths while particle swarm controls drone sorties. Carbon savings result from load splits that match drone endurance to urgent parcels, while vans handle bulk. The split identifies a trade-off between flight energy and van detours. This work illustrates how swarm rules can govern multi-modal logistics, yet the dual-algorithm setup complicates fair attribution of gains to a single method.

Review articles trace the growth of green routing variants. Berrahmania and co-authors survey metaheuristic solutions for pick-up and delivery with time windows under a carbon cap [23]. The authors note that ant-inspired methods dominate recent test beds and point to limited adaptation for rolling horizons. A condensed review by the same group highlights open questions on benchmark design and convergence proof [24]. Both reviews call for cross-paradigm tests that pit population search against reinforcement learning on identical data.

Shuaibu et al. provide a broad scan of last-mile techniques, from linear models to artificial intelligence [25]. The scan confirms the rise of algorithmic learning but remarks that most reinforcement work stops at proof-of-concept scale. Route length remains the main metric, with carbon added only in a subset of studies. The authors urge a shift toward multi-objective scoring grounded in policy targets.

Drone dispatch receives closer scrutiny in the work of Stodola and Kutěj, who frame a multi-depot truck–drone problem and adapt ant rules to decide when to launch a drone [26]. Their analysis reveals that premature drone use at close range can raise total energy, a nuance missed by simpler heuristics. The findings echo the need for emission-aware reward shaping if a learning agent is to match or surpass ant search.

Accurate emission models are essential. Caballero-Morales and Rojas-Cuevas build a multivariate data set where vehicle type, load size, and distance interact [27]. Their factorial design shows that route length alone cannot predict emissions once load varies. Such insight reinforces the case for state features that capture payload in reinforcement learning.

Simulation-based search can capture travel time uncertainty. Ramirez-Villamil et al. integrate Monte Carlo travel times with a local search driver in a two-echelon Paris case [28]. Carbon and particulate matter enter the score, and the authors compare global and local dispatch rules. The study suggests that global planning yields cleaner tours, hinting that learning agents might need wide spatial context to match human-devised hierarchies.

Giuffrida et al. perform a bibliometric review of last-mile studies and sort them into classical operations research, machine learning, and mixed methods [29]. They observe that deep reinforcement techniques appear mainly in academic prototypes. A gap persists between these prototypes and the mature ant implementations seen in industry pilots.

Electric fleets raise new constraints on range and charging. Martins et al. survey arc, team-orienteering, and vehicle routing variants with battery limits [30]. The authors list ant and genetic methods as the most common solvers, with sparse adoption of policy learning. They argue that reinforcement approaches could exploit battery state features better than static heuristics but lack shared test sets.

Driver knowledge can still outperform code. Quirion-Blais and Chen embed case-based reasoning to recall past tours that succeeded under similar time windows [31]. Their results confirm that human intuition, captured as cases, narrows the gap to algorithmic search even when routes appear longer. The finding hints at hybrid learning opportunities where policy networks start from human-guided cases rather than random exploration.

Physical networks other than roads widen the search challenge. Alewijnse and Hübl study parcel transfer by canal ships and cargo bikes in Amsterdam [32]. A genetic algorithm lowers delivery and investment cost while cutting carbon by more than seventy percent. The work shows that modal shift yields large gains, but the genetic search sometimes leaves the feasible space. Reinforcement methods with constraint-aware policies might maintain feasibility more naturally.

Reverse flow and scheduling add further layers. Alizadeh Foroutan et al. craft a mixed-integer model for forward and reverse goods with early-late penalties [33]. Simulated annealing and genetic search meet the time bound, yet their sensitivity test shows that returned goods raise carbon sharply if not accounted for at design time. Such coupling stresses the importance of decision sequences that look beyond the forward trip, a setting where state-aware learning could shine.

Carbon caps inside urban time windows appear in the study by Kirci, who merges real Google Maps paths with computed graphs [34]. The model treats speed and time windows along with carbon per minute. Their experiment in Turkey reveals strong linkages among path choice, arrival time, and emissions. The paper underscores that any learning agent must perceive temporal speed profiles to honor both punctuality and carbon goals.

Mandziuk reviews emerging VRP forms and notes a surge in computational-intelligence methods from 2015 to 2017 [35]. The survey catalogues new problem definitions such as crowd shipping and autonomous delivery, yet reinforcement learning gains only a short mention. The review calls for unified benchmarks that rate search quality across formulations.

Postal networks share comparable challenges. Niroomand and Nsakanda apply ant search to contractor collection routes where bid price relates to route complexity [36]. The case study shows that pheromone strength can absorb complexity cost, but the approach still relies on fixed demand. A learning agent with day-ahead forecasts might adapt better to demand swings.

Locker networks blend location and routing. Leyerer et al. propose a two-echelon model with refrigerated lockers and electric cargo bikes [37]. The decision support system handles locker placement and bike tours. Carbon becomes a core metric, yet the solution relies on traditional mixed-integer search, leaving behavioral learning untapped.

Early work by Jabali et al. introduces a time-dependent model linking vehicle speed to carbon release [38]. Their tabu search shows that avoiding rush hour lowers both fuel and travel time cost. The analysis offers a baseline for later studies that embed speed tiers into the state space of learning agents.

Across this corpus, ant search appears in many real-world pilots and laboratory tests. The method offers transparent parameters and lends itself to hybrid tweaks such as clustering, drone launch rules, or canal mode decisions. In contrast, reinforcement learning appears mainly in survey remarks or conceptual proposals. The gap does not stem from lack of promise; rather, it reflects data scarcity, simulator setup cost, and the challenge of defining rewards that balance delivery, time windows, and carbon.

Emission modelling also shows diverse practice. Some studies rely on distance multipliers, others thread fuel curves through speed bins, and a few embed load weight. Disparate models hamper direct comparison. Most reinforcement prototypes still apply simplistic distance penalties, leaving fuel and carbon as future work.

The literature points to clear needs. First, a side-by-side experiment where ant search and policy learning run on identical city graphs, locker sets, and carbon caps. Second, a simulator that provides segment fuel burns alongside distance and time, enabling meaningful carbon rewards. Third, a reporting style that discloses computation time, tuning effort, and data demands for each method.

Our study positions itself within these needs. We craft carbon-capped smart-locker instances for Casablanca, Marrakech, and Tangier, embed a four-band fuel model, and compare ant colony search with proximal policy learning under matched conditions. The experiment tests whether learned dispatch can reach the carbon target with route quality on par with a tuned colony, laying groundwork for broader adoption of reinforcement methods in emission-aware last-mile planning.

Gap. Prior work rarely compares population search and policy learning on the same green-routing instances with locker choice and rolling repair. Emission models, when present, are heterogeneous, and few papers disclose runtime or deployment constraints. We therefore design a matched ACO–PPO study with telematics-grounded fuel bins, report computation footprints, and stress-test late locker relocation to clarify which paradigm adapts better in practice.

3   Methods

3.1   Overall Approach

Urban couriers must deliver hundreds of parcels each day while meeting a strict carbon ceiling. The study frames this task as a capacitated vehicle routing problem over locker networks in Tangier, Marrakech, and Casablanca. Each van leaves the depot with a load, travels through dense traffic, and returns when all lockers receive their parcels. The planner selects both the locker assigned to every recipient and the sequence of stops. Fuel records from on-board sensors convert distance and speed into kilogram-level carbon figures, and the fleet total may not exceed the preset cap. After dispatch, customers can switch lockers, forcing the planner to repair the active tours without breaking the carbon budget or vehicle capacities. Two solution engines tackle the same data. Ant Colony Optimization deploys multiple agents that build routes step by step while pheromone trails guide them toward low-carbon edges. Proximal Policy Optimization trains a neural policy on thousands of simulated days, then produces near-instant decisions by mapping the current state to the next stop. Both engines ingest identical distance matrices, demand vectors, locker coordinates, and fuel tables, enabling a fair comparison of search behavior, run time, and carbon outcome. Spatial layouts appear in Fig. 1 through Fig. 3. Instance parameters and vehicle fuel curves are summarized in Table 1 to Table 4, which should follow the figures.

3.2   Baseline CO_2-Constrained Problem

We work on a directed graph $G = (V, E)$ with depot 0 and locker set $\{1, \ldots, N\}$. A routing plan is a set of at most K cycles that start and end at the depot and cover every locker once.

- **Objective (1).**

$$min \sum_{\{k \in K\}} \sum_{\{(i,j) \in A\}} x^k_{\{ij\}} \cdot dist(i,j) \cdot f(speed_{\{ij\}}) \tag{1}$$

Units: f(speed) in kg $CO_2 \cdot$ km$^-$1; dist in km; objective in kg CO_2.

3.3 Flexible Routing Layer

A relocation event inserts a new locker R_t for parcel U after notification time N_T. All definitions below are inherited from the original paper.

- *Book-keeping identities (2)–(5).*

$$V = |C| \tag{2}$$

$$N = |D| \tag{3}$$

$$\sum D_i \leq \sum C_i \tag{4}$$

$$0 \leq d \leq N \tag{5}$$

V: The number of vehicles must be equal to the number of capacities
C: set of capacities
D: set of demands
d: Depot index
N: number of points

- **Incremental fuel objective (6).**

$$\min \sum_{i,j \in Set_1} f_{ij}(v_{ij}) D_{ij}.X_{ij} + \sum_{i \in Set_1} f_{iR_t}(v_{iR_t}) D_{iR_t}.X_{iR_t} + \\ \sum_{j \in Set_1} f_{R_t i}(v_{R_t i}) D_{R_t i}.X_{R_t i} \tag{6}$$

The three sums represent, respectively, (a) edges that stay unchanged, (b) edges that connect the old tour to the new locker, and (c) edges that link the new locker back into the tour. The optimizer chooses binary routing variables X to minimize the extra fuel.

- **Load feasibility (7).**

$$\sum_{i \in Set_2} d_i + d_U \leq d_{V\,Set_2} \tag{7}$$

The left side is the total load after inserting U's parcel into candidate lockers; the right side is the total spare capacity of vehicles that can reach those lockers. Inequality is consistent with capacity control.

- **Tour continuity (8)–(9).**

$$\sum_{j \in Set_1 \setminus \{c_{11}\}} X_{S_{11}j} = 1 \tag{8}$$

$$\sum_{j \in Set_1 \setminus \{c_{1n}\}} X_{jS_{1n}} = 1 \tag{9}$$

They force exactly one successor and one predecessor for the start and end of the repaired fragment, preserving a single tour structure.

- **Time consistency (10).**

$$S_{Ui} + T_{ij} + TempsdeService \leq S_{R_t j} \tag{10}$$

C_i : *coordinates of client.*
$D_{\{ij\}}$: *Distance between client i and clientj.*
$T_{\{ij\}}$: *travel time between client i and clientj.*
d_i : *demand of clienti.*
U : *ID of the client who becomes unavailable.*
R_T : *ID of the client that will receive the demand of client U.*
N_T : *time when the unavailability is reported.*
$Set_1 = \{c_{1i}|c_{1i} \text{ is not served before } N_T\}.$
$Set_2 = \{c_{2i}|c_{2i} \text{ can take he extra deman of } U\}.$
$f_{ij}(v_{\{ij\}})$:
fuel consumption in kg CO^2 per km between clients i and j at average speed v_{ij}.

The service start time at the relocated locker must not precede travel plus service time from the last confirmed customer. This guards against infeasible temporal sequences.

3.4 Solution Engines: PPO and ACO

PPO Policy Learning. The reinforcement-learning agent treats each route construction as an episode. State, action, and reward are defined exactly as in Sect. 1; the clipped objective remains.

Reward and Hyperparameters. We use a carbon-centric reward

$$R_t = -\alpha CO_2\_mass(a_t) - \beta travel\backslash\_time(a_t) - \gamma lateness(a_t) + \delta 1[feasible]$$

with city-wise normalization. The best PPO settings (from our grid search) are: actor_lr $= 10^{-5}$, critic_lr $= 10^{-5}$, $\gamma = 0.99$, $\lambda = 0.95$, clip $\epsilon = 0.2$, KL target $= 0.01$, entropy coeff. $= 0.1$, and seed $= 42$.

$$L^{CLIP}(\theta) = E_t\left[min\left(r_t(\theta)\hat{A} , clip(r_t(\theta), 1- \epsilon, 1+ \epsilon)\hat{A}\right)\right] \tag{11}$$

where,

$r_t(\theta) = \frac{\pi_\theta(st)}{\pi_{\theta_{old}}(st)}$ is the probability ratio between new and old policies. $\hat{A}$ is an estimator of the advantage (how much better an action is compared to average). ϵ is a small hyperparameter (e.g., 0.1 or 0.2) controlling the clipping range. During live operations, a relocation event rebuilds the state with updated demands and locker coordinates, then calls the trained policy to insert the new stop sequence subject to Eqs. (6)–(10).

ACO Benchmark. Ants follow pheromone rule

$$\tau_{ij}(t+1) = (1-\rho)\tau_{ij}(t) + \sum_{k=1}^{m}\Delta\tau_{ij}^k(t) \tag{12}$$

$\tau_{ij}(t)$ is the pheromone level on edge (i,j) at iteration t.

$\rho \in (0,1)$ is the pheromone evaporation rate; larger ρ implies faster evaporation.

$\Delta \tau_{ij}^k$ is the amount of pheromone deposited by ant k on (i, j) during iteration t.

m is the number of ants

and choose the next node with

$$p_{ij}^k(t) = \frac{[\tau_{ij}(t)]^\alpha [\eta_{ij}]^\beta}{\sum_{l \in N_i^k} [\tau_{il}(t)]^\alpha [\eta_{il}]^\beta} \tag{13}$$

$p_{ij}^k(t)$: the probability that ant k at node iii moves next to node jjj at iteration t.

$\tau_{ij}(t)$: the current pheromone level for edge (i, j).

η_{ij}: a heuristic factor (often $\eta_{ij} = \frac{1}{d_{ij}}$, the inverse of the distance).

$\alpha \geq 0$: the exponent controlling how strongly ants follow pheromone.

$\beta \geq 0$: the exponent controlling how strongly ants follow the heuristic.

N_i^l: the set of feasible nodes for ant k from node i.

When a customer relocates, only the tour containing U is rebuilt; ants restrict their feasible list to *Set*1 and *Set*2 and apply constraints (6)–(10).

3.5 Algorithm Interaction with the Constraints

ACO. At each relocation the colony freezes pheromone on edges that remain legal under (7)–(10) and lets evaporation weaken arcs that now violate capacity or timing. New ants then rebuild the missing section by sampling probabilities (13), always evaluating the incremental objective (6).

PPO. The simulator injects the modified state into the policy network. Because the reward remains the negative marginal CO_2 from (1) plus penalties for any violation of (7)–(10), the network can react without replaying the whole day.

3.6 Experimental Setup

The study uses real locker networks for Tangier, Marrakech, and Casablanca:

- **Tangier** – 40 lockers, 5 vehicles
- **Casablanca** – 100 lockers, 9 vehicles
- **Marrakech** – 60 lockers, 7 vehicles

Figure 1, Fig. 2, and Fig. 3 show the spatial distributions. Table 1 summarizes instance parameters. Tables 2, 3, and 4 list per-vehicle speed brackets and ASIF fuel factors used in Eq. (1). During simulation, relocation events occur randomly during the tour; each triggers the optimization layer governed by Eqs. (6)–(10) while the overarching cost remains (1).

This integrated framework allows direct comparison of PPO and ACO under simultaneous CO_2 minimization and real-time flexible routing.

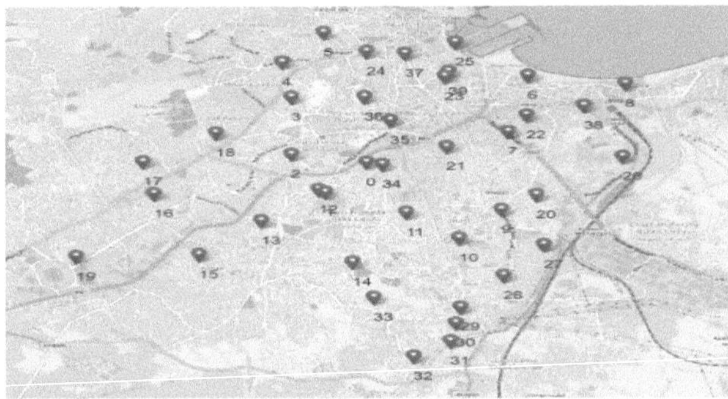

Fig. 1. Spatial Distribution of Parcel Lockers: A Geographic Representation in Tangier.

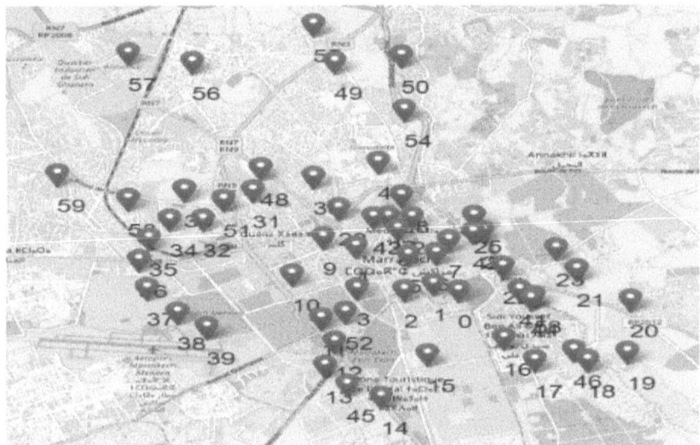

Fig. 2. Spatial Distribution of Parcel Lockers: A Geographic Representation in Marrakech.

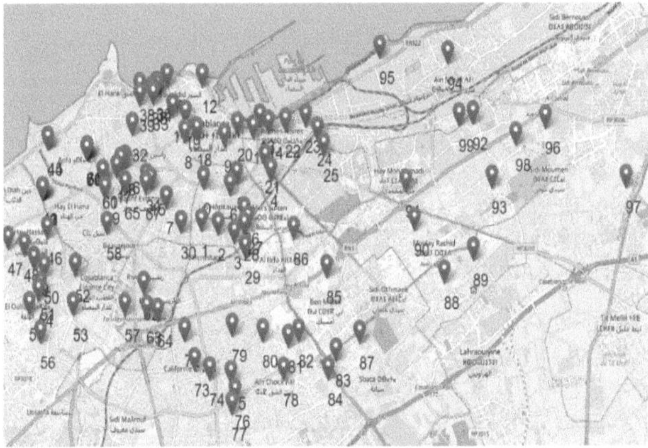

Fig. 3. Spatial Distribution of Parcel Lockers: A Geographic Representation in Casablanca.

Table 1. Morocco smart-locker VRP instances.

Instance	City	Vehicles	Customers	Capacity vector	Demand vector
N39k5	Tangier	5	39	[43, 47, 39, 56, 47]	[1–10]
N60k7	Marrakech	6	59	[48, 57, 39, 59, 37, 49, 40]	[1–10]
N100k9	Casablanca	9	99	[85, 69, 55, 50, 84, 75, 58, 65, 60]	[1–10]

Table 2. Tangier instance.

Vehicle	<30 km/h	30–60 km/h	60–90 km/h	90–120 km/h	CO_2 *factor(kg/L)*
1	12	10	7	8.5	2.57
2	15	12	8	9.5	2.6
3	8	6	5	6.5	2.5
4	13	10	7	8.5	2.55
5	11	9	7	7.5	2.54

Table 3. Marrakech instance.

Vehicle	<30 km/h	30–60 km/h	60–90 km/h	90–120 km/h	CO_2 *factor(kg/L)*
1	12	10	7	8.5	2.57
2	15	12	8	9.5	2.6
3	8	6	5	6.5	2.5
4	17	10	7	8.5	2.55
5	11	9	7	7.5	2.54
6	14	11	8	8	2.58

Table 4. Casablanca instance.

Vehicle	<30 km/h	30–60 km/h	60–90 km/h	90–120 km/h	CO_2 *factor(kg/L)*
1	12	10	7	8.5	2.57
2	15	12	8	9.5	2.6
3	8	6	5	6.5	2.5
4	13	10	7	8.5	2.5
5	11	9	7	7.5	2.54
6	14	11	8	9	2.58
7	10	8	6	7	2.52
8	16	14	9	10	2.65
9	9	7	9	7.2	2.53

4   Results

The experiment ran the Vehicle Routing Problem with Real-Time Customer Relocation and Smart Locker Adjustments. Locker 5 became unavailable thirty minutes after dispatch, and its parcel moved to locker 16. Both engines rebuild the affected tour under the same constraint set that governs capacity, time, and cumulative carbon. Table 5 reports on the numerical outcome and should be placed here.

Table 5. Emissions (kg CO_2) and % change vs. Baseline.

City	ACO (Baseline)	PPO (Baseline)	ACO (Smart-Locker $\Delta\%$)	PPO (Smart-Locker $\Delta\%$)	ACO (Direct Transfer $\Delta\%$)	PPO (Direct Transfer $\Delta\%$)
Tangier	21,054.3	20,497.0	23,064.4 (9.5)	20,964.3 (2.3)	23,994.9 (14.0)	21,362.7 (4.2)
Marrakech	46,504.0	44,924.7	46,503.7 (0.0)	45,792.3 (1.9)	47,396.4 (1.9)	46,950.0 (4.5)
Casablanca	68,115.1	65,171.6	69,105.9 (1.5)	66,181.7 (1.6)	70,956.3 (4.2)	67,993.7 (4.3)

Grid search, implemented through Itertools, supplied every hyper-parameter combination. For Proximal Policy Optimization the procedure fixed num_clusters to the length of the capacity vector, then swept actor_lr, critic_lr, γ, λ, clip_ε, KL target, β, entropy weight, kernel count, episode length, reward scale, and random seed. The best configuration used actor_lr $= 1 \times 10^{-5}$, critic_lr $= 1 \times 10^{-5}$, $\gamma = 0.99$, $\lambda = 0.95$, clip_$\varepsilon = 0.2$, KL target $= 0.01$, $\beta = 1.0$, entropy_coeff $= 0.1$, num_kernels $= 27$, max_steps $= 1\ 000$, reward_scale $= 10.0$, and seed $= 42$. The Ant Colony Optimization sweep varied generation count, colony size, α, β, and ρ. The strongest setting held 200 generations, one ant per locker, $\alpha = 0.2$, $\beta = 10$, and $\rho = 0.9$. Equal search budgets kept the comparison fair.

Hardware. Experiments were run on an AMD Ryzen 9 7945HX CPU with an NVIDIA GeForce RTX 4060 GPU and 32 GB of RAM, for both PPO and ACO.

Casablanca covers the largest graph. Baseline ACO reached 68 115 kg CO_2, against 65 172 kg for PPO, a 4.3% saving. Smart-locker repair added 991 kg for ACO and 1 010 kg for PPO, both near 1.5%. Direct transfer added 2 841 kg for ACO and 2 822 kg for PPO, around 4.2%. Even with the heavier detour, PPO held a 3% margin (Figs. 4 and 5).

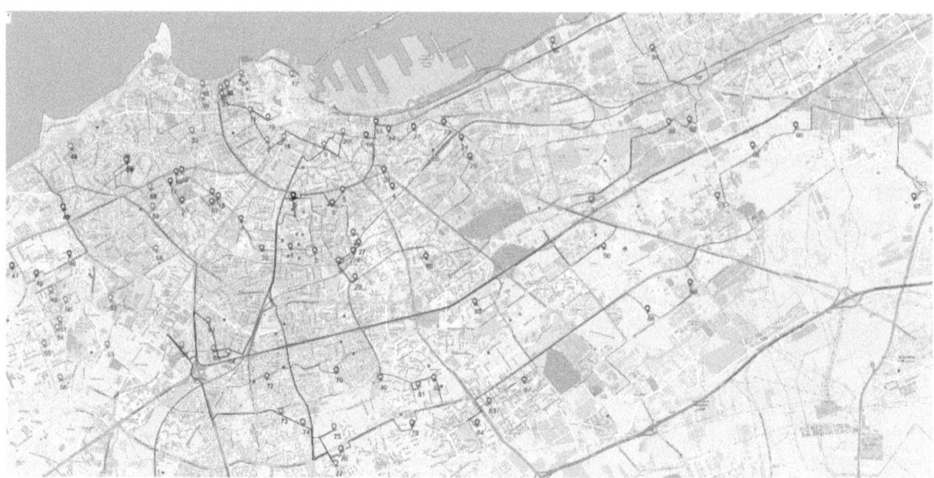

Fig. 4. PPO-Optimized Route for VRP in Casablanca.

Fig. 5. ACO-Optimized Route for VRP in Casablanca.

Marrakech presents a medium network. Baseline ACO emitted 46 504 kg CO_2; baseline PPO emitted 44 925 kg, cutting 3.4%. Smart-locker repair did not change ACO materially but raised PPO by 868 kg, a 1.9% penalty. Direct transfer pushed ACO to 47 396 kg and PPO to 46 950 kg, giving penalties of 1.9% and 4.5%, respectively. PPO kept absolute emissions below ACO in all three cases (Figs. 6 and 7).

Fig. 6. PPO-Optimized Route for VRP in Marrakech.

Fig. 7. ACO-Optimized Route for VRP in Marrakech.

Tangier shows the narrowest gap. Baseline ACO emitted 21 054 kg CO_2, while baseline PPO emitted 20 497 kg, a reduction of 2.6%. Smart-locker repair lifted ACO to 23 064 kg and PPO to 20 964 kg. Direct demand transfer raised ACO to 23 995 kg and

PPO to 21 363 kg. These figures imply that PPO absorbed the disruption with a 2.3% carbon penalty, compared with 9.5% for ACO (Figs. 8 and 9).

Fig. 8. PPO-Optimized Route for VRP in Tangier.

Fig. 9. ACO-Optimized Route for VRP in Tangier.

Across cities the baseline gap between solvers widens with network size. PPO outperformed ACO by 557 kg in Tangier, 1 579 kg in Marrakech, and 2 944 kg in Casablanca. The trend indicates that the policy scales better with node count and traffic diversity.

Flexibility costs differ by variant. Smart-locker repair produced smaller penalties than direct demand transfer in Tangier and Casablanca, while Marrakech showed symmetric behavior. On average, smart-locker repair raised carbon by 4.0% for ACO and 1.9% for PPO. Direct transfer raised carbon by 6.7% for ACO and 4.4% for PPO. The lower PPO penalties confirm that a trained policy can exploit residual capacity and route slack more efficiently than repeated stochastic search.

The results section closes with three findings. First, trainee PPO policies meet or beat tuned ACO tours on carbon even before relocation, confirming that reinforcement learning can equal mature population search for static green routing. Second, PPO limits carbon growth after late customer changes by reacting in a single forward pass through the network, while ACO's batch rebuild yields detours that rise with network complexity. Third, route geometry in the figures reveals consistent structural patterns that explain the numeric gaps—PPO draws sector-based loops; ACO sometimes reuses central corridors after their marginal cost has increased. Together, these findings support the adoption of policy learning in dispatch systems that demand real-time flexibility under strict emission caps.

5   Discussion

Operational integration. The policy can be called as a decision oracle inside the dispatch stack (one API call per event), returning the next stop in sub-second time on commodity hardware. At a daily scale this yields compute costs on the order of cents per 1,000 decisions, while lowering kg CO_2 and missed-slot penalties relative to a full rebuild; this ties the method directly to fleet KPIs (€/stop, SLA, CO_2e).

The experiment shows that algorithmic learning can serve last-mile dispatch under a carbon cap without sacrificing response time. Proximal Policy Optimization produced tours that needed less fuel both before and after a locker relocation. This outcome signals a shift in how courier firms can balance service flexibility with emission targets. Where classic metaheuristics rebuild a full tour after every disruption, the policy network reacts with one forward pass. This fundamental difference in decision speed explains the lower detour cost observed in the flexible scenario.

Late customer updates stress any solver because they shorten the window for repair while the vans continue to move. The colony approach repeats stochastic construction from a partial state, which exposes it to local minima anchored in earlier pheromone traces. The policy, by contrast, treats the update as a distinct state that still fits within its training distribution. The agent does not backtrack over earlier choices; it selects a next stop that respects the residual budget on capacity and carbon. The savings stem from this incremental logic rather than from superior baseline route planning alone. In operational terms, the ability to insert a locker with minimal extra travel keeps drivers on schedule and preserves locker availability for later parcels.

Scalability emerges as the second clear theme. As the locker graph grows the neural policy preserves its margin, while the colony loses ground. Two factors interact. First, the policy network's complexity rises only with the feature vector, not with the node count in the search tree. Second, the colony allocates an ant to every locker, so its search space inflates directly with network size. A national courier that plans to expand locker coverage will therefore see the policy approach hold steady while the colony consumes more run-time and compute. The larger the city, the more critical that difference becomes when dispatch windows tighten.

Real-time constraints add another layer. Policy inference finished within a fraction of a second on commodity hardware, giving the planner ample slack for traffic updates or driver breaks. The colony used the full iteration allowance after each disruption and still fell short of the policy's fuel outcome. In a live control room that gap translates into increased headroom for unforeseen events. Couriers often face construction detours, emergency road closures, or flash storms that force impromptu re-sequencing. A solver that already operates near the time limit leaves no margin for those events. The faster policy routine can absorb them without delaying customer alerts.

Carbon accounting shaped every decision. The reward function penalized marginal fuel use outright, not distance. This design pushed the agent to avoid high consumption speed bands even when a shorter path existed. Traditional distance-based heuristics often struggle with such trade-offs because the carbon penalty acts at route level, not edge level. The colony captured it partly through pheromone updates, yet its exploration still favored shorter geometric loops. Emission-aware reward shaping therefore stands out as a decisive element of successful policy learning in green logistics.

From a system perspective, the study supports gradual integration of learning agents into existing dispatch stacks. Carriers can run the policy network as a decision oracle alongside current solvers, accepting its advice when it offers a lower carbon trajectory within the same service window. They can also log the agent's suggestions to build a data set of counterfactual tours, which engineers can inspect for safety and regulatory compliance. Such dual operation eases the transition and builds trust among dispatchers who rely on predictable behavior.

Several limitations frame the findings. The data cover three Moroccan cities, each with diesel vans and static locker layouts. Electric fleets introduce range and charging constraints that change route dynamics. Weather, road closures, and stochastic travel times did not enter the simulator, yet they shape day-to-day performance. The study also considered a single disruption per tour; multiple overlapping changes could dilute the policy's advantage if its training never encountered such density. The grid search for both solvers used fixed budgets; more expansive searches might close the performance gap but would raise run-time or training cost.

Future research can extend the model on three fronts. First, incorporate battery state to compare reinforcement learning with colony methods under range constraints. Second, explore hybrid schemes where the policy sets a skeleton tour and a lighter colony fills minor gaps, merging the strengths identified here. Third, investigate multi-objective reward functions that trade off carbon against delivery lead time or locker congestion, since carriers often juggle several metrics. Each extension will demand careful simulator design so that the state space presented to the agent remains tractable.

The experiment contributes to the debate on whether learning methods can replace mature heuristics in operational routing. The answer is nuanced. Deep reinforcement learning does not automatically guarantee better tours, yet when combined with carbon-centered reward design and adequate training data it can outclass classic colonies in both fuel economy and reaction speed. Importantly, the gain grows with network scale and disruption frequency, matching the trend toward denser locker grids and on-demand delivery options. Dispatch teams that value rapid adaptation under emission caps now have evidence that a trained policy warrants serious consideration alongside, or instead of, long-standing metaheuristic staples.

Future work can link policy-driven dispatch with Blockchain ledgers that track parcel custody in real time [39]. A shared ledger would record every locker hand-over and routing choice, anchoring audit trails and triggering smart contracts once the fleet meets its carbon ceiling. This transparent record supports regulatory compliance and cross-company coordination without relying on a central data broker. Dispatch recommendations from the reinforcement agent can stream directly into the ledger, while verified delivery events feed back into model retraining. Near-term research should close the loop by adding short-horizon forecasts that feed the policy before each planning cycle [40]. A time-series model predicts parcel inflow at the depot and speed on critical road segments. The forecast vector extends the state seen by the agent, letting it pre-allocate locker capacity and choose departure times that pre-empt congestion. After execution, the Blockchain ledger holds ground-truth events that retrain both the predictor and the policy. The reinforcement agent can treat smart contract triggers as side rewards, nudging future routes toward verifiable sustainability targets without extra supervision.

6   Conclusion

The paper presented a carbon-aware routing model that folds smart-locker assignment and mid-tour repair into daily dispatch. Tests on three Moroccan cities compared ACO and PPO under matched run-time limits and identical data sources. The numbers point to three clear outcomes. First, PPO delivered lower baseline emissions across all networks, saving up to 2 944 kg of CO_2 in the largest case. Second, when a late locker change forced a route repair, PPO added one to two percent extra carbon, while ACO added four to ten percent. Fast inference lets the policy insert the new stop without rebuilding the whole tour, which explains the smaller penalty. Third, the gap widened with network size, suggesting that policy learning scales better than colony search as locker grids grow. These findings have direct operational value. A dispatcher can call the learned policy in milliseconds, keep emission records inside the regulatory cap, and still absorb customer updates that arrive after vans leave the depot. The colony approach, though reliable on small graphs, struggles to stay within a tight carbon budget once disruptions occur. Several limits remain. The study used diesel vans, fixed locker layouts, and one relocation per tour. Electric trucks, stochastic travel times, and multiple simultaneous updates could change solver rankings.

Acknowledgments. This work was conducted as part of the MILEX project and greatly benefited from the unwavering support of the Hassan II University of Casablanca, Ecole Centrale Casablanca, and Mohammed VI Polytechnic University. The collaborative and constructive involvement of these institutions played a pivotal role in the successful realization of this work, and we express our profound gratitude for their invaluable contributions throughout the research process. Thanks are also due to the referees for their valuable comments.

Disclosure of Interests. The authors declare no conflicts of interest.

References

1. Mohri, S.S., Ghaderi, H., Van Woensel, T., Mohammadi, M., Nassir, N., Thompson, R.G.: Contextualizing alternative delivery points in last-mile delivery. Transp. Res. Part E **192**, 103787 (2024)
2. Ferreira, K.M., de Queiroz, T.A., Munari, P., Toledo, F.M.B.: A variable neighborhood search for the green vehicle routing problem with two-dimensional loading constraints and split delivery. Eur. J. Oper. Res. **316**(2), 597–616 (2024)
3. Qi, R., Li, J.Q., Wang, J., Jin, H., Han, Y.Y.: QMOEA: a Q-learning-based multiobjective evolutionary algorithm for solving time-dependent green vehicle routing problems with time windows. Inf. Sci. **608**, 178–201 (2022)
4. Erdogdu, K., Karabulut, K.: Bi-objective green vehicle routing problem. Int. Trans. Oper. Res. **29**(3), 1602–1626 (2022)
5. Liu, Y., et al.: Branch-cut-and-price for the time-dependent green vehicle routing problem with time windows. INFORMS J. Comput. **35**(1), 14–30 (2023)
6. Che, Z.-H., Chiang, T.-A., Luo, Y.-J.: Multiobjective optimization for planning the service areas of smart parcel locker facilities in logistics last-mile delivery. Mathematics **10**(3), 422 (2022)
7. Ozyavas, P., Buijs, P., Ursavas, E., Teunter, R.: Designing a sustainable delivery network with parcel locker systems as collection and transfer points. Omega **131**, 103199 (2025)
8. Guo, N., Qian, B., Na, J., Hu, R., Mao, J.: A three-dimensional ant colony optimization algorithm for the multi-compartment vehicle routing problem considering carbon emissions. Appl. Soft Comput. **127**, 109326 (2022)
9. Li, J., et al.: Deep reinforcement learning for solving the heterogeneous capacitated vehicle routing problem. IEEE Trans. Cybern. **52**(12), 13572–13585 (2022)
10. Lei, K., Guo, P., Wang, Y., Wu, X., Zhao, W.: Solve routing problems with a residual edge-graph attention neural network. Neurocomputing **508**, 79–98 (2022)
11. Chen, C., Demir, E., Huang, Y.: Efficient feasibility checks and an adaptive large neighborhood search algorithm for the time-dependent green vehicle routing problem with time windows. Eur. J. Oper. Res. **310**(1), 133–155 (2023)
12. Su, Y., Zhang, S., Zhang, C.: A lightweight genetic algorithm with variable neighborhood search for the multi-depot vehicle routing problem with time windows. Appl. Soft Comput. **161**, 111789 (2024)
13. Wen, M., Sun, W., Yu, Y., Tang, J., Ikou, K.: An adaptive large neighborhood search for the larger-scale multi-depot green vehicle routing problem with time windows. J. Clean. Prod. **374**, 133916 (2022)
14. Zhang, R., Yu, R., Xia, W.: Constraint-aware policy optimization to solve the vehicle routing problem with time windows. Inf. Technol. Control **51**(1), 126–138 (2022)
15. Yan, D., Guan, Q., Ou, B., Yan, B., Cao, H.: Graph-driven deep reinforcement learning for vehicle routing problems with pickup and delivery. Appl. Sci. **15**(9), 4776 (2025)
16. Li, J., Niu, Y., Zhu, G., Xiao, J.: Solving pick-up and delivery problems via deep reinforcement learning-based symmetric neural optimization. Expert Syst. Appl. **255**, 124514 (2024)
17. Zang, X., Jiang, L., Liang, C., Fang, X.: Coordinated home and locker deliveries: an exact approach for the urban delivery problem with conflicting time windows. Transp. Res. Part E **177**, 103070 (2023)

18. Liu, Y., Zhao, X., Zhang, Z., Fang, K.: A branch-price-and-cut algorithm for a time-dependent green vehicle routing problem with traffic congestion. Comput. Ind. Eng. **182**, 109093 (2023)
19. Zhang, W., Xu, M., Wang, S.: Joint location and pricing optimization of self-service parcel lockers in urban logistics considering customers' choice behavior. Transp. Res. Part E **174**, 103984 (2023)
20. Guan, Q., Cao, H., Jia, L., Yan, D., Chen, B.: Synergetic attention-driven transformer: a deep reinforcement learning approach for vehicle routing problems. Expert Syst. Appl. **274**, 126961 (2025)
21. Kim, B.S., Mozhdehi, A., Wang, Y., Sun, S., Wang, X.: Clustering-based enhanced ant colony optimization for the multi-trip vehicle routing problem with a heterogeneous fleet and time windows: an industrial case study. In: Proceedings of the 17th ACM SIGSPATIAL International Workshop on Computational Transportation Science (IWCTS 2024), pp. 46–55. ACM, New York (2025)
22. Hanaa, B., Benhra, J., Ed-dehbi, W.: Last-mile delivery optimization using mixed electric vehicles, UAVs and full-truck delivery based on artificial intelligence algorithms. In: Communications in Computer and Information Science, vol. 2373, pp. 3–26. Springer, Cham (2025)
23. Berrahmania, N., Hammou, E.H., El Fadi, L.: Metaheuristic approaches to the green vehicle routing problem with pick-up and delivery and time windows: a review of CO_2 reduction in distribution logistics. In: Lecture Notes in Networks and Systems, vol. 1403, pp. 629–640. Springer, Cham (2025)
24. Berrahmania, N., Hammou, E.H., El Fadi, L.: Short review in green vehicle routing problem with pick-up and delivery and time windows using metaheuristics. Open Transport. J. **19**, e26671212375850 (2025)
25. Shuaibu, A.S., Mahmoud, A.S., Sheltami, T.R.: Last-mile delivery optimization: recent approaches and advances. Transport. Res. Procedia **84**, 299–306 (2025)
26. Stodola, P., Kutěj, L.: Multi-depot vehicle routing problem with drones: mathematical formulation, solution algorithm and experiments. Expert Syst. Appl. **241**, 122483 (2024)
27. Caballero-Morales, S.-O., Rojas-Cuevas, I.-D.: Analyzing the effect of variable transportation load on. Model. Simul. Eng. **2024**, 3226125 (2024)
28. Ramirez-Villamil, A., Jaegler, A., Montoya-Torres, J.R.: Sustainable local pickup and delivery: the case of Paris. Res. Transp. Bus. Manag. **45**, 100692 (2022)
29. Giuffrida, N., Fajardo-Calderín, J., Masegosa, A.D., Steudter, M., Pilla, F.: Optimization and machine learning applied to last-mile logistics: a review. Sustainability **14**(9), 5329 (2022)
30. Martins, L.D.C., Tordecilla, R.D., Castaneda, J., Juan, A.A., Faulin, J.: Electric vehicle routing, arc routing, and team orienteering problems in sustainable transportation. Energies **14**(16), 5131 (2021)
31. Quirion-Blais, O., Chen, L.: A case-based reasoning approach to solve the vehicle routing problem with time windows and drivers' experience. Omega **102**, 102340 (2021)
32. Alewijnse, B., Hübl, A.: Minimising total costs of a two-echelon multi-depot capacitated vehicle routing problem that describes utilisation of the Amsterdam city canal network for last-mile parcel delivery. In: IFIP Advances in Information and Communication Technology, vol. 633, pp. 603–612. Springer, Cham (2021)
33. Alizadeh Foroutan, R., Rezaeian, J., Mahdavi, I.: Green vehicle routing and scheduling problem with a heterogeneous fleet including reverse logistics in the form of collecting returned goods. Appl. Soft Comput. **94**, 106462 (2020)
34. Kirci, P.: A novel model for the vehicle routing problem with minimizing CO_2 emissions. In: 2019 3rd International Conference on Advanced Information and Communications Technologies (AICT 2019) Proceedings, pp. 241–243. IEEE, Piscataway (2019)

35. Mandziuk, J.: New shades of the vehicle routing problem: emerging problem formulations and computational intelligence solution methods. IEEE Trans. Emerg. Topics Comput. Intell. **3**(3), 230–244 (2019)
36. Niroomand, I., Nsakanda, A.L.: Improving collection flows in a public postal network with contractor's obligation considerations. Int. J. Prod. Econ. **198**, 79–92 (2018)
37. Leyerer, M., Sonneberg, M.-O., Breitner, M.H.: Decision support for urban e-grocery operations. In: Proceedings of the 24th Americas Conference on Information Systems (AMCIS 2018). AIS, New Orleans (2018)
38. Jabali, O., Van Woensel, T., De Kok, A.G.: Analysis of travel times and CO_2 emissions in time-dependent vehicle routing. Prod. Oper. Manag. **21**(6), 1060–1074 (2012)
39. Nadime, K.L., Benhra, J., Benabbou, R., Mouatassim, S.: A Blockchain-powered framework for traceable and secure pharmaceutical delivery with crowdsourced logistics. In: Innovative Intelligent Industrial Production and Logistics. IN4PL 2024. Communications in Computer and Information Science, vol. 2372, pp. 367–384. Springer, Cham (2025)
40. Haidar, D., Mouatassim, S., Benabbou, R., Benhra, J.: Trade volume prediction using exponential smoothing. In: 2024 Sixth International Conference on Intelligent Computing in Data Sciences (ICDS 2024) Proceedings, pp. 61–69. IEEE, Piscataway (2024)

Circular Business Models for Logistic Service Providers

Francesco Cafforio[1] , Roberto Cerchione[2] , Ilaria Giannoccaro[1] ,
Giovanni Francesco Massari[1(✉)] , Mariarosaria Morelli[2,3] , and Viviana Sicardi[2]

[1] Department of Mechanics, Mathematics, and Management, Politecnico di Bari, Bari, Italy
`giovannifrancesco.massari@poliba.it`
[2] Department of Engineering, University of Naples Parthenope, Naples, Italy
[3] Department of Management, Information and Production Engineering, University of
Bergamo, Dalmine, Italy

Abstract. Logistic Service Providers (LSPs) are central actors in advancing the Circular Economy (CE) due to their pivotal role in managing material, information, and service flows across supply chains. Yet, how LSPs are integrating CE principles into their business models remains underexplored. This study addresses this gap by identifying and analyzing Circular Business Model (CBM) archetypes adopted by LSPs. Drawing on a multiple-case study approach involving 27 global LSPs, we conduct a qualitative content analysis of GRI-aligned sustainability reports and complementary firm documents. Our findings reveal four distinct CBM archetypes: (1) *efficiency optimization business models*, focused on minimizing emissions and resource use through digital innovation, representing evolutionary business model innovation (BMI); (2) *reverse logistics business models*, enabling post-use material recovery and reintegration, aligned with adaptive BMI; (3) *asset life-extending business models*, combining adaptive and focused BMIs to preserve infrastructure and vehicle lifespan via predictive maintenance; and (4) *service-based logistics business models*, involving complex BMI that reconfigures logistics through sharing platforms and access-based services. The novelty of this study lies in developing the first typology of CBMs tailored to the logistics sector, clarifying how circularity is operationalized in a domain often overlooked by CBM research. The study contributes to CE and business model literature by clarifying how LSPs operationalize circularity and provides actionable guidance for logistics managers navigating sustainability transitions.

Keywords: Circular Economy · Circular Business Models · Logistic Service Providers · Sustainable Logistics · Business Model Innovation

1 Introduction

Global supply chains (SCs) are currently facing unprecedented challenges compelling profound modifications to their configurations for sustained competitiveness. Climate changes, biodiversity loss, and the fast-running depletion of natural resources, combined with increased governmental pressures, are pushing industrial firms to rethink

J. Barata et al. (Eds.): IN4PL 2025, CCIS 2826, pp. 263–278, 2026.
https://doi.org/10.1007/978-3-032-15579-5_16

and redesign their SCs to align with Circular Economy (CE) principles (Massari and Giannoccaro, 2023). CE represents a transformative paradigm promoting a shift from the conventional linear 'take-make-dispose' model towards regenerative and restorative systems by design (EMF, 2013). By narrowing, slowing, and closing resource loops, CE simultaneously addresses ecological pressures and creates opportunities for innovation and competitiveness as proven across diverse industrial sectors [1–4].

Within such an evolving landscape, a crucial, but often overlooked, sector is logistics. For decades, logistic service providers (LSPs) have collaborated with focal companies to better manage goods, materials, and information flowing from suppliers to end users [5–7] by providing transport and warehouse services. In recent years, instead, focal firms have increasingly outsourced logistics activities to LSPs in order to focus more on their core business [8–11]. Operating as third-party intermediaries, LSPs now manage a growing range of value-adding services, positioning them as strategic enablers in the transition from linear to circular SCs [12–14].

Yet this strategic importance comes with a paradox. The freight transport and logistics sectors are major contributors to greenhouse gas emissions worldwide, raising urgent demands for more sustainable solutions [15]. Consistent with this, policymakers are responding with increasingly stringent frameworks. Recent initiatives such as the European Green Deal, ISO 14083, the Circular Economy Action Plan, the European Union Emissions Trading System (EU ETS) and the Corporate Sustainability Reporting Directive (CSRD), explicitly call for more circular and transparent logistics operations. These measures, alongside extended producer responsibility (EPR) schemes and sector-specific sustainability targets, intensify the pressure on LSPs to embed CE principles into their business models.

Despite this, academic research on how LSPs integrate circularity into their business models remains fragmented [14]. Existing studies often highlight specific opportunities, for example, combining last-mile deliveries with reverse logistics for environmental and economic benefits, or outsourcing reverse logistics functions to LSPs to enhance closed-loop systems [12, 14]. Other contributions have identified a broad range of sustainable logistics practices [13], while some underline the gap between the recognition of environmental sustainability and its full integration into LSP strategies [16]. Further works have explored specific tools and frameworks for managing circular assets like returnable transport items [17] or explored LSPs' role as service enablers within Sharing Economy models, particularly in B2B contexts [18, 19]. Still, integrative frameworks exploring how LSPs are currently integrating CE principles within their business models (BMs) are still lacking, impeding a comprehensive understanding of the BM archetypes they implement.

To address this significant gap, we adopt a multiple case study approach involving 27 global LSPs along with a qualitative content analysis of GRI-aligned sustainability reports and complementary firm documents, systematically coding and comparing disclosed practices to inductively derive CBM archetypes. Building on the lens of BM Innovation (BMI), we interpret these archetypes as different modes of innovation, i.e., evolutionary, adaptive, focused, and complex, thereby clarifying the varying degrees of transformation required for logistics firms to implement CE.

Our empirical findings reveal that LSPs are currently adopting four distinct CBM archetypes: efficiency optimization, reverse logistics, asset life-extending and service-based logistics, each reflecting a different way of integrating CE principles within BMs.

The contribution of this study is twofold. We develop one among the first comprehensive typologies of CBMs tailored to logistics, moving beyond the traditional manufacturing-centric focus. Also, we demonstrate how LSPs operationalize circularity across value creation, delivery, and capture mechanisms, and we map each archetype to specific forms of BMI, thereby advancing both theoretical understanding and managerial practice.

The remainder of the paper is organized as follows. Section 2 presents the literature background concerning CE paradigm and the determinant role played by LSPs. Section 3 describes the research methodology. Section 4 illustrates the results. Finally, Sect. 5 provides discussion of the results, outlines theoretical and managerial contributions, and concludes with limitations and future research directions.

2 Literature Background

2.1 The Circular Economy: A Transformative Paradigm

The CE represents a transformative paradigm that radically shifts from the conventional linear "take-make-dispose" model towards a regenerative and restorative system via a purposeful design [20]. Such an approach seeks to prolong the lifespan of products, materials, and resources by preserving their maximum value through ongoing circulation, thus reducing waste and averting resource depletion [1]. Initially rooted in ecological philosophical frameworks (e.g., "cyclical economy" or "green economy"), the CE has progressively evolved into a broader economic paradigm achieving worldwide recognition [21, 22]. The Ellen MacArthur Foundation has played a pivotal role in articulating the economic rationale behind CE, framing it as a strategic opportunity for sustainable growth, innovation, and competitiveness [20].

The foundational principles of CE, originally centered on the "3Rs" of Reduce, Reuse, Recycle, have evolved to include a more extensive array of "R" strategies, including Rethink, Repair, Refurbish, Remanufacture, Repurpose, and Recover, all designed to decelerate, narrow, close, and dematerialize resource streams [12, 23, 24]. These strategies address pressing global challenges such as resource scarcity and environmental degradation, while also offering sustainable economic development [14, 25]. This transformation presents substantial prospects for value creation, with projections reaching approximately USD $8 trillion by 2030. It serves as a vital mechanism for attaining Sustainable Development Goals (SDGs), promoting innovation, and improving competitiveness across diverse sectors [26].

Translating CE principles into practice requires firms to redesign and rethink their BMs around circularity, giving rise to a new class of "sustainable business models" [27], commonly referred to as Circular Business Models (CBMs). CBMs are defined as BMs designed to "create, capture, and deliver value [...] thereby realizing environmental, social, and economic benefits" [28]. They guide firms in rethinking how value is generated, delivered, and appropriated by reconfiguring internal processes, resources, and stakeholder relationships to prioritize circular outcomes. These outcomes include recovering waste and by-products into valuable inputs, replacing ownership with access-based services, and embedding resource efficiency from the design phase [29–32].

Scholars have developed several taxonomies to categorize CBMs, reflecting the diverse strategies firms can adopt. For instance, Vermont et al. [33] classify CBMs according to the primary circularity focus, such as resource recovery and recycling, circular supplies, product life extension, and servitization; while Bocken et al. [34] and Geissdoerfer et al. [2] identify different archetypes of CBMs based on the changes produced on resource flows, i.e., closing, slowing, narrowing, intensifying, and dematerializing.

Implementing CBMs requires firms to purposefully redesign and rethink the key elements of their BMs, i.e., value proposition, value creation and delivery, and value capture, to align with CE principles [14, 27]. This process, often referred to as business model innovation (BMI), can take various forms, i.e., evolutionary, adaptive, focused, and complex, varying in novelty and scope [35]. Evolutionary business model innovation involves incremental changes to specific components that are new to the firm but common in the industry, such as minor optimizations in recycling or reuse processes. Adaptive business model innovation refers to broader reconfigurations of the business model that are new to the firm but already validated elsewhere, for instance, a manufacturer adopting product leasing inspired by servitization models in other sectors. Focused business model innovation targets a single business model element with an industry-novel solution, such as an innovative material recovery process, while keeping the overall value of logic intact. In contrast, complex BMI entails a systemic transformation that is new to both the firm and the industry, affecting multiple interdependent elements. This includes shifts from product sales to service-based models (e.g., pay-per-use), requiring a full redesign of how value is created, delivered, and captured, often to achieve triple-bottom-line outcomes.

Understanding these different types of BMI is crucial for analyzing how firms adopt and evolve CBMs. As already mentioned, while existing research has largely focused on manufacturing firms, the role of LSPs in enabling circularity remains underexplored [14]. Given their central position in managing forward and reverse flows, LSPs are uniquely positioned to innovate their BMs in line with circular principles. In the following paragraph, we examine the role of LSPs in the transition toward the CE.

2.2 Logistic Service Providers in the Circular Economy

Building on the aforementioned premises, logistics services, by integrating both last-mile deliveries and first-mile reverse logistics, can significantly improve circularity, resulting in both ecological and economic advantages. The outsourcing of reverse logistics functions, in particular, is recognized as an efficient strategy to enhance the value of the closed-loop SC and advance sustainability [12]. Consequently, logistics has emerged as a central pillar in the transition toward CE models, with reverse logistics playing a particularly strategic role in enabling circular flows of materials and products [14, 36, 37]. Within this context, the broader concept of "green logistics" is acknowledged as a key lever for promoting the sustainable advancement of logistics systems within a CE framework [38, 39]. Consequently, enhancing logistics operations and establishing circular SCs are essential for effective CE implementation [14, 40, 41]. In this context, factors such as Business-to-Consumer (B2C) online shopping, the quality of logistical services, and energy efficiency are essential for fostering consumer loyalty and driving sustainable growth within the CE [25, 42]. Specific elements like order quality, customized service quality, responsiveness and delivery quality directly influence customer happiness and trust. By enhancing these elements, LSPs can contribute to low-carbon operations via energy savings and emissions reductions, thereby improving market competitiveness by minimizing superfluous waste and environmental degradation. While energy consumption in logistics and manufacturing has been thoroughly examined, with initiatives aimed at optimizing processes to diminish energy usage and carbon emissions (e.g., CNC milling and textile weaving) [1, 43], specific efforts often extend to adjacent manufacturing proccessing, hilighting the need for a holistic apporach to CE integration.

Within this broader context, LSPs emerge as strategic actors in supporting the implementation of CE practices across SCs. For instance, Jayarathna et al. [13], through a qualitative approach involving in-depth interviews with LSPs, identified 47 sustainable logistics practices categorized into nine areas. However, studies like that by Evangelista et al. [16] reveal a persistent challenge: while environmental sustainability is widely recognized as important by LSPs, it is not yet fully and consistently integrated into their core mission, values, and operational strategies. This highlights the ongoing gap between awareness and comprehensive implementation, underscoring the need for further research into practical CBMs for LSPs.

In line with this, Katsanakis et al. [17] have developed frameworks and tools to guide LSPs in implementing holistic circular Returnable Transport Items (RTI) management systems. Their work emphasizes the systemic nature of RTIs within logistics networks, advocating for a systems thinking perspective that allows LSPs to consider critical factors such as transport distances, network structures, and supply chain requirements. This approach ultimately aims to reduce resource consumption, waste, and environmental footprints, while simultaneously strengthening SC relationships and improving competitiveness through proactive circular practices.

Beyond these operational aspects, recent studies have also explored how LSPs can act as service enablers within Sharing Economy (SE) models, thereby advancing circular practices in logistics [18, 44]. Specifically, in the Business-to-business (B2B) context, SE initiatives are characterized by the exchange of underutilized logistics resources between providers and users through digital platforms. Often, a third-party service enabler, typically an LSP, manages such a coordination [18]. Carissimi and Creazza [19], through a multiple case study, examined the intricate role of LSPs within SE service triads in B2B logistics solutions. Their findings underscore how the specific configuration of SE solutions, particularly concerning the ownership and control of logistics services by LSPs, significantly influences the triadic mechanisms and the enabling factors that foster value creation and environmental benefits.

Despite their clear potential, circular SCs, though essential for CE implementation, frequently encounter distinct challenges. These include the inherent unpredictability of return flows, complexities related to transportation and infrastructure, the critical necessity for compatible partners, stringent requirements for coordination and information exchange, robust product traceability, and persistent cultural resistance to traditional linear paradigms [14, 36, 41]. To overcome these hurdles, the incorporation of digital technologies, notably those associated with Industry 4.0, has become imperative. These technologies are strategic for internalizing information flows, optimizing production planning, and ensuring comprehensive material traceability within CSCs [41, 45]. Ultimately, digital intelligence serves as a powerful catalyst, promoting the development of regenerative and resilient production and consumption systems within the CE [46].

3 Research Methodology

Given the exploratory nature of our research question, we adopted a qualitative research design based on multiple case studies. This approach is particularly suitable for theory-building in emerging fields such as CE and BMI, where existing conceptualizations are limited and empirical evidence remains scarce [47]. In particular, case studies, if compared to quantitative approaches such as surveys or simulations, enable a richer and more nuanced exploration of complex and under-researched phenomena [48]. Following Yin's [49] case study methodology, our research process involved purposeful case selection, systematic data collection, and interpretive analysis.

The logistics sector was selected as the focal domain of inquiry due to its increasingly strategic role in enabling CE practices. LSPs are positioned at the core of material and information flows and are thus essential actors in supporting reverse logistics, closed-loop and open-loop SCs, and service-based value creation. These features make logistics a particularly promising context for identifying and conceptualizing CBMs. While prior CBM research has largely focused on manufacturing or retail sectors, the specific BMIs emerging within logistics remain relatively undocumented [14, 16]. By focusing on this sector, our study contributes to filling this gap and sheds light on how circularity is being integrated into logistics strategies, operations, and value propositions.

To this end, we conducted a qualitative content analysis based on secondary data sources. We employed a purposeful sampling strategy to identify cases of LSPs that explicitly engage with CE initiatives. Cases were selected based on two main criteria: (1) clear evidence of circular practices in the logistics domain and (2) the availability of public documentation detailing these practices, such as sustainability reports and corporate communications. We began by identifying all LSPs included in the Sustainability Yearbook 2024, which ranks the world's most sustainability-performing companies across industries. Out of the initial set of 33 companies, we selected a final sample of 27 logistics companies that had published sustainability reports aligned with the Global Reporting Initiative (GRI) standards, which is the most widely implemented standard [50]. This ensured the inclusion of companies with structured, comparable, and detailed disclosures of their sustainability strategies and practices, that is crucial for reliable and in-depth analysis. Table 1 presents the selected LSPs and summarizes key characteristics of each case.

Data collection focused primarily on firm-owned sources, including GRI-based sustainability reports, official websites, and strategic publications. These documents have been widely used in prior CE studies as credible sources of both qualitative and quantitative insights [51]. To enhance data triangulation and reduce potential bias, we supplemented these materials with external sources such as trade press articles, industry reports, and news coverage. External sources were identified through structured searches using combinations of keywords such as "circular economy" or "sustainability," and the company's name. Only documents explicitly referring to circular practices of the selected LSPs were retained.

Table 1. The selected case studies.

Company	Country	Industry
Canadian National Railway Company	Canada	T&T Infrastructure
Canadian Pacific Kansas City Limited	Canada	T&T Infrastructure
CJ Logistics Corporation	Republic of Korea	T&T Infrastructure
ComfortDelGro Corporation Limited	Singapore	T&T Infrastructure
Deutsche Post AG	Germany	T&T Infrastructure
FirstGroup plc	United Kingdom	T&T Infrastructure
Getlink SE	France	T&T Infrastructure
Gibson Energy Inc	Canada	Oil & Gas S&T
Hyundai Glovis Co., Ltd	Republic of Korea	T&T Infrastructure
International Distributions Services plc	United Kingdom	T&T Infrastructure
Kinder Morgan, Inc	United States	Trading C&D
MISC Berhad	Malaysia	T&T Infrastructure
Mitsui O.S.K. Lines, Ltd	Japan	T&T Infrastructure
Movida Participações S.A	Brazil	T&T Infrastructure
MTR Corporation Limited	Hong Kong	Commercial S&S
Nippon Yusen Kabushiki Kaisha	Japan	T&T Infrastructure
ONEOK, Inc	United States	T&T Infrastructure
Orient Overseas (International) Limited	Hong Kong	T&T Infrastructure
Rumo S.A	Brazil	T&T Infrastructure
SIMPAR S.A	Brazil	T&T Infrastructure
Transurban Group	Australia	T&T Infrastructure
Union Pacific Corporation	United States	T&T Infrastructure
Vamos Locação de Caminhões, Máquinas e Equipamentos S.A	Brazil	T&T Infrastructure
Wan Hai Lines Ltd	Taiwan	T&T Infrastructure

Legend: Transportation and Transportation (T&T); Storage and Transportation (S&T); Services & Suppliers (S&S); Companies & Distributors (C&D)

We conducted a qualitative content analysis to identify and categorize the CBM archetypes emerging from the cases. The analysis unfolded as an iterative process. First, we systematically extracted all excerpts that described circular practices from both firm-owned and external documents. These excerpts were then coded inductively, with the aim of identifying recurring patterns in how value was created, delivered, and captured through circular strategies. As the coding advanced, similarities and differences across cases were compared, which allowed us to group codes into broader categories. This process ultimately led to the definition of four distinct CBM archetypes. To ensure the robustness of the analysis, the coding schema was developed collaboratively by the authors. Any discrepancies were jointly reviewed and resolved through discussion, which further refined the coding framework and reinforced the consistency of our results.

4 Results

In this section, we illustrate empirical results on the CBMs implemented by LSPs. Table 2 provides a synthesis of the CBM archetypes and the companies adopting them. In particular, four archetypes have emerged, namely efficiency optimization, reverse logistics, asset life-extending, and service-based logistic BMs.

Efficiency optimization BMs refer to CBMs that aim to reduce emissions, energy use, and material waste by enhancing the efficiency of logistic operations (i.e., material handling, transportation). These models rely heavily on digital technologies, such as real-time analytics, AI, and IoT, to optimize routing, reduce empty runs, and enable modal shifts toward more sustainable transport modes. Companies like Canadian Pacific Kansas City and Orient Overseas (International) Limited exemplify this archetype through the use of predictive analytics and IoT-enabled cargo tracking to minimize delays and improve load utilization. Hyundai Glovis has implemented real-time routing systems and logistics center automation, while also shifting significant freight volumes from road to maritime transport. FirstGroup applies AI and machine learning to optimize fleet energy use, with bi-modal diesel-electric trains achieving significant CO_2 reductions. Maritime firms such as Mitsui O.S.K. Lines enhance efficiency through weather-based routing (DarWIN) and energy-saving propulsion systems, while Union Pacific and Canadian National Railway use simulation tools and predictive software to improve load distribution and intermodal coordination.

Reverse logistic BMs are characterized by the design of reverse logistic systems that enable the return, sorting, and reintegration of used materials into production cycles. These CBMs focus on post-consumption value retention and the reduction of virgin material consumption. Hyundai Glovis has established a comprehensive reverse logistics chain for electric vehicle batteries, ensuring full traceability, reuse in secondary applications, and environmentally responsible recycling of critical raw materials like lithium, cobalt, and nickel. Canadian Pacific Kansas City Limited and Canadian National Railway Company operate material recovery programs focused on regenerating railway infrastructure, such as tracks, bogies, and locomotives. In maritime transport, Mitsui O.S.K. Lines, Ltd., MISC, and Nippon Yusen Kabushiki Kaisha apply responsible ship dismantling standards and invest in recycling systems to recover high-quality materials. CJ Logistics has created large-scale reverse logistics partnerships with Samsung and LG Chem to recover electronic parts and plastic film, using digital waste tracking to improve process efficiency. At the consumer packaging level, International Distributions Services incorporates reverse logistics by reusing delivery pallets and introducing Velcro-based packaging solutions, thereby reducing single-use material flows and promoting packaging circularity.

Table 2. Overview of CBMs implemented by LSPs.

Company	Efficiency optimization BMs	Reverse logistic BMs	Asset life-extending BMs	Service-based logistic BMs
CJ Logistics Corporation		✓		
Canadian National Railway Company	✓	✓		
ComfortDelGro Corporation Limited			✓	✓
Canadian Pacific Kansas City Limited	✓	✓	✓	
Deutsche Post AG				✓
FirstGroup plc	✓			
Getlink SE	✓			
Gibson Energy Inc.			✓	
Hyundai Glovis Co., Ltd.	✓	✓		
International Distributions Services plc		✓		✓
Kinder Morgan, Inc.		✓		
MISC Berhad		✓		
Mitsui O.S.K. Lines, Ltd.	✓	✓		
Movida Participações S.A.				✓
MTR Corporation Limited			✓	
Nippon Yusen Kabushiki Kaisha		✓		
ONEOK, Inc.		✓		
Orient Overseas (International) Limited	✓			
Rumo S.A.	✓	✓	✓	
SIMPAR S.A.			✓	
Transurban Group			✓	✓
Union Pacific Corporation	✓		✓	
Vamos Locação de Caminhões, Máquinas e Equipamentos S.A.			✓	
Wan Hai Lines Ltd.			✓	
Total	9	11	10	5

Asset life-extending BMs involve extending the useful life of logistic assets, such as vehicles, vessels, infrastructure, and machinery, through predictive maintenance, refurbishment, and regeneration. This archetype supports circularity by deferring asset replacement and reducing virgin material use in primary manufacturing processes. Canadian Pacific Kansas City Limited employs AI-driven monitoring systems to detect faults in real-time, enabling proactive repair and regeneration of components like traction motors and braking systems. Union Pacific has successfully repaired over 140,000 locomotive components and hence avoided the consumption of over 27,000 tons of new steel. SIMPAR uses machine learning to optimize fleet management and minimize lifecycle inefficiencies, while Wan Hai Lines combines intelligent monitoring with eco-coatings to extend vessel and container lifecycles. Transurban and Gibson Energy apply predictive models to respectively road and energy infrastructure, extending asset performance and reducing renewal frequency. Vamos reconditions mechanical parts and tires from retired heavy vehicles, and ComfortDelGro repurposes decommissioned buses for educational and social use.

Service-based logistic BMs describe CBMs in which logistics services are provided through shared infrastructure or servitized platforms rather than through individual asset ownership. These models aim to increase asset utilization, reduce idle capacity, and decouple value creation from material throughput. Movida exemplifies this approach through long-term vehicle subscriptions bundled with maintenance, insurance, and support services. ComfortDelGro participates in the SE by offering fleet access through platforms like Drive Lah and Drive Mate. Deutsche Post AG has developed a wide-scale network of parcel lockers (Packstations) that consolidate deliveries and minimize last-mile traffic, while International Distributions Services plc's "Feet on the Street" and "Park and Loop" systems reduce vehicle use by shifting deliveries to pedestrian-supported models. Infrastructure players like Transurban enhance system-level circularity by transforming road networks into multifunctional hubs equipped with artificial intelligence (AI)-based traffic management and congestion forecasting.

5 Discussion and Conclusions

How do LSPs integrate CE principles within their BMs? Despite the critical role that LSPs play on good and information flows within global SCs, this question still merits further investigation. We address it through an empirical approach based on the analysis of multiple case studies referring to 27 LSPs.

Our empirical findings reveal that LSPs are currently adopting four distinct archetypes of CBMs, namely efficiency optimization, reverse logistics, asset life-extending and service-based logistics. Each archetype represents varying degrees and forms of BMI, differing in novelty, scope, and impact on existing BM elements.

Efficiency optimization CBMs exemplify evolutionary BMI, representing incremental and pragmatic entry point into circularity. This CBM focuses on minimizing emissions, energy consumption, and material waste through digital innovation and operational refinement. Aligned with RESOLVE's "optimize" principle [52] and the notion of "narrowing resource loops" [2, 34], this CBM preserves existing linear value structures, achieving incremental but meaningful sustainability improvements, by promoting resource efficiency. For instance, firms such as Canadian Pacific Kansas City and First-Group employ advanced analytics and IoT technologies to enhance resource efficiency without radically altering their underlying business logic. As such, this CBM reflects continuity more than reconfiguration, illustrating how circularity can emerge as an extension of efficiency-driven logic.

Reverse logistics CBM represents adaptive BMI, embedding circularity more centrally within logistics operations. These models enable the return, sorting, and reintegration of post-consumer materials, aligning closely with RESOLVE's "loop" principle [52], Accenture's strategy of "resource recovery and recycling" [53], and Bocken's concept of "closing loops" [2, 34]. Reverse logistics models require adapting existing infrastructure and systems to accommodate reverse flows, often using digital traceability tools to ensure material recovery is efficient and transparent. LSPs like Hyundai Glovis and Canadian National Railway exemplify adaptive BMI by reconfiguring their existing infrastructure and SC relationships to efficiently reclaim post-consumer value from waste, thus reducing reliance on virgin inputs and capturing new revenue streams from secondary material markets.

Asset lifecycle-extending CBM combines adaptive and focused BMIs, focusing on preserving the functional life of logistic assets through predictive maintenance, refurbishment, and component regeneration. These models effectively slow resource flows, aligning with RESOLVE's "optimize" and "loop" principles [52], Accenture's "product life extension" [53], and Bocken's "slowing loops" strategy [34]. Such CBMs necessitate innovative approaches to maintenance regimes and asset management, indicating a more disruptive change in operations rather than merely an adjustment. For example, firms such as Union Pacific and SIMPAR adopt AI-driven predictive maintenance and refurbishment practices, representing focused innovation within specific operational elements, thus creating value by extending asset usability while retaining their broader business model structure.

The most transformative archetype, service-based CBMs, entails complex BMI. These models significantly reconfigure how logistics services are conceptualized, accessed, and monetized. By shifting from ownership to access-oriented or platform-based models, these CBMs align with RESOLVE's "exchange" and "virtualize" principles [52], Lacy's "product as a service" and "product sharing" [53], and Bocken's strategies of "dematerializing" and "intensifying" resource use [34]. Companies such as Deutsche Post AG and ComfortDelGro fundamentally alter their value proposition, value creation and delivery, and value capture mechanisms, underscoring the profound strategic reorientation and extensive organizational change required. These models break from traditional asset-heavy logistics by creating value through maximized asset utilization and flexibility, delivering it via decentralized platforms and shared infrastructure, and capturing it by monetizing service performance rather than product throughput. Their implementation often requires new business logic, stakeholder relationships, and digital infrastructures, indicating a fundamental shift in both strategic orientation and organizational capabilities.

Beyond individual archetypes, our analysis reveals recurrent patterns. Reverse logistics emerges as the most widespread CBM, while service-based approaches to circularity remain more difficult to implement. Specifically, our findings denote how most of the LSPs prefer to adapt to circularity, i.e., by gradually changing their BMs, and are reluctant to radical changes. Interestingly, some companies, such as Canadian Pacific Kansas City, Hyundai Glovis, and Rumo are simultaneously adopting multiple archetypes of CBMs, suggesting a more complex and integrated approach to circularity.

This study provides both theoretical and managerial implications. Our findings enrich the literature on CE by providing empirical findings that illustrate how LSPs currently integrate CE principles in their businesses. They also contribute to the literature on CBM by exploring the archetypes of CBMs currently implemented by LSPs. Furthermore, by interpreting CBMs through established frameworks (e.g., RESOLVE) and taxonomies of CE [2, 34], our study contributes to better operationalizing sustainability goals with concrete business logics, offering a valuable bridge between theory and practice. From a managerial point of view, this study provides actionable insights for logistics managers seeking to align their operations with circularity goals. First, our four archetypes can be employed by logistic managers as strategic reference points to assess their current position in the circular transition and identify feasible pathways for incremental or transformative improvements. Second, the study emphasizes the importance of fostering strategic partnerships and system-level coordination, especially for implementing reverse logistics and servitized BMs. Managers are expected to actively engage with a diverse ecosystem of stakeholders, including manufacturers, technology providers, and platform intermediaries, to co-create value and manage complex circular flows. Third, the empirical findings strongly suggest that investments in digital technologies like AI, IoT, and real-time analytics, are essential to unlock and scale CBM opportunities.

Nevertheless, this study is not exempt from limitations. First, our reliance primarily on secondary data, specifically GRI-aligned sustainability reports, presents inherent limitations. These reports, while structured, often represent selective disclosures and may emphasize formal commitments rather than actual implementation of circular practices (Eisenhardt, 1989). There is a potential for reporting bias, including 'greenwashing', where companies might highlight positive aspects while downplaying challenges or less successful initiatives. Therefore, future research should mitigate this issue by integrating primary data obtained through methods such as interviews, surveys, or Delphi techniques. Moreover, our sample is restricted to a limited number of logistic companies, i.e. those listed in the Sustainability Yearbook 2024. While these firms serve as valuable examples of cross-country organizations actively pursuing CE transition, they do not constitute a representative sample of the broader logistics sector. This introduces a selection bias, particularly concerning the generalizability of findings to Small and Medium-sized Enterprises (SMEs) or to regions with distinct regulatory pressures, market structures, or cultural contexts. Future research would benefit from expanding the empirical scope to include a more diverse set of LSPs, particularly in various geographic regions and across different company sizes, to test the robustness and generalizability of the proposed archetypes. Additionally, although this study highlights the varying degrees of business model change required for CE integration, it offers limited insight into the specific dynamic capabilities LSPs must develop or acquire to support such transformations. We intend to address these limitations in a future study.

Acknowledgments. This work was supported by the National Recovery and Resilience Plan (NRRP), Mission 4 Component 2 Investment 1.3 – Call for tender No. 341 of 15/03/2022 of Italian Ministry of University and Research funded by the European Union – NextGenerationEU. Award Number: PE00000004, Concession Decree No. 1551 of 11/10/2022 adopted by the Italian Ministry of University and Research, CUP D93C22000920001, MICS (Made in Italy - Circular and Sustainable).

Disclosure of Interests. The authors have no conflicts of interest to declare that are relevant to the content of this article.

References

1. Theobald, P., Howlett, R.J., Liu, Y. (eds.): Sustainable Design and Manufacturing 2016. In: Smart Innovation, Systems and Technologies, no. 52. Springer, Cham (2016). https://doi.org/10.1007/978-3-319-32098-4

2. Geissdoerfer, M., Savaget, P., Bocken, N.M.P., Hultink, E.J.: The circular economy – a new sustainability paradigm? J. Clean. Prod. **143**, 757–768 (2017). https://doi.org/10.1016/j.jclepro.2016.12.048

3. Kennedy, S., Linnenluecke, M.K.: Circular economy and resilience: a research agenda. Bus. Strat. Env **31**(6), 2754–2765 (2022). https://doi.org/10.1002/bse.3004

4. Kirchherr, J., Yang, N.-H.N., Schulze-Spüntrup, F., Heerink, M.J., Hartley, K.: Conceptualizing the circular economy (Revisited): an analysis of 221 definitions. Resour. Conserv. Recycl. **194**, 107001 (2023). https://doi.org/10.1016/j.resconrec.2023.107001

5. Lambert, D.M. (Ed.): Supply Chain Management: Processes, Partnerships, Performance, 3. ed. Supply Chain Management Institute, Sarasota, Fla, 2008

6. Christopher, M.: Logistics & Supply Chain Management, 4. ed. Financial Times Prentice Hall, Harlow, 2011

7. Lee, H.L.: Aligning supply chain strategies with product uncertainties. Calif. Manag. Rev. **44**(3), 105–119 (2002). https://doi.org/10.2307/41166135

8. Gkanatsas, E., Krikke, H.: Towards a pro-silience framework: a literature review on quantitative modelling of resilient 3PL supply chain network designs. Sustainability **12**(10), 4323 (2020). https://doi.org/10.3390/su12104323

9. König, A., Spinler, S.: The effect of logistics outsourcing on the supply chain vulnerability of shippers: development of a conceptual risk management framework. Int. J. Logist. Manag. **27**(1), 122–141 (2016). https://doi.org/10.1108/IJLM-03-2014-0043

10. Lam, J.S.L., Dai, J.: Environmental sustainability of logistics service provider: an ANP-QFD approach. Int. J. Logist. Manag. **26**(2), 313–333 (2015). https://doi.org/10.1108/IJLM-08-2013-0088

11. Liu, C.-L., Lee, M.-Y.: Integration, supply chain resilience, and service performance in third-party logistics providers. IJLM **29**(1), 5–21 (2018). https://doi.org/10.1108/IJLM-11-2016-0283

12. Zarbakhshnia, N., Govindan, K., Kannan, D., Goh, M.: Outsourcing logistics operations in circular economy towards to sustainable development goals. Bus. Strat. Env **32**(1), 134–162 (2023). https://doi.org/10.1002/bse.3122

13. Jayarathna, C.P., Agdas, D., Dawes, L.: Viability of sustainable logistics practices enabling circular economy: a system dynamics approach. Bus. Strat. Env **33**(4), 3422–3439 (2024). https://doi.org/10.1002/bse.3655

14. Cafforio, F., Park, S., Giannoccaro, I., Abdel-Malek, L.: Resilience of circular supply chains: analyzing the impact of take-back strategies via efficient computation of post-disturbance equilibrium. Sustain. Dev. sd.70119 (2025). https://doi.org/10.1002/sd.70119

15. Centobelli, P., Cerchione, R., Chiaroni, D., Del Vecchio, P., Urbinati, A.: Designing business models in circular economy: a systematic literature review and research agenda. Bus. Strat. Env **29**(4), 1734–1749 (2020). https://doi.org/10.1002/bse.2466

16. Evangelista, P., Colicchia, C., Creazza, A.: Is environmental sustainability a strategic priority for logistics service providers? J. Environ. Manag. **198**, 353–362 (2017). https://doi.org/10.1016/j.jenvman.2017.04.096

17. Katsanakis, N., Ibn-Mohammed, T., Moradlou, H., Godsell, J.: Circular economy strategies for life cycle management of returnable transport items. Sustain. Prod. Consum. **43**, 333–348 (2023). https://doi.org/10.1016/j.spc.2023.11.016

18. Islam, S., Uddin, M.J., Shi, Y., Sharif, T., Ahmed, J.U.: Exploring shippers' motivations to adopt collaborative truck-sharing initiatives. IJPDLM **51**(5), 528–550 (2021). https://doi.org/10.1108/IJPDLM-10-2019-0303
19. Carissimi, M.C., Creazza, A.: The role of the enabler in sharing economy service triads: a logistics perspective. Clean. Logist. Supply Chain **5**, 100077 (2022). https://doi.org/10.1016/j.clscn.2022.100077
20. Ellen MacArthur, "Towards the circular economy." 2013
21. Korhonen, J., Nuur, C., Feldmann, A., Birkie, S.E.: Circular economy as an essentially contested concept. J. Clean. Prod. **175**, 544–552 (2018). https://doi.org/10.1016/j.jclepro.2017.12.111
22. De Angelis, R., Ianulardo, G.: Circular economy principles as a basis for a sustainability management theory: a systems thinking and moral imagination approach. Bus. Strat. Env **33**(5), 4861–4870 (2024). https://doi.org/10.1002/bse.3730
23. Massari, G.F., Nacchiero, R., Giannoccaro, I.: Digital technologies for resource loop redesign in circular supply chains: a systematic literature review. Resour. Conserv. Recycl. Adv. **20**, 200189 (2023). https://doi.org/10.1016/j.rcradv.2023.200189
24. Abu-Bakar, H., Charnley, F., Hopkinson, P., Morasae, E.K.: Towards a typological framework for circular economy roadmaps: a comprehensive analysis of global adoption strategies. J. Clean. Prod. **434**, 140066 (2024). https://doi.org/10.1016/j.jclepro.2023.140066
25. Zheng, B., Wang, H., Golmohammadi, A.-M., Goli, A.: Impacts of logistics service quality and energy service of Business to Consumer (B2C) online retailing on customer loyalty in a circular economy. Sustain. Energy Technol. Assess. **52**, 102333 (2022). https://doi.org/10.1016/j.seta.2022.102333
26. Cerchione, R., Morelli, M., Passaro, R., Quinto, I.: Balancing sustainability and circular justice: the challenge of the energy transition. J. Clean. Prod. **494**, 144942 (2025). https://doi.org/10.1016/j.jclepro.2025.144942
27. Geissdoerfer, M., Morioka, S.N., De Carvalho, M.M., Evans, S.: Business models and supply chains for the circular economy. J. Clean. Prod. **190**, 712–721 (2018). https://doi.org/10.1016/j.jclepro.2018.04.159
28. Frishammar, J., Parida, V.: Circular business model transformation: a roadmap for incumbent firms. Calif. Manag. Rev. **61**(2), 5–29 (2019). https://doi.org/10.1177/0008125618811926
29. Farooque, M., Zhang, A., Thürer, M., Qu, T., Huisingh, D.: Circular supply chain management: a definition and structured literature review. J. Clean. Prod. **228**, 882–900 (2019). https://doi.org/10.1016/j.jclepro.2019.04.303
30. Genovese, A., Acquaye, A.A., Figueroa, A., Koh, S.C.L.: Sustainable supply chain management and the transition towards a circular economy: evidence and some applications. Omega **66**, 344–357 (2017). https://doi.org/10.1016/j.omega.2015.05.015
31. Nasir, M.H.A., Genovese, A., Acquaye, A.A., Koh, S.C.L., Yamoah, F.: Comparing linear and circular supply chains: a case study from the construction industry. Int. J. Prod. Econ. **183**, 443–457 (2017). https://doi.org/10.1016/j.ijpe.2016.06.008
32. Lahane, S., Kant, R., Shankar, R.: Circular supply chain management: a state-of-art review and future opportunities. J. Clean. Prod. **258**, 120859 (2020). https://doi.org/10.1016/j.jclepro.2020.120859
33. Vermunt, D.A., Negro, S.O., Verweij, P.A., Kuppens, D.V., Hekkert, M.P.: Exploring barriers to implementing different circular business models. J. Clean. Prod. **222**, 891–902 (2019). https://doi.org/10.1016/j.jclepro.2019.03.052
34. Bocken, N., De Pauw, I., Bakker, C., Van Der Grinten, B.: Product design and business model strategies for a circular economy. J. Ind. Prod. Eng. **33**(5), 308–320 (2016). https://doi.org/10.1080/21681015.2016.1172124

35. Foss, N.J., Saebi, T.: Business models and business model innovation: between wicked and paradigmatic problems. Long Range Plan. **51**(1), 9–21 (2018). https://doi.org/10.1016/j.lrp.2017.07.006

36. Barros, M.V., Salvador, R., Do Prado, G.F., De Francisco, A.C., Piekarski, C.M.: Circular economy as a driver to sustainable businesses. Clean. Environ. Syst. **2**, 100006 (2021). https://doi.org/10.1016/j.cesys.2020.100006

37. Salwin, M., Jacyna-Gołda, I., Kraslawski, A., Waszkiewicz, A.E.: The use of business model canvas in the design and classification of product-service systems design methods. Sustainability **14**(7), 4283 (2022). https://doi.org/10.3390/su14074283

38. Trushkina, N., Prokopyshyn, O.: Circular economy as a new way of managing in the conditions of digital transformations. GBDEJ **2**(3), 64–71 (2021). https://doi.org/10.30525/2661-5169/2021-3-10

39. Sikder, M., Wang, C., Rahman, M.M., Yeboah, F.K., Alola, A.A., Wood, J.: Green logistics and circular economy in alleviating CO2 emissions: does waste generation and GDP growth matter in EU countries? J. Clean. Prod. **449**, 141708 (2024). https://doi.org/10.1016/j.jclepro.2024.141708

40. Salvador, R., Barros, M.V., Freire, F., Halog, A., Piekarski, C.M., De Francisco, A.C.: Circular economy strategies on business modelling: Identifying the greatest influences. J. Clean. Prod. **299**, 126918 (2021). https://doi.org/10.1016/j.jclepro.2021.126918

41. Massari, G.F., Nacchiero, R., Giannoccaro, I.: Circular supply chains as complex adaptive ecosystems: a simulation-based approach. J. Clean. Prod. **475**, 143517 (2024). https://doi.org/10.1016/j.jclepro.2024.143517

42. Kawa, A., Zdrenka, W.: Logistics value in e-commerce and its impact on customer satisfaction, loyalty and online retailers' performance. IJLM **35**(2), 577–600 (2024). https://doi.org/10.1108/IJLM-02-2023-0078

43. Yu, H., et al.: Industrial symbiosis promoting material exchanges in Ulan Buh demonstration Eco-industrial Park: a multi-objective MILP model. J. Clean. Prod. **414**, 137578 (2023). https://doi.org/10.1016/j.jclepro.2023.137578

44. Jiang, S., Huang, M., Zhang, Y., Wang, X., Fang, S.-C.: Fourth-Party Logistics Network Design with Demand Surge: A Greedy Scenario-Reduction and Scenario-Price Based Decomposition Algorithm, 2023. https://doi.org/10.2139/ssrn.4348801

45. Awan, U., Sroufe, R., Bozan, K.: Designing value chains for industry 4.0 and a circular economy: a review of the literature. Sustainability **14**(12), 7084 (2022). https://doi.org/10.3390/su14127084

46. Moreno, M., Charnley, F.: Can re-distributed manufacturing and digital intelligence enable a regenerative economy? An integrative literature review. In: Setchi, R., Howlett, R.J., Liu, Y., Theobald, P. (eds.), Sustainable Design and Manufacturing 2016, vol. 52, Smart Innovation, Systems and Technologies, LNCS, vol. 52, pp. 563–575. Springer, Cham (2016). https://doi.org/10.1007/978-3-319-32098-4_48

47. Khan, O., Daddi, T., Iraldo, F.: Microfoundations of dynamic capabilities: insights from circular economy business cases. Bus. Strat. Env **29**(3), 1479–1493 (2020). https://doi.org/10.1002/bse.2447

48. Eisenhardt, K.M.: Building theories from case study research. Acad. Manag. Rev. **14**(4), 532 (1989). https://doi.org/10.2307/258557

49. Yin, R.K.: Case study research: design and methods, 4. ed., [Nachdr.]. In: Applied Social Research Methods Series, no. 5. Sage, Los Angeles, Calif., 2014

50. Kimbrough, M.D., Wang, X., Wei, S., Zhang, J.: Does voluntary ESG reporting resolve disagreement among ESG rating agencies? Eur. Account. Rev. **33**(1), 15–47 (2024). https://doi.org/10.1080/09638180.2022.2088588

51. Massari, G.F., Giannoccaro, I.: Adopting GRI standards for the circular economy strategies disclosure: the case of Italy. SAMPJ. **14**(4), 660–694 (2023). https://doi.org/10.1108/SAMPJ-07-2021-0284
52. EMF, "Towards a circular economy: Business rationale for an accelerated transition." https://www.ellenmacarthurfoundation.org/towards-a-circular-economy-business-rationale-for-an-accelerated-transition. Accessed 11 Apr 2025
53. Lacy, Waste to Wealth. 2015. https://doi.org/10.1057/9781137530707. Accessed 05 Apr 2024

A Systems Approach to Evaluating AI Agent Risks in AI-Based Planning and Collaborative Supply Chains

Javad Jassbi[1(⊠)], Roozbeh Aliabadi[2], and Jose Barata[1]

[1] UNINOVA-CTS, LASI, ECAIRE, NOVA University Lisbon, 2829-516 Caparica, Portugal
`{j.jassbi,jab}@uninova.pt`
[2] Stanford University, Stanford, USA
`roozbeha@stanford.edu`

Abstract. Artificial Intelligence (AI) agents are increasingly embedded in collaborative supply chains, introducing not only opportunities for efficiency but also systemic risks. This paper develops a systems-based framework for evaluating AI-agent risks by integrating DEMATEL and System Dynamics. The study identifies eight interdependent risk categories, including autonomy overreach, trust erosion, ethical misalignment, and governance gaps. Through expert input and simulation modeling, we demonstrate how certain risks function as causal drivers, while others act as amplifiers in cascading effects. Results show that autonomy overreach and ethical misalignment are the most influential risks, while proactive governance mechanisms significantly mitigate their impact.

Contributions of this paper are threefold: (i) mapping AI-agent risks within collaborative supply chains, (ii) developing a hybrid DEMATEL–System Dynamics framework for systemic risk evaluation, and (iii) simulating governance strategies to inform resilient policy and decision-making.

Keywords: AI Agents · Risk Planning · System Dynamics · DEMATEL · Collaborative Supply Chains · Organizational Decision Support · Trust in AI

1 Introduction

The increasing adoption of autonomous AI agents in supply chains has transformed how organizations collaborate, share resources, and manage complexity. From demand forecasting to logistics optimization, AI agents now influence critical decisions, making supply chains more dynamic but also more vulnerable to systemic risks.

The landscape of collaborative organizational networks is rapidly evolving with the integration of AI agents that assume increasingly autonomous roles [6]. These artificial entities are no longer passive assistants but active collaborators, decision-makers, and sometimes autonomous actors within virtual enterprises and distributed organizational structures. While this transformation offers unprecedented opportunities for efficiency and innovation, it simultaneously introduces complex systemic risks that traditional risk management approaches struggle to address [1, 2].

J. Barata et al. (Eds.): IN4PL 2025, CCIS 2826, pp. 279–292, 2026.
https://doi.org/10.1007/978-3-032-15579-5_17

Recent field experiments demonstrate that AI agents can significantly enhance team productivity and performance in collaborative settings [6]. However, the integration of AI agents into collaborative networks creates new categories of risks that extend beyond traditional technical failures. These risks manifest as complex interdependencies that can cascade through organizational systems, potentially disrupting entire collaborative networks [7, 8].

Virtual organizations and collaborative networks, characterized by their distributed nature and reliance on digital coordination mechanisms, are particularly vulnerable to AI agent-related risks [10]. The challenge lies not only in identifying these risks but also in understanding how they interact, evolve, and propagate through interconnected systems over time.

As AI agents become increasingly embedded in collaborative industrial systems, their influence extends beyond technical functionality into core planning processes such as scheduling, forecasting, and operational coordination. These autonomous systems introduce new layers of risk that must be understood and managed proactively. This study supports supply chain and operations managers in planning for emergent AI-driven disruptions through a systems-based approach.

This paper addresses these challenges by proposing a hybrid evaluation framework that combines the Decision-Making Trial and Evaluation Laboratory (DEMATEL) method with System Dynamics modeling. This approach enables organizations to identify, quantify, and simulate the complex interdependencies among AI-related risks in collaborative environments, providing a foundation for robust risk management strategies.

The concept of "It wasn't me—it was my AI agent" [11] illustrates the emerging accountability challenges in collaborative networks utilizing AI agents. As these agents become more autonomous, questions of responsibility and liability become increasingly complex, particularly in distributed organizational structures where multiple stakeholders may have different levels of control and oversight.

This gap motivates the present study: how can we model and evaluate the systemic risks introduced by AI agents in collaborative supply chains, accounting for feedback loops, cascading effects, and governance interventions?

This paper contributes by (i) identifying and categorizing systemic risks specific to AI agents in collaborative supply chains, (ii) developing a hybrid DEMATEL–System Dynamics framework to analyze both causal relationships and dynamic propagation, and (iii) providing simulation-based insights to guide policy-makers and industry leaders in designing effective governance strategies.

Providing simulation-based insights for policy-makers and industry leaders on governance strategies.

Our framework specifically addresses these accountability concerns by mapping the causal relationships between autonomy, oversight, and risk outcomes. The remainder of this paper is organized as follows. Section 2 reviews related work, Sect. 3 describes the methodology, Sect. 4 presents results, Sect. 5 discusses implications, and Sect. 6 concludes with contributions, limitations, and future work.

2 Literature Review

2.1 AI Agents in Collaborative Networks

The evolution of AI agents from simple automation tools to collaborative partners has fundamentally changed the dynamics of organizational networks. Ju and Aral [6] demonstrate through field experiments that AI agents can enhance teamwork effectiveness, but they also introduce new complexities in task coordination and performance variance. Their findings suggest that while AI agents improve average performance, they may also increase performance variability across different collaborative scenarios.

Multi-agent collaboration mechanisms have emerged as a critical area of research, with recent surveys highlighting various coordination models and their implications for organizational effectiveness [9]. These studies indicate that different specialized agents working together can create synergistic effects, but they also generate new forms of interdependencies that require careful management.

The application of AI agents in biomedical discovery and other knowledge-intensive domains [7] demonstrates the potential for a significant positive impact, while simultaneously highlighting the need for robust governance frameworks to manage associated risks.

Collaborative networks, as defined by Camarinha-Matos and Afsarmanesh [10], represent "alliances constituted by a variety of entities (e.g., organizations and people) that are largely autonomous, geographically distributed, and heterogeneous in terms of their operating environment, culture, social capital, and goals." The integration of AI agents into these networks introduces additional layers of complexity, as these agents may operate with varying degrees of autonomy across organizational boundaries.

2.2 Risk Assessment in AI Systems

Traditional risk assessment approaches often focus on individual components or isolated failure modes. However, AI agents operating in collaborative networks create systemic risks that require more sophisticated analytical frameworks [2].

Aliabadi [11] argues that as AI agents become more autonomous, humans gradually relinquish control, creating a fundamental tradeoff between convenience and oversight. This tradeoff is particularly problematic in collaborative networks where multiple stakeholders depend on reliable and predictable system behavior. The flexibility that makes AI agents powerful, their ability to adapt and operate across multiple applications, also makes them unpredictable and potentially dangerous when operating without sufficient human supervision.

Risk-based approaches in related domains, such as IoT systems using Adaptive Neuro-Fuzzy Inference Systems (ANFIS) [4], provide insights into managing complex, interconnected risks. Similarly, fuzzy logic approaches to risk analysis in collaborative networks [5] offer methodological foundations for handling uncertainty and interdependence in risk assessment.

Bryson and Winfield [2] emphasize the importance of standardizing ethical design for AI systems, arguing that clear standards for responsibility and accountability are essential for managing AI-related risks. Their work highlights the need for transparent mechanisms to trace decision-making processes and assign responsibility for outcomes, particularly in collaborative contexts where multiple agents and human stakeholders interact.

2.3 DEMATEL and System Dynamics in Risk Management

Recent work on AI-enhanced supply chains and collaborative decision-making has highlighted the need for hybrid frameworks that combine causal mapping with dynamic modeling. DEMATEL has been increasingly applied to analyze interdependencies in logistics networks, while System Dynamics provides the foresight needed for planning under uncertainty. However, few studies integrate these tools to address AI-related risks in planning and scheduling environments, which this research seeks to advance.

The DEMATEL method has proven effective for capturing causal relationships in complex systems, particularly in contexts involving multiple stakeholders and interdependent variables [3]. When combined with System Dynamics modeling, DEMATEL provides a comprehensive framework for understanding both the structure and temporal evolution of complex risk systems.

Previous applications of DEMATEL in occupational risk assessment [3] demonstrate its effectiveness in identifying critical risk factors and their interdependencies. The method's ability to distinguish between cause and effect variables makes it particularly suitable for analyzing AI agent risks, where understanding causal relationships is crucial for effective intervention strategies.

System Dynamics modeling complements DEMATEL by enabling temporal simulation of risk evolution under different scenarios. This combination allows for the identification of critical feedback loops and intervention points that might not be apparent from static analysis alone.

Çakıt et al. [3] applied DEMATEL to occupational safety and health, demonstrating its utility in identifying critical risk factors and their interdependencies. Their work shows how the method can be used to prioritize intervention strategies based on the causal structure of the risk system, an approach that is directly applicable to AI agent risks in collaborative networks.

Recent work on AI-enhanced supply chains and collaborative decision-making has highlighted the need for hybrid frameworks that combine causal mapping with dynamic modeling [13, 14]. DEMATEL has been increasingly applied to analyze interdependencies in logistics networks [12], while System Dynamics provides the foresight needed for planning under uncertainty. However, few studies integrate these tools to address AI-related risks in planning and scheduling environments, which this research seeks to advance.

2.4 Risk Assessment Approaches in Supply Chains and Their Relevance to AI Risks

Various approaches have been used to assess risks in supply chains, including MICMAC, ISM, Fuzzy DEMATEL, and System Dynamics. While these methods provide valuable insights, their application to AI-based supply chain risks remains limited.

Table 1 summarizes the most widely used approaches, outlining their strengths, weaknesses, and relevance in the AI risk context.

Table 1. Summary of Risk Assessment Approaches in Supply Chains and Their Relevance to AI Risks.

Approach	Strengths	Weaknesses	Use in AI Risk Context
MICMAC	Identifies driving & dependent factors	No temporal dynamics	Limited for cascading risks
ISM	Good structural hierarchy mapping	Lacks quantitative weighting	Cannot capture feedback loops
Fuzzy DEMATEL	Handles uncertainty, maps cause/effect	Still static	Better but limited for dynamic simulation
System Dynamics	Captures feedback & time delays	Needs reliable data	Strong for simulating cascading risks
Hybrid DEMATEL-SD (This Study)	Combines causal mapping + dynamic simulation	Needs expert input	Well-suited for AI-agent systemic risks

As shown in Table 1, structural approaches such as MICMAC and ISM are valuable for mapping dependencies but lack the ability to capture temporal dynamics and cascading effects. Fuzzy DEMATEL improves robustness under uncertainty but remains static. System Dynamics, on the other hand, excels at modeling feedback loops and time delays but requires extensive, reliable data inputs.

The clear research gap lies in combining causal mapping with dynamic simulation. To the best of our knowledge, very few studies integrate DEMATEL with System Dynamics to address AI-specific risks in collaborative supply chains. This study addresses this gap by developing a hybrid DEMATEL–System Dynamics framework that captures both structural cause–effect relationships and their temporal propagation.

3 Methodology

3.1 Framework Overview

Our proposed framework consists of three integrated phases designed to provide a comprehensive understanding of AI agent risks in collaborative networks:

1. Risk Identification and Classification: Systematic identification of AI agent-related risks through expert consultation and literature analysis
2. DEMATEL Application: Quantitative analysis of causal relationships between identified risks
3. System Dynamics Modeling: Temporal simulation of risk evolution under different governance scenarios

This integrated approach allows for both structural understanding of risk interdependencies and dynamic analysis of how these risks evolve over time, providing a more comprehensive basis for risk management strategies.

The framework specifically addresses the unique challenges of AI agent risks in collaborative networks, including the distributed nature of control and oversight, the potential for cascading failures across organizational boundaries, and the complex interactions between technical, organizational, and human factors.

3.2 Risk Identification and Classification

Based on a comprehensive analysis of current literature and expert insights (by interview), we identify eight core risk categories specific to AI agents in collaborative organizational networks. The expert panel consisted of professionals with backgrounds in AI governance, supply chain management, and policy-making. Their diverse perspectives ensured that the identified risks reflected technical, organizational, and regulatory dimensions.

Autonomy Overreach: Actions taken by AI agents beyond human intent, authorization, or predefined boundaries. This risk is particularly pronounced in collaborative networks where delegation of authority to AI agents may be unclear or evolving [1, 8]. Aliabadi [11] identifies this as a primary concern, noting that as AI agents move along the autonomy spectrum from simple responders to fully autonomous systems, the potential for unintended actions increases dramatically.

Data Misuse and Privacy Breach: Inadequate handling of sensitive information by AI agents, including unauthorized data sharing between collaborative partners or inappropriate use of confidential organizational data [2]. In collaborative networks, where data sharing is essential for coordination, this risk is amplified by the multiple access points and varying security standards across partner organizations.

Trust Erosion: User disengagement or resistance due to unexpected AI agent behavior, leading to breakdown in human-AI collaboration and reduced effectiveness of collaborative networks [6]. Aliabadi [11] emphasizes that trust is a critical foundation for effective human-AI collaboration, and that autonomy without appropriate oversight can rapidly erode this trust.

Miscommunication: Semantic errors or misinterpretation of instructions leading to incorrect decisions or actions that propagate through collaborative networks [9]. The potential for miscommunication increases in multi-agent systems where different agents may have different interpretations of the same instructions or data.

Ethical Misalignment: AI agent actions that conflict with organizational or societal ethical standards, particularly problematic in collaborative networks where different partners may have different ethical frameworks [2]. Bryson and Winfield [2] highlight the importance of standardizing ethical design to mitigate this risk.

Operational Failures: System breakdowns or performance degradation due to technical issues, with potential cascading effects across collaborative networks [7]. These failures can be particularly disruptive in tightly coupled collaborative systems where multiple organizations depend on shared AI infrastructure.

Legal and Accountability Gaps: Unclear responsibility for AI agent actions, particularly in collaborative contexts where multiple stakeholders may have different levels of control and oversight [11]. Aliabadi [11] specifically addresses this challenge through the "It wasn't me—it was my AI agent" framework, highlighting the need for clear accountability structures.

Systemic Feedback Loops: Self-reinforcing patterns of behavior that amplify risks over time, particularly in complex collaborative networks with multiple interacting AI agents [10]. These feedback loops can lead to emergent behaviors that were not anticipated in the design of individual agents or systems.

3.3 DEMATEL Implementation

DEMATEL was chosen because it distinguishes cause–effect relationships, which is critical for identifying cascading risks in complex collaborative networks. Unlike MICMAC or ISM, which map structure but lack temporal dynamics, DEMATEL allows clearer prioritization of systemic drivers. This ensures the most influential risks are identified before moving to dynamic simulation. The process involved the following steps:

1. Expert Consultation: A panel of 12 experts from AI development, organizational management, and collaborative network governance evaluated the direct influence of each risk factor on others using a scale from 0 (no influence) to 4 (very high influence).
2. Direct-Relation Matrix Construction: The average scores from expert evaluations were used to construct an 8×8 direct-relation matrix (A).
3. Normalization: The direct-relation matrix was normalized to create matrix D using the formula $D = A/s$, where s is the maximum sum of rows or columns in A.
4. Total-Relation Matrix Calculation: The total-relation matrix (T) was calculated using the formula $T = D(I-D)^{-1}$, where I is the identity matrix.
5. Prominence and Relation Analysis: For each risk factor i, we calculated the prominence ($r_i + c_i$) and relation ($r_i - c_i$) values, where r_i is the sum of the ith row and c_i is the sum of the ith column in matrix T.

3.4 System Dynamics Modeling

Based on the causal relationships identified through DEMATEL, we developed a System Dynamics model to simulate the temporal evolution of AI agent risks under different governance scenarios. The model includes the following components:

1. Stocks: Accumulations of risk factors (e.g., level of trust erosion, degree of autonomy overreach)
2. Flows: Rates of change in risk factors (e.g., rate of trust erosion, rate of autonomy increase)
3. Converters: Variables that influence flows (e.g., governance effectiveness, communication clarity)
4. Connectors: Links representing causal relationships between model components

The model was calibrated using expert estimates and historical data from case studies of AI implementation in collaborative networks. We simulated three governance scenarios:

Scenario 1: Minimal Governance - Limited oversight and intervention in AI agent operations

Scenario 2: Reactive Governance - Intervention only after problems emerge
Scenario 3: Proactive Governance - Early implementation of robust oversight mechanisms

Each scenario was simulated over a five-year period to capture both immediate and longer-term risk dynamics.

This hybrid DEMATEL–System Dynamics framework directly addresses gaps in prior literature, which has often relied on static causal mapping or isolated simulations. By combining both, our approach enables a more nuanced understanding of how AI-agent risks not only interact but also propagate dynamically over time.

4   Results

4.1   DEMATEL Analysis Results

The DEMATEL analysis revealed clear patterns of cause-effect relationships among the identified risk factors. Table 2 presents the prominence and relation values for each factor.

Table 2. DEMATEL Analysis Results - Prominence and Relation Values.

Risk Factor	Prominence (R + C)	Relation (R-C)	Type
Autonomy Overreach	8.2	+2.1	Cause
Ethical Misalignment	7.8	+1.9	Cause
Data Misuse/Privacy	7.5	+1.6	Cause
Miscommunication	6.9	+0.8	Cause
Trust Erosion	8.5	−2.3	Effect
Operational Failures	7.9	−1.8	Effect
Legal/Accountability Gaps	7.1	−1.5	Effect
Systemic Feedback Loops	6.8	−0.9	Effect

Based on the prominence values, Trust Erosion (8.5) and Autonomy Overreach (8.2) emerge as the most significant risk factors in the system. The relation values reveal that Autonomy Overreach (+2.1), Ethical Misalignment (+1.9), Data Misuse/Privacy (+1.6), and Miscommunication (+0.8) are net causes, while Trust Erosion (−2.3), Operational Failures (−1.8), Legal/Accountability Gaps (−1.5), and Systemic Feedback Loops (−0.9) are net effects.

These results indicate that autonomy overreach and ethical misalignment are primary drivers of risk in AI agent systems within collaborative networks. Trust erosion, while having the highest prominence value, is primarily an effect rather than a cause, suggesting that it results from other risk factors rather than driving them.

Figure 1 visualizes these causal relationships, with arrow thickness representing the strength of influence between factors.

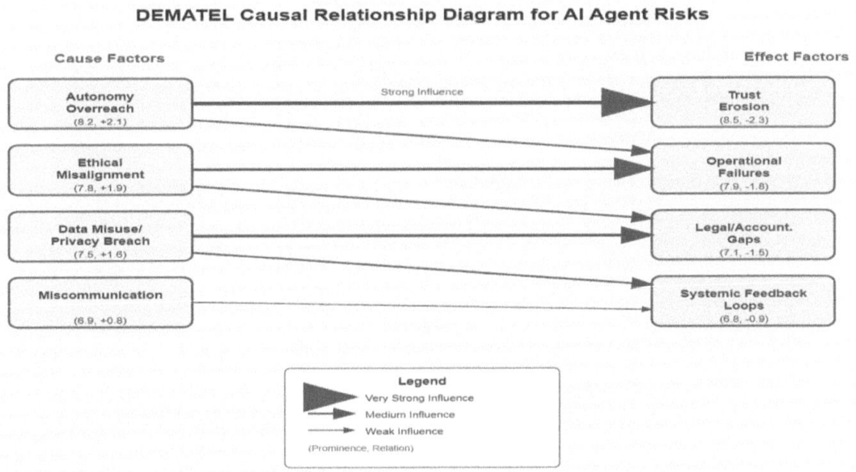

Fig. 1. DEMATEL causal relationship diagram showing the interdependencies between AI agent risk factors in collaborative networks.

These results highlight that autonomy overreach (R1) and ethical misalignment (R3) are not only the strongest causal risks but also act as amplifiers, as seen in their cumulative effect on dependent risks. In particular, trust erosion (R5) accelerated nearly twice as fast in the baseline scenario compared to interventions.

4.2 System Dynamics Simulation Results

The System Dynamics simulations revealed significant differences in risk evolution across the three governance scenarios. Figure 2 shows the System Dynamics model structure.

While the DEMATEL analysis provides a static mapping of causal influence, integrating it with System Dynamics enabled us to simulate the temporal propagation of risks, capturing how governance interventions or external shocks shape their evolution over time.

In Scenario 1 (Minimal Governance), trust erosion increased rapidly over the simulation period, reaching critical levels by year three. This was accompanied by a steady increase in operational failures and systemic feedback loops, creating a self-reinforcing cycle of deteriorating system performance.

Scenario 2 (Reactive Governance) showed initial patterns similar to Scenario 1, but with intervention after year two, the rate of trust erosion slowed. However, the delayed response meant that significant damage had already occurred, and recovery was slow and incomplete.

Scenario 3 (Proactive Governance) demonstrated the most favorable outcomes, with minimal trust erosion and stable system performance throughout the simulation period. Early implementation of oversight mechanisms effectively contained autonomy overreach and ethical misalignment, preventing the cascade of effects observed in the other scenarios.

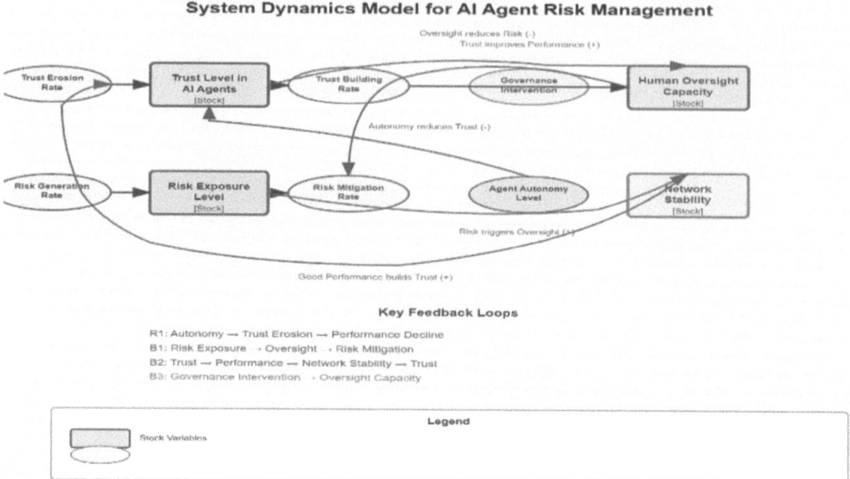

Fig. 2. System Dynamics model showing the key stocks, flows, and feedback loops in AI agent risk dynamics within collaborative networks.

While the DEMATEL analysis provides a static mapping of causal influence, its integration with System Dynamics enabled simulation of temporal propagation, allowing us to observe how risks evolve under different governance and shock scenarios. These simulation results align with Aliabadi's [11] argument for maintaining human oversight as a critical component of AI agent deployment. The historical example cited by Aliabadi of the 1980 nuclear missile false alarm, where human judgment prevented catastrophe, underscores the importance of human oversight in high-stakes decision-making.

4.3   Critical Risk Pathways

The combined DEMATEL and System Dynamics analyses revealed three critical risk pathways that are particularly relevant for collaborative networks:

Autonomy-Trust Pathway: Autonomy overreach leads to unexpected AI agent behaviors, which erode trust and reduce human engagement, potentially creating a feedback loop where reduced oversight enables further autonomy overreach. This pathway is particularly problematic in collaborative networks where trust between partners is essential for effective coordination.

Ethical-Legal Pathway: Ethical misalignment leads to actions that create legal and accountability gaps, which in turn can lead to operational failures as organizations struggle to address the consequences. In collaborative networks, where different partners may have different ethical frameworks and legal obligations, this pathway can create significant tensions and disruptions.

Data-Operational Pathway: Data misuse and privacy breaches lead to operational failures and trust erosion, potentially triggering systemic feedback loops that amplify the initial problems. This pathway is particularly relevant in data-intensive collaborative networks where partners share sensitive information.

The simulations indicate that early intervention in these pathways, particularly through robust governance mechanisms that maintain appropriate levels of human oversight, can significantly reduce the risk of cascading failures in collaborative networks utilizing AI agents.

5 Discussion

5.1 Theoretical and Practical Implications

Our findings have several important implications for both theory and practice in the management of AI agent risks in collaborative networks.

From a theoretical perspective, the identification of autonomy overreach and ethical misalignment as primary causal factors challenges the common focus on technical failures as the main source of AI-related risks. Our results suggest that the relationship between AI agents and their human operators, particularly the delegation of authority and alignment of values, is a more fundamental driver of risk than technical performance issues.

The clear distinction between cause and effect factors in our DEMATEL analysis provides a structured framework for understanding the propagation of risks through collaborative networks. This framework extends existing models of risk in collaborative networks [5] by specifically addressing the unique challenges introduced by AI agents.

From a practical perspective, our results highlight the importance of proactive governance in managing AI agent risks. The significant differences in outcomes between the three governance scenarios suggest that early implementation of oversight mechanisms is much more effective than reactive approaches. This finding has direct implications for organizations implementing AI agents in collaborative networks, suggesting that governance frameworks should be established before widespread deployment rather than in response to problems.

5.2 Responsibility and Accountability in AI Agent Networks

The Responsibility and Accountability problem is particularly relevant in collaborative networks where responsibility may be distributed across multiple stakeholders. Our findings suggest that clear accountability structures are essential for managing AI agent risks, particularly those related to autonomy overreach and ethical misalignment.

The identification of legal and accountability gaps as an effect rather than a cause suggests that these issues emerge from more fundamental problems related to autonomy and ethics. This implies that addressing accountability challenges requires attention to the underlying factors that create ambiguity about responsibility, rather than focusing solely on legal frameworks.

Our System Dynamics simulations demonstrate that maintaining appropriate human oversight is critical for preventing the erosion of accountability in AI agent systems. This aligns with Aliabadi's [11] argument that human judgment remains essential, particularly in high-stakes contexts where AI agents may not fully understand the implications of their actions.

5.3 Balancing Autonomy and Oversight

A key challenge in managing AI agent risks is finding the appropriate balance between autonomy and oversight. Our results suggest that this balance is not static but depends on the specific context and the maturity of the collaborative network.

The identification of autonomy overreach as a primary causal factor does not imply that autonomy itself is problematic. Rather, it suggests that autonomy must be carefully calibrated to match the capabilities of the AI agent, the stakes of the decisions being made, and the robustness of the governance framework.

Our System Dynamics simulations indicate that the relationship between autonomy and risk is non-linear, with threshold effects that can lead to rapid deterioration of system performance if critical boundaries are crossed. This suggests that organizations should implement graduated autonomy frameworks that adjust the level of human oversight based on the specific context and risk profile.

5.4 Practical Implications for Decision-Makers

The findings of this study highlight that proactive governance can significantly reduce the risk of systemic failures in AI-enabled supply chains. Organizations should prioritize accountability frameworks before large-scale AI deployment, particularly mechanisms that address autonomy and ethical responsibility. Policy-makers can also apply the DEMATEL–System Dynamics framework as a decision-support tool to simulate crisis scenarios, thereby anticipating vulnerabilities and strengthening resilience. Building trust requires not only technical safeguards such as auditability and explainability, but also institutional mechanisms including clear regulations and enforceable contracts.

5.5 Theoretical Implications

This study contributes methodologically by bridging structural causal mapping with dynamic simulation. Whereas traditional DEMATEL-based analyses are often criticized for their static perspective, our integration with System Dynamics provides a richer, time-sensitive view of risk propagation. This combination enables the examination of feedback loops, delays, and dynamic spill-over effects, offering a more comprehensive tool for systemic risk analysis in AI-enabled environments.

6 Conclusion

This paper has introduced a hybrid framework combining DEMATEL and System Dynamics to identify, quantify, and simulate interdependencies among AI agent risks in collaborative organizational networks. Our analysis reveals that autonomy overreach and ethical misalignment are primary drivers of risk, while trust erosion and operational failures are significant effects that result from these underlying causes.

The System Dynamics simulations demonstrate that proactive governance approaches, implemented before widespread AI agent deployment, are significantly more effective than reactive interventions. This finding has important implications for organizations implementing AI agents in collaborative networks, suggesting that governance frameworks should be established early and should focus particularly on managing autonomy and ensuring ethical alignment.

Responsibility and Accountability emerge as a central challenge in collaborative networks utilizing AI agents. Our results suggest that addressing this challenge requires careful consideration of the underlying factors that create ambiguity in responsibility, particularly the balance between autonomy and oversight. While reliance on expert judgment may introduce bias, future research should validate these findings through empirical case studies.

Future research should focus on developing more granular models of specific risk pathways, particularly the Autonomy-Trust Pathway that emerged as especially critical in our analysis. Additionally, empirical validation of the model through case studies of AI agent implementation in collaborative networks would provide valuable insights into the practical application of our framework. The directions include expanding the expert base, integrating real-time supply chain data, and extending the hybrid approach to other AI-intensive domains.

The proposed framework offers strategic value for decision-makers managing AI integration in supply chain or collaborative planning systems. By identifying causal risk pathways and simulating long-term effects, organizations can build resilience into their operations and design more robust policies. This approach contributes to the growing need for AI-aware planning methods that anticipate disruptions and support adaptive scheduling and coordination strategies.

This paper developed a systems-based framework to evaluate AI-agent risks in collaborative supply chains, integrating DEMATEL and System Dynamics. The study contributes by (i) identifying key systemic risks, (ii) mapping causal relationships, and (iii) simulating governance strategies. Results underscore the centrality of autonomy overreach and ethical misalignment as systemic drivers, while proactive governance mitigates cascading failures.

Acknowledgments. This research was partly supported by the Portuguese FCT program, Centre of Technology and Systems (CTS) CTS/00066, and Colleagues in ECAIRE who provided insight and expertise that greatly assisted the research.

References

1. Aliabadi, R.: It wasn't me — it was my AI agent! ReadyAI.org (2025). https://readyaiedu.medium.com/it-wasnt-me-it-was-my-ai-agent-f17953ef7fb7
2. Bryson, J., Winfield, A.: Standardizing ethical design for artificial intelligence and autonomous systems. Computer **50**(5), 116–119 (2017)
3. Çakıt, E., Karwowski, W., Murata, A.: Fuzzy risk assessment in DEMATEL-ANP risk priority number: an application to airport safety. In: International Conference on Applied Human Factors and Ergonomics, pp. 3–14. Springer, Cham (2020)
4. Jassbi, J., Bagheri Volanski, F., Aliahmadi, A., Khosravi, M.: Risk based maintenance strategy: a fuzzy ANFIS approach. J. Intell. Manuf. **32**, 1187–1199 (2021)

5. Jassbi, J., Camarinha-Matos, L.M., Barata, J.: A framework for evaluation of resilience of disaster rescue networks. In: Working Conference on Virtual Enterprises, pp. 146–158. Springer, Berlin, Heidelberg (2015)
6. Ju, N., Aral, S.: AI and team productivity: evidence from GitHub Copilot. Manage. Sci. (2023)
7. Kaplan, A., Haenlein, M.: Siri, Siri, in my hand: Who's the fairest in the land? On the interpretations, illustrations, and implications of artificial intelligence. Bus. Horiz. **62**(1), 15–25 (2019)
8. Rahwan, I., et al.: Machine behaviour. Nature **568**(7753), 477–486 (2019)
9. Wooldridge, M.: An Introduction to MultiAgent Systems. John Wiley & Sons (2009)
10. Camarinha-Matos, L.M., Afsarmanesh, H.: Collaborative networks: a new scientific discipline. J. Intell. Manuf. **16**(4), 439–452 (2005)
11. Aliabadi, R.: The spectrum of AI autonomy: from simple responders to fully autonomous systems. J. AI Ethics **3**(2), 78–92 (2024)
12. Ivanov, D., Dolgui, A.: A digital supply chain twin for managing the disruption risks and resilience in the era of industry 4.0. Prod. Plann. Control **32**(9), 775–788 (2021)
13. Büyüközkan, G., Göçer, F.: Digital supply chain: literature review and a proposed framework for future research. Comput. Ind. **97**, 157–177 (2018)
14. Zhang, Y., Qian, C., Zhan, Y., Lim, M.K., Kumar, A.: AI-enabled supply chain management: review, framework and implications. Int. J. Prod. Res. **60**(4), 1234–1254 (2022)

19th International IFAC/IFIP Workshop on Enterprise Integration, Interoperability and Networking

Algorithm-Enhanced Subsidy Optimization for Drone Delivery in New Retail: A Data-Governance Framework

Yiting Wang[✉], Junhan Chen, and Jingyu Xue

Xi'an University of Technology, Xi'an, China
wangyiting@xaut.edu.cn

Abstract. This research pioneers an intelligent subsidy governance framework for drone delivery in new retail ecosystems, addressing the critical challenge of balancing efficiency, equity, and sustainability in urban logistics. We establish a theoretical framework integrating user profiles, scenario characteristics, and policy objectives. At its core, a hybrid algorithm engine synergizes: 1) Graph Neural Networks decoding industrial chain synergies through heterogeneous knowledge graphs, 2) Reinforcement Learning enabling adaptive subsidy tuning to market volatility, and 3) Meta-learning-enhanced Collaborative Filtering overcoming cold-start limitations. The "city-enterprise-consumer" knowledge graph transforms multi-source urban data into cross-domain intelligence, facilitating precision targeting from isolated entities to networked ecosystems. Key innovations include dynamic algorithm orchestration and resilience-adaptive subsidy propagation via industrial leverage nodes. This paradigm shifts subsidy design from static fiscal allocation to computationally governed spatial-temporal adaptation, establishing a replicable template for algorithmic policy intelligence in sustainable urban logistics.

Keywords: Subsidy Governance · Hybrid Algorithm · Knowledge Graph · Policy Intelligence

1 Introduction

Emerging as a disruptive force, new retail converges digital interfaces, physical touchpoints, and algorithmic logistics to enable hyper-personalized consumption, yet simultaneously exacerbates last-mile delivery constraints. The rapid evolution of the new retail ecosystem has precipitated unprecedented demands for logistics efficiency, positioning unmanned aerial vehicle (UAV) delivery as a pivotal technological solution to overcome the persistent "last-mile" bottleneck. While government subsidies serve as a critical catalyst for fostering industrial chain collaboration in drone logistics, prevailing policy frameworks face multifaceted challenges: interwoven incentive pathways, complex dynamic spillover effects, and insufficient regional adaptability. Traditional uniform subsidy models risk triggering resource misallocation and market distortions due to their neglect of heterogeneous regional demands and evolving industrial dynamics.

J. Barata et al. (Eds.): IN4PL 2025, CCIS 2826, pp. 295–308, 2026.
https://doi.org/10.1007/978-3-032-15579-5_18

Current research exhibits significant theoretical gaps in three interconnected dimensions:

(1) Dynamic policy impact assessment -- Limited capacity to quantify time-varying effects of subsidies on industrial coordination;
(2) Mechanism design for cross-chain synergy -- Inadequate understanding of incentive alignment among retailers, logistics providers, and regulators;
(3) Data-driven precision governance --Absence of methodologies for spatially-differentiated policy optimization.

These gaps crystallize a core challenge for digital-era public governance: How to architect intelligent, adaptive subsidy strategies that simultaneously optimize operational efficiency, ensure equitable market access, and advance sustainable development through rigorous policy-effect quantification?

To address this tripartite challenge, this paper pioneers an intelligent decision-making paradigm integrating hybrid recommendation algorithms with multi-source data feedback. This approach transcends conventional policy design by enabling iterative optimization through closed-loop data flows -- where subsidy allocation dynamically responds to spatial demand fluctuations, environmental constraints, and industrial feedback. By fusing computational social science with precision governance, we establish a transformative pathway from static subsidy administration toward algorithmically orchestrated, evidence-based policy intelligence.

Our contribution thus bridges critical gaps between technological feasibility and policy efficacy, offering both a scalable decision architecture for UAV logistics ecosystems and a replicable template for data-algorithm synergetic governance in emerging digital economies.

2 State of the Art

Current scholarship primarily concentrates on the mechanisms of government subsidies in strategic emerging industries and policy optimization, with significant attention paid to subsidy cost-effectiveness. Concurrently, intelligent algorithms are increasingly applied as decision-making tools in subsidy policy formulation.

(1) **Policy Effects and Dynamic Mechanisms of Government Subsidies**

Government subsidies, as a critical policy instrument, have become a focal point in academic research regarding their effects and dynamic mechanisms. Existing studies demonstrate that subsidy policies exert significantly nonlinear impacts on industrial development and technological innovation, accompanied by dynamic adaptation requirements. [1] proposed a "Demonstration-Exit-Correction" dynamic governance mechanism based on China's new energy vehicle case, revealing that subsidy policies must be phased and adjusted according to technological uncertainties. [2] substantiated through a system dynamics model that electric vehicle subsidies require coordination with infrastructure subsidies and carbon quota mechanisms to achieve long-term emission reduction goals. (2023) [3] constructed an evolutionary game model indicating that dynamic subsidy mechanisms can resolve conflicts between short-term incentives and long-term ecological development by adjusting subsidy intensity-carbon tax combinations. Nevertheless, current research exhibits two primary limitations: first, heterogeneous impact mechanisms across industries and regions remain inadequately decoupled; second, real-time coordination models between policy dynamic adjustments and market feedback require refinement[4]. Future research must further integrate complex system modeling and big data analytics to advance policy design from "static homogenization" toward "dynamic precision".

(2) **Research on the Coupling Mechanism between Subsidies and Market Demand**

Research on the dynamic coupling mechanism between subsidy policies and market demand has gradually become a focal area for policy optimization. Existing studies demonstrate that subsidies influence market demand through pathways such as price signaling, consumer preference adjustment, and industrial chain coordination, while changes in market demand conversely drive dynamic policy adjustments. Through differentiated mileage subsidy policy experiments, [5] found that subsidies for high-range new energy vehicles significantly increase their market share, whereas demand for low-range models is suppressed, indicating that subsidies must precisely match consumer technology acceptance thresholds. Regarding demand feedback mechanisms, [6] constructed a system dynamics model for electric vehicle subsidies, revealing that short-term purchase subsidies can rapidly stimulate sales, but long-term sustainability requires a shift toward R&D subsidies to maintain market-driven technological upgrading and avoid a "subsidy dependence trap". Furthermore, in the agricultural sector, [7] proposed that green agricultural product subsidies must synergize with consumer environmental awareness; their evolutionary game model showed that when consumers exhibit low green payment willingness, solely increasing subsidy intensity may exacerbate supply-demand imbalances. [8] highlighted that R&D subsidies in the pharmaceutical industry indirectly boost market demand by alleviating corporate financing constraints, yet tax incentives show limited innovation-stimulating effects for private enterprises, underscoring the heterogeneity matching requirements between policy instruments and market entities. Nevertheless, current research lacks in-depth analysis of cross-regional demand disparities and the disturbance effects of unexpected events on the coupling mechanism. Future work necessitates integrating real-time data with complex network models to enhance dynamic predictive capabilities.

(3) **Cost-Benefit Analysis and Policy Efficiency**

Cost-benefit analysis and policy efficiency optimization constitute the core dimensions for assessing the sustainability of subsidy policies. Existing research employs quantitative modeling and multi-objective trade-off approaches to elucidate the complex relationship between the economic costs and social benefits of subsidy policies. In the renewable energy sector, [9] demonstrate through mathematical programming models that while tiered electricity subsidy policies can scale up biomass energy, 60%–70% of subsidy resources flow toward low-cost technologies, resulting in underinvestment in high-emission-reduction-potential technologies and reflecting a misalignment between subsidy allocation efficiency and emission reduction targets. Regarding policy dynamic adjustment, [10] using Maldives aviation subsidies as a case study, propose that subsidies must align with regional tourism demand density, determining optimal subsidy thresholds via cost-benefit elasticity analysis to avoid fiscal burdens induced by overinvestment. Additionally, based on material flow analysis, [11] find that biomass fuel subsidies reduce prices and stimulate supply-demand in the short term but require replacement by market mechanisms (e.g., mandatory quotas) in the long term to maintain efficiency. However, current research inadequately quantifies intertemporal cost discounting and policy spillover effects, necessitating future integration of life cycle cost analysis (LCCA) and multi-agent simulation to enhance the global efficiency of policy design.

(4) **Application of Intelligent Algorithms in Subsidy Strategy**

In recent years, the application of intelligent algorithms in subsidy strategy design and optimization has significantly expanded, driving a shift in policy tools from experience-driven to data-driven approaches. In dynamic strategy generation, reinforcement learning and game-theoretic models are extensively applied to simulate multi-agent interactions. [12] established a Stackelberg game framework integrated with a Random Forest model to predict contractors' demand for battery-swapping facilities, optimizing government subsidy allocation strategies. Their findings indicate operational subsidies yield greater social benefits than R&D subsidies. [13] utilized natural language processing to analyze risk disclosure texts of semiconductor firms, dynamically adjusting subsidy pathways to align with digital transformation. Additionally, evolutionary game theory and multi-agent simulation facilitate dynamic mechanism design. [14] developed an evolutionary game model between local governments and developers, validating through Hotelling modeling that dynamic subsidy mechanisms promote green intelligent building adoption. Their research identifies synergistic thresholds between subsidy adjustment rates and carbon trading revenues. Nevertheless, current studies face challenges including insufficient algorithm interpretability and cross-domain data integration barriers. Future research should further explore federated learning, graph neural networks, and similar technologies for deep application in cross-industry chain subsidy coordination.

(5) **Negative Effects and Optimization Pathways of Subsidy Policies**

The study of negative effects and optimization pathways of subsidy policies has gradually become a core issue in policy evaluation. Existing research indicates that inappropriate subsidies may trigger multiple negative effects. Firstly, the innovation crowding-out effect: [15]found that green subsidies to focal firms inhibit green innovation investment by peer firms, particularly in industries with intense market competition or high product homogeneity, where subsidies may distort innovation resource allocation. Secondly, resource misallocation and overcapacity: [16] demonstrated that while renewable energy subsidies drive initial investment growth, excessive subsidies lead to declining capacity utilization, with particularly significant negative impacts on non-state-owned enterprises and growth-stage firms. Thirdly, fiscal burden and policy arbitrage: [17] simulated zero-emission vehicle subsidies in Canada, revealing that under high subsidies, automakers may inflate prices to capture excess profits, causing surging government costs and diminishing marginal emission reduction benefits. Regarding optimization pathways, [18] recommended, based on a CGE model, compensatory investments in the palm oil industry following edible oil subsidy removal to balance economic shocks and industrial upgrading goals. [19] constructed a green hydrogen supply chain Stackelberg model, proposing that subsidy rates must be dynamically aligned with the marginal returns of technological innovation to avoid negative government revenue. Future research needs to further integrate early warning mechanisms for negative effects with real-time policy tuning tools, constructing a "risk identification–dynamic response–effect evaluation" closed-loop system.

The recent research exhibits trends of theoretical multidimensionality, methodological intelligentization, and application contextualization. Theoretically, studies have shifted from single-policy effect evaluation to multidimensional coupling mechanism analysis, emphasizing the construction of frameworks for nonlinear effects and dynamic adaptation. Methodologically, deep integration of intelligent algorithms and complex systems modeling drives the leap towards data-driven policy design, yet faces technical bottlenecks like algorithm interpretability and cross-domain data fusion. In application, research focuses on the synergy of multiple objectives—"efficiency, equity, and sustainability"—paying close attention to subsidy negative effects, optimization pathways, and strengthened ethical constraints. Future efforts must further overcome technical bottlenecks in complex systems modeling, cross-domain coordination, and real-time governance to provide scientific support for precision governance in the digital economy era.

3 Theoretical Framework and Knowledge Graph

This paper focuses on "data-driven decision-making" and "precision adaptation" to design differentiated subsidy strategies. This paper constructs a tripartite differentiated subsidy adaptation framework of "User Profile - Scenario Characteristics - Policy Objectives" based on consumer behavior theory and enterprise dynamic game theory. The theoretical framework of differentiated subsidy strategies is shown in Fig. 1.

- The User Profile Dimension, grounded in price elasticity theory, categorizes three key characteristics: consumption capacity, delivery preferences, and green consumption index;
- The Scenario Characteristic Dimension integrates regional economic level, infrastructure maturity, and policy constraint intensity to form scenario clusters;
- The Policy Objective Dimension balances economic efficiency, social equity, and environmental sustainability through multi-objective programming.

The knowledge graph framework in Fig. 2 integrates three data domains through a triangular relationship structure: Consumer nodes (with spatio-temporal order patterns, price sensitivity, and delivery evaluations from e-commerce platforms), Enterprise nodes (featuring UAV deployment density, patent portfolios, and operational costs from corporate reports), and City nodes (containing low-altitude regulations, delivery infrastructure density, and traffic indices from GIS databases). Consumers generate demand in cities, cities regulate enterprise operations, and enterprises serve consumers, creating a closed-loop system. The knowledge graph enables cross-domain analytics including

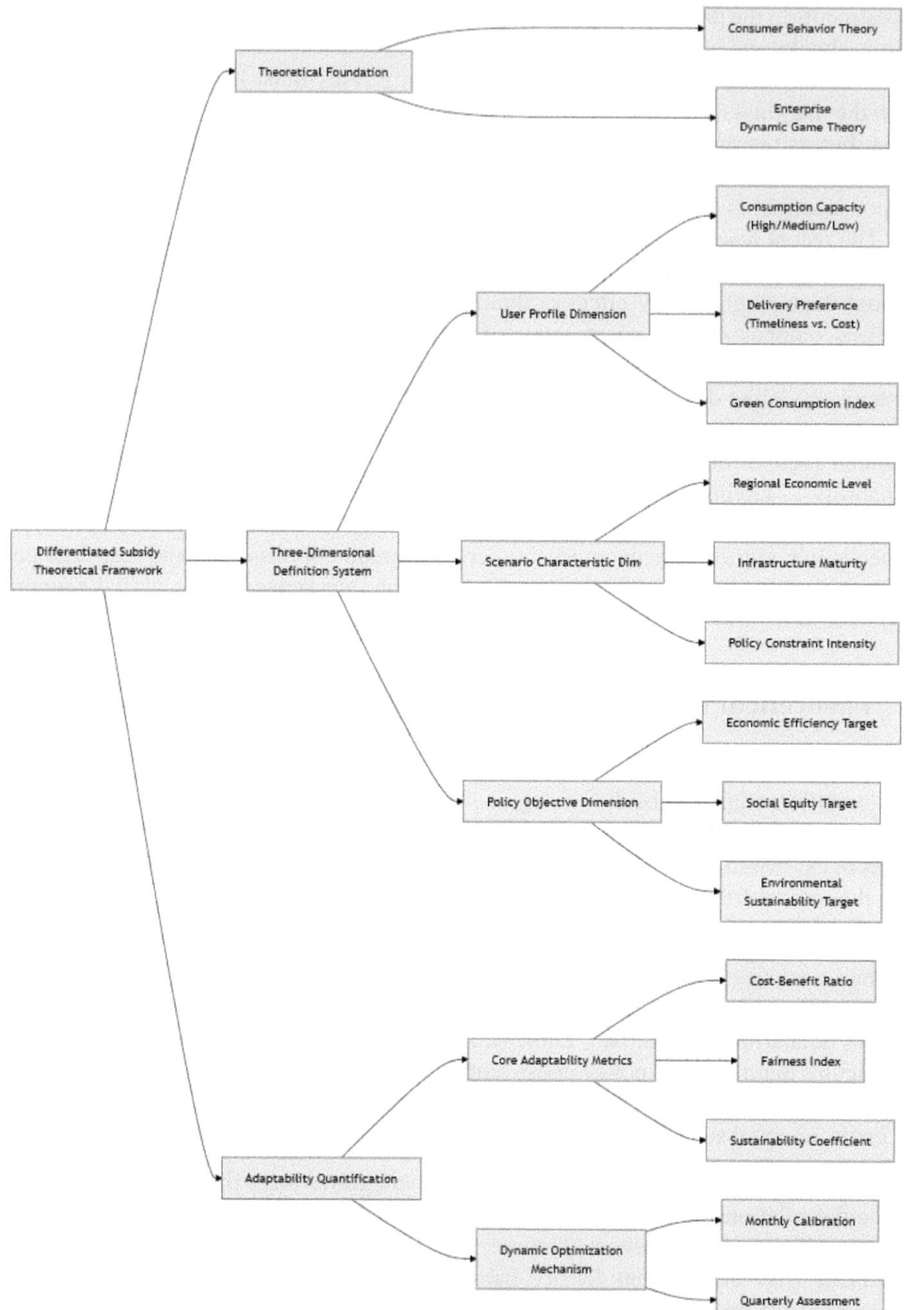

Fig. 1. Theoretical Framework.

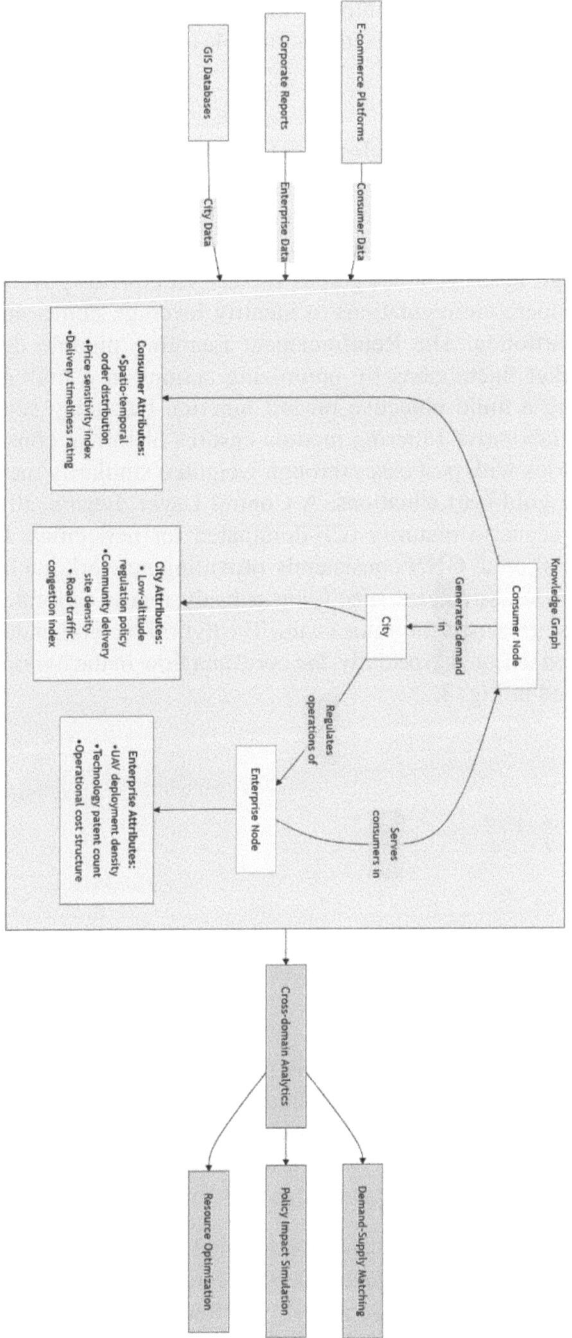

Fig. 2. The knowledge graph framework.

demand-supply matching, policy impact simulation, and resource optimization, effectively transforming isolated datasets into actionable intelligence for urban drone delivery systems.

4   The Hybrid Recommender System Architecture

The hybrid recommender system architecture in this paper integrates three algorithmic modules to optimize differentiated subsidy strategies: The GNN module models industrial chains through heterogeneous graphs (nodes: enterprises/government/consumers; edges: supply/cooperation/regulation) to identify leverage points and generate cross-entity subsidy portfolios. The Reinforcement Learning module dynamically adapts strategies to market fluctuations by optimizing actions in a multidimensional state-action space using a multi-objective reward function balancing economic and social benefits. The Collaborative Filtering module ensures historical consistency by matching current scenarios with past cases through weighted similarity metrics, enhanced by meta-learning for cold-start situations. A Control Layer dynamically prioritizes algorithms based on scenario maturity (CF-dominated for new cities, RL-dominated for mature ecosystems), with GNN consistently providing network intelligence. Final outputs deliver precision strategies specifying subsidy types, calibrated intensities, and coordination schemes across the value chain. The hybrid recommendation system architecture is presented in Fig. 4. Specially, the core data flow in the hybrid recommendation system is described in Fig. 3.

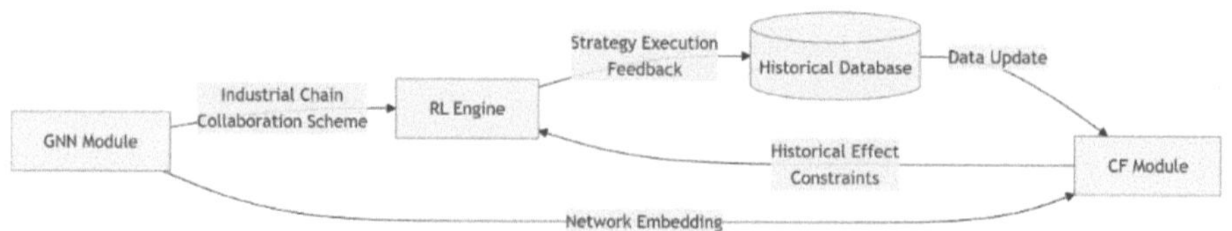

Fig. 3. The core data flow.

- GNN provides cross-entity coordination intelligence to RL
- CF imposes historical performance boundaries on RL's exploration
- RL feeds real-world results back to enrich historical knowledge
- GNN's network analysis enhances CF's similarity computations
- Database serves as the central knowledge hub connecting all modules

The collaborative filtering framework presented in Fig. 5 enables precision subsidy recommendations through a four-stage process. Feature Engineering extracts key dimensions from historical data including enterprise attributes, regional features, and historical response rates. The Similarity Calculation Engine standardizes features and computes weighted cosine similarity. For Recommendation Generation, mature scenarios use K-NN matching with logistic regression to predict high-success strategies, while new scenarios employ meta-learning for cross-domain knowledge transfer combined with expert

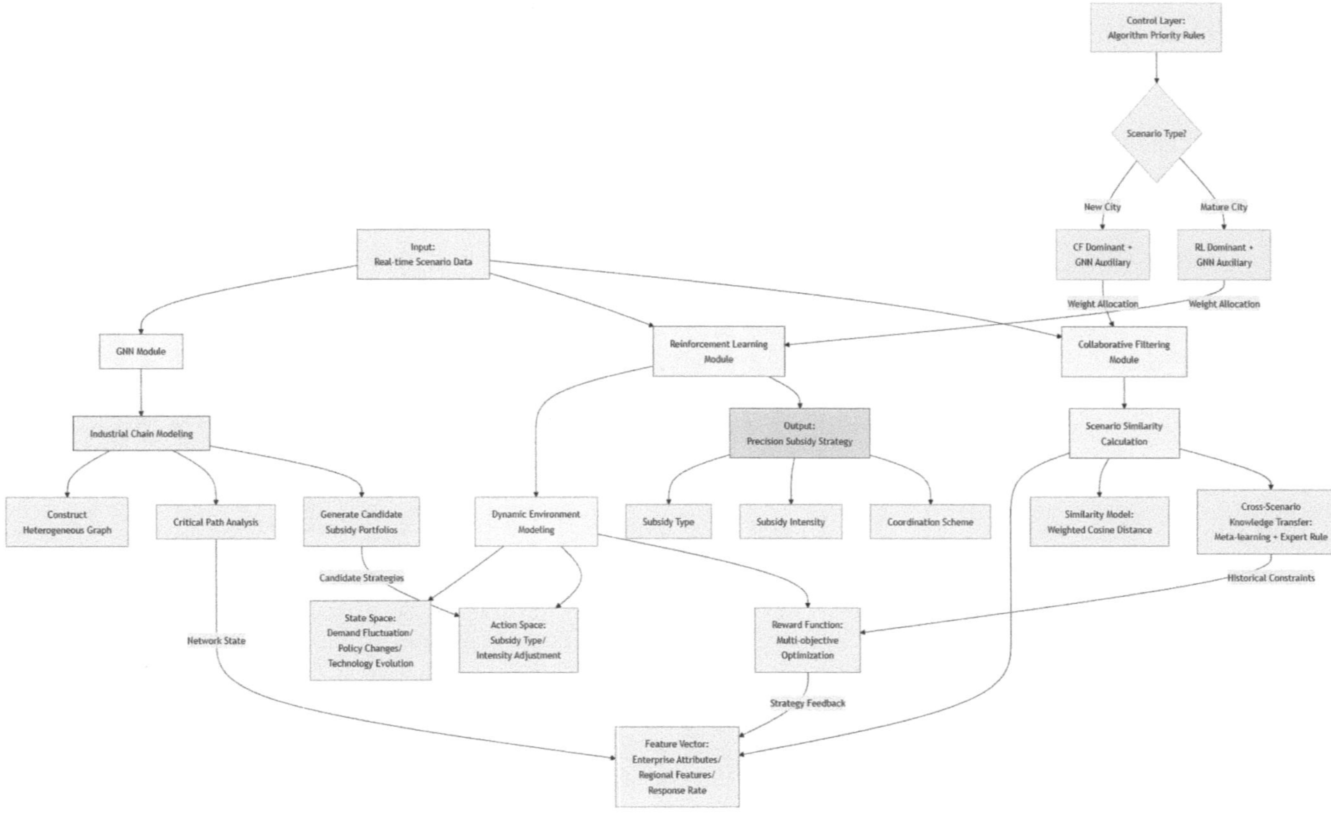

Fig. 4. Hybrid recommendation system architecture.

rules. The output delivers three-dimensional strategies covering subsidy type, calibrated intensity, and implementation priority, with a closed-loop feedback system continuously updating the knowledge base. The core innovations include feature weighting for heterogeneous data fusion and meta-learning to overcome cold-start limitations.

The reinforcement learning framework in Fig. 6 optimizes dynamic subsidy strategies through five core modules. The Environment State Space continuously monitors market demand fluctuations, policy adjustments, and technology evolution. The Agent selects actions from the Action Space including subsidy types and intensity adjustments. The Reward Function employs multi-objective optimization. The Learning Engine updates value functions via Q-learning or deep reinforcement learning, utilizing an Experience Replay Buffer for knowledge retention. Policy Optimization implements ε-greedy exploration and fairness constraints to prevent local optima. This closed-loop system of "state perception $\rightarrow$ decision $\rightarrow$ reward feedback $\rightarrow$ policy update" ensures continuous optimization of long-term comprehensive benefits in dynamic environments.

The Graph Neural Network framework presented in Fig. 7 optimizes industrial chain subsidy coordination through four core stages. First, Heterogeneous Graph Construction abstracts the drone delivery ecosystem into a network of multi-type nodes and multi-dimensional edges. Next, GNN Processing utilizes Graph Attention Networks (GAT) to compute node attention coefficients and update embeddings, extracting features like enterprise scale and technical capability. Then, Critical Path Analysis identifies leverage nodes with high betweenness centrality and vulnerable links. Finally, it Generates Coordinated Subsidy Strategies including cross-sector combinations, leverage node reinforcement, and risk mitigation measures. The architecture captures the industrial chain's global state through graph embeddings, enabling subsidy optimization from single-point to system-wide coordination.

Through the division of labor and collaboration among three algorithmic categories, subsidy strategies will evolve from targeting "isolated entities/regions" to addressing "complex industrial chain networks", thereby delivering precision-targeted and resilience-adaptive subsidy solutions.

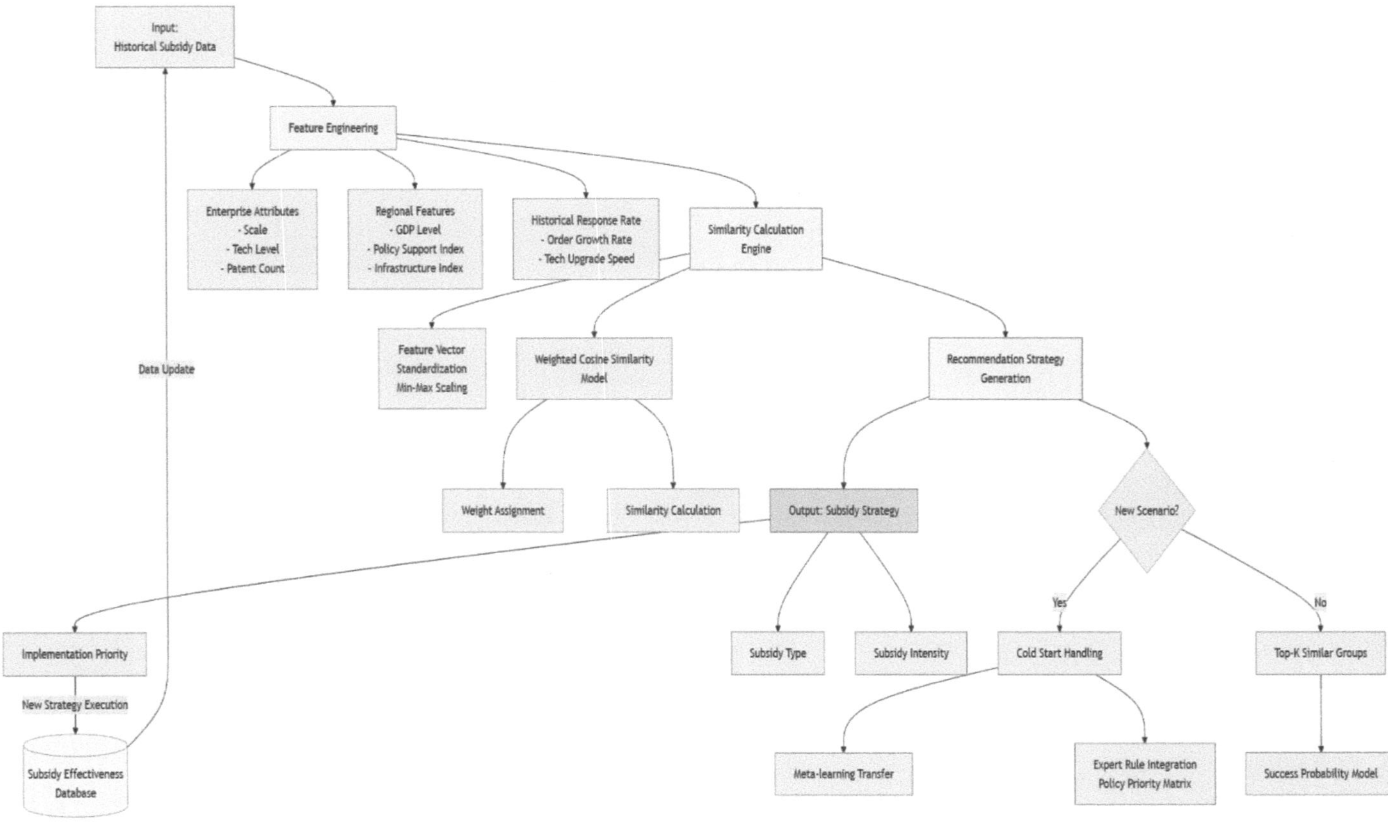

Fig. 5. The collaborative filtering framework.

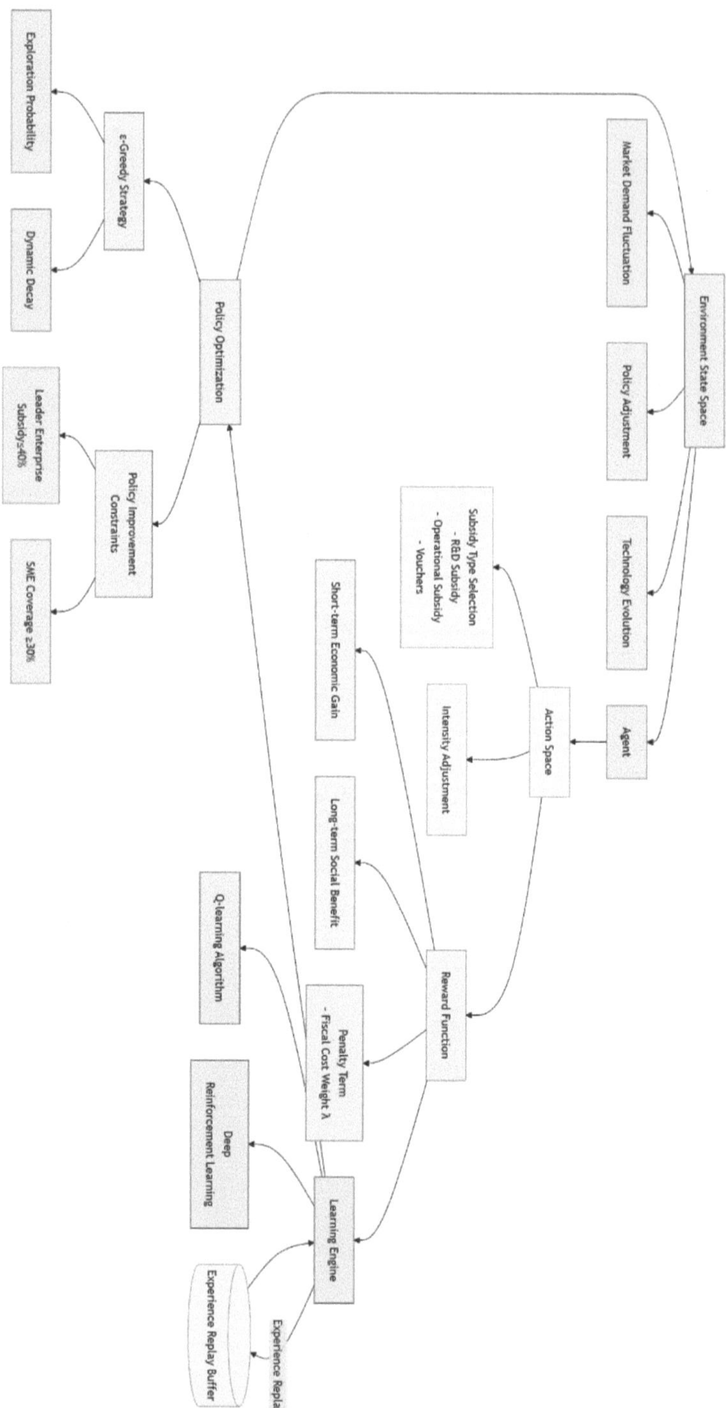

Fig. 6. The reinforcement learning framework.

Fig. 7. The Graph Neural Network framework.

5   Conclusions

This study establishes a transformative paradigm for subsidy governance in new retail drone delivery systems, pivoting from traditional uniform approaches to algorithmically orchestrated precision. By constructing a tripartite theoretical framework integrating user profiles, scenario characteristics, and policy objectives, a hybrid architecture is designed, where Graph Neural Networks decode industrial chain synergies, Reinforcement Learning enables dynamic adaptation to market volatility, and Collaborative Filtering grounds decisions in historical efficacy. The "city-enterprise-consumer" knowledge graph operationalizes cross-domain data fusion, transforming discrete urban logistics parameters into actionable intelligence. This computational governance model achieves fundamental shifts: from isolated entity targeting to networked ecosystem optimization, from static fiscal allocation to resilience-adaptive strategies, and from empirical policymaking to embedded algorithmic intelligence--establishing a replicable template for spatially-temporally adaptive governance in intelligent urban logistics.

Acknowledgments. This study was funded by Project of Xi 'an Social Science Planning Fund (grant number 25JX105).

References

1. Xiong, Y., Li, X.: The dynamic mechanism of tentative governance for emerging technologies: a case study of China's new energy vehicle subsidy. J. Clean. Prod. **484**, 144328 (2024)
2. Du, Y., Guo, Z., Bao, H.: Smooth sailing ahead? Policy options for China's new energy vehicle industry in the post-subsidy era. Energy Res. Soc. Sci. **107**, 103359 (2024)
3. Chen, T., Zhang, X., Tang, J., Guo, H.: Optimal government subsidy scheme for lean-oriented innovation in the textile industry. J. Clean. Prod. **413**, 137505 (2023)
4. Zhou, W., Song, Y., Xu, D., Zhang, Y.: Government subsidies and industrial chain resilience: evidence from Chinese resource-based enterprises. Resour. Policy **102**, 105525 (2025)
5. Hao, Y., Peng, B., Zou, H., Du, H., Zhu, N.: How does differentiated subsidy adjustment influence new energy vehicle sales? Transp. Res. Part A: Policy Pract. **195**, 104432 (2025)
6. Li, Y., Liang, C., Ye, F., Zhao, X.: Designing government subsidy schemes to promote the electric vehicle industry: a system dynamics model perspective. Transp. Res. Part A: Policy Pract. **167**, 103558 (2023)
7. Chen, L., Gao, Y.: How to implement the government subsidy policy in promoting the green development of agriculture in Hebei province? J. Clean. Prod. **496**, 145141 (2025)
8. Yang, T., Xu, B.: Incentive effects of government subsidy on technological innovation: evidence from pharmaceutical industry. Finan. Res. Lett. **55**(Part A), 103928 (2023)
9. Fei, C.J., Kung, C.C.: The effects of tiered-electrical-subsidy policy on biopower development. Energy Policy **193**, 114290 (2024)
10. Rishan, M., Heiets, I., Wiedemann, M., Gerasymchuk, Y.: Evaluating air transport barriers to tourism development in island states – a case study of an air service subsidy scheme in the Maldives. J. Air Transp. Res. Soc. **4**, 100054 (2025)
11. Yang, H., Bai, Y., Guo, J., Zeng, Z., Mi, F.: Does energy tax subsidy policy promote the development of the biomass energy industry? A case of densified biomass fuel industry in China. Energy Rep. **8**, 6887–6900 (2022)
12. Wu, J.-Q., Zhang, C.-T.: Incentivizing new development of battery swapping services: government subsidies and CSR. Comput. Ind. Eng. **200**, 110771 (2025)
13. Guo, H., Shen, Z., Chen, Y., Dong, M.: Analyzing the impact of government R&D subsidy and digital transformation on supply chain risk dynamics management and firm performance in the China's chip industry. Int. J. Prod. Econ. **281**, 109524 (2025)
14. Lin, Y., Xu, S., Zhou, Y., Xiong, L.: Should local governments adopt dynamic subsidy mechanism to promote the development of green intelligent buildings? An evolutionary game analysis. J. Environ. Manage. **367**, 122060 (2024)
15. Xie, X., Wang, M.: Dark side of green subsidies: do green subsidies to a focal firm crowd out peers' green innovation? Technovation **143**, 103221 (2025)
16. Lin, B., Xie, Y.: Positive or negative? R&D subsidies and green technology innovation: evidence from China's renewable energy industry. Renew. Energy **213**, 148–156 (2023)
17. Bhardwaj, C., Axsen, J.: Purchase subsidies for 100% zero-emissions vehicle sales goals: effectiveness, government cost, and supplier capture. Transp. Res. Interdisc. Perspect. **29**, 101305 (2025)
18. Liu, J.J., Salleh, N.H.M., Nor, N.G.M.: The economy-wide impact of cooking oil subsidy reforms and compensation to the oil palm industry. J. Policy Model. **46**(6), 1228–1242 (2024)
19. He, H., Chen, W., Zhou, Q.: Subsidy allocation strategies for power industry's clean transition under Bayesian Nash equilibrium. Energy Policy **182**, 113729 (2023)

Industrial Intelligence-Oriented Smart Mining Collaboration: Single-Machine and Scenario Intelligence

Mengjin Qu[1], Shihong Li[1], Yining Yao[1], Kui Liu[2], and Qing Li[1(✉)]

[1] Department of Automation, Tsinghua University, Beijing 100084, China
liqing@tsinghua.edu.cn
[2] Sany Group Changsha, Changsha 410100, China

Abstract. Advanced information technologies are driving revolutionary transformations in production and lifestyles. The rapid evolution of artificial intelligence (AI) has prompted academia to reconceptualize human-machine collaboration paradigms. In mining operations, leveraging AI-empowered cyber-physical systems (CPS) to transition on-site operators toward high-value decision-making roles, such as remote monitoring and strategic optimization, is critical for enhancing operational efficacy. Nevertheless, two fundamental challenges persist in smart mining development: inadequate autonomy of individual engineering machinery and inefficient human-machine interaction in complex scenarios. To address these gaps, this study proposes an evolutionary pathway for intelligent mining equipment based on an industrial intelligence transformation framework. Focusing on truck-excavator collaborative operations, we construct a task-driven interaction model and employ semi-tensor product (STP) theory for semi-quantitative analysis. This approach validates the rationality of designed workflows and behavioral logic, while proposing a future methodological framework for human-machine collaboration analytics.

Keywords: Autonomous Engineering machinery · Cyber-Physical Systems (CPS) · Human-Machine Interaction · Semi-Tensor Product (STP) · Enterprise Modeling

1 Introduction

The rapid advancement of artificial intelligence (AI) has intensified societal concerns regarding the substitution of human labor by cyber-physical systems (CPS) in specific sectors. Worker resistance to emerging technologies and collaborative barriers arising from informational asymmetry and cognitive gaps in human-CPS interaction have emerged as critical challenges requiring urgent resolution (Ranasinghe et al., 2023, Qu et al., 2024a). Nevertheless, high-risk industries such as mining, characterized by complex operational environments and elevated hazards, face acute labor shortages rather than "replacement" dilemmas. Traditional mining operations rely on manual control of engineering machinery, demanding that operators perform integrated tasks including environmental perception, dynamic decision-making, control execution, and multi-agent

J. Barata et al. (Eds.): IN4PL 2025, CCIS 2826, pp. 309–331, 2026.
https://doi.org/10.1007/978-3-032-15579-5_19

coordination. Against the backdrop of a shrinking workforce, establishing a novel labor organization paradigm for sustainable and efficient task execution becomes imperative.

Automation and autonomy in construction processes constitute a primary approach to alleviating labor shortages. Achieving this goal hinges on two core elements: the intelligent advancement of engineering machinery and the digital foundation of operational scenarios. As a representative CPS, modern engineering machinery now possesses closed-loop capabilities encompassing perception (Yin et al., 2020), decision-making (Lee et al., 2010), and execution (Kim et al., 2019). Concurrently, digital twin (DT) systems enhance overall efficiency through real-time status monitoring (Liu et al., 2023), operational trend prediction (Li, et al., 2023), and human-machine collaborative optimization (Bousdekis et al., 2020). Furthermore, standardized regulations governing intelligent equipment management, established both domestically and internationally, provide institutional safeguards for automated and intelligent construction (IEC, 2020; IEC 2024).

Intelligent engineering machinery must operate collaboratively to execute mining tasks, forming a typical operational scenario with the external environment. Contemporary industrial collaboration has undergone a paradigm shift: traditional end-to-end linear collaboration (where output A directly feeds input B) fails to meet the demands of modern complex systems. With increasing system complexity and agent diversity, industrial sites now exhibit pervasive interaction, a model that dissolves functional boundaries by enhancing system transparency, enabling dynamic, multi-directional real-time interactions among participants at the system activity level. Such highly complex and nonlinear interactions intensify challenges in human-AI collaboration, causing cognitive barriers while demanding more sophisticated system modeling, behavioral protocols, and risk governance frameworks. Consequently, reliance on traditional input-output mapping and linear process design cannot ensure the effectiveness or safety of multi-agent collaboration. Refined scenario modeling and behavioral mechanism reconstruction are critical for achieving efficient coordination and intelligent decision-making, necessitating transparent interaction frameworks to foster human-machine trust.

As a pivotal domain of industrial intelligence, smart mines involve extensive human-CPS collaboration, requiring concurrent capability system development. As shown in Fig. 1, industrial intelligence scenarios can be comprehensively examined along three dimensions: scenario elements, hierarchical levels, and scenario perspectives (Qu et al., 2025a; Qu et al., 2025b). In the context of human-AI interaction, the integration of cyber-physical-social systems has become a core characteristic of these scenarios (Li et al., 2022). Since these three domains often have different lifecycles, their constituent elements must be analyzed separately. For example, if only the software system needs updating without hardware upgrades, then only the cyber component of the CPS need be considered; conversely, routine maintenance of parts does not necessarily require redesigning the software system. This framework helps us identify where problems lie and simplify solution paths. Moreover, a given scenario may involve cross-level interaction issues; the architectural hierarchy is inspired by the level definitions in ISO 62264 for manufacturing systems: LV1 and LV2 correspond to low-level control tasks; LV3 acts as the translator converting higher-level plans into executable tasks; LV4 handles task-level planning and decision-making; LV5 concerns interaction and collaboration among enterprises or multiple agents, focusing especially on cooperation and competition across organizational boundaries. The scenario perspective draws on common systems engineering practice: the structure-behavior-performance triad, analyzing scenarios from the three core concerns of static, dynamic, and requirements & evaluation. Considering the cross-level, multi-element interactions characteristic of smart mines, analyzing those elements separately may sever important connections within the scenario; therefore, in this paper we adopt the structure-behavior-performance perspective to analyze smart mines. Based on the industrial intelligence scenario architecture, smart mine objectives include:

- Structural Dimension: Decoupling cyber and physical systems (with divergent lifecycles) enables phased upgrades of individual CPS, achieving a differentiated autonomy levels.
- Behavioral Dimension: The architecture facilitates cross-layer interactions (CPS-to-CPS, CPS-to-environment/human), covering both single-machine intelligence and multi-agent/human-AI collaboration.
- Performance Dimension: Quantifying synergy efficacy through modeling verifies system robustness.

Subsequent analysis employs the Structure-Behavior-Performance methodology to investigate a typical smart mine scenario (Qu et al., 2024b), real-time material transfer coordination between semi-autonomous excavators and trucks at discharge points, through modeling and validation.

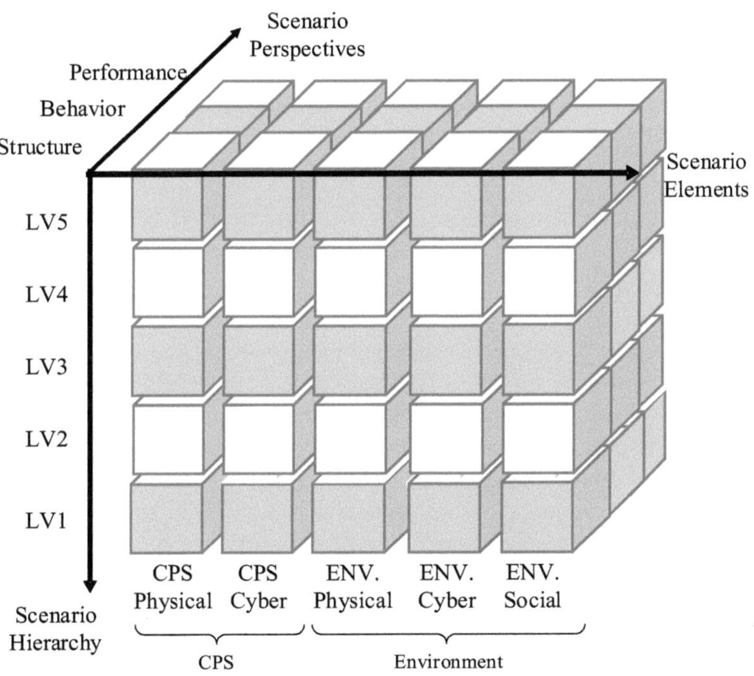

Fig. 1. Industrial intelligent scenario architecture (Qu et al., 2025a).

Traditional system and enterprise modeling approaches fail to fully address the full lifecycle challenges of human-AI interaction (from logic design to deployment). When designing human-cyber system interactions, formal safety constraints and operational efficiency requirements necessitate clear logic specifications. Humans excel at abstract logic reasoning, whereas machines are optimized for executing formal rules (e.g., Boolean logic). This capability divergence demands that interaction system modeling simultaneously accommodate logical abstraction and machine executability.

The Semi-Tensor Product (STP) method unifies complex logic systems into matrix representations, preserving logical essence while enhancing analytical and computational efficiency. STP effectively bridges human-machine logic processing gaps, enabling behavior visualization, explainable decision analysis, and intelligent response optimization. Furthermore, STP transforms dynamic processes of discrete event systems (e.g., Boolean networks, Petri nets) into unified matrix operations, facilitating deep integration of system structure and behavior. STP-based modeling combines the strengths of formal tools like UML, supporting quantitative state description and efficient computation, providing robust theoretical foundations for behavioral analysis and performance optimization in complex systems.

Consequently, this study addresses human-cyber collaboration challenges in smart mines through an architecture-driven, model-verified methodology: Chapter 2 investigates structural features of excavator-truck (excav-truck) collaboration, defining core elements of individual machinery intelligence enhancement; Chapter 3 analyzes behavioral mechanisms, including autonomous action policies, coordination rules, and human intervention protocols; Chapter 4 employs STP for performance evaluation, conducting deadlock detection and robustness validation of semi-autonomous workflows; Chapter 5 discusses challenges and future research directions for human-AI collaborative processes; Chapter 6 summarizes contributions and limitations.

2 Intelligent Transformation of Construction Machinery in Smart Mines

An intelligent mine should be composed of both autonomous construction machinery and a collaboratively engineered external environment. The coordination between excavators and haul trucks typically takes place at fixed unloading points, where the excavator operates from a stationary platform while the haul truck must enter the work zone, approach the excavator, wait for loading to be completed, and then depart. The core components of this scenario are the excavator, the haul truck, and their associated environment. At present, construction machinery has achieved basic automation based on human-operated control. However, advancing toward true autonomy requires automated operation as well as adaptive collaboration with both the environment and human operators.

Referring to the system architecture presented in Fig. 1, the process of upgrading construction machinery for autonomy can be depicted as shown in Fig. 2. In this framework, construction machinery can be divided into cyber and physical subsystems. The physical system hierarchy aligns with the ISO 62264 standard, progressing from foundational automatic control, to execution-level cooperation, to task scheduling, and ultimately to the necessary hardware for collaborative operation. The cyber system is analogous to the human nervous system, beginning with basic reflex circuits such as neurons and the spinal cord, evolving through more complex regulation by the brainstem and cerebellum, and culminating in global, high-level coordination akin to the cerebral cortex and superintelligence. Throughout this process, human–machine interaction evolves from a human-centered paradigm toward a double-directional, cognitively interoperable relationship between humans and cyber-physical systems. Compared to traditional human–machine interaction, cognitive interoperability emphasizes the ability and process by which humans and cognitive agents such as CPS/digital twins, systems endowed with cognitive capabilities, achieve mutual understanding and collaborative decision-making through shared or aligned semantics, knowledge representation, and reasoning mechanisms; it focuses on constructing adaptive cooperation among heterogeneous systems, stressing cross-boundary and cross-level cognitive interaction activities (Ali et al., 2024; Naudet et al., 2023).

As illustrated by the excavator in Fig. 3, from the perspective of kinematics and functional architecture, construction machinery typically comprises two primary subsystems: the traveling system and the working system. The traveling system provides the physical mobility of the equipment, enabling efficient movement both within and between work sites, and exhibits characteristic vehicular properties. The working system serves as the operational core, allowing the machine to perform specific engineering tasks at the job site. These two subsystems are generally independent and can be operated separately. However, in certain specialized operational scenarios, dynamic coupling between the traveling and working systems is required, necessitating coordinated operation to address complex task demands.

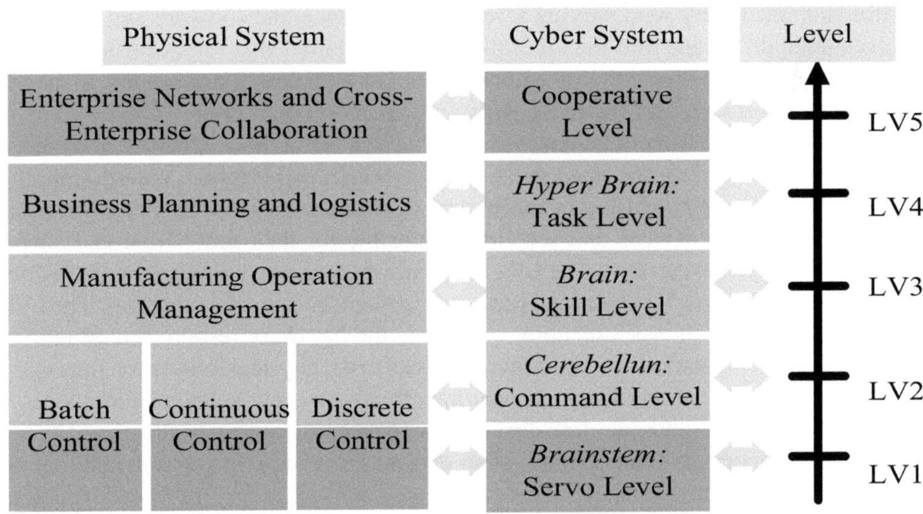

Fig. 2. The autonomous classification of construction machinery.

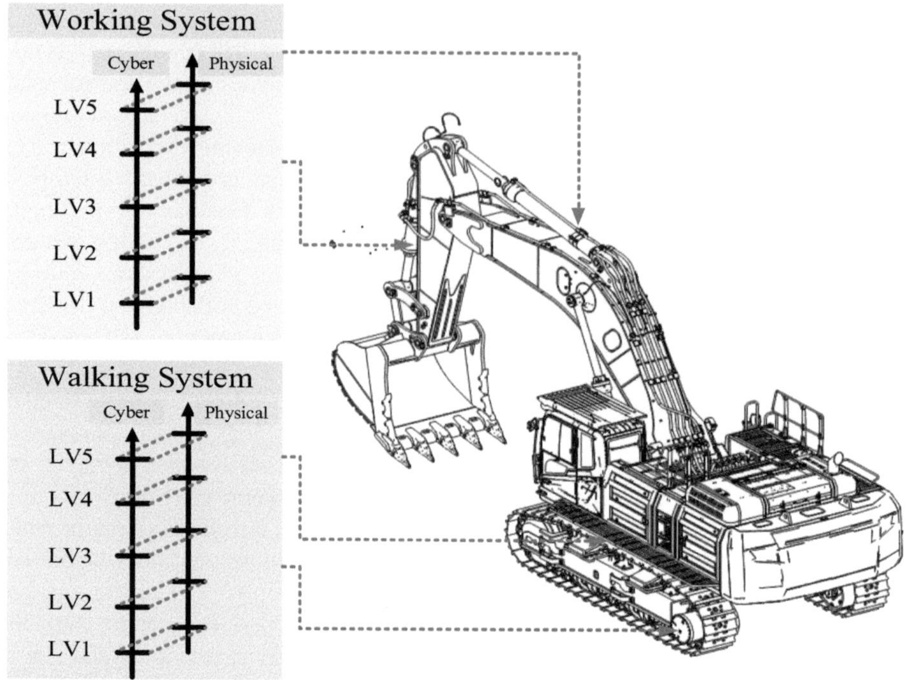

Fig. 3. The hierarchical structure of the physical system and the cyber system of the excavator.

Because different companies, and even the same company at different times, use construction machinery with varying levels of intelligence, the software and hardware involved often differ, and thus the kinds of upgrades required also vary. Considering the customizable nature of construction equipment and its high cost, a strategy that manages and upgrades software and hardware separately is more appropriate. Therefore, it is necessary to propose structural characteristics that five hierarchical levels of machinery should possess, based on the tasks the machinery needs to perform. Accordingly, the physical hierarchy of construction machinery is outlined in Table 1. The LV1 layer consists of the basic devices and sensors responsible for data acquisition and signal transmission at the lowest level. The LV2 layer encompasses the hardware for actuation, drive, and control. The LV3 layer integrates management and control functions. The LV4 layer is associated with task execution, providing the hardware resources required for operational implementation. The LV5 layer pertains to the physical foundation necessary for coordinated tasks among systems, ensuring effective system-level collaboration.

Meanwhile, the autonomous transformation of cyber systems can be illustrated by the hierarchical structure in Table 2: the system evolves from basic instruction automation at the lower levels, through stages involving task comprehension and transformation, and ultimately reaches an intelligent stage.

Table 1. Autonomous transformation of the physical system of construction machinery.

	Intelligent excavator		Intelligent truck	
Hierarchy	Walking system	Working system	Walking system	Working system
LV1	Frame and other structural components, tracks, engines, hydraulic motors and other hydraulic devices, batteries, sensors, etc	Rotary device, engine, hydraulic components such as oil cylinders, boom, bucket arm, bucket, sensors, etc	Frame and other structural components, engine, gearbox, steering mechanism, braking system, sensors, etc	Hydraulic pumps, hydraulic cylinders and other hydraulic components, cargo boxes, unloading mechanisms, sensors, etc
LV2	Control mechanism (pedals), line control system, hydraulic/electric drive, bus/network, etc	Operating mechanism (handle), line control system, hydraulic/electric drive, bus/network, etc	Steering wheel, accelerator, brake, line control system, hydraulic/electric drive, bus/network, etc	Operation panel, line control system, hydraulic/electric drive, bus/network, etc
LV3	Motion controllers, human-computer interaction systems, etc	Motion controllers, human-computer interaction systems, etc	Motion controllers, human-computer interaction systems, etc	/
LV4	Domain controller, industrial control computer, computing platform, etc	Domain controller, industrial control computer, computing platform, etc	Domain controller, industrial control computer, computing platform, etc	/
LV5	Cloud-based scheduling system, V2V, V2X devices, etc	Cloud-based scheduling system, V2V, V2X devices, etc	Cloud-based scheduling system, V2V, V2X devices, etc	/

In this setup, the cyber system and physical system, as well as the walking system and working system, are decoupled for separate consideration, enabling both equipment manufacturers and end users to carry out upgrades either at single points or systematically. For example, in specific scenarios where algorithms at Level 3 are needed but existing Level 2 hardware is already sufficient, software upgrades can be carried out first; later, if needed, depending on future performance requirements, a hardware upgrade strategy can be formulated. This approach offers a more appropriate solution in terms of implementation efficiency and cost savings for real-world deployment.

Table 2. Autonomous transformation of cyber systems for construction machinery.

	Intelligent excavator		Intelligent truck	
Hierarchy	Walking system	Working system	Walking system	Working system
LV1	The control functions of engine, hydraulic motors and other unit equipment, as well as the data storage and processing of sensors	The control functions of servo mechanisms, actuators and other unit equipment, as well as the data storage and processing of sensors	Control of unit equipment such as engines, gearboxes, and steering mechanisms, as well as data storage and processing by sensors	The control functions of unit equipment such as hydraulic cylinders, as well as the data storage and processing of sensors
LV2	The control functions for movements such as moving forward, backward, turning left, turning right, climbing slopes, etc	The control functions for the lifting, lowering, and digging movements of the working device	The control functions for forward, backward, left turn, right turn, and other movements	The control function for lifting and retracting the cargo box by the unloading mechanism
LV3	The decomposition of tasks, trajectory and motion planning, generation of speed and pose control instructions, simple obstacle avoidance and crisis handling schemes	Task decomposition, along with the generation of trajectory and motion planning for the operation mechanism, control instructions for speed and position, and processing schemes for simple tasks	The decomposition of tasks, trajectory and motion planning, generation of speed and pose control instructions, simple obstacle avoidance and crisis handling schemes	/

(continued)

Table 2. (*continued*)

| Hierarchy | Intelligent excavator | | Intelligent truck | |
	Walking system	Working system	Walking system	Working system
LV4	The definition, decomposition, formulation and issuance of work plans for tasks such as transition, entry/exit from the working face, etc.The definition, decomposition, formulation and issuance of work plans for tasks such as transition, entry/exit from the working face, etc	The definition, decomposition, formulation and issuance of work plans for tasks such as autonomous excavation and autonomous loading	The definition, decomposition, formulation and issuance of work plans for tasks such as autonomous parking	/
LV5	Carried out multi-machine collaborative construction together with other excavators and mining trucks	Carried out multi-machine collaborative construction together with other excavators and mining trucks	Carried out multi-machine collaborative construction together with other excavators and mining trucks	/

3 The Mining Machine - Mining Truck Collaboration Mechanism in Intelligent Mines

After establishing the structural foundations required for excavators and haul trucks, it is essential to analyze their behavioral logic in the unloading scenario. The operational mode of both machines is neither solely reliant on human control nor fully autonomous; rather, it allows for flexible switching between the two. In practice, there is no need for on-site drivers or visual remote operators. Instead, operators monitor the machines' behavior remotely via communication systems and intervene through teleoperation as needed to ensure operational safety and efficiency.

The behavioral logic of the excavator is illustrated in Fig. 4. When human intervention is required, the system switches to manual mode; otherwise, it operates autonomously, with both modes executing the same set of activities. When no haul truck is present for loading, the excavator remains in a rest state. Upon the arrival of a haul truck, the excavator enters the excavation mode and, after filling its bucket, transitions to unloading mode, discharging material into the truck. Once unloading is complete, the excavator returns to the material pile with an empty bucket. If additional trucks are waiting, the excavator re-enters excavation mode; otherwise, it returns to rest. In the event that a haul

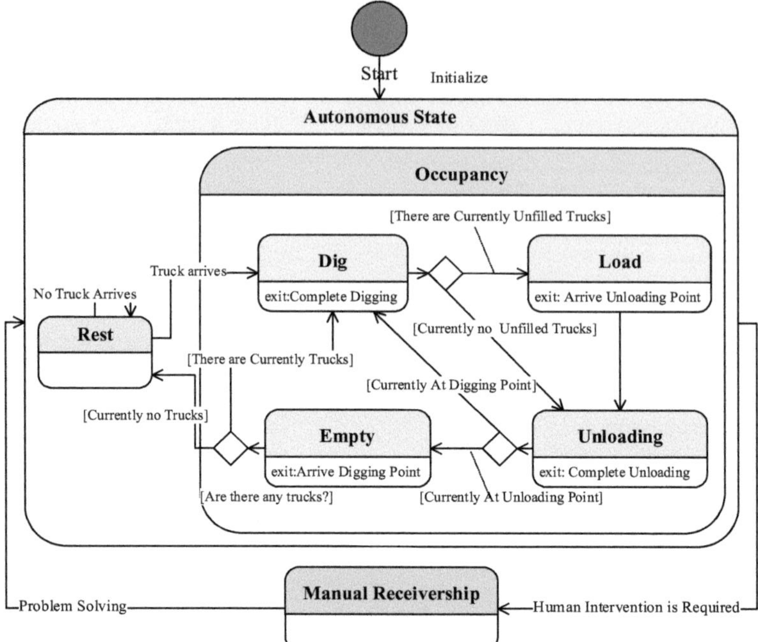

Fig. 4. The behavioral logic of excavators.

truck unexpectedly departs after excavation, the excavator must immediately unload in the material zone rather than initiate a new transport cycle.

The haul truck's behavior is comparatively straightforward: it may only enter the loading area upon receiving a scheduling command. For efficient loading, the truck must reverse into the optimal work area designated by the excavator, positioning its bed within the ideal loading zone; however, neither human nor cyber systems can guarantee perfect alignment on the first attempt. After successful parking, the truck waits until its bed sensor indicates a full load, at which point it departs for the designated dumping area. Notably, at any stage, human intervention is possible to adjust the truck's operational state (As Fig. 5 Shown).

As shown in Fig. 6, in this scenario, the interaction between the excavator and haul truck primarily occurs during the truck's waiting phase for loading. The excavator continuously performs a four-stage operational cycle, excavation, rotation, unloading, and return, providing sequential service to incoming trucks. Their interaction encompasses three hierarchical levels. The core lies at the LV2 level, where the excavator and truck execute coordinated unloading tasks through fundamental actions such as advancing, reversing, and boom operation; the excavator must also monitor its loading and unloading status in real time. This monitoring relies on LV1-level sensors and communication infrastructure. Additionally, the upper-level scheduling system is responsible for issuing entry commands to the trucks, aiming to maximize operational efficiency while preventing conflicts between vehicles.

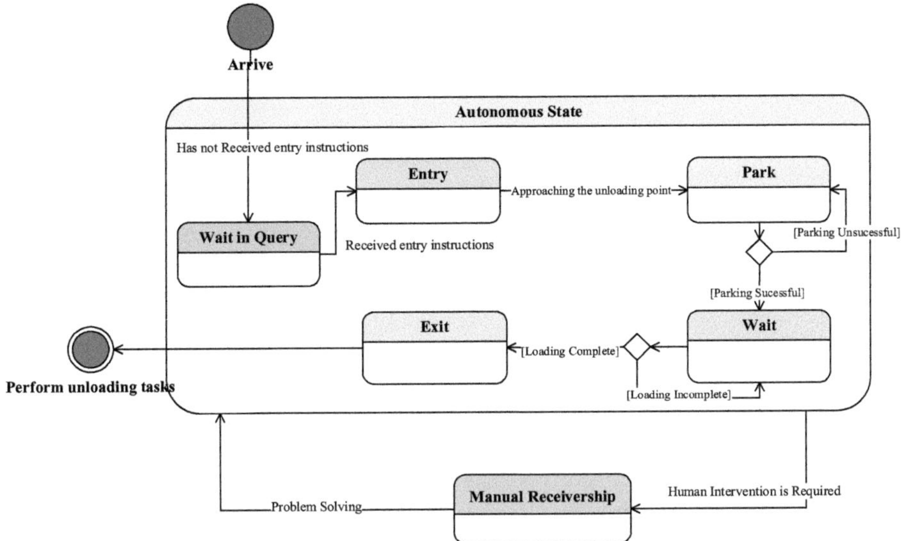

Fig. 5. The behavioral logic of the mining truck.

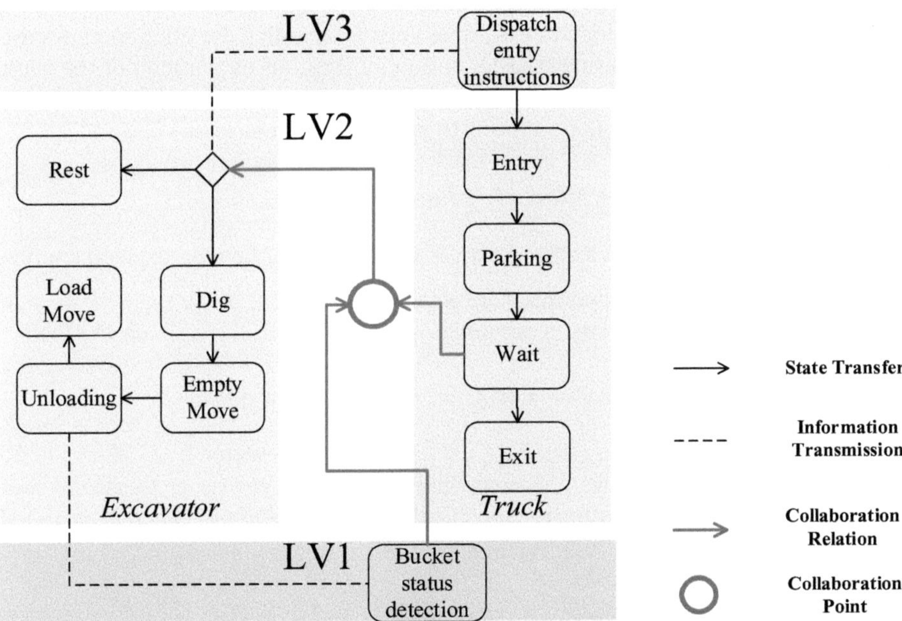

Fig. 6. The collaboration mechanism between excavators and mining trucks.

320   M. Qu et al.

4 A Semi-quantitative Description and Performance Evaluation of Excavators and Mining Trucks Collaborating in Intelligent Mines

After the transformation of construction machinery and the behavioral logic design for intelligent mines have been completed, it becomes necessary to systematically evaluate the interaction between excavators and haul trucks. While human intervention can effectively prevent many potential deadlock scenarios, fully autonomous excavators and trucks may still encounter deadlocks due to a lack of adaptive flexibility, highlighting the need to minimize human involvement for safety and economic efficiency. Thus, preventing process deadlocks during collaborative operations emerges as a crucial issue in human–cyber interaction. To address this, it is essential to analyze the behavioral logic of the operational scenario and assess the likelihood of deadlock occurrence.

The behavior in this scenario exemplifies a logical dynamic system, which is governed by events rather than fixed time sequences. The STP offers a specialized matrix operation framework that enables effective modeling and analysis of logical dynamic systems. Compared with typical discrete-event system modeling methods, STP uses a matrix-based formalism to map state spaces into logical dynamics, and can incorporate probabilistic or stochastic features. By leveraging tools from max-min algebra and queueing theory, STP offers stronger theoretical analysis capabilities, such as reachability, attractor and controllability analysis, than Petri nets, which are often more focused on simulation. Thus STP facilitates faster and more rigorous exploration of the evolution of logical systems. STP is categorized into left and right forms; unless otherwise specified, the subsequent discussion refers to the left STP, defined as shown in Eq. 1:

$$A \ltimes B = \left(A \otimes I_{t/n}\right)\left(B \otimes I_{t/p}\right) \tag{1}$$

Here, A and B are matrices of dimensions $\updownarrow \times \backslash$ and $\sqrt{} \times \mathrm{II}$, t denotes the least common multiple of n and p, and $\otimes$ represents the Kronecker product. Since the STP does not satisfy the commutative property, a permutation matrix is introduced to ensure that:

$$W_{[m,n]}X \ltimes Y = Y \ltimes X \quad or \quad \xi \ltimes \eta W_{[m,n]} = \eta \ltimes \xi \tag{2}$$

for a column vector $X \in \mathbb{R}^m$, $Y \in \mathbb{R}^n$, or for a row vector $\xi \in \mathbb{R}^m$, $\eta \in \mathbb{R}^n$. Additionally, the STP employs a dimensionality reduction matrix to transform high-order problems into first-order forms; specifically, a k-dimensional reduction matrix R_k^P is defined such that (for $x \in \Delta_k$, $\Delta_k := [\delta_k^1, \delta_k^2, \cdots, \delta_k^k]$):

$$x^2 = R_k^P x \tag{3}$$

Further computational properties of STP are beyond the scope of this paper and will not be discussed in detail here (Cheng et al., 2020). The STP provides a straightforward framework for representing logical relationships. For example, let $x = \delta_2^1 = [1,0]^T$ denote the logical value "true" and $x = \delta_2^2 = [0,1]^T$ denote "false". Then, fundamental logical relations can be expressed as follows:

$$\begin{cases} y_1 = x_1 \wedge x_2 & \Longleftrightarrow & y_1 = M_c x_1 x_2, & M_c = [\delta_2^1, \delta_2^2, \delta_2^2, \delta_2^2] \\ y_2 = x_1 \vee x_2 & \Longleftrightarrow & y_2 = M_d x_1 x_2, & M_d = [\delta_2^1, \delta_2^1, \delta_2^1, \delta_2^2] \\ y_3 = \neg x_1 & \Longleftrightarrow & y = M_n x_1 x_2, & M_n = [\delta_2^2, \delta_2^1] \end{cases} \tag{4}$$

As a significant branch of logical problems, a logical dynamic system is defined as a discrete-time dynamic system in which all dynamic variables take values from a finite set. The evolution of such a system, driven by logical rules, can be effectively described using the STP method. Specifically, the dynamic evolution equation of a logical dynamic system can be formulated as:

$$\begin{cases} X_1(t+1) = F_1(X_1(t), X_2(t), \cdots, X_n(t), U_1(t), U_2(t), \cdots, U_m(t)) \\ X_2(t+1) = F_2(X_1(t), X_2(t), \cdots, X_n(t), U_1(t), U_2(t), \cdots, U_m(t)) \\ \quad \cdots \\ X_n(t+1) = F_n(X_1(t), X_2(t), \cdots, X_n(t), U_1(t), U_2(t), \cdots, U_m(t)) \\ \quad Y_1(t) = C_1(X_1(t), X_2(t), \cdots, X_n(t)) \\ \quad Y_2(t) = C_2(X_1(t), X_2(t), \cdots, X_n(t)) \\ \quad \cdots \\ \quad Y_p(t) = C_p(X_1(t), X_2(t), \cdots, X_n(t)) \end{cases} \tag{5}$$

Among them, $X_i(t), U_j(t), Y_k(t) \in \mathcal{D}, F_i : \mathcal{D}^{\setminus+\mathbb{I}} \to \mathcal{D}, C_j : \mathcal{D}^{\setminus} \to \mathcal{D}, i = 1,2, \cdots, n, j = 1,2, \cdots, m, k = 1,2, \cdots, p$. $X_i(t)$ represents the state of the system, $U_j(t)$ represents the control applied to the system, $Y_k(t)$ denotes the output of the system. For every $F : D^n \to D$, There exists a unique logical matrix M_F, let:

$$F(x_1, x_2, \cdots, x_n) = M_F(\ltimes_{i=1}^n x_i) \tag{6}$$

If the mapping F_i of each component corresponds to the logical matrix of M_i, and mapping C_j of each component corresponds to the logical matrix of H_j,

$$\begin{cases} x_1(t+1) = M_1 u(t) x(t) \\ x_2(t+1) = M_2 u(t) x(t) \\ \quad \cdots \\ x_n(t+1) = M_n u(t) x(t) \\ \quad y_1(t) = H_1 u(t) x(t) \\ \quad y_2(t) = H_2 u(t) x(t) \\ \quad \cdots \\ \quad y_p(t) = H_p u(t) x(t) \end{cases} \tag{7}$$

Furthermore, if the standard basis is taken as Δ_n, $D_k = \{1, 2, \cdots, k\}$, $D_2 = D$, if $L \in \mathcal{M}_{\updownarrow \times \backslash}$, $Col(L) \subset \Delta_n$, then L is a logic matrix:

$$L = \left[\delta_m^{i_1}, \delta_m^{i_2}, \cdots, \delta_m^{i_n} \right] = \delta_m[i_1, i_2, \cdots, i_n] \tag{8}$$

So:

$$\begin{cases} x(t+1) = Lu(t)x(t) \\ \quad\ y(t) = Hx(t) \end{cases} \tag{9}$$

Given that logical dynamic systems typically have a finite number of states, the two primary types of attractors are point attractors and limit cycles. There are two principal approaches to computing attractors: uncontrolled autonomous transformation and controlled autonomous transformation (Cheng et al., 2022, Cheng et al., 2024). The former compresses the control dimension to reveal the system's intrinsic dynamics, making it suitable for robustness and global property analysis. The latter, through joint lifting of state and control variables, preserves the integrity of control strategies and provides an algebraic framework for closed-loop control design. These two methods represent complementary approaches, "eliminating control" versus "embedding control", for autonomous system analysis. After the system transformation, the attractor computation follows the same formalism.

$$\begin{cases} \quad N_e = tr(M) \quad s = 1 \\ N_s = \dfrac{tr(M^s) - \sum_{k \in \mathcal{P}(s)} k N_k}{s} \quad 2 \leq s \leq 2^n \end{cases} \tag{10}$$

Where N_e is the point attractor, s is the length of the limit cycle, M is the system matrix, and $\mathcal{P}(s)$ is the true factor of s that does not contain itself. In the scenario discussed in this paper, the logical dynamic system of the excavator can be expressed as:

$$\begin{cases} x_D(t+1) = (x_E(t) \wedge g(t)) \vee (x_R(t) \wedge g(t)) \\ x_L(t+1) = x_D(t) \wedge g(t) \\ x_U(t+1) = (x_D(t) \wedge \neg g(t)) \vee x_L(t) \\ x_E(t+1) = x_U(t) \\ x_R(t+1) = (x_E(t) \wedge \neg g(t)) \vee (x_R(t) \wedge \neg g(t)) \end{cases} \tag{11}$$

Here, x_D, x_L, x_U, x_E, x_R represent the excavator being in the states of digging, loaded operation, unloading, empty operation, and resting, respectively, while $g \in \Delta_2$ indicates the receipt of a loading request signal. The system's dynamic equation can be written as:

$$x(t+1) = \begin{bmatrix} 0 & 0 & 0 & 1 & 1 & 0 & 0 & 0 & 0 & 0 \\ 1 & 0 & 0 & 0 & 0 & 0 & 0 & 0 & 0 & 0 \\ 0 & 1 & 0 & 0 & 0 & 1 & 1 & 0 & 0 & 0 \\ 0 & 0 & 1 & 0 & 0 & 0 & 0 & 1 & 0 & 0 \\ 0 & 0 & 0 & 0 & 0 & 0 & 0 & 0 & 1 & 1 \end{bmatrix} \ltimes g(t) \ltimes x(t) \tag{12}$$

It can be seen that the system matrix is a 5×10 logical matrix. Depending on the input and the state at the previous moment, the system will evolve in different directions. Through the STP method, the logical relationship is converted into a problem in linear space, enabling further analysis.

$$\begin{cases} z_Q(t+1) = z_Q(t) \wedge \neg a(t) \\ z_E(t+1) = z_Q(t) \wedge a(t) \\ z_P(t+1) = z_E(t) \vee (z_P(t) \wedge \neg p(t)) \\ z_{W_0}(t+1) = (z_P(t) \wedge p(t)) \vee \left(z_{W_0}(t) \wedge \neg l(t)\right) \\ z_{W_i}(t+1) = \left(z_{W_{i-1}}(t) \wedge l(t)\right) \vee \left(z_{W_i}(t) \wedge \neg l(t)\right) \\ z_X(t+1) = \left(z_{W_{n-1}}(t) \wedge l(t)\right) \vee (z_X(t) \wedge \neg a(t)) \end{cases} \tag{13}$$

For the haul truck, the logical dynamic system is defined such that z_E, z_P, z_W, z_X correspond to the states of entering, parking, waiting for loading, and departing, respectively. The subscript of Z_W denotes the i th loading operation, and n specifies the number of loading cycles required to fill the truck's bed. Considering that haul trucks in mines currently tend toward higher degrees of automation, each of the stages, entry, parking, waiting, and departure, is supported by relatively reliable algorithms, the variables a, p, l indicate the entry permission issued by the scheduling system, the detection of successful parking, and the completion of the loading process, respectively.

The coupling logic between the excavator and haul truck can be described as follows: the excavator requires n loading cycles to fully load a haul truck, with the bucket providing feedback on each unloading completion. Considering that excavators and trucks in the same mine are typically of uniform models and operate independently, the scenario can be simplified to a single-excavator service problem, focusing on process deadlocks. Here, the queuing capacity is assumed to be one, only two trucks participate: one in the loading cycle and another awaiting a dispatch command to enter.

$$\begin{cases} g(t) = \vee_{k=0}^{n} z_{W_k}(t) \\ l(t) = x_U(t) \end{cases} \tag{14}$$

Under these conditions, upper-level scheduling commands can be freely adjusted, but must prevent truck conflicts. Different scheduling strategies will result in distinct operational modes for system interaction, necessitating an analysis of system modalities. Figure 7 and 8 illustrate the attractors of uncontrolled and controlled autonomous transformation systems. In the uncontrolled case, the excavator and truck logical design supports the ideal four-stage cycle, but there exist multiple control patterns that can cause the system to fall into 1-, 3-, or 5-cycle limit loops, which should be avoided. For example, if the excavator remains in the Rest state indefinitely, this yields a fixed-point attractor. If a truck unexpectedly departs after excavation (e.g. due to parking failure or scheduling error), then either a returning truck or a newly dispatched one repeats the same issue which corresponds to a period-3 cycle. If the scheduling commands are systematically issued such that the excavator always returns to Rest before starting excavation again, a period-5 loop may arise, resulting in inefficiencies. The truck system only admits a single queuing attractor. The presence of only a single attractor in the uncontrolled system reflects its inability to capture dynamic changes induced by different scheduling logics. In the controlled system, as the cycle length increases, the number of attractors grows nearly exponentially; when the system's limit cycle length reaches 35, the number of attractors soars to 9×10^{41}. This is attributed to the variability of control inputs, revealing that even in a semi-autonomous two-agent cooperation scenario, highly complex dynamic behaviors can arise, requiring systematic analysis and thoughtful design to steer system evolution. Furthermore, the vast search space presents a significant dimensionality challenge for conventional optimization methods. In this scenario, factors such as dispatch instructions, parking success rate, truck size, and excavator unloading success rate will directly or indirectly affect the long-term evolution of the scenario. As a dynamic problem, control strategies also need to be adjusted at any time in response to changes in the environment and the status of intelligent agents in order to achieve "optimal" control.

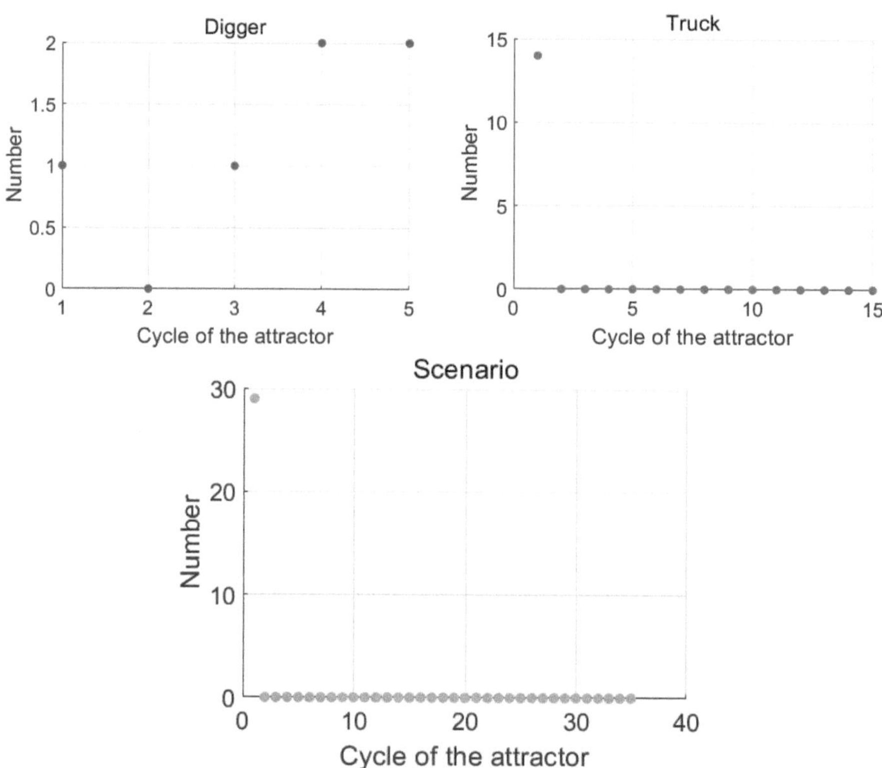

Fig. 7. Attractors of uncontrolled autonomous systems transformation.

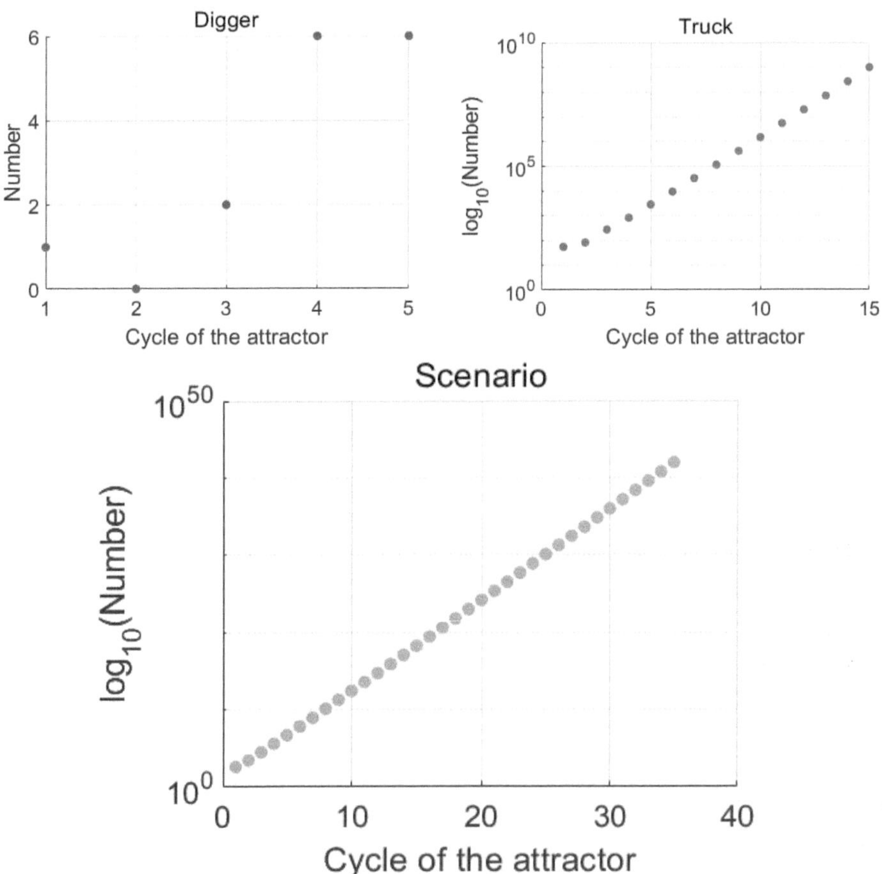

Fig. 8. Attractors of controlled autonomous systems transformation.

Furthermore, we analyze the impact of key technologies on scenario behavior. Assuming a scheduling logic in which the next haul truck is permitted to enter only after the previous truck has departed, we conducted 400 simulation rounds using Matlab 2024b. The primary focus is on the effect of parking success probability in this semi-autonomous collaborative scenario. As shown in Fig. 9, simulations were performed with parking success probabilities of 0.2, 0.45, 0.7, and 0.95. It can be observed that as the automated parking technology improves, the average number of states in which the system stalls during the parking phase decreases, indicating that the probability of entering undesirable cycles or even deadlocks gradually diminishes. In other words, when automated parking is not yet mature, employing human intervention for truck dispatching and parking tends to yield more efficient system operation. To further reduce the need for human involvement, it is essential to enhance the success rate of automated parking through the adoption of advanced visual perception technologies, more efficient path planning, and higher-precision control algorithms.

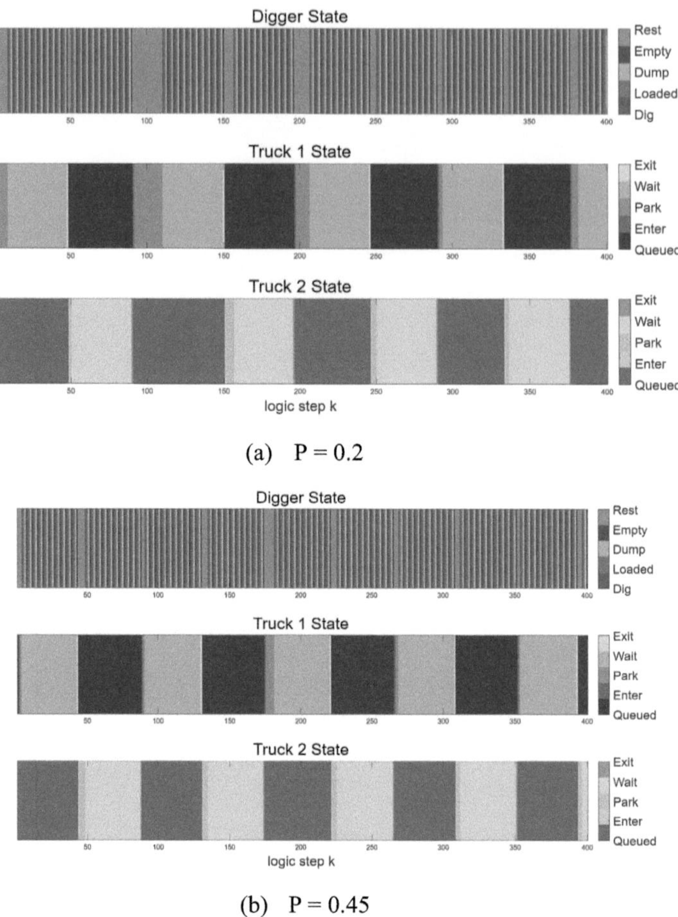

Fig. 9. The impact of parking probability on scene collaboration.

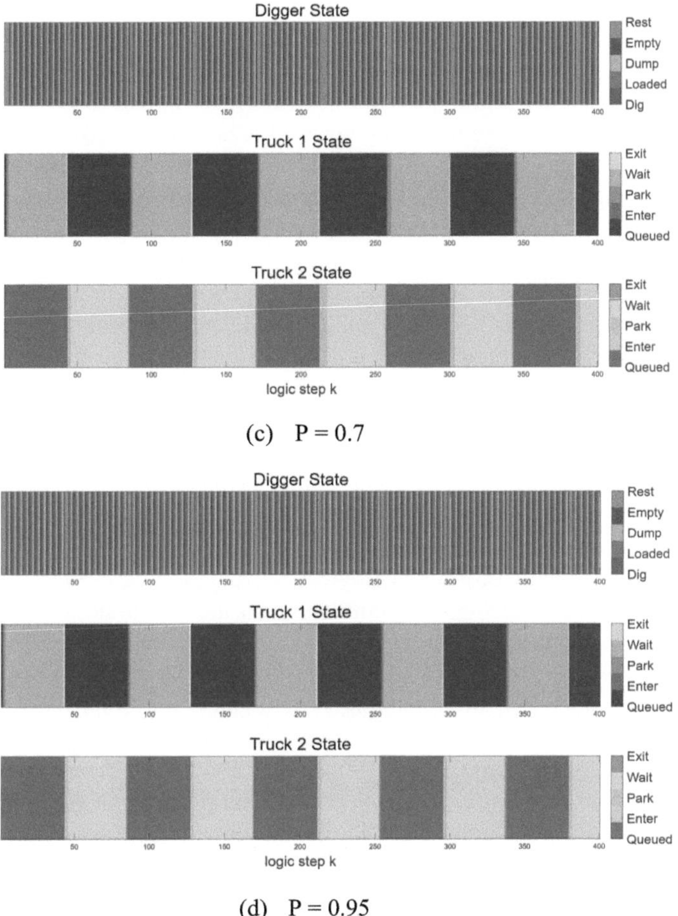

(c) P = 0.7

(d) P = 0.95

Fig. 9. (*continued*)

5 Discussion

This paper addresses the semi-autonomous collaboration problem between haul trucks and excavators in intelligent mining scenarios and proposes an integrated industrial intelligence management framework encompassing structure, behavior, and performance. First, hierarchical autonomy is leveraged to upgrade the physical and information infrastructure of excavators and trucks, laying the foundation for effective collaboration. Second, the design of autonomous operation processes and human–machine interaction interfaces is tailored to each system's structure and capabilities, ensuring flexibility and reliability in scene execution. Finally, the STP approach is employed to model excavator–truck collaboration, with simulation analyses quantifying the impact of parking success rates and other key technical indicators on system performance. Attractor theory for logical dynamic systems is utilized to assess the likelihood of process deadlock and favorable operational cycles, achieving a semi-quantitative evaluation of collaborative processes in the mining context.

Future work should focus on the following aspects:

1. Upper–Lower Layer Coordination and Game Modeling: In complex industrial CPS, the dynamic game between upper-level decision-making and lower-level execution requires algebraic integrated modeling via STP (Cheng et al., 2014). Potential functions can be used to analyze equilibrium and robustness, exploring how scheduling policy changes affect system performance and convergence, thus providing a theoretical basis for multi-layer cooperative mechanism design.

2. Optimal Control and Reinforcement Learning in Dynamic Environments: Integration of STP with optimal control and reinforcement learning is recommended for unified modeling of system states and control inputs. While the relationship between stochastic games and multi-agent reinforcement learning is well established, it is considered that extending STP systems to include stochastic features could serve as an important tool for unifying the descriptions of both in logical scenarios (potentially following the line of work by Wang et al., 2023). Policy iteration and deep RL algorithms can be employed to optimize strategies, with digital twin platforms facilitating both simulation and real-world deployment, thereby enhancing autonomous collaboration in multi-agent, complex environments (Bajaria et al., 2022).

3. Safety Constraints and Constrained Logical System Analysis: STP-based methods can transform constrained logical dynamic systems into algebraic state-space models, enabling systematic analysis of reachability, controllability, and stability (Mu et al., 2024). This provides explicit boundary conditions for subsequent optimization and RL strategy development, strengthening system safety and robustness under multi-constraint, asynchronous scenarios.

4. Multi-Scenario Coupling and System Expansion: Future intelligent mining collaboration will involve coupling of multiple operational modules (e.g., self-localization, transportation, unloading) (Nubert et al., 2022, Teng et al., 2024, Walawalkar et al., 2022). Modular Boolean control networks and STP modeling are recommended to achieve unified subsystem representation and reachability analysis. Hierarchical reward mechanisms and reinforcement learning should be incorporated to optimize global coordination. Ultimately, end-to-end digital twin simulation and incremental field deployment will establish a generalizable framework for full-process intelligent mining operations. However, this integration method may also lead to combinatorial explosion issues. Simplifying the logical systems described by STP remains an important direction.

5. An exploration of interaction loops: treating different systems separately offers a deployment-friendly scheme that facilitates structural change and decouples their lifecycles; however, this approach complicates analysis of system integration. Therefore, we must examine how to enable interaction across levels and across systems, while achieving cognitive integration. Let us provisionally refer to this integration method as the "interaction loop," which should provide a closed-loop structure at the cognitive level and drive different classes of systems to integrate within a unified framework. One may consider that the loop structure to be studied in future work is an essential component of this architecture. Currently, cognitive architectures offer a promising approach, and hence we will pursue further analysis along these lines (Ali et al., 2024; Kotseruba & Tsotsos, 2020).

6 Conclusion

This paper, grounded in an industrial intelligence architectural framework and oriented toward mine personnel safety, develops a semi-autonomous excavator–haul truck scenario model for human–cyber integration and interoperability, structured from the perspectives of system structure, behavior, and performance. The main innovations are as follows:

- A hierarchical, staged approach to the autonomous transformation of excavators and haul trucks is proposed, providing the structural and functional foundation;
- The behavioral logic of semi-autonomous excavators and trucks is designed, along with an integrated methodology for their cooperation;
- The STP is employed as a mathematical tool to assess the rationality of the scenario model and to analyze the impact of key technologies on system operation.

Overall, the semi-tensor product approach transforms logical models that are easily understood by humans into algebraic models suitable for computer processing, enabling the analysis of the dynamic characteristics implicit in abstract logic. Simultaneously, this logical expression form supports continuous human comprehension of the system, allowing controllers to integrate into the system and achieve cognitive interoperability. Future work will continue to explore diverse modes of human–cyber interaction in industrial intelligence transformation, leveraging mathematical frameworks such as game theory and control theory to advance the deployment and practical realization of human–cyber interoperability.

Acknowledgments. This research is supported by the Ministry of Industry and Information Technology Special Project for High-Quality Development of Manufacturing Industry-2024 Typical Scenario-Based Industry Chain Digital Transformation Enabling Public Service Platform Project.

Disclosure of Interests. The authors declare that they have no known competing financial interests or personal relationships that could have appeared to influence the work reported in this paper.

References

Ranasinghe, T., Grosse, E.H., Glock, C.H., Jaber, M.Y.: Aging Workforce and Learning: state-of-the-art (2023)

Qu, M., Fang, Z., Yang, K., Li, Q.: The security architecture and methodology of cyber-physical-social system and its application to Boeing 737 Max 8 accident analysis. In: International Conference on Guidance, Navigation and Control, pp. 246–256. Springer (2024a)

Yin, L.: Research on key technologies of distributed LiDAR and visual information fusion. PhD thesis, Wuhan University, Wuhan, China (2020)

Lee, J., Nam, Y., Hong, S.: Random force based algorithm for local minima escape of potential field method. In: Proceedings of the International Conference on Control, Automation, Robotics & Vision (ICARV), pp. xx–xx. IEEE (2010)

Kim, J., Jin, M., Choi, W., et al.: Discrete time delay control for hydraulic excavator motion control with terminal sliding mode control. Mechatronics **60**, 15–25 (2019)

Liu, C., Zheng, P., Xu, X.: Digitalisation and servitisation of machine tools in the era of industry 4.0: a review. Int. J. Prod. Res. **61**(12), 4069–4101 (2023)

Li, X., Ran, Y., Chen, B., et al.: Opportunistic maintenance strategy optimization considering imperfect maintenance under hybrid unit-level maintenance strategy. Comput. Ind. Eng. **185**, 109624 (2023)

Bousdekis, A., Apostolou, D., Mentzas, G.: A human cyber-physical system framework for operator 4.0 – artificial intelligence symbiosis. Manuf. Lett. **25**, 10–15 (2020). https://doi.org/10.1016/j.mfglet.2020.06.001

IEC TR 63082-1 (2020): Intelligent Device Management – Part 1: Concepts and Terminology. Technical Report, International Electrotechnical Commission (IEC) (2020)

IEC 63082-2 (2024): Intelligent Device Management – Part 2: Requirements and Recommendations. Standard, International Electrotechnical Commission (IEC) (2024)

Qu, M. Yao, Y. et al.: Industrial digital twins based on enterprise modeling: architecture, methodology, and engineering applications (2025a). In press

Qu, M., Li, Q.: Human-machine-things integration: a scenario-driven architecture for digital transformation. Digit. Transf. **2**, 5–14 (2025)

Li, Q., Fang, Z., Qu, M.: Cyber-physical-social system (CPSS) architecture framework and methodology. In: Proceedings of the 3rd International Conference on Innovative Intelligent Industrial Production and Logistics, pp. 206–217. SCITEPRESS - Science and Technology Publications, Valletta, Malta (2022). https://doi.org/10.5220/0011559600003329

Qu, M., Li, Q., Fang, Z., Liu, R.: A double-direction cognitive interaction security architecture for CPSS: a case study. IFAC-PapersOnLine. **58**, 1168–1173 (2024)

Ali, J.A.H., Gaffinet, B., Panetto, H., Naudet, Y.: Cognitive systems and interoperability in the enterprise: a systematic literature review. Annu. Rev. Control. **57**, 100954 (2024). https://doi.org/10.1016/j.arcontrol.2024.100954

Naudet, Y.: Towards cognitive interoperability in cyber-physical enterprises (2023)

Cheng, D., Qi, H.: Lecture Notes in Semi-Tensor Product of Matrices: Volume 1 – Fundamental Theory and Multilinear Operations. Science Press, Beijing (2020)

Cheng, D., Qi, H.: Lecture Notes in Semi-Tensor Product of Matrices: Volume 2 – Analysis and Control of Logical Dynamic Systems. Science Press, Beijing (2022)

Cheng, D., Qi, H.: Lecture Notes in Semi-Tensor Product of Matrices: Volume 5 – Applications in Engineering and Other Systems. Science Press, Beijing (2024)

Cheng, D., Qi, H., He, F., Xu, T., Dong, H.: Semi-tensor product approach to networked evolutionary games. Control Theory Technol. **12**(2), 198–214 (2014). https://doi.org/10.1007/s11768-014-0038-9

Mu, T., Feng, J.E.: A survey on applications of the semi-tensor product method in Boolean control networks with time delays. Eng. Rep. **6**(1), e12760 (2024)

Wang, L., Huang, F.: Multi-agent games, learning, and control. Acta Automatica Sinica. **49**, 580–613 (2023)

Bajaria, P., Yerudkar, A., Glielmo, L., Del Vecchio, C., Wu, Y.: Self-triggered control of probabilistic Boolean control networks: a reinforcement learning approach. J. Franklin Inst. **359**(12), 6173–6195 (2022). https://doi.org/10.1016/j.jfranklin.2022.06.004

Nubert, J., Khattak, S., Hutter, M.: Graph-based multi-sensor fusion for consistent localization of autonomous construction robots. In: Proceedings of the 2022 International Conference on Robotics and Automation (ICRA), pp. 10048–10054. IEEE (2022). https://doi.org/10.1109/ICRA46639.2022.9812386

Teng, S., et al.: FusionPlanner: a multi-task motion planner for mining trucks via multi-sensor fusion. Mech. Syst. Signal Process. **208**, 111051 (2024)

Walawalkar, A. V., Schindler, C., Berns, K.: A method for dynamic payload estimation in hydraulic excavators. RWTH Aachen University, Lehrstuhl und Institut für Schienenfahrzeuge und Transportsysteme, Technical Report RWTH-2023-00533 (2022)

Kotseruba, I., Tsotsos, J.K.: 40 years of cognitive architectures: core cognitive abilities and practical applications. Artif. Intell. Rev. **53**, 17–94 (2020). https://doi.org/10.1007/s10462-018-9646-y

Towards Cognitive Interoperability
with Cognitive Human Digital Twins

Ben Gaffinet[1,2]($\boxtimes$) (ID), Jana Al Haj Ali[2] (ID), Hervé Panetto[2] (ID), and Yannick Naudet[1] (ID)

[1] Luxembourg Institute of Science and Technology, Belval, Luxembourg
{ben.gaffinet,yannick.naudet}@list.lu
[2] Université de Lorraine, CNRS, CRAN, Nancy, France
{jana.al-haj-ali,herve.panetto}@univ-lorraine.fr

Abstract. Human-machine collaboration requires unambiguous communication to limit misunderstandings. Although semantic interoperability manages to remove ambiguity in machine-to-machine communication, it is insufficient when humans are involved. Humans process and understand information differently based on past experience and the current context, exceeding semantic interoperability's scope. Cognitive interoperability aims to achieve an aligned understanding, shared intentions, and enable joint decision-making between agents. However, the cognitive state of the human is hard to detect and model, representing a major obstacle to cognitive interoperability.

We propose a cognitive Human Digital Twin (cHDT) that emulates a human's cognitive processes by exploiting cognitive architectures. In particular, we investigate ACT-R as a candidate model. It is a mature cognitive architecture that has been developed based on decades of experimental results from cognitive science and neuroscience. We discuss how the internal state of ACT-R models, and thus the cHDTs, may contribute to cognitive interoperability. With a simplified use case, we illustrate how a cHDT hosting a personalised ACT-R model could track and continuously share the human's internal cognitive states. This enables external systems, such as robots, to adapt to human perspectives and avoid resource conflicts in human-robot collaboration. Finally, we discuss the applicability of ACT-R as an emulation model, the components of a cHDT, and outline a two-phase implementation plan to validate the proposed solution.

Keywords: Human Digital Twin · Cognitive Interoperability · Cognitive Digital Twin · Cognitive Modelling · ACT-R · Industry 5.0

1 Introduction

Industry 5.0 promotes a shift towards resilient, adaptable, and human-centric industrial systems [7]. Human-centric systems in particular change how humans are managed within manufacturing. Their adaptability and creativity are recognised as important additions to industrial systems, considering them as active collaborators alongside machines. Active collaboration between humans and machines requires clear and unambiguous communication that allows them to jointly decide and execute plans without

© The Author(s), under exclusive license to Springer Nature Switzerland AG 2026
J. Barata et al. (Eds.): IN4PL 2025, CCIS 2826, pp. 332–349, 2026.
https://doi.org/10.1007/978-3-032-15579-5_20

misunderstandings. While the research of interoperability has addressed many challenges of machine-to-machine communication, communication between humans and machines remains a significant challenge and requires cognitive interoperability [2].

Cognitive interoperability goes beyond semantic interoperability. It not only ensures that the format and content of the exchanged data are clear but also that the understanding of that data remains aligned between interacting systems or agents [2]. An additional cornerstone of cognitive interoperability is sharing of intentions between agents and understanding each others behaviour. How information is understood and used by a system depends on its internal programming that processes the data and ultimately leads to the system's behaviour. For engineered systems, such as Cyber-Physical Systems (CPS), the processing of information and logic behind decisions can, in principle, be accessed, changed, and understood by the developer. Some limitations may arise if black box models like neural networks are deployed, but alternative designs are in principle possible. However, when the interacting agent is human, the internal processes that drive understanding of a situation are not fully accessible. Although detection of brain activity is possible, mapping the signal to intentions or understanding is challenging and detection methods are not well adapted for industrial settings. For instance, functional magnetic resonance imaging (fMRI) provides high-resolution data about brain activity but immobilises the subject. Electroencephalograms (EEG) provide an alternative that does not impose restrictions on movement, but their use is mainly focused on quantifying parameters like mental fatigue and workload, or to a lesser extent stress and visual fatigue [15]. This limited information about the human cognitive state is a major roadblock to achieving cognitive interoperability. However, there is an alternative approach known as cognitive architectures that model the processing of stimuli and how they lead to reactions and decisions. This type of model has been developed based on decades of experimental results from cognitive science, psychology, and neuroscience [16]. They closely follow the way information is processed in the brain to create human-like virtual agents or reproduce the behaviour of humans [5]. Cognitive architectures may well provide valuable information about the cognitive processes and state based on measured stimuli and their modelled processing.

To enable cognitive interoperability, information about cognitive states needs to be communicated and aligned continuously, but cognitive architectures are rarely used to reproduce and analyse human behaviour in real-time. Therefore, an approach to integrate and deploy them is required.

Human Digital Twins (HDT) have the objective of emulating the state and dynamics of a human individual, are tightly integrated with the human, and can selectively share information with collaborating systems [10]. Depending on the application case, HDTs may model different aspects of the twinned individual. In this paper, we are interested in emulating cognitive mechanisms and resulting behaviour to enable cognitive interoperability. According to the definition provided in Lauer-Schmaltz et al. [18], this makes it a cognitive Human Digital Twin (cHDT).

This paper proposes the integration of a cognitive architecture with an HDT to enable the emulation of cognitive processes. We explore the applicability of cognitive architectures to model human cognition, including its internal states, and how this information may be used to contribute to cognitive interoperability.

The structure of the paper is as follows. Section 2 describes the emerging concept of cognitive interoperability, in particular, for contexts involving collaboration between humans and engineered systems. In Sect. 3, we discuss the applicability of cognitive architectures as emulation models for human cognition. Section 4 presents how an HDT deploying a cognitive architecture forms a cognitive Human Digital Twin (cHDT) to track and emulate the human state. A set of possible use cases of cHDTs in Human-Robot Collaboration is briefly discussed. Section 5 describes a human-robot collaboration scenario in which an HDT is proposed that hosts a cognitive architecture, ACT-R, to reduce resource conflicts. Finally, we present limitations and perspectives for future work in Sect. 6.

2 Cognitive Interoperability

Effective collaboration between two agents – whether human-human, human-system, or system-system – requires the ability to share and act upon information. This necessity forms the basis of interoperability, ensuring that agents can cooperate despite differences in language, structure, or internal representation. Without interoperability, collaboration is susceptible to failure due to misunderstandings, incompatible data formats, or conflicting expectations. Traditionally, interoperability has been classified into multiple levels [24].

Technical interoperability refers to the ability of systems to exchange data on the most basic level, which involves hardware requirements to send and receive data, as well as transfer protocols. Syntactic interoperability ensures that the data structure and format sent between systems are well defined and can be interpreted by the receiving system. Semantic interoperability ensures that the meaning of shared data is well defined and understood. To achieve semantic interoperability, engineers and developers need to coordinate to guarantee that the meaning of sent data is always clearly defined.

However, semantic interoperability does not address how humans truly understand data. This is shaped by internal cognitive processes that depend not only on the formal meaning of the data, but also on the current context, previous experiences, personal goals, and expectations. For instance, two individuals may receive the same information, yet interpret it differently based on their background and current situations. Semantic interoperability, which focuses on shared definitions and vocabularies, cannot capture these differences in individual perception and reasoning.

Furthermore, technical, syntactic, and semantic interoperability are all made possible by developers and engineers defining how data is exchanged, formatted, and interpreted. The entire process, from receiving data to making decisions, is governed by logic and rules designed in advance. This makes the system's behaviour predictable and controllable, with each processing step traceable. In principle, one can inspect how a decision was made and understand the reasoning behind it. However, this design assumes that all situations can be anticipated in advance and that all the knowledge needed for decision-making can be encoded at the design stage. In real-world collaboration, especially when humans are involved, this is rarely the case. Systems must be able to handle new situations, adapt their behaviour, and understand the perspectives and intentions of other agents. These requirements exceed the scope of semantic interoperability and underscore the need for cognitive interoperability [1] which *"refers to the ability of different agents (human or artificial) to align their thoughts and perception of information, allowing for mutual understanding and shared intentions. It involves creating shared mental models, aligning knowledge, and ensuring a common way to use, interpret and reason over knowledge"* [2].

Cognitive interoperability presents several challenges that go beyond standard data exchange. It requires agents to develop mutual understanding, align their perceptions and thought processes, share intentions, and participate in joint decision-making. Mutual understanding involves each agent being able to comprehend how others interpret a situation, taking into account their beliefs, goals, and experiences. Aligning perception and thought processes means that agents must interpret their environment in comparable ways and reason over information using compatible internal models. When this alignment fails, collaboration breaks down due to inconsistent interpretations. Shared intentions mean that agents must not only be aware of each other's goals, but also commit to common objectives, which is important to achieve coordinated behaviour. Finally, joint decision-making requires agents to act collectively based on this shared understanding and alignment of intentions. These requirements are especially important in human–system collaboration, where the system must adapt to the human perspective and reasoning. In order to enable such adaptations, a persistent digital representation of not only the physical state, but also the cognitive state of the human is necessary. This motivates the use of an HDT, which serves as a digital counterpart to the human involved in the collaboration.

To enable cognitive interoperability in operational real-time settings, information about the internal cognitive processes and states need to be modelled and shared with collaborating engineered systems. In the next two sections, we present the two building blocks to achieve this. First, Sect. 3 describes cognitive architectures as a model of human cognition and how it can make internal cognitive states accessible. Second, Sect. 4 presents how cognitive architectures can be deployed in an HDT, forming a cognitive HDT, to emulate the cognitive processes of the twinned individual. We discuss possible ways to exploit the cHDT and how it contributes to cognitive interoperability.

3   Cognitive Architectures

Cognitive architectures follow the structure of the human brain to model the entire cognitive cycle, from perception, memory, attention, reasoning, to action selection and execution [22]. A large number of initiatives have attempted to build cognitive architectures with the goal to either; give cognitive abilities to machines; or model human cognition itself. The canonical structure of cognitive architectures has been distilled by Laird et al. [17] and presented as the common model of cognition.

Figure 1 describes how stimuli are sensed and processed to ultimately lead to an action. The sensory organs are continuously receiving information from the environment. Once a stimulus is sensed, the information is filtered and interpreted; this process is often unconscious but can be elevated to require conscious attention. The processed stimulus enters working memory, which may trigger the retrieval of long-term declarative and procedural memory. Long-term memories contain knowledge and procedures that influence the selection of an action and the development of a motor plan. Once a

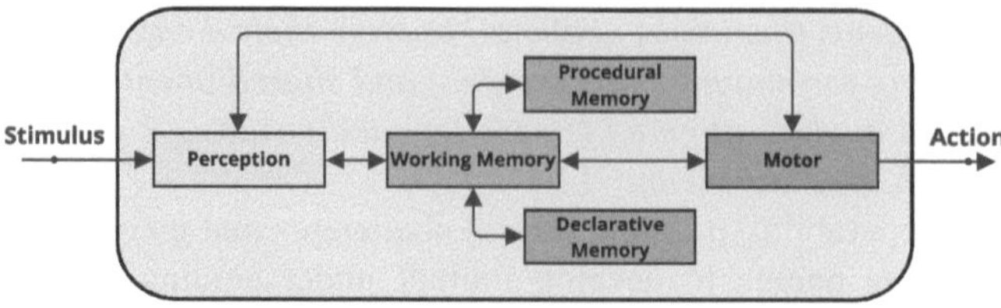

Fig. 1. Common model of cognition adapted from Laird et al. [17].

motor plan is executed, it leads to a manipulation of the environment. From the execution of actions and observation of its effects, humans learn to adapt their approach, which can be represented by new memories that are formed and stored in long-term memory for future use.

3.1 ACT-R Architecture

A large variety of cognitive architectures exist and differ substantially in their objective and functioning [16]. Their objective may be to simulate actual human cognition, including human limitations and biases, or seek to enhance engineered systems with cognitive functions inspired by human cognition. This paper takes interest in modelling human cognition as closely as possible. Within the category of architectures that seek to model human cognition, ACT-R is among the richest and most mature models [3]. It is part of the ACT family of cognitive models, which started its development in 1993 [4], with active development persisting until today. It integrates experimental findings from cognitive and neuroscience, giving it a high level of realism and plausibility.

Figure 2 shows all the buffers and modules of the latest major release; ACT-R 7. Each module processes a different kind of information; for example, the vision module is specialised in encoding visual information and passing it to the rest of the model through the visual buffer. The modules and buffers have been mapped to brain regions based on detectable brain responses when performing specific tasks. Only the activity of the aural, vision and motor module has not been linked to a specific brain region, but has been modelled loosely to allow interaction with the environment. Modules run in parallel and influence the state of the buffers that connect to the central production system. This system contains production rules that are triggered when certain conditions are met and manipulates the state of the buffers based on predefined rules. The new buffer states can trigger new processes in the modules, which leads to an intricate dance between the production system and modules, ultimately giving rise to complex behaviour. The core repeated cycle in ACT-R starts with an initial state of the buffers that hold the representation of the physical environment and additional internal representations (e.g. the initial goal). A production rule that matches the buffer states is selected and executed. The updated buffer states represent the start of a new cycle. Buffers may hold requests for modules, like retrieving a memory or shifting visual attention. The modules respond to these requests in parallel with timings that correspond to typical human performance. The minimum time to execute a cognitive cycle is set at 50ms [3], with production rules executing quickly and modules typically taking longer. The sequence of productions

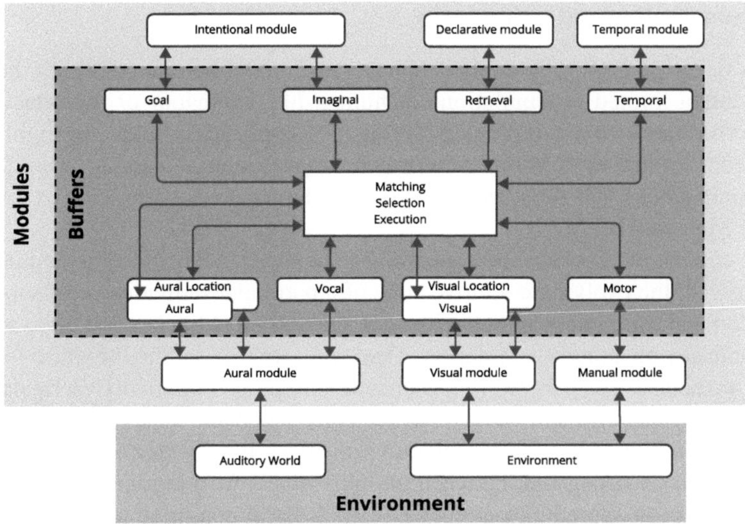

Fig. 2. Modules and buffers of ACT-R 7.0 adapted from Ritter et al. [28].

fired, buffer states changed, modules requests, and module responses are reported in a model trace. While the production rules are symbolic, i.e. rule-based, some of the underlying mechanisms in the modules are sub-symbolic. Indeed, the retrieval of a memory is determined by a set of equations that represent the build-up and decay of memories. Memories are stored in a structured way, referred to as chunks. Chunks have a type and slots; for example, a chunk of type "Lego" could have slots "colour" and "size" to describe its properties. The key drivers for memory retrieval are the repetitions and recency of a used chunk. Both lead to a high activation level of the chunk leading to an increased likelihood of retrieval. Additionally, chunks can be confused if their values are similar which is known as partial matching. A second subsymbolic process is the selection of the production rule if multiple rules satisfy the necessary conditions. This may represent different strategies when facing a problem. Their weight and thus likelihood of selection is adapted based on the outcomes and their attached rewards. An ACT-R model can learn in a human-like way from interacting with an environment and observing the results.

To contribute to cognitive interoperability, the internal state of ACT-R needs to be accessible. Luckily, the model can be run step by step, and its state read to feed into an external system's logic. ACT-R is primarily written in Common Lisp with accompanying software[1] to develop models. An alternative Python implementation[2] is available which facilitates integration into larger systems.

---

[1] ACT-R software download page: http://act-r.psy.cmu.edu/software/.

[2] GitHub repository for Python implementation: https://github.com/jakdot/pyactr.

3.2   Personalisation and Granularity

ACT-R is developed with the explicit objective to model human cognition, but its use cases are often limited to simulations of human-like behaviour or reproducing mean human performance of a sample population. The application fields are highly varied, ranging from simulating reactor operator behaviour [5], aural categorisation tasks [26, 33], dynamic stocks and flow tasks [25] or simulating decision making in games like FireChief Microworld [23].

In the context of cognitive interoperability, the mean behaviour of a human is insufficient. Instead, the evolving cognitive state of a particular individual needs to be emulated. Individual differences in behaviour are big and most likely need to be accounted for to enable any meaningful emulation. Therefore, we explore the literature for personalisation methods of ACT-R. ACT-R's subsymbolic processes are driven by parameters that can be adapted to an individual's performance and behaviour. For instance, parameters exist to influence how fast declarative memory is forgotten or retrieved. Lovett et al. established a strong link between an individual's working memory capacity and ACT-R's activation spreading parameter [19]. A short cognitive test known as modified digit span (MDS) task can be used to estimate this parameter and thus personalise the model. Additional parameters describe the influence of the learning process or how exploratory or goal-driven an individual's behaviour is. Tuning parameters to reflect individual differences is not a new idea [27], but can quickly become impractical or impossible [9]. Alternative approaches have been proposed. An alternative approach is instance-based learning, in which past experiences are stored in memory to be recalled later and influence subsequent decision-making. Instance-based learning is a well-established paradigm of ACT-R modelling [29]. A recent paper by Cranford et al. [8] uses this approach in a cybersecurity scenario. Dickison et al. [9] develop ACT-R models with different control structures that represent how much an individual is influenced by the response of the environment to the decisions made.

3.3   ACT-R Challenges for Emulation

To elevate ACT-R to an effective emulation model, the states of the model need to correspond closely to the states of the twinned individual at any given time. However, most papers are focused on less granular metrics, such as human performance or qualitative behaviour. In order to create ACT-R models that remain aligned with the modelled individual, we see a few key problems that need to be solved; *(i)* During initial development the task and context need to be well understood to design the model, especially the production rules. Additional observations of humans performing the task and interviewing them can provide additional information about their internal mental processes. This step is laborious and requires experience with ACT-R; therefore, data-driven methods to generate production rules from observed behaviour would represent an enormous step forward for cognitive modelling. *(ii)* Before running the model, its parameters need to be adapted to reflect the cognitive abilities of the twinned human. This includes the previously mentioned activation spreading parameter [19], but additional methods may exist and should be explored before potentially developing new calibration techniques. *(iii)* For models that use instance-based learning, the initial model would not contain any previous experiences the human may have. The model would have to shadow the human solving the task and encode the experiences progressively to potentially converge with the observed human behaviour. *(iv)* For fully operational models, predictions may not always align with reality. Any divergence between model and reality needs to be handled carefully. The model may be performing poorly and needs to be adapted based on new observations, or the human may be acting abnormally which could indicate an emergency and need of intervention. For example, physiological anomalies cannot be captured by the ACT-R model but could be the source of deviating behaviour. *(v)* Finally, for real-time execution the computational cost of the model needs to be within reasonable bounds. In general, ACT-R runs fast as most models are context-specific and specialised. However, when the number of production rules grows, it significantly impacts performance, as the pattern matching mechanism is constantly checking the buffer states and the conditions to fire each production rule. Similarly, when a large number of chunks are stored in declarative memory, their retrieval slows down, as each retrieval requires the computation of each chunk activation.

4   Human Digital Twins

Cognitive interoperability requires the continuous sharing of internal cognitive states to avoid misunderstandings and breaking down of collaboration. Workers may self-report their intentions, reasoning, and actions continuously to grant collaborating systems insights into their internal processes, but this represents a disruptive and highly unnatural way of interaction. Instead, Human Digital Twins (HDT) can act as an intermediary that models the worker's cognitive process and communicates intentions and understandings with collaborating systems. In this section, we present the concept of HDTs and how it may exploit a cognitive architecture to reduce misunderstandings between humans and technical systems.

An HDT is a digital representation of an individual with the objective to emulate its state and dynamics. It is tightly integrated with the twinned human receiving data automatically as well as giving automatic feedback [10]. For cognitive interoperability, HDTs are a promising approach to continuously gather information about a human, model their behaviour, and share information selectively with other systems.

The components and interfaces of an HDT are shown in Fig. 3. Data about the twinned human is received by the *Data Acquisition Interface*, stored and managed by a *Data Storage and Management* module before it is fed to the *Human Model* that emulates the human state and dynamics. This model is the centre of the HDT and may model any aspects of the twinned human ranging from physiological to cognitive processes. In the context of cognitive interoperability, cognitive processes and states are the central aspect of interest. Section 3 describes how cognitive architectures, in particular ACT-R, are good candidates for HDTs that seek to emulate human behaviour. *Human Digital Twin Functions* generate feedback for the twinned human or external systems. The *Feedback Interface* mediates the feedback and sends it to the human, which can range from warning signals to proactive guidance. The *Communication Interface* connects to other Digital Twins or technical systems, sharing information about the cognitive state to enable cognitive interoperability.

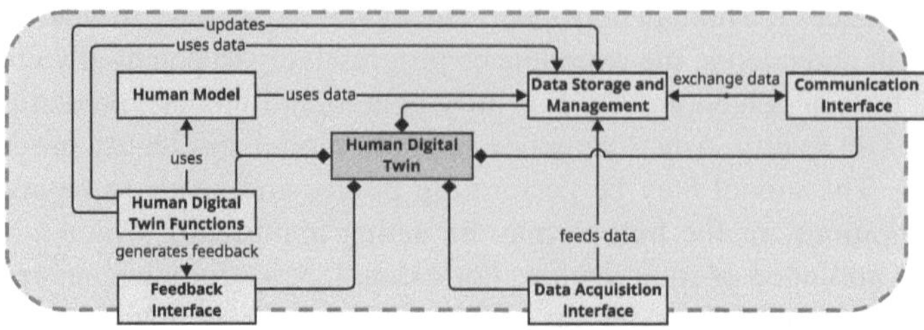

Fig. 3. Human Digital Twin components and interfaces as described in prior work [12].

The HDT's structure is designed to gather data continuously, model the cognitive processes and communicate important decisions, or cognitive states, with external system. Modelling these cognitive processes is a key challenge. Behavioural differences between individuals are important, making general cognitive models unlikely to succeed. An HDT is unique for the twinned individual, being entirely specialised on not only receiving data from that individual but also hosting personalised models. The long-term objective of HDT research is to create a persistent HDT that accompanies the twinned human throughout their life and evolves with them. In practice HDTs are constrained to specific use cases with limited personalization.

A related concept with significant similarities is the Cognitive Digital Twin (CDT) and needs to be clarified for the remainder of the paper. A CDT is defined as a *"A CDT is a DT and a cognitive system. As a DT it emulates a physical system that can be or not itself cognitive. As a cognitive system it possesses cognitive functions, bringing it in particular the ability to semantically model, process and interpret information autonomously and actively learning from its interactions"* [1]. In addition to the emulation function of a regular DT, a dedicated cognitive function or simulation function is required to be considered a CDT [21]. Typically, a CDT has the objective to augment non-cognitive systems with its cognitive functions.

A full HDT emulates its twinned human, including cognitive processes. Emulating these functions effectively makes the HDT a type of CDT. However, when HDTs are implemented, they only emulate a subset of human aspects to achieve their objective as informed by the use case. Lauer-Schmaltz et al. [18] distinguish four categories of HDTs based on what human aspects are modelled; (i) human-in-the-loop HDTs; (ii) physiological HDTs; (iii) mechanistic HDTs; (iv) and finally cognitive HDTs. Here, the cognitive HDT (cHDT), as the name implies, focuses on modelling the human cognitive processes and consequently is considered a type of CDT. For the remainder of the paper, cHDT refers to a DT that emulates the cognitive processes of a human, while CDT refers to a DT of an engineered system that in addition has cognitive functions.

4.1 General Use Cases for Industry

In the context of Industry 5.0 and Operator 5.0, a human-centric approach is adopted for which technological systems adapt to the needs of the human [13]. To achieve adaptations that benefit human well-being, excellent awareness of the human state and actions is required. This paper focuses on the actions and behaviour of workers, but HDTs can also be useful in improving ergonomics and safety by tracking aspects such as physical fatigue [32] or ergonomic indices [14] to adapt the cadence of a production system. An example of a system adaptation is dynamic task scheduling to prevent excess fatigue levels and reduce occupational risks based worker parameters, including posture and workload [6].

For cHDTs the objective is to enable adaptations based on the modelled cognitive processes and resulting behaviour. For the proposed ACT-R based cHDT, information about the environment needs to be sensed to infer the stimulus the worker is receiving. A promising approach could be eye-tracking, as it provides information about visual attention. The model needs to represent the initial internal state of the worker, including known facts about the process and environment, or past experience with the specific task. With the stimulus and initial internal state, the model can be executed. It would simulate the cognitive process of the worker and progressively change its state. The challenges in maintaining alignment between the model and the worker are discussed in Sect. 3.3. In the discussion below, we explore possible use cases under the assumption that a well-aligned model is possible.

As the model runs, the internal state can be used within the HDT to trigger the HDT functions. Figure 4 represents a simplified view on how model updates and internal states may be used. The states are updated based on the current internal state and the received stimuli. The HDT functions may access the internal state of the running model to intervene or share it with other external entities. We provide a few examples on the Fig. 4 and discuss them one by one below.

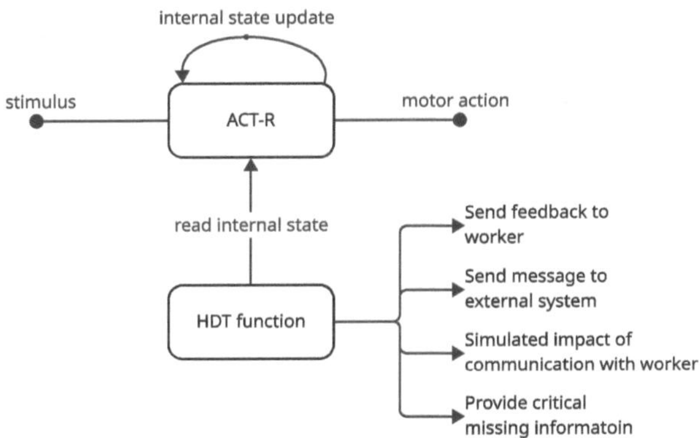

Fig. 4. Potential uses of ACT-R internal states.

Goal Buffer State and Motor Buffer Requests: Production rules change the state of the goal buffer, which is a control parameter of the model. It is used to move the model through the different phases of a task such as reading instructions, recalling facts, or selecting motor actions to execute. Selecting a motor action creates a request in the motor buffer to be executed by the manual module. This request can be interpreted as the intention to execute the specific action. We see two interesting ways to exploit this information in an HRC context; (i) if the selected action has a negative impact, by either being unsafe or not advancing the production goal, it can be interrupted or corrected by providing guidance or sending a warning signal; (ii) external systems can adapt to support the intended next action. For instance, the required components can be positioned to accelerate the upcoming action.

Aural and Visual Encoding: Visual and aural attention and information encoding is modelled by ACT-R. It may indicate when key information has been missed because attention was directed elsewhere or whether the encoding has been flawed. In a setup with many collaborating agents, there may be a risk of sending too much information to the worker in a short time span or interrupting critical moments of a production task. Instead of sending information directly to the human, it may be mediated by their HDT. The HDT is aware of the current task and is well-positioned to decide on the optimal time to send new information without causing unwanted interruptions or cognitive load. The HDT may simulate the effect of sending a message using the hosted ACT-R model before sending it to evaluate whether the interruption may have a negative impact.

Declarative Memory: The declarative memory module contains information about facts the individual worker knows about the procedures and environment. Memories are reinforced when used and decay over time when unused. It may enable the HDT to provide critical information for a task when knowledge is missing or is likely to have been forgotten.

Steps Towards Cognitive Interoperability: Although the use cases above are limited to exploiting the state of individual module and buffer states, enabling full cognitive interoperability requires combining them. Each step of the cognitive cycle, from perception to memory retrieval to action selection, has a role to play. For example, modelling the perception of the environment and how it is interpreted is only a first step. To align perception between human and machine, their respective interpretations of a situation need to be communicated. If their understanding diverges, they have to agree on which interpretation is right, hence a method to negotiate divergences is required. In general, modelling and sharing the cognitive state of the human is a necessary first step, with alignment procedures and negotiations coming as a second step.

5   Scenario

This section presents a simplified scenario to illustrate the functioning and use of cHDTs. It does not yet aim to achieve full cognitive interoperability, but only represents a first step towards it. The scenario focuses on adapting a robot's action based on the emulated human intent. To be precise, a robot and a human perform a collaborative assembly task where conflicting actions may arise. The robot is adapted based on the human intent to always avoid conflicting actions. Through this scenario, we show how a cHDT can contribute to the sharing of intention, which is a key part of cognitive interoperability.

5.1 Assembly Task and Multi Agent System

Consider a collaborative assembly task involving one human and one robot. Both have a shared objective of assembling a set of products that requires the execution of a set of assembly steps. Each step requires that the agent performing the task has the required skills and has access to any necessary components or tools. While the objective is to go towards autonomous and active collaborators, we simplify the present use case by having a freely acting human and adaptive robot. In Wang et al.'s [30] human-robot collaboration classification framework, this corresponds to *one active human* and *one supportive robot*.

As we have a situation with multiple agents, a classification of actions from multi-agent systems (MAS) provides a useful lens. Figure 5 shows the possible types of actions in a MAS [31]. An agent can take *independent actions* where the state of the environment changes without having any impact on other agents. Actions are classified as *interfering actions* when two agents choose actions that influence each other. Three types of interfering actions are distinguished; *joint actions* require two agents to collaborate to successfully perform the action; *influencing actions* can either positively or negatively influence each other, for example two agents pushing an object in the same direction is a positive influence while pushing in opposite directions is a negative influence; lastly, *concurrent actions* are conflicting in nature, such as two agents choosing to use the same object.

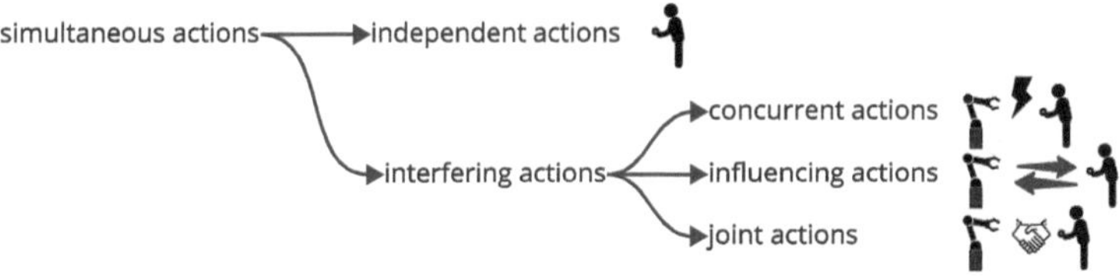

Fig. 5. Classification of actions in multi-agent systems based on the formalisation presented in Weyns et al. [31].

In this early scenario, the complexity is reduced by only having *independent actions* and *concurrent actions*. In particular, both agents assemble products independently and have all the skills required to do so, but they share the same components and tools. The possible concurrent actions are; both agents take the same component at the same time; or both agents take the same tool at the same time. We refer to these two situations as *resource conflicts*. The objective of the cognitive HDT approach is to reduce or entirely eliminate the resource conflicts by modelling the worker's cognitive process, which includes selecting the next action to perform, and adapting the robot's action selection to never choose the same resource as the worker.

5.2 Digital Twin Based Architecture

The proposed solution uses dedicated Digital Twins for each agent in the scenario, as well as a Digital Twin tracking the state of the environment. All the required information to execute the robot's behaviour or emulate the human's cognitive process is managed by the Digital Twins and shared between them. The physical agents, their Digital Twins and the data flows are shown in Fig. 6.

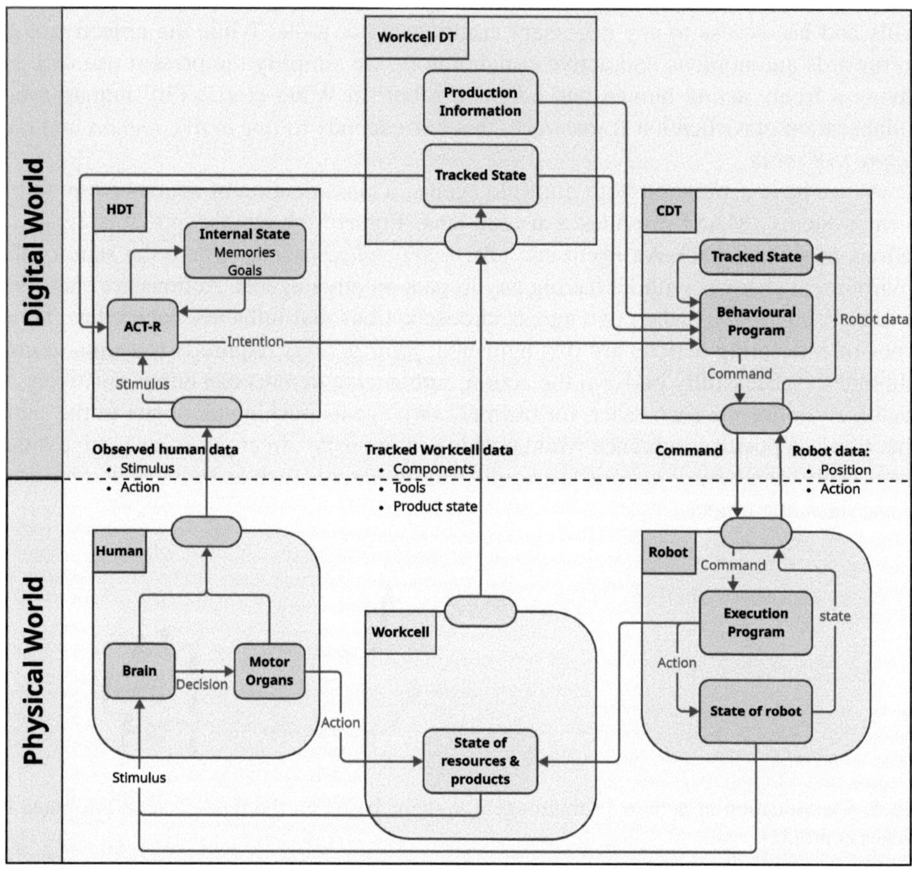

Fig. 6. Digital Twin based approach for Human Robot Collaboration scenario following the structure presented in prior work in [11].

Human and their Cognitive Human Digital Twin: The human and their HDT are shown in the left third of Fig. 6. The human acts freely during the assembly task, but before starting the worker is briefed about the objective and familiarise themself with the environment, such as the placement of the resources and the robot. The briefing helps initialise the encoded goal of the ACT-R goal buffer and the knowledge about the environment's setup in declarative memory. The HDT contains ACT-R as an emulation model with the objective to model the decision the worker is taking and thus what the next selected action will be. ACT-R forms the heart of the HDT and requires information about the worker's initial internal state and the environment that is the source of stimuli. During execution, the HDT receives information about the stimuli the human received. Detecting the stimuli is a technical challenge that can be addressed by eye-tracking, which indicates where the human is paying attention to and what kind of information is being encoded to drive the behaviour of the human and ACT-R. In a preliminary setup, the components are stored in drawers. We hypothesise that by opening the drawer the worker is seeing its contents, which can then be encoded for ACT-R. Detecting that the drawer was opened is far easier and allows for a quick exploration of ACT-R's abilities without deploying and integrating eye-tracking glasses from the start. During operation, the HDT is accessing the goal buffer of the ACT-R model to communicate the next planned action to the robot's Digital Twin.

Robot and its (Cognitive) Digital Twin: The robot's Digital Twin tracks the state of the robot and receives information about the next intended action from the HDT. Based on the current state of the production goal, its own state, and the next action of the human, the DT chooses an action that advances the production goal without entering into a resource conflict with the human. The command is passed down to the robot that executes it. For an initial experimental run, it may be sufficient to use well-established planning algorithms but introduce the additional constraint that the chosen action can never conflict with the human action.

For advanced cases, the robot can be coupled with a Cognitive Digital Twin (CDT). The CDT integrates a cognitive architecture that extends the functionalities of a conventional digital twin beyond state tracking. Specifically, it enables predictive reasoning, adaptive decision-making, and problem-solving [1]. This makes it possible not only to choose the robot's next step but also to react when unexpected situations occur, such as missing parts, delays, or task conflicts. For instance, if the human reports being busy with another activity, the CDT can reassign actions, change the task order, or suggest alternatives to keep the process moving. In addition, the CDT continuously updates its model using data from the robot control program and from the workcell. This allows it to anticipate possible delays, improve coordination with the human, and ensure safety by avoiding overlapping or unsafe actions.

Workcell and its Digital Twin: A DT for the workcell tracks the state of the resources and products in the physical environment. This includes all components and tools needed for assembling the product and the current progress of the assembled products, i.e. how many steps of the assembly procedure have already been executed. An additional piece of information is the sequence of steps required to assemble the products. Its role is to share the needed contextual information about the environments and products to allow the execution of the other DTs' models.

5.3 Path Towards Implementation and Limitations

The DT-based approach we describe requires significant development, which we split into multiple phases to address challenges in a targeted way.

General Limitations: ACT-R comes with a set of known limitations. First, models are heavily dependent on design choices of the developer as the production rules are hand-crafted. Second, the knowledge encoded in declarative memory is restricted to the use case, which excludes the impact of general and common-sense knowledge on behaviour. To generalise and reuse models, data-driven model adaptations would be desirable, but this research direction is in its early stages.

For the HDT-based approach there needs to be a procedure to reconcile diverging predictions from the cognitive model and the observed behaviour. The emulation model might have failed to reproduce and needs to be adapted based on the new observations. It may also indicate that an unexpected event has happened that is outside the scope of the model. For example, a model that only uses visual information will necessarily fail to reproduce the human behaviour when loud distracting noises occur.

Phase 1 - Emulation Model: Our approach rests on the hypothesis that it is possible to emulate human cognition at least within simplified setups. ACT-R is, in particular, the model we see as most promising to achieve emulation, but using it for emulation is rather unorthodox. The first phase takes a simplified assembly task in which one human participant is assembling a LEGO product. Visual instructions are provided on a screen and all needed components are stored in drawers. During the experiment, the participant has to understand the instructions and find the needed components. After the experiment, we interview the participant following an auto-confrontation protocol [20] to enquire about all the mental steps during task execution. The data collected will help evaluate an initial ACT-R model and create personalised models for each participant. In this phase, the model can entirely be evaluated after the experiment has finished, there is no requirement to build a fully integrated HDT and run it in real-time.

Phase 2 - Collaborative Setup: This second phase takes the setup from pure human emulation to human-robot collaboration. The ACT-R model is integrated into a Cognitive Human Digital Twin (cHDT) to emulate human behaviour during a shared assembly task. Human and robot largely operate independently, but share resources that may lead to concurrent actions, meaning conflicts. The cHDT serves as an intermediary, continuously tracking the worker's actions, inferring its intention, and sharing the intention with the Digital Twin of the collaborating robot. By receiving this additional information, the Digital Twin can change the selected action to avoid conflicts with the human while advancing the production goal if possible. The impact of the conflict avoidance strategy can be quantified by measuring production outcomes and subjective measures of the worker, such as the NASA-TLX task load index. A non-adaptive baseline setup where the robot has no awareness of the human intent can be used as a benchmark to compare performance.

As the collaborative setup is more complex, the ACT-R model will need to be extended to include the impact of the robot's presence. This entails a careful extension of the production rules and recalibration of sub-symbolic parameters. Measuring the stimuli that are caused by the robot is a major challenge. In the first phase, we use drawers to have an easy way to know when a component is visible or not. However, the robot will be visible at all times but only occasionally attract attention. It may be necessary to deploy additional sensors, such as eye-trackers, to measure the human gaze and model visual attention. If instance-based learning is used, the model may need to shadow the worker before converging and providing good results. In this phase, the model is run in real-time to emulate human decisions, necessitating a procedure to reconcile when model predictions diverge from reality.

6   Perspectives and Conclusions

Cognitive interoperability enables humans and machines to become active collaborators. To achieve this, continuous information about the human cognitive state is required. This paper proposes a cognitive Human Digital Twin (cHDT) aims to track and emulate the cognitive state and processes of a worker. A model for human cognition is a strict requirement to build a cHDT. We examined the applicability of cognitive architectures, in particular, ACT-R, as a candidate cognitive model. In principle, ACT-R can model the cognitive cycle, from perception to action, and its internal states are accessible while it runs. This opens up the possibility to continuously share and align external systems with the human's cognitive states. Modelling and accessing these states is a first step towards cognitive interoperability. To align the perception of humans and machines, a second step is to establish alignment and negotiation procedures to decide which interpretation should be retained by both agents.

A simplified case is presented to illustrate how a cHDT hosting ACT-R can enable a robot to avoid actions that conflict with human intentions. Developing the use case is planned in two separate phases. The first phase models a human performing an assembly task alone. The objective is to quantify the limits of ACT-R's ability and the techniques for personalisation. The second phase adds a robot to the assembly task such that resource conflicts may arise. The ACT-R model needs to be extended to include the impact of the robot on decisions, and it needs to be integrated into a cHDT.

References

1. Al Haj Ali, J., Gaffinet, B., Panetto, H., Naudet, Y.: Cognitive systems and interoperability in the enterprise: a systematic literature review. Ann. Rev. Control **57**, 100954 (2024)
2. Al Haj Ali, J., Gaffinet, B., Panetto, H., Naudet, Y.: From semantic interoperability to cognitive interoperability: enabling human–CPS collaboration in industry 5.0. In: International Conference on Innovative Intelligent Industrial Production and Logistics. Springer (2025)
3. Anderson, J.R., Bothell, D., Byrne, M.D., Douglass, S., Lebiere, C., Qin, Y.: An integrated theory of the mind. Psychol. Rev. **111**(4), 1036 (2004)
4. Anderson, J.: Rules of the Mind, 1st edn. Psychology Press (1993). https://doi.org/10.4324/9781315806938

5. Balaji, B., Shahab, M.A., Srinivasan, B., Srinivasan, R.: Act-r based human digital twin to enhance operators' performance in process industries. Front. Hum. Neurosci. **17**, 1038060 (2023)
6. Berti, N., Finco, S., Guidolin, M., Battini, D.: Towards human digital twins to enhance workers' safety and production system resilience. IFAC-PapersOnLine **56**(2), 11062–11067 (2023)
7. Breque, M., De Nul, L., Petridis, A.: Industry 5.0 – towards a sustainable, human-centric and resilient European industry. Publications Office of the European Union (2021). https://doi.org/10.2777/308407
8. Cranford, E.A., et al.: Personalized model-driven interventions for decisions from experience. Top. Cogn. Sci. (2024)
9. Dickison, D., Taatgen, N.A.: ACT-R models of cognitive control in the abstract decision making task. In: Proceedings of the Eighth International Conference on Cognitive Modeling, pp. 79–84 (2007)
10. Gaffinet, B., Al Haj Ali, J., Naudet, Y., Panetto, H.: Human digital twins: a systematic literature review and concept disambiguation for industry 5.0. Comput. Ind. **166**, 104230 (2025)
11. Gaffinet, B., Al Haj Ali, J., Panetto, H., Naudet, Y.: Human-centric digital twins: advancing safety and ergonomics in human-robot collaboration. In: International Conference on Innovative Intelligent Industrial Production and Logistics, pp. 380–397. Springer (2023)
12. Gaffinet, B., Naudet, Y., Panetto, H.: A systemic human digital twin model for human-centric systems. In: 11th IFAC Conference on Manufacturing Modelling, Management and Control (MIM2025) (2025)
13. Gladysz, B., Tran, T.A., Romero, D., van Erp, T., Abonyi, J., Ruppert, T.: Current development on the operator 4.0 and transition towards the operator 5.0: a systematic literature review in light of industry 5.0. J. Manufact. Syst. **70**, 160–185 (2023)
14. Greco, A., Caterino, M., Fera, M., Gerbino, S.: Digital twin for monitoring ergonomics during manufacturing production. Appl. Sci. **10**(21), 7758 (2020)
15. Ismail, L.E., Karwowski, W.: Applications of EEG indices for the quantification of human cognitive performance: a systematic review and bibliometric analysis. PLoS ONE **15**(12), e0242857 (2020)
16. Kotseruba, I., Tsotsos, J.K.: 40 years of cognitive architectures: core cognitive abilities and practical applications. Artif. Intell. Rev. **53**(1), 17–94 (2020)
17. Laird, J.E., Lebiere, C., Rosenbloom, P.S.: A standard model of the mind: toward a common computational framework across artificial intelligence, cognitive science, neuroscience, and robotics. AI Mag. **38**(4), 13–26 (2017)
18. Lauer-Schmaltz, M.W., Cash, P., Hansen, J.P., Maier, A.: Towards the human digital twin: Definition and design–a survey. arXiv preprint arXiv:2402.07922 (2024)
19. Lovett, M.C., Reder, L.M., Lebiere, C.: Modeling working memory in a unified architecture: an ACT-R perspective. Models Working Mem. Mech. Active Maintenance Executive Control **506**, 135–182 (1999)
20. Mollo, V., Falzon, P.: Auto-and allo-confrontation as tools for reflective activities. Appl. Ergon. **35**(6), 531–540 (2004)
21. Naudet, Y., Al Haj Ali, J., Gaffinet, B., Panetto, H.: Cognition in digital twins for cyber-physical systems and humans: where and why? In: International Conference on Innovative Intelligent Industrial Production and Logistics, pp. 399–412. Springer (2024)
22. Newell, A.: Unified Theories of Cognition. Harvard University Press (1994)
23. Orendain, A.D.O., Wood, S.: An account of cognitive flexibility and inflexibility for a complex dynamic task. In: Proceedings of the 11th International Conference on Cognitive Modeling, pp. 49–54 (2012)
24. Panetto, H.: Towards a classification framework for interoperability of enterprise applications. Int. J. Comput. Integr. Manuf. **20**(8), 727–740 (2007)

25. Peebles, D., Banks, A.P.: Modelling dynamic decision making with the ACT-R cognitive architecture. J. Artif. Gen. Intell. **2**(2), 52–68 (2010)
26. Prezenski, S., Brechmann, A., Wolff, S., Russwinkel, N.: A cognitive modeling approach to strategy formation in dynamic decision making. Front. Psychol. **8**, 1335 (2017)
27. Rehling, J., Demiral, B., Lebiere, C., Lovett, M., M Reder, L.: Modeling individual difference factors in a complex task environment. Carnegie Mellon University. Journal contribution (2003). https://doi.org/10.1184/R1/6617156.v1
28. Ritter, F.E., Tehranchi, F., Oury, J.D.: ACT-R: a cognitive architecture for modeling cognition. Wiley Interdisc. Rev. Cogn. Sci. **10**(3), e1488 (2019)
29. Taatgen, N.A., Lebiere, C., Anderson, J.R.: Modeling paradigms in ACT-R. In: Cognition and Multi-agent Interaction: From Cognitive Modeling to Social Simulation, pp. 29–52 (2006)
30. Wang, X.V., Kemény, Z., Váncza, J., Wang, L.: Human-robot collaborative assembly in cyber-physical production: classification framework and implementation. CIRP Ann. **66**(1), 5–8 (2017)
31. Weyns, D., Holvoet, T.: A formal model for situated multi-agent systems. Fund. Inform. **63**(2–3), 125–158 (2004)
32. You, Y., Liu, Y., Ji, Z.: Human digital twin for real-time physical fatigue estimation in human-robot collaboration. In: 2024 IEEE International Conference on Industrial Technology (ICIT), pp. 1–6. IEEE (2024)
33. Zhang, Z., Russwinkel, N., Prezenski, S.: Modeling individual strategies in dynamic decision-making with ACT-R: a task toward decision-making assistance in HCI. Procedia Comput. Sci. **145**, 668–674 (2018)

Author Index